ANDERSON'S
Law School Publications

ADMINISTRATIVE LAW ANTHOLOGY
by Thomas O. Sargentich

ADMINISTRATIVE LAW: CASES AND MATERIALS
by Daniel J. Gifford

APPELLATE ADVOCACY: PRINCIPLES AND PRACTICE
Cases and Materials
by Ursula Bentele and Eve Cary

A CAPITAL PUNISHMENT ANTHOLOGY
by Victor L. Streib

CASES AND PROBLEMS IN CRIMINAL LAW
by Myron Moskovitz

THE CITATION WORKBOOK
by Maria L. Ciampi, Rivka Widerman and Vicki Lutz

COMMERCIAL TRANSACTIONS: PROBLEMS AND MATERIALS
Vol. 1: Secured Transactions Under the Uniform Commercial Code
Vol. 2: Sales Under the Uniform Commercial Code and the Convention on
International Sale of Goods
Vol. 3: Negotiable Instruments Under the Uniform Commercial Code
and the United Nations Convention on International
Bills of Exchange and International Promissory Notes
by Louis F. Del Duca, Egon Guttman and Alphonse M. Squillante

A CONSTITUTIONAL LAW ANTHOLOGY
by Michael J. Glennon

CONTRACTS
Contemporary Cases, Comments, and Problems
by Michael L. Closen, Richard M. Perlmutter and Jeffrey D. Wittenberg

A CONTRACTS ANTHOLOGY
by Peter Linzer

A CRIMINAL LAW ANTHOLOGY
by Arnold H. Loewy

CRIMINAL LAW: CASES AND MATERIALS
by Arnold H. Loewy

CRIMINAL PROCEDURE: TRIAL AND SENTENCING
by Arthur B. LaFrance and Arnold H. Loewy

ECONOMIC REGULATION
Cases and Materials
by Richard J. Pierce, Jr.

ELEMENTS OF LAW
by Eva H. Hanks, Michael E. Herz and Steven S. Nemerson

ENDING IT: DISPUTE RESOLUTION IN AMERICA
Descriptions, Examples, Cases and Questions
by Susan M. Leeson and Bryan M. Johnston

ENVIRONMENTAL LAW
Vol. 1: Environmental Decisionmaking: NEPA and the Endangered Species Act
Vol. 2: Water Pollution
Vol. 3: Air Pollution
Vol. 4: Hazardous Wastes
by Jackson B. Battle, Mark Squillace, Maxine I. Lipeles and Robert L. Fischman

FEDERAL INCOME TAXATION OF PARTNERSHIPS AND OTHER PASS-THRU ENTITIES
by Howard E. Abrams

FEDERAL RULES OF EVIDENCE
Rules, Legislative History, Commentary and Authority
by Glen Weissenberger

Continued

FIRST AMENDMENT ANTHOLOGY
by Donald E. Lively, Dorothy E. Roberts and Russell L. Weaver

INTERNATIONAL HUMAN RIGHTS: LAW, POLICY AND PROCESS
Problems and Materials
by Frank Newman and David Weissbrodt

INTERNATIONAL LAW ANTHOLOGY
by Anthony D'Amato

INTRODUCTION TO THE STUDY OF LAW: CASES AND MATERIALS
by John Makdisi

JUSTICE AND THE LEGAL SYSTEM
A Coursebook
by Anthony D'Amato and Arthur J. Jacobson

THE LAW OF MODERN PAYMENT SYSTEMS AND NOTES
by Fred H. Miller and Alvin C. Harrell

PATIENTS, PSYCHIATRISTS AND LAWYERS
Law and the Mental Health System
by Raymond L. Spring, Roy B. Lacoursiere, M.D., and Glen Weissenberger

PROBLEMS AND SIMULATIONS IN EVIDENCE
by Thomas F. Guernsey

A PROPERTY ANTHOLOGY
by Richard H. Chused

THE REGULATION OF BANKING
Cases and Materials on Depository Institutions and Their Regulators
by Michael P. Malloy

A SECTION 1983 CIVIL RIGHTS ANTHOLOGY
by Sheldon H. Nahmod

SPORTS LAW: CASES AND MATERIALS
by Raymond L. Yasser, James R. McCurdy and C. Peter Goplerud

A TORTS ANTHOLOGY
by Lawrence C. Levine, Julie A. Davies and Ted Kionka

TRIAL PRACTICE
Text by Lawrence A. Dubin and Thomas F. Guernsey
Problems and Case Files with *Video* Presentation
by Edward R. Stein and Lawrence A. Dubin

Administrative Law Anthology

ADMINISTRATIVE LAW ANTHOLOGY

EDITED WITH COMMENTS BY
THOMAS O. SARGENTICH

Professor of Law
Washington College of Law
The American University

ANDERSON PUBLISHING CO.

ADMINISTRATIVE LAW ANTHOLOGY

© 1994 by Anderson Publishing Co.

All rights reserved. No part of this book may be used or reproduced by any means without written permission from the publisher and author.

Library of Congress Cataloging-in-Publication Data

An Administrative law anthology / edited with comments by Thomas O.
  Sargentich.
       p.   cm.
   Includes bibliographical references.
   ISBN 0-87084-803-8
   1. Administrative law—United States.   I. Sargentich, Thomas O.
KF5402.A5A27   1994
342.73'06—dc20
[347.3026]   94-9982
                                                                           CIP

Contents

Preface   xi

PART I   Major Controversies Implicating the Dominant Rule of Law Vision of Administrative Legitimacy   1

A.   Controversies About Substantive Legal Limits on Agencies   1

    1.   The Debate About Reviving the Delegation Doctrine   1

Theodore J. Lowi, *Two Roads to Serfdom: Liberalism, Conservatism and Administrative Power*, 36 AM. U. L. REV. 295 (1987)   3

Richard B. Stewart, *Beyond Delegation Doctrine*, 36 AM. U. L. REV. 323 (1987)   9

Thomas O. Sargentich, *The Delegation Debate and Competing Ideals of the Administrative Process*, 36 AM. U. L. REV. 419 (1987)   14

Jerry L. Mashaw, *Prodelegation: Why Administrators Should Make Political Decisions*, 1 J. LAW, ECON. & ORGAN. 81 (1985)   20

Additional Sources   27

    2.   Debates About the Interpretation of Statutory Authorizations of Agencies   28

       a.   Statutory Interpretation in General   28

William N. Eskridge, Jr., *Dynamic Statutory Interpretation*, 135 U. PA. L. REV. 1479 (1987)   29

Nicholas S. Zeppos, *Judicial Candor and Statutory Interpretation*, 78 GEO. L.J. 353 (1989)   36

Cass R. Sunstein, *Interpreting Statutes in the Regulatory State*, 103 HARV. L. REV. 405 (1989)   42

Stephen Breyer, *On the Uses of Legislative History in Interpreting Statutes*, 65 S. CAL. L. REV. 845 (1992)   44

Additional Sources   53

       b.   Judicial Deference to Agency Interpretations   55

Richard J. Pierce, Jr., *Chevron and its Aftermath: Judicial Review of Agency Interpretations of Statutory Provisions*, 41 VAND. L. REV. 301 (1988)   56

Thomas W. Merrill, *Judicial Deference to Executive Precedent*, 101 YALE L.J. 969 (1992)   59

Antonin Scalia, *Judicial Deference to Administrative Interpretations of Law*, 1989 DUKE L.J. 511   69

Cynthia R. Farina, *Statutory Interpretation and the Balance of Power in the Administrative State*, 89 COLUM. L. REV. 452 (1989)   71

Additional Sources   80

B.   Controversies About Procedural Legal Limits on Agencies   81

    1.   Debates About Procedural Due Process   81

Edward L. Rubin, *Due Process and the Administrative State*, 72 CAL. L. REV. 1044 (1984)   82

Jerry L. Mashaw, *The Supreme Court's Due Process Calculus for Administrative Adjudication in* Mathews v. Eldridge: *Three Factors in Search of a Theory of Value*, 44 U. CHI. L. REV. 28 (1976) — 97

Cynthia R. Farina, *Conceiving Due Process*, 3 YALE J.L. & FEMINISM 189 (1991) — 108

Additional Sources — 128

2. The Debate About Nonlegislative Rule Exemptions to Notice-and-Comment Rulemaking Procedures — 130

Robert A. Anthony, *Interpretive Rules, Policy Statements, Guidances, Manuals, and the Like—Should Federal Agencies Use Them to Bind the Public?*, 41 DUKE L.J. 1311 (1992) — 131

Peter L. Strauss, *The Rulemaking Continuum*, 41 DUKE L.J. 1463 (1992) — 137

Michael Asimow, *Nonlegislative Rulemaking and Regulatory Reform*, 1985 DUKE L.J. 381 — 142

Additional Sources — 149

3. The Debate About Alternative Dispute Resolution in Administrative Procedure — 150

Philip J. Harter, *Negotiating Regulations: A Cure for Malaise*, 71 GEO. L.J. 1 (1982) — 151

William Funk, *When Smoke Gets in Your Eyes: Regulatory Negotiation and the Public Interest—EPA's Woodstove Standards*, 18 ENVTL. L. 55 (1987) — 153

Philip J. Harter, *Points on a Continuum: Dispute Resolution Procedures and the Administrative Process*, 1 ADMIN. L.J. 141 (1987) — 159

Owen M. Fiss, *Against Settlement*, 93 YALE L.J. 1073 (1984) — 161

Additional Sources — 164

PART II   Major Controversies Implicating Other Visions of Administrative Legitimacy — 165

A. Controversies About the Instrumental Rationality of Administration in the Pursuit of Public Values — 165

1. The Debate About Comprehensive Regulatory Analysis — 165

Thomas O. McGarity, *Regulatory Analysis and Regulatory Reform*, 65 TEX. L. REV. 1243 (1987) — 166

Steven Kelman, *Cost-Benefit Analysis: An Ethical Critique*, REGULATION 33 (Jan./Feb. 1981) — 177

Additional Sources — 183

2. The Debate About Judicial Assessment of the Rationality of Agency Decisionmaking: Hard-Look Review — 184

Merrick B. Garland, *Deregulation and Judicial Review*, 98 HARV. L. REV. 505 (1985) — 185

Stephen Breyer, *Judicial Review of Questions of Law and Policy*, 38 ADMIN. L. REV. 363 (1986) — 195

Sidney A. Shapiro and Richard E. Levy, *Heightened Scrutiny of the Fourth Branch: Separation of Powers and the Requirement of Adequate Reasons for Agency Decisions*, 1987 DUKE L.J. 387 — 200

Additional Sources — 208

B. Controversies About the Openness and Political Oversight of Administration in the Pursuit of a More Democratic Process — 209

1. Debates About Openness in Government: Freedom of Information — 209

Antonin Scalia, *The Freedom of Information Act Has No Clothes*, REGULATION 15 (March/April 1982) — 210

Patricia M. Wald, *The Freedom of Information Act: A Short Case Study in the Perils and Paybacks of Legislating Democratic Values*, 33 EMORY L.J. 649 (1984) — 211

Robert G. Vaughn, *Federal Information Policy and Administrative Law, in* HANDBOOK ON REGULATION AND ADMINISTRATIVE LAW 467 (David Rosenbloom & Richard Schwartz eds., 1994) — 216
Additional Sources — 226

2. Debates About the Supervision of Agencies by Congress — 227
a. The Legislative Veto of Administrative Action — 227

Harold H. Bruff and Ernest Gellhorn, *Congressional Control of Administrative Regulation: A Study of Legislative Vetoes*, 90 HARV. L. REV. 1369 (1977) — 228

E. Donald Elliott, INS v. Chadha: *The Administrative Constitution, the Constitution, and the Legislative Veto*, 1983 SUP. CT. REV. 125 — 234

Stephen Breyer, *The Legislative Veto After* Chadha, 72 GEO. L.J. 785 (1984) — 241
Additional Sources — 243

b. Congressional Oversight of Administrative Action — 245

James B. Pearson, *Oversight: A Vital Yet Neglected Congressional Function*, 23 KAN. L. REV. 277 (1975) — 246

Peter M. Shane, *Legal Disagreement and Negotiation in a Government of Laws: The Case of Executive Privilege Claims Against Congress*, 71 MINN. L. REV. 461 (1987) — 247
Additional Sources — 261

3. The Debate About the Supervision of Agency Rulemaking by the President — 262

Harold H. Bruff, *Presidential Management of Agency Rulemaking*, 57 GEO. WASH. L. REV. 533 (1989) — 263

Alan B. Morrison, *OMB Interference with Agency Rulemaking: The Wrong Way to Write a Regulation*, 99 HARV. L. REV. 1059 (1986) — 269

Peter L. Strauss and Cass R. Sunstein, *The Role of the President and OMB in Informal Rulemaking*, 38 ADMIN. L. REV. 181 (1986) — 271

Charles Tiefer, *The Quayle Council: "No Fingerprints" on Regulation, in* THE SEMI-SOVEREIGN PRESIDENCY: THE BUSH ADMINISTRATION'S STRATEGY FOR GOVERNING WITHOUT CONGRESS 61 (1994) — 274
Additional Sources — 279

4. Debates About the Constitutional System of the Separation of Powers — 281
a. The Constitutional Position of Administrative Agencies — 281

Geoffrey P. Miller, *Independent Agencies*, 1986 SUP. CT. REV. 41 — 282

Peter M. Shane, *Independent Policymaking and Presidential Power: A Constitutional Analysis*, 57 GEO. WASH. L. REV. 596 (1989) — 296

Peter L. Strauss, *The Place of Agencies in Government: Separation of Powers and the Fourth Branch*, 84 COLUM. L. REV. 573 (1984) — 300
Additional Sources — 311

b. The Parliamentary Critique of the Separation of Powers — 313

Lloyd N. Cutler, *To Form a Government, in* SEPARATION OF POWERS: DOES IT STILL WORK? 1 (Robert A. Goldwin & Art Kaufman eds., 1986) — 314

Thomas O. Sargentich, *The Limits of the Parliamentary Critique of the Separation of Powers*, 34 WM. & MARY L. REV. 679 (1993) — 321
Addtional Sources — 334

Part III Other Major Controversies About the Role of Courts Implicating Competing Visions of Administrative Legitimacy — 335

A. The Controversy About the Reviewability of Agency Decisionmaking — 335

Ronald M. Levin, *Understanding Unreviewability in Administrative Law*, 74 MINN. L. REV. 689 (1990) — 336
Additional Sources — 344

x CONTENTS

B. The Controversy About the Plaintiff's Standing to Sue an Agency   **345**

Antonin Scalia, *The Doctrine of Standing as an Essential Element of the Separation of Powers*, 17 Suffolk U. L. Rev. 881 (1983)   347

Cass R. Sunstein, *What's Standing After* Lujan? *Of Citizen Suits, "Injuries," and Article III*, 91 Mich. L. Rev. 163 (1992)   349

William A. Fletcher, *The Structure of Standing*, 98 Yale L.J. 221 (1988)   360

Gene R. Nichol, Jr., *Rethinking Standing*, 72 Cal. L. Rev. 68 (1984)   363

Additional Sources   366

C. The Controversy About Agency Nonacquiescence to Judicial Rulings   **367**

Samuel Estreicher and Richard L. Revesz, *Nonacquiescence by Federal Administrative Agencies*, 98 Yale L.J. 679 (1989)   368

Matthew Diller and Nancy Morawetz, *Intracircuit Nonacquiescence and the Breakdown of the Rule of Law: A Response to Estreicher and Revesz*, 99 Yale L.J. 801 (1990)   377

Additional Sources   381

D. The General Controversy About the Role of Courts in Administrative Law   **382**

Keith Werhan, *The Neoclassical Revival in Administrative Law*, 44 Admin. L. Rev. 567 (1992)   383

R. Shep Melnick, *Administrative Law and Bureaucratic Reality*, 44 Admin. L. Rev. 245 (1992)   392

Additional Sources   396

Part IV Competing Theoretical Perspectives on the Administrative Process   **397**

George J. Stigler, *The Theory of Economic Regulation*, 2 Bell J. of Econ. & Mgmt. Sci. 3 (1971)   399

Mark Seidenfeld, *A Civic Republican Justification for the Bureaucratic State*, 105 Harv. L. Rev. 1511 (1992)   404

Gerald E. Frug, *The Ideology of Bureaucracy in American Law*, 97 Harv. L. Rev. 1276 (1984)   412

Thomas O. Sargentich, *The Reform of the American Administrative Process: The Contemporary Debate*, 1984 Wis. L. Rev. 385   432

Additional Sources   450

Preface

Administrative law—the study of general legal norms governing federal agency structures, procedures, and powers—is in a period of considerable intellectual ferment. This anthology's chief purpose is to capture central elements of that ferment. The compilation reflects the premise that a full understanding of administrative law requires more than an exposure to particular cases, for throughout the field the doctrine is deeply affected by competing visions of law and government.

This collection of recent writings is designed as a supplement for a basic course in administrative law, in which it can provide general perspectives to enrich classroom analysis. It also should be useful for specialized courses or seminars. Moreover, it is intended for others—including judges, practitioners, and students of public administration or government—who are interested in major controversies about administrative law in the United States.

This book of readings covers nineteen key topics, as follows:

- the delegation doctrine;
- statutory interpretation in general;
- judicial deference to agencies' statutory interpretations;
- procedural due process;
- nonlegislative rule exemptions from notice-and-comment rulemaking;
- alternative dispute resolution in the administrative context;
- comprehensive regulatory analysis;
- hard-look judicial review;
- Freedom of Information Act debates;
- the legislative veto;
- congressional oversight of agencies;
- presidential review of agency rulemaking;
- the constitutional position of administrative agencies;
- the parliamentary critique of the separation of powers;
- reviewability;
- the plaintiff's standing to sue;
- agency nonacquiescence to judicial rulings;
- the general role of courts in administrative law; and
- competing theoretical perspectives on the administrative process.

To be sure, other subjects could usefully be included in an anthology of this sort; their exclusion is due primarily to the constraint of space.

Let me add a few words about classroom usage. The nineteen sections are self-contained and can be assigned in a variety of sequences. The collection can supplement any administrative law casebook, and it can be used without a casebook. To aid the reader, introductions highlight some of the themes of each section. Moreover, lists of additional sources are provided for those wishing to do further work on a topic.

Thanks are due to the authors and publishers whose work is excerpted here. Thanks also are owed to colleagues who provided helpful comments, including Peter Shane, Geoffrey Miller, Robert Vaughn, Gary Edles, and Charles Tiefer; my administrative law students and my student research assistants, especially Eva Loser and Pamela Strauss; as well as Robert Kelso and others in the Washington College of Law Secretariat.

I hope that readers will send me their comments and suggestions. Intellectual life at its best involves an ongoing dialogue.

Thomas O. Sargentich [*]

---

[*] Business Address: Washington College of Law, American University, 4400 Massachusetts Ave., N.W., Washington, D.C. 20016; Phone: 202-885-2614; Fax: 202-885-3601; e-mail: Sargenti@PostOffice.WCL.American.Edu.

Part I

Major Controversies Implicating the Dominant Rule of Law Vision of Administrative Legitimacy

A. Controversies About Substantive Legal Limits on Agencies

1. The Debate About Reviving the Delegation Doctrine

The delegation doctrine requires Congress to provide intelligible principles in statutes empowering agencies to act. The Supreme Court has not imposed a demanding version of the doctrine since the 1930s. For years, however, some critics have called on the Court to revitalize the delegation principle as a serious constitutional check on Congress.

Professor Theodore Lowi, a political scientist, became well-known for taking this view in his book, *The End of Liberalism*. In the first excerpt below, Professor Lowi again calls for the doctrine's revival. He associates the existence of extremely broad delegations to agency bureaucrats with what he calls "derangements" in the American political system. He also criticizes legal scholars such as Professor Stewart—whose excerpt follows Professor Lowi's—who oppose the delegation doctrine's renewal.

Professor Richard Stewart, in contrast, urges that broad delegations provide the flexibility that agencies need in order to do their jobs. He also questions whether the courts are the appropriate decisionmaking bodies to determine the necessary degree of specificity in statutes. In Professor Stewart's eyes, the chief problem with the modern regulatory system is not the existence of broad delegations, but is rather an undue emphasis on centralized regulatory power that, he believes, would be made worse by the delegation doctrine's revival. Professor Stewart contends that centralization of regulatory power leads to rigidities, excessive costs, and inefficiencies in the relations between the government and social and economic actors. He supports reconstitutive strategies that would shift power to states and localities as well as rely more on market forces than on centralized prescriptive regulations.

In my piece commenting on Professors Lowi and Stewart, I situate their remarks in a broader context of ongoing debates involving competing ideals of administrative legitimacy. Professor Lowi's position, I suggest, implicates a rule of law ideal that, however difficult it is to achieve, has considerable normative force in our administrative state. Professor Stewart's piece, on the other hand, borrows elements of competing ideals focusing on economic and political visions of regulatory legitimacy. I suggest that aspects of a public purposes ideal and a democratic process ideal are implicated in Professor Stewart's critique. More generally, I argue that those seeking to revive the delegation doctrine, and those opposing it, are unlikely to persuade one another because they tap into such fundamentally clashing yet powerful justificatory theories.

In the final excerpt, Professor Jerry Mashaw offers an overview of the revival literature, including work by Professor Lowi and others. Professor Mashaw organizes the revival position in terms of two claims: first, that broad delegations tend to delegitimate the administrative process and, second, that they foster welfare-reducing behavior. After criticizing these claims, Professor Mashaw asks how one would make an affirmative case for broad delegations. He suggests that such delegations may, strangely enough as he puts it, be a mechanism for enhancing the government's responsiveness to the public. This argument depends on the notion that the president has more power in a system with generous delegations than in one with narrow delegations, given the president's role as chief executive and thus as overseer of agency policymaking. To that extent, broad delegations can be said, Professor Mashaw suggests, to improve the potential for electoral wishes to be imposed on governmental bureaucratic organizations. In making this argument, Professor Mashaw raises major issues in a larger debate about the role of the president in the administrative process.*

---

* The topic of presidential oversight of agency rulemaking is discussed in section II.B.3 below.

Theodore J. Lowi, *Two Roads to Serfdom: Liberalism, Conservatism and Administrative Power*, 36 AM. U. L. REV. 295, 297-312, 314-18, 321-22 (1987)*

* * *

As I began arguing twenty years ago, liberalism was undoing itself not because its policy goals would alienate the American people but because its failure to appreciate that the constitutional and political limitations inherent in broad delegation would interfere with their attainment of those policy goals by contributing to the impression and the reality of patronage, with privilege and private goods going not to the deserving but to the best organized. The reasoning was that: every delegation of discretion away from electorally-responsible levels of government to professional career administrative agencies is a calculated risk because politics will always flow to the point of discretion * * *.

Such arguments in the 1960s were largely disregarded or ridiculed as unrealistic. The biggest horse laugh was given to the idea of considering the revival of the [*A.L.A. Schechter Poultry Corp. v. United States*] rule. Consequently, government by broad and undefined delegated discretionary power was given a forty-year test. As liberal programs advanced toward completion of the New Deal agenda, so did the breadth of delegated discretion. My 1969 critique coincided with the first year of a five-year binge in the enactment of important regulatory policies. Depending on who is doing the counting, an argument can be made that Congress enacted more regulatory programs in the five years between 1969 and 1974 than during any other comparable period in our history, including the first five years of the New Deal. It is possible to identify 130 major regulatory laws enacted during the decade of 1969-79. Moreover, an even stronger argument can be made that the regulatory policies adopted during that period were broader in scope and more unconditional in delegated discretion than any other programs in American history.

What makes this epoch of policy creativity all the more significant is that the national government during that decade was comprised of two right-of-center Republican administrations and one Democratic administration elected on an explicit anti-Washington campaign. Yet, most of the votes for these programs in the House and the Senate were overwhelmingly favorable, with dissents coming from both parties. Although there was occasional grumbling heard from the White House, no important bills passed by Congress were vetoed by these three presidents.

In other words, the goals and methods, and the broad, virtually unconditional delegations of power were supported by strong, bipartisan consensus. Moreover, no evidence can be found that opposition to any of these programs included arguments about unduly or dangerously broad delegations of power. Thus, those who rose then and rise now to defend delegated legislative power have had their way. Also, oblivious to the consequences that might flow from broad delegation, the lawyers and the policy makers would naturally search for other explanations when the collapse of regulatory government came. And it did come, at the very time of the regulation binge itself. I recognize that many factors may have contributed to the constitutional derangements observed here; but this in no way reduces the possibility of the causal linkage between these derangements and the rise of delegated power.

I. Constitutional Derangement and the Delegation of Power

A. From Congressional to Presidential Government

In the 1880s, political science professor Woodrow Wilson characterized American national government as "congressional government," and he published an important book under that title. At some point toward the end of the 1930s, a book characterizing American national government as "presidential government" would have been equally appropriate. Recognized by virtually all, and embraced by most, the rise of presidential government has been explained by any number of factors, ranging from the growth of the large economy to the expansion of the media of mass communication. But the factor most immediately and obviously involved in the transformation from congressional to presidential government was the voluntary, self-conscious rendering of legislative power to the President, thence to the agencies in the executive branch. I call the process "legiscide."

The conversion to presidential government directly contributed to the transformation of national politics, broadly defined. The most noticeable aspect of that was the decline of national political parties and their loss of control of the presidency. The transition can be understood as one from party democracy to mass democracy, where consent is conveyed

---

* Reprinted with permission of the American University Law Review and Theodore J. Lowi. All rights reserved.

not merely by election but by regular plebiscite, expressed in weekly and monthly public opinion polls. The center of initiative has become the presidency, the center of gravity has become the executive branch, and the focus of expectations on the part of the American people follows accordingly.

B. Undermining the Welfare State Consensus

The last of the great expansions of the welfare state, Supplemental Security Income and the indexing of social security benefits on top of a twenty-percent boost in those benefits, occurred in 1972. These were followed within a year by official recognition of a fiscal crisis in the welfare state. The problem was less one of financing, however, than of political support. There had been considerable political support for medicare and medicaid, adopted in 1965. There had been initial support for the boost in social security benefits and for indexing pegged to the cost of living. But over the years after 1965, many corporate and middle class supporters of welfare were one-by-one jumping ship, despite the fact that many of the expansions of the welfare state had been aimed at benefiting the middle classes themselves. They were jumping ship largely because of the welfare programs of Aid to Families with Dependent Children, public assistance, welfare-in-kind, and other "means tested" programs associated with the War on Poverty. Why? Because these were discretionary welfare programs, in contrast to the first several social security titles adopted after 1935, which were relatively nondiscretionary.

The abandonment of the relatively clear categoric criteria of the original social security titles in favor of the highly discretionary, open-ended approach of the newer programs contributed to grievous insecurity among the very persons that welfare sought to assist, cut a deep wedge between the minority poor and city hall, and alienated large segments of formerly middle class supporters. During the 1970s, it became *de rigeur* to attack the welfare state. Ironically, efforts to establish welfare as a right were coming just in the wake of the successful efforts to render the very concept of welfare increasingly vague.

C. Undermining Regulation

To a great extent, the undermining of the welfare categories contributed to the undermining of regulation because the problems with welfare were the most important reasons for the binge of regulatory programs and the vast expansion of the scope of each. Regulatory programs adopted in this period have been referred to as "social regulation," for the very good reason that they had to be society-wide in scope in order to control the costs of the welfare state. Cost containment in welfare can only go so far by such things as controlling rate charges and cleansing the welfare roles of chiselers. If the welfare state assumes responsibility for indemnifying all injuries and the dependencies attributable to them, then a maximum effort had to be made to reduce cost by reducing the number of injuries themselves. This meant more regulation. In each instance, the purpose was good; an ounce of prevention may be worth a pound of cure. But legislation merely ordaining a desired goal was bound to undermine the process itself. Demands for remedies escalated from demands for relief against specific conduct to demands for the general outcome itself as a collective right—not a right asserted by an individual to a specific remedy for a specified act of damage, but a generalized "class action" right to the safe water, the safe machine, etc.

D. Interest-Group Liberalism, Continued

The long established pattern of officially sponsored interest group access and representation in agency decisionmaking processes continued, but with some new twists in the 1970s. New groups, emerging in what is now called the new politics or public interest politics, achieved close coalitional relationships with some agencies, especially the new regulatory agencies with the broadest discretion. Many of the new groups adopted a "politics of rights," attempting to put their own interests in a safe position beyond the access of majoritarian politics. This was not an illogical development and in fact was a predictable one, considering that all legislation tends to convey some rights to some and the new, broad "goals statutes" convey some rights absolutely. Although this gave some agencies an adversarial environment that they had not before had, the general pattern of privileged relations between groups and agencies continued, and so did the declining consensus for regulation itself. There were no regular political forces or processes in the national government that had the capacity of regularly pushing interest groups back toward the more public and generalized legislative process, where confrontations and competition among groups might tend to contribute to the self-regulation of which Madison spoke so longingly in *The Federalist No. 10*.

E. Derangements in the Judiciary

Widespread and generally critical references to activist courts and the imperial judiciary are entirely misleading. The federal courts have been activist, perhaps imperial, but only in regard to state actions. At the national government level, virtually the reverse is true. As national executive power has grown and federal agencies have grown larger as well as more numerous, the federal courts have acted as though they are seeking to maintain their power as a coordinate branch of government by joining, supplementing, and generally embracing agency powers—often by pushing agencies beyond where agency chiefs want to go and by pushing agencies to act more vigorously than agency chiefs wish to act. Relaxation of the rules of standing to sue and the filing of class action suits seem to me to be as often as not motivated by willingness to accommodate new politics groups who are seeking to push agencies more vigorously in a direction of statutory obligations. There may be a few instances where federal courts resist federal agencies, but the fact remains that this resistance has rarely been articulated at the level of constitutional discourse. The federal courts follow the rule of statutory construction that will render the statute constitutional, and then they proceed to interpret the statute in order to help dispose of the issues brought forth in the case being litigated. The logic of this situation is generally to expand agency powers because in most instances, especially involving social regulation, the terms of the delegation from Congress to the agency are so broad, containing such high-flown rhetoric about the goals, that any but an expansive interpretation would be contrary to the spirit of the statute. Among other things, this leads me to ask a very important question of commentators such as Professor Richard Stewart: Why is a court that is competent to interpret existing statutes and to develop rules from its decisions within the context of this broadly and ill-defined statute institutionally incompetent to judge the absence of enforceable rules in the statute? And why is it politically more acceptable and less hazardous for judges to create an operational statute out of an empty legislative enactment than it is for judges to state honestly and forthrightly that the original statute is too empty to permit judges to enforce it?

F. Derangement of Agency Professionalism

The derangement of agency professionalism takes two paradoxical forms. First, substantive specialization and the reputation for professional judgment are displaced by formula decisionmaking, formalistic analysis, and the appearance of theoretical science. Second, law is replaced by economics as the language of the state. The delegation of power from the legislature is not merely a straightforward grant of authority to an agency. It is that and more. The language of these broad statutes is a systems language, a language that attempts to incorporate all of the variables that characterize the problem and might tend to explain the existence of the problem and provide a lead toward a solution of the problem. We talk about a systems analysis today as though that were an established fact and a phenomenon capable of being analyzed. In fact, a system is a figment of imagination, an artifact of someone's theory. This has become so much a part of our thinking that it takes on the appearance of reality and loses its connection with the hypothetical and, basically, the mysterious. Embracing the system as the universe of analysis led policy makers to think of regulation as embracing that entire system. This imposed upon the perspective of the law maker and the administrator a complexity beyond human capacity * * *. * * *

* * *

Although some skeptical scholars * * * have tried to demonstrate the limits of formal reasoning in policymaking, the science/technology methodologies, ranging from aggregate quantitative indices and benefit-cost analysis to zero-based budgeting are replacing the very professional judgments for which Congress claims to be so respectful when it leaves its statutes so inadequately constructed. The involvement of science/technology as a decisionmaking methodology can be explained in part by America's faith in science and technology. However, another important part of the explanation is that the provision for science/technology methodology *tends to compensate for the absence of legal integrity*. Once a systems concept is combined with general, aggregate, theoretical science with generalized cookbook decisionmaking formulas, the boundaries of agencies are surpassed or eradicated, as the case may be. At this point, who needs the agency at all? To whom is the legislative authority being delegated? Or, I should ask, to *what* is agency authority being delegated?

G. Derangement of Procedure

There has been an important transition from procedure to proceduralism. * * * Just as Congress has relied upon science/technology, so Congress also has used procedure as an effort to compensate for the absence of legal integrity in its legislative draftmanship. On the eve of the 1970s regulatory policy binge, the leading student of administrative law, Kenneth Culp Davis, observed that broad administrative discretion is unavoidable, but that safeguards are available, thereby making administrative discretion desirable, as long as discretion is "guided by administrative rules adopted through procedure like that prescribed by the federal Administrative. Procedure

Act." That is the classic rationalization for broad delegations and poor legislative drafting.

It is certainly better to have procedure than to have nothing. But a closer look at the politics of Congress' adoption of regulatory policies will reveal that there are at least four other reasons why procedures are provided and why, in the period of the regulation binge, procedures went *well beyond* the requirements of the Administrative Procedure Act (APA). First, as already suggested, the procedural provisions that go well beyond the APA are adopted to compensate for unconstitutionally vague and unguided delegations of power. Second, certain kinds of procedures are adopted to open access to agency decisionmaking in order to co-opt citizens and to add legitimacy to their processes. Although some observers are dubious that broad delegations of legislative power to administrative agencies endanger legitimacy, Congress and the agencies themselves operate as though that is a real problem, and both go out of their way to use procedure to shore up legitimacy with the various organized constituencies. Third, and closely related to the second, procedures that provide for easy access and participation by citizens and groups to the rulemaking process enable officials to encourage or channel citizens and groups into the administrative process rather than to pursue the same issues prematurely in a court. This procedure-laden rulemaking process has had a significant impact on interest group politics, shifting more and more of it from the lobbies of Congress to the corridors of agencies. We need a new word for the administrative equivalent to lobbying. I propose "corridoring." Fourth, and finally, many of the procedural provisions that go beyond the APA are proposed by *opponents* of the legislation in order to reduce the effectiveness of the programs themselves.

For all of these reasons, the time span of agency decisionmaking, from the moment a rule is proposed to the point where it is adopted and published in the *Federal Register* is now exceeding an average of thirty-five months. This is used in the arguments against the legitimacy and efficiency of administrative agencies when in fact a good part of that decisionmaking span is attributable to the deliberate, strategic antagonistic or dilatory imposition of procedures.

H. Derangement of Presidential Power

Presidential government was a direct and immediate product of the 1930s delegations of power from Congress. The development of the office in practice and in theory took longer, although it began in 1937 with the appeal of the President's Committee on Administrative Management whose second sentence was "[t]he President needs help." Help was forthcoming, to such an extent that observers were very soon referring to the "institutional presidency" and to management as an essential feature of the presidency. It did not stop there, and it has not stopped since that time. Every president has said, or has appointed a commission to say for him, that the president continues to need help; and every president has gotten virtually all the help he has asked for, without eliminating any of the innovations and additions inherited from his predecessors.

Presidential power has been given the stamp of approval by scholarly and journalistic experts and also by the Supreme Court. One of the greatest sources of derangement has been from the scholars, many of whom stepped forward in the 1940s, '50s and '60s to proclaim that the presidency was not only part of democratic theory, but was a superior form of democracy to democracy based upon the legislature. In effect, the presidency represents the "real majority." This view was reflected in decisions of the Supreme Court. Even in the historic steel seizure case, although the Supreme Court denied President Truman's claim that the president had inherent powers to seize the steel mills, the justices otherwise actually strengthened the presidential power by the dictum that the president could very probably have succeeded in the seizure if he had claimed the authority to do so under an existing statute.

Another important case, *United States v. Nixon,* also advanced presidential power while appearing to delimit it. The court rejected President Nixon's claim to executive privilege as a constitutional protection against delivery of the Watergate tapes; but at the same time, the court stated only that the claim to executive privilege did not protect documents from a subpoena in a criminal prosecution. In all other instances, such as when there is a specific need to protect military, diplomatic, or sensitive national security secrets, executive privilege for the presidency was a privilege—qualified, but nonetheless a privilege.

The constitutional basis of presidential power was advanced again in 1983 when the Supreme Court declared the legislative veto unconstitutional. The purpose of this device, which Congress had applied to 295 provisions in 196 laws, was to take back in bits and pieces what Congress had given away since the 1930s in increasingly large chunks of delegated legislative power. Although not of fundamental importance, the decision tipped the balance between the two branches still further toward the presidency. * * *

This suggests that both Congress and the Court,

having respectively granted and approved the enormous delegations of discretion in a long series of enactments and decisions, have locked themselves into a kind of imperative to grant additional powers, constitutional validation, and ideological embrace to the presidency in order to accomplish the impossible task of meeting the obligations that the statutes impose. If lawyers would spend half as much time expressing concern over the impossibility of presidential control of administrative agencies as they do on the impossibility of Congress' formulating decent rules of law, both presidential control and congressional lawmaking would improve immeasurably.

II. The Conservative Reaction

As predicted in 1969, liberalism was eventually its own undoing, and a major, if not the major, contribution to its shrinking consensus. Liberalism's electoral collapse was due to the structure of its laws, the increasingly discretionary character of its administrative agencies, and the disappointment and indignation that arose out of frustrated expectations built on high-flown rhetoric about collective rights to statutory goals. There were actually two reactions to liberal excesses. One was libertarianism and the other conservativism. Libertarians and conservatives made common cause against big national government. Both sought to make the domestic part of the government smaller, especially in the area of the regulatory agencies. The two reactions, however, are far from identical.

The libertarian reaction was a genuine demand for deregulation. Libertarians are the descendents of the 19th century, free-market liberals, and had been screaming, pretty much in the wilderness, against all forms of government intervention since the 1930s. The size and strength of the libertarian critique did not really begin to grow until the liberalism of the New Deal was already in a virtual shambles in the 1970s. The growth of the popularity of the libertarian position must be attributed more to the failure of New Deal liberalism than to the strength of the libertarian position itself. * * *

* * *

* * * Contrary to the expectations of most people, there was more real deregulation in the four years of the Carter administration than in the [first] six years of the Reagan administration, up until the time of this writing. President Reagan has not once confronted Congress with requests for legislation actually terminating any regulatory authority. * * * Instead, the Reagan administration has sought and has taken on significant increases in managerial power. President Reagan has sought to use this managerial power to reduce the regulatory burden not by terminating or shrinking any of the authority now held in the executive branch, but by retaining the power and using it to control the agencies so as to reduce or delay the output of rules. The difference here is quite significant and is consonant with the history of the growth of executive power. President Reagan can reduce significantly the level and intensity of government intervention while leaving the *capacity for intervention* intact for himself and his successors. * * *

* * *

III. The Two Roads to Serfdom

The governmental and political institutions shaped during the nearly fifty years between 1933 and 1981 have not been put under siege by the first serious alternative to liberalism this century. Whatever the "Reagan Revolution" may amount to as a change of policy direction, it will not amount to a revolution against liberal institutions because nothing about the Reagan Revolution was aimed at the overly powerful presidency, the mass base of the presidency, the peripheral (albeit occasionally pesky) Congress, the discretionary agencies, or the cooperative courts.

President Reagan has for at least two very compelling reasons accepted the liberal national institutions. First, they suit him. The presidency was already a star system before it got its first star. Reagan's conservatism should have led him to resist and to try to tone down if not to decentralize the vulgar, mass democracy of the plebiscitary presidency and the immense size and power of the executive branch. As a conservative, President Reagan should have wanted to bring it down to human proportion. But genuine conservatives also need a bully pulpit; and if it happens to have been built by liberalism, so be it.

This points to the second reason why this genuinely conservative administration has embraced liberal institutions. This is simply that conservatives are *not* libertarians. Conservatives need a solid structure, just as modern liberals do, but a structure with a different orientation. George F. Will, one of the few writers who grasps the difference between conservatism and libertarianism made the point best. Conservatives have no interest, Will points out, in dismantling the strong national government. Rather, according to Will, they believe in strong government, "including the essentials of the welfare state." Conservatives, however, in Will's view, reject liberal "uncertainty about. . . human nature . . . ." In other words, Will argues, "statecraft" must attempt "soulcraft." Let there be regulatory policy—but for the purpose of restoring moral hegemony to traditional elites. Let there be welfare policy—but for the primary purpose of teaching the moral lessons required to bring the poor and self-indulgent classes into the realm of proper comportment within proper authority. Justice William Rehnquist * * * is the correct personification of the Reagan administration: the free market comes second to a strong state capable of exercising moral leadership, moral education, moral mobilization, and moral authority.

Because 1980s conservatives need a large discretionary state as much as the liberals, there is at present no constituency for the rule of law. Interest group liberals have been impatient to get on with goals defined by sentiment and by the claims of the best organized groups. New politics groups are most concerned with getting a favorable administrative environment. Conservative groups seek economic goals for the national government and moral hegemony for their new federalism. But why should that be otherwise? The surprising thing is that the legal experts offer no counterpoise. In their struggle for the power they have enjoyed as a profession throughout most of their history, lawyers have joined the flow rather than fight or shape it. Defense of the rule of law by old fashioned lawyers and older liberals was wiped away as a mask for the status quo. Legal realists debunked the rule of law as a mere rationalization for private values. * * * [M]ainstream legal scholars hammer more nails in the coffin of the rule of law by providing reasoned arguments for why the effort to establish the rule of law, especially in legislative drafting, is unrealistic, unnecessary, counterproductive, and, in some instances, downright undesirable.

Let us take Stewart's position [which is enunciated in the immediately following excerpt] as an illustrative (and illustrious) case in point. First, to make his case for broad delegation, Stewart posits a false dichotomy: Congress cannot "write detailed commands" or "precise rules of conduct," *therefore*, broad and undefined delegation is the only alternative. Stewart then adds to this a second false dichotomy: federal courts are not "institutionally competent" to "invalidate wholesale" congressional statutes, *therefore*, broad delegation to administrative agencies is not only desirable but unreviewable. That is, the judiciary, for reasons not given, would have to condemn entire statutes on the grounds that the policies are too important to be left to administrators or that such delegations are not necessary and proper, and because this would "usurp judgments which we as a nation have concluded ever since 1937 ought to be resolved through political mechanisms . . .," *therefore*, courts must not review the propriety of a delegation at all.

It is inexplicably ideological not to examine any middle points or other alternatives. Stewart leaves no room whatsoever for a bad first effort to be improved by successive efforts, unless he believes that Congress cannot learn from the experience of the administrative agencies in trying to implement the vague first effort at lawmaking. Good legislation ought to be a matter of successive approximations—through later amendments, and, best of all, through codification. Stewart, like so many others, apologizes for congressional incompetence by telling us how busy Congress is already (doing what?), and by telling us how much more complex our society is today. Because no data or arguments are given to support such an apology, it remains in the realm of pure ideology. In fact, to the state legislators of the 1840s, society must have seemed immeasurably more complex than ours is to us today. They were, after all, living in the midst of the Industrial Revolution; there was not yet any established economic theory of capitalism, no clear grasp of fractional reserve banking or insurance, and, according to the legal historians I read, even the tort law was only barely emerging. Meanwhile, there was less continuity among legislators and less education. They had less staff and a smaller budget with which to buy expertise and research. There were also problems such as greater party domination and more corruption. Yet, there was much more legal integrity in the average statute produced by the state legislatures of the 1840s than in the average statute coming out of Congress today.

Turn now to that part of the apology where Stewart and others argue that it is next to impossible to formulate good rules of law for such a "vast and varied nation." The fact is that *proposals* for legislation are usually very clear and provide a very sound basis for articulating a general rule. When organized interest groups come before Congress, they tend to know exactly what they want and can generalize their wants into a rule that would be clearly understood and applicable to a known category of people or conduct. It is true that the rules they would have Congress adopt tend to be much too self-serving and often patently contrary to the public interest. It is the job of Congress to take these proposals and to work out compromises with the various contrary and conflicting proposals until a majority is ready to vote final passage. Thus, the burning question here is not why Congress is unable to formulate legislation with clear rules, but why Congress, in the process of compromise, takes proposals that embody clear rules and turns them into the vague and meaningless delegations of power that apologists call inevitable. All of this gives the ring of eternal verity to the observation that "those who love laws and sausages would do well not to watch either one being made." * * *

* * *

Conclusion

* * *

Serfdom is a condition of dependency on patronage. Patronage in the medieval sense, as in "to patronize," is a relationship between holders of resources (patrons) and seekers of resources (clients), where the holders have the discretion or power to share their resources—material goods or privileges—on a personal basis. This can be in response to meritorious personal claims, or on a personal basis where the patron seeks to recruit the client's loyalty or the general reputation for virtue or goodwill. In our modern context, patronage remains the same. It includes, however, a great deal more that has been governmentalized. The greater the discretion that accompanies the delegation of power, the greater the capacity of agencies to become patrons because the discretion enables them to convert regulatory or welfare policies into resources for group or individual patronage.

The antidote to government by patronage is not termination of the policies or the agencies, but *reduction of their discretion*. Otherwise, conservatism and liberalism speak to each other with nothing better than alternative roads to serfdom. * * *

Richard B. Stewart, *Beyond Delegation Doctrine*, 36 AM. U. L. REV. 323, 326, 328-43 (1987)*

* * *

For the courts to invalidate wholesale congressional statutes on the basis of judicial conclusions that the issues of policy left statutorily unresolved are too important to be delegated to administrators, or that such delegations are not "necessary and proper" and are therefore politically irresponsible, is to usurp judgments that we as a nation have concluded ever since 1937 ought to be resolved through political mechanisms of representative government. The courts have refused to second guess legislative decisions on the appropriate extent of delegation for the same reasons that they properly have refused to second guess political decisions on the scope of the commerce power or the content of the general welfare on which the federal government's taxing and spending powers rest. Contrary to Dean Ely, the moribund state of the delegation doctrine since 1937 is not a case of "death by association."* It reflects the same basic institutional conclusions that have led the courts to renounce other forms of general superintendency over social and economic legislation.

* * *

Even if workable judicial doctrine could be formulated, vigorous enforcement of the delegation doctrine would be undesirable for a variety of reasons, including the fact that detailed decisionmaking often is done more responsibly by executive officials (subject to hearing requirements and judicial review) than by legislators. Rather than repeating the reasons why I continue to adhere to these conclusions, I will use them as the starting point for a new thesis: the delegation problem is created, in large part, by the federal government's reliance on prescriptive strategies of centralized regulation. The "command and control" approach to regulation exerts enormous strain on decisional and political capacities at the center. Vigorous application of the delegation doctrine * * * is likely to increase rather than relieve this strain. Delegation doctrine merely focuses on a symptom: congressional delegation to administrators of the power to formulate central directives. Instead, we should focus on the underlying problem of excessive reliance on centralized directives to legislate conduct throughout a vast and varied nation. This reliance on centralized directives inevitably produces policy dysfunctions and political irresponsibility regardless of whether the directives are formulated by federal administrators, federal legislators or, indeed, federal judges.

In some areas, the cure for the present excess of central prescription is outright deregulation. In many other areas, however, we cannot rely on the market or on state and local government to meet important societal needs. As developed below, new reconstitutive strategies of regulation are appropriate in these areas. Adoption of these strategies will require major new federal legislation. The ultimate solution to the

---

* Reprinted with permission of the American University Law Review and Richard B. Stewart. All rights reserved.

* Professor John H. Ely, Jr. (formerly dean), in DEMOCRACY AND DISTRUST 133 (1980), associated the moribund status of the delegation doctrine with the death of the substantive due process approach of the pre-1937 era—hence, "death by association."

delegation problem thus lies with the political branches, not with constitutional adjudication in the courts.

II. The Transactional and Political Overload Generated by Centralized Prescription

It is no accident that the revival of interest in the delegation doctrine in recent years has coincided with a sweeping expansion of centralized federal command and control regulation. We have become addicted to federal rules and orders that attempt to minutely prescribe conduct throughout our complexly differentiated society. This addiction has created severe decisionmaking and political overload at the center. In turn, overload has resulted in a massive transfer of decisional power to federal administrative bureaucracies, provoking calls for vigorous enforcement by the courts of the delegation doctrine in order to restore "juridical democracy."*

For the past several decades we as a nation have relied increasingly on centralized command and control regulation to achieve national goals of social and economic justice. This reliance has created serious institutional strains. One is peculiar to Congress. Faced with a crowded agenda and relatively high costs of reaching agreement on specific measures, Congress has often delegated the formulation of regulatory commands to federal administrators. Such delegation, however, cannot cure the more general institutional problems involved in reliance on centralized directives to achieve national goals.

We are a vast, varied, and dynamic nation composed of many diverse institutions, including state and local governments, corporations and labor unions, and a huge variety of nonprofit religious, educational, charitable, social, and advocacy organizations. Central formulation of rules and orders to control in detail conduct within these diverse institutions involves exorbitant information-gathering and decisionmaking costs. These costs are especially severe in the case of the various environmental, health, safety, and antidiscrimination "social" regulatory programs that have arisen during the past two decades. Such programs seek wholesale change throughout the entire society, in contrast to earlier "economic" regulation which was often limited to particular industries such as banking, transportation, or communications.

The officials responsible for implementing these comprehensive, centralized programs of command and control regulation have sought to reduce the high costs of making decisions by using rulemaking to adopt relatively crude and uniform prescriptions. Central decision makers would face intolerable burdens if they sought to adjust general commands to the individual circumstances of each actor in each regulated business firm or other organization. Standardized, inflexible prescriptions, however, are bound to be excessively costly, burdensome, impractical, or simply irrational in many particular applications, creating widespread resentment on the part of those regulated. On the other hand, the errors and distortions involved in devising and implementing centralized blueprints and their rapid obsolescence often prevent command and control regulation from delivering the swift and sure changes in conduct promised, creating pervasive "implementation gaps" and corresponding resentment on the part of regulatory beneficiaries.

Regulation through centralized directives also creates serious problems of political overload. Under the model of juridical democracy proposed by advocates of the delegation doctrine, Congress itself must formulate the prescriptions governing conduct within regulated organizations. The fundamental principle is that government may not coerce citizens except in accordance with legal authority granted through politically responsible processes of representative government. The importance of this principle has been reinforced by impressive evidence, marshalled by Professor Lowi and others, showing that when Congress has delegated to federal administrators the power to make prescriptive rules, parochial economic and ideological factions often dominate the process through which the delegated power was exercised. * * *

Using the delegation doctrine to restore juridical democracy, however, would not solve these problems and could make them worse. The demands on Congress' agenda far exceed its capacity to make collective decisions. Securing agreement by a majority of 435 representatives, a majority of 100 senators, and the President is typically an arduous, time-consuming, and difficult process. This eighteenth-century legislative procedure is incapable of responsibly making even the more basic of the myriad decisions entailed by a regulatory strategy of centralized prescription. In these circumstances, vigorous enforcement of delegation doctrine would likely produce one of two outcomes.

First, requiring that all regulatory statutes contain detailed rules of conduct would increase substantially the costs and difficulty of legislative agreement and greatly reduce the amount of legislation enacted. Those who view legislation as generally pernicious might welcome this development. * * * [H]owever, this result would represent a sweeping, open-ended,

---

* This term—juridical democracy—is used by Professor Lowi in his book calling for revival of the delegation doctrine. *See* THE END OF LIBERALISM 298-301 (2d ed. 1979).

and institutionally unacceptable judicial veto on the political process.

Second, and in my view much more likely, Congress would respond by subdelegating the legislation function to congressional committees or subcommittees whose decisions would in most cases be ratified with little or no review by the entire Congress. Because the costs of agreement would be lower at the subcommittee level than in Congress as a whole, internal delegation would enable Congress to maintain its legislative output despite the greater specificity required by the courts. * * *

Subdelegation, however, creates serious problems of political responsibility. Decisional power is shifted to congressional subcommittee chairmen and staff and their bureaucratic and interest group allies. Policy is made through a submerged micropolitical process without open and regular procedures. The hazards of subdelegation are apparent already in highly detailed tax or environmental regulatory statutes. * * *

* * *

Does internal delegation to congressional subcommittees produce sounder, more responsible government than delegation to agencies backed by hearing requirements and judicial review? Although I doubt that any firm, general conclusions can be reached, there are good grounds for supposing that internal delegation does not on balance lead to more desirable results. Unlike administrative decisionmaking, subdelegated congressional decisionmaking often is not subject to public input through regularly established procedures. It is not required to be based on a public record, and is not subject to "hard look" judicial review. These requirements are not imposed on legislators because of the supposed efficacy of political checks. These checks, however, are weakened grievously when decisions are made through congressional subdelegation.

It is true * * * that there are difficulties in securing effective representation for weakly organized interests in administrative decisionmaking. Those difficulties, however, apply to legislative decisionmaking with at least equal force. * * *

On the other hand, the courts' use of administrative law to oversee command and control decisionmaking by bureaucrats is no panacea. The transaction costs of the current system of administrative central planning through litigation are enormous, as witnessed by lengthy proceedings, swollen records, and mammoth opinions. Whatever limited capacity might otherwise exist to coordinate the various prescriptions issued by the central government has been sapped by the tendency of the litigation system to deal with each controversy in isolation. Moreover, shifting power to judges and litigants is hardly a promising recipe for enhancing political responsibility.

These problems have led some to favor an increased role for the presidency. * * * Although I am not unsympathetic to such efforts, which would move the United States closer to the practices of other industrialized democracies, I do not believe that they can solve the basic problems of central overload produced by excessive reliance on prescriptive regulation.

OMB has only a limited capacity to evaluate, supervise, and coordinate the myriad specialized decisions made by the ranks of federal agencies. More important, this limited capacity can only be achieved by extensive subdelegation within the institutional presidency. The "Commander-in-Chief" rationale for increased OMB review power is an appealing one. The harsh reality, however, is that the presidency can no more escape the iron law of transaction costs than can Congress. The many specific decisions that must be made by subordinates within OMB and other subunits within the White House are too remote from the attention and commitment of the President and his chief lieutenants, and too vulnerable to real or apparent infection by bureaucratic or interest group parochialism, to provide adequate guarantees of political responsibility for the mass of regulatory commands that continue to gush forth from the Federal Register. OMB review cannot effectively ameliorate the inescapable rigidities, inefficiencies, and inequities involved in attempting to mandate conduct throughout a vast nation through central directives. The only real solution is to forswear our excessive addiction to centralized prescription.

III. Reconstitutive Strategies of Regulation

The delegation dilemmas created by centralized prescription can be greatly alleviated by transferring responsibility for detailed decisionmaking out of the central government to other institutions and organizations such as the market, collective bargaining, or state and local government. Outright deregulation and devolution is one version of this strategy. Deregulation at the federal level has achieved significant success in several areas, including communications and airline transportation. A number of continuing economic regulatory programs, such as agricultural marketing orders, should also be scrapped. As presently constituted, however, the market and the federal system of decentralized state and local government cannot adequately secure important societal goals in such areas as the environment, health, and safety. Command and control regulation by federal officials, whether legislative, executive, or judicial, is the prevailing response to these institutional deficiencies. It is not, however, the only possible response. The alternative is to reconstitute such institutions in order to ensure that national goals are served without detailed central prescription of conduct.

Constitutional law consists of rules that make legally recognized practices possible. Examples of such practices include the making of contracts, the holding of elections, or the adjudication of disputes. Legal and social institutions, such as the market or the federal structure of our government, are composed of such practices. Constitutive rules thus create or establish institutions.

Prescriptive law consists of rules or orders specifying conduct that is prohibited or mandated within the context of a particular practice or institution. Examples of prescriptive law include prohibitions on the misappropriation of trade secrets or the taking by government of private property without just compensation.

Constitutive rules necessarily have prescriptive elements. Prescriptions are needed in order to define and protect constituent endowments, ensure compliance with decisional rules, and limit the jurisdictional authority of the various institutions and organizations that make up the greater society. For example, markets are constituted in important part by prescriptions against theft, duress, and the selling of votes. On the other hand, prescriptive rules are created by constitutive processes, such as those established by contract law or article I of the Constitution.

There remains, however, a key difference between prescriptive and constitutive rules that is of great importance in the choice of strategies to harmonize institutional decisions and national norms. Prescriptive rules specify and dictate required conduct. Accordingly, the use by federal authorities of prescriptive directives inevitably involves preemption of the values of those regulated. Regulated decision makers must act as federal officials direct. Constitutive rules, by contrast, explicitly contemplate and allow institutional decision makers a substantial measure of discretion that permits incorporation of institutional interests and values in their decisions.

Reconstitutive strategies promote institutional adherence to national goals by restructuring the constitutive law of such institutions rather than simply preempting it by dictating outcomes. Such reconstitution may be achieved by altering the definition or allocation of endowments within an institution, changing its decisionmaking rules, or modifying its jurisdictional competence. One option is to retain an institution's existing decisional procedures but modify constituent endowments. For example, innovation within competitive markets can be encouraged by congressional enactment of patent, copyright, and trade-secret laws that create incentives for such innovation. Similarly, the national government may impose a tax on pollution or offer matching grants for specific local services. Another option is to modify institutions' decisionmaking procedures by, for example, adopting a one-person, one-vote rule for state and local elections, requiring administrators to afford hearings to those affected before making decisions, or promoting collective bargaining. As a final option, subsystem jurisdictions may be altered. For example, the areas of economic life governed by markets policed by antitrust laws may be expanded or contracted in relation to competing regimes of regulation or collective bargaining.

Although reconstitutive strategies for promoting national goals are more indirect than command and control regulation, directness is not synonymous with efficacy, as the record of federal antitrust law and labor law demonstrates. Reconstitutive strategies have a number of advantages over prescriptive ones. They reduce centralized information processing overload. Once reconstitution is achieved, most of the relevant decisions are made within subsystems rather than at the center. Reconstitution also avoids the dysfunctional rigidities and uniformities of centralized prescription while furthering decentralization and diversity. Reconstitutive strategies also promote greater political responsibility at the center. By reducing the need for federal officials to prepare and enforce detailed blueprints for conduct, reconstitutive strategies respect the iron law of transaction costs. Rather than being overwhelmed with countless prescriptive details, Congress and the President can assume and exercise responsibility for choosing basic national goals and selecting means of reconstituting subsystems to achieve them.

* * *

* * * [R]econstitutive strategies could be developed to replace the current reliance on centralized directives in federal regulatory programs. For example, the current system of federal command and control regulation of air and water pollution could in large part be replaced by a system of transferable pollution permits. The current system relies on uniform federal rules and implementing orders to dictate the degree of pollution control required of each of hundreds of thousands of sources. Under an alternative reconstitutive strategy, the federal government would determine the maximum amount of pollution permitted in a given region or state. Permits to discharge pollution would be issued in numbers equal to this amount and allocated among pollution sources by auction or otherwise. Thereafter, permits could be bought and sold freely. Each source would be free to decide how much to clean up and how many permits to buy. This flexibility would allow sources that can clean up more cheaply to assume more of the abatement burden, saving society tens of billions of dollars over the existing system of uniform prescription.

The fact that sources would have to pay for the pollution they emit would provide a continuing incentive to develop environmentally superior production and control technologies. Limiting the number of permits issued would ensure that the aggregate pollution emitted by all firms does not exceed the chosen maximum. Future decreases in pollution could be achieved by amortizing the permits on a fixed schedule. By making the air and water property interests created by the existing prescriptive system transferable, this alternative would harness the mechanisms of the market to serve new social concerns. A similar strategy eventually might be developed to deal with other environmental harms, such as the risks created by pesticides, toxic chemicals, and toxic wastes.

Other economic incentive systems, relying either on the creation of new forms of transferable property interests or on taxes or subsidies, have been or could be developed to replace prescriptive controls over commercial activity in such areas as waste treatment and recycling, land and water resource use, employment safety, unemployment, and inflation. New tax or liability rules could be used to discourage socially undesirable conduct, such as the operation of unsafe workplaces. Expanded use of vouchers and similar systems could replace command and control federal regulation in housing, education, health care, and other social service programs.

Economic incentives, moreover, are but one form of reconstitutive strategy. Other forms require or encourage new decisionmaking procedures and structures. Occupational risks provide a case in point. Occupational safety and health regulation by the federal government is thought to be necessary because workers are often poorly informed about occupational hazards and may lack the collective resources and bargaining power to deal effectively with them. Centralized OSHA directives are not, however, the only means of dealing with this problem. The federal government could require employers to disclose information about occupational hazards to workers or undertake the job itself. Employers could be required to hire occupational health and safety professionals, chosen jointly by employers and employees, to monitor risks and correct hazards. Occupational health and safety could be made a mandatory subject of collective bargaining or employment contracts. The current system of labor law could be reconstituted to promote unionization. These steps could well be more effective in reducing workplace hazards than the current patchwork and inherently clumsy system of centralized regulation. They would decentralize decisionmaking responsibility to those most directly affected, enabling employers to choose the most cost-effective means of dealing with hazards and giving workers a collective voice in deciding the appropriate levels of risk in their workplace.

A third reconstitutive approach is to alter the jurisdictional competence of different constitutive legal systems. Deregulation is one example of this approach, replacing administrative governance of particular sectors of the economy with governance by market laws. Straightforward deregulation is an appropriate and desirable form of reconstitution in some sectors. In other sectors, however, economies of scale and other considerations dictate more complex forms of restructuring. * * *

These reconstitutive strategies affirm the need for national initiative to deal with major social and economic problems. Unlike the prevailing reliance on centralized prescription, they respect institutions' legitimate interests in autonomy and reduce overload at the center. Congress' need to delegate decisions to central bureaucracies would be reduced. Detailed implementation decisions would be shifted from federal administrators to business firms, workers, and state and local governments. This shift would greatly reduce the current reliance on adversary processes and judicial review to control the myriad detailed economic, engineering, and scientific decisions made by federal administrators. * * *

Proponents of the delegation doctrine often seem to have assumed that prescription is the only or principal means of regulating conduct. Professor Lowi's demand for "juridical democracy" and "democratic formalism" seems to envisage a statutory universe of detailed prescriptions. * * *

We need broad delegations to achieve national goals. The delegations required by prescriptive regulation, however, are the wrong type of delegation to the wrong people. Rather than giving federal agencies and reviewing courts the responsibility for designing detailed conduct blueprints or subdelegating power within Congress and the presidency, we should give decisional power back to the various decision makers within the various economic, governmental, and social institutions of our society, transmitting the delegation through new structures that will align their decisions with national goals.

Reconstitutive law is not the appropriate means of scrutinizing national objectives in all cases. Prescriptive law is far more appropriate for securing core civil rights, such as the right to be free from racial discrimination. Such rights should be nationally uniform, and are vindicated most appropriately by imposition of correlative legal duties. * * * In still other areas of regulation, such as airline safety, prescriptive regulation may be preferable because it is more reliable and effective than other approaches. But in many other contexts there are opportunities for far greater use of reconstitutive strategies to advance federal regulatory goals.

It will not necessarily be easy to devise and win political support for congressional legislation to eliminate existing prescriptive systems of regulation and adopt reconstitutive alternatives. Increasing congressional reliance over the past two decades on prescriptive strategies is the product of powerful political forces, including the incentives of legislators to use legislation to target benefits to particular interest groups. This targeting often can be achieved most effectively through centralized prescription, rather than more generalized reconstitutive strategies. Regulatory agencies, regulated firms, and environmental and consumer advocacy groups have invested heavily in the prevailing system of regulation. * * * Hard work will be needed to devise and secure the adoption of reconstitutive solutions to the central overload and political irresponsibility generated by our prevailing reliance on command law. The energies of academic lawyers, policy analysts, political scientists, and others should be centered on this task, not on supposed constitutional solutions that, in the end, can solve nothing. Here as elsewhere administrative law must escape its preoccupation with what judges say and do, and embrace a broader perspective and responsibility.

Thomas O. Sargentich, *The Delegation Debate and Competing Ideals of the Administrative Process*, 36 AM. U. L. REV. 419, 423–42 (1987)*

* * *

I. The Rule of Law Ideal of Administration and the Call to Revive the Nondelegation Doctrine

A. *The Rule of Law Ideal and the Nondelegation Doctrine*

The rule of law ideal of administration is a well-known and powerful vision in administrative law and liberal democratic theory. This ideal holds that power should be seen to be restrained by legal norms announced, in particular by the legislature, as much as possible in advance.

To be sure, agencies "make" law as well as policy in any ordinary sense of the meaning of words. In many instances, their formulations have retroactive implications. Yet although agencies make law, their actions under the rule of law ideal are presumed to be grounded in and guided by prior legal norms emanating from statutes and the Constitution. On that basis, the rule of law proponent feels able to urge that legal principles provide the animating authority for, and ultimately constrain the use of, agency power.

As the rule of law's supporters and detractors often point out, a formalist division of the normative universe into "law" and other matters such as politics lies at the center of much traditional theory. The critical idea is not the facially implausible one that somehow law is walled off from, or wholly untainted by, warring moral and political conceptions. Rather, the ideal's main defense relies on the premise that once broader social forces have created a legal regime, as in a statute, it becomes possible to say that reasoning can proceed with reference to the law itself, as distinct from the diverse political forces that generated it. The critical element of such faith is that law has integrity of its own. However difficult the task may be in any given case, the ideal requires that one acknowledge and confirm this integrity in structuring the use of administrative power.

The nondelegation doctrine is directly linked with this key formalist conviction. In essence, the doctrine importantly restates, in the terms of a constitutional precept, the main tenets of the formalist rule of law ideal of administration. The doctrine holds that Congress, as the article I lawmaker, has a basic and nondelegable duty to be the primary source of public legal norms. When agencies "make" law or policy, they generally should be seen to be acting pursuant to some intelligible legal principle emanating from the legislature. If Congress does not fulfill its job by clearly specifying the legal boundaries of agency discretion, the would-be delegation violates the guiding picture of the rule of law, and is unconstitutional.

Thus one can see rather quickly the considerable normative power underlying the principle against overly broad delegations. It does not only reflect a commitment to a separation of powers between the legislative and executive branches. It also resonates deeply with a traditional liberal commitment to the rule of law that seeks to be faithful to the norms of

---

* Reprinted with permission of the American University Law Review and Thomas O. Sargentich. All rights reserved.

consensual decisionmaking. It would be surprising, given such an alliance, for proponents of the nondelegation principle not to take advantage of this association of ideas.

B. The Use of Rule of Law Idealism in Calling for the Nondelegation Doctrine's Revival

One of the most outspoken proponents of the nondelegation doctrine's revival is Theodore Lowi. In his activist defense of the doctrine, he is strikingly explicit in his reliance on the rule of law ideal. This is clear in his classic study, *The End of Liberalism*, which takes a decidedly dim view of tendencies toward fragmentation that pervade the modern American polity. In his book, Lowi explores various institutional and historical factors that contribute to what he sees as the destabilization of American pluralism. One of the chief *bêtes noires* in his story is what he considers to be the unduly open-ended, all-things-to-all-persons character of much modern legislation.

As Lowi writes with evident concern, "the complexity of modern life forces Congress into vagueness and generality in drafting its statutes." Lowi, however, is ultimately undaunted by contemporary realities. He enlists the rhetorical energies of the rule of law in arguing vigorously for judicial rediscovery of the need for rigorous delegations. As he sees it, "the first and most important step" toward a democracy under meaningful guidance by law—which he calls "juridical democracy"—would be the reinvigorated use by the courts of the latent rigors of article I's limit on overbroad delegations.

Lowi's * * * contribution [in the article excerpted above] reaffirms his longstanding faith, even as it seeks to avoid the charge of undue rigidity in its embrace. His critical application to the modern state of the notion of patronage, with its connotations of servility, is a striking case in point. To claim that we risk a life of patronage, rather than of vigorous citizenship, is precisely to call to mind the contrast between dependency on government and independent, self-critical participation in a law-governed polity. What Lowi calls the "governmentalization" of patronage is seen to result in large measure because we have turned over so many diverse social problems to the government for its solution, without constraining its discretion by rules that sufficiently specify what we, as distinct from our public keepers, want done.

Lowi evinces concern about more than general rule of law idealism. Indeed, his discussion touches on a number of phenomena in contemporary American politics—for instance, the growth of the administrative state, the vagueness of legislative directives, the development of a powerful presidency, the fractionalization of power in Congress—in a richly textured portrayal of the complexities, deadlocks, and limits of modern pluralism. Nevertheless, with regard to the broader debate about administration's legitimacy, his themes are notably unified: he returns over and over again to a guiding commitment to a rule of law, not of persons or interests.

Accordingly, Lowi's defense of the juridical democracy model is his most fundamental contribution to the theory of administrative legitimacy. He is a striking figure in American political science: he is actually a strong believer in law and its formalist aspirations. Lowi's position ultimately forces us to consider not only the premises, but also the limits, of the rule of law ideal itself.

II. The Functionalist Critique of the Rule of Law Ideal and the Rejection of the Call to Revive the Nondelegation Doctrine

A. The Functionalist Critique and the Nondelegation Doctrine

Critiques of the rule of law ideal in the administrative context take different forms. For present purposes, I will concentrate on a functionalist view that does not seek to question the liberal vision of the rule of law in general, but rather challenges the legal formalism that informs it. This critique implicitly recognizes that the rule of law itself is central to liberal theory. Rather than take on the ideal in toto, this critique probes the limits of its specifically legal implementation as a guiding image of bureaucracy. It generates a number of familiar themes, both in general and in relation to attacks on proposals for revitalizing the nondelegation doctrine.

For many functionalist critics, the chief problems with the legal formalism informing a rule of law vision derive from the fact that it is awfully abstract and removed from the actual operation of law in everyday institutional life. The difficulty is not that a rule of law approach has no theoretical appeal. Rather, it is that, as a pure notion, the formalist program is not seen to be practical. This critique has become so central to so much legal discourse that * * * merely to describe a legal position as "formalistic" is for many seriously to condemn it.

Such an assault is hardly unanticipated by rule of law proponents. Lowi himself is at pains to address the charge—to be expected from many in his own professional domain of political studies—that a formalist program for juridical democracy represents something of a flight of fancy. Indeed, the burden of much of his analysis is to convince the reader that a concern about broad delegations is not necessarily a fruitless preoccupation, but could lead to practical change if the legal system were to alter its premises. It therefore would be inaccurate to consider Lowi's approach heedless of the criticism that a formalist program is impractical. At the same time, however, one can criticize Lowi for not exploring more closely than he does the formalist foundation on which his prescriptions tend to rest. Will it really carry the weight he places on it?

Many functionalist critics of rule of law idealism think not. Such doubts are grounded in a regard for what are seen as the inevitable institutional limitations of the governmental bodies—agencies, Congress, courts—that would be called upon to change their ways under a newly formalist regime. Basically, the functionalist critic holds that modern administrative realities are so complex and governmental institutions are so dependent on broad authorizations that it is highly unrealistic, if not also likely to be counterproductive, to seek to achieve a regime of narrow delegations.

B. The Use of Functionalist Criticism in Rejecting the Call to Revive the Nondelegation Doctrine

* * * This section will briefly summarize major functionalist criticisms of Lowi's proposal that go beyond the general claim of impracticality.

First, the argument is often made that broad delegations are essential for flexible, effective, and fair administrative decisionmaking in a complex modern society. This view rests partly on the notion that agencies are unable to respond adequately to new and unforeseen problems unless their authorizations afford them considerable room for maneuvering. Moreover, agencies are thought unable to tailor solutions appropriate to particular problems, or to achieve equitable applications of law, unless they have a good deal of flexibility to respond to specific circumstances. After all, the flip side of justice through rule-governed behavior is allowance for the exceptional, special, or merely concrete. Such allowance may be seen to presuppose a significant amount of discretion.

Even if agencies could do without broad delegations, the functionalist critic often insists that Congress is unlikely either to be able or moved to do so. As Stewart notes [in the article excerpted above], incentives operating on Congress favor increasing, not decreasing, the scope of agency power. This is not only due to Congress' appreciation of the needs of administrators, but more pointedly because it allows Congress, in effect, to have its cake and eat it, too. That is, capacious delegations serve Congress' interests of appearing to address public problems through legislation and thereby to respond to whatever constituent interests support the legislation. At the same time, Congress maintains the ability to distance itself from unpopular policies implemented by agencies by claiming that those, after all, were not what it had in mind. This best of both worlds attraction is particularly understandable given the tendencies toward fractionated power in our complex political system, which make specific legislative policymaking especially difficult.

Furthermore, even if a call for narrower delegations would not be institutionally problematic from the perspectives of agencies and Congress, functionalists often question whether the impetus for such a move should ever come from judicial activism under the nondelegation doctrine. The key premise here is that judicial legitimacy in a democratic system is inherently tenuous. On this view, courts should be rigorously self-restrained. Otherwise, they may squander their power. Stewart reasons along these lines that courts should be especially cautious about employing constitutional norms like the nondelegation principle in striking down statutes. If they are not, he urges, they will be ignoring the necessary counsel of prudence.

In addition, functionalists contend that the capacities of courts are not likely to include precise knowledge about the optimal degree of specificity in statutory authorizations. Judgments about such specificity that are raised to a level of constitutional mandate, Stewart objects, are likely to be seen as "subjective" or perhaps frankly partisan. As he writes [in an earlier article]:

> Such judgments [about delegations] are necessarily quite subjective, and a doctrine that made them determinative of an administrative program's legitimacy could cripple the program by exposing it to continuing threats of invalidation and encouraging the utmost recalcitrance by those opposed to its effectiveness. *Given such subjective standards, and the controversial character of decisions on whether to invalidate legislative delegations, such decisions will almost inevitably appear partisan, and might often be so.*

These several concerns, taken as a whole, reveal a thoroughgoing lack of confidence in the idea of revitalizing the nondelegation doctrine. Just as Lowi's support for the idea is nurtured by his embrace of a formalist rule of law ideal, Stewart's opposition to revitalization of the nondelegation doctrine finds support in functionalist skepticism about the abilities of law to overcome the asserted constraints of governmental institutions.

III. Alternative Ideals of Administration in Relation to the Debate About Reviving the Nondelegation Doctrine

A. The Major Alternative Ideals of Administration

Functionalist critics of the formalist program of reviving the nondelegation doctrine confront the challenge of developing an alternative picture of administrative legitimacy that can serve as a counterweight to the powerful rule of law vision. In the present terms of reformist discourse about the administrative process, at least two such alternative visions exist. They move away from legal formalism and embrace central premises of modern political science and economics. To distinguish their main concentrations, I will call them, respectively, the public purposes and the democratic process ideals.

These two alternatives, although in some respects complementary to the rule of law, differ fundamentally in their emphases. I will first consider their major themes. I will then explore the ways in which aspects of each are blended by Professor Stewart.

1. The public purposes ideal

The public purposes ideal takes for granted that the mission of agencies is to be instrumentalist in the broad sense of rationally and efficiently pursuing statutory objectives. This ideal has a superficial similarity to the rule of law ideal because it looks to statutes for reference points by which to assess an agency's compliance with its mission. * * * [H]owever, there are major differences between a rules oriented jurisprudence and one that is founded on the instrumental pursuit of goals or ends.

The former often tends, as with the traditional rule of law ideal reflected in Lowi's work, to stress the need for some formally realizable integrity in law itself as the chief constraint on agency power. The latter emphasizes the general objectives or purposes of laws. It sees agencies as the instruments of policymaking empowered and, sometimes, well-attuned to advance given objectives in a hopefully rational manner. The distinction between rules and goals touches on the related distinction noted by Lowi between law as formally conceived and various types of "systems analysis" or policy frameworks that go beyond legal constraints on agencies.

The thrust of the public purposes ideal is to view agencies not in terms of any particular policy framework, but generally as rational managers in pursuit of public values encoded in statutes. This larger ideal, like the rule of law vision, has had a long and distinguished history in administrative law. James Landis, a New Deal proponent of agency expertise, advanced key elements of its basic framework. Our current debates often take for granted that Landis' view of administrative expertise is unduly optimistic in its pursuit of disinterested managerialism. Yet the public purposes ideal in general has not declined in importance. Rather, it has undergone various metamorphoses. It has supported a range of developments in administrative theory emphasizing, for instance, cost-benefit balancing or market-oriented economic critiques in the regulatory setting.

* * *

2. The democratic process ideal

The third major competing ideal is the democratic process vision. This notion idealizes the very pluralism that Professor Lowi so deeply suspects. The democratic process ideal envisions a happy coincidence between the competing issue networks and interests of our social world, and the responsiveness to interest pressures that is thought to characterize our governmental structures. This ideal seeks to promote interest group competition and representation in the administrative process itself.

The democratic process ideal, like the rule of law and public purpose ideals, has a prominent history in administrative theory. Among its leading expositors is Richard Stewart. His 1975 article heralded the coming of an interest representation model of administrative law as a unifying perspective from which to consider a number of legal doctrines.[70] Yet the notion of direct interest representation in administrative decisionmaking is not the only theme of the democratic process ideal. It also includes a commitment to oversight of the administrative system by politically responsible actors, including Congress and the President. Oversight proposals embody the thrust of the democratic process vision by embracing democratic accountability, not legal formalism or instrumental management, as the guidepost by which to assess agency behavior.

Like the public purposes ideal, the democratic process ideal superficially resembles rule of law idealism in its emphasis on the role of statutes in structuring agency behavior. This superficial coincidence belies a deeper tension. That tension may be highlighted by contrasting the democratic process picture of administration with the image of the role of courts presented by Dean John Hart Ely in his discussion of judicial review in constitutional law.[72]

---

[70] *See generally* [Richard Stewart, *The Reformation of American Administrative Law*, 88 HARV. L. REV. 1667, 1760-90 (1975).]

[72] *See generally* [JOHN ELY, DEMOCRACY AND DISTRUST 131-34 (1980).]

For Dean Ely, the American democratic system generally works to produce majoritarian outcomes so long as its channels are kept free of constricting or skewing influences. The basic task for judicial review, as Ely elaborates in detailed arguments * * *, is to guarantee the fidelity of the process to its own premises. When some important process defect may be reasonably thought to exist—as in the case of systematic denials of the right to vote—judicial correction is seen as fully justified, if not mandated.

This picture of the role of courts has at least one significant advantage not shared by a democratic process vision of administration. In particular, Ely's process theory builds on an implicit alliance with the rule of law ideal's general distinction between law and politics. For Ely, politics quite naturally inheres in the political system. Law, in the form of constitutional adjudication, is seen as the domain of courts. The task of judicial review in the constitutional setting is to "perfect" the political process under guiding legal principles. Even without elaborately developing the formalist theory that informs this picture, Ely invokes what for many is its reassuring image of law's special place.

In rather sharp contrast, the democratic process ideal of administration represents a basic challenge to the rule of law ideal. At its core, the democratic process vision presupposes that agency decisions * * * consist essentially of political compromises among varying interests. This process theory considers that politics, not law, animates administrative decisionmaking. It deemphasizes law as such. To be sure, an overdrawn opposition should be avoided. Yet * * * the democratic process ideal significantly conflicts with the rule of law vision of bureaucracy.

Moreover, the democratic process approach is also in tension with the public purposes ideal. The democratic process approach does not stress supposedly objective markers of efficiency. Instead, it sees the governmental system as inherently one of interest competition which, at its best, can lead to democratically responsive decisions. Efficiency is not the goal of the democratic process ideal; accountability and political compromise are. Of course, some may argue that the ideas of democratic responsiveness and efficiency should be linked, as Richard Stewart does * * *. Such an argument, however, tends to reaffirm the distinctness of the ideas themselves.

B. The Reflection of the Two Alternative Ideals in Argumentation about the Nondelegation Doctrine

* * * Professor Stewart borrows heavily from the normative artillery furnished by the public purposes and democratic process ideals, although he does not cast the debate in these terms. In so doing, his position raises two major questions * * *. First, how does Stewart's position account for the tension that exists between the two main ideals from which it borrows? Second, does it deal fully with the challenge of the rule of law vision that Professor Lowi advances? Before considering these matters, I will briefly summarize Professor Stewart's position * * *.

Stewart's argument is that the costs of centralized regulation of the economy and society at the national level are so great that we would do better to decentralize power. A decentralization strategy would turn over to societal "subsystems" the job of advancing national goals. The costs to which Stewart refers include burdens associated with complex collective decisionmaking, such as those of obtaining information in order to regulate, as well as burdens on the regulated community. The latter become especially clear when one presupposes with Stewart that rigidities and near-term obsolescence inhere in national standard setting.

The subsystems to which power should devolve, in Stewart's view, include the free market, the sphere of administratively overseen bargaining (such as collective bargaining under labor statutes and competition pursuant to the antitrust laws), and state and local governments. Stewart considers that these economic, social, and political subsystems are naturally closer to the people. The subsystems involve either voluntary interactions or action by governments below the national level.

Both Stewart's critique of national regulatory standard setting and his proposal to decentralize decisionmaking power rest on premises central to the public purposes and the democratic process ideals. * * *

For instance, in criticizing national standard setting, Stewart stresses an "iron law of transaction costs" that generates inefficiencies in national regulatory programs. His concern about such purported inefficiencies depends on the larger instrumentalist idea that federal agencies should be rational pursuers of national objectives. They should not trip over their own feet as they go about their jobs. Stewart believes, however, that such tripping is inevitable in a complex society. On this view, the instrumentalist underpinning of the public purposes vision is relied upon in arguing for a new way to achieve legislative objectives.

In related fashion, Stewart's economic argument for decentralization strategies—including deregulation in some instances and the use of economic incentives in remaining regulatory systems (such as one that might allow the trading of legislatively authorized pollution permits)—may be seen to reflect a commitment to efficient managerialism. In these respects as well, Stewart's analysis builds on key elements of the public purposes alternative to the rule of law ideal.

Stewart's argument for decentralization also reflects the democratic process ideal. This notion is particularly clear in the context of Stewart's advocacy of the transfer of power to state and local governments. Stewart defends this federalist strain in his proposal as a means of advancing democratic responsiveness to the particular wants and needs of citizens throughout the country. He posits that federal standard setting cannot be equally responsive because of the requirement in this context for uniformity across the nation.

* * *

To summarize, Stewart's efficiency critique of national regulatory standard setting, as reflected in his arguments for decentralization, echoes the public purposes ideal. At the same time, his democratic responsiveness critique and associated arguments for decentralization reflect key elements of the democratic process ideal. In these ways, Stewart participates in deep theoretical debates about administrative legitimacy and reform. * * *

Yet in so doing, Stewart does not take full account of the tensions between the ideals he implicitly invokes. It is true that an efficiency critique and a democratic responsiveness argument are not so inconsistent that they could not logically be linked. Nevertheless, the two ideals, as normative constructs of administrative activity, do present deeply competing images. They cannot easily or magically be harmonized.

For instance, the public purposes vision emphasizes efficiency. It does not welcome efforts to make the administrative process more democratically responsive to the extent that such efforts might slow down or otherwise make more inefficient the administrative process. In reciprocal fashion, the democratic vision emphasizes process values. It does not welcome the public purpose ideal's efficiency orientation to the extent that such orientation might undermine the pursuit of democratic responsiveness. Stewart, by focusing on alternatives to Lowi's formalism, does not undertake to explore these matters and, therefore, does not fully develop his own theoretical position in the contemporary debate.

In addition, Stewart's analysis, although rich and intriguing, understates the importance of the rule of law ideal on which Lowi draws. Stewart's * * * argument does implicitly embrace the functionalist critique of formalism and the main reformist alternatives to the rule of law. But it does not directly answer Lowi's concern that decentralization in the name of economics or localism is—if not legally empty—not sufficiently attentive to the need to uphold the chief legal ideal of modern liberalism.

The concern here is one often generated by functionalism. The functionalist critic, by stressing the practical limits of legal formalism, gradually narrows the debate to one about the method of decisionmaking by legal actors. As methodological debaters, functionalists may claim victory after characterizing their opponents as crabbed, narrow, and out of touch with reality. The larger problem with such a critique, however, is that it may miss the most powerful point of formalism, which is not methodological, but is normative. It is that, as a matter of legitimacy in a liberal state, one cannot escape the rule of law no matter how problematical its embrace may be. That appears to be the point of Lowi's expressions of frustration at what he calls the "apologetics" of law professors in the face of seemingly intractable reality. He is essentially saying that intractability is not reason enough to shrink from the challenge of liberal legalism. For Lowi, that challenge is to develop the conceptual and doctrinal bases for what we claim to be the rule of law, as opposed to persons or interests.

The difficulties presented by that challenge of course are enormous. It would be facile to suggest that a critique of centralized regulation lacks value because it does not complete the herculean task of fashioning a modern day rule of law. That is not my point. The point is that Stewart's decentralization proposals do not sufficiently recognize the seriousness of this task given the liberal premises he embraces. Lowi's preoccupations are central to liberal theory, and on those tenets the concerns about the rule of law ultimately cannot be evaded simply by allegations of their present institutional impracticality.

Conclusion: A Competing Ideals Perspective on the Debate about the Nondelegation Doctrine

It is necessary * * * to back away from the particular arguments of Professors Lowi and Stewart to consider the advantages of analyzing their debate in terms of competing reformist ideals. There are at least two major advantages.

First, this approach shows why the controversy about the nondelegation doctrine is not properly viewed as parochial or passe. To the contrary, it is of central importance to the theory of our administrative system. Wholly apart from the practical impact that any revival of the doctrine would have, it also has critical normative significance.

Second, this approach clarifies what is ultimately at stake in the debate over nondelegation. There is no clear and uncontestable doctrinal answer for or against revival of the nondelegation doctrine because there is deep theoretical disagreement about the premises one should employ. What is at war here are broader currents in liberal theory itself.

The competing ideals perspective shows that one's position on the nondelegation controversy will depend in significant measure on which larger ideal one embraces. One who agrees with Lowi that the rule of law ideal should dominate will be more prone to emphasize the revitalization of the nondelegation doctrine or will, at least, be more sympathetic with Lowi's concerns about the problem of vague delegations. On the other hand, one who accepts the functionalist critique of legal formalism or otherwise embraces alternatives to the rule of law ideal may well be drawn to a position similar to Stewart's.

Does the competing ideals perspective allow one to go further and decide, in terms of this theoretical debate, which of the ideals is the "right" one? Hope for such resolution is surely understandable. It is often frustrating to work in a system of ideas so internally riven that each affirmative proposal encounters well-established lacuna in argument.

Yet in my view, the competing ideals cannot be reduced to the dominance of a single vision of administration. That result, even if desirable, would misrepresent the character of the normative debates that inform contemporary liberal theory. My point is not just that liberalism has multiple strands, although that is true. My point is that the structure of contemporary argument about administrative reform is based on a delicate balance among competing ideals. To impose on it the hegemony of one view would be to misrepresent the character of the structure itself.

In this sense, the debate between Lowi and Stewart gives us winners and losers, but they are the same: each "wins" under certain premises, and each "loses" under competing premises. * * *

All of this suggests that we should continue to explore the normative underpinnings of our administrative system. We should consider more directly than we often tend to do the theoretical justifications of administrative power and its reform. To be sure, we should avoid seeing in the foundations of our system such complexity that we cannot achieve a sense of it as a whole, and thus cannot understand it more completely and systematically. At the same time, we need to avoid oversimplification, a constant risk in any theoretical discussion of the great diversity of administrative life. With such caution, we should continue to explore openly the strengths and weaknesses not just of particular normative frameworks, but of the major competing ideals of administrative law and government.

Jerry L. Mashaw, *Prodelegation: Why Administrators Should Make Political Decisions*, 1 J. LAW, ECON. & ORGAN. 81, 82-91, 95-100 (1985)*

I. Introduction
* * *

As a means of approaching an affirmative case for broad statutory delegations, we shall examine the multiple reasons why contemporary critics have been opposed to such delegations. For the moment, at least, we will leave aside the question of what constitutes a vague versus a specific conferral of administrative authority. That question is not without its own difficulty, but the antidelegation commentary views the distinction as nonproblematic. We shall also attempt to avoid the closely connected question of whether a vigorous constitutional nondelegation doctrine, enforced via judicial review, would be desirable, even if it were clear that vague delegations of authority to administrators were undesirable. Issue is to be joined on questions of political organization, not on questions of judicial competency or of the conceptual possibility of providing a functional definition of "vague" or "specific."

2. The Positions of the Antidelegation Fraternity

Among contemporary critics, Theodore Lowi is perhaps the earliest and most persistent antidelegation theorist. In *The End of Liberalism*, Lowi argues that the modern toleration of broad delegations of decisionmaking authority to administrators is part of a political tradition that is at base antithetical to *law*.

> In brief, law, in the liberal view, is too authoritative a use of authority. Authority has to be tentative and accessible to be acceptable. If authority is to be accommodated to the liberal

---

* Reprinted with permission of the Journal of Law, Economics & Organization and Jerry L. Mashaw. All rights reserved.

myth that it is not power at all, it must emerge out of individual bargains.

Moreover, Lowi finds this timid approach to legal authority pernicious. The legislature's failure to make clear choices inevitably, in Lowi's view, results in the failure of government to develop coherent policy. Ultimately law is replaced by ad hoc bargaining. Lowi believes that most intelligent people involved with this form of "gutless" and contentless administration will hold administrators and government in contempt. It is unclear whether Lowi believes that a more authoritative use of law—meaning legislatively specified rules—would produce better public policy, but he certainly seems to believe that it would produce government whose legitimacy was more widely recognized by the electorate.

Although largely concerned with defining an appropriate role for judicial review, John Hart Ely echoes Lowi's dissatisfaction in his * * * book *Democracy and Distrust*. While building a theory of judicial review whose main purpose is to reinforce the representativeness of governance, Ely has some especially unkind words to say about the practice of broad delegation of authority. Indeed, he views the failure of "legislators [i.e., Congress] to legislate [i.e., to decide policy questions]" as one of the major obstacles to a truly representative democracy. * * *

A similar concern with the breakdown of representative government seems to underlie recent opinions by Justice Rehnquist. (*See Industrial Union Department, AFL-CIO v. American Petroleum Institute*, 448 U.S. 607, 671 (1980) (Rehnquist, J., concurring); *American Textile Manufacturers' Institute v. Donovan*, 452 U.S. 490, 543 (1981) (Rehnquist, J., dissenting, joined by Burger, C. J.).) Justice Rehnquist apparently would send Section 6(b)(5) of the Occupational Safety and Health Act back to the Congress for further specification of the criteria by which the Occupational Safety and Health Administration (OSHA) should balance the objectives of protecting worker health and maintaining a vibrant economy. Section 6(b)(5) directs OSHA, when regulating worker exposure to toxic chemicals, to prescribe standards that "most adequately assure, to the extent feasible . . . that no employee will suffer material impairment of health or functional capacity even if such employee has regular exposure to the hazard . . . for the period of his working life." Union representatives had claimed that this instruction obliged OSHA to require the use of whatever available technology an industry might be able to afford to install without bankrupting itself. Employer groups, on the other hand, contended that the agency was required to weigh the costs of controls against health benefits in deciding what standard was "feasible."

Abstractly considered, either position was plausible. The real world differences in these two approaches to the statute might determine the necessity for hundreds of millions of dollars of industry investment in safety equipment as well as specify vastly different levels of risks of illness for workers exposed to toxic chemicals. OSHA's choice of interpretation would thus entail significant economic and social consequences. The question also obviously implicated significant political and moral values.

According to Justice Rehnquist's opinion in *Industrial Union Department*,

> In drafting §6(b)(5), Congress was faced with a clear, if difficult, choice between balancing statistical lives and industrial resources or authorizing the Secretary to elevate human life above all concerns save massive dislocation. . . . That Congress chose . . . to pass this difficult choice on to the Secretary is evident from the spectral quality of the standard it selected.

In the later case, *American Textile Manufacturers' Institute*, Justice Rehnquist and the Chief Justice suggested that the "special" language of §6(b)(5) indeed masked a disagreement so profound, that had the Congress been required to resolve it, "There would have been no bill for the President to sign." The Congress had thus passed on to the agency (OSHA) precisely the legislative issue that the Constitution called upon the legislative branch to decide.

The Lowi-Ely-Rehnquist critique dramatizes an apparently serious flaw in American government—a legislature fleeing from choice on critical issues, not by refusing to act, but by adopting vacuous statutes conferring policymaking power on administrators whose legitimacy and efficacy will be deeply compromised by their lack of clear statutory authority. Thus, it is suggested, we blunder our way into an administrative state that has traded its democratic values for little or no increase in effective governance.

Other scholars have gone further to claim that broad legislative delegations are not only antidemocratic, they tend to reduce public welfare as well. The most elaborate exposition of this view * * * is by Aranson, Gellhorn, and Robinson * * *. The Aranson, Gellhorn, and Robinson thesis is fairly straightforward. The authors first ask when one should expect that legislators would be willing to confer broad authority to determine policy on administrators. They discern two such situations. In the first, legislators recognize that legislation is likely to benefit one group of constituents while imposing substantial costs on another group. In order to claim credit with the former constituency, while avoiding potentially energetic opposition from the second group in the next election, legislators pass a vague statute. They can then claim credit for the general action benefiting the first constituency, while shifting the responsibility for focused harms to the implementing decisions of administrators.

The second set of circumstances yielding vague statutes is one in which legislators again confront opposing groups in their constituencies. But all groups favor some action to the status quo. They merely are unable to agree on any single course of action. Passing a vague statute in effect creates a public policy lottery: an action preferred by all the opposing groups to no action at all. Who gains and who loses among these contending interests will then be determined by administrative action.

Having identified circumstances under which they would predict vague statutes—that is, statutes conferring broad discretionary authority on administrators—Aranson, Gellhorn, and Robinson then ask whether these are circumstances that are likely to produce welfare-enhancing legislation. Their answer is a resounding "No." In their view, virtually all legislation is designed to produce "private goods at public expense." Moreover, they consistently imply that the net benefits of these "private goods" are negative, that is, the public costs of producing the private goods are greater than the benefits received by the private-interest groups who receive them. Because vague delegations reduce the cost to legislatures of legislating, we get more of this "private goods" legislation than we otherwise would. A reinvigorated nondelegation doctrine would increase the costs of legislating, reduce the number of private goods bills that were enacted and thereby enhance general welfare. Aranson et al. recognize that prohibiting vague delegations would also inhibit some "public interest" legislation. But given their belief about the relative incidence of private interest versus public interest legislation, these losses would be more than offset by the gains from reduced legislative output.

3. The Critics Criticized

The critical literature is thus of two general types: one predicts that vague delegations will delegitimize representative governance; the other suggests that statutory vagueness leads to an overall reduction in public welfare. Either effect would be serious; taken together they are perhaps calamitous.

Interestingly, none of the literature surveyed provides more than anecdotal support for the hypotheses offered. Indeed, none of the literature is sufficiently precise about the difference between vague and specific legislation to permit confident assignment of legislation to one or another category. But before worrying about empirical testing and better specification of the behavioral hypotheses, we should consider the plausibility of the normative claims that are being made.

3.1. Vagueness and Legitimacy

The delegitimation critics might be divided further into two camps. Lowi seems to make an argument from authoritativeness; Ely and Justice Rehnquist seem to be making arguments about the need for accountability. Let us examine these arguments in turn.

Lowi's position is certainly familiar. A consistent strain of our constitutional politics asserts that legitimacy flows from "the rule of law." By that is meant a system of objective and accessible commands, law which can be seen to flow from collective agreement rather than from the exercise of discretion or preference by those persons who happen to be in positions of authority. By reducing discretion, and thereby the possibility for the exercise of the individual preferences of officials, specific rules reinforce the rule of law.

Yet, while focusing on the rule of law and its undeniable importance in maintaining liberty, we should not forget the apparent equal importance of a contradictory demand: the demand for justice in individual cases. Moreover, the demand for justice seems inextricably linked to the flexibility and generality of legal norms, that is, to the use of vague principles (reasonableness, fairness, fault, and the like) rather than precise rules. Were one to doubt either the ubiquitous human desire for justice or its connection to general norms, Thibout and Walker have demonstrated, in an impressive series of cross-national clinical trials, a demand for the absence of law in the sense (legal rules) that Lowi uses that term. Indeed, these findings lead Thibout and Walker to argue that law must consist exclusively of these broad general principles in order for any adjudicatory system to appear just. And, of course, any set of general principles that would allow elaborate contextualization of circumstances before authoritative judgment would, of necessity, also allow the exercise of broad discretion by those charged with developing middle-level policies and deciding concrete cases.

This is not to say that Lowi is wrong to remind us about the demand for authoritativeness. But it is surely not the case that legitimacy is subsumed in authority, even were we to agree that the latter is nonproblematically implemented by statutory precision.

The Ely-Rehnquist demand for legislative decisionmaking as a prerequisite to accountability is similarly incomplete, and even more perplexing. * * * The dynamics of accountability apparently involve voters willing to vote upon the basis of their representative's record in the legislature. Assuming that our current representatives in the legislature vote for laws that contain vague delegations of authority, we are presumably holding them accountable for that at the polls. How is it that we are not being represented?

* * *

The sort of specific issue accountability that Ely seems to applaud, indeed to advocate, is hardly transparently desirable. Do we really want to choose our representatives (or hold them accountable) on the basis of specific votes concerning specific legislation which, but for constitutional necessity (a nondelegation doctrine with bite), they would have cast in more general terms? How exactly does it help us in choosing legislators to judge them on the basis of preference expressions that are not the expressions they would give but for the constitutional necessity of being specific?

Even if we were to imagine that statutory precision is informative, it is hard to envisage how rational voter calculation is improved appreciably. When one votes for Congressman X, presumably one votes on the basis of a prediction about what X will do in the next time period in the legislature. How much better off are voters likely to be in making that prediction—that is, in determining how well Congressman X is likely to represent them over a range of presently unspecified issues—by knowing that he or she voted yes or no on the specific language in certain specific bills in some preceding legislature? After all, the voter will also know that X could not have controlled all or even a substantial portion of the language of those bills. Votes must have been cast "all things considered." Therefore, when making a general appraisal of X's likely behavior in the future, it is surely much more important that voters know the general ideological tendencies that inform those votes (prolabor, probusiness, prodisarmament, prodefense) than that X votes for or against particular language of a particular bill. I know of no one who argues that statutory vagueness prevents the electorate from becoming informed on the general proclivities of their representatives. * * *

3.2. Vagueness and the General Welfare

The Aranson et al. thesis fills in the behavioral gaps in Ely's account and goes on to claim that negative welfare effects flow from vague delegations. This is truly heroic theorizing. Unproven behavioral hypotheses are combined with welfare assumptions to produce determinate policy recommendations. For present purposes, we will assume that Aranson, Gellhorn, and Robinson's hypotheses are generally true. The crucial question is whether the asserted welfare consequences of these behavioral predictions are at all plausible even if their predictions about political behavior are accurate.

Assume first the hypothetical scenario in which the legislature creates a public policy lottery by charging an agency to do something about some issue, but without charging it specifically with what to do. In the Aranson account the legislature does this in order to satisfy diverse demands for action when there is no consensus on what the action should be. By hypothesis all the actors demanding that the legislature do *something* are risk acceptant, that is, they prefer the lottery to the status quo. Assuming rational expectations (as Aranson et al. seem to do), this implies that every actor will favor giving implementing decisions to administrators within the bounds of the legislatively established lottery.

Aranson and his colleagues present this situation as one of pernicious legislative action. Yet it is extremely difficult to discern why. The legislature has been perfectly responsive (representative) and has by definition enhanced general welfare (everyone preferred the lottery to the status quo). To be sure the administrative agency's implementing action may not be pareto optimal, or even pareto superior. Perhaps they believe that if forced to act specifically the legislature would act pareto optimally, or at least in a pareto superior fashion, thus eliminating the possibility of administrative error. Given these authors' general views of legislative behavior, however, one is hard-pressed to imagine how their argument would proceed.

The welfare argument flowing from the alternative Aranson et al. scenario is less puzzling. Here, remember, the reelection-oriented legislator attempts to take credit for the beneficial outcomes of legislation while avoiding responsibility for the legislation's costs—what numerous authors refer to as the creation of a "fiscal illusion." (How politicians achieve this illusion year after year without being discovered by the electorate is left unexplained. But that is mere carping; we agreed that we would accept the behavioral hypotheses as true.)

What then are the welfare consequences of this credit-claiming, blame-avoiding behavior on the part of legislators? Aranson, Gellhorn, and Robinson argue that it is negative. That claim rests on a much more general proposition—that the free play of political life, assuming self-interested constituents and self-interested legislators, makes all legislation disbeneficial (or most of it, anyway). Indeed, given the generality of the premises, Aranson et al. should advocate a constitutional rule which somehow requires that the legislature be limited to specific legislation whenever it would be vague and vague legislation whenever it finds it easier to be specific.

What are the bases for this pessimistic view of legislation? The first proposition is that legislators are oriented primarily to their own reelection. Thus they will consider legislative actions from the perspective of their ability to claim credit with relevant constituencies. Second, because legislators represent different constituencies with different interests, all of them will find it useful to make trades with each other (logrolling) so that the demands of a wide variety of constituencies can be satisfied. Finally, even where the costs of legislation affect all constituencies equally, bare majority coalitions of the beneficiaries of legislation remain possible, provided that the benefits of legislation exceed one half its costs. Given this possibility, all legislation (or, sometimes, most legislation) can be presumed to be the satisfaction of some coalition of private groups at a public cost that exceeds the legislation's benefits to the coalition. Notwithstanding these routinely negative results, voters will not chuck the legislators out because of something called "high voter perceptual thresholds." Voters can see the direct benefits to them but are relatively impervious to the high indirect costs to them of benefits to others.

The empirical gaps and logical leaps in this model are quite wonderful. First, all politics is interest-group politics. All legislation and all legislator-constituency relationships are "pure pork barrel." Legislation with respect to abortion, prayer in the public schools, environmental protection, and river and harbor improvements can all be modeled in precisely the same way. More critically, a possibility theorem (it can happen) is transformed into a behavioral prediction (it will happen). Because bare majority coalitions *could* pass disbeneficial legislation, they do. The system is maintained by a combination of logrolling (allowing all legislators to play the same game) and electoral ignorance (fiscal illusion). In this worst-case scenario, neither the balkanization of power in subcommittees nor the decline of party discipline seem to inhibit logrolling. Ideology (a belief in civil rights or environmental protection) neither broadens the benefits of legislation beyond bare majority coalitions nor limits (for example, a general belief in individual autonomy or small government) the legislators' ability to pass (remember the presidential veto?) welfare reducing statutes.

Quite apart from the doubts engendered by modest reflection on the empirical bases of this attempt to extract welfare consequences from (sometimes axiomatically diverse) public choice theorems, the analysis presented appears quite incoherent when placed in the context of a choice between vague or specific legislation. Presumably, vague delegations foster the march toward pareto pessimal results by reducing legislative decision costs. But there is a problem. Logrolling is one of the major driving forces behind the proposed worst-case scenario. Vague delegations, however, would seem to inhibit logrolling, for delegations of power transfer policy decisions to the jurisdiction of administrative agencies who have grave legal difficulties, and little apparent incentive, to trade values across programs. Any delegation thus restricts the policy space across which logrolling can be orchestrated and thereby limits the number of deals available to legislators in the next time period. The only way to cure this defect—to keep policy within the legislative space where logrolling can continue—would be to maintain all apparently delegated policy questions continuously on the legislative agenda. But if that were true, there would in fact be no delegation and no savings in legislative decision costs. Delegation would be irrelevant because nonexistent.

This difficulty might be solved if all possible legislative deals could be constructed within a particular piece of legislation. If there is, indeed, wide diversity of interests, there seem to be two techniques available for accomplishing all logrolling within a single bill. The first is a breathtakingly broad delegation: a pure policy lottery—completely standardless legislation that restricts neither policy choice nor jurisdiction. For even a determinate subject matter would restrict some trades, thus excluding some legislators and their constituents from logrolling. This would in turn produce incentives to blow the whistle on the fiscal illusion, and then the whole story begins to unravel. Ignoring for present purpose the obvious nonexistence of such delegations, there is, as I have noted, no a priori basis for presuming that the welfare consequences of pure policy lotteries are negative. Indeed, if demanded by voters with rational expectations, continuous play in such lotteries should produce net general welfare gains.

A moment's reflection, however, reveals why the pure policy lottery is likely to remain a mere conceptual category. It seems extremely unlikely that all groups will prefer any conceivable change with respect to every possible issue to the status quo. Logrolling by special interests in the presence of fiscal illusions seems much more likely to produce a disparate set of *specific* statutory provisions. Such statutes can give everyone something while confining the bargain to a particular time period, thus leaving open fulsome opportunities for multilateral trades in the future.

In short, while Aranson's general theory of legislation may capture the dynamics and welfare consequences of certain classes of legislation—appropriations bills for defense installations or for river and harbor improvements—it is a theory which seems to explain specific, not vague, legislation. And to the extent that we believe that such "Christmas tree bills" are indeed instances of private interest legislation that reduce general welfare, we perhaps should favor statutory vagueness as a potential correction. Perhaps the Defense Department or the Corps of Engineers could avoid at least some of the worthless projects that pure-pork-barrel politics produce. Thus, without exploring further the empirical naivete of this apparently hard-headed approach * * *, it appears that the theory has nothing to offer that would support a limitation on the legislature's capacity to delegate discretion to administrators. For the theory cannot make out even a plausible theoretical case for the systematically negative welfare effects of vague delegations.

4. The Affirmative Case for Broad Delegations

* * * The case against broad delegations thus seems quite weak. But is there anything that can be said that would tend to favor broad delegations of authority to administrators? Or is this perhaps a debate in which whoever has the burden of persuasion loses?

* * *

6. The Legitimation Value of Broad Delegations

Strangely enough it may make sense to imagine the delegation of political authority to administrators as a device for improving the responsiveness of government to the desires of the electorate. This argument can be made even if we accept many of the insights of the political and economic literature that premises its predictions of congressional and voter behavior on a direct linkage between benefits transferred to constituents and the election or reelection of representatives. All we need do is not forget there are also presidential elections and that * * * presidents are heads of administrations.

Assume then that voters view the election of representatives to Congress through the lens of the most cynical interpretation of the modern political science literature on congressional behavior. In short, the voter chooses a representative for that representative's effectiveness in supplying governmental goods and services to the local district, including the voter. The representative is a good representative or a bad representative based upon his or her ability to provide the district with at least its fair share of governmental largesse. In this view, the congressperson's position on various issues is of modest, if any, importance.

The voter's vision of presidential electoral politics is arguably quite different. The president has no particular constituency to which he or she has special responsibility to deliver benefits. Presidents are hardly cut off from pork-barrel politics. Yet issues of national scope and the candidates' positions on those issues are the essence of presidential politics. Citizens vote for a president based almost wholly on a perception of the difference that one or another candidate might make to general governmental policies.

If this description of voting in national elections is reasonably plausible, then the utilization of vague delegations to administrative agencies takes on significance as a device for facilitating responsiveness to voter preferences expressed in presidential elections. The high transactions costs of legislating specifically suggests that legislative activity directed to the modification of administration mandates will be infrequent. Agencies will thus persist with their statutory empowering provisions relatively intact over substantial periods of time. Voter preferences on the direction and intensity of governmental activities however, are not likely to be so stable. Indeed, one can reasonably expect that a president will be able to affect policy in a four-year term only because being elected president entails acquiring the power to exercise, direct, or influence policy discretion. The group of executive officers we commonly call "the Administration" matters only because of the relative malleability of the directives that administrators have in their charge. If congressional statutes were truly specific with respect to the actions that administrators were to take, presidential politics would be a mere beauty contest. For, in the absence of a parliamentary system or a system of strict party loyalty, specific statutes would mean that presidents and administrations could respond to voter preferences only if they were able to convince the legislature to make specific changes in the existing set of specific statutes. Arguments for specific statutory provisions constraining administrative discretion may reflect therefore a desire merely for conservative, not responsive, governance.

Of course, the vision of a president or an administration having to negotiate with the Congress for changes in policy is not one that is without its own attractiveness. Surely, we desire some limits on the degree to which a president can view a national election as a referendum approving all the president's (or the president's colleagues') pet projects, whether disclosed or undisclosed during the campaign. Those who abhor the policies of the Reagan administration, for example, might surely be attracted to a system that would have required that particular president to act almost exclusively through proposals for legislative change. Yet it seems likely that the flexibility that is currently built into the processes of administrative governance by relatively broad delegations of statutory authority permits a more appropriate degree of administrative, or administration, responsiveness to the voter's will than would a strict nondelegation doctrine. For, if we were to be serious about restricting the discretion of administrators, we would have to go much beyond what most nondelegation theorists seem to presume would represent clear congressional choices.

This last point is so neglected in the nondelegation literature that it is worth spelling out in some detail. While most discussions of the nondelegation doctrine focus on the question of substantive criteria for decision, establishing criteria is but one aspect of the exercise of policy discretion. In the formation of regulatory policy, for example, at least the following general types of questions have to be answered: What subjects are to be on the regulatory agenda? What are their priorities? By what criteria are regulations to be formulated? Within what period of time are they to be adopted? What are the priorities for the utilization of enforcement machinery with respect to adopted policies? What are the rules and procedures by which the relevant facts about the application of legal rules will be found? What are the rules by which facts and law will be combined to yield legal conclusions, that is, "findings" that there have or have not been violations of the regulations? What exceptions or justifications are relevant with respect to noncompliance? If violations are found, what corrective action or remedies will be prescribed?

Each of these questions can, of course, be broken down into a multitude of others and the answer to each question is a policy choice. Virtually any issue that can be specifically controlled by legislative answers to one of these questions can be reopened and redetermined when considering another. * * *

Were the Congress to attempt to make statutory meaning uniform over time, it would have to specify the most extraordinarily elaborate criteria for exercising enforcement initiative, for finding facts, for engaging in contextual interpretation, and for determining remedial action. Indeed, to insure uniformity it would have to specify some objective criteria for all these judgments and some algorithm by which they were unified into decisions. Squeezing discretion out of a statutory-administrative system is indeed so difficult that one is tempted to posit a "Law of Conservation of Administrative Discretion." According to that law the amount of discretion in an administrative system is always constant. Elimination of discretion at one choice point merely causes the discretion that had been exercised there to migrate elsewhere in the system. * * *

Nor will it do to suggest that activities beyond the setting of substantive criteria really do not raise the broad policy issues that concern nondelegation theorists. How the facts will be found often determines who wins and who loses. What cases are important enough to pursue entails policy discretion of the broadest sort. When to withhold remedial sanctions or alternatively to make an example of some offender raises issues of basic moral and political values. In short, as Aranson, Gellhorn, and Robinson recognize, making legislation specific and congressional choice determinative means addressing all these issues in great detail.

Such a strategy would, of course, result in wonderfully wooden administrative behavior and on that ground alone be highly objectionable. More important for present purposes, were Congress forced to repeal the Law of Conservation of Administrative Discretion in order to comply with a reinvigorated nondelegation doctrine, it would thereby eliminate executive responsiveness to shifts in voter preferences. For in this scenario, the high transaction costs of specific legislation will give an enormous advantage to the status quo, and the status quo will be susceptible to change only by a statute of the same kind.

Responsiveness to diversity in voter preferences is not limited to changes through time. It is surely plausible to imagine that, with a large land area and a heterogeneous citizenry, governmental responsiveness also entails situational variance at any one time. If our laws were truly specific, this would also be impossible. We could not, for example, have local draft boards exercising their discretion in accordance with their perceptions of the tolerance of the local population for particular attempts at mobilization, or granting exceptions based upon their understanding of the legitimacy of particular excuses from the local point of view. We could not have a Social Security Disability program which harnesses the national government's advantage in the collection of taxes for redistributional purposes and employs a national general criterion of disability, while permitting flexible application that takes account of local attachment to the work ethic, local employment opportunities, and other variations that are likely to be peculiar to particular regions of the country. In short, we could not have laws that say "Do something, but be reasonable and take account of local differences." Or at least we could not have them if our idea of democratic responsiveness is that the Congress as a body should make all the decisions necessary to give determinant meaning to the statutes that it passes.

In fact, as the fraternity of antidelegation theorists often laments, Congress seldom enacts such statutes. The extraordinary delegitimizing effect of rules that are so specific that they cannot be made responsive across either space or time suggests to me that this "failure" is a major benefit. Responsiveness to the will of the people is not a unitary phenomenon that can be embodied in a single institution. Broad delegations recognize that tight accountability linkages at one point in the governmental system may reduce the responsiveness of the system as a whole.

* * *

Additional Sources

Peter H. Aranson, Ernest Gellhorn, & Glen O. Robinson, *A Theory of Legislative Delegation*, 68 Cornell L. Rev. 1 (1982)

Lisa A. Cahill & J. Russell Jackson, *Nondelegation After* Mistretta: *Phoenix or Phaethon?*, 31 Wm. & Mary L. Rev. 1047 (1990)

Kenneth Culp Davis, *A New Approach to Delegation*, 36 U. Chi. L. Rev. 713 (1969)

Kenneth Culp Davis, Discretionary Justice: A Preliminary Inquiry (1969)

James O. Freedman, *Delegation of Power and Institutional Competence*, 43 U. Chi. L. Rev. 307 (1976)

Henry J. Friendly, The Federal Administrative Agencies: The Need for Better Definition of Standards (1962)

Ernest Gellhorn, *Returning to First Principles*, 36 Am. U. L. Rev. 345 (1987)

Theodore J. Lowi, The End of Liberalism: The Second Republic of the United States (2d ed. 1979)

Richard J. Pierce, Jr., *Political Accountability and Delegated Power: A Response to Professor Lowi*, 36 Am. U. L. Rev. 391 (1987)

David Schoenbrod, *The Delegation Doctrine: Could the Court Give It Substance?*, 83 Mich. L. Rev. 1223 (1985)

Sidney A. Shapiro & Robert L. Glicksman, *Congress, the Supreme Court, and the Quiet Revolution in Administrative Law*, 1988 Duke L.J. 819

2. Debates About the Interpretation of Statutory Authorizations of Agencies

a. Statutory Interpretation in General

In recent years, there has been a vigorous debate about how a court or other interpreter should analyze an agency's statutory authority. In the first excerpt, Professor William Eskridge argues that statutes should be interpreted "dynamically," by which he means not only in terms of their text, structure, purposes, and legislative history, but also in light of present societal, political, and legal contexts. He elaborates a model of dynamic interpretation and defends it against the charge of illegitimacy. Professor Eskridge also urges that courts are institutionally competent to perform the role he envisions.

In the second excerpt, Professor Nicholas Zeppos criticizes Professor Eskridge's call for dynamic interpretation.* Professor Zeppos questions whether dynamic interpretation adequately respects the need both to limit the role of courts and to distinguish courts from other branches of government. Moreover, he criticizes the recommendation that courts should be more candid when they do consider current political and societal conditions, suggesting that a certain lack of candor may be essential for preserving judicial legitimacy.

In the third excerpt, Professor Cass Sunstein discusses the notion that the text of the relevant statutory provision should be the basis of any interpretation. Professor Sunstein describes the main premises underlying a textualist approach, and then offers his own skeptical view of textualism.

In the final excerpt, U.S. Court of Appeals Judge Stephen Breyer addresses the claim that courts generally should avoid relying on legislative history when interpreting a statute. Legislative history includes the committee reports that accompany a reported bill as well as other materials, such as pertinent statements by key members of Congress during floor debates in the House of Representatives or the Senate. While acknowledging that legislative history can be misused, Judge Breyer argues that, in many circumstances, not to consult it would be inappropriate.

---

* Professor Zeppos also discusses a dynamic model expounded by Professor Guido Calabresi, whose work is noted in the list of additional sources at the end of this section.

William N. Eskridge, Jr., *Dynamic Statutory Interpretation*, 135 U. PA. L. REV. 1479, 1479-80, 1482-84, 1497-1503, 1506-11, 1523-24, 1526-29, 1533-38 (1987)*

Federal judges interpreting the Constitution typically consider not only the constitutional text and its historical background, but also its subsequent interpretational history, related constitutional developments, and current societal facts. Similarly, judges interpreting common law precedents normally consider not only the text of the precedents and their historical context, but also their subsequent history, related legal developments, and current societal context. In light of this, it is odd that many judges and commentators believe judges should consider only the text and historical context when interpreting statutes, the third main source of law. Statutes, however, should—like the Constitution and the common law—be interpreted "dynamically," that is, in light of their present societal, political, and legal context.

Traditional doctrine teaches that statutes should not be interpreted dynamically. Prevailing approaches to statutory interpretation treat statutes as static texts. Thus, the leading treatise states that "[f]or the interpretation of statutes, 'intent of the legislature' is the criterion that is most often cited." This "intentionalist" approach asks how the legislature originally intended the interpretive question to be answered, or would have intended the question to be answered had it thought about the issue when it passed the statute. A "modified intentionalist" approach uses the original purpose of the statute as a surrogate for original intent, especially when the latter is uncertain; the proper interpretation is the one that best furthers the purpose the legislature had in mind when it enacted the statute.

Theoretically, these "originalist" approaches to statutory interpretation assume that the legislature fixes the meaning of a statute on the date the statute is enacted. The implicit claim is that a legislator interpreting the statute at the time of enactment would render the same interpretation as a judge interpreting the same statute fifty years later. This implication seems counterintuitive. Indeed, the legal realists argued this point earlier in the century. For example, gaps and ambiguities exist in all statutes, typically concerning matters as to which there was little legislative deliberation and, hence, no clear intent. As society changes, adapts to the statute, and generates new variations of the problem which gave rise to the statute, the unanticipated gaps and ambiguities proliferate. In such circumstances, it seems sensible that "the quest is not properly for the sense originally intended by the statute, [or] for the sense sought originally to be put into it, but rather for the sense which can be quarried out of it in the light of the new situation." Moreover, as time passes, the legal and constitutional context of the statute may change. Should not an interpreter "ask [her]self not only what the legislation means abstractly, or even on the basis of legislative history, but also what it ought to mean in terms of the needs and goals of our present day society[?]"

* * *

I. A Model of Dynamic Statutory Interpretation

The static vision of statutory interpretation prescribed by traditional doctrine is strikingly outdated. In practice, it imposes unrealistic burdens on judges, asking them to extract textual meaning that makes sense in the present from historical materials whose sense is often impossible to recreate faithfully. As doctrine, it is intellectually antediluvian, in light of recent developments in the philosophy of interpretation. Interpretation is not static, but dynamic. Interpretation is not an archeological discovery, but a dialectical creation. * * *

The dialectic of statutory interpretation is the process of understanding a text created in the past and applying it to a present problem. This process cannot be described simply as the recreation of past events and past expectations, for the "best" interpretation of a statute is typically the one that is most consonant with our current "web of beliefs" and policies surrounding the statute. That is, statutory interpretation involves the present-day interpreter's understanding and reconciliation of three different perspectives, no one of which will always control. These three perspectives relate to (1) the statutory text, which is the formal focus of interpretation and a constraint on the range of interpretive options available (textual perspective); (2) the original legislative expectations surrounding the statute's creation, including compromises reached (historical perspective); and (3) the subsequent evolution of the statute and its present context, especially the ways in which the societal and legal environment of the statute has materially changed over time (evolutive perspective).

Under dynamic statutory interpretation, the textual perspective is critical in many cases. The tradi-

---

* Reprinted with permission of the University of Pennsylvania Law Review, Fred B. Rothman & Co., and William N. Eskridge, Jr. All rights reserved.

tional understanding of the "rule of law" requires that statutes enacted by the majoritarian legislature be given effect, and that citizens have reasonable notice of the legal rules that govern their behavior. When the statutory text clearly answers the interpretive question, therefore, it normally will be the most important consideration. Exceptions, however, do exist because an apparently clear text can be rendered ambiguous by a demonstration of contrary legislative expectations or highly unreasonable consequences. The historical perspective is the next most important interpretive consideration; given the traditional assumptions that the legislature is the supreme lawmaking body in a democracy, the historical expectations of the enacting legislature are entitled to deference. Hence, when a clear text and supportive legislative history suggest the same answer, they typically will control.

The dynamic model, however, views the evolutive perspective as most important when the statutory text is not clear and the original legislative expectations have been overtaken by subsequent changes in society and law. In such cases, the pull of text and history will be slight, and the interpreter will find current policies and societal conditions most important. The hardest cases, obviously, are those in which a clear text or strong historical evidence or both, are inconsistent with compelling current values and policies.

* * *

II. Justification for Reading Statutes Dynamically

* * * There are * * * arguments that have been advanced in favor of a static view of statutory interpretation. * * * The formalist argument is that the creation of law by federal judges is beyond the authority given them in the Constitution, for it trenches upon the lawmaking power given to Congress. * * * The traditional legal process argument is that such judicial lawmaking is "countermajoritarian" and so ought to be avoided in a democracy, where important policy decisions ought to be made by the majoritarian branches of government.

I shall articulate and respond to * * * these arguments in turn, but there are certain themes which run through all my responses. One theme is a Madisonian view of the Constitution. Historical scholarship suggests that our constitutional system of government was not meant to be one of rigid separation of powers or pure majoritarianism. Instead, the polity created by the Constitution requires a government that is deliberative and promotes the common good, at least on important matters. Judicial lawmaking from statutes has a constructive role to play in such a polity, especially in light of the tendency of the legislature to produce too little up-to-date public-seeking policy and not to produce well-integrated policies. The vision of a tripartite government and the legitimacy of the system are not served by a straitjacketed theory of statutory interpretation but are better served by a flexible approach that is sensitive to current policy concerns. The final theme is jurisprudential. Interpretation is no longer automatically seen as an objective and mechanical process of "discovering" historical meaning; instead, the emerging view among historians, literary theorists, and legal scholars is that interpretation itself inevitably involves the "creation" of meaning from the interaction of the text, historical context, and evolutive context.

A. *The Formalist Argument*

When the Supreme Court interprets statutes, it often invokes a strict formalist-sounding separation of responsibilities among the three branches of government, with the role of courts merely being to discern and apply the "intent" of the legislature. Professor Thomas Merrill has recently synthesized the Supreme Court's ad hoc approach and has presented a more systematic formal defense of intentionalist statutory interpretation.[68] In brief, his argument is that the Constitution's separation of powers gives all lawmaking power to Congress and none to the federal courts and that intentionalism is the only mode of statutory interpretation that is consonant with this constitutional division of functions.

This is an unusually strong statement of the formalist argument, because it denies courts any lawmaking functions. Indeed, the most striking thing about the argument is how little support it derives from the text and structure of the United States Constitution. Nowhere does the Constitution say that Congress shall have all lawmaking power. It only says, in article I, that "[a]ll *legislative* Powers" shall be vested in Congress and, in article III, that the "judicial Power of the United States" shall be vested in the Supreme Court and whatever inferior courts Congress might create. The commonly accepted meaning of "legislative Powers"—in 1789 as well as today—is the power to enact statutes, which can override the common law that is part of the "judicial Power."

The specification in article III, section 2 of what the "judicial Power" might encompass supports the view that the Framers assumed federal courts would have common law-making powers. The first para-

---

[68] Merrill, *The Common Law Powers of Federal Courts*, 52 U. CHI. L. REV. 1 (1985).

graph of section two lists nine areas of federal jurisdiction, and only one of those areas of potential federal jurisdiction, "Cases, in Law and Equity, arising under this Constitution, *the Laws of the United States*, and Treaties," explicitly contemplates that federal statutes would define the substantive rights of the parties. The Supreme Court was vested with original jurisdiction over two of these categories, that is, "Cases affecting Ambassadors, other public Ministers and Consuls, and those in which a State shall be a Party," with the implicit power to make law to resolve these disputes. In practice the Court in its original jurisdiction cases has deferred to relevant federal statutes but has often created federal common law.

Several of the areas of federal jurisdiction over which the Supreme Court has appellate jurisdiction similarly contemplate the creation of federal common law. For example, "Cases of admiralty and maritime Jurisdiction" had traditionally been governed by English judge-made law before American independence, and there is no reason to believe that the Framers intended to reject the traditional approach. "Controversies to which the United States shall be a Party" might involve federal statutory law, but it is unlikely that the Framers expected Congress to regulate all aspects of federal government affairs, such as government contracting. Even "Controversies . . . between Citizens of different States" were considered to be appropriate occasions for federal judicial lawmaking in the nineteenth century.

Merrill disapproves of much of this lawmaking by federal courts or explains it away as "preemptive," but the fact remains that the structure of the Constitution, the apparent expectations of the Framers, and two hundred years of Supreme Court practice establish the authority of federal courts to make law, subject to legislative override. Nor does this undercut the constitutional precept of "separation of powers." The Framers' conception of separation of powers was inspired in large part by Montesquieu's *De L'Esprit des Lois* and is best explained in *The Federalist*. Montesquieu had argued that tyranny was certain when the legislative, executive, and judicial powers were all combined in one authority, and the main purpose of separate powers in the Constitution was to protect against this certain abuse of federal power. Madison, echoing Montesquieu, argued in *The Federalist* that only "where the *whole* power of one department is exercised by the same hands which possess the *whole* power of another department, the fundamental principles of a free constitution are subverted." Thus, branches that are separate can still have some "partial agency in" or "control over"

one another * * *. In short, the Framers contemplated the existence of shared, rather than concentrated, lawmaking. * * *

For these reasons, Merrill's articulation of the formalist argument for intentionalist statutory interpretation is not persuasive. The formalist argument, however, does not have to deny federal courts all lawmaking powers. A weaker statement of the formalist argument would simply posit that the Framers and their contemporaries generally agreed that when a statute, not the common law, is at issue, the "judicial Power" is limited to "giving effect to the will of the Legislature." I believe this to be a more persuasive version of the formalist argument, but it only supports the proposition that the federal courts must respect statutory language, not the broader proposition that the courts must always replicate the original intent, or purpose, of the legislature. My response to this weaker version of the formalist argument rests upon historical * * * and jurisprudential analysis.

1. The Historical Response

The irony of modern formalism is that in limiting statutory interpretation to seeking out original legislative intent, it substitutes late nineteenth century assumptions for those that the Framers would have intended to guide the "judicial Power." Intentionalist statutory interpretation is probably not what the Framers had in mind when they defined the "judicial Power" in article III. Educated lawyers in 1789 would have considered statutory texts binding on courts, but would not have dogmatically argued that statutory interpretation involves nothing more than divining the intent of the legislature. The evidence suggests, moreover, that the Framers were no more intentionalist than their contemporaries.

Sir William Blackstone's *Commentaries* describe judges as "depositories of the law," whose job is to "determine not according to his private judgment, but according to the known laws and customs of the land; not delegated to pronounce a new law, but to maintain and expound the old one."[90] While Blackstone did not fully appreciate the creative role of judges, neither did he advocate slavish devotion to original legislative intent. He urged that "the most universal and effectual way of discovering the true meaning of a law, when the words are dubious, is by considering the *reason* and *spirit* of it . . . [f]or when this reason ceases, the law itself ought likewise to cease with it." While Blackstone refused to allow courts to substitute their judgment for that of the

---

[90] 1 W. BLACKSTONE, [COMMENTARIES ON THE LAWS OF ENGLAND 68-70 (1765).]

legislature, even when the legislature has "positively enact[ed] a thing to be done which is unreasonable," he did allow judges "to expound the statute by equity" to reject unreasonable consequences "where some collateral matter arises out of the general words" of the statute. To the extent that Blackstone had a theory of statutory interpretation, it was that judges should enforce the textual commands of statutes, though not to the detriment of the statute's overall purposes and the current demands of equity. That theory is closer to my model of dynamic interpretation than it is to any original intent approach.

Several of the influential Framers of the Constitution were at least as flexible as Blackstone in their approach to statutes. Alexander Hamilton went beyond Blackstone in *The Federalist No. 78* in favoring a fairly broad power of federal courts to declare congressional enactments void and unconstitutional, and in arguing that courts should also have the power to control "unjust and partial laws" by "mitigating the severity and confining the operation of such laws." His arguments derive from the checks and balances concept found in the Constitution: judicial frustration of unjust laws would force the legislature to "qualify" the severity of future laws. Hamilton further contended that everyone ought to support such judicial power, because "no man can be sure that he may not be tomorrow the victim of a spirit of injustice, by which he may be a gainer today" and "every man must now feel that the inevitable tendency of such a spirit is to sap the foundations of public and private confidence."

* * * It was not until the second half of the nineteenth century that the formalist approach—the role of a court interpreting a statute is only to divine and apply legislative intent—became the prevailing doctrine. This was part of a general shift in Anglo-American law that emphasized the importance of will and choice. Just as scholars and judges redefined punitive damages in tort and criminal prohibitions in terms of malicious "intent," so legislative scholars redefined statutory interpretation as a search for legislative intent. In short, the formalist argument for strictly intentionalist statutory interpretation is ultimately not grounded in any constitutional vision held by the Framers. Rather, it reflects constitutional theory that was fashionable a hundred years later, and which has little persuasive power for our society today.

* * *

3. The Jurisprudential Response

The historical * * * analysis developed above suggests * * * [another] response to the formalist argument. Intentionalist statutory interpretation has not been the product of the separation of powers idea; both the Framers in 1789 and modern civil law commentators have envisioned a system of separate powers, with legislative supremacy, but have contemplated dynamic interpretation of statutes to adapt to changed circumstances. Instead, intentionalist statutory interpretation has been the product of the "mechanical jurisprudence" of the late nineteenth century. Mechanical jurisprudence posits that law consists of rules promulgated by the sovereign legislature and mechanically applied by judges. The conception that the legislature has a specific "intention" on a wide range of interpretive questions, and that courts "objectively" determine that intention, is central to mechanical jurisprudence.

Therefore, a central problem with intentionalist rhetoric is that subsequent jurisprudence in both the United States and Europe has rejected the assumptions of mechanical jurisprudence and, concomitantly, liberated judges to read statutes dynamically. The sociological and legal realist movements of the early twentieth century rejected the divorce of law from policy associated with mechanical jurisprudence and, more importantly, delegitimated the essential metaphors of intentionalist statutory interpretation.

* * *

Just as the realists debunked the mechanical ideal of the passive judge, so they derided the anthropomorphism of legislative "intent." Max Radin argued that the concept of a single "will" for a collective body is incoherent and, in any event, is not even necessary for a thoroughgoing formalism.[113] According to Radin, the constitutional task of the legislature is not to have a "will," but only to write statutes, which are then interpreted and applied by judges and administrators to specific circumstances. Statutes are instruments of social policy, not ends in themselves, argued Radin. Other thinkers of the period developed the insight that percipient statutes, those responsive to genuine social and economic needs, would have an expansive influence on society and the common law itself.

The criticisms made by the legal realists are accepted widely today. Scholars from a variety of viewpoints agree that the idea of legislative intent is incoherent and that judges have substantial lawmaking discretion in applying statutes. But the realists

---

[113] *See* Radin, *Statutory Interpretation*, 43 HARV. L. REV. 863, 871-72 (1930). *But see* Landis, *A Note on "Statutory Interpretation,"* 43 HARV. L. REV. 886, 892 (1930) * * *.

were not successful in replacing the obsolete theory of statutory interpretation with a modern one. Radin himself proposed that statutory interpretation should start with the text, which will often provide determinate answers. Where the text does not provide a clear answer, the court should determine what "mischief" the legislature had targeted in passing the statute and then should interpret the statute to attack that mischief as it is manifested under current circumstances.

* * * [D]evelopments in the new "jurisprudence of interpretation" of the last two decades decisively undermine the coherence of the formalist argument for intentionalist interpretation and support my dynamic model. For the hard cases, interpretation will inevitably be affected by the current context of the judicial interpreter, and the greater the distance between the current and the historical context of the statute the more unlikely it is that intentionalist interpretation is even possible.

* * *

* * * A persuasive, though still controversial, body of modern aesthetic theory rejects the concept that a text has a single "true" meaning and posits that meaning is constructed by the interaction of readers and text. One leading theorist, Hans-Georg Gadamer, has argued that interpretation of a historical text involves a "fusing of horizons," in which the reader reaches out to the past perspective, understanding that her present context conditions her comprehension of that text.[123] Gadamer and subsequent critics further emphasize that interpretation of a canonical text is an ongoing dialectical process. Interpretation is a contemporary interpreter's dialogue with the text and with the tradition that surrounds it.

* * *

Although debated in their respective disciplines, these theories of subjective interpretation represent a growing academic consensus that different interpreters over time are likely to interpret the same text differently. * * *

Even the moderate form of contextualist interpretation theory is fatal to the formalist argument for originalist statutory interpretation. It denies the possibility of consistent and objective interpretations of the same statute by different judges—or even by the same judges under different circumstances. On the other hand, moderate contextualism does not assert that the interpreter is entirely unconstrained. One interpretation can still be "better" than another, because it is more consistent with the historical or evolutive perspectives, or with both. In most cases—the "easy cases"—the text and the interpretive history of the statute will provide relatively determinate answers, or at least narrow the range of permissible debate. * * *

* * *

C. The Countermajoritarian Difficulty with Reading Statutes Dynamically

A legal process objection to dynamic interpretation is suggested by the "countermajoritarian difficulty" that the late Alexander Bickel raised in connection with judicial review.[171] Although some of the Framers and subsequent scholars have tried to slide over the difficulty by characterizing judicial review as nothing more than the assertion of the constitutional superiority of "the power of the people" over the "will of the legislature," the fact remains that it is a nonelected judge asserting lawmaking power over the duly elected representatives of the people. Even though Bickel did not claim that the Republic was in imminent danger because of active judicial review and did not tie his argument rigorously to a vision of the Constitution, his argument was persuasive because it articulated the anxiety remaining from the discredited period of Lochnerian judicial review. Bickel's challenge to the "legitimacy" of judicial activism was based upon his view that activist judges may thereby be substituting their own "personal values" for legislatively determined values. This is inconsistent with our society's fundamental commitment to democracy.

Bickel's concerns may apply to statutory interpretation that slights the original value choices of the legislature. The countermajoritarian difficulty, however, ought not to be the basis for rejecting a cautious model of dynamic interpretation such as that set forth here. For example, when there has been a significant change in circumstances, the countermajoritarian difficulty presents slight justification for continuing to treat old statutory majorities as decisive and controlling. Additionally, other political values, apart from majoritarianism, are important in our constitutional

---

[123] H. GADAMER, [TRUTH AND METHOD 337 (G. Barden & F. Cumming trans., 1975).] While Gadamer's work has provoked debate, it has drawn a solid group of influential defenders. * * * Taking Gadamer's theory several steps further, Stanley Fish, in *Is There a Text in This Class?* 94 (1980), argues that readers are not "passive and disinterested comprehenders of a knowledge external to them" and are "at every moment creating the experiential spaces into which a personal knowledge flows."

[171] * * * A. BICKEL, THE LEAST DANGEROUS BRANCH 16 (1962) * * *.

polity. The legitimacy of government is ultimately based upon the continued responsiveness of the whole government to the objective needs of the evolving society. Under this view of legitimacy, the constructive role of courts in interpreting statutes by reference to current problems and policies can be quite substantial. * * *

1. Is Dynamic Statutory Interpretation Significantly Countermajoritarian?

In defending his thesis that courts should have the power to overrule statutes, just as they overrule common law decisions, * * * Guido Calabresi has analyzed several responses to the countermajoritarian concern.[174] While I find none of the responses completely dispositive of that concern, they do effectively minimize it and suggest that my cautious model of dynamic interpretation is not significantly countermajoritarian.

One response analyzed, but not endorsed, by Calabresi is that non-constitutional judicial treatment of statutes is only conditional, for it may be "corrected" by legislative action. This argument seems intuitively inconsistent with the primacy accorded legislative policy making. More importantly, the possibility of legislative correction is not a true majoritarian check because it is not regularly invoked. Political theory and experience suggest that because of the many procedural obstacles to legislation in our bicameral committee-dominated Congress, the tendency of interest groups to block rather than advance legislation, and the deference that legislators and their staffs will typically give to virtually any decision of the Supreme Court, such legislative correction will rarely occur. * * *

* * *

A second response, accepted by Calabresi as the best solution to the countermajoritarian difficulty, is that judicial lawmaking is justified by "the subservience of courts to principles, to rational decisionmaking, and to the whole fabric of the law." Because such "principled decisionmaking within a legal landscape [is] the primary judicial task," courts may, consistent with majoritarian democratic theory, be given lawmaking tasks based upon "the belief that the legal fabric, and the principles that form it, are a good approximation of one aspect of the popular will, of what a majority in some sense desires." This response, however, is not as persuasive as some commentators consider it to be, in part because it is rooted in the outdated rhetoric of mechanical jurisprudence, associating courts with reasoned, timeless "principle," and legislatures with irrational, contingent "politics." After its critique by the legal realists, that rhetoric has lost much of its cogency, and critical scholarship during the 1980's has rendered it increasingly controversial.

More important, Calabresi's equation of the "legal landscape" with "one aspect of the popular will" is incoherent. On the one hand, the majority appears at times to be quite at odds with the legal landscape. The legal landscape, after all, is mostly created by lawyers and other affluent groups in our society, and it would appear that its upper middle class values would frequently be at odds with those of mainstream America. On the other hand, even if it were true that the legal landscape enjoys majoritarian support, that does not prove that a majority of people would favor the existing legal landscape over other alternatives if such alternatives were explained to them. People accept most existing legal rules because they are the rules, not because people positively prefer them.

Perhaps the primary insight to be drawn from Calabresi's argument is a negative one: the majoritarian position cannot object to dynamic statutory interpretation unless it appears that the original majority which sought enactment, and had a discernible intent on the interpretive issue, persists. Of course, this is all but impossible to demonstrate. Where societal and legal circumstances have decisively changed since the enactment of the original statute, there is usually good reason to believe that the historical majority has vanished.

A third response, not explored by Calabresi, justifies dynamic statutory interpretation * * * where it is likely that the majority will has not changed. This response challenges the primacy that traditional legal process thinkers have given to the countermajoritarian difficulty. While it is routinely assumed by scholars such as Calabresi that our society is committed to majoritarian government, this is only true in the most general sense. Notwithstanding the one-person, one-vote cases, political gerrymandering and other devices ensure that elections will not reflect true majority preference. Once these representatives are in office, public choice theory predicts that their incentives will lead them away from majoritarian preferences and that, in any event, the rules created by a legislature will often fail to reflect majority preferences because of procedural manipulations. * * *

Had the Framers favored, and the Constitution embodied, a strict majoritarianism, the system of

---

[174] G. CALABRESI, [A COMMON LAW FOR THE AGE OF STATUTES 92-97 (1982).]

"direct democracy," in which people vote on statutory proposals, might have been appropriate. Yet direct democracy was considered and rejected in favor of representative democracy. A Madisonian vision of the Constitution explains this result and suggests that the deliberative process of lawmaking seeks to transform private preferences, not just reflect them. * * *

The deliberative democracy envisioned by the Framers, therefore, is one in which "the public voice" will speak beyond the private preferences of citizens. The Civil Rights Act of 1964, for example, was a great statute not only because it embodied a fundamental public value, but because the process of educating the American people both before and after enactment transformed private values as well. * * *

In short, under this third response, the Constitution seems to envision a dynamic policy creation in which majoritarian preferences are filtered and transformed through the deliberations of their representatives. In Congress, the preferences of members of the House, the most accountable representatives, are tempered by further deliberation by members of the Senate, the less accountable representatives, who originally were not even popularly elected. The role of the courts, therefore, is to be further deliberative filters, as envisioned by Hamilton, mitigating the effects of unwise laws and exploring their full consequences. Under this more complex view of the countermajoritarian difficulty, dynamic statutory interpretation is not problematic unless courts are not appropriate representatives or are not accountable for their mistakes. * * *

* * *

3. Courts Are Institutionally Competent to Perform the Lawmaking Role Implicit in the Task of Dynamic Statutory Interpretation

When circumstances have significantly changed and the statutory text is indeterminate, the countermajoritarian difficulty fails to provide a sufficient basis to deny courts the power to interpret statutes dynamically. Indeed, dynamic interpretation may contribute to the overall legitimacy of government. However, a central concern remains unaddressed: whether judges can be entrusted with this sort of lawmaking. It is questionable whether it is proper that value choices made by nonelected judges displace choices made by elected legislators. The specter of *Dred Scott* and *Lochner* and other past misjudgments raise doubts about any theory that openly accepts this type of judicial lawmaking.

These charges, that courts are incompetent to perform implicit lawmaking, are entirely overstated * * *. First, our polity already gives enormous lawmaking power to administrative agencies. In a vast range of statutes, agencies are empowered to update ongoing policy, often with virtually no congressional standards to confine administrative discretion. Although an agency's choice of policy is subject to judicial review, courts typically uphold an agency's choice when it is not contrary to the text of the statute and is reached after a deliberative process. Moreover, bureaucrats, like judges, are not elected. To give them power to update statutes seems no more legitimate than to recognize a similar power in judges. If anything, judges who update statutes are more trustworthy. They are not only removed from the political process but are also in positions that give them few incentives to slant their interpretations, as bureaucrats often do, in favor of regulated groups.

Second, judges can be trusted with greater discretion. Our polity already gives much broader lawmaking power to judges in nonstatutory situations than the power I advocate here for statutory interpretation. A good example of this judicial discretion is structural injunction litigation, in which courts preside over the reconstruction of public or private institutions. * * *

According to its supporters, structural litigation is justified because, substantively, it contributes to our society's need for social justice and public values and because, procedurally, it reveals that judges are much better at policy creation than traditionally supposed. In structural litigation, the old bromides extolling judicial independence from political pressures and the professional ideal of reflective and dispassionate analysis of focused problems have been demonstrated in the most trying circumstances in which judges are tempted to become personally involved in their cases. * * * Indeed, the nonbureaucratic nature of the judiciary has had some advantages. Unlike bureaucrats, judges must deliberate about problems brought before them; they cannot simply ignore problems. Also unlike bureaucrats, judges make law in the context of specific fact situations, thereby enabling them to focus their policy and to change it incrementally.

The first two responses to concerns about judicial imposition of personal values have an analogical appeal: if we allow lawmaking by agencies in statutory matters and by courts in nonstatutory matters, we should allow lawmaking by courts in statutory matters. The third response is that the adjudicative process will minimize the imposition of values idiosyncratic to individual jurists, because it is incremental and conventional. * * * The slowness and deliberateness of judicial lawmaking ensures that it will never be a threat to legislated lawmaking as the main source of policy preference and priorities in the United States.

The judge's interpretation will not be idiosyncratic, moreover, because it must be justified by a written opinion which relies on sources other than the judge's personal values. Although judges can find reasons and facts to support a variety of interpretations, their professional reputations depend in part on the persuasiveness of their justifications to readers with different values. Adjudication has been likened to an extended legal conversation, in which the interpreter is both constrained and legitimated by her need to explain and justify her interpretations to the interpretive community of other jurists, legislators, scholars, and lawyers.

* * *

III. Dynamic Statutory Interpretation Applied

Theoretically, my model of dynamic statutory interpretation offers quite a different focus from traditional theories of statutory interpretation because it treats the evolutive context as a persuasive source of statutory meaning which should be considered in addition to the statute's text and legislative history.
* * *

I do not argue that the model of dynamic statutory interpretation will produce different results in a large number of cases. After all, as literary theory teaches us, the current context and public values always exercise some influence on the interpretive enterprise. Instead, the model is appealing because it rests upon a realistic vision of the legislative and interpretive processes *and* because it promotes more candid decisionmaking in statutory interpretation cases. * * *

* * *

Nicholas S. Zeppos, *Judicial Candor and Statutory Interpretation*, 78 Geo. L.J. 353, 358–62, 379–86, 388, 393–95, 400–02, 404–07 (1989)*

* * *

The purpose of this article is to examine critically

---

* Copyright 1982 The Georgetown Law Journal Association. Reprinted with permission of The Georgetown Law Journal Association, Georgetown University, and Nicholas S. Zeppos. All rights reserved.

the theories that call for abandoning originalism in statutory interpretation and adopting judicial candor in its place. Although candor in judging is frequently invoked as a value to which judges should aspire, scholarly debate in general—and on statutory interpretation in particular—contains little critical debate about the need for or possibility of such candor. This article argues that judicial candor in statutory interpretation is far more problematic than it seems because of the legitimacy concerns that arise when a court candidly declares its power to refuse either to apply a statute or to interpret a statute according to its own vision of society's current demands or needs. This article further argues that theories of candid interpretation inadequately address the potential conflict between judicial candor and the checking function played by courts. In particular, theories of candid dynamic interpretation fail to take into account the effect on the judiciary's established role in supervising the activities of administrative agencies.

* * *

I. Judicial Candor and Dynamic Statutory Interpretation

For years, the dominant scholarly and judicial tradition in statutory interpretation focused on discovering original legislative intent. This approach required courts to ask how the enacting legislature resolved (or would have resolved) the particular interpretive problem. New theories of statutory interpretation challenge this model. Their proponents see no reason why the intent of the enacting legislature, which often cannot even be discovered, should be used to resolve important questions of law that significantly affect the structure and governance of present day society. In place of this search for legislative intent, new theories of statutory interpretation urge courts to interpret statutes in light of society's present day needs and demands, and to be candid in declaring the factors that lead courts to adopt updated readings of statutes.

* * *

A. Theories of Dynamic Interpretation

The works of Guido Calabresi and William Eskridge make the most compelling case for candid dynamic statutory interpretation. Each condemns the originalist theory and in its place offers a model in which the judge asks how a particular statute can be read to meet the needs of present day society. Calabresi and Eskridge acknowledge that this process of updating goes on today but assert that it is masked by courts that continue to invoke originalist rhetoric to justify dynamic results. In place of this masking process, both Calabresi and Eskridge argue for candor in judging.

Calabresi's theory is the more far-ranging. He urges courts faced with a problem of statutory interpretation to ask whether the statute fits the current fabric of society. According to Calabresi, a judge undertaking this inquiry should consider political, social, and economic values of society, as well as any related legal or technological developments that shed light on how the statute could advance societal goals and needs. If the statute as written fails to meet the present day needs of society, Calabresi argues for judicial modification, much like judicial updating of outdated common law precedents.

Calabresi argues that his model of judging is frequently used by courts but that courts mask their decisions in traditional originalist rhetoric. He condemns this technique of covert judicial updating. Calabresi urges that judicial policymaking by subterfuge should be replaced by judicial candor, in which court opinions explicitly state those factors—economic, social, political, and technological—that in fact shaped their results. Calabresi concludes by stating that the continued lack of candor in statutory interpretation will eventually undermine the judiciary's legitimacy and credibility.

Eskridge's theory of dynamic statutory interpretation is similar to Calabresi's. Eskridge argues that statutes should be interpreted in a dynamic fashion, taking into account new developments and changes in the legal framework as well as in society in general. Unlike Calabresi, Eskridge does not envision courts refusing to enforce statutes that fail to meet the present day needs of society. Instead, he proposes a model of interpretation that requires courts to weigh three perspectives: the text of the statute (textual perspective); the legislative expectations surrounding the statute's creation (historical perspective); and the subsequent evolution of the statute, with a particular focus on whether the societal and legal environment has changed since the statute's enactment (evolutive perspective). According to Eskridge, these three perspectives allow cases to be placed on a continuum. When the statute at issue is of recent origin or is particularly detailed, the textual or historical perspective will most likely control. When the statute is older or there has been a significant shift in public values, however, the evolutive perspective will usually be most important.

Eskridge argues for a complex and sophisticated balancing of perspectives to tell courts when they are free to depart from the statute's text or historical basis and instead use current public values as a basis for interpretation. Like Calabresi's approach, Eskridge's ambitious model is both prescriptive and descriptive. Eskridge not only recommends his model for future use by the courts, but also argues that it largely captures the present method by which courts reach evolutionary results. He argues that his model's main advantage is that by expressly making the evolutive perspective part of their decisions, courts will enhance candor in judging. Thus, like Calabresi, Eskridge foresees that judicial candor can be a positive byproduct of a dynamic model of interpretation.

* * *

II. Solving the Countermajoritarian Problem in Statutory Interpretation

Under our constitutional system, policy judgments in the crafting of legislation are attained through interaction between Congress and the President. The Constitution prescribes no role for the judiciary in the process by which a bill becomes law. Courts deal with legislation produced by the elected branches only as a byproduct of the case or controversy requirement of article III. When a party is injured by the application of the statute and seeks relief in court, the court engages in the process of statutory interpretation. Traditionally, a court interpreting a statute cannot question the solution enacted by the elected branches. Once the law passes through the constitutionally prescribed procedure—passage by both houses of Congress and presentment to the President—and absent any constitutional infirmity, the court has no choice but to enforce the statute.

Obviously, this is a highly idealized description of the judicial role in interpreting statutes. Even the most ardent defenders of judicial restraint have admitted that ambiguity in statutes is inevitable, and that courts are left unguided by any specific congressional intent. The legal realists go even further and demonstrate that judges necessarily play a creative policymaking role in interpreting statutes. Recent scholarship on the role of language as a guiding source in interpretation has further revealed the lawmaking power of judges in statutory interpretation.

The idealized separation of powers model, in which the court simply enforces the statute enacted by the elected branches, is in obvious tension with the creative lawmaking function of the courts. As much as in constitutional interpretation, judicial interpretation of statutes raises a problem of legitimacy, i.e., justification for unelected and unrepresentative judges making law in a representative democracy.

A. A Critique of Prior Efforts

Theories of dynamic interpretation raise the problem of legitimacy in a particularly stark context. They seek to assign to the courts the task of adjusting statutes to economic, technological, and social developments, a matter usually reserved for the legislature. By urging a judicial role in updating statutes, Calabresi and Eskridge thrust themselves directly into this debate.

As the title to his book suggests [A COMMON LAW FOR THE AGE OF STATUTES (1982)], Calabresi seeks to justify his bold approach for judicial repudiation of obsolete statutes by analogizing it to the accepted judicial role of modifying the common law. Reviewers of the book quickly pointed out that Calabresi's legitimacy theory suffers from a fatal flaw. The common law is judge-made, and thus appropriately modified or even discarded by a judge. In contrast, statutory law is created by the legislature. Thus, it may be changed only by the legislature. The analogy to the common law is simply inapposite because the source of constitutional authority for the creation of statutory law is different. It is apposite only if one assumes that the legislature is not supreme to the court—an assumption, of course, that assumes away the basic legitimacy problem.

Calabresi's critics identified a second weakness in his common law analogy: the inability of a judge to perform the tasks Calabresi's theory requires. In Calabresi's scheme, the court, in deciding whether to overturn an obsolete statute, measures the statute against the current "legal landscape." This requires the court to examine other related legal developments and current social, economic, moral, and political values. Through this comparative inquiry of the old and the new, Calabresi forecasts that democratic values will be furthered by bringing law into harmony with the people's demands for a coherent body of legal principles. Critics of the book commented upon the Herculean nature of this undertaking. The judge's limited abilities and resources suggest that no matter how well-intentioned, a court is simply not up to this monumental task.

Finally, critics identified a third weakness in Calabresi's theory of legitimacy. Calabresi justifies judicial repudiation or modification of statutes by claiming that the end product will be a more coherent body of law—a goal of a democratic society. But such a theory wrongly assumes that statutory law must be principled and coherent. The bartering and negotiation among interest groups in the legislative process virtually assures that the end product will be unprincipled, with favored groups getting special exemptions or treatment in the statutory scheme.

Eskridge's justification for a judicial role in updating statutes begins with an argument similar to Calabresi's. He first reasons that the Constitution contemplates that judges will make law in certain areas. Specifically, he refers to the numerous areas in which federal courts have made common law. Eskridge, however, goes beyond this analogy to judicial lawmaking through the common law and challenges the fundamental premise of the countermajoritarian problem. He argues that those seeking to legitimate a lawmaking role for courts in a democratic society mistakenly assume that our constitutional scheme is purely a democratic one.

Eskridge draws support for this view from various sources. He first points to writings contemporaneous to the drafting of the Constitution to justify nonoriginalist interpretation. Specifically, Eskridge argues that eighteenth century legal theorists endorsed nonoriginalist statutory interpretation. Thus, at the time the Constitution was adopted, it was accepted that courts could interpret statutes in a nonoriginalist fashion without violating majoritarian values. Eskridge also relies upon the description of the legislative process found in *The Federalist No. 10*, authored by James Madison. According to Madison (and Eskridge), our constitutional system builds in many constraints against a direct democracy or pure majoritarianism. Primary among these restraints are a bicameral legislature with an upper house whose membership is not based on proportional representation and whose members serve six year terms, an electoral college, and the presidential veto. The purpose of these structural restraints is to check and filter the shifting (and often capricious) whims of the majority through a deliberative process. For Eskridge there is no legitimacy problem in having an unelected, unrepresentative judiciary help perform this filtering function.

Eskridge elaborates on this theme of countermajoritarian democracy by tying the judicial role in updating statutes to the goals of a representative democracy. His argument suggests that a representative democracy draws its legitimacy not simply from its ties to the electorate, but also from how it serves the electorate. When the politically elected branches fail to adjust statutes to the current needs of society, they act contrary to the ultimate goals of a representative democracy. And, when a court, interpreting a statute, takes into account the current needs of society, the court is acting consistent with the goals of a representative democracy and thus contributing to the overall legitimacy of government.

Although Eskridge's justifications for judicial updating of statutes differ from those offered by Calabresi, they have common attributes. Both attempt to resolve the countermajoritarian problem by pointing to other nonmajoritarian features of our system. This theory of legitimacy may be challenged in two respects. First, many of the countermajoritarian elements in our constitutional lawmaking process are themselves subject to direct political control. Senators, although serving six years and distributed equally among the fifty states, do run for reelection. Similarly, a presidential veto may be overridden by a popularly elected legislature. Judges, on the other hand, are not subject to these same forms of political check or control. Second, many of the nonmajoritarian elements in our legislative process—bicameralism, a House of Representatives accountable through biennial elections, a Senate accountable every six years, and a presidential veto—are found in the text of the Constitution. Other than through a rather generous reading of the "case or controversy" requirement of article III, the power of judges to update statutes simply cannot be found in the Constitution. Although it may be useful to have article III judges serve as a filter in the legislative process, absent some better evidence it is difficult to justify this judicial power by relying on other nonmajoritarian procedures that can be found in the text of the Constitution and that remain subject to some check by the people.

It is also difficult to justify the judicial role in statutory updating by focusing entirely on the end product. Eskridge, like Calabresi, ultimately claims that judicial updating is not antidemocratic because the courts will reach results that reflect the values of a just society. One must obviously ask whose vision of justice applies? * * *

* * *

B. Judicial Candor and Legitimacy: The Values of Limitation and Distinction and the Problem of Indeterminacy

This critique of previous efforts to legitimate a judicial lawmaking role in interpreting statutes should not be taken to mean that the reasons offered by proponents of judicial lawmaking are irrelevant. To the contrary, they do shed some light on the acceptance of a policymaking or lawmaking role for judges in the context of statutory interpretation. However, by focusing on analogies to other nonmajoritarian aspects of our constitutional system or on the just results reached in a particular case, these theories only partially legitimate judicial lawmaking in statutory interpretation.

First, theories that rely solely on other nonmajoritarian procedures in our system or on just results contain no obvious rule of limitation. In asserting a judicial power to override the legislative process, they contain no criteria for determining when, if ever, the legislative command should be followed.

Second, these theories ignore another indispensable aspect of legitimating judicial decisions. If what the courts do appears to be exactly like what Congress and the executive branch do—assess the legal landscape and reach what each considers to be the best result—one might well ask why judicial decisions should be obeyed over the determinations of the political branches. To overcome these problems, a theory of legitimacy must restrain the judiciary and articulate how the judicial decisionmaking process can be distinguished from that employed by the other branches.

Significantly, both Calabresi and Eskridge recognize that the notions of restraint and distinction are integral to legitimating judicial lawmaking. Calabresi relies on the interstitial nature of judicial lawmaking, the need for judges to act according to principle, and the need for judges to give reasons for their decisions as central to legitimating judicial invalidation of obsolete statutes. Eskridge limits his theory of dynamic interpretation to cases in which statutory text and historical considerations do not provide a clear answer. Thus, both ultimately seek to ground the legitimacy of dynamic interpretation by courts in the principles of limitation and distinction. But neither looks further to see if these legitimating principles can coexist with judicial candor.

* * *

Critical to Eskridge's theory legitimating dynamic interpretation is his assertion that in some cases, dynamic interpretation will not be possible because traditional originalist sources provide for determinate results. If, however, the entire interpretive process is more indeterminate than Eskridge suggests, his model of limited candid dynamic interpretation may be indistinguishable from Calabresi's—whose model Eskridge rejects as "difficult to justify in light of current assumptions about legislative supremacy. . . ."

As Eskridge recognizes, he may well overstate the extent to which the text or historical background of a statute provides for determinate results. When faced with an argument for dynamic interpretation, the court by definition must read the statute in an entirely new context shaped by significant cultural, societal, technological, or economic changes. Yet, these cultural and societal contexts give meaning to the statutory text. Once the reader's context changes, raising the initial need for dynamic interpretation, determinate results may disappear.

Reliance on determinate statutory text is further complicated by the settled interpretive technique of invoking the "spirit" or purpose of the statute over statutory language. Resort to statutory text to dispose of cases in which dynamic interpretation is urged seems to carry with it the same shortcomings identified by critics of the "plain meaning" rule. It denies that an element of choice exists when choice seems obvious.

* * *

In sum, even a limited theory of candid dynamic interpretation like Eskridge's may compromise the values of limitation and distinction, which seem to be crucial to legitimating judicial lawmaking in statutory interpretation. Distinctions between the judicial process and the legislative or administrative processes may be blurred because the court will decide based on what it deems to be best for society. Further, every case may be an invitation to dynamic interpretation. If that is so, limitations may also be eased because the court will repeatedly invoke its own power to choose.

C. Legitimacy and the Persistence of Legislative Supremacy

I have sketched a legitimacy theory that is hardly unassailable or the *only* theory of legitimating the process of statutory interpretation. The values of limitation and distinction are normatively linked to a particular vision of separation of powers and legislative supremacy.

One could, of course, challenge these norms and urge a theory of legitimacy that is tied to other values. Yet dynamic theorists never quite break from legislative supremacy in their own theories of legitimacy. Eskridge goes down this path to a certain extent when he argues that dynamic interpretation is legitimate because legitimacy is not defined solely by process, but by results that respond to the needs of society. He argues that when a legislature fails to meet these needs, it lacks legitimacy and the court responds appropriately by engaging in dynamic interpretation. But, as discussed above, by limiting candid dynamic interpretation to "unclear" cases, Eskridge seeks to preserve a role for originalist interpretation at the expense of dynamic results.

* * *

Ultimately, then, the interesting question is why proponents of dynamic theories of statutory interpretation challenge the traditional legitimacy values drawn from legislative supremacy, yet always manage nonetheless to preserve a role for originalism (as Eskridge does) * * *. Their arguments to the contrary, dynamic theorists seem to share the interest in legislative supremacy that forms the very basis for originalist rhetoric.

* * *

III. The Values of Judicial Candor: A Critique

The countermajoritarian problem may at least partially explain why originalism continues to dominate in statutory interpretation. The tenacity of originalism seems all the more remarkable when measured against the repeated calls for candor in the judging process. But, although judicial candor is frequently invoked as an exalted value, proponents rarely provide a full explanation of why candor should be a part of judging. Perhaps those who urge adoption of judicial candor view it as a self-evident truth of uncompromising importance.

Further analysis of judicial candor seems indispensable. There must be some reason why candor is currently sacrificed in the judging process. We cannot expect courts to suddenly adopt a more honest approach to dynamic statutory interpretation without providing some explanation for why they should abandon originalism. Candor—or its absence—in statutory interpretation can be understood only if the values associated with it are spelled out and subjected to critical discussion.

A. The Values Associated with Judicial Candor

Candor can be readily associated with other values the law strives to achieve. First, candor in judging seeks to make the law predictable. When a court is candid, it gives the parties notice of the basis for its ruling and allows the parties to plan their transactions based on the court's actual rationale. By striving to make the law more predictable, candor appeals to basic notions of fairness embodied in our legal system. * * *

The predictability accompanying judicial candor is important in another respect. A candid judicial decision allows future courts to know the grounds upon which the ruling was based. This is particularly important in a hierarchical judicial system. * * *

The second value associated with judicial candor, which seems to form the unspoken premise for almost all of the prior calls for candor, is that deception in judging undermines the integrity of the judiciary. The almost universal condemnation of lying suggests that those who call for judicial candor have staked out the moral high ground. The moral dilemma faced by courts is compounded by their role as authority figures with lawmaking power. A court that lays claim to the power to pronounce legal rights and remedies cannot expect obedience if its process is corrupted by lying.

B. The Viability of a Candid Approach

These two values—predictability of the law for litigants and judges, and the morality of truthfulness—explain why candor seems to have such a strong claim on our legal system. Candor's link to fair notice and truth appeals to the higher aspirations of the law and society in general. It seems odd that a system of judging could long exist that apparently has contravened these cherished values. But, the covert process of dynamic statutory interpretation criticized by Calabresi and Eskridge * * * is evidence that candor has perhaps made fewer inroads than one might expect. This discrepancy between the calls for candor and the current practice of judging perhaps may be explained by looking at whether a candid approach * * * actually would [further] the values associated with candor.

1. Predictability

It is doubtful that judicial candor leads to greater predictability for litigants or the courts. Proponents of candor urge the court to resolve questions of statutory interpretation by consulting economic, social, and technological developments, as well as any related legal developments that would shed light on the question. But, any system of dynamic interpretation that requires the judge to make decisions based on considerations that are coextensive with the public good cannot easily claim that candor in one case will make for predictable results in the next.

* * *

2. Candor and Judicial Integrity

The strongest argument in favor of judicial candor is that candor avoids undercutting the integrity of the judiciary. Yet, it appears that the moral force of candor has not caused courts to abandon originalism in statutory interpretation. The reasons for this may rest on the judiciary's interest in preserving what it perceives as the established judicial function in our society.

As discussed above, there seems to be a link between adherence to originalism in statutory interpretation and resolution of the countermajoritarian difficulty. By appearing to erase limitations on the judicial power to construe statutes and to blur distinctions between the judicial, legislative, and administrative processes, candor may threaten the accepted lawmaking role for judges. Thus, for a judge, the choice between candor and originalist rhetoric may represent a choice between rejecting or accepting the judge's traditional role.

One can cynically view originalist rhetoric as the judiciary's selfish effort to avoid responsibility and at the same time retain power. Yet, this may not be an entirely fair or accurate characterization. Others outside the judiciary—most notably legal scholars—have come to regard courts as essential actors in enforcing both constitutional and statutory restrictions on the other branches. By threatening the legitimacy of the judicial role, candor may jeopardize the courts' performance of this checking function. Indeed, exalting the judicial role may place the courts in a "Catch-22" situation. The increased importance of the courts only heightens the demands for judicial candor. Yet, candor may diminish the courts' ability to perform their checking role and thereby diminish their overall importance.

The moral case for candor is compelling and poses the greatest problem for preserving originalist rhetoric. But for the judiciary, other values—such as preserving the court's checking function—may outweigh the value of candor. * * *

The potential that candor could undermine the judiciary's established checking function suggests that the problem of candor in judging is quite complex. Until theories advocating candor become more convincing, and until the courts' checking function can be reconciled with the effects of total candor, originalism may continue to dominate statutory interpretation.

IV. Judicial Candor and the Complexity of Judicial Decisionmaking

Originalist interpretation is subject to a basic challenge as a legitimating force for judges. How can originalism really solve the countermajoritarian difficulty if it is all a ruse or charade? Any careful outside observer can demonstrate the doctrinal incoherence of and hidden policy bases for non-candid, originalist judicial decisions.

There are at least two responses to this challenge. On one level, illusions and myths can serve useful purposes. As long as courts cultivate the perception that they are constrained and distinguishable from the political branches, their legitimacy will remain intact. On another level, originalist interpretation may be legitimated, or at least defended, by examining the process by which judges make decisions based on originalist sources.

Proponents of candid dynamic interpretation implicitly characterize originalist decisionmaking as a two-step process. First, there is the process by which the judge actually makes a decision. Second, there is the separate process by which the judge justifies the decision in a written opinion. Candor in statutory interpretation requires judges to eliminate the disconnection between these two steps and use the reasons for the result as the basis for the written opinion.

The problem is, however, that this demarcation into two discrete steps may be an oversimplification of the judging process. The judicial decisionmaking process is a complex blend of conscious and unconscious factors. On an elementary level, a judge interpreting a statute considers the traditional array of evidentiary sources, including statutory text, legislative history, and prior cases construing the same or similar statutes. But, as much as the judge may want to limit consideration to these evidentiary sources, other factors inevitably enter into the judging process. Based on the facts, the statutory backdrop, or personal experiences, the judge may form personal notions of justice or social welfare in a particular context. Added to this may be the judge's views about the court's role in relation to that of the legislature, and doubts or questions about competency.

The interplay of these various and conflicting stimuli explains why legal realists sought to portray the judging process as more than a mechanical exercise. Yet, the complexity of the process may also belie the notion that the judge can separate out the "false" reasons for a decision (i.e., statutory language, legislative history, or canons of interpretation) from the "real" reasons (the impulse to do what is right for society under the circumstances). As much as any other product of human decisionmaking, the judge's work is subject to the complex ways in which the human mind orders, explains, and processes information.

* * *

Cass R. Sunstein, *Interpreting Statutes in the Regulatory State*, 103 HARV. L. REV. 405, 415–24 (1989)*

* * *

A. Courts As Agents

* * *

1. Textualism.—It is sometimes suggested that statutory language is the source of judicial power and the only legitimate object of judicial concern. Textualism appears to be enjoying a renaissance in a number of recent cases, and perhaps in the academy as well, partly because of dissatisfaction with alternative interpretive strategies * * * which counsel courts to rely on "purpose" or to produce "reason" in regulatory regimes.

Several considerations argue in favor of textualist

---

* Copyright 1989 by the Harvard Law Review Association. Reprinted with permission of the Harvard Law Review Association and Cass R. Sunstein. All rights reserved.

strategies. First, textualism contains an important and often overlooked truth. Statutory terms are the enactment of the democratically elected legislature and represent the relevant "law." Statutory terms—not legislative history, not legislative purpose, not legislative "intent"—have gone through the constitutionally specified procedures for the enactment of law. Second, resort to the text promotes goals associated with the rule of law: citizens have access to the statutory words and can most readily order their affairs in response to those words. Third, the words of a statute, considered in light of widely shared conventions about how they should be understood, often have only one plausible interpretation, or at least sharply constrain the territory of legitimate disagreement. Finally, an emphasis on the primacy of the text serves as a salutary warning about the potential abuses of judicial use of statutory "purpose" and of legislative history.

Some textualists emphasize the "plain meaning" or dictionary definition of statutory terms; others are more sensitive to the particular settings. In its purest form, however, the textualist approach is inadequate. The central problem is that the meaning of words (whether "plain" or not) depends on both *culture* and *context*. Statutory terms are not self-defining, and words have no meaning before or without interpretation. To say this is emphatically not to say that words used in statutes or elsewhere can mean anything at all. But it is to say that statutory terms are indeterminate standing "by themselves," and, even more important, they never stand by themselves. The significance of congressional enactments necessarily depends on the context and on background understandings about how words should be understood. Moreover, reliance on ordinary or dictionary definition, without reference to context, will sometimes lead to interpretive blunders.[35]

Usually the context does not prevent reliance on ordinary meaning, and usually the background prin-

---

[35] Courts have conspicuously rejected literalism on many occasions. *See* Missouri v. Jenkins, 109 S. Ct. 2463, 2471 (1989) (holding that "attorney's fee" should be read to include award of paralegal fees); and Hensley v. Eckerhart, 461 U.S. 424, 429 n.2, 433 (1983) (observing that under § 1988, which provides attorney's fees to the "prevailing party," prevailing plaintiffs may recover if they prevail on any significant issue, but defendants may recover only if the plaintiff's suit was groundless) (dictum); United States v. Colon-Ortiz, 866 F.2d 6, 11 (1st Cir. 1989) (refusing to adhere to an obvious drafting error); *In re* House Bill No. 1,291, 178 Mass. 605, 60 N.E. 129 (1901) (holding that a requirement in the Massachusetts Constitution of a "written vote" allows a voting machine involving no writing); Riggs v. Palmer, 115 N.Y. 506, 22 N.E. 188 (1889) (refusing to allow a testator's murderer to recover under the will) * * *.

ciples are so widely shared—for example, that Congress is speaking in English, that Congress is not joking or attempting to mislead, that statutes have purposes, or that judges should not decide cases simply according to their predilections—that they are invisible. Even in easy cases, however, courts must resort to background principles. * * *

* * *

(a) Ambiguity or Vagueness.—The most familiar problem with textualism is that statutory language is sometimes ambiguous or vague. To say that courts should rely on the words or on their ordinary meaning—the plain meaning approach—is unhelpful when statutory words have more than one dictionary definition, or when the context produces interpretive doubt. It is not clear, for example, whether the term "feasible" contemplates a cost-benefit analysis, or whether a prohibition of "discrimination" bars voluntary race-conscious measures designed to counteract the effects of past and present discrimination against blacks. In both of these cases, moreover, it is uncertain whether the language should be taken to refer to the original meaning of those words for the enacting legislature (assuming that idea can be made intelligible in light of the problems of aggregating the views of numerous actors) or should instead take account of contemporary understandings of what the words mean. Indeed, it is not even clear what bearing the desires, or interpretive instructions, of the enacting legislature should have for judicial interpretation. By itself, textualism cannot answer these questions. Nor can the agency conception of the judicial role resolve such problems.

(b) Overinclusiveness.—If textualism is taken, as it often is, to call for reliance on the literal language of statutory words—their dictionary definition or meaning in ordinary settings—it will sometimes suggest an outcome that makes little or no sense. For example, suppose that a state law says that no vehicles are permitted in public parks, and a city proposes to build in a park a monument consisting of tanks used in World War II. The literal language must yield, for the statute could not reasonably be taken to forbid a monument, which causes none of the harms the statute could be thought to prevent.

A passage from Wittgenstein indicates the basic difficulty: "Someone says to me: 'Shew the children a game.' I teach them gaming with dice, and the other says 'I didn't mean that sort of game.' Must the exclusion of the game with dice have come before his mind when he gave me the order?" The example shows that sometimes the best interpretation of a textual command is one that runs counter to its apparent literal meaning—even if the author did not have in mind the case at issue, or make a judgment about how that case should be resolved.

Courts encounter the problem of overinclusiveness frequently. The Supreme Court recently held that a statute exempting state and local public housing obligations "from all taxation . . . imposed by the United States" should not be interpreted to include an exemption from federal estate tax. The Court held that the exemption did not mean what it appeared to say in light of the contemporaneous understanding that an excise tax was not ordinarily comprehended within the category of "taxation." As another example, suppose that the legislature has said that an employer may discharge an employee "for any reason." Is the employer thereby authorized to fire workers who have refused to commit crimes on his behalf? If a state law says that one spouse will inherit from another "in all circumstances," may a husband who has murdered his wife make a claim against the estate? These are examples of what might be described as the overinclusiveness of a prominent version of textualism: the possibility that statutory language, read without sufficient regard to context or its intended field of application, will reach situations that it could not reasonably cover.

(c) Underinclusiveness.—Although it arises less frequently, there is also a possibility that textualism will be underinclusive. Justice Holmes warned that "[c]ourts are apt to err by sticking too closely to the words of a law where those words import a policy that goes beyond them." A particular difficulty here is that a statute may be "evaded" by private ingenuity. The literal language of the statute does not cover the situation, but because the private conduct causes all of the harms that the statute could be thought to prevent, courts sometimes hold a statute applicable notwithstanding its literal terms. The problem of evasion should not be an excuse for judicial stretching of statutes (to be sure, a most ill-defined concept in this setting), but the problem has elicited judicial responses in a number of areas, most notably taxation.

(d) Delegation, Gaps, and Implementing Rules.—The incompleteness of textualism is most conspicuous when Congress has explicitly or implicitly delegated lawmaking power to the courts or when Congress has simply left a gap. In cases of delegated power or gap-filling, the problem is not that words are susceptible to more than one construction, but instead that the words necessarily require courts to look to sources outside of the text.

The Sherman Act, for example, raises a serious gap-filling problem. The language of the Act does not answer the question of what practices amount to "conspiracies in restraint of trade." The legislative history is suggestive but unclear, and the courts have inevitably taken the Act as a delegation of policymaking power pursuant to quite open-ended criteria. Similarly, section 1983 is silent on many important questions, including available defenses, burdens of pleading and persuasion, and exhaustion requirements. Because of the textual silence, judges must fill the gaps. To this extent, the statute delegates power to make common law.

Judicial implementation of title VII of the Civil Rights Act of 1964 can be understood in similar terms, though this example is more controversial. The basic prohibition of "discrimination" provides no guidance on the role of discriminatory effects, the appropriate burdens of proof and production, and the mechanisms for filtering out discriminatory treatment. Judicial answers to these questions sometimes purport to be relatively mechanical responses to congressional commands, but in fact they amount to judge-made implementing devices that reflect the judges' own, inevitably value-laden views. In light of the existence of textual gaps on many questions, this approach is hardly an embarrassment or a usurpation, but instead an inevitable part of interpretation. Much of the law of title VII is an unavoidable, and therefore legitimate, norm-ridden exercise in developing gap-filling rules. In this respect, the Sherman Act and title VII are closely analogous.

When the language of a statute does not specify its implementing rules, textualism is incomplete: courts must look elsewhere. When Congress has delegated power or left a gap, the line between interpreting and creating federal common law becomes quite thin.

(e) Changed Circumstances.—The discussion thus far has assumed that circumstances have not changed significantly since the statute was enacted. Textualism becomes even more problematic when time has affected the assumptions under which the statute was originally written. Changed circumstances may produce ambiguity or interpretive doubt in the text where neither existed before.

* * *

The discussion thus far suggests two principal points. First, and most fundamentally, there is no such thing as an acontextual "text" that can be used as the exclusive guide to interpretation. In easy cases, interpretive norms—on which there is wide or universal consensus—and context both play a part in the process of ascertaining statutory meaning. Because such norms are so widely shared, they are invisible and are not an object of controversy. Only in these cases can meaning ever be said to be "plain." With these qualifications, textualism is generally appropriate. In hard cases, however, courts must resort to a highly visible background norm, or a contestable one, or some gap-filling device in order to resolve an interpretive dispute. In these settings, and in this sense, textualism is incomplete.

Second, it is by no means obvious that courts should always rely solely on the text or on the "plain meaning" of its words even in cases in which such reliance leads to determinate results. Although textualism properly draws on the democratic primacy of the legislature, legislative instructions are often unclear and the claim of a command is a myth. An interpretive strategy that relies exclusively on the ordinary meaning of words is precisely that—a strategy that reflects a choice among competing possibilities—and it will sometimes produce irrationality or injustice that the legislature did not intend. Textualism of this sort is not incomplete but instead pernicious.

In cases of overinclusiveness, underinclusiveness, changed circumstances, or divergence between ordinary meaning and contextual or legislatively intended meaning, textualism—with its disregard of the irrational, unjust, and often unintended outcomes produced by literalism in hard cases—is best defended as a fighting faith, an inference from the system of separation of powers, rather than as a necessary understanding of statutory interpretation. On this view, reliance on ordinary meaning and indifference to context, irrationality, and injustice will discipline the judges, limit their discretion, hold them to Congress' actual words, and warn the lawmakers to be careful about statutory language. It is by no means clear, however, that a system of textualism, so defended, will lead to a superior system of law, and there is considerable reason to suspect otherwise. Even the most attractive form of textualism, emphasizing not literalism but the meaning of words read in context and against shared interpretive norms, is inadequate in light of the need to use contestable norms in hard cases and the interpretive difficulties produced by unintended irrationality and injustice.

* * *

Stephen Breyer, *On the Uses of Legislative History in Interpreting Statutes*, 65 S. CAL. L. REV. 845, 845-48, 850-67, 872-74 (1992)*

I. Introduction

Until recently an appellate court trying to interpret

---

* Reprinted with permission of the Southern California Law Review and Stephen Breyer. All rights reserved.

unclear statutory language would have thought it natural, and often helpful, to refer to the statute's "legislative history." The judges might have examined congressional floor debates, committee reports, hearing testimony, and presidential messages in an effort to determine what Congress really "meant" by particular statutory language. Should courts refer to legislative history as they try to apply statutes correctly? Is this practice wise, helpful, or proper? Lawyers and judges, teachers and legislators, have begun to reexamine this venerable practice, often with a highly critical eye. Some have urged drastically curtailing, or even totally abandoning, its use. Some argue that courts use legislative history almost arbitrarily. Using legislative history, Judge Leventhal once said, is like "looking over a crowd and picking out your friends." Others maintain that it is constitutionally improper to look beyond a statute's language, or that searching for "congressional intent" is a semi-mystical exercise like hunting the snark.

These and other criticisms are taking their toll. Judge Wald has pointed out that the Supreme Court relied on legislative history in almost every statutory case it decided in 1981. And although Justice White has recently commented that "the Court's practice of utilizing legislative history reaches well into its past, [and we] suspect that the practice will likewise reach well into the future,["] the Supreme Court's actual use of legislative history is in decline. By 1989, the Court decided a significant number of statutory cases (ten out of about sixty-five) without any reference to legislative history at all; and, in the 1990 Term, the Court decided nineteen out of about fifty-five such statutory cases without its use. Referring to legislative history to resolve even difficult cases may soon be the exception rather than the rule.

Although I recognize the possible "rearguard" nature of my task, I should like to defend the classical practice and convince you that those who attack it ought to claim victory once they have made judges more sensitive to problems of the abuse of legislative history; they ought not to condemn its use altogether. * * *

* * *

I concede at the outset that my arguments are more pragmatic than theoretical. They rest upon two important assumptions. First, I assume that appellate courts are in part administrative institutions that aim to help resolve disputes and, while doing so, interpret, and thereby clarify, the law. Second, I assume that law itself is a human institution, serving basic human or societal needs. It is therefore properly subject to praise, or to criticism, in terms of certain pragmatic values, including both formal values, such as coherence and workability, and widely shared substantive values, such as helping to achieve justice by interpreting the law in accordance with the "reasonable expectations" of those to whom it applies. If you do not accept these assumptions, then I am unlikely to convince you of the legitimate role of legislative history in the judicial process. * * *

II. The Usefulness of Legislative History: Examples

Using legislative history to help interpret unclear statutory language seems natural. Legislative history helps a court understand the context and purpose of a statute. Outside the law we often turn to context and purpose to clarify ambiguity. Consider, for example, a sign that says "no animals in the park." The meaning of even so simple a sign depends heavily on context and purpose. Does "animal" include a squirrel, a dog, or an insect? If you think of an ordinary sign outside New York City's Central Park, you will arrive at one answer. But if I create an unusual context you may reach a different answer. Suppose the sign appears outside a parking lot in a city where much of the population rides donkeys or elephants. Does it then include dogs? Suppose the sign appears in a laboratory in England (where people call insects "animals") next to the rack where the microbiologists "park" their test tubes. The meaning of the sign, the scope of its rule, depends on context, on convention, and on purpose. Is this fact not true of words in statutes as well? Should one not look to the background of a statute, the terms of the debate over its enactment, the factual assumptions the legislators made, the conventions they thought applicable, and their expressed objectives in an effort to understand the statute's relevant context, conventions, and purposes?

* * *

A. Avoiding an Absurd Result

Blackstone himself, more than two hundred years ago, pointed out that a court need not follow the literal language of a statute where doing so would produce an absurd result. He said that if "collaterally . . . absurd consequences, manifestly contrary to common reason," arise out of statutes those statutes "are, with regard to those collateral consequences, void." Blackstone further explained:

> Where some collateral matter arises out of the general words [of a statute], and happens to be unreasonable; there the judges are in decency to conclude that this consequence was not foreseen by the parliament, and therefore

they are at liberty to expound the statute by equity . . . .[8]

* * *

B. Drafting Error

Legislative history can also illuminate drafting errors. A statute's language might seem fairly clear. The language might produce a result that does not seem absurd. Yet, legislative history nonetheless might clearly show that the result is wrong because of a drafting error that courts should correct. Consider the following example:

A federal criminal statute says "whoever . . . possesses *any* false, forged, or *counterfeit coin*, with intent to defraud any person" is guilty of a crime. The question in a case the First Circuit decided in 1982 was whether the statute covers a person who (with the requisite fraudulent intent) possesses, in the United States, false Krugerrands, gold coins used as currency in South Africa, but not in the United States. Does this particular statutory provision protect against fraudulent use of South Africa's currency in the United States? The language indicates that it does. It refers to *"any . . . counterfeit coin,"* and a false Krugerrand is a counterfeit coin.

The history of this statute, however, shows a narrower meaning. In 1965 Congress reorganized, and slightly rewrote, a set of anti-counterfeiting statutes, of which this particular provision was one. During the 150 years that preceded the reorganization, this provision constituted a small part of a statutory paragraph, most of which prohibited the *making* of counterfeit coins. This older paragraph contained an important qualifying phrase, indicating clearly that the provision applied to American coins and not to foreign coins. When Congress rewrote the statutes in 1965, it kept the qualifying phrase in the reorganized provision that governs the *making* of counterfeit coins. That provision now says that "whoever falsely makes . . . any coin . . . in resemblance of" any United States coin or any foreign gold or silver coin that is *"current in the United States or in actual use and circulation as money within the United States"* is guilty of a crime. But when Congress separated the "possession" provision from the larger paragraph, it did not include the qualifying provision that limited its application to coins "current" as money in the United States.

Now the question seems more difficult. Without this history, one might think that a false Krugerrand obviously falls within the scope of the statute's words "any . . . counterfeit coin." But does it? After all, the word "any" in a statute rarely means "any at all in the universe." It almost always has some context-implied limitation. Moreover, for 150 years this particular statute explicitly did not apply to ancient coins, Krugerrands, or counterfeits of any other coin not currently used as American currency. Should a court read the provision to continue this limitation, reading the word "any" as so limited, or should it assume that the "possession" statute, unlike its near cousin, the "making" statute, includes false Krugerrands? Either answer seems reasonable.

In answering this question, would you not want to know just what Congress had in mind in 1965 when it reorganized and rewrote the preexisting statutes? More specifically, would you not want to know why the human being who drafted the new "possession" language left out the qualifying phrase? Was it an accident? Did someone tell the drafter to leave it out? If so, did the legislator who told the drafter to omit the phrase have some policy change in mind? If so, what sort of change?

The 1965 House and Senate Reports on the counterfeiting legislation provide fairly clear answers. They specify that the congressional reenactment of the law, reorganizing it and rewriting some of it, was intended to serve purely organizational objectives. They say that Congress expected, after the changes, that the law would remain what it was before the changes. These reports reveal that the individual staff members who rewrote the law thought that the legislators wanted them to accomplish a purely technical, non-substantive drafting objective. The reports thereby indicate that no one in Congress intended to change substantive law or to rewrite federal counterfeiting law so that it helped protect the currency of all nations, including South Africa, or ancient Greece and Rome.

If a court has such good evidence that no one in Congress intended to change the law substantively, is that not grounds for saying, "Congress did not intend any substantive change?" And is this not grounds for reading the preexisting limitation back into the word "any?" The First Circuit used legislative history to uncover, and then to undo, a drafting error. This use seems to me perfectly appropriate and desirable.

C. Specialized Meanings

Even the strongest critics of the use of legislative history concede that a court should take full account of any special meaning that a statutory word may have. The word "standing," for example, means

---

[8] 1 WILLIAM BLACKSTONE, COMMENTARIES ON THE LAWS OF ENGLAND 90-91 (15th ed. 1809).

something quite different in a statute than on a subway poster because the word carries with it a host of technical meanings growing out of context, case law, and history more generally. Presumably the critics see nothing wrong with looking to history to help determine whether a particular word has a specialized meaning and, if so, what sort. But why should that history specifically exclude legislative history?

Consider *Pierce v. Underwood*, a recent Supreme Court opinion authored by Justice Scalia. One of the legal questions in the case concerned the meaning of the phrase "substantially justified," as used in the Equal Access to Justice Act. A private party who wins a suit against the government is entitled to attorneys' fees unless the government's position was "substantially justified." The Court considered whether "substantially justified" means "better than reasonable," or even "less than reasonable."

The Court held that the word "substantial," in effect, means "reasonable." In reaching this conclusion, Justice Scalia made various comparisons with other areas of law, including the following:

> Judicial review of agency action, the field at issue here, regularly proceeds under the rubric of "substantial evidence" set forth in the Administrative Procedure Act, 5 U.S.C. § 706(2)(E). That phrase does not mean a large or considerable amount of evidence but rather "such relevant evidence as a reasonable mind might accept as adequate to support a conclusion." [citing *Consolidated Edison Co. v. NLRB*]

For present purposes, the interesting part of this quotation is the date of the *Consolidated Edison* case, namely 1938. The reason it is interesting is that Justice Scalia uses that case to help explain the somewhat technical meaning of a word in the Administrative Procedure Act, which did not become law until *1946*. It is worth asking how Justice Scalia knew that the meaning of the word in the 1946 statute was given in a case decided eight years earlier.

The well-known answer to this question is that the 1946 House and Senate Reports make clear that in the Administrative Procedure Act, Congress intended to enact into law recommendations contained in the Report of the Attorney General's Committee on Administrative Procedure. That report cites the *Consolidated Edison* definition, as does a later report by the Attorney General, which focused specifically on the bill that Congress enacted into law in 1946. This later report appears as an appendix to the Senate Report on the bill, and in the *Congressional Record*, as an extension of remarks made during floor debate. That is how the administrative law community knows, and is very certain, that the APA's term "substantial evidence" means just what Justice Scalia says it means.

This example demonstrates a fairly common function of legislative history—explaining specialized meanings of terms or phrases in a statute which were previously understood by the community of specialists (or others) particularly interested in the statute's enactment. * * *

D. Identifying a "Reasonable Purpose"

A court often needs to know the purpose a particular statutory word or phrase serves within the broader context of a statutory scheme in order to decide properly whether a particular circumstance falls within the scope of that word or phrase. * * *

How does a court determine the purpose of a statutory phrase? Sometimes it can simply look to the surrounding language in the statute or to the entire statutory scheme and ask, "Given this statutory background, what would a reasonable human being intend this specific language to accomplish?" Often this question has only one good answer, but sometimes the surrounding statutory language and the "reasonable human purpose" test cannot answer the question. In such situations, legislative history may provide a clear and helpful resolution.

Consider, for example, Congress's 1984 revision of federal bankruptcy law. The statute contained a phrase, "core proceeding," not previously used in a federal statute. The statute authorized a federal Article I bankruptcy judge to hear and determine "core proceedings" without the consent of the parties. For non-core matters the bankruptcy judge could make binding decisions only with the parties' consent. What is a core proceeding? What is a non-core proceeding? The statute lists fifteen examples of core proceedings, but also says that "core proceedings include, but are not limited" to the fifteen enumerated examples. Why did Congress not set forth a complete list? Probably because those who drafted this provision feared they would not be able to imagine, in advance, every possible kind of proceeding that should be included. Such a reason is a common cause of generality, or lack of precision, in statutes. However, it is not a basis for criticizing the legislature. Were human vision not limited, if we could specify in advance all possible future circumstances, we would need to give courts only fact-finding power, not the power to interpret statutes.

The First Circuit found itself faced with a circumstance not on the fifteen-item list. We had to decide whether an Article I bankruptcy court could decide a debtor's post-petition state-law contract claim—a claim that arose *after* the debtor filed for bankruptcy—without the parties' consent.[27] Was such a post-petition state-law controversy a core or non-core proceeding?

The legislative history of the 1984 legislation provided the answer. First, it clearly stated that Congress passed the Act in response to the Supreme Court's decision in *Northern Pipeline Construction Co. v. Marathon Pipe Line Co.*, which held that the Constitution's separation-of-powers principles did not permit Article I bankruptcy courts to adjudicate a debtor's pre-petition state-law contract claim—a claim that arose *before* the debtor filed its bankruptcy petition.

Second, floor statements made by the bill's sponsors, Democratic Representative Kastenmeier, and Republican Representative Kindness, clarified the relation of the word "core" in the statute to the *Marathon* case. They explained in detail that they intended the words "core proceedings" (over which the bankruptcy courts would have full decision-making powers) to encompass as many different kinds of proceedings as the Constitution would permit. They referred to proceedings outside the "core" as "*Marathon*-type" cases, and explained that "jurisdiction in core bankruptcy proceedings is broader than the summary jurisdiction under pre-1978 law."

These two aspects of the statute's history led our court to consider the constitutional question first. Did the Constitution permit an Article I bankruptcy court to consider a "*post*-petition" contract claim? We concluded that "post-petition" and "pre-petition" claims differed significantly from a constitutional perspective and that the Constitution permitted the bankruptcy courts to determine the post-petition state-law claims. Did the "post-petition" claim fall within the statute's word "core"? The legislative history tying that word to the *Marathon* case suggested that it did. The reference to pre-1978 summary jurisdiction offered further support, for "summary jurisdiction under pre-1978 law" included jurisdiction over "post-petition" state-law contract claims. Consequently we concluded that the word "core" covered the circumstance before us.

Without the legislative history, without the floor statements, we might have reached a different result. After all, state-law contract claims, whether pre- or post-petition, look very much alike, and both sorts of claims are only peripherally related to bankruptcy itself. But the result suggested by any such "purpose-free" analogy would be pointless and wrong, for it would not comport with the legislators' basic statutory objectives.

More importantly, the incompatibility between the result we could have reached (but did not) and those congressional objectives, seen from a general institutional or governmental perspective, would be undesirable. The undesirability consists, not simply of the fact that Representatives Kastenmeier and Kindness were democratically elected, but also of the fact that the statute's general objectives (and the detailed provisions needed to implement the objectives) reflect far more than the work of the two Representatives themselves. The objectives, and the detailed provisions, reflect the work of all the representatives of the bankruptcy community involved in the legislative process that produced the bankruptcy bill, namely bankruptcy judges, practitioners, teachers, and many others who worked on the details of the law. Their knowledge and experience, likely communicated through staff, with or without compromises, is embodied both in particular statutory phrases and in reports and floor statement language. To take from the courts the power to refer to legislative history in a case such as this one is to cut an essential channel for communications with these informed communities of groups and individuals, a channel that runs from those affected by a law's implementation, through courts and legislators, to those involved in the law's creation. To reach a result inconsistent with their work denies the public a significant part of the benefit of their expertise—an important matter in so technical an area where the knowledge of informed groups is likely to produce a more workable, legally "better" statute. More significantly, reaching such an inconsistent result defeats the reasonable expectations of the many individuals and groups involved in the legislative process. As long as we believe that one important goal of a legal system is to maintain rules of law consistent with the reasonable expectations of those who live within it, this result is undesirable.

E. Choosing Among Reasonable Interpretations of a Politically Controversial Statute

Consider as a final example a statute that evoked strong political support and opposition in Congress and was enacted with language that is unclear or silent about an important issue that faces a court. Judicial use of legislative history to determine meaning in this context seems to cause critics the greatest concern, for it is the kind of situation in which courts risk elevating the testimony to the level of a statute.

---

[27] *See* In re Arnold Print Works, Inc., 815 F.2d 165 (1st Cir. 1987).

Consider a 1981 case in our court that arose out of the Urban Mass Transportation Act of 1964.[30] That Act provided financial aid for urban mass transit systems, and it foresaw that the states receiving aid would likely acquire privately owned mass transit systems. The Act, in section 13(c), said that if a state received aid the federal Secretary of Labor had to certify that the state had made "fair and equitable arrangements . . . to protect the interests of employees affected" by the transit funding. The Secretary of Labor issued various regulations under section 13(c), the thrust of which was that the Secretary would consider an arrangement "fair and equitable" if the employees and the state employer agreed to them.

The case before us asked whether this provision of federal law, section 13(c), preempted a Massachusetts state statute that instructed its Transit Authority not to negotiate away its power to insist upon productivity-enhancing work-rule changes whenever it negotiated new contracts with the transit unions. The Authority previously had, in effect, given up this power to the unions and promised not to take it back, not even when the old contracts expired. The federal Secretary of Labor had approved the "arrangement" under which the Authority would never try to take the work-rule-change power back. Could Massachusetts, by statute, instruct its Authority to act contrary to this Secretary-approved arrangement? If section 13(c) and regulations promulgated pursuant to it preempted conflicting state law, the answer to this question was "no."

The text of the statute does not answer the preemption question. It simply says that the Secretary must certify that the "arrangements" between employer and employee are "fair and equitable." The legislative history of section 13(c), however, did suggest an answer.

First, the Secretary of Labor, Willard Wirtz, testified about the draft bill that became section 13(c) in the committee hearings that preceded its enactment into law. He said that when the Labor Department drafted the bill it had consulted the Amalgamated Transit Workers' Union and the AFL-CIO, and that section 13(c) would not supersede state law. Second, the preemptive effect of section 13(c) was discussed on the floor of Congress just prior to the bill's enactment. Senators hostile to the entire bill, such as Senator Barry Goldwater, asked whether or not it would preempt state law. Senators favoring the bill, such as Senator Pete Williams and Senator Jacob Javits,

replied that section 13(c) would not preempt state law. Secretary Wirtz's testimony, and the floor debate, seemed clear and definite, and they helped our court decide that the provision did *not* preempt the Massachusetts law.

Were we right to rely upon legislative history in this way? The bill itself, and section 13(c) in particular, were controversial in Congress. But the legislative history with respect to preemption was fairly clear. Of course, the legislators themselves may not have written that history. But suppose that a civil servant actually wrote Secretary Wirtz's testimony after consulting with the unions. Suppose that legislative staff wrote the Goldwater/Williams floor colloquy after consulting with counsels for the Transit Workers' Union, employers groups, and the states. Indeed, suppose that union lawyers, or employer lawyers, wrote the debate word for word. Should that fact make the use of legislative history significantly less legitimate?

Before answering this question "yes," consider, for a moment, how Congress actually works. Congress is no longer (was it ever?) made up of part-time citizen-legislators, extemporaneous orators, who burn the midnight oil as they themselves draft the laws needed to resolve the social and political problems revealed during the day's interchange of spontaneous debate. Rather, Congress is a bureaucratic organization with twenty thousand employees, working full-time, generating legislation through complicated, but organized, processes of interaction with other institutions and groups, including executive branch departments, labor unions, business organizations, and public interest groups. These other institutions and groups (including interest groups) through their representatives (including lobbyists) often initiate legislation; they typically make clear to congressional staff just what they are trying to achieve, and why; they may suggest content and text, not only for statutes, but also for reports or floor statements; they review proposed changes; and they negotiate and compromise with staff, with legislators and with each other. The staff, working with these groups, the legislators, and other staff members, will do the same.

When this process works properly, staff members for each legislator carefully review statutory language, report language, and significant proposed language for floor statements (of the staff member's own, and of other legislators), checking for consistency with the legislator's own objectives and positions, suggesting changes, and negotiating compromises. The staff member flags matters of significant substantive or political controversy, brings them to

---

[30] *See* Local Div. 589 v. Massachusetts, 666 F.2d 618 (1st Cir. 1981), *cert. denied*, 457 U.S. 1117 (1982).

the legislator's attention, discusses them with the legislator, and obtains instructions from the legislator about how to proceed. On important matters, staff members for legislators who are directly involved will examine with care each word and proposed change, often with representatives of affected interest groups or institutions not only in the language of the statute, but also in each committee report and the many floor statements. Significant matters will again be brought to the attention of the legislators for development of their individual positions, and for them to discuss and resolve with other legislators. The process involves continuous interaction among legislators, staff members, and representatives of those institutions or groups most likely to be affected by the proposed legislation. This process requires each legislator to rely upon staff, in the first instance, to separate the matters that are significant from those that are not; it requires each legislator to make decisions about, and to resolve with other legislators, each significant matter; and it requires each legislator further to rely upon drafters and negotiators to carry out the legislator's decisions.

The process I have just described is an institutional one, in which the legislator relies in part upon the work of staff. In this process, no legislator reads every word of every report or floor statement or proposed statute, which may consist of hundreds of pages of text. However, in this process those words are carefully reviewed by those whom they will likely affect and by the legislator's own employees. Moreover, in this process the legislator makes the significant decisions and takes responsibility for the outcome.

This institutional process, in which the legislator serves as a kind of manager, should seem familiar to those who manage other large institutions such as businesses, labor unions, and government departments. No one expects the top officials in such institutions to have read every document they generate. Yet those top officials typically are held responsible for those documents, and the outside world typically treats those documents as genuine reflections of the institution's position, whether or not the top officials actually read them. Many, if not most, institutions work through downward delegation, with responsibility flowing upward. Of course, the judicial branch, in principle, does not work this way. It is perhaps, then, understandable that law professors, judges and lawyers might hope that the legislative branch would function in a similarly centralized fashion. But, after a little reflection, this hope seems unachievable and perhaps undesirable. The judge's staff is smaller and the judge's involvement in the making of legal decisions is more direct and detailed. Why should the judicial ideal be the model for Congress? Why should the fairly public congressional legislative process, which involves checking with those whom the legislation will most likely affect, and then perhaps publicly adopting and explaining their related points of view, diminish the legitimacy of the resulting legislative history? * * *

* * *

In sum, these * * * examples identify five different circumstances in which courts might turn to legislative history for help in interpreting a statute: (1) avoiding an absurd result; (2) preventing the law from turning on a drafting error; (3) understanding the meaning of specialized terms; (4) understanding the "reasonable purpose" a provision might serve; and (5) choosing among several possible "reasonable purposes" for language in a politically controversial law. The first three are not very controversial. The last two are controversial. The last two examples suggest, however, how in certain contexts reference to legislative history can promote interpretations that more closely correspond to the expectations of those who helped create the law (and whom the law will likely affect). To that extent, its use seems likely to promote fair and workable results.

III. The Criticisms of the Use of Legislative History

I have tried to group the many different arguments made against the use of legislative history into five categories of criticism. Although many of these criticisms have considerable logical and practical force, the question you should ask is whether they are strong enough to force us to abandon, or significantly to curtail, the often useful practice of looking to legislative history in circumstances such as those I have previously described. Why, of all the many tools judges use to help interpret unclear statutory language (context, tradition, custom, precedent, dictionary meanings, administrability, and so on), should they not use this one?

A. Lack of Utility

The argument most frequently heard against the use of legislative history is that it does not help. Critics quote Justice Jackson's remark that "legislative history here, as usual, is more vague than the statute we are called upon to interpret." Again they will point to Judge Leventhal's comment that searching congressional documents for a statute's legislative history is like "looking over a crowd and picking out your friends." One can easily find examples of vague or conflicting legislative history. The critics do so, and they cite them.

This kind of argument is strongest when aimed at "misuse" of history. But, how strong a case can it make for abandonment? Logically, the argument is open to the response, "If the history is vague, or seriously conflicting, do not use it." No one claims that history is *always* useful; only that it *sometimes* helps.

Moreover, those who oppose the use of legislative history often illustrate their arguments with Supreme Court cases, for unlike lower courts, the Supreme Court frequently interprets statutory provisions arising out of serious political disagreement. The warring legislative parties, in such cases, often leave no legislative history stone unturned in their efforts to influence subsequent judicial interpretations.

Federal courts of appeals, however, consider many more cases each year, and many more less important cases, than does the Supreme Court. Indeed, they decide about nine thousand cases by written opinion, compared to about 150 in the Supreme Court. Their workload includes many unclear statutory provisions where lack of clarity does *not* reflect major political controversy. Such cases usually do not involve conflicting legislative history; in fact, the history itself often is clear enough to clarify the statute—as in the examples I have provided already.

B. Constitutional Arguments

Two types of constitutional arguments are made against the use of legislative history. The first concerns the Constitution's requirements for enacting a law. A bill must pass both houses of Congress and obtain the President's signature or a veto override. The result, says the Constitution, is a statute; and that statute, not a floor speech or committee report or testimony or presidential message or congressional "intent," is the law. The use of legislative history, according to this argument, tends to make these other matters—report language and floor speeches—the "law" even though they had received neither a majority vote nor a presidential signature.

Second, the Constitution vests "legislative" power in a Congress made up of elected members. It does not vest legislative power in congressional staff or in lobbyists. Yet these unelected individuals write the floor statements, testimony, reports, and messages that make up legislative history. Indeed, the elected members may not even read these materials. Thus, to use legislative history not only makes "law" out of that which is not law, but also permits the exercise of legislative power by those who do not constitutionally possess it.

These arguments overstate their case. The "statute-is-the-only-law" argument misses the point. No one claims that legislative history is a statute, or even that, in any strong sense, it is "law." Rather, legislative history is helpful in trying to understand the meaning of the words that do make up the statute or the "law." A judge cannot interpret the words of an ambiguous statute without looking beyond its words for the words have simply ceased to provide univocal guidance to decide the case at hand. * * *

The delegation argument ("the Senator did not write, or even read, the report") is susceptible to the same type of criticism. After all, no one elected lexicographers or agency civil servants to Congress. The Constitution nowhere grants them legislative power. Yet, judges universally seek their help in resolving interpretive problems.

More importantly, this argument misunderstands how Congress works as an institution. The relevant point here is that nothing in the Constitution seems to prohibit Congress from using staff and relying upon groups and institutions in the way I have described. * * *

C. The Problem of Congressional "Intent"

Critics sometimes argue that the use of legislative history depends upon a mistaken belief that behind every statute lies a congressional "intent." Congressional intent, they say, is a myth; some say that the concept itself lacks intellectual coherence. How can a document written by a committee staffer indicate the inner workings of the mind of even one legislator, let alone the several hundred who voted for the law, perhaps each for different individual reasons? Moreover, a branch of political science, called "public choice" theory, argues that legislation simply reflects the conflicting interactions of interest groups; the resulting law sometimes reflects their private, selfish interests, and sometimes serves no purpose at all. Does it make any sense in such circumstances to ascribe a responsible-sounding purpose to the statute's words?

Conceptually, however, one can ascribe an "intent" to Congress in enacting the words of a statute if one means "intent" in its, here relevant, sense of "purpose," rather than its sense of "motive." One often ascribes "group" purposes to group actions. A law school raises tuition to obtain money for a new library. A basketball team stalls to run out the clock. A tank corps feints to draw the enemy's troops away from the main front. Obviously, one of the best ways to find out the purpose of an action taken by a group is to ask some of the group's members about it. But, this does not necessarily mean that the group's purposes and the members' motives or purposes must be identical. The members of the group participating in the group activity—indeed, whose actions are necessary conditions for its action—may have different, private *motives* for their own actions; but that fact does not necessarily change the proper characterization of the group's purpose. Perhaps several key members of the faculty voted for the tuition increase, not because they cared about the library, but simply in order to please the Dean. Is a better library any the less the object of the *law school's* action? Indeed, must it always matter if many, or even most, of the group do not fully understand the group objective of the specific action? Perhaps the basketball team is simply reacting instinctively with long-practiced, set plays, the basic function of which the individual members do not have time to consider, or perhaps have forgotten. Is the purpose of those plays any the less the running of the clock? Perhaps the members of the tank corps do not understand why they head in the direction they take; indeed, perhaps even the commanding general does not understand fully the function of each specific action, the exact purposes of which are spelled out only in a memorandum written by a lowly intelligence officer at brigade headquarters (which officer himself was killed sometime before the attack began). Does this story make any difference at all in respect to the purpose of the individual troop movements?

All this is to say that ascribing purposes to groups and institutions is a complex business, and one that is often difficult to describe abstractly. But that fact does not make such ascriptions improper. In practice, we ascribe purposes to group activities all the time without many practical difficulties.

Of course, the relationship between individual group members' purposes and the group's purpose itself may (depending on the type of group) be particularly complex. * * * A legislator, for example, may vote for language that the legislator believes will extend a statute of limitations solely to obtain campaign contributions, to gain political support, or to defeat the bill on the floor. Those personal motives, however, do not change the purpose of the bill's language, namely, to extend the limitations period. A legislator may vote for technical language that the legislator does not understand, knowing that committee members believe (perhaps because of their faith in the drafting process) that it has a proper function. That fact does not necessarily *change* its function or its purpose. Professors Hart and Sacks, many years ago, described in detail how knowledge of the institutional workings, internal understandings, and soci-etal role of Congress helps to determine Congress's purpose in enacting a statutory word, a phrase, a section, a title, or an entire statutory scheme.[46] If I am correct in believing that ascribing a purpose to a human institution is an activity related to, but different from, ascribing a purpose to an individual, then I do not see how one can criticize courts that use legislative history on *conceptual* grounds. * * *

The public choice theory arguments against the use of legislative history are more substantial, for they seek to dissolve our belief that ascribing purpose serves any useful descriptive function. Public choice theory describes legislative outcomes in terms of interest-group interaction. The description resembles a psychoanalytic explanation of an individual's actions. Normally such an explanation can coexist with, but not replace, a person's own ordinary purposive account of his behavior. But if an individual's behavior is quite bizarre, if his own long, ordinary-purpose-related accounts of what he is doing do not seem to make much sense, and if the psychoanalytic account is good enough, observers will begin to disregard the individual's own purposive accounts as mere window-dressing, and they will begin to consider the psychoanalytic account as the only (or the most) accurate description and explanation of what is going on. Such is the hope of public choice theorists in respect to their explanation of congressional behavior.

Public choice theory, however, does not yet seem able to explain legislation well enough to warrant abandoning the use of legislative history. Public choice proponents sometimes seem to say that a legislature cannot enact laws in the "public interest" if those laws lack strong private interest group support and face strong private interest group opposition. Empirically, however, this seems wrong. The deregulation movement, for example, began in the airline and trucking industries with virtually no interest-group support. The relevant industries were, in fact, strongly opposed to deregulation and the positions of key labor unions ranged from the unenthusiastic to the adamantly opposed. At other times, the theory's proponents seem to deduce from the fact that legislation was enacted that strong private interest groups supported the legislation. As so used, however, the theory becomes tautological.

Moreover, the experience of those who have worked in legislatures does not confirm many public choice theorists' descriptions of the legislative pro-

---

[46] *See* [H.L.A. HART & A. SACKS, THE LEGAL PROCESS: BASIC PROBLEMS IN THE MAKING AND APPLICATION OF LAW 1242-86 (10th ed. 1958).]

cess. Chief Judge Mikva of the District of Columbia Circuit, a congressman for many years, writes:

> The politicians and other people I have known in public life just do not fit the "rent-seeking" egoist model that the public choice theorists offer.... Not even my five terms in the Illinois state legislature—that last vestige of democracy in the "raw"—nor my five terms in the United States Congress, prepared me for the villains of the public choice literature.

My experience running the staff of the Senate Judiciary Committee led me to conclude that elected officials seriously consider public interest arguments and act upon them far more often than the press, the public choice theorists, or the cynics would lead one to believe.

Finally, one should recall that legislative history is a *judicial* tool, one judges use to resolve difficult problems of judicial interpretation. It can be justified, at least in part, by its ability to help judges interpret statutes, in a manner that makes sense and that will produce a workable set of laws. If judicial use of legislative history achieves this kind of result, courts might use it as part of their overarching interpretive task of producing a coherent and relatively consistent body of statutory law, even were the "rational member of Congress" a pure fiction, made up out of whole cloth.

* * *

The complex legislative process I have described relies heavily upon interactions of legislators, staff, and interest groups to create, review, criticize, and amend legislative language, reports, and floor statements. The process is reasonably open and fair so long as those whom the legislation will likely affect have roughly equal access to the legislative process. However, critics of the congressional process challenge this assumption strongly and often. Most critics concede that trade associations, labor unions, executive departments, and certain public interest groups, all under the watchful eye of the press, participate fully in the process on behalf of those they represent. But they ask several familiar questions. For example, are there not many disadvantaged groups who are excluded from the legislative process? Indeed, is the ordinary citizen adequately represented as a "typical citizen" rather than as a member of some organized interest group? Moreover, does ideology drive congressional staff more than the desire to reflect the will of the voter? Perhaps because we are all familiar with such criticism, my description of the legislative process did not fully dispel doubts about the legitimacy of the use of legislative history.

If these questions disturb you, then you might ask yourself whether judicial abandonment of the use of legislative history would make matters better or worse. Certainly abandonment would eliminate one factor that favors public hearings, public reports vetted by staff, and fairly detailed floor debates. It would also make it easier for legislators to justify amending legislation after it leaves committee, while it is on the floor of the House or Senate, or even while both Houses of Congress confer upon the bill after it passed each in different versions. To the extent that a change weakens the publicly accessible committee system and diminishes the need for public justification, it increases the power of the "special interests" (and here I use that term pejoratively) to secure legislation that is not in the "public interest." Thus, if judges abandon the use of legislative history, Congress will not necessarily produce better laws.

To the contrary, insofar as courts discourage Congress from using the regular committee, floor debate, and conference process, the technical quality of statutory law is likely to deteriorate significantly. The statutory language inserted by amendment on the floor of Congress produces absurd, anomalous, or unfair results. * * *

* * *

I did not dwell upon the problems of the legislative process, however, because my focus was the judiciary. I have simply argued that, viewed in light of the judiciary's important objective of helping to maintain coherent, workable statutory law, the case for abandoning the use of legislative history has not yet been made. * * * The "problem" of legislative history is its "abuse," not its "use." Care, not drastic change, is all that is warranted.

Additional Sources

T. Alexander Aleinikoff, *Updating Statutory Interpretation*, 87 Mich. L. Rev. 20 (1988)

Guido Calabresi, A COMMON LAW FOR THE AGE OF STATUTES (1982)

Colin S. Diver, *Statutory Interpretation in the Administrative State*, 133 U. Pa. L. Rev. 549 (1985)

Frank H. Easterbrook, *The Role of Original Intent in Statutory Construction*, 11 Harv. J.L. & Pub. Pol'y 59 (1988)

Frank H. Easterbrook, *Statutes' Domains*, 50 U. Chi. L. Rev. 533 (1983)

William N. Eskridge, Jr., *The New Textualism*, 37 UCLA L. Rev. 621 (1990)

William N. Eskridge, Jr. & Philip P. Frickey, *Statutory Interpretation as Practical Reasoning*, 42 Stan. L. Rev. 321 (1990)

William N. Eskridge, Jr. & Philip P. Frickey, *Legislation Scholarship and Pedagogy in the Post-Legal Process Era*, 48 U. Pitt. L. Rev. 691 (1987)

Daniel A. Farber, *Statutory Interpretation and Legislative Supremacy*, 78 Geo. L.J. 281 (1989)

Geoffrey P. Miller, *Pragmatics and the Maxims of Interpretation*, 1990 Wis. L. Rev. 1179

Eben Moglen & Richard J. Pierce, Jr., *Sunstein's New Canons: Choosing the Fictions of Statutory Interpretation*, 57 U. Chi. L. Rev. 1203 (1990)

Richard A. Posner, *Legislation and Its Interpretation: A Primer*, 68 Neb. L. Rev. 431 (1989)

Kenneth W. Starr, *Observations About the Use of Legislative History*, 1987 Duke L.J. 371

Cass R. Sunstein, *Interpreting Statutes in the Regulatory State*, 103 Harv. L. Rev. 405 (1989)

Cass R. Sunstein, AFTER THE RIGHTS REVOLUTION: RECONCEIVING THE REGULATORY STATE (1990)

Patricia M. Wald, *The Sizzling Sleeper: The Use of Legislative History in Construing Statutes in the 1988-89 Term of the United States Supreme Court*, 39 Am. U. L. Rev. 277 (1990)

b. Judicial Deference to Agency Interpretations

A central issue in statutory construction is the extent to which a reviewing court should defer to an agency's view of its legal authority. Traditionally, courts have looked at a number of factors in determining in particular cases whether to defer to an agency's interpretation. In general, the multifactor approach confers on courts a good deal of discretion in the matter. Yet the debate took a new turn in 1984 when the Supreme Court decided *Chevron*. The excerpts in this section deal with *Chevron*'s implications.

In the first excerpt, Professor Richard Pierce supports a strong reading of *Chevron*, which would foster a high degree of judicial deference to agencies' statutory constructions. Pierce defends this reading in terms of a sharp distinction between issues of law and issues of policy. He suggests that Congress typically resolves very few legal questions when it enacts a statute, and thus leaves most matters—which he sees as issues of policy—for agencies to decide. Professor Pierce argues that courts should play a quite limited role in reviewing policy issues.

In the second excerpt, Professor Thomas Merrill takes a more skeptical view of *Chevron*. He underscores the degree to which *Chevron*, if read in a strong sense, would change the law of judicial review. He also highlights a number of weaknesses in *Chevron*'s analysis. Furthermore, he suggests that the Supreme Court has not followed *Chevron* in many subsequent cases and that the multifactor approach has been retained in numerous instances in the post-*Chevron* era.*

Next, Justice Antonin Scalia defends *Chevron* as an attempt to achieve some degree of resolution of the question "what Congress intended courts to do when statutes are ambiguous." Part of his defense rests on the premise that the search for genuine legislative intent is "probably a wild goose-chase anyway." Toward the end of his discussion, Justice Scalia suggests that *Chevron* will be most disturbing to judges who are unable to reach a conclusion based on a statute's language and structure, for such judges may be forced to go along with a reasonable agency interpretation with which they personally disagree. Justice Scalia indicates that this problem is less likely to plague judges, such as himself, who find more often than not that the meanings of statutes are discernible from their texts and relationships with other laws.

In the last excerpt, Professor Cynthia Farina launches a broad assault on *Chevron* in terms of the balance of authority in the administrative system. She points out that the controversy about judicial deference is essentially about the allocation of decisional power, and she defends a reasonably assertive judicial role. Professor Farina argues that allocating to the courts the principal responsibility for interpreting regulatory statutes advances important values of checks and balances by counterbalancing the concentration of regulatory authority in the executive.

---

* Because the excerpts in this section are directed at the analysis of *Chevron*, Professor Merrill's discussion of his alternative "executive precedent" model has been deleted. Readers interested in pursuing this subject should refer to the full article.

Richard J. Pierce, Jr., Chevron *and its Aftermath: Judicial Review of Agency Interpretations of Statutory Provisions*, 41 VAND. L. REV. 301, 301-08, 312-14 (1988)*

In its 1984 opinion in *Chevron U.S.A., Inc. v. Natural Resources Defense Council, Inc.*, the Supreme Court attempted to resolve the long standing conflict concerning the proper scope of judicial review of agency interpretations of statutory provisions. *Chevron* concerned the Environmental Protection Agency's (EPA) interpretation of the Clean Air Act, which requires the EPA to limit emissions from all "stationary sources." The EPA interpreted the statutory term "stationary source" to mean an entire plant, rather than an individual piece of combustion equipment. That statutory interpretation was adopted as part of the EPA's "bubble concept," which is based on the EPA's belief that it can simultaneously further the inherently conflicting goals of the Clean Air Act—improved air quality and continued economic growth—most effectively by imposing emission limitations on an entire plant, and by conferring upon the owner of the plant both the obligation and discretion to determine the means by which to reduce plant emissions.

In defining the proper scope of judicial review of agency interpretations of statutory provisions, the *Chevron* Court established what one judge calls the "*Chevron* two-step." The first step requires the court to determine "whether Congress has directly spoken to the precise question at issue," in which case "the court, as well as the agency, must give effect to the unambiguously expressed intent of Congress." If the court concludes, however, that "Congress has not directly addressed the precise question at issue," the court must refrain from any statutory interpretation of its own and must simply determine "whether the agency's answer is based on a permissible construction of the statute." The *Chevron* test established a simple approach to a traditionally complicated issue in administrative law. The court first decides whether the statute resolves the specific issue or is silent or ambiguous with respect to the issue. If it determines that the statute is silent or ambiguous, the court then affirms the agency's interpretation of the statute if that interpretation is "reasonable."

* * *

* Reprinted with permission of the Vanderbilt Law Review and Richard J. Pierce, Jr. All rights reserved.

This Essay views *Chevron* as an exceedingly important development in administrative law that represents a dramatic improvement over prior attempts to grapple with the proper scope of judicial review of agency interpretations of statutory provisions. This Essay argues that the strong reading of *Chevron* is the proper interpretation because agencies are the best equipped institutions to resolve policy questions in the statutes that grant the agency its legal power. In addition, a strong reading of *Chevron* will result in a number of positive consequences in the process of policy making in the modern administrative state.

The forceful criticisms of *Chevron* and the attempts to limit or redefine the *Chevron* test are predicated on a misunderstanding of the nature of the statutory interpretation issues that agencies and courts frequently must resolve. Historically, interpretation of terms used in a regulatory statute has been characterized as an issue of law. Thus, some commentators distinguish between the proper scope of judicial review of issues of law, including all agency interpretations of statutory provisions, and judicial review of issues of policy. Professor Sunstein argues that *Chevron* is inconsistent both with *Marbury v. Madison* and the Administrative Procedure Act because courts possess the exclusive responsibility to decide issues of law.

This characterization of *Chevron* is based on a serious misunderstanding of the legislative process and the nature of the issue before a court when it reviews an agency's interpretation of a provision in a regulatory statute. Many instances of statutory interpretation require an agency to resolve policy issues, rather than legal issues. Viewed in this light, the first step in the *Chevron* test requires a court to determine whether the issue of statutory interpretation in question is an issue of law or an issue of policy. If the court determines that it is reviewing an agency's resolution of a policy issue, the court then moves to the second part of the test and affirms the agency's interpretation of the statutory provision—and its resolution of the policy issue—if the agency's interpretation is "reasonable."

In determining whether an agency's interpretation of a statute involves an issue of law or policy, it is useful to analyze and characterize the issue prior to Congress' enactment of the statute in question. For example, in *Chevron* most would agree that, prior to the enactment of the Clean Air Act, the question of whether to limit emissions at the plant level or the level of each piece of combustion equipment is a pure question of policy. This question is but one of hundreds of policy issues that some institution of government must resolve in order to implement any regulatory program to reduce air pollution. In the process of enacting the Clean Air Act, or any other regulatory statute, Congress invariably resolves some policy issues but leaves to some other institution of government the task of resolving many other policy issues.

As the Court recognized in *Chevron*, Congress declines to resolve policy issues for many different reasons: Congress simply may have neglected to consider the issue; Congress may have believed that the agency was in a better position to resolve the issue; or finally, Congress may not have been able to forge a coalition or simply may have lacked the political courage necessary to resolve the issue, given that a resolution either way might damage the political future of many members of Congress. The general proposition that Congress cannot and does not resolve all the policy issues raised by its creation of a regulatory scheme probably is not at all controversial.

A more controversial point, however, may be that Congress resolves very few issues when it enacts a statute empowering an agency to regulate. Rather, Congress typically leaves the vast majority of policy issues, including many of the most important issues, for resolution by some other institution of government. Congress accomplishes this through several different statutory drafting techniques, including the use of empty standards, lists of unranked decisional goals, and contradictory standards. Thus, Congress declines to resolve many policy issues by using statutory language that is incapable of meaningful definition and application.

When a court "interprets" imprecise, ambiguous, or conflicting statutory language in a particular manner, the court is resolving a policy issue. Courts frequently resolve policy issues through a process that purports to be statutory interpretation but which, in fact, is not. For lack of a better term, this process will be referred to as "creative" interpretation. Judicial decisions under the Sherman Act provide a good example of judicial policy making through creative statutory interpretation. Whether through congressional inadvertence or by design, courts have interpreted the substantive standard stated in the Sherman Act—whether a restrictive practice should be prohibited as imposing an unreasonable "restraint of trade or commerce"—in many different and inconsistent ways.

As long as courts follow a process of reasoned decision making, judicial policy making through creative interpretation and application of ambiguous statutory provisions is generally appropriate. The function of a court is to resolve cases or controversies. By enacting a statute that raises but does not resolve myriad policy issues, and by permitting parties to bring judicial actions pursuant to that statute, Congress has created a large number of cases or controversies that courts have no choice but to resolve through a process that can only be characterized as judicial policy making. In the context of the Sherman Act, for example, courts and commentators seem increasingly to recognize that judges make antitrust policy. Because Congress has declined to resolve many of the policy decisions raised by the Sherman Act, and because no other institution of government is available to fill that policy making void, the courts regularly must make policy decisions in the guise of interpreting the Sherman Act.

Some judicial policy making in the guise of statutory interpretation seems superficially different from the typical judicial opinion interpreting the Sherman Act. Occasionally courts interpret statutory provisions through lengthy discussions of congressional goals and legislative history. In some cases, this analysis undoubtedly is an exercise in what may be termed "real" statutory interpretation; the judge is honestly convinced from reading the language of the statute and its legislative history that Congress resolved a policy issue in a particular manner. When Congress has resolved a policy issue, the court is dealing with an issue of law, in which case the court's role is limited to implementing congressional intent.

In a high proportion of cases, however, an honest analysis of the language, the congressional goals, and the legislative history of the statute will not support a holding that Congress actually resolved the policy issue presented to the court. This situation often arises because Congress frequently uses ambiguous or conflicting statutory language and invariably promulgates inconsistent congressional goals. While sometimes helpful, the legislative history of a statute is often unclear, inconsistent, or untrustworthy.

In many cases in which a search for congressional intent is futile, courts nevertheless purport to resolve conflicts concerning the meaning of specific provisions in a statute through the process of statutory interpretation. In actuality, however, these courts are resolving a policy issue that Congress raised but declined to resolve. The judge's personal political philosophy influences greatly his resolution of the policy issue. As in the context of the Sherman Act, policy making is an appropriate and inevitable judicial role, because the judiciary, as the only institution empowered to resolve cases or controversies, must make the policy decisions necessary to decide a particular case or controversy. The exception to this proposition is in the context of administrative law.

Like a court, an agency frequently makes policy when it interprets ambiguous or imprecise terms in the statute that grants the agency its legal powers. *Chevron* provides a good illustration. In defining "stationary source" to mean a plant, rather than an individual piece of combustion equipment, the EPA did not "interpret" the statutory language by determining that Congress intended "stationary source" to mean a plant. Congress used the imprecise term "stationary source" without defining the term at all. The EPA decided, as a matter of policy, that it would interpret "stationary source" to mean a plant because, in the agency's view, such an interpretation would further Congress' conflicting goals. In addition, as the Supreme Court recognized, the agency's choice of policy was influenced by the President's political philosophy.

Once a court realizes that it is reviewing an agency's resolution of a policy issue, rather than an issue of law, comparative institutional analysis demonstrates that the agency is a more appropriate institution than a court to resolve the controversy. Because agencies are more accountable to the electorate than courts, agencies should have the dominant role in policy making when the choice is between agencies and courts. A court's function in reviewing a policy decision made by an agency should be the same whether the agency policy decision is made by interpreting an ambiguous statutory provision or by any other means of agency policy making. The court should affirm the agency's policy decision, and hence its statutory interpretation, if the policy is "reasonable." The court should reverse the agency's policy decision if the policy is arbitrary and capricious. Of course, in deciding whether the agency's policy decision is "reasonable," the court should review the agency's decision making process by which the agency determined that its choice of policy was consistent with statutory goals and the contextual facts of the controversy in question.

This characterization of the nature of statutory interpretation by an agency is entirely consistent with the Court's two-step approach to judicial review of agency interpretations of statutory provisions established in *Chevron*. The first step under *Chevron* is for the court to determine if Congress has resolved the policy issue that corresponds to the interpretive issue resolved by the agency. The court should engage in "real" statutory interpretation to determine whether Congress resolved the specific issue that the agency purported to resolve through statutory interpretation. If Congress resolved the specific issue presented, the court is dealing with an issue of law, and the case is at an end because the court is limited to implementing congressional intent.

In the process of applying *Chevron*'s first step, the court should refrain from teasing meaning from the statute's ambiguous or conflicting language and legislative history; it should eschew the process of "creative" statutory interpretation that is otherwise essential and appropriate in judicial decision making. Creative statutory interpretation is not appropriate in the administrative law context because creative statutory interpretation permits judges to make policy decisions that should be made instead by agencies. If the process of "real" statutory interpretation does not produce a determination that Congress resolved the specific issue, the court is dealing with a policy decision made by an agency. Although the court still must insure that the agency made its policy decision through a process of reasoned decision making, the court's role should be influenced greatly by the recognition that it is reviewing a policy decision made by another branch of government.

* * *

Several consequences logically follow from this Essay's interpretation of *Chevron* and characterization of the nature of the issues presented to courts when they review agency interpretations of statutory terms. First, courts should apply the *Chevron* test to all agency interpretations of provisions in the statutes that grant the agency its legal power. Courts should not confine the test to the unique context of agency applications of statutory terms to specific factual situations. Indeed, according agencies deference when they apply statutory terms to specific facts but not when they define terms in general rules would create incentives for an agency to make policy through adjudication rather than through rule making. Yet, virtually all judges and administrative law scholars agree that agencies should make policy through rule making procedures rather than through adjudication.

Second, courts should refrain from attempting to tease meaning from ambiguous statutory language and legislative history if the statute at issue establishes a regulatory scheme that is to be implemented by an agency. Agencies are more appropriate institutions to resolve policy issues than courts, which should avoid "creative" interpretation of regulatory statutes administered by agencies.

Third, when a court concludes that Congress left unresolved a policy issue in a statute that is not administered by an agency, the court should acknowledge explicitly that it must resolve the policy issue Congress raised but declined to resolve. In resolving that policy issue, the court should refer to Congress' goals. This is not to say, however, that the court's job is to determine congressional intent. If Congress did not resolve the policy issue, the court must undertake its own resolution of the issue in light of Congress' goals. Forthright recognition by a court that it is resolving a policy issue is likely to yield better policy than judicial resolution of policy issues through a process disguised as statutory interpretation.

Fourth, since many statutory interpretation issues are actually issues of policy rather than issues of law, an agency should have the ability to change its prior "interpretation" of a statutory provision. For example, an agency should possess the legitimate power to reassess its goals and policies in light of a change in presidential administrations. This power to reassess an agency's policies should apply to agency policy making through interpretation of ambiguous statutory provisions as well as through the rule making process. Thus, if the next President appoints an EPA administrator who believes that the bubble concept requires an inordinate sacrifice of air quality goals, the administrator should have the discretion to redefine "stationary source" to refer to each piece of combustion equipment. Because Congress chose not to resolve that policy issue, the agency head may appropriately resolve the policy question in a manner consistent with the President's political philosophy "[a]s long as [he] remains within the bounds established by Congress." Different agency heads appointed by Presidents with different political philosophies might reasonably reach different conclusions with respect to that policy issue.

Fifth, if courts apply the Chevron test universally, judges will have less room to infuse their personal political philosophies in the Nation's policy making process. The Chevron test will allow judges of widely differing political perspectives to agree in a large number of cases that Congress did or did not resolve a particular policy issue. This agreement should reduce the unfortunate tendency of judges to engage in policy making disguised as interpretation of ambiguous statutory language. The traditional approach to judicial review of agency interpretations frequently required judges to search for congressional intent with respect to a policy issue when, in fact, Congress had not made a decision on that policy issue. Such a search is illusory, of course, and invites judges to "interpret" creatively ambiguous language in accordance with their own political philosophies.

Sixth, the Chevron test notwithstanding, courts still will confront difficult cases in the process of reviewing agency interpretations of statutory provisions. In some instances courts will legitimately disagree as to whether Congress resolved the specific policy issue addressed by the agency's interpretation.

The second part of the Chevron test also will present some difficulty. Often judges will differ on the question of whether an agency's decision to adopt a particular policy is reasonable or arbitrary and capricious.

The conceptual framework established by Chevron will not eliminate all difficult cases; nor will it eliminate completely the influence of each judge's personal political philosophy on the process of judicial review of agency actions. Those goals are unattainable through any means. They are important goals, however, and the Chevron framework provides a means to further those goals incrementally. The Chevron framework can reduce the number of difficult cases that courts must face and limit the influence of each judge's personal political philosophy on the process of policy making in the modern administrative state.

Thomas W. Merrill, *Judicial Deference to Executive Precedent*, 101 YALE L.J. 969, 969-85, 990-91, 993-98, 1000-02, 1032-33 (1992)*

In 1984, the Supreme Court adopted a new framework for determining when courts should defer to interpretations of statutes by administrative agencies. Previous decisions had looked to multiple contextual factors in answering this question. *Chevron U.S.A., Inc. v. National Resources Defense Council, Inc.* appeared to reject this approach and require that federal courts defer to any reasonable interpretation by an agency charged with administration of a statute, provided Congress has not clearly specified a contrary answer. The Court justified this new general rule of deference by positing that Congress has implicitly delegated interpretative authority to all agencies charged with enforcing federal law.

Chevron is widely regarded as a kind of "counter-*Marbury*" for the administrative state. Indeed, read for all it is worth, the decision would make administrative actors the primary interpreters of federal statutes and relegate courts to the largely inert role of enforcing unambiguous statutory terms. This in turn would have enormous implications for the overall balance of power among the three branches of gov-

---

* Reprinted with permission of The Yale Law Journal Company, Fred B. Rothman & Company, and Thomas W. Merrill. All rights reserved.

ernment. Executive branch agencies would gain new power to achieve rapid changes in policy through reinterpretation of their legislative authority; courts would play a diminished role in checking agency aggrandizement and in protecting reliance interests associated with past interpretations; and Congress, unable to rely on the courts to honor unstated institutional understandings, could react by enacting excruciatingly detailed statutes or intensifying the use of oversight hearings.

* * * It turns out that the Court does not regard *Chevron* as a universal test for determining when to defer to executive interpretations: the *Chevron* framework is used in only about half the cases that the Court perceives as presenting a deference question. Nor have the multiple factors identified in the pre-*Chevron* period disappeared; to the contrary, the Court continues to rely upon them in many cases, despite their apparent irrelevance under *Chevron*. Perhaps most strikingly, in recent Terms the application of *Chevron* has resulted in *less* deference to executive interpretations than was the case in the pre-*Chevron* era. Thus, instead of functioning as a "counter-*Marbury*," there are signs that *Chevron* is being transformed by the Court into a new judicial mandate "to say what the law is." I will argue that the failure of *Chevron* to perform as expected can be attributed to the Court's reluctance to embrace the draconian implications of the doctrine for the balance of power among the branches, and to practical problems generated by its all-or-nothing approach to the deference question.

* * *

I. *Chevron*: The Revolution on Paper

* * *

A. *Pre-*Chevron: *The Multiple Factors Regime*

Prior to 1984, the Supreme Court had no unifying theory for determining when to defer to agency interpretations of statutes. The approach was instead pragmatic and contextual. One feature of the Court's practice was that deference could range over a spectrum from "great" to "some" to "little" (although no attempt was ever made to calibrate different degrees of deference with any precision). A particularly common approach was to cite the views of those charged with administration of the statute as one of several reasons for adopting a particular construction. Thus, the Court might embrace a particular interpretation (1) because it was supported by the language of the text, (2) because it was consistent with the legislative history, and (3) because it was the longstanding construction of the administrative agency. To be sure, there were also decisions at the polar extremes during this era—either ignoring the agency view or treating it as virtually dispositive. But in practice, deference existed along a sliding scale, bridging these outer limits.

In addition, in deciding what degree of deference to give an executive interpretation, the Court relied on an eclectic cluster of considerations. Although there was no explicit rationale linking the various factors together, the overall approach had an implicit logic. The default rule was one of independent judicial judgment. Deference to the agency interpretation was appropriate only if a court could identify some factor or factors that would supply an affirmative justification for giving special weight to the agency views. Admittedly, the factors tended to be invoked unevenly. But in this respect, they probably functioned in a manner not too different from the way the canons of interpretation operate in statutory interpretation cases.

The pre-*Chevron* deference factors may be classified in various ways. For present purposes, I will group them into three categories: (1) factors addressed to Congress' interpretative intent (that is, whether Congress intended courts to defer to an agency's interpretation of a statutory provision); (2) factors addressed to the attributes of the particular agency decision at issue; and (3) factors thought to demonstrate congruence between the outcome reached by the agency and congressional intent regarding that specific issue.

The first factor focused on Congress' probable interpretative intent. The important distinction was between "legislative rules" and "interpretative rules." Legislative rules were the product of a specific delegation of authority from Congress to an administrative agency to interpret a specific statutory term or fill in a statutory gap. Interpretative rules were executive interpretations not backed by this type of specific delegated authority. The Supreme Court on several occasions suggested that interpretations in the former category were entitled to great deference, but those falling within the latter category were entitled only to whatever persuasive effect they might have.

A second group of factors focused not on the agency's authority, but rather on various attributes of its decision. One factor was whether the issue fell within an area of agency "expertise." The idea was that courts are generalists, whereas agencies are specialists. Specialists usually have a better grasp of technical terms or the practical consequences of a decision, and thus their views should be given deference by generalists. Another important factor was the notion that "longstanding," "consistent," or "uniform" administrative interpretations (the terms were used more or less interchangeably) are entitled to special deference. A third factor in this category was that interpretations supported by a reasoned analysis were entitled to deference. The most prominent statement to this effect is found in *Skidmore v. Swift & Co.*, where the Court stated that the weight to be given to an agency interpretation will depend upon "the thoroughness evident in its consideration, the validity of its reasoning, its consistency with earlier and later pronouncements, and all those factors which give it power to persuade, if lacking power to control." A final decision-related factor, encountered less often, was whether multiple agencies agreed or disagreed about the correct interpretation of the statute.

A third set of factors was designed to measure the degree to which the specific outcome reached by an agency was likely to reflect the intent of Congress. One old idea was that an executive interpretation is entitled to extra weight "when it involves a contemporaneous construction of a statute by the men charged with the responsibility of setting its machinery in motion." Contemporaneous interpretations were thought to be especially probative of congressional intent, either because the administrators had themselves participated in the drafting process or because such an interpretation was "itself evidence of assumptions—perhaps unspoken by either the administrators or Congress—brought to a regulatory problem by all involved in its solution." In addition, there was the recurrent notion that executive interpretations are entitled to special deference if they have been ratified in some fashion by Congress. The notion of what would count as a ratification was never very precise. The paradigm situation was when Congress, after being informed of an agency's construction, reenacted a statute without any relevant modification.

Standing alone, these factors did not comprise, either individually or collectively, what could be described as a coherent doctrine. No attempt was made to connect the various factors together or to explain their relevance in terms of a model of executive-judicial relationship. Indeed, my own attempt to organize them in functional categories may impose a greater sense of order than the cases themselves warrant. Moreover, there is little evidence that the factors had much predictive or constraining power. * * *

* * *

B. *The* Chevron *Framework*

* * *

Chevron's first important innovation was the prescription of a procedural formula for courts to follow in determining whether to defer to agency interpretations. Each case, the Court suggested, should proceed in two steps. At step one, the court would operate in the independent judgment mode. It would ask, using traditional tools of statutory construction, whether Congress had "directly spoken to the precise question at issue." If the court concluded that Congress had a "specific intention" with respect to the issue at hand, it would adopt and enforce that answer. But if the court failed to uncover any such intention, it would move on to step two, where it would shift into the deference mode. Here, the question would be whether the agency's position was "a reasonable interpretation" of the statute.

On its face, the two-step formula seems innocuous enough. Indeed, after the formlessness of the previous era, it offers the beguiling promise of an orderly method for resolving a wide variety of controversies. What was unclear at the time, however, was that the two-step inquiry as framed by *Chevron* would have profound consequences for the way in which courts approach the deference question. There are several reasons for reaching this conclusion.

First, in contrast to the previous approach, the two-step structure makes deference an all-or-nothing matter. If the court resolves the question at step one, then it exercises purely independent judgment and gives no consideration to the executive view. If it resolves the question at step two, then it applies a standard of maximum deference. In effect, *Chevron* transformed a regime that allowed courts to give agencies deference along a sliding scale into a regime with an on/off switch.

Second, the Court's new framework inverted the traditional default rule. In the pre-*Chevron* period, deference to executive interpretations required special justification; independent judgment was the default rule. Under *Chevron*, the court must initially establish whether the issue is suitable for independent judicial resolution; if it is not, the court automatically shifts into a deferential mode. As a result, independent judgment now requires special justification, and deference is the default rule. If, as the Court seemed to suggest, the circumstances justifying independent judgment were defined narrowly, this inversion portended a major transfer of interpretative power from courts to agencies.

Third, the two-step framework has important implications for the kinds of considerations that enter into judicial decisionmaking. In particular, the framework appears to exclude any examination of the multiple factors historically relied upon by courts. The most immediate basis for this conclusion is the Court's decision to defer to the EPA's definition of "stationary source" even though it arguably represented a "sharp break with prior interpretations of the Act." Thus, the decision appeared to downgrade the frequently cited factor stressing the importance of agency views that were longstanding and consistent. More importantly, none of the traditional factors fits under step one or step two of the new framework. They are clearly irrelevant under step one, which focuses entirely on what happened in Congress, not on the agency or its decision. The factors could conceivably enter into the calculus at step two, where the court asks if the executive interpretation is "reasonable." But by "reasonable," the Court seemed to mean reasonable in light of the text, history, and interpretative conventions that govern the interpretation of a statute by a court; at least, this was the way the Court conducted the reasonableness inquiry in *Chevron* and subsequent cases. The question whether an interpretation is reasonable in light of these traditional norms of judicial interpretation likewise provides no place for the various contextual factors that played such an important role in the pre-*Chevron* era.

In addition to its novel framework, *Chevron* also broke new ground by invoking democratic theory as a basis for requiring deference to executive interpretations. Congress, Justice Stevens reasoned, is the ultimate source of lawmaking authority in a democracy. "If the intent of Congress is clear, that is the end of the matter; for the court, as well as the agency, must give effect to the unambiguously expressed intent of Congress." If the intentions of the primary lawgiver are not clear, however, then we are presented with a choice: who should undertake to fill in the gap in the understanding of congressional will, the court or the agency? *Chevron* declared that the agency is the preferred gap filler. Judges "are not part of either political branch"; they "have no constituency." An agency, on the other hand, while "not directly accountable to the people," is subject to the general oversight and supervision of the President, who is accountable. Thus, it is fitting that agencies, rather than courts, resolve "the competing interests which Congress itself either inadvertently did not resolve, or intentionally left to be resolved by the agency charged with the administration of the statute in light of everyday realities."

This new emphasis on democratic theory was important to the doctrinal framework because it supplied the justification for switching the default rule from independent judgment to deference. Under the pre-*Chevron* regime, not every agency decision would qualify for deference in the face of an ambiguous statute. In order to make deference a general default rule, the Court had to come up with some *universal* reason why administrative interpretations should be preferred to the judgments of Article III courts. Democratic theory supplied the justification: agency decisionmaking is always more democratic than judicial decisionmaking because all agencies are accountable (to some degree) to the President, and the President is elected by the people.

Chevron's heavy reliance on democratic theory left one major problem. Congress presumably ranks higher on the democracy scale than do the agencies. After all, Congress is directly elected by the people; agencies are at most indirectly accountable to the electorate through the President. Yet how do we know that Congress, the ultimate democratic trump card, wants ambiguities and gaps to be resolved by agencies rather than by courts?

Chevron solved this potential quandary by adopting its third and probably most controversial innovation: a presumption that whenever Congress has delegated authority to an agency to administer a statute, it has also delegated authority to the agency to interpret any ambiguities present in the statute. Previous cases, as we have seen, suggested that deference was appropriate if Congress had expressly delegated to an executive agency the power to define a particular term. *Chevron* in effect adopted a fiction that assimilated all cases involving statutory ambiguities or gaps into the express delegation or "legislative rule" model.

In short, the *Chevron* opinion can be understood as a prescription for resolving questions of statutory interpretation through a series of presumptions about primary and delegated lawmaking. Congress is presumed to be the primary lawmaking institution, and where it has spoken, its will must prevail. But when Congress has not addressed the precise issue in dispute and has delegated authority to an administrative agency, then we presume that interpretative authority has been delegated to the agency. Only if Congress is silent and has failed to designate an agency to administer the statute do we presume that power to interpret ambiguous law has been delegated to an Article III court.

* * *

II. *Chevron*: The Revolution in Practice

* * *

A. *The Incomplete Revolution*

One way to measure the impact of *Chevron* is to examine the Court's own post-*Chevron* deference cases in the aggregate. In order to make such an assessment, I reviewed all Supreme Court decisions from the 1981 Term to the end of the 1990 Term. The results for the seven post-*Chevron* Terms (*Chevron* was decided near the end of the 1983 Term) are summarized in Table 1.

Column A reports the total number of cases each Term in which at least one Justice recognized the presence of a question (concerning either a primary or a subsidiary issue) about whether to give deference to an administrative interpretation of a statute. Column B indicates how many of these decisions accepted the executive interpretation. Column C shows how many of the total cases applied the two-step *Chevron* framework or its equivalent; column D reports how many of the cases following the *Chevron* framework accepted the executive interpretation; column E reveals the number of *Chevron* cases that gave some consideration to the reasonableness of the executive view (step two of the framework) as opposed to stopping at step one. Finally, column F indicates how many controlling opinions in the cases rely on one or more of the traditional factors applied in the pre-*Chevron* period, such as longstanding and consistent interpretation, contemporaneous interpretation, congressional ratification, and so forth. In order to provide a basis for comparison, Table 2 reproduces data for some of these variables (total deference cases, cases accepting the administrative interpretation, and cases applying traditional factors) for the three pre-*Chevron* Terms, 1981-83.

Table 1. *Post*-Chevron *Terms*

Term	A Total Cases Involving Deference Question	B Agency View Accepted	C Chevron Framework Applied	D Chevron Framework: Agency View Accepted	E Chevron Framework: Decided At Step Two	F Cases Citing Traditional Factors
1990	11	8 (73%)	6 (55%)	4 (66%)	2 (33%)	6 (55%)
1989	14	8 (57%)	9 (62%)	4 (44%)	2 (25%)	4 (29%)
1988	9	4 (44%)	3 (33%)	1 (33%)	1 (33%)	6 (66%)
1987	14	9 (64%)	5 (36%)	3 (60%)	3 (50%)	3 (21%)
1986	9	5 (55%)	2 (22%)	1 (50%)	1 (50%)	2 (22%)
1985	14	11 (78%)	6 (43%)	5 (83%)	4 (66%)	6 (43%)
1984	19	18 (94%)	1 (5%)	1 (100%)	1 (100%)	7 (35%)
Total 1984-90	90	63 (70%)	32 (36%)	19 (59%)	14 (44%)	34 (37%)

Table 2. *Pre*-Chevron *Terms*

Term	A Total Cases Involving Deference Question	B Agency View Accepted	F Cases Citing Traditional Factors
1983	19	13 (68%)	11 (57%)
1982	15	11 (73%)	11 (73%)
1981	11	10 (90%)	8 (73%)
Total 1981-83	45	34 (75%)	30 (66%)

A number of interesting conclusions can be derived from the figures in Tables 1 and 2. First, it is clear that *Chevron* is often ignored by the Supreme Court. Although the *Chevron* opinion purports to describe a universal standard by which to determine whether to follow an administrative interpretation of a statute, the two-step framework has been used in only about one-third of the total post-*Chevron* cases in which one or more Justices recognized that a deference question was presented. Although *Chevron* began to be used more frequently after the 1987 Term, it is still far from the monolithic norm the opinion seems to describe. If we look solely at the 1987-90 period, the two-step framework was still applied in only half of the deference decisions.

Although some of the failure to rely on *Chevron* may be attributed to time lag, as awareness of the decision slowly disseminated through the administrative bar, this cannot account for the persistent resistance to using the framework in the Supreme Court. By the end of the 1987 Term, for example, the Court had applied the *Chevron* framework in fifteen different cases in a wide variety of areas. Any Justice who was paying attention to the Court's own work product should have been thoroughly versed in the tenets of *Chevron* by this time. Moreover, even if administrative lawyers in specialized areas like tax and labor law were late in coming to an awareness of *Chevron*, the federal agencies were represented in the Supreme Court almost exclusively by the Solicitor General's office—a small group of "generalists" who have been very conscious of *Chevron*. Thus, by 1987 at the latest, the agencies could be expected to take maximum advantage of *Chevron* in the Supreme Court. Yet in the 1988-90 Terms, the Court continued to apply the *Chevron* framework in only half the cases presenting a deference question. The persistent spottiness of *Chevron* during this period strongly suggests that the Court in many cases was simply not prepared to abide by the type of analysis dictated by *Chevron*—although apparently it was not prepared to abandon it or explain why it ought not to be controlling either.

Second, although *Chevron* is generally regarded as directing that courts give greater deference to executive interpretations, there is no discernible relationship between the application of the *Chevron* framework and greater acceptance of the executive view. Indeed, cases applying the *Chevron* approach have on the whole produced *fewer* affirmances of executive interpretations than those that do not follow *Chevron*. Although the number of cases is too small to attribute significance to the precise percentages, the general phenomenon is apparent when we compare the rate of acceptances in the cases actually applying the *Chevron* framework in the post-*Chevron* period—59% adopting the agency view—with either the overall acceptance rate in the post-*Chevron* period (70%) or the rate in the pre-*Chevron* era (75%). Paradoxically, it appears that adoption of the *Chevron* framework has meant, if anything, a decline in deference to agency views.

The suggestion that *Chevron* has had little discernible influence on the Supreme Court contrasts sharply with the only other published empirical study of *Chevron*'s impact. Professors Peter Schuck and Donald Elliot undertook a survey of *Chevron*'s influence on lower courts and found that deference to agency interpretations increased sharply after *Chevron*.[60] Their findings, however, are not necessarily inconsistent with my data suggesting no such change in the Supreme Court. Lower courts probably take Supreme Court opinions more seriously than does the Court itself. Moreover, one would predict that as it became increasingly evident over time that the Supreme Court employs the *Chevron* approach only sporadically, lower courts would begin to revert to their old habits. And indeed, there is evidence in the Schuck and Elliot study that suggests the "*Chevron* effect" in the lower courts may have been only temporary.

Third, the tables indicate that the emergence of *Chevron* has caused a decline in reliance on the traditional contextual factors for determining whether deference is appropriate. Again, the numbers are too small to attribute significance to precise percentages, but in the pre-*Chevron* period (1981-83 Terms) 66% of the deference cases cited one or more of these traditional factors. In the post-*Chevron* period, in contrast, the percentage of cases citing one of these factors declined to 36% overall. Still, it is obvious that the Court's invocation of these factors persists, with no visible trend pointing toward their complete extinction. This is not what one would expect to find if *Chevron* had completely transformed the practice of deciding when to defer.

* * *

C. *The Revolution Transformed*

Perhaps the most significant post-*Chevron* development * * * is a subtle but important modification in the statement of the relevant inquiry at step one. As we have seen, *Chevron* formulated that inquiry in terms of whether the court could "clearly" discern

---

[60] Peter H. Schuck & E. Donald Elliott, *To the* Chevron *Station: An Empirical Study of Federal Administrative Law*, 1990 DUKE L.J. 984.

that Congress "had an intention on the precise question at issue." If this threshold requirement were faithfully followed, there is little doubt that it would mark a major shift of interpretative power toward the executive branch: it is a rare case where a court can fairly say that Congress thought about, let alone formulated a clear view on, the precise issue in controversy. The "specific intentions" formulation therefore operates as an engine of judicial deference. By the same token, however, if the threshold determination for independent judicial resolution at step one were described differently—for example, if courts were instructed to ask whether the statute has a general meaning that resolves the controversy, even if Congress has not specifically addressed the issue at hand—then the balance might shift back toward independent judgment. In short, under the two-step *Chevron* framework, everything turns on the theory of judicial interpretation adopted at step one.

Post-*Chevron* cases have in fact begun to change the formulation of the step-one inquiry. The first sign of change was when opinions began to drop any reference to "specific intentions" or whether Congress had "clearly spoken to" the issue at hand and instead described the threshold inquiry simply in terms of whether the statute was "ambiguous" or "unclear." Then, beginning in 1988 * * * a more dramatic change emerged: the Court began to describe the inquiry at step one in terms of whether the statute has a "plain meaning." This rubric, an offspring of the "new textualism" espoused more generally by Justices Scalia and Kennedy, has not been followed uniformly. Some opinions continue to quote the language of *Chevron* about whether Congress has spoken to the precise question at issue. The trend, however, has been strongly away from the original *Chevron* formulation of step one.

What are the consequences of substituting textualism for intentionalism at step one? By itself, such a shift does not necessarily reduce deference. Indeed, if the inquiry at step one is formulated in terms of whether the statutory text discloses that Congress has spoken to the precise question at issue, this results in *even greater* deference to agency views, because Congress has undoubtedly "spoken to" fewer issues in text than it has through some combination of textual and nontextual sources. But at the same time that the Court has dropped the language of intent and substituted the language of plain meaning, it has also dropped the reference to "the precise question at issue." * * * [T]he "plain meaning" inquiry has tended in practice to devolve into an inquiry about whether the statute as a whole generates a *clearly preferred* meaning.

The movement from "specific intention" to "plain meaning" to "plain meaning considering the design of the statute as a whole" is but one short step away from "best meaning." In other words, with a shift at step one from the "specific intentions" rubric to the "plain meaning" rubric, the Court has moved the threshold inquiry a long way toward the exercise of independent judgment. * * *

* * *

III. What's Wrong with *Chevron*?

Chevron's adoption of a general theoretical framework for structuring the choice between independent judgment and deference was an important advance over the formlessness of the previous era. Unfortunately, evidence is mounting that the Court picked the wrong framework. I have already described the primary symptom of dysfunction: the lack of congruence between *Chevron* and the actual practice of the Supreme Court in determining whether or to what extent to defer to administrative interpretations of statutes. Theory and practice diverge in many ways: the failure to apply *Chevron* in at least half the cases in which, by its own terms, it should govern; the continuing use of traditional factors of deference which *Chevron* appears to render irrelevant; the creation of numerous exceptions to *Chevron* that do not seem to cohere with the decision's rationale; the development of a different version of the *Chevron* doctrine that greatly expands the judicial role at step one.

It is possible to argue that these manifold deviations simply reflect lapses of judgment on the part of the Court, and that the proper response is to identify the "true" version of *Chevron* and exhort the Justices to follow it consistently. But the divergences between theory and practice * * * are so pervasive that it is difficult to attribute the problem simply to judicial backsliding. Supreme Court Justices are practical individuals, sensitive to the traditions of American constitutionalism, and the Court's persistent refusal to abide by the narrow strictures of *Chevron* suggests that there must be something wrong with either *Chevron*'s implicit theory of deference, or its practical implications, or both. In this part, I will attempt to spell out why *Chevron* is incompatible with fundamental tenets of American public law, and why the framework proves to be so unsatisfactory in practice.

A. Chevron *Theory*

Chevron raises issues that go [to] the heart of our understanding of the judicial role under a system of separation of powers. In terms of formal separation of powers theory, interpretation of law is often said to be the exclusive province of the judiciary. This raises the "*Marbury* problem": if it is the role of courts "to say what the law is," then how can courts defer to the views of another branch of government on the meaning of the law? In terms of a functional theory of separation of powers, the purpose of an independent judiciary is often described in terms of its capacity for checking arbitrariness and aggrandizement by the other branches of government. This raises the problem of agency accountability: how can we structure judicial review of agency action so that agencies have enough discretion to implement complex regulatory programs, and yet assure that they do not become a tyrannical "Fourth Branch" of government, immune from popular control?

One of the strengths of the *Chevron* doctrine is that it offers, if only implicitly, answers to the *Marbury* and agency accountability problems. The answers it provides, however, are radically different from those that were put forth in the past, and are difficult to square with other, more enduring commitments about the proper role of the courts in a system of separated powers.

In the early days of modern administrative law, the *Marbury* and agency accountability dilemmas were usually resolved by borrowing from longstanding notions about the relationship between judges and juries. Courts would defer to agency findings of fact, but would decide all questions of law de novo. Under such a division of labor, courts would clearly retain final authority to "say what the law is." And by independently ascertaining the meaning of the agency's statutory authority in all cases, courts would provide a powerful constraint against arbitrariness and aggrandizement.

This solution was short lived, however. The comparative advantage of agencies is not limited to finding facts (or applying the law to facts), but extends to resolving many questions of law as well. And if courts decide all questions of law de novo—even where the meaning of the law is uncertain—then the price of containing agency aggrandizement is very likely to be judicial aggrandizement. In response to these shortcomings, the Court abandoned the judge-jury model soon after the Administrative Procedure Act was enacted, gradually developing the multifactored contextual approach that, as we have seen, dominated the pre-*Chevron* era.

Chevron in effect advances a third solution to the *Marbury* and agency accountability problems. The *Marbury* problem is resolved by a theory of congressionally mandated deference. Courts reconcile their duty to "say what the law is" with the practice of deferring to agency interpretations of law by positing that Congress, in conferring authority on an agency to administer a statute, has implicitly directed courts to defer to the agency's legal views. Accountability is achieved under *Chevron* by reducing the role of judicial review and relying instead on Presidential oversight.

Both halves of the *Chevron* solution are problematic at best. The mandatory deference solution to the *Marbury* problem rests entirely on the presumption that when Congress delegates the authority to administer a statute to an agency, it wants courts to defer to that agency's interpretations of law. The evidence that would support such a presumption is weak. Congress has never enacted a statute that contains a general delegation of interpretative authority to agencies. The very practice of enacting specific delegations of interpretative authority suggests that Congress understands that no such general authority exists. Moreover, the one general statute on point, the Administrative Procedure Act, directs reviewing courts to "decide *all* relevant questions of law." If anything, this suggests that Congress contemplated courts would always apply independent judgment on questions of law, reserving deference for administrative findings of fact or determinations of policy.

The strongest evidence in support of the Court's presumption is the fact that Congress knows about the practice of judicial deference to agency interpretations and has not acted to prohibit it. But in order to establish that Congress has mandated the practice of deference, the Court should be able to point to more than a debatable inference from congressional inaction. *Chevron* itself, in defining the judicial role in the interpretation of statutes, suggested that courts have no authority to impose decisional rules that cannot be traced to an authoritative judgment of Congress. Yet the Court could point to no statute indicating that Congress has required that agencies, rather than courts, interpret ambiguities and gaps in statutes. A decisional framework that rests on two foundations, one of which contradicts the other, is difficult to regard as sound.

Chevron's solution to the agency accountability problem is also unsatisfactory. Unlike previous discussions of the accountability problem, which tended to assume that popular control comes about only through the election of representatives who pass statutes that are then enforced by courts, *Chevron* perceives a dual channel of popular control: one operating through the election of representatives who pass statutes; the other through the election of the President who directs the agents who implement those statutes. The Court sought to forge a formula that would allow both channels of popular control to operate by limiting courts to the enforcement of unambiguous legislative directives, leaving all discretionary decisions to be disciplined by Presidential oversight.

The Court's perception that there is a dual channel of control is an important insight. But Presidential oversight has inherent limitations. Many administrative entities—including the "independent" regulatory agencies and "legislative" or Article I courts—enjoy various degrees of statutory immunity from direct Presidential control. Several prominent separation of powers decisions handed down since *Chevron* have legitimized these immunities, diluting the power of the President to assure overall direction of those agents who administer the law. But even without the Court's sanction for these immunities, it is simply unrealistic, given the vastness of the federal bureaucracy, to expect that the President or his principal lieutenants can effectively monitor the policymaking activities of all federal agencies. Nor does it seem wise or appropriate to leave control of agency behavior to congressional oversight hearings. In the end, the primary protection against arbitrary or aggrandizing action by agencies must remain the fundamental constitutional limitation on all executive action—that it "comport with the terms set in legislative directives." And the only effective institutional mechanism for preserving this constraint is judicial review.

* * *

In sum, *Chevron* seeks to resolve the central theoretical problems of the modern administrative state by adopting a dubious fiction of delegated authority and by reducing the role of the courts to a point that threatens to undermine the principal constitutional constraint on agency misbehavior. Given these failings, it is small wonder that the Court often seems wary of the *Chevron* doctrine, applying it inconsistently at best.

B. Chevron *Practice*

The Court's general failure to abide by the teachings of *Chevron*—whether by acts of omission or commission—also suggests that the framework frequently generates unwanted results. There are a number of reasons why *Chevron* does not function well as a guide to determining the relative weight to be given to judicial and agency views.

1. *The Sequential Inquiry*

Perhaps the most basic problem stems from the fact that *Chevron* casts the relevant determinants in a sequential hierarchy: consideration of judicial competence first, consideration of administrative competence second. By sequencing the inquiry in this fashion, *Chevron* almost guarantees that in every case the independent views of the judiciary will be given either too much or too little weight, and concomitantly, that the views of the agency will be given either too little or too much deference. If the issue is resolved at step one, then the court gives no consideration to the views of the executive and decides the matter independently. If the issue is resolved at step two, then the court regards the agency view as dispositive, unless it can say that it is unreasonable. In other words, *Chevron* inevitably generates "one-sided" decisions. In those cases where the Court feels that one-sidedness is appropriate, *Chevron* will do fine. But if the Court perceives that a more refined approach is called for, *Chevron* is a source of awkwardness. The predominant solution in the latter situation appears to be to ignore *Chevron*.

* * *

2. *The Dividing Line*

A second set of problems is generated by the method for determining the dividing line between the two steps in the sequential inquiry. As we have seen, the balance is determined by the theory of interpretation adopted at step one. As originally formulated, *Chevron* described the judicial inquiry in such a way that it would almost certainly produce routine deference to agency views.

Chevron's theory of the judicial role at step one is the statutory analogue of what in constitutional law has been called "strict intentionalism." As Dean Paul Brest has put it, "Strict intentionalism requires the interpreter to determine how the adopters would have applied a provision to a given situation, and to apply it accordingly."[130] The problem with such a theory of interpretation is that no matter how precise the meaning of the text, unanticipated questions will invariably arise about how the text is to apply in different circumstances. In the familiar example, if the statute says "no vehicles are permitted in the park," does this language apply to bicycles? Or, if the legislature anticipates this application, and provides that "no *motor* vehicles are permitted in the park," does this version apply to motorized wheel chairs? Given the limits of human imagination, it is virtually impossible for the legislature to formulate a specific intention about how a provision should be applied to all or even most situations. The process

---

[130] Paul Brest, *The Misconceived Quest for the Original Understanding*, 60 B.U. L. Rev. 204, 222 (1980). * * *

of application, especially over time, will always outrun the understanding of even the most farsighted legislature. For this reason, to ask the interpreter to "ascertai[n] that Congress had an intention on the precise question at issue," as *Chevron* demands, is to ask a question that will yield an affirmative answer—at least an honest affirmative answer—in only a tiny number of cases.

Under the *Chevron* framework, there is only one way to expand the small judicial role contemplated by the specific intentions theory—reformulate the nature of the inquiry at step one. The cure, unfortunately, may be as bad as the disease. As we have seen, recent decisions have begun to drop the specific intentions requirement in favor of a "plain meaning" formulation. But this leaves unanswered several critical questions about what kinds of interpretative aids courts may consult at step one. Must the court find the statute plain on its face? Or may it be plain after consulting extrinsic sources, like dictionary definitions, definitions contained (explicitly or implicitly) in other statutes, or considerations of the structure of the act? In its more latitudinarian versions, where the court looks to considerations of structure and purpose in deciding whether the meaning is "plain," the plain meaning inquiry tends to converge with a "clearly preferred meaning" approach. If this happens, then *Chevron* would suffer from the exact opposite of the problem that plagued the original formulation: if step one does not completely swallow step two, at least it will have dramatically expanded—perhaps too far—in the opposite direction.

On other occasions the Court has not committed to either a "specific intentions" method, or to a textualist method, but has stated the relevant inquiry simply in terms of whether the statute is "ambiguous" or "unclear." This formulation leaves even more questions unanswered. To what extent may the court resolve the meaning of the statute at step one based on inferences drawn from legislative history or considerations of statutory purpose? May it use canons of construction based on linguistic usage? Canons based on substantive policy considerations? Given the wide range of possible answers to these questions, the *Chevron* framework becomes at best unpredictable, and at worst a vehicle for complete substitution of judicial judgment for the views of the agency.

* * *

VI. Conclusion

From the perspective of this Article, the long controversy over judicial deference to administrative interpretations of statutes can be seen as a rivalry between two competing models: the mandatory deference model and the discretionary deference model. The rivalry has been largely unconscious because the assumptions of the mandatory deference model are often unstated, and the theoretical basis for the discretionary deference model has never been previously articulated. Still, we can see these ideas struggling for dominance in judicial practice.

In the pre-*Chevron* era, the two models coexisted uneasily. Courts applied the mandatory deference model to interpretations backed by express delegations of regulatory authority from Congress. But in the absence of an express delegation, they applied something that in retrospect looks very much like the discretionary deference model—examining various contextual factors that could be applied just as easily to a precedent of a court of coordinate jurisdiction as to the construction of an executive branch agency. The *Chevron* era on paper represents a rejection of the discretionary approach and an embrace of a pure mandatory regime. Now, however, the realm of mandatory deference has vastly expanded to include a presumption of delegation in all cases where a federal statute is ambiguous or unclear. As we have seen, however, in practice the discretionary approach has lived on, in the shadows of *Chevron*, and in considerable tension with its expanded delegation theory.

Chevron's many failings are largely those of the mandatory deference model that it incorporates. Although the idea of express delegation is straightforward enough, the concept of an implied delegation of interpretative authority is difficult to characterize as a congressional command. The focus on delegation also makes the decision about whether to defer subordinate to the resolution of a question of judicial interpretation: Did Congress (constructively) delegate, or did it not? In this fashion, consideration of the executive view becomes ensnared in controversies over the legitimate scope of judicial interpretation. Finally, the idea of delegation requires that deference be viewed in either/or terms: either Congress delegated authority, or it did not; no intermediate possibilities make sense. The either/or nature of the mandatory deference theory based on delegated power pushes the doctrine toward extremes of either too little or too much deference.

I have argued that a better solution to the uneasy mixture of the pre-*Chevron* period would have been to move to a pure discretionary regime, what I have called the executive precedent model. The idea of delegation would not disappear in such a regime. It would simply revert to its original scope of express delegation, and it would become one of several factors that courts would examine in determining the "strength" of an executive precedent. Because the practice of deference under the executive precedent model is grounded in a conception of the judicial power rather than in a fiction of delegation, it avoids the major theoretical failings of the *Chevron* doctrine. In addition, it allows courts to consider various attributes of the executive decision that seem undeniably relevant to the question of how much weight it should be given: such as whether the agency's interpretation is supported by careful reasoning, whether its interpretation has generated reliance interests that should be protected, and whether its construction has been approved by Congress. The executive precedent model also permits a flexible response to the question of deference, allowing courts to give various degrees of deference to executive interpretations, depending on the strength of the contextual factors involved and on the court's conviction about the clarity of the statute as an original matter.

* * *

Antonin Scalia, *Judicial Deference to Administrative Interpretations of Law*, 1989 DUKE L.J. 511, 513-17, 520-21*

* * *

It is not immediately apparent why a court should ever accept the judgment of an executive agency on a question of law. Indeed, on its face the suggestion seems quite incompatible with Marshall's aphorism that "[i]t is emphatically the province and duty of the judicial department to say what the law is." Surely the law, that immutable product of Congress, is what it is, and its content—ultimately to be decided by the courts—cannot be altered or affected by what the Executive thinks about it. I suppose it is harmless enough to speak about "giving deference to the views of the Executive" concerning the meaning of a statute, just as we speak of "giving deference to the views of the Congress" concerning the constitutionality of particular legislation—the mealy-mouthed word "deference" not necessarily meaning anything more than considering those views with attentiveness and profound respect, before we reject them. But to say that those views, if at least reasonable, will ever be *binding*—that is, seemingly, a striking abdication of judicial responsibility.

---

* Reprinted with permission of the Duke Law Journal and Antonin Scalia. All rights reserved.

* * *

What, then, is the theoretical justification for allowing reasonable administrative interpretations to govern? The cases, old and new, that accept administrative interpretations, often refer to the "expertise" of the agencies in question, their intense familiarity with the history and purposes of the legislation at issue, their practical knowledge of what will best effectuate those purposes. In other words, they are more likely than the courts to reach the correct result. That is, if true, a good practical reason for accepting the agency's views, but hardly a valid theoretical justification for doing so. * * * If it is, as we have always believed, the constitutional duty of the *courts* to say what the law is, we must search for something beyond relative competence as a basis for ignoring that principle when agency action is at issue.

One possible validating rationale * * * is that the constitutional principle of separation of powers requires *Chevron*. The argument goes something like this: When, in a statute to be implemented by an executive agency, Congress leaves an ambiguity that cannot be resolved by text or legislative history, the "traditional tools of statutory construction," the resolution of that ambiguity necessarily involves policy judgment. Under our democratic system, policy judgments are not for the courts but for the political branches; Congress having left the policy question open, it must be answered by the Executive.

Now there is no one more fond of our system of separation of powers than I am, but even I cannot agree with this approach. To begin with, it seems to me that the "traditional tools of statutory construction" include not merely text and legislative history but also, quite specifically, the consideration of policy consequences. Indeed, that tool is so traditional that it has been enshrined in Latin: *"Ratio est legis anima; mutata legis ratione mutatur et lex."* ("The reason for the law is its soul; when the reason for the law changes, the law changes as well.") Surely one of the most frequent justifications courts give for choosing a particular construction is that the alternative interpretation would produce "absurd" results, or results less compatible with the reason or purpose of the statute. This, it seems to me, unquestionably involves judicial consideration and evaluation of competing policies, and for precisely the same purpose for which (in the context we are discussing here) *agencies* consider and evaluate them—to determine which one will best effectuate the statutory purpose. Policy evaluation is, in other words, part of the traditional judicial tool-kit that is used in applying the first step of *Chevron*—the step that determines, *before* deferring to agency judgment, whether the law is indeed ambiguous. Only when the court concludes that the policy furthered by *neither* textually possible interpretation will be clearly "better" (in the sense of achieving what Congress apparently wished to achieve) will it, pursuant to *Chevron*, yield to the agency's choice. But the reason it yields is assuredly *not* that it has no constitutional competence to consider and evaluate policy.

* * *

In my view, the theoretical justification for *Chevron* is no different from the theoretical justification for those pre-*Chevron* cases that sometimes deferred to agency legal determinations. As the D.C. Circuit, quoting the First Circuit, expressed it: "The extent to which courts should defer to agency interpretations of law is ultimately 'a function of Congress' intent on the subject as revealed in the particular statutory scheme at issue.'" An ambiguity in a statute committed to agency implementation can be attributed to either of two congressional desires: (1) Congress intended a particular result, but was not clear about it; or (2) Congress had no particular intent on the subject, but meant to leave its resolution to the agency. When the former is the case, what we have is genuinely a question of law, properly to be resolved by the courts. When the latter is the case, what we have is the conferral of discretion upon the agency, and the only question of law presented to the courts is whether the agency has acted within the scope of its discretion—i.e., whether its resolution of the ambiguity is reasonable. As I read the history of developments in this field, the pre-*Chevron* decisions sought to choose between (1) and (2) on a statute-by-statute basis. Hence the relevance of such frequently mentioned factors as the degree of the agency's expertise, the complexity of the question at issue, and the existence of rulemaking authority within the agency. All these factors make an intent to confer discretion upon the agency more likely. *Chevron*, however, if it is to be believed, replaced this statute-by-statute evaluation (which was assuredly a font of uncertainty and litigation) with an across-the-board presumption that, in the case of ambiguity, agency discretion is meant.

It is beyond the scope of these remarks to defend that presumption (I was not on the Court, after all, when *Chevron* was decided). Surely, however, it is a more rational presumption today than it would have been thirty years ago—which explains the change in the law. Broad delegation to the Executive is the hallmark of the modern administrative state; agency rulemaking powers are the rule rather than, as they once were, the exception; and as the sheer number of modern departments and agencies suggests, we are awash in agency "expertise." If the *Chevron* rule is not a 100% accurate estimation of modern congressional intent, the prior case-by-case evaluation was not so either—and was becoming less and less so, as the sheer volume of modern dockets made it less and less possible for the Supreme Court to police diverse application of an ineffable rule. And to tell the truth, the quest for the "genuine" legislative intent is probably a wild-goose chase anyway. In the vast majority of cases I expect that Congress *neither* (1) intended a single result, *nor* (2) meant to confer discretion upon the agency, but rather (3) didn't think about the matter at all. If I am correct in that, then any rule adopted in this field represents merely a fictional, presumed intent, and operates principally as a background rule of law against which Congress can legislate.

If that is the principal function to be served, *Chevron* is unquestionably better than what preceded it. Congress now knows that the ambiguities it creates, whether intentionally or unintentionally, will be resolved, within the bounds of permissible interpretation, not by the courts but by a particular agency, whose policy biases will ordinarily be known. The legislative process becomes less of a sporting event when those supporting and opposing a particular disposition do not have to gamble upon whether, if they say nothing about it in the statute, the ultimate answer will be provided by the courts or rather by the Department of Labor.

* * *

There is one final point I wish to discuss: What does it take to satisfy the first step of *Chevron*—that is, when is a statute ambiguous? *Chevron* becomes virtually meaningless, it seems to me, if ambiguity exists only when the arguments for and against the various possible interpretations are in absolute equipoise. If nature knows of such equipoise in legal arguments, the courts at least do not. The judicial task, every day, consists of finding the *right* answer, no matter how closely balanced the question may *seem* to be. In appellate opinions, there is no such thing as a tie. If the judicial mentality that is developed by such a system were set to answering the question, "When are the arguments for and against a particular statutory interpretation in equipoise?," I am certain that the response would be "almost never." If *Chevron* is to have any meaning, then, congressional intent must be regarded as "ambiguous" not just when no interpretation is even marginally better than any other, but rather when two or more reasonable, though not necessarily equally valid, interpretations exist. This is indeed intimated by the opinion in *Chevron*—which suggests that the opposite of "ambiguity" is not "resolvability" but rather "clarity." Here, of course, is the chink in *Chevron*'s armor—the ambiguity that prevents it from being an absolutely clear guide to future judicial decisions (though still a better one than what it supplanted). How clear is clear? It is here, if *Chevron* is not abandoned, that the future battles over acceptance of agency interpretations of law will be fought.

* * *

I cannot resist the temptation to tie this * * * [article] into an impenetrable whole, by observing that where one stands on this last point—how clear is clear—may have much to do with where one stands on the earlier points of what *Chevron* means and whether *Chevron* is desirable. In my experience, there is a fairly close correlation between the degree to which a person is (for want of a better word) a "strict constructionist" of statutes, and the degree to which that person favors *Chevron* and is willing to give it broad scope. The reason is obvious. One who finds *more* often (as I do) that the meaning of a statute is apparent from its text and from its relationship with other laws, thereby finds *less* often that the triggering requirement for *Chevron* deference exists. It is thus relatively rare that *Chevron* will require me to accept an interpretation which, though reasonable, I would not personally adopt. Contrariwise, one who abhors a "plain meaning" rule, and is willing to permit the apparent meaning of a statute to be impeached by the legislative history, will more frequently find agency-liberating ambiguity, and will discern a much broader range of "reasonable" interpretation that the agency may adopt and to which the courts must pay deference. The frequency with which *Chevron* will require *that* judge to accept an interpretation he thinks wrong is infinitely greater.

* * *

Cynthia R. Farina, *Statutory Interpretation and the Balance of Power in the Administrative State*, 89 COLUM. L. REV. 452, 456-57, 464, 466-72, 499-526 (1989)*

* * *

I. Deference According to *Chevron*: In Search of Clear Statements and a Constitutional Cure-All

---

* Reprinted with permission of the Columbia Law Review and Cynthia R. Farina. All rights reserved.

When the Supreme Court in *Chevron* chastised the D.C. Circuit for failing to defer to the Environmental Protection Agency's (EPA) "reasonable" reading of the Clean Air Act, it did more than merely declare the victor in a forty-year war between advocates of the deferential model and defenders of independent judgment. First, *Chevron* defined deference in a way that, while not entirely unprecedented, was far more extreme than earlier articulations of the model had been. Second, it justified its commitment to deference in terms resonant with revealed constitutional truth. The combination—a strong formulation of the concept of deference with an apologia invoking fundamental constitutional principles—generated a powerful new image of the appropriate functions of court and agency in the administrative state.

* * *

B. *The Appeal of Deference*

By its very extremism, the *Chevron* * * * articulation of deference underscores a critical point: the choice of interpretive model is ultimately a choice about allocating power, the power that results from ambiguity. When Congress has failed to speak clearly or comprehensively, who gets to decide what the law is? If a *nonregulatory* statute is obscure or silent on a dispositive issue, the court proceeds to construct legal meaning out of whatever the enactors did supply. Although we continually debate how this process of meaning elaboration ought to occur, we rarely question the appropriateness of the judiciary's undertaking it—perhaps because no other option readily exists. When a *regulatory* statute is ambiguous, however, the agency stands as a potential alternative recipient of the power inevitably created by the legislature's finite capacity for prescience and precision in expression. The rigid, literalistic approach *Chevron* * * * adopt[s] towards whether Congress has expressed a judicially cognizable "intent" simply increases the quantum of power at stake in the selection of interpretive model.

* * *

* * * Deference is necessary, *Chevron* argues, to avoid judicial usurpation of functions Congress wished to entrust to the agency. If the judiciary displaces the conclusions of the legislature's chosen administrative delegate with its independent views on statutory meaning, it frustrates the will of a coordinate branch for its own aggrandizement. From this same concern for power seeping into the wrong institutional hands, *Chevron* derives an additional justification for deference. The process of statutory interpretation inevitably involves some lawmaking, as

well as law finding, component. Because the judiciary is the branch least accountable to the people, *Chevron* reasons, the court is not a suitable organ for exercising policy-making power. Agencies, of course, are not elected entities either. But, *Chevron* asserts, they are answerable to the political branches. If the judiciary substitutes its judgment on questions of statutory meaning for the views of the agency, even this secondary link to the electorate will be lost.

Both of these justifications for deference are rooted in the central constitutional principle of separation of powers. The first (hereinafter referred to as the "judicial usurpation" argument) condemns the independent judgment model as judicial interference with the legislature's prerogative to advance the public good in the way it deems fit—that is, by giving interpretive leeway to expert agencies. The second (hereinafter the "interference with legitimate political control" argument) emphasizes the importance of each branch exercising the governmental function for which it is peculiarly suited. The judiciary, it asserts, is an inappropriate body to make the kinds of policy choices that are unavoidable in construing contemporary regulatory statutes. In addition to reflecting separation of powers considerations, this second justification for deference voices fundamental concerns about legitimacy. It echoes the Lockean view that the exercise of power in a democratic government can be defended only through accountability to its source, the electorate.

Because they respond directly to our collective unease about the growth of regulatory authority, *Chevron*'s two justifications for choosing the deferential model are deeply appealing. If deference is indeed the ally of separation of powers and legitimacy, then the rejection of independent judgment represents the triumph of fundamental constitutional values in an area riddled with constitutional doubts.

In the end, however, *Chevron*'s solution to the puzzle of allocating the interpretive power is only as sound as its premises. The balance of this Article scrutinizes those premises. It suggests that the "judicial usurpation" and "interference with legitimate political control" arguments rest on factual assumptions that are, at best, dubious and on theoretical assumptions that work extraordinary, yet unacknowledged, alterations in the constitutional ground rules.

II. Independent Judgment as Judicial Usurpation?

Chevron's conclusion that deference is necessary to prevent the judiciary from arrogating power Congress wished to place in administrative hands requires acceptance of two propositions: First, Congress intends, as a factual matter, that agencies take principal responsibility for determining what regulatory statutes mean; and second, Congress is unconstrained, as a matter of constitutional doctrine, in choosing to entrust such responsibility to agencies. While both these propositions are critical to the "judicial usurpation" justification for deference, neither is self-evident—and neither is critically examined by the *Chevron* Court. In fact, the first proves to be extremely problematic, while the second can be accepted only by repudiating fundamental aspects of existing theory.

A. *Chasing the Will-o'-the-Wisp of "Interpretive Intent"*

If Congress, when it enacts regulatory legislation, intends that the implementing agency will resolve a particular question of statutory meaning, then a court would indeed be contravening the legislative will to treat the issue as a matter for independent judicial determination. On these facts, the validity of the "judicial usurpation" justification for deference would turn solely on whether any constitutional principle prevents effectuation of the legislature's "interpretive intent." However, this set of facts—in which Congress *both* perceives the need for future interpretation *and* formulates an intent * * * [to] be accomplished by the agency—is only one of four logically possible scenarios.

Alternatively, Congress may recognize that its words will require interpretation and assume that the *court* will resolve questions of statutory meaning in the normal course of appropriate litigation. In this scenario, the legislature has an interpretive intent, but its principal object is the judiciary, not the agency. A third possibility is that Congress means to provide the substantive answer itself, but instead unwittingly creates an interpretive question by failing to express its answer clearly. In such a case, the legislature's intention—unsuccessfully implemented—is not to delegate to any other entity the power to determine meaning. Finally, Congress may have no intent whatsoever about interpretive responsibility or its allocation. This could occur because the substantive question is unknowable or, if theoretically knowable, is unrecognized at the time the legislature acts, or because the question is lost or deliberately bypassed in the process of hammering out the regulatory package.

Whenever one of these latter three scenarios accurately describes the state of Congress's "intent" on a given issue of statutory meaning, it is simply inaccurate to suggest that the independent judgment approach would constitute judicial usurpation of power legislatively designated for another. Of course, discerning, for each statutory provision requiring interpretation, which scenario correctly describes the enactors' intent is likely to be a formidable, if not an impossible, task. *Chevron* sidesteps this difficulty by announcing a presumption. If Congress has not itself *unambiguously* resolved the *precise* substantive issue, then we are to assume that it either "explicitly" or "implicitly" delegated to the agency the interpretive task. Apparently, this presumption—that ambiguity equals legislative intent to empower the agency—is irrebuttable.

Perhaps *Chevron* cannot be faulted for resorting to the device of a presumption. Given the predictable difficulty of making individualized determinations of the state of legislative intent for each new question of statutory meaning, even a court dedicated to vindicating Congress's interpretive will might be forgiven for selecting the model of statutory interpretation according to which of the four scenarios most commonly occurs. The problem is that, even though there is no a priori connection between substantive ambiguity and interpretive intent, *Chevron* offers no evidence to support its conclusion that silence or unclarity in a regulatory statute typically represents Congress's deliberate delegation of meaning-elaboration power to the agency. If conclusions about the "typical" legislative will are going to be based on nothing more than intuition, many observers would opine that Congress rarely formulates an intent about who will decide particular questions of statutory meaning. If they are correct, then the choice between the two interpretive models cannot sensibly be framed as a matter of obeying or defying the legislative will.

If we want to move beyond intuition, solid evidence of what, if anything, Congress "typically" intends with respect to statutory interpretation is hard to come by. Some commentators have urged that Congress's choice of "inherently broad" language in many regulatory statutes raises an inescapable inference of legislative intent to delegate the power of meaning elaboration to the agency. Others—even including some who generally advocate the deferential model—have disapproved such an inference, and the presence of equally expansive language in statutory schemes committed to judicial oversight would seem to undermine any notion of some generic legislative disinclination to trust courts with interpreting broad statutory mandates. Another aspect of regulatory statutes that could conceivably be relevant is the frequently included catchall authorization to make all rules and orders necessary for carrying out the purposes of the act. Such a provision obviously manifests a legislative judgment that the agency should have considerable discretion to flesh out the regulatory scheme. From the fact that so much power was given, some observers would deduce that the grant of full interpretive authority was intended. Others conclude that the matter cannot be resolved so simply. For example, Judge Stephen Breyer * * * has argued that the enactors' interpretive intent is likely to have varied, even within a single regulatory statute, depending on the importance of a given question to the administrative scheme, the nature of the substantive issues involved, and the ability and orientation of the particular agency.[80]

* * *

III. Independent Judgment as Interfering with Legitimate Political Control?

Chevron's depiction of deference as a necessary judicial affirmation of democratic decision making strikes a deep constitutional chord. After observing that "[j]udges are not experts in the field, and are not part of either political branch of the Government," the Court writes:

> When a challenge to an agency construction of a statutory provision, fairly conceptualized, really centers on the wisdom of the agency's policy, rather than whether it is a reasonable choice within a gap left open by Congress, the challenge must fail. In such a case, federal judges—who have no constituency—have a duty to respect the legitimate policy choices made by those who do. The responsibilities for assessing the wisdom of such policy choices and resolving the struggle between competing views of the public interest are not judicial ones: "Our Constitution vests such responsibilities in the political branches."

The reasoning is adroit. Construing ambiguous regulatory statutes is really just a species of policy making. Policy making is the province of the elected branches, not the judiciary. Therefore, the constitutionally appropriate interpretive model is one that turns the problem of statutory meaning over to the political process and confines the role of unelected judges to asking merely whether the interpretation/policy choice that emerges is a "reasonable" one. Deference thus becomes a way to assuage another of the prime constitutional anxieties bred by broadly delegative statutes: the fear that the power to define public policy is passing out of the hands of the people's elected representatives.

---

[80] Breyer, [*Judicial Review of Questions of Law and Policy*, 38 ADMIN. L. REV. 363, 370 (1986).]

Appealing as it seems, this "interference with legitimate political control" justification for deference can nonetheless be challenged on many levels. In the first place, treating the interpretation of regulatory statutes as simply an exercise in policy making has troubling implications * * *. In particular, when this view of interpretation is superimposed on *Chevron*'s rule that a statute is "ambiguous" (and hence fair game for "interpretation") whenever it does not provide unequivocal direction on the precise point at issue, great potential is created for overlooking substantive directions and limitations that the enactors had intended, and attempted, to incorporate in the statute. Even in the unlikely event that the "meaning" selected by the agency accurately reflects the wishes of the people's current elected representatives, the prospect that regulatory statutes will routinely be amended or even repealed by "interpretation" should at least give us pause. In the second place, the Court's reasoning reflects a singularly narrow conception of the judicial function. *Chevron* implies that the shaping of public policy is so foreign to the judiciary's proper task that courts must avoid responsibility for resolving policy questions whenever possible. The primacy of the political branches in establishing domestic and foreign policy is beyond dispute; surely, however, it overstates theory and distorts reality to suggest that the judicial role in defining public policy is an extraordinary one, legitimately undertaken only as a last resort. Far-reaching policy resolutions are a regular part of both common-law and constitutional adjudication. Even if common-law examples are dismissed as irrelevant to the federal courts and constitutional adjudication is distinguished as sui generis, the federal judiciary has long administered sweeping yet open-textured statutes in such areas as antitrust, labor and civil rights. Whatever one's views of the wisdom of this, it simply cannot be considered aberrant for federal courts to resolve policy questions as part of deciding cases properly before them.

Even if we were to accept that interpretation is merely policy making and that public policy can legitimately be shaped only by the political branches, the most fundamental problems with *Chevron*'s second justification for deference remain. The proposition that deference is constitutionally compelled in order to legitimate regulatory policy making rests on two assumptions. First, if courts follow the deferential model, agencies will exercise the interpretive power subject to the direction of the political branches; second, the direction agencies receive will indeed respond to the constitutional concerns raised by the delegation of regulatory power. Once again, neither of these critical assumptions is self-evidently correct, and neither is scrutinized by the Court. In fact, the first assumption may be wholly unfounded and certainly is misleading to the extent it implies that *Congress* will regularly play an active directory role in agencies' interpretive decisions. And since the President is the "political branch" most likely to achieve control over such decisions, the second assumption is also inaccurate—at least in view of how principles of legitimacy and separation of powers traditionally have been framed.

A. *Congress, the President, and Control of Agency Discretion*

* * *

Many observers of the growth of the administrative state would respond that administrative discretion is rarely directed, on a consistent or sustained basis, by any person or institution outside the agency. The fear that agencies—particularly the independent agencies—have moved beyond the effective control of the political branches was voiced at the height of the New Deal, and continues to be expressed, in varying degrees of intensity, by judges, academics, practitioners and politicians. It reflects the very plausible skepticism that either Congress or the President can penetrate the immense size and bewildering complexity of the federal bureaucracy to reach the decision makers who matter or overcome the volume and technical complexity of regulations to affect their content to any significant extent. If this fear is well-founded, then *Chevron*'s "interference with legitimate political control" argument founders on the facts at the very outset. For the deferential model to result in interpretive choices being made under the direction of elected officials, Congress and/or the President must exert meaningful direction over agency decisions. * * *

Other observers believe, however, that the "headless fourth branch" metaphor overstates the autonomy of agencies. They note that administrative decision makers are often keenly aware of and responsive to their political environment. But the fact that agencies may keep an attentive ear on emanations from Capitol Hill and the White House does not mean that Congress and the President compete on an equal footing in the struggle to influence administrative discretion. Rather, a potent combination of constitutionally granted powers, congressional acquiescence (taking the form of both custom and statute) and institutional and organizational factors have contributed to the emergence of the President as the dominant force in regulatory policy making. A few examples of this synergy can demonstrate the point without belaboring it.

The appointment of agency heads illustrates how custom has combined with the Constitution to strengthen the President's hand. Control over the power to appoint key government officials was an issue of intense concern for the Framers. Article II, section 2 of the Constitution, providing for presidential appointment of major officers with Senate consent, represented a deeply considered and much debated attempt to balance executive and legislative involvement in the selection process. However, although the power to withhold consent could have made the Senate a powerful (if not quite equal) partner with the President in choosing top administrators, the confirmation process has, by custom, rarely interfered with his preferences. As a consequence, the appointment power has come to represent a significant opportunity for a skillful and determined President to extend his influence by placing in critical agency positions those who share his regulatory philosophy.

The way in which the President's constitutional powers have been enhanced by Congress's statutory cooperation and subsequent acquiescence is exemplified by the evolution of the Office of Management and Budget (OMB). Created by statute in 1921 as the accountant for the executive branch, the OMB underwent a dramatic reorganization in 1970. It emerged with significant managerial functions that have enabled it to become a powerful device for imposing the President's stamp on the regulatory process. Possessing almost mythic stature as "the Cerberus at the gate of any program" an agency proposes to undertake or strengthen, the OMB now serves as a filter between agencies and Congress. Except for certain agencies that have been statutorily exempted from the requirement, agencies must obtain OMB clearance of proposals for legislation and even legislative testimony. In addition, the OMB presses the President's view of the relative priorities to be accorded various regulatory activities through its control over the budget. Although the coercive potential of budget clearance has been vitiated for some agencies by statutory requirements that their original funding requests be transmitted to Congress, the overall policy-shaping effect of the OMB's budgetary power is significant. Perhaps most important, the OMB serves as a powerful conduit for injecting the President's views directly into the rule-making process. This is accomplished in part through the agency's formal responsibility to monitor proposed rules for compliance with applicable Executive Orders. Additionally, the OMB maintains an active practice of informally communicating the White House position to agency personnel during the rule-making process. Highly controversial and heavily scrutinized as the OMB has been in the last few years, it has escaped any meaningful legislative curb on its activities.

* * *

This [presidential] "power to act" stems not simply from constitutional and statutory grants and congressional acquiescence, but also from the very structure of the presidency. After intense debate about the proper organization of the executive branch, the drafters of the Constitution settled on a unitary President who would be capable of the dispatch, coordination, initiative and consistency necessary to maintain law and order and conduct foreign policy. Not surprisingly, those deliberately cultivated qualities can prove just as effective when turned to shaping domestic policy. In the struggle to direct administrative discretion, a single, highly visible, constantly present Chief Executive is at a considerable structural advantage when compared with a collegial legislative body that assembles only periodically, must act through a complex set of procedures by consensus of its several hundred members and is vulnerable to substantial turnover in membership every two years.

The practical constraints that flow from the institutional structure of Congress were as deliberately cultivated as the practical advantages that flow from the structure of the presidency. The Framers perceived the lawmaking power as necessarily large and concomitantly dangerous. Accordingly, they designed the branch which would hold this power in a manner that disabled it from making or changing public policy too quickly or too often. What they did not foresee, however, was the movement of vast portions of the lawmaking power from that original, carefully structured repository into another part of government. Now, although Congress possesses two of the most potentially powerful devices for controlling agency behavior—the power of the purse and the power to amend or even repeal the agency's organic statutes—the same cumbersome organization and time-consuming process upon which the Framers relied to constrain the legislative branch in *itself* establishing or amending policy hinders it from using those devices effectively or extensively to direct the policy making of its delegees. * * *

There are, of course, control devices outside the formal legislative process. Oversight hearings by standing or special committees can subject agency personnel to sufficient harassment and embarrassment that the agency comes to heel, at least temporarily. These sorts of exercises are relatively infrequent, although they can be sufficiently spectacular when they do occur that agencies other than the "victim" are sensitized to messages emanating from Capitol Hill. Agency action can be publicly castigated on the House or Senate floor, and members of Congress or their staffs can importune agency decision makers. The principal difficulty with these informal control devices, however, is that whatever policy direction they represent tends to be direction by individual legislators, not by the legislative branch. The control over agency policy wielded by a powerful committee or chairperson may in some cases be substantial, but it is neither the practical nor the constitutional equivalent of policy direction by Congress.

In sum, although Congress theoretically holds ultimate power over the content of regulatory policy, in fact the President has a singular ability to exploit the opportunity for social and economic policy making presented by broadly delegative statutes. Of course, disparities in the personal and political skills of individual Presidents and their key advisors will cause variations in the tenor and level of White House direction. The sheer magnitude of federal regulation will resist comprehensive management by even the most formidable Chief Executive. Whether or not the full potential for presidential control is actually achieved, however, few observers would disagree that the President is likely to come out significantly ahead of any other branch in harnessing and directing the stream of regulatory policy-making power.

For these reasons, whatever supervision "the political branches" will exert over agencies' exercise of the authority to interpret regulatory statutes is most likely to emanate from the Chief Executive, not from the legislature. * * * Thus, *Chevron*'s exaltation of deference as the ordained course of a dutiful judiciary demurring to representative democracy ultimately comes to rest on the proposition that *presidential* control of regulatory policy addresses the constitutional concerns generated by the administrative state.

B. *The Constitutional Implications of Presidential Control*

Those constitutional concerns * * * are twofold. The legislative delegation of regulatory authority implicates separation of powers by threatening to undermine structural protections against the accumulation (and consequent abuse) of power. In addition, delegation implicates what might be called the "legitimacy ideal" by alienating the power to define public policy from the people's elected representatives. *Chevron* offers presidential direction of administrative discretion (including the power to select among the set of rational statutory meanings) as responsive to this latter concern. But presidential control over domestic regulatory policy cannot cure the legitimacy problems posed by delegation *unless* the traditional conception of the legitimacy ideal is fundamentally altered. And any such effort at reconceptualization must confront the severe separation of powers dangers posed by the convergence of regulatory power in the hands of the Chief Executive.

1. *The Legitimacy Ideal and Presidential Control of Regulatory Policy.*—* * * From the premise that the right to legislate resides initially in every member of the community, Locke reasoned that government could legitimately establish binding social policy only because, and to the extent that, the people confer such power in the constitution by which they create the state. The terms of this original grant simultaneously create and constrain government's lawmaking authority:

> The power of the legislative, being derived from the people by a positive voluntary grant and institution, can be no other than what that positive grant conveyed, which being only to make laws, and not to make legislators, the legislative can have no power to transfer their authority of making laws and place it in other hands.

The legitimacy ideal thus forms a second major conceptual root of the nondelegation doctrine, a root independent of (although in sympathy with) the separation of powers root. As the guardian of legitimacy, nondelegation focuses on the type of power at issue and the nature of the entity exercising it; the doctrine, in its pristine form, insists that decisions of public policy be made only by the legislature to whom the people chose to entrust lawmaking power. As nondelegation analysis evolved, however, the perceived needs of the legitimacy ideal, like those of separation of powers, were gradually and subtly redefined.

The approach the Court took in the early, formalistic delegation cases neatly accommodated the legitimacy ideal. So long as the sort of power delegated could be characterized as not "legislative," the lawmaking authority remained safely in its original constitutional repository. With the emergence of "intelligible principle" analysis, however, this easy response was no longer possible, for the analysis conceded that some lawmaking power was indeed being transferred out of the legislature. In this intermediate stage of nondelegation development, legitimacy was secured through the requirement that Congress itself perform the "essential legislative function" of setting the "primary standards." Although the people's designated representatives might no longer make *all* policy choices, they would continue to make the kinds of choices that really matter. When *Yakus* [*v. United States*] finally restated the nondelegation standard in terms of the control, rather than the nature, of power, the Court's conception of the needs of the legitimacy ideal again modulated. A delegation is permissible under *Yakus* so long as it contains standards "sufficiently definite and precise to enable Congress, the courts and the public to ascertain whether the [agency] . . . has conformed to those standards." Thus, from an original emphasis on the *generation* of policy choices, the legitimacy focus shifted to the *oversight* of policy choices.

The maturation of nondelegation analysis strained the legitimacy ideal, but the central thread was not broken. Oversight of agency policy making, *Yakus* asserted, would come from the people and from the legislature, with courts assisting "in a proper proceeding to ascertain whether the will of Congress has been obeyed." * * *

Yakus's assumptions—that Congress possessed the will and the ability to keep pace with the growth of regulatory power; that the process of interpreting regulatory statutes would be a simple matter of finding and enforcing the legislative "will"—may now seem sheer Pollyannaism. Nevertheless, a vision of the administrative state that retained *Congress* as the control center of domestic public policy making was, if ultimately unrealistic, essentially true to the legitimacy ideal. A vision of the administrative state that would place *the President* in this position—*Chevron*'s vision—cannot make the same claim.

* * * [T]he President does not become the interchangeable stand-in for Congress as domestic policy maker simply because he also is elected. On the most pragmatic level, the Chief Executive reflects a very different political base, and speaks with a very different political voice, than does the legislature. More fundamentally, in our constitutional scheme the legitimacy ideal has not reduced—at least until now—to the epithet "popularly elected." Rather, the archetype of legitimate formulation of public policy has been Congress acting through a majority of each House with the President's concurrence or through two-thirds of each House without his concurrence. The proposition that when Congress fails to speak clearly on a regulatory issue the President is constitutionally warranted, in his own right, to take over the task must be recognized for what it is: the advocacy of a profoundly different conception of legitimacy.

Given our seemingly irreversible commitment to the administrative state and Congress's apparent inability to direct it meaningfully, a reconception of legitimacy principles to support an independent presidential domestic policy-making prerogative should perhaps be attempted. However, *Chevron*'s facile pronouncement that deference is necessary because the President's elected status entitles him to direct the course of regulatory policy—to the point of constitutionally disabling the judiciary from exercising even the modest slice of policy-making power represented by statutory interpretation—appears not even to recognize that a major theoretical transformation has occurred. In such obliviousness there is danger. Constructing a new legitimacy ideal would be essential to support this radical reconception of the President's constitutional role, but would not, of itself, be sufficient. Advocates of this revised view of the appropriate allocation of policy-making responsibility must also be prepared to explore what it would mean for the balance of power in government.

2. *Separation of Powers and Presidential Control of Regulatory Policy.*—* * * [W]e might use the phrase "dynamic equilibrium" to describe the constitutional structure which emerged from the uniquely American understanding of separation of powers. Characterizing the equilibrium as "dynamic" implies that shifts in the balance of power among the branches will not necessarily be either constitutionally improper or politically unhealthy. Our history has seen cycles in which first Congress, and then the President, has enjoyed relative ascendancy. Sometimes the will of the people is expressed more clearly through one branch than through another, and then a change in the balance appropriately serves the democratic process. Indeed, the capacity for such adjustments and readjustments is itself an important part of the functioning of separation of powers. However, several factors now operating to affect the balance of power have little to do with differing degrees of political responsiveness. The commitment to pervasive intervention in the economic and social order that has vastly increased the level of extant federal power, the implementation of this commitment through broad delegations of power to entities outside Congress * * *, and the structural and customary factors that favor the President in any struggle for control of the regulatory bureaucracy have coalesced to create a persistent and decided tilt toward presidential dominance of large sections of domestic policy.

This shift in the balance of power might be defended by observing that the Framers were determined to secure a strong Chief Executive vis-à-vis the legislature. Without doubt, this concern is evident in the Convention debates and the Federalist Papers. The conclusion does not follow, however, that the gradual emergence of the President as chief architect of social policy was part of the constitutional plan.

* * *

* * * The delegates who met in Philadelphia to structure the new government began with the assumption that the legislative branch would, by the nature of things, be the most powerful. As Madison argued, the lawmaking power is intrinsically "more extensive and less susceptible of precise limits" than the executive or judicial powers. Determined to provide against the danger that ineluctably follows power, the Framers divided the legislature within itself and set out to create an executive that could serve as a meaningful external counterweight. Their emphasis on shoring up the President's position arose not from the expectation that he would emerge as the dominant domestic policy-making force, but rather from sad experience that no branch could be trusted with too much power. That they aimed to correct a perceived imbalance in favor of the legislature rather than to facilitate a reversion to executive supremacy is underscored by various choices they made during the drafting process. Although they gave the President the appointment power, they required him to find Senate concurrence when filling important vacancies in the executive branch. Although they granted him the authority to veto legislation, they rejected the proposal that this power be absolute. And, ultimately, they subjected him to an impeachment process controlled by Congress.

Thus, history affords no basis for assuming that the constitutional structure was set up to favor a predominant role for the President. Indeed, to divorce the Framers' concern for establishing a strong Chief Executive from its context poses a grave risk of using their words to sanction precisely the sort of harm they had determined to avoid: a dangerous concentration of authority in one power center of government. Those who drafted and defended the Constitution perceived in Congress the threat of overreaching because the legislative power was difficult to delimit and, hence, to control. When large portions of this power move away from Congress through delegation, however, Madisonian fears of encroachment should shift correspondingly from the original repository of the lawmaking power to its new possessor—especially when the delegated power tends to flow towards a recipient that already holds the considerable power to execute the laws and that has been structured to maximize the potential for resolute, consistent exercise of power. As Madison reminded Jefferson in the early days of the new constitutional government, "Wherever the real power in a Government lies, there is the danger of oppression."

One might concede this history yet nonetheless advocate presidential assumption of the role of chief regulatory policy maker by observing, as the Justices are wont to do, that the Framers were "practical statesmen" who intended, above all, to establish an effective system of government. Regulatory programs of ever increasing scope and complexity have grown like Topsy, creating, in the view of many observers, a desperate need for coordination and prioritization. The movements of the 535-member Congress, at best elephantine, are too frequently paralyzed by the competing demands of a plethora of interest groups. By contrast, the President, with his national constituency and outlook and his position as the unitary head of a hierarchy of policy analysts and technical experts, is said to have both the perspective and the structural ability to undertake the difficult task of shaping an integrated regulatory policy.

Looking once again to history, such utilitarian arguments for the allocation of power among the branches are not constitutionally irrelevant. Montesquieu had offered two distinct justifications for organizing government on principles of separation of powers: such a structure prevents the concentration of power, thereby discouraging tyranny; in addition, it makes possible specialization of function, thereby furthering efficient government. The American vision of separation of powers enthusiastically embraced the efficiency as well as the control strand of Montesquieu's theory. The unitary executive was praised as possessing the capacity for resolve, expeditiousness and secrecy needed to maintain domestic order and conduct foreign affairs, while the bicameral legislature was lauded for reflecting the diversity of interests needed to craft sound policy. In spite of these paeans, though, one is left with the sense that the Framers' insistence on the efficiency of the constitutional structure was part of their almost Panglossian captivation with separation of powers. This organizational principle was the best of all possible worlds because it thwarted tyranny and, at the same time, enhanced efficiency by enabling specialization of function. When they actually came down to choosing between control and efficiency, however, the former won out. The best evidence of this is the structure they ultimately created. If they perceived efficiency to flow from the opportunity for specialization and from the molding of each part's organizational structure to suit the demands of a particular governmental task, then their deliberate decision to depart from absolute division of powers—their conscious choice to cause each branch to share its power with an "unsuited" and hence "inefficient" branch—reveals the Framers' priorities.

That the equilibrium of government power was expected by those "practical statesmen" to be dynamic rather than static, to be capable of shifting to provide effective government in the face of the changing demands of a developing society, cannot obscure the fact that the core idea *was* equilibrium: a balance and counterbalance of power centers in government. * * * Efficiency, though a powerful card, was not to be a trump. * * * [I]n a constitutional system built upon separation of powers, "good" government is defined not simply in terms of efficient government, but also in terms of government restrained. That the President may be the branch best suited to pilot the administrative state is not constitutionally irrelevant, but, as a constitutional justification for the allocation of power, it is by no means enough.

In sum, the dominance of the executive that has followed the delegation of regulatory power cannot be squared with the original commitment to separation of powers, any more than the emergence of the President as chief architect of regulatory policy can be justified under the traditional understanding of the legitimacy ideal. We might, then, simply reject the relevance of those original principles to the demands of contemporary government, abandoning separation of powers in favor of some new structural conception at the same time that we fashion a new theory of legitimacy. A decision of this magnitude, however, ought not be made by default, through an incremental acquiescence to presidential control of the regulatory process that is oblivious to the larger structural consequences.

Those original principles were central to a political theory that had been crafted by men who systematically canvassed the forms of government and self-consciously dissected their own experience with both executive and legislative dominance. Surely it is something more than "envelop[ing] ourselves in the mythology of the superhuman wisdom of the Founding Fathers" to suggest that, before we discard their conclusions, we should think very carefully about what we are doing. Have we indeed good reason for believing that the Framers were wrong to assess the danger of concentrated power as greater, in the long run, than the danger of inefficiency? The Confederation period led them to conclude that government which moved too quickly in establishing and altering policy was, over time, less likely to make wise choices and more likely to threaten individual liberty. Therefore, they deliberately created a lawmaking process that was slow, even cumbersome. In pursuing the vision of a forceful Chief Executive who can cut resolutely through regulatory policy dilemmas, minimizing the delay of consensus building and the frustration of political impasse, are we really ready to dismiss their fears as groundless, their precautions as unnecessary?

Moreover, even if we are now prepared to rate efficiency more highly as a structural objective than control, are we so sure that encouraging presidential dominance of the regulatory process will yield better results? We have gradually become disillusioned with the idea that regulatory policy dilemmas have an objectively "correct" answer, discernible through the aggregation of enough information and the application of enough expertise. That disillusionment would seem to leave a democratic society little choice but to define "good" policy as that which represents the consensus of the citizenry. Led by their own experience to conclude that no single part of government could be trusted to speak authoritatively for the people, the Framers split the legislature into two houses and strengthened the executive so that several different expressions of the will of the governed might be heard. This original judgment that no one power center fully embodies the interests of the people seems to be borne out by contemporary observations of the different constituencies of Congress and the President. Can we nevertheless comfortably conclude that the quality of regulatory policy choices will be improved by legal rules that promote the convergence of policy direction in the President's hands?

Unless we are confident that these questions can be answered in the affirmative, and until we are prepared to undertake and justify a redefinition of the constitutional ground rules, invoking a presidential prerogative to direct agency policy making as a principle of decision in cases that concern the allocation of regulatory power is, at a minimum, foolishly premature. If we remain committed to separation of powers as a central structural credo, then choices such as the one made in *Chevron* are steps in the wrong direction. At stake in *Chevron* was the fate of one relatively small but not insignificant slice of the regulatory power pie: the authority to interpret the statutes that define the policy-making universe. The Court's resolution deliberately moves that power squarely into the President's domain. By relinquishing the authority to determine statutory "meaning" to agencies whenever Congress has failed to speak clearly and precisely, *Chevron* enlarges the quantum of administrative discretion potentially amenable to direction from the White House. It then goes even further and exhorts agencies to exercise this discretion, *not* by attempting to intuit and realize the objectives of the statute's enactors, but by pursuing the regulatory agenda of the current Chief Executive.

Had the Court instead chosen the independent judgment model, this slice of power would have been placed beyond the reach of the executive in the hands of another branch. The negative act of withholding authority from a power center that tends to have too much could have yielded positive constitutional benefit. Concededly, independent judgment is not a constitutional panacea. To the extent that giving meaning to regulatory statutes involves law*making* as well as law *finding*, judicial control over the interpretive process does not satisfy the legitimacy ideal any better than does presidential control. However, as the ideal has traditionally been defined, it can be satisfied by little short of some mechanism for remanding important policy questions raised by interpretation to the legislative process for clarification. Several commentators have called for such a remand mechanism, and this would, at least in theory, be the most direct response not only to legitimacy but also to separation of powers concerns. While searching for the optimal solution, though, we ought to be alert to take what we can get. Allocating principal responsibility for interpreting regulatory statutes to the judiciary would significantly further separation of powers by placing power where it will counterbalance, rather than contribute to, the concentration of regulatory authority in the executive. In the interminable struggle to make peace between the Constitution and the administrative state, that would be no small victory.

* * *

Additional Sources

Clark Byse, *Judicial Review of Administrative Interpretation of Statutes: An Analysis of* Chevron's *Step Two*, 2 Admin. L.J. Am. U. 255 (1988)

Stephen G. Breyer, *Judicial Review of Questions of Law and Policy*, 38 Admin. L. Rev. 363 (1986)

Maureen B. Callahan, *Must Federal Courts Defer to Agency Interpretations of Statutes?: A New Doctrinal Basis for* Chevron U.S.A. v. Natural Resources Defense Council, 1991 Wis. L. Rev. 1275

Ronald M. Levin, *Identifying Questions of Law in Administrative Law*, 74 Geo. L.J. 1 (1985)

Abner J. Mikva, *How Should the Courts Treat Administrative Agencies?*, 36 Am. U. L. Rev. 1 (1986)

Richard J. Pierce, Jr., *The Role of the Judiciary in Implementing an Agency Theory of Government*, 64 N.Y.U. L. Rev. 1239 (1989)

Thomas O. Sargentich, *The Scope of Judicial Review of Issues of Law:* Chevron *Revisited*, 6 Admin. L.J. Am. U. 277 (1992)

Peter H. Schuck and E. Donald Elliott, *To the* Chevron *Station: An Empirical Study of Federal Administrative Law*, 1990 Duke L.J. 984

Laurence H. Silberman, Chevron—*The Intersection of Law & Policy*, 58 Geo. Wash. L. Rev. 821 (1990)

Kenneth W. Starr, *Judicial Review in the Post-*Chevron *Era*, 3 Yale J. on Reg. 283 (1986)

Cass R. Sunstein, *Law and Administration After* Chevron, 90 Colum. L. Rev. 2071 (1990)

B. Controversies About Procedural Legal Limits on Agencies

1. Debates About Procedural Due Process

Procedural due process doctrine is among the most fundamental in constitutional and administrative law. In general, the doctrine seeks to prevent arbitrary government, to avoid mistaken deprivations, to allow persons to know about and respond to charges against them, and to promote a sense of the legitimacy of official behavior.

The modern roots of procedural due process trace to the leading decisions of *Londoner v. Denver* (1908) and *Bi-Metallic Investment Co. v. State Board of Equalization* (1915), which distinguish between two types of situations. In the first situation, the government singles out an individual for detrimental treatment based on facts associated with that person; this raises due process hearing issues. In the second case, a broad policy affects large numbers of people; this situation generally does not trigger a due process hearing. In addition, courts ask whether the government has deprived an individual of protected "liberty" or "property." If so, courts will then proceed to determine whether the procedures provided by the agency are constitutionally adequate.

In the first excerpt, Professor Edward Rubin criticizes the concepts of liberty and property as substantive threshold triggers of procedural due process protection. He suggests that the concepts do not in any clear sense define the situations that should prompt constitutional protection. In Professor Rubin's view, due process requirements should apply to all demonstrable and direct governmental deprivations of individuals in adjudicatory contexts. He elaborates the principles of due process in terms of what he calls the norms of rule obedience and fair procedures.

In the second excerpt, Professor Jerry Mashaw criticizes the Supreme Court's discussion in *Mathews v. Eldridge*, a leading case establishing the framework for determining as a constitutional matter how much process is due when the government does deprive an individual of liberty or property. Professor Mashaw analyzes the decision itself, its doctrinal underpinnings, and its theoretical presuppositions.

In the last excerpt, Professor Cynthia Farina generally examines arguments to the effect that due process should apply only in certain circumstances. She suggests that various efforts to find a reasonably unproblematical mechanism for triggering due process fail because of their underlying association with a set of premises fundamental to liberal legal theory. Professor Farina describes these premises and appraises them critically, posing as a possible alternative a feminist vision of the individual and the government, which, she suggests, could be the starting point for a new way in which to conceive of procedural due process.

Edward L. Rubin, *Due Process and the Administrative State*, 72 Cal. L. Rev. 1044, 1044-52, 1060-63, 1065-69, 1072-1110, 1114-19, 1123-28 (1984)*

If ever a constitutional doctrine has fallen from grace, it is the doctrine of procedural due process. By far the oldest of our civil rights, its content seemed so clear to prior generations that they included the term "due process" in the fifth and fourteenth amendments virtually without discussion. Although great controversy arose about the applicability of due process to nonprocedural or substantive matters, procedural due process doctrine evolved quietly and steadily * * *. * * *

* * * The procedural due process doctrine is now the subject of intense debate, with its central meaning regularly questioned by both courts and commentators. This descent into uncertainty is largely the result of the Supreme Court's conscious effort to define the interests to which the due process clause relates. While the answer seems clear enough for criminal and civil trials, it has proved to be a dark conundrum for newer forms of government activity, such as benefits programs, licensing, mass employment, education, and corrections. The Court's answer in these areas has been that procedural protections must be triggered by some underlying "liberty" or "property" right—a right that is generated either by the state's positive law or by constitutional provisions other than the due process clause itself. Dissenters on the Court, and virtually all of the early commentators, objected vigorously, arguing that this underlying rights approach undermines the essential nature of the protection that procedural rights provide.

* * *

* * * The notion that the scope of due process protection can be derived from definitions of the terms "liberty" and "property" is unprecedented. The subsidiary notion, also prominent in current doctrine, that specific due process protections can be determined by balancing a series of policy-related factors is equally unprecedented. Both notions, moreover, indicate a desire to start from first principles and proceed by means of logical argument. Although an admirable effort, such an approach aspires to a level of certainty that is generally denied to legal doctrine and raises risks of unexpected consequences to which legal doctrine is uniquely subject.

Combined with the Court's unconstrained ambition, as so often is the case, is a substantial element of naivete. The Court seems to have assumed that it could reach solid ground by invoking the terms "liberty" and "property." Unfortunately, these terms have had no fixed boundaries since the decline of legal formalism, and they lack even an intuitive core when applied to modern administrative situations. As a result, the effort to determine whether a prisoner can be subjected to solitary confinement by discussing "liberty" or to determine whether a student can be suspended from school by discussing "property" is little more than arid conceptualism. It either conceals the real issues behind a screen of unrelated terms or, worse still, uses the unrelated connotations of those terms to control the real issues. What it clearly fails to do is to provide a coherent, realistic doctrine for applying our notion of procedural due process to the recently developed features of the administrative state.

* * *

I. The Evolution of Current Doctrine

A. *The Rise and Fall of the Right-Privilege Approach*

* * *

1. *The Administrative State and the Problem of Due Process*

The rise of the administrative state in the late nineteenth and early twentieth centuries created major complexities for the procedural due process doctrine. To begin with, some administrative agencies were empowered to make decisions in areas previously governed by the common law. The Supreme Court applied the concept of due process * * *. [T]he Court not only found that due process imposed traditional procedural restrictions upon administrative decisions, but also that it imposed absolute limits on the scope of an agency's power.

During the 1940's, however, the latter part of this doctrine was significantly eroded. Perhaps the New Deal had persuaded the Court, if by no other means than by having populated it, that administrative agencies were essential to the operation of a modern state. To put the matter in more principled terms, the Court had accepted the notion that an administrative agency, when subjected to procedural standards, could function as fairly as a judicial decisionmaker.

Besides traditional adjudicative powers, administrative agencies were granted two other types of

---

* Copyright 1984 by California Law Review Inc. Reprinted with permission of California Law Review Inc. and Edward L. Rubin. All rights reserved.

power that raised procedural due process issues. First, agencies could make rules governing the substance of their adjudicative decisions. Second, agency adjudicative powers included decisionmaking about matters that had never before been adjudicated by courts, but that resembled judicial adjudications in certain ways. This posed the question whether the requirement of due process should extend to either of these powers, as it had to the agency's powers to adjudicate traditional judicial questions. Courts ultimately decided that the due process clause was not applicable in either context. Administrative rulemaking was treated as equivalent to legislation, and was thus exempt from procedural requirements. The problem was to distinguish such rulemaking from the adjudications to which procedural due process applied. Addressing this question in *Londoner v. City of Denver*, the Supreme Court held that the enactment of a streetpaving ordinance was not controlled by due process standards, even though the legislative body had apparently violated legally established rules in passing the ordinance. In contrast, the assessment of the cost to individual property owners was held to violate the clause, because the property owners had not been given notice and a hearing before the assessment became final.

The Court clarified the *Londoner* principle several years later in *Bi-Metallic Investment Co. v. State Board of Equalization*. *Bi-Metallic* involved a due process challenge to an order of the State Board of Equalization that increased the valuation of all taxable property in the City of Denver by forty percent. In rejecting this challenge, Justice Holmes wrote: "Where a rule of conduct applies to more than a few people it is impracticable that every one should have a direct voice in its adoption." *Londoner* was a different case, he continued, because a "relatively small number of persons was concerned, who were exceptionally affected, in each case upon individual grounds." While the precise rule of *Bi-Metallic* is not entirely clear, the idea appears to be that procedural controls do not apply when rules of general applicability are declared, but do apply to binding legal determinations regarding specified individuals. Thus, a generally worded provision that applies to only a few persons need not conform to due process requirements, but governmental action determining the rights or obligations of numerous specified persons is invalid unless the mandates of due process are satisfied.

As for the powers of administrative agencies to adjudicate matters not traditionally dealt with by common law courts, the Court again held that the due process clause did not apply. The rationale for this conclusion was the now notorious right-privilege distinction. * * * [C]ommon law causes of action were regarded as defining the fundamental rights of liberty and property, the natural law entitlements of individuals. These rights received procedural due process protection against government deprivation, just as they received substantive due process protection against regulation. If a matter lay beyond the limits of these rights, however, any interest that the individual could claim was necessarily a government creation that could be abolished by the same power that created it. It seemed chimerical to hold that a person had a right to such contingent, temporal creations. * * *

Although the right-privilege distinction was deeply ingrained in the judicial consciousness, it was not followed with absolute consistency. * * *

* * *

3. Goldberg v. Kelly *and the Welfare Rights Cases*

* * *

In 1970, the Supreme Court finally decided a paradigmatic welfare rights case. *Goldberg v. Kelly* addressed the specific issue whether the due process clause required New York City to give welfare recipients an evidentiary hearing before terminating their benefits. With the creative spirit that comes from ultimate authority, the Court * * * advanced a new rationale to decide the case. The opinion, written by Justice Brennan, began with the familiar declaration that "[t]he constitutional challenge cannot be answered by an argument that public assistance benefits are 'a "privilege" and not a "right."'" The opinion suggested instead that the entire distinction be abandoned, since "[i]t may be realistic today to regard welfare entitlements as more like 'property' than a 'gratuity.'" The proper basis for decision, the opinion continued, should be "whether the recipient's interest in avoiding [the] loss outweighs the governmental interest in summary adjudication." Applying this test, Justice Brennan concluded that even a temporary deprivation of one's welfare benefits is sufficiently serious to require an evidentiary hearing before termination.

* * *

* * * The only issue, as Justice Brennan emphasized, was whether a hearing was required prior to the termination. On the crucial question whether an individual is entitled to any hearing, or to due process rights in general, the opinion is essentially silent. Its direct contribution in this area was only to deal one

more blow—the fatal one, as it turned out—to the already moribund right-privilege distinction. Indirectly, of course, *Goldberg* was profoundly influential. It signaled the Court's willingness to extend due process protections to the daily operations of virtually every state and federal administrative agency, and thus to a vast range of government benefits that had not been explicitly protected by due process prior to that time.

* * *

B. The Rise and Falter of the Liberty-Property Approach

1. Board of Regents v. Roth

The current approach of the Supreme Court, and the current agony of procedural due process, began * * * in *Board of Regents v. Roth*. At issue in *Roth* were the procedures that administrators of a public university had to follow before refusing to renew an untenured faculty member's contract. Justice Stewart's opinion for the Court proceeded in three basic steps. First, he declared that only certain types of interests constituted the sort of "liberty or property" protected by the due process clause. Next, he defined the liberty interest and concluded that Roth's interest in renewal did not qualify. Finally, he defined the property interest and concluded that Roth did not have a property interest either.

In declaring that due process protection applied "only to the deprivation of interests encompassed by the Fourteenth Amendment's protection of liberty and property," Justice Stewart seemed simply to restate the text of the amendment itself. The district court, he wrote, had held due process protection applicable "by assessing and balancing the weights of the particular interest involved." But Justice Stewart found that approach unacceptable: "[T]o determine whether due process requirements apply in the first place, we must look not to the 'weight' but to the *nature* of the interest at stake."

This analysis represented a marked change from *Goldberg*, which had indeed focused on the weight of the individual's interest. Moreover, the interest in *Goldberg* was the hardship of a temporary financial deprivation, which did not fit very well under the rubric of either liberty or property. But *Roth* did much more than repudiate *Goldberg*. *Goldberg* had assessed the individual's interest only to determine the proper timing of due process rights whose basic existence was conceded. In shifting from the weight of the interest to the nature of the interest, *Roth* also shifted from the question of when the hearing was required to the question of whether the hearing was required at all.

* * *

The real explanation for the *Roth* analysis may lie in the extent to which the Burger Court majority, which was just taking shape at this time, was troubled by the expansive nature of the Warren Court doctrines it had inherited. Its response was to limit rather than overturn these doctrines, by establishing well-defined boundaries that restricted the number of cases in which they would operate. The Court's decisions on standing are perhaps the most notable example of this response. * * *

Given this general predilection for restrictive boundaries, the Court's search for a limitation on the categories of interests protected by due process seems natural. Conscious of the power that administrative agencies wield in the modern state, it was not prepared to revive the right-privilege distinction and thereby insulate most administrative actions from due process review. But it was also clearly anxious to limit *Goldberg*, whose vast implications for administrative law were already being felt. * * *

Having established that only certain categories of individual interests merit due process protection, Justice Stewart assumed, without discussion, that those categories are identified by the terms "liberty" and "property" as they appear in the text of the fourteenth amendment. He then proceeded to consider whether *Roth* could assert any such interest. He defined liberty expansively, quoting the resounding language of *Meyer v. Nebraska*, a noneconomic substantive due process case. In assessing the factual situation of *Roth*, however, he identified two more discrete and carefully defined strands of protected liberty: the right to one's good name, and the right to pursue one's chosen occupation.

Turning to the property interest, Justice Stewart adopted a notably different approach. Instead of articulating specific illustrations of interests inherent in the concept, he assessed the nature of the property concept itself: "To have a property interest in a benefit, a person clearly . . . must have more than a unilateral expectation of it. He must, instead, have a legitimate claim of entitlement to it." Justice Stewart was then able to define the sort of entitlements that would constitute property interests with surprising ease: "Property interests, of course, are not created by the Constitution. Rather they are created and their dimensions are defined by existing rules or understandings that stem from an independent source such as state law." For this proposition, he offered no support at all. He could have referred back to the right-privilege cases, since they held that interests beyond the scope of the common law were not protected. Being unwilling to do so, * * * he was compelled to recognize that administrative regulations were as much a source of law as judicial decisions. He then had to create a new, and indeed unprecedented distinction: not between private and public rights, but between rights defined by some positive law and rights, or nonrights, that were not.

2. The "Underlying Rights" Cases of the Mid-1970's

The *Roth* opinion had an immediate impact. It was new, it was written in definitive terms, and it served the Supreme Court's purposes. What was not apparent at the time were its far-reaching implications.

* * *

* * * When Justice Stewart held in *Roth* that the due process clause's property interest was determined by positive law, it apparently did not occur to him that the liberty interest should be similarly determined. Instead, he invoked a substantive due process case to define the fundamental interest in liberty and then articulated two aspects of liberty that were clearly federal in origin. * * *

The case that initiated the movement toward a positive law definition of "liberty" was probably *Wolff v. McDonnell*, though the holding actually extended the scope of due process protection. In *Wolff*, prison officials had denied inmates good-time credits that they would otherwise have been entitled to, on the grounds of misconduct. The Court conceded that there was no constitutional guarantee of good-time credit. But "having created the right to good time and itself recognizing that its deprivation is a sanction authorized for major misconduct," the state acknowledged the liberty interest involved and could not deny the credit without minimum procedures. The Court could have found that the state's failure to employ its own procedures rendered the state's action arbitrary. Instead, the Court reasoned that the existence of rules governing good-time credits had created a liberty interest, and that "[t]his analysis as to liberty parallels the accepted due process analysis as to property."

What Justice White probably meant was that liberty interests over and above those inherent in the due process clause could be created by state law, just as property interests of all kinds were created. But once the parallel between liberty and property interests had been articulated, it was a small step for the Court to find that the liberty interest, like the property interest in *Roth*, could be created only by state law. That step was taken in 1976 in *Paul v. Davis* and *Meachum v. Fano*. These cases modify *Wolff* much the same way *Roth* modified *Goldberg*. In both, the Court began by extending the guarantee of minimum procedures to additional, statutorily created interests, and ended by holding that it applied only to such interests.

Paul v. Davis is one of the most peculiar opinions in due process jurisprudence. A police department had compiled a list of "active shoplifters" largely on the basis of arrest records, and had distributed it to local merchants. It seemed apparent, based on the existing precedents, that such an action would be held unconstitutional as arbitrary "stigmatization" of an individual. But Justice Rehnquist's majority opinion insisted that a positive law liberty interest was required before due process protection applied, and he found no such interest. State law, he wrote, "does not extend to [an individual] any legal guarantee of present enjoyment of reputation which has been altered as a result of [the police department's] actions." Admittedly, the plaintiff might have been able to sue the police department for defamation, a state law cause of action. But to regard this as a due process interest, Justice Rehnquist argued, "would make of the Fourteenth Amendment a font of tort law to be superimposed upon whatever systems may already be administered by the States."

The most obvious difficulty with *Paul* was the unbroken line of cases, extending back to the loyalty-security era, that had imposed due process requirements on government action when that action stigmatized a person. Justice Rehnquist expended substantial energy distinguishing these cases by asserting that they all had involved the loss of something more than reputation. * * * But perhaps the most difficult task, as Justice Rehnquist seemed to recognize, was to distinguish *Roth*, the mother case. *Roth* involved dismissal—admittedly something more than reputation—but it discussed stigmatization as a government action quite distinct from dismissal. Because *Roth* spoke the same language as *Paul*, its delineation of stigma avoidance as a separate interest established by the Constitution was quite clear and quite difficult to explain away. Justice Rehnquist did not succeed in doing so. His opinion, in fact, represents a new departure—the application of *Roth*'s property analysis to what was previously the federal preserve of liberty.

The true peculiarity of the case, even accepting this state law based approach to property interests, is its notion that a tort cause of action does not qualify as a state law interest for due process purposes. After all, the state did grant individuals the right to sue for defamation. But, in Justice Rehnquist's view, such a tort interest is somehow different from a job—

essentially a contract law cause of action—although he did not really explain the distinction. One might well ask whether any common law right would qualify under this approach, since the principal indication of such a right is the existence of a cause of action. *Paul* would thus appear to be much more restrictive than any of the right-privilege cases, all of which granted protection to common law rights. The effect is to eliminate many situations for which minimal procedures are required, and to shrink the scope of due process to the requirement that the government follow applicable rules. * * *

The Court was back on statutory ground in the other liberty interest decision of 1976, *Meachum v. Fano*. Pursuant to statutory authority, correction officials transferred a prisoner from one state facility to another, allegedly for disciplinary reasons, without prior notice or hearing. The Court upheld the transfer, observing that the legislative scheme gave prison officials complete discretion to transfer prisoners without requiring any specific factual determination. Thus, the prisoner had no state law right, no fourteenth amendment liberty interest and, as a result, no due process protection.

Meachum is notable for its clear refusal to give the liberty notion any independent force. The state may eliminate any liberty interest, and thus escape any minimum procedures requirement, by statutory negation or by not specifying positive criteria for decision. To be sure, the result is less controversial in relation to prison inmates * * * but the language of the opinion suggests no such qualification. *Meachum* treated liberty just like property; both interests had to be created by a positive state law or an independent constitutional provision. This submersion of the liberty concept proved to be too much for Justice Stevens, * * * who replied in dissent: "I had thought it self-evident that all men were endowed by their Creator with liberty as one of the cardinal unalienable rights."

3. Partial Retreat from Underlying Rights

* * * *Paul v. Davis* and *Meachum v. Fano* represent the high water mark of the underlying rights approach to the due process clause. * * * [They] were close decisions, drawing spirited dissents, and subsequent fact patterns have made their specific holdings appear untenable. This is not to suggest that the Court has abandoned the liberty-property analysis, for it has not. But it has ceased to maintain that liberty is exclusively the product of state law or independent constitutional provisions, as it did in *Paul* and *Meachum*; * * * and it has certainly abandoned *Paul*'s view that a common law right is not sufficient to constitute a fourteenth amendment interest. Instead, the Court has fashioned criteria that, while maintaining the underlying rights framework, provide a significantly broader scope for due process protection.

The first major departure from *Paul* and *Meachum* came one Term later when the Court acknowledged that the due process clause itself gives rise to certain liberty interests. In *Ingraham v. Wright*, the Court held that the corporal punishment of school children constitutes a deprivation of liberty, and thus requires minimally adequate procedural protection. Justice Powell's opinion cast away the underlying rights requirement with a rousing citation of *Meyer v. Nebraska*, Blackstone, and the Magna Carta—only the Almighty was absent from the list. "It is fundamental," he wrote, "that the state cannot hold and physically punish an individual except in accordance with due process of law." The Court was unanimous on the point. Indeed, it seems inconceivable that the Court would permit a state to establish an administrative scheme where people were restrained and beaten simply because the state legislature declared that there was no positive law right to avoid such treatment.

Subsequent cases have confirmed and extended *Ingraham*'s basic principle. In *Vitek v. Jones*, the Court reiterated that the right to personal security was inherent in the due process clause. Moreover, it found a right to avoid being stigmatized by the government in the clause, and gave *Paul v. Davis* a taste of its own medicine by ignoring it. In *Hewitt v. Helms*, Justice Rehnquist conceded that the due process clause itself creates certain liberty interests, although he declined to find that those interests include a right to parole. * * *

Another major change since the mid-1970's was the Court's more charitable interpretation of administrative statutes in areas where it continued to employ the underlying rights approach. * * *

* * *

Several of these post-1976 cases have granted due process protection on the basis that the relevant statutory criteria for agency decisionmaking created a property interest. In *Memphis Light, Gas & Water Division v. Craft*, for example, the Court found such an interest in the requirement that a public utility not terminate service "'except for good and sufficient cause.'" In *Barry v. Barchi*, the Justices all agreed that a property interest arose from a licensing statute that permitted revocation "only upon proof of certain contingencies." A third property case, *Logan v. Zimmerman Brush Co.*, merits particular attention. Logan had filed a complaint with the Illinois Fair Employment Practices Commission, pursuant to a statute that gave the Commission 120 days after the date of the complaint to convene a factfinding panel. When the Commission failed to meet its deadline, the Illinois Supreme Court held that the statute's mandatory language deprived it of jurisdiction. Thus, Logan had no remedy because the Commission had delayed. This result was obviously untenable, and the Supreme Court reversed it unanimously as a violation of due process. The Court held that Logan was deprived of a property interest because "a cause of action is a species of property protected by the Fourteenth Amendment's Due Process Clause."

Another line of cases, mainly in the prison administration context, found that statutory limitations on administrative discretion created protectable liberty interests. Nebraska's parole statute was held to create a liberty interest in *Greenholtz v. Inmates of the Nebraska Penal and Correctional Complex*, although the Court ultimately found that the statute allowed administrators sufficient discretion so that no procedures beyond those already provided were required. Similarly, in *Vitek v. Jones*, Nebraska's statute for transferring prisoners to a mental hospital was held to require due process protection because the statute grounded transfer on a finding of mental disease or defect. And *Hewitt v. Helms* held that a Pennsylvania statute created a liberty interest for inmates in avoiding administrative segregation. The crucial factor was that certain procedures were made mandatory by the statute, so that inmates were to be segregated only on the occurrence of "specified substantive predicates."

The trend of these cases has been to expand the range of due process protection. Their rationale, however, is * * * unstable * * *. All of them are grounded on the Court's interpretation of state statutes. * * * Consequently, their holdings are vulnerable to more authoritative statutory constructions. If the federal courts do not happen to get the case before a state court has interpreted the relevant statute, federal inquiry into administrative discretion will be precluded.

* * *

Moreover, Court review of agency discretion is also subject to legislative declarations that apparent statutory limits on agency discretion—through, say, specified decisionmaking criteria—are advisory. While the legislature could simply eliminate the criteria, such an approach has its costs, most notably the loss of control over the agency, and a simple declaration may be deemed preferable. The negation of due process implications is disturbing, however, because it again allows a state the power to establish any procedures it wishes, free of constitutional restraint.

Finally, administrative agencies themselves interpret statutes. When an agency fails to provide certain procedural rights, it can argue that it is interpreting the criteria and procedures prescribed in its statute as purely advisory in nature. It is not at all obvious why the Supreme Court should not defer to such agency interpretation of state statutes. If a state court would defer, the federal courts would seem obligated to do so, since they are supposed to interpret state statutes in accordance with state law. Even without a state court interpretation, it would seem that the federal courts should defer to state agency interpretations as a matter of federal law. * * *

II. The Nature and Limits of Procedural Due Process

The procedural due process cases of the post-*Roth* (or perhaps the post-*Goldberg*) era, although not impressive examples of legal reasoning, generally represent serious efforts to deal with a complex legal issue: the relationship between procedural due process and the activities of an administrative state. * * *

* * *

The difficulty with these cases lies in the rationale by which the Court reached its results. They take garden-variety constitutional issues and, in the process of rationalizing fairly unsurprising results, create a jurisprudential Armageddon. Of course, genuine controversy exists over the results in these cases, but that controversy is much more limited in scope. Decisions about whether notice and a hearing are required before a university can refuse to renew a probationary teacher's contract, or before a prison can transfer its inmates to another prison in the state, should produce minor variations in procedural due process doctrine, not shake it to its very foundations.

* * *

A. Beyond the Roth *Analysis*

1. Beyond Liberty and Property

It is perhaps useful to begin this discussion with a definition of procedural due process. The ultimate definition, of course, is what all of the cases and commentaries are striving for; but the concept must have some agreed-upon core, however debatable its boundaries and operation. Presumably, that core is the notion of "procedure," which is generally viewed as referring to governmental methods of adjudication. To say that procedural due process is required, therefore, means that some set of standards must be imposed on those adjudicatory methods.

* * *

The *Roth* opinion's starting point is that "[t]he requirements of procedural due process apply only to the deprivation of interests encompassed by the Fourteenth Amendment's protection of liberty and property." This statement actually contains two distinct premises, each of which was relatively new with *Roth*: first, that some type of individual interest must be present before the due process clause is applicable; and second, that this interest can be described by the terms "liberty" and "property."

The opinion treats both premises as self-evident, but they are in fact problematic. First, there is a basic ambiguity in the way the terms "liberty" and "property" are used in the *Roth* opinion: their generalized invocation, without more, could have at least two entirely different meanings. The terms could refer to a federally defined standard, which would mean that federal courts will apply the clause only to those interests they themselves regard as liberty or property. Alternatively, the terms could refer to a state-defined standard, which would mean that federal courts will apply the clause only to those interests that state courts recognize as within these concepts.

One might expect that this ambiguity would have been resolved when the *Roth* opinion discussed the general meaning of liberty and property, and applied both of these concepts to Roth's claim. With respect to liberty, it was. Justice Stewart unquestionably referred to a federal standard in his discussion of stigma and opportunity. With respect to property, however, the ambiguity was carefully preserved. The crucial sentences read: "Property interests, of course, are not created by the Constitution. Rather, they are created and their dimensions are defined by existing rules or understandings that stem from an independent source such as state law . . . ." Again, this fails to specify whether the term "property" refers to a federal standard that serves to characterize state law, or to a state standard that derives its content from state law. Given the contrasting treatment of liberty, however, it seems likely that a state-law standard was intended.

If the Court was relying on the state-standard approach, it must have concluded that state law contains definitions of liberty and property. The most obvious place to look for such definitions is the common law. But common law does not define liberty and property in any useful way. Instead, the decisions define legal causes of action. Once a cause of action has been established, the liberty or property label attaches automatically, to the extent that such labels are employed at all. Nor can it be asserted that concepts of liberty or property serve as the origin of common law causes of action. The common law is a far more complex system than that, deriving its provisions from social policy, tradition, and elaborated analogies.

Moreover, whatever limited control the terms "liberty" and "property" exerted over legal issues has been largely eliminated by the decline of legal formalism. The legal realist movement rejected such doctrinal formulas in favor of social policy analysis, while those who defend the integrity of the doctrine regard it as composed of principles that go well beyond mere terminology. Thus, it is now commonplace to acknowledge that property is simply a label for whatever "bundle of sticks" the individual has been granted.

As remote as the concepts of liberty and property are from the articulation of common law causes of action or their codified equivalents, they are even more remote from state administrative statutes. Because such statutes create new types of legal relationships, even current common law concepts are often inapplicable, to say nothing of archaic ones. Consequently, the Court's efforts to characterize the rights created by these statutes as liberty or property have been notably strained. For example, in *Vitek v. Jones*, the Court described a prisoner's statutory right to avoid transfer to a mental hospital as a liberty interest. That such a right was granted is perhaps significant, but it is difficult to perceive its connection with the common law concept of liberty.

Similarly, in *Goss v. Lopez*, the Court treated a child's right to a free public education as a property interest. There is something extremely unhelpful about such a description, however, since the right in question has few of the indicia that real or personal property possess at common law. It is not alienable, devisable, or descendible, and cannot be altered by the owner, or saved for later use. Indeed, Justice White, writing for the Court, seemed aware that the property designation was meaningless. The central statement in his property interest analysis was: "Having chosen to extend the right to an education to people of appellees' class generally, Ohio may not withdraw that right on grounds of misconduct, absent fundamentally fair procedures to determine whether the misconduct has occurred." In effect, then, the imposition of due process protection had nothing to do with the characterization of the right to education as property.

Perhaps the most convoluted opinion of all is *Logan v. Zimmerman Brush Co.*, where the plaintiff was deprived of a state-created cause of action by the challenged administrative rules. True to *Roth*, the Court held that a state law cause of action is a property interest, thus rendering due process protection applicable. In reality, all the Court needed to say was that the existence of a state law cause of action satisfied the individual interest requirement it perceived in the due process clause. To hold that the cause of action is a property right and that the property right then triggers the protection adds nothing useful to the analysis, since it is the cause of action that creates the property right in the first place. Even the state-law standard requires nothing more than the assertion that a federal cause of action under the due process clause exists only if there is an underlying state law cause of action. Liberty and property are simply not useful concepts in this context.

It is possible, however, that *Roth* was referring to a federal standard for the underlying interest, and it is clear that a number of more recent procedural due process cases do so. That would seem to restore meaning to the terms liberty and property; even if state law creates only causes of action, federal law might employ the two terms to determine whether such causes of action merit due process protection. The difficulty here is determining the source of the federal definitions of those terms. They cannot really come from an analogy to common law, since common law, as previously indicated, does not provide adequate definitions of the terms. Nor can they be derived from other provisions of the Constitution. Outside of the due process clauses themselves, the terms "liberty" and "property" do not appear anywhere else in the Constitution, except for the reference to liberty in the preamble, to the property of the United States in article IV, and to private property in the closely related and equally mysterious just compensation clause.

There appear to be two remaining sources from which federal standards for liberty and property could be derived. The first is general jurisprudence, a realm in which these terms enjoy a primacy they lack in the workaday world of common law. The second is the due process clause itself. Perhaps Justice Stewart had some jurisprudential notion in mind when he conceded in *Roth* that "'[l]iberty' and 'property' are broad and majestic terms." The difficulty is that their jurisprudential meaning is substantially too broad and majestic. By simply invoking these terms, the Court was plunging itself into a prodigious, age-old debate about the nature of civil government, of man, and possibly the universe-at-large.

From a purely strategic viewpoint, this seems like an unpromising way to determine whether a probationary college teacher is entitled to a nonrenewal hearing.

* * *

With respect to property, the Court has refused to articulate any constitutionally based standards apart from the notion that property is not created by the Constitution. * * * [A]s long as the Court insists that due process protection requires a property interest and that state law is the only standard for property, it is virtually committed to accepting the state's control over the content of due process protection.

With respect to liberty, the Court has articulated an independently derived definition. It has held that state actions—administrative actions in particular—that invade personal security or impose a stigma implicate the liberty interest. This approach, which originated with *Board of Regents v. Roth* and *Morrissey v. Brewer*, avoids the collapse of procedural protection in those circumstances where it is used, but it raises the same question as the Court's circuitous treatment of state law causes of action. If the Court has decided to create a right to avoid certain types of stigma or restraint, what value is served by characterizing these rights as liberty? The term is nothing more than a label for rights that the Court has decided to recognize and protect, useful only if it has some independent force. It is, moreover, a confusing label, for it has been used in due process doctrine to explain a multitude of sins, most notably the doctrine of substantive due process. *Roth*'s identification of specific factors is preferable to reliance on the general term liberty precisely because it excludes some of the "liberties" that have previously been found in the fourteenth amendment.

2. Beyond Textual Literalism

In short, the second premise of the *Roth* decision seems difficult to maintain. The terms "liberty" and "property" simply fail to define the individual interest that triggers due process protection. There is, however, an argument for the use of the terms "liberty" and "property" that is independent of their usefulness: the argument that the text of the due process clause includes them. And as Justice Stewart said in *Roth*, perhaps inadvertently, "the words 'liberty' and 'property' in the Due Process Clause of the Fourteenth Amendment *must* be given some meaning."

One may well concede that every constitutional phrase must be given some meaning, if only in the interest of maintaining the legitimacy of the judicial enterprise. A further argument for treating the Constitution's language as the determinative factor is based on one theory of judicial review, sometimes referred to as interpretivism. Its underlying rationale is that modern courts should implement the intent of the Framers, as revealed in the constitutional text or other sources. Even if one accepts the theory—and it is a source of serious controversy—it hardly compels reliance on the literal words of a provision like the due process clause. The clause was enacted twice, each time with little, if any, discussion or debate. While this does not necessarily suggest that the Framers were unaware of its meaning, it should caution against overinterpretation of the specific language. One might look to the general understanding of the guarantee at the time of its enactment, although even that is a matter of uncertainty. In all likelihood, the major external referent was chapter 39 of the Magna Carta, which would suggest that the emphasis was on the concept of due process, not on liberty or property.

As soon as one moves away from a strict interpretivist approach, a literal reading of the terms liberty and property becomes decidedly untenable. There have been at least two major changes since 1791 or 1868 that preclude any direct translation of prior liberty and property ideas into modern legal doctrine. The first is the jurisprudential change in the concept of rights; the second is the historical change in the nature of government.

When the Framers used the terms "liberty" or "property," they probably had in mind some definitive set of interests fixed by natural law. But modern courts and modern jurisprudence * * * tend to treat these terms as legal conclusions, rather than as independent arguments. As a result, their literal use now results in the abolition of fixed restraints, and gives the states extensive power to control the scope of due process protection. A natural rights approach would do exactly the reverse; it would suggest a rather vigorous federal standard that places absolute limits on state power. Of course, we have lost faith in the existence of such natural-law rights, probably as a result of the substantive due process doctrine, but we cannot conclude that this change in attitude about liberty and property requires an equivalent change in attitude about due process. That syllogism would hold only if the primary concern of the clause were liberty and property, rather than fair procedures.

Beginning from the notion that the clause guarantees fair procedures, the logical approach would be to interpret the terms liberty and property by seeking some concept that fulfills the same function now as liberty and property did previously. Presumably, that concept would be the dominant view about the proper type of interaction between government and individuals. Those views, which are in some sense "natural" to this society, represent society's general sense of the fixed limits on state power.

Second, adoption of the fifth and fourteenth amendments preceded the development of the administrative state. When these amendments were drafted, adjudications by states—to which due process clearly applied—were carried out almost exclusively by courts. The words "life, liberty, or property" were sufficient to include the entire range of issues that courts adjudicated; their effect, therefore, was to describe, not to exclude.

Today, most adjudications are carried out by administrative agencies rather than courts. And these agencies perform many functions that courts did not and probably could not fulfill, most notably the distribution of benefits. A literal reading of the terms "liberty" and "property" in this modern context excludes many administrative adjudications from the scope of due process protection. Again, this makes sense only if some independent significance attaches to the fact that these adjudications involve issues that are not readily described in terms of traditional common law interests. If one focuses instead on the concept of procedural fairness, the fact is that due process originally applied to all government adjudications; the only adjudications were court decisions about "life, liberty, or property," as those terms were understood at the time. Consequently, a strong argument can be made to preserve that inclusive effect. Instead of reading "life, liberty, or property" as referring to a particular group of interests, it could be read as referring to the entire, now-expanded range of government adjudications.

* * *

* * * [T]he real issue is one of values. Should the inevitably ambiguous language of the constitutional text be read to represent a fixed set of protections, whose content remains constant even when the surrounding society changes? Or should it be read to create an open-ended principle, capable of expanding so that its relative scope remains constant as those changes occur? If one adopts the former view, one will read "life, liberty, or property" as words of limitation: that no interest should be granted constitutional protection unless the Framers would have regarded it as falling within those terms. If one adopts the latter view, however, the same phrase becomes one of inclusion: that as large a proportion of government actions should be granted protection

as was granted protection at the time the due process clause was enacted.

The text of the due process clause itself does not inform us which interpretation is correct. It does not compel a particular definition of "liberty" or "property." Rather, it simply poses the issue for us, leaving us free to make the type of choices that all moral action requires.

3. Beyond the Underlying Rights Standard

The unpersuasive nature of Roth's second premise—that "liberty" and "property" define a meaningful set of individual interests—naturally casts some doubt on its first premise—that the notion of an individual interest limits the applicability of the due process clause. Some minimal level of individual interest is required to confer standing on the plaintiff, of course, at least in a federal action. Article III as presently interpreted prohibits federal courts from deciding a case unless a definable interest of the moving party is at stake. But in declaring that an individual interest is necessary for due process purposes, Roth could hardly have been restating the standing requirement. Instead, the Court must have been saying that once a plaintiff has standing, some additional interest must be identified, some underlying right that will support the imposition of due process requirements.

But why is this so? If one cannot rely on liberty and property to give content to the underlying rights concept, its link to the constitutional text disappears. So does its potential for restricting the open-ended character of due process decisions by means of the certainty of its limiting effect. Of course, it might be possible to identify some other underlying rights, and thus reinfuse this notion with preclusive force. But it seems like a large expenditure of effort to reconstruct an abstract principle without its main support.

Nonetheless, the effort has been made. Dean Ely suggests that the individual interest or underlying rights notion should be reinterpreted to include any significant injury suffered by the individual.[267] However, since that virtually restates the standing requirement, its real effect is to drain "underlying rights" of any content or significance. Ely virtually concedes this; the major question is why he felt the need to cast the argument in terms of underlying rights in the first place. * * *

Another effort to locate underlying rights apart from liberty and property is derived from the dignitary theory of due process. This theory holds that procedures are valuable in their own right, apart from the interests they protect, because they indicate a basic governmental respect for individuals. When Professor Kadish articulated this idea in the 1950's, he saw it as a basis for determining the content of due process itself.[270] While various scholars have continued to advance this approach, the theory has also been enlisted as another interest of the individual that can be used to expand the scope of procedural protection beyond the Court's liberty and property analysis.[272]

In reality, this latter notion is simply another product of the general obsession with underlying rights. In its pure form, the dignitary theory deals with the purpose and significance of procedural protection itself. To translate it into the idea that there exists an individual interest in "dignity" is to separate it from its due process moorings and reduce it to a psychological observation of questionable validity. Some of our society's most "dignified" members, such as corporate presidents or cabinet secretaries, are entitled to no procedural protection; conversely, the dreary realities of local court procedures are often a continuing affront to the dignity of those involved in them. In fact, the dignitary theory has very little to do with the notion of the individual's interest in "dignity." Properly conceived, it is a theory about the stance that government should take toward the people it rules.

The problem with the underlying rights standard, however, goes beyond the difficulty of defining it. There is an archaic quality about the whole idea; its implicit assumptions belong, at the most basic level, to a style of legal thinking that has been largely abandoned. The essence of the procedural due process enterprise, after all, is to identify those procedural protections to which individuals have a constitutional right. The insistence on finding an underlying right springs from the idea that such protections must be attached to some substantive interest. But this seems compelling only if one starts from the assumption

---

[267] See J. Ely, [DEMOCRACY AND DISTRUST 18-19 (1980).]

[270] See Kadish, Methodology and Criteria in Due Process Adjudication—A Survey and Criticism, 66 YALE L.J. 319, 347-48 (1957).

[272] See, e.g., L. Tribe, [American Constitutional Law 502-03 (1978)]; Saphire, Specifying Due Process Values: Toward a More Responsive Approach to Procedural Protection, 127 U. PA. L. REV. 111, 144-48 (1978); cf. Monaghan, [Of "Liberty" and "Property," 62 CORNELL L. REV. 405, 433 (1977)] (liberty "should be read to embrace . . . any governmental conduct which so invades a decent respect for a person's personal integrity that, if not fairly justified, the result would outrage public sensibility") (footnote omitted) (emphasis in original).

that all rights are contained within the individual. That assumption excludes purely procedural protections that unlike the ownership of objects or the freedom to move about at will, do not seem so contained.

If one starts instead from the assumption that rights usually represent relationships between human beings, or between human beings and government, the need to find underlying rights within individuals simply dissolves. It is perfectly sensible to place limits on the government's behavior toward individuals, quite apart from any independent rights those individuals may possess. We may want to say, for example, that the government may not operate segregated golf courses or coffee shops, even though we recognize no independent right to public facilities of this nature. Similarly, we may want to say that the government must provide notice and a hearing before it takes certain types of actions, regardless of the existence or nonexistence of an independent right. We might even want the government to provide notice and a hearing before it takes any action at all. That may not be required by our common understanding of due process and it may not be advisable, but there is nothing illogical or incomprehensible about it.

The notion that rights must be contained within the individual has no modern jurisprudential basis. At best, it is a restatement of the formalist view that people have certain natural-law rights independent of the social order. It may be related to the view that Professor Macpherson has labeled "possessive individualism"—the seventeenth-century notion that the individual should be regarded "neither as moral whole, nor as part of a larger social whole, but as an owner of himself."[275] But the realist tradition, the methodology of which has been described by Professor Summers as our "dominant general theory about law," definitively rejects any notion of inherent rights.[276] Like positivism generally it treats rights as products of the social order, that is, of relationships between the government and its citizens.

* * *

---

[275] C. MACPHERSON, [THE POLITICAL THEORY OF POSSESSIVE INDIVIDUALISM: HOBBES TO LOCKE 3 (1962).]

[276] Summers, *Pragmatic Instrumentalism in Twentieth Century American Legal Thought—A Synthesis and Critique of Our Dominant General Theory About Law and Its Use*, 66 CORNELL L. REV. 861 (1981). Professor Summers' characterization applies to realist methodology, rather than the realist program in its entirety. For the realist's rejection of inherent rights, see, e.g., J. FRANK, COURTS ON TRIAL 9-13 (1949); Holmes, *The Path of the Law*, 10 HARV. L. REV. 457 (1897); Llewellyn, *Some Realism About Realism—Responding to Dean Pound*, 44 HARV. L. REV. 1222 (1931).

The Court's view that procedural protection must be attached to some underlying right is thus based on a conception of rights that is at odds with modern legal and philosophic thought. Nothing supports the Court's position other than the natural rights philosophy of the *Lochner v. New York* era that modern doctrine has so definitively rejected. The Court realizes this difficulty, which is why it has been so hesitant to establish independent federal definitions of "liberty" and "property." But because it insists on the form, if not the content, of the underlying rights concept, it has continued to search for some method of defining those mythological entities. The only obvious place to find them, once the search begins, is positive state law, which has the previously noted effect of undermining the federal nature of the due process guarantee.

Abandoning the notion of inherent rights, however, resolves this particular problem. Rights can be defined in terms of interpersonal relationships without being separately contained in, or owned by, any of the participants in those relationships. Such rights, including the right to procedural protection, can be found either in positive law or in social principles, depending on one's view. Fortunately, there is no need to choose a view at this stage of the analysis, because the right to procedural protection is grounded in the concept of due process, which is incontrovertibly both a positive enactment and a generally accepted social principle.

The individual interest or underlying rights idea, therefore, can simply be abandoned. This is hardly an extreme position, since it constitutes the general state of procedural due process doctrine between the time the right-privilege distinction fell into desuetude and the articulation of the liberty-property approach in *Roth*. Nor does it mean that the importance of the individual's interest need be entirely ignored. Courts might continue to treat that interest, in appropriate circumstances, as one element in determining the extent of procedural protection that would be imposed. What courts would not do, however, is give the individual's interest a preliminary and preclusive role in determining the applicability of the due process clause. Finally, eliminating the underlying rights notion does not mean that the phrase "life, liberty, or property" must be read out of the constitutional text. It may simply mean that the phrase should be read as characterizing the nature of the government's interaction with the individual, rather than the nature of the nonprocedural right that triggers procedural protection.

B. The Standard of Procedural Fairness
1. The Basis of the Standard

The *Roth* liberty-property approach, though heavily criticized, is so familiar as the foundation of due process doctrine that the possibility of its elimination may produce a sense of vertigo. It is not difficult, however, to articulate the requirements for an alternative theory. The starting point should be the prevailing modern view that rights are derived from relationships between people, or between people and government, rather than from inquiries into the inherent qualities of either. The fourteenth amendment, at least if one accepts the state action concept in its present form, is exclusively directed toward relations between people and the government. Thus, the basic enterprise of interpreting "procedural due process" is to determine the procedures that the government must employ in dealing with individuals.

Despite the agonies of * * * [recent due process jurisprudence], a consensus exists about the purpose of these procedures: to ensure accurate decisionmaking in government adjudications. An accurate decision is defined as one that finds the facts as they actually are and applies the law to those facts in accordance with prevailing doctrine. Underlying this concern for accuracy is a notion that inaccurate determinations are unfair to individuals. * * * The concern, therefore, must be that an inaccurate decision impinges on some basic value, the constitutional significance of which is defined either independently, or in terms of other values, or in terms of a democracy's inability to protect it.

This basic value is essentially the rule of law—that is, the treatment of individuals in accordance with legal standards. An accuracy requirement imposes standards on the decisionmaker, both as a finder of fact and as an interpreter of law. It thus limits the individual discretion of state agents. The danger of unfettered discretion is that individuals can be subjected to personalized tyranny, no matter how democratic the system as a whole may be. State agents may demand bribes, seek unreasonable obeisance, take revenge, or act on the basis of caprice or inadvertence. It is the one-to-one interaction between the state agent and the individual that generates the danger. Such interactions call forth emotions that would otherwise be absent: antipathy based on the individual's appearance or personality traits, antagonism based on the individual's general attitude or particular interaction with the agent, and—perhaps the greatest danger in a mass bureaucracy—annoyance based upon the mere necessity of having to deal with yet another individual. These one-to-one interactions, moreover, create the opportunity for the state agent to act upon whatever emotions are called forth. They generally occur in the obscure and dusty corners of the bureaucratic state, far away from public scrutiny, and often insulated from internal review by their perceived insignificance.

Procedure is our traditional method for ensuring that the decision in question is accurate, thus protecting individuals from the potential oppressions of direct interaction with state agents. The explanation for the special status that the Constitution confers on this protection, therefore, is simply that the danger of such oppression is too great and its consequences too severe to leave the matter to the political process.

* * *

Having identified the generally accepted purpose of due process protection, the next question is whether identifiable limits on due process protection exist, particularly in relation to administrative decisionmaking. The Court's adoption of the liberty-property approach was almost certainly motivated by a desire to contain the genie *Goldberg* had released. Eliminating the underlying rights test as a trigger for due process protection necessarily raises that concern again. The problem is to describe a boundary that is both workable and close to society's intuitive consensus about the appropriate level of due process protection. There is, of course, no need for the boundary to follow the precise contour of existing decisions; indeed, no consistent rationale could do so.

2. The Content of the Standard

With these considerations in mind, it is now possible to explore what we mean by due process or fair procedure. * * *

a. *The Rule-Obedience Principle*

The rule-obedience principle simply establishes our basic concept of legality. Suppose a decisionmaker announces: "I recognize that the rules, that is, the law, grant you a particular benefit, but I decline to apply those rules in deciding your particular case." * * * [S]uch a decision is obviously improper—lawless one might say. By definition it violates the substantive rule that has been ignored. It also violates the principle of procedural due process; it is the very antithesis of accurate decisionmaking, since accuracy is the proper application of the law to the case at hand. Nothing leaves a state agent as much room for venality, hatred, caprice, or carelessness as the power to ignore the applicable rules. And from a dignitary perspective, the failure to follow applicable rules subjects individuals to a totally arbitrary regime, thereby denying them any possible control over their fate. Therefore, even if the state provides no cause of action for the decisionmaker's violation of a substantive law, the federal Constitution does.

Despite its intuitive appearance, the rule-obedience principle has a counterintuitive element. If government is not obligated to enact rules, as it obviously is not, why should it be obligated to obey those rules it chose to enact? One answer * * * is simply the common understanding of the word "rules": it would mislead people to declare rules if they did not carry with them the obligation of obedience. More important, since people might learn to be wary, such rules would also confer on the government's actions a legitimacy to which they were not entitled.

A second answer is that the counterintuitive element results from a perception that rules generally contract the power of state officials by placing limits on their actions. In the modern state, however, this notion is often incorrect. Rules frequently expand official power, creating governmental functions that did not previously exist. It seems appropriate, therefore, to require obedience to the limiting principles that accompany these general grants of power.

Still another answer is that "the government" is a combination of different functional units, not a monolithic entity. In the traditional model of government, one unit—the legislature—makes the rules while another unit—the judiciary—adjudicates. Under this model, there is nothing problematic about permitting the legislature to alter preexisting rules while requiring the judiciary to obey them. While the structural difference between rulemaking and adjudicatory units has disappeared in the modern administrative agency, the functional distinction between the two activities remains. Requiring administrative agencies to abide by their own rules, therefore, preserves the appropriate separation of functions.

The most basic answer, however, is the identified purpose of procedural due process: to provide people with protection when state officials act directly upon them as individuals. Due process applies, therefore, only when the state acts in this way—not when the state chooses not to act. And when it applies, it governs only the manner by which the state brings its force to bear. The failure to follow preexisting rules is an arbitrary use of that force, one that allows precisely the oppressive action that the clause is designed to prevent. Therefore, because the legitimacy of state power is conditioned upon a norm that governs the legitimate exercise of power, it is hardly surprising that the rule-obedience principle takes effect only when that power is exercised.

The rule-obedience principle tends to be overlooked because it is not typically a demanding requirement. Since it governs the way in which a state applies its own laws, primarily a question for the state to resolve, federal review is necessarily based upon a standard of minimum rationality. Either the state must concede that it is not following its own rules, or the interpretation of the rule the state claims to be following must be patently irrational. The rule-obedience principle is, therefore, essentially equivalent to the minimum rationality requirement of equal protection.

* * *

b. The Minimum-Procedures Principle

The second principle * * * is that a state must provide certain minimum procedures in various adjudicatory contexts. These procedures are generally identified as notice, a hearing, and an impartial decisionmaker. The connection between them and the due process goal of accurate decisionmaking is virtually self-evident, since the trial-type interaction that these procedures establish reflects our basic model of decisional accuracy.

Any substantive requirement for accurate decisionmaking would require us to decide how much accuracy we want, but setting acceptable accuracy levels is a daunting task—one for which courts are notably ill suited. Procedure eliminates this problem, at least in the nonadministrative realm, because we have a general consensus about the proper amount of procedure—specifically those procedures associated with civil and criminal trials—that substitutes for the absence of consensus about accuracy levels.

There are, of course, numerous other grounds on which the imposition of minimum procedures can be justified. While accurate decisionmaking has been characterized, quite properly, as "instrumental," it is not the only instrumental justification. Procedures might be imposed for heuristic purposes, either because they are themselves instructive or because they provide the individual with sufficient information to alter future behavior. This might be particularly useful in certain contexts such as school suspensions. Procedures might also be employed to reconcile people to unfavorable decisions, thus serving the very instrumental purpose of keeping the decisionmaker alive. In this context, they might be viewed as an alternative to compromise, thus freeing decisionmakers to act more definitively and speak more resoundingly in certain situations.

Minimum procedures might also have noninstrumental or inherent justifications. The most common is the dignitary theory that these procedures indicate respect for human beings, and a commitment to treat people as ends rather than means. There is also the notion that Professor Rawls refers to as pure procedural justice: the use of procedures to reach a decision may be the most reliable way to define fairness in that situation, particularly if we have no external standard for the fairness of the result.[315]

c. The Due Process Cause of Action

The two principles of rule obedience and minimum procedures establish the basic content of "procedural due process" or, more precisely, the elements of a due process cause of action. Since both are necessary, denial of either will constitute a constitutional violation. To state the cause of action, the plaintiff must allege that he or she was denied the protection that these principles afford: that the government failed to follow applicable rules, or to provide minimum procedures in a situation where such procedures are required. According to our general consensus, that is what we mean when we say that the person was denied due process of law.

* * *

3. Specificity as a Limit on the Standard

Even if the standard of procedural fairness, as embodied in the principles of rule obedience and minimum procedures, is a necessary component of a due process cause of action, it may not be a sufficient component. In addition, a due process theory must possess identifiable limits. * * *

By focusing on the content of procedural due process, it is possible to generate a workable limiting principle. What makes a particular use of the due process clause "procedural," after all, is that it imposes standards on the means of government adjudication. Procedural due process, then, is necessarily limited to adjudicatory contexts. Instead of determining whether the individual can assert a liberty or property interest, it is only necessary to determine the nature of the government's action about which the individual is complaining. If the action is adjudicatory, the due process clause applies. That does not mean that governmental rules that must be obeyed necessarily exist, or that minimum procedures must be required; rather, it means that due process doctrine is the proper mode of analysis and that any decision to impose, or not impose, due process standards must be made by assessing the proper scope of those two basic principles.

a. Adjudication as a Limit

* * *

Limiting procedural due process protection to adjudicatory action is certainly consistent with the modern concept of rights. This is reflected in the current law regarding rule obedience and minimum procedures. There is no due process requirement that the government follow its own rules, unless it is performing an adjudicative function. Obviously a legislature's or an agency's rulemaking activities are not bound by the rules that it has previously promulgated. It can always change its own rules, subject to the restrictions on ex post facto actions.

* * *

b. The Definition of Adjudication

Procedural due process, then, is limited by its nature to adjudicatory contexts. In order for the limitation to be precise, however, "adjudication" must be defined with greater specificity. A century ago the definition would have been an intuitive and unchallenged one. Adjudication was what courts did, as compared with rulemaking, which was what legislatures did. Legal doctrine both reflected and maintained this definition. * * *

The growth of the administrative state complicated this situation, for it produced governmental agencies that both made rules and conducted adjudications. As a result, the distinction between these two basic modes of governmental action could no longer be based on the nature of the actor, and a more theoretical solution became necessary. *Londoner v. City of Denver* and *Bi-Metallic Investment Co. v. State Board of Equalization* provided the solution: rules are governmental actions affecting relatively large groups of people, whereas adjudications are applications of the law or determinations of fact concerning specific individuals. Moreover, the cases explicitly linked this distinction to the imposition of due process requirements. *Londoner* found that the absence of minimum procedures in assessing taxes against specified individuals violated due process, while the failure of the government to follow its own rules in deciding to build a road did not. *Bi-Metallic* clarified this distinction, holding that an across-the-board tax increase, even if based on what purported to be a factual determination, was not subject to the notice and hearing requirements of the due process clause.

While *Londoner* and *Bi-Metallic* are not necessarily binding precedent today, the distinction they articulate between rulemaking and adjudication has been carried forward into modern administrative law. In *United States v. Florida East Coast Railway*, the Court emphasized the general applicability of an Interstate Commerce Commission ratesetting regulation in holding that the Administrative Procedure Act

---

[315] J. Rawls, [A Theory of Justice § 14 (1971).]

(APA) and the Interstate Commerce Act required only the quasi-legislative procedures of informal rulemaking, rather than the quasi-judicial procedures of rulemaking on the record. Justice Rehnquist's opinion for the Court explicitly analogized this quasi-legislative/quasi-judicial distinction to the rulemaking/adjudication distinction *Londoner* and *Bi-Metallic* made in interpreting the due process clause.
* * *

The force of the general-specific distinction is that it reflects the values that underlie procedural due process: action against specified individuals carries with it the potential for particularized abuse. This potential is due to both the nature of the interaction, which permits illegitimate motives to arise, and the lack of other protections for the individual. In other words, the theoretical definition of adjudication that is needed in the modern administrative state is fully congruent with due process concepts. The central purpose of procedural due process—to provide protection against individualized oppression by the government—thus constitutes the limiting principle for the clause's operation by informing the definition of adjudication.

* * *

4. The Definitional Difficulties of the Specificity Concept

Like every legal dichotomy, the general-specific distinction is not without its difficulties. First, there is the universal difficulty of fixing the boundary between the two parts of the dichotomy. Once that is achieved, there remains the possibility that general rulemaking can be equivalent to particularized adjudication in certain circumstances, most notably when a purportedly general rule applies to a very small number of individuals. There is also the possibility that certain types of general rules, although not equivalent to adjudication, can affect due process rights by altering the nature of all adjudications in a given area. In essence, the task is to establish a boundary between general and specific action that is both sufficiently clear to be usable, and sufficiently fixed to withstand attempts at circumvention.

a. Defining the Boundary

The notion of general and specific action is fairly abstract. One way to fix the boundary between the two is to translate the distinction into operational terms. Professor Davis' dichotomy between legislative and adjudicative facts, now a fixture in administrative law, represents perhaps the leading effort to do so. Davis defines adjudicative facts as those that "answer the questions of who did what, where, when, how, why, with what motive or intent," and legislative facts as those that "do not usually concern the immediate parties but are the general facts which help the tribunal decide questions of law and policy and discretion."[369] While these definitions work well in certain circumstances, the dichotomy has been criticized because it does not really yield a workable distinction.

In any event, this dichotomy presents several problems in the present context. First, it focuses on the nature of the facts, rather than the nature of the government action. While this does not create the same conceptual problems presented by focusing on individual interest, it does shift attention away from the modern view of rights as relationships, and toward the assessment of inherent characteristics. Second, this dichotomy has no real connection with the policy arguments for distinguishing general and specific action. Actions that affect a large group, which has full access to the political process, can be based on adjudicative facts, for example. Finally, Professor Davis' distinction provides little guidance in cases where the state claims the power to act in a purely discretionary manner, without reference to facts.

A different operational principle can be generated by considering the nature of the government's action in reaching adjudicatory decisions. Such decisions generally involve two components: finding facts about an individual, and applying the law on the basis of those facts. In a true adjudication of the sort that we would generally want to subject to due process requirements, the facts found must have direct and demonstrable consequences for the individual. Absent such consequences, the purpose underlying accurate decisionmaking disappears, since there can be no oppressiveness toward individuals when there are no particular consequences for them. Thus, no procedural protection is generally required when a person appears in a legislative hearing, even if a general statute is passed based on facts derived from that person's direct experience. The issue would arise only if the testimony had some adverse consequences for that person * * *. * * * [For] example, the most extensive factfinding activity of the federal government is the census, but since it has no direct effect on individuals, there is no due process right to insist on an accurate assessment of oneself. On the other hand, a right to accuracy exists if the government is making factual assessments about an individual in order to grant benefits or impose burdens,

---

[369] 2 K. DAVIS, [ADMINISTRATIVE LAW TREATISE 413 (2d ed. 1978).]

or if the government action will have significant collateral consequences.

The second aspect of adjudication is the application of the law to a specified individual on the basis of the facts that have been found. According to the rule-obedience principle, the law to be applied must be valid, and it must cover the case under consideration. Thus, due process requires that the individual have the opportunity to challenge the law on substantive grounds, although it does not provide any substantive grounds of its own force. In addition, it requires the opportunity to argue that the established facts do not justify the application of the legal consequences in question.

General action, to which due process protection is not applicable, can now be operationally defined as action that neither makes factual determinations about a particular individual that have direct consequences for that individual, nor determines how the law is to be applied to a particular individual. If these elements are present, however, the action is an adjudication and must be analyzed in due process terms. Many adjudications involve both these elements; in others, however, the facts will be stipulated or the validity and applicability of the law conceded, so that one element of adjudication will operate separately.

b. Avoiding Particularized Rulemaking

This operational distinction between general and specific action may begin to break down as the group to which a general rule relates becomes increasingly small. At some point, such a rule effectively applies the law to an individual, even if it purports to be achieving a more generalized effect. Once that point is reached, there is a danger that the action was motivated by a desire to punish that one individual. This possibility is unquestionably a real problem for procedural due process analysis. But the Court's underlying rights approach provides no solution at all; it simply abandons the individual to the legislative will.

Restating the scope of procedural due process in terms of the general-specific distinction suggests a possible solution to the problem. When the affected group is sufficiently small and the danger of improper governmental action sufficiently great, the due process clause may be read to impose certain limits on general action.

* * *

c. Presumptions and Procedural Fairness

The general-specific distinction also breaks down when rulemaking alters the nature of adjudications subject to the rulemaking authority. This alteration can occur directly. In *Goldberg v. Kelly*, for example, the government had adopted general rules that granted a subsequent hearing but denied a prior one. A more subtle approach is to establish a factual presumption, as a matter of general law, essentially short-circuiting the factfinding stage of the adjudication process. Both types of actions take advantage of the government's control of the substantive law to achieve procedural effects. The first operates against the form of the adjudication, while the second operates against its underlying content.

These cases cannot be resolved by refining the general-specific distinction, or on any other definitional basis. The answer necessarily rests on the independent determination of what procedural fairness means: the content of the principle of rule obedience and, more significantly, the extent of minimum procedures. Once this determination is made, due process can be treated like any other constitutional right. A general rule that reduces procedural protection below the established minimum is invalid, just as a general rule that prohibits protected speech would be. Both answers are totally unsatisfying because they leave open the only important question: what is the required minimum of procedural protection, or what is protected speech? But that is precisely the point: the problem posed by general rules governing adjudication is to give content to our notion of procedural fairness. No particular difficulty is created because the primary focus of the guarantee involved is specific governmental action as opposed to some other area of law. Whatever due process governs, it shares with all other constitutional rights the power to invalidate governmental acts of any kind that conflict with the protections it provides.

* * *

Jerry L. Mashaw, *The Supreme Court's Due Process Calculus for Administrative Adjudication in* Mathews v. Eldridge: *Three Factors in Search of a Theory of Value*, 44 U. CHI. L. REV. 28, 30–59 (1976)*

* * *

The thesis of this article is that the *Eldridge* approach is unsatisfactory both as employed in that

---

* Reprinted with permission of the University of Chicago Law Review and Jerry L. Mashaw. All rights reserved.

case and as a general formulation of due process review of administrative procedures. The failing of *Eldridge* is its focus on questions of technique rather than on questions of value. That focus, it is argued, generates an inquiry that is incomplete because unresponsive to the full range of concerns embodied in the due process clause.

* * *

I. *Mathews v. Eldridge*
A. The Disability Determination Process

The plaintiff George Eldridge first filed an application for disability benefits with the defendant Social Security Administration (SSA) on March 10, 1967. His claim was processed through an adjudicatory system which is massive and complex—and increasingly unmanageable. The complexity of the system can be attributed to two factors: first, the problematic statutory definition of "disability" and, second, the division of labor among a variety of administrative bodies—(1) the Bureau of Disability Insurance of the SSA, (2) state vocational and rehabilitation agencies, (3) administrative law judges, and (4) the Appeals Council of the SSA.

The statutory definition of disability requires that a worker demonstrate his "inability to engage in any substantial gainful activity by reason of any medically determinable physical or mental impairment which can be expected to result in death or which has lasted or can be expected to last for a continuous period of not less than 12 months . . . ." To satisfy that test the worker bears a continuing burden of showing by means of "medically acceptable clinical and laboratory diagnostic techniques" that his impairment is of such severity that he is unable not only to do his previous work but,

> considering his age, education, and work experience, [to] engage in any other kind of substantial gainful work which exists in the national economy, regardless of whether such work exists in the immediate area in which he lives, or whether a specific job vacancy exists for him, or whether he would be hired if he applied for work.

Except to the extent that the Social Security Administration has by regulation designated certain impairments as per se disabilities, the effect of a medical impairment on functional capacity for employment must be evaluated in light of various nonmedical factors.

This elaborate determination is made through the following sequence of procedures. First an applicant applies at a district office of the SSA. There a claims official determines, on the basis of the claimant's prior earnings and contributions to the Social Security system, whether he is eligible for Social Security benefits. The case is then referred to a state agency, usually the state vocational and rehabilitation service, where an adjudication unit composed of a doctor and a lay "vocational specialist" develops medical and vocational evidence and makes an initial decision on the claim. If the state agency denies the claim and the SSA affirms that denial, the claimant is notified that he is entitled to a de novo reconsideration of his claim by the state agency. If a reconsideration is requested, the claim is reviewed by a different state agency unit.

Should the claim again be denied, the claimant is informed that he is entitled to a de novo hearing before an administrative law judge appointed pursuant to the federal Administrative Procedure Act. The administrative law judge is usually the first person to decide the case who has seen the claimant or heard any oral testimony or argument. If the claimant loses before the administrative law judge, he is entitled to request discretionary review by the Appeals Council of the Social Security Administration. If the Appeals Council dismisses the request or denies the claim on the merits, the claimant may then seek judicial review in a federal district court. At every stage prior to judicial review the record remains open and the claimant may adduce new evidence.

In order to ensure continued beneficiary eligibility, disability awards are reviewed periodically by an adjudication unit within the state agency. The procedures for the termination of benefits are essentially the same as those for the initial determination of eligibility, except that the state unit rather than the claimant initiates the process. Once the initial state unit recommendation has been reviewed and accepted by an examiner in the SSA Bureau of Disability Insurance, benefits are terminated effective two months after the month in which medical recovery is determined to have occurred. The beneficiary is notified of termination at the time he is notified of his right to a de novo reconsideration by a different state unit. If the beneficiary prevails at any stage after benefits have been terminated, he is entitled to retroactive payments. Alternatively, the Secretary of HEW has a statutory right under certain conditions to recover payments which are later determined to be illegitimate.

B. The Plaintiff: George Eldridge

George Eldridge's experience exemplifies the operation of the foregoing sequence of procedures. After Eldridge first filed an application, a state agency review team in Virginia found him not to be disabled within the meaning of the Social Security Act. He requested a reconsideration, which affirmed the prior finding. He then filed a request for a hearing. The hearing examiner found Eldridge disabled and ordered disability insurance benefits paid to him. Notice of this award was sent to Eldridge in June 1968, accompanied by a statement that his claim would be reexamined in one year because by that time he might show a medical improvement justifying termination of the benefits. In 1969, accordingly, Eldridge's claim was reexamined, and in February 1970 the SSA determined that his disability had ceased and suspended his benefits. Eldridge requested a reconsideration of this determination. He also filed suit in federal district court, alleging that the SSA's failure to provide him with a hearing prior to the suspension of his benefits violated due process. The court ordered that payments be continued pending its decision. Meanwhile, the SSA affirmed the state agency's reconsideration decision sustaining the prior determination against Eldridge. Eldridge requested a hearing, and in March 1971 the hearing examiner found that his disability had not ceased. Shortly thereafter the district court suit was dismissed as moot.

In March 1972 the Virginia agency responsible for processing Social Security disability awards sent Eldridge a form letter and questionnaire concerning the current condition of his disability. Eldridge completed this questionnaire and returned it to the state agency indicating that in his opinion he had not improved. The state agency received medical reports from Eldridge's treating physician and from a psychiatric consultant. On May 16, 1972, Eldridge received a letter from the state agency stating, with reasons, that the medical evidence in his case indicated that he was able to work as of May 1972. The letter also stated that benefits would terminate after July 1972 if the agency's findings were affirmed by the SSA, but that a reasonable time would be granted him to obtain and submit additional information. Eldridge responded to this letter as follows:

> In regards to your letter of May 16, 1972 asking for more evidence to prove my disability, I think you should already have enough evidence in my files to prove the disability already. Besides if I was able to work I would have worked because if I was able to work I could make more money than social security paid me. Another thing, if you will check my reports a little closer I think you will find that I have arthritis of the spine rather than a strained back as you stated in your letter. The people at the disability section in Richmond have never made a yes decision in my case, I have always had to have a hearing in order to get the decision made properly. Even at the last hearing that was held in my case I had to employ an attorney, and the examiner made his decision wholly in my favor and stated in his decision for me for my checks to continue without interruption. So go ahead and make your own decision in the case, I know I'm not able to work, if I ever get able to work I will, I will get by some way without the social security even though I've paid into it while I was able to work.

In June the SSA affirmed the state's findings that Eldridge's disability had ceased and, accordingly, that benefits should terminate after July 1972. Eldridge was notified of this determination on July 7, and was advised of his right to request a reconsideration within six months.

In August Eldridge again filed suit, alleging that the Secretary of HEW, in whose name Social Security determinations are made, had no authority to stop his benefit payments without first affording him an opportunity to be heard. The gist of Eldridge's argument was that his experience clearly showed that he could not get a proper determination on his disability claim except at an oral hearing before a hearing examiner (now called an administrative law judge).

* * *

II. The Due Process Calculus as Applied in *Mathews v. Eldridge*

A. The Private Interest

Because the SSA makes retroactive payments when it reinstates a recipient after a hearing, the *Eldridge* Court articulated the plaintiff's substantive interest as an interest merely "in the uninterrupted receipt of his source of income pending final administrative decision of his claim." The Court conceded that this was the same interest as that of the welfare recipient in *Goldberg v. Kelly*, but it then distinguished the *Eldridge* facts on the ground that *Goldberg* had involved an income maintenance scheme of last resort for those in financial need, while the Social Security disability system in *Eldridge* made payments to the disabled irrespective of financial necessity.

Justice Powell conceded that "[although] the potential deprivation here is generally likely to be less than in *Goldberg* . . . the degree of difference can be overstated." He went on to note that the possible length of wrongful deprivation is one consideration in judging the impact of official action on private interests and that the Social Security hearing process * * * is "torpid." The Court also noted the typically modest resources of a physically disabled worker and the significant possibility that ineligibility for federal disability payments would also render a recipient ineligible for the most logical welfare program, Supplemental Security Income (SSI), which uses the same definition of disability. Notwithstanding these observations, however, the Court concluded that since a disability recipient might have access to private resources and other forms of government assistance beyond those normally available to welfare recipients like the one in *Goldberg*, there was "less reason here than in *Goldberg* to depart from the ordinary principle, established by our decisions, that something less than an evidentiary hearing is sufficient prior to adverse administrative action."

Despite its fairly careful analysis, the Court's approach to weighing the private interest is incomplete and problematic. If the objective, as the Court's due process calculus suggests, is to compare the monetary value of the private interests in avoiding wrongful terminations prior to hearing with the monetary value of the governmental interest in summary termination, the Court should have computed the total value of terminated SSA disability claims. Given the current success rate on appeal, that figure might then be discounted by about 50%. This discounted value would also have made an interesting comparison with the total value of terminated welfare claims, discounted by perhaps 75% to reflect the lesser success rate of appellants from adverse welfare determinations. For purposes of comparing the social loss from erroneous termination of welfare and disability benefits, the Court might also have wanted to know the median and mean values of disability benefit claims as compared with welfare benefit claims. Yet, neither the briefs nor the Court's opinion discuss these questions.

Rather the Court's approach is subjective and impressionistic. Its stated concern is the potential desperation resulting from adverse administrative action, a concern that is obviously germane but that raises some rather severe analytic difficulties. First, the Court assumes that interpersonal comparisons of utility, or disutility, are possible—a position which, though intuitively appealing, has no scientific support. Second and more importantly, the Court assumes that these interpersonal comparisons hold across the total populations of welfare and disability recipients when it assumes that disability recipients are less dependent on income support than welfare recipients. This assumption is buttressed only by the notion that welfare is for the needy and disability insurance is for prior taxpayers. The simple rejoinder is that in both cases a recipient's most important residual asset is his or her human capital; since a terminated welfare recipient has never been adjudged unable to perform any substantial gainful activity in any region of the country, he or she might a priori be considered better off than a terminated disability recipient. In fact, any number of circumstances might make a terminated welfare recipient's plight less desperate than that of his disabled SSA counterpart,[42] or vice versa. But any wholesale assumption in favor of either group so grossly overgeneralizes the positions of individual recipients that it masks grave potential injustice.

B. The Value of Additional Procedural Safeguards

The Court's analysis of the reliability of existing pretermination procedures and the probable value of additional procedural safeguards is as unsatisfactory as its analysis of the private interest at stake. The Court reached substantially three conclusions: (1) that it was dealing with an essentially medical determination, (2) that oral presentation would add little reliability to the existing written procedures, and (3) that the statistics on reversal rates at hearings, although noteworthy, did not by themselves impugn the reliability of the procedure.

First, the Court characterized the "nature of the relevant inquiry" as essentially a medical assessment of a worker's physical or mental condition. This assessment, as the Court viewed it, was "a more sharply focused and easily documented decision than the typical determination of welfare entitlement." Pursuing this comparison, the Court suggested that whereas welfare determinations involved issues of witness credibility and veracity, disability determinations turned on "routine, standard and unbiased medical reports by physical specialists." Relying on its language in *Richardson v. Perales*, the Court stated that "[t]he spectre of questionable credibility and veracity is not present."

The Court then dealt with, and dismissed, the *Goldberg* decision's requirement of an oral presentation to the decisionmaker. While noting that the

---

[42] The terminated AFDC [Aid to Families with Dependant Children] recipient may have access to home or general relief depending upon his residence, whereas the disability claimant in a different state or locality may not. The disability claimant may be totally dependent for his livelihood on the disability payments, whereas the welfare recipient who is terminated may have been receiving a small AFDC payment to supplement inadequate family earnings.

Goldberg decision had relied on the limited educational attainment and deficient writing ability of welfare recipients, the Court did not attempt to distinguish disability recipients from welfare recipients on this basis. Rather, the Court emphasized two other aspects of the disability process that suggested the sensibleness and reliability of a written presentation of evidence. The first was that a disability claimant was likely to have much more information than a welfare claimant concerning the precise issues that were relevant to an entitlement decision. Second, evidence in the disability case, according to the Court, derived primarily from other sources other than the claimant: physicians' written reports and records, supplemented by X-rays and documents reflecting other clinical or laboratory tests. The Court was also impressed that the agency informed the recipient of its tentative assessment and then provided an opportunity to submit additional written evidence, thus enabling the recipient to challenge directly the agency's information as well as its tentative conclusions.

The Court was nevertheless troubled, though not ultimately persuaded, by the apparently high reversal rate (58.6%) for appealed reconsideration decisions, that is, decisions that go to hearing before an administrative law judge. What was unclear, however, was whether the reversal rate should be computed from the standpoint of appealed reconsideration decisions or from the standpoint of the overall adjudicatory process, including appealed and unappealed decisions. Under the latter approach, the reversal rate was only 3.3%. Furthermore, the Court was uncertain about the meaning of the reversal rate in terms of the reliability of initial and reconsideration decisions, since the "open file" concept in disability determinations means that the decision at the hearing may be based on additional or new medical evidence that was unavailable at the time of the initial or reconsideration decision.

Again, the Court's analysis is problematic. First, its characterization of the type of decision involved is incomplete. Certainly the definition of "disability" in the Social Security Act requires that disability be the result of a determinable physical or mental impairment. But the question whether the complaining party is disabled often requires the decision maker to translate this medical impairment into functional limitations and to evaluate the effect of those functional limitations on the claimant's capacity to engage in substantial gainful activity, given his age, education, and work experience. Thus a procedure that begins with routine medical reports concerning clinical diagnosis and treatment becomes a highly judgmental process requiring at least the following additional determinations: (1) the degree to which disease or trauma has produced impairments, that is, abnormalities in the claimant's physical or mental structure; (2) the degree to which these impairments result in activity losses or restrictions, usually characterized as functional limitations; (3) the degree to which the claimant's impairments and functional limitations affect the required capacities for the performance of normal roles and activities, including an analysis of attendant therapeutic limitations, environmental restrictions, energy reserve losses, and psychological overlays; (4) the interaction of the claimant's age, education, and prior work experience with his functional limitations and his response to them, and the effect of this combination of factors on his capacity for work available in the national economy. The importance of live testimony in this decision process, particularly by the claimant, has been recognized by several circuit courts of appeal.

Furthermore, according to recent studies by the staff of the House Ways and Means Committee, only 29% of the awards to those persons who are awarded disability benefits are made on the basis of medical condition alone. The basis of the remaining decisions to award benefits is either that impairments are functionally equivalent to those medical conditions which are per se disabling (45%) or that, although the impairment does not meet or functionally equal the medical listings in the regulations, vocational factors specific to the individual justify a determination of total disability (26%).

George Eldridge's fundamental complaint, therefore, might well be that the state agency was making a "medical" decision when it should have made a "disability" decision. His concern is not necessarily with the "veracity" of the medical evidence but rather with the capacity of a disability adjudicator to make a decision about his disability without seeing him and his response to his medical problem. If that is Eldridge's claim, the Court's characterization of the decision as medical and its discussion of the importance of an oral presentation are rather unresponsive: Eldridge might sensibly claim that his disability could not be reliably determined by an adjudicator who had not seen and heard him even if, as a general matter, disability claimants were substantially different socioeconomically from welfare recipients—which they are not—and even if the notice of the SSA's preliminary determinations gave a claimant a good idea of the precise issues upon which his case had turned—which they do not. Three studies by the Social Security Administration have all confirmed that a face-to-face encounter with the claimant has a substantial positive correlation with acceptance of the claim.

The Court might respond, of course, that the purpose of administrative adjudication is not to give an income maintenance claimant the best chance of winning. The question is whether the procedure he has been accorded gives a reasonable chance of producing reliable decisions. The Court's approach to the question of reliability, however, is no more thorough than its analysis of the nature of the decision.

Perhaps the best evidence of reliability is whether the decisions that are made, through whatever procedures, are in fact accurate. But what does "accuracy" mean in the disability system? The fact that over 50% of appealed cases are reversed was not sufficient in the Court's view to indicate that the SSA's underlying process produces inaccurate decisions. This may be perfectly sensible: not only might a finding of disability on appeal simply reflect the worsening of a previously nondisabling impairment, but more fundamentally there is no external standard for determining whether the initial or the appeal decision was accurate. There is also reason to believe that decisions made at the state agency level and at the appeal level may differ because the two sets of adjudications do not act wholly within the same legal framework. The Disability Insurance State Manual, which attempts to objectify the disability standard in order to render state disability decisions more consistent, is not used by the administrative law judges who hold hearings in disability insurance cases. Instead, these judges apply the statutory standard, embellished only by the regulatory medical listings—listings that are almost always irrelevant to cases that reach the hearing stage. The discrepancy, then, between administrative law judges and state agency personnel may be one that flows from the difference between a hierarchical, bureaucratic decision-making system with relatively specific standards and a hearing process designed to provide individualized justice pursuant to general statutory criteria.

Given the absence of an objective external standard for accuracy and the possible noncomparability of decisions by state agencies and those by administrative law judges, the reliability of state agency decisionmaking should be measured by some means other than the percentage of decisions that successfully withstand appeal. The nearest approximation to an index of accuracy is consistency in adjudication: if like cases are being treated alike by state agencies, then claimants are at least receiving formal justice through the existing procedures. In a closed hierarchical structure with no external referents consistency and accuracy tend to merge.

The General Accounting Office (GAO) recently completed a consistency survey of state agency disability determinations, and the results are not encouraging. By random sample the GAO selected 221 SSA and SSI disability claims that had been adjudicated by a state agency; it then transmitted copies of the claims files to ten other state agencies and to federal adjudicators in the Bureau of Disability Insurance in Baltimore. There was significant lack of agreement among state agencies and between state agencies and the federal adjudicators. More importantly, in nearly 50% of the cases, state agencies and federal adjudicators believed that the furnished documentation was insufficient to reach a decision.

If "accuracy" is meaningless and consistency unachievable—or at least unachieved— what does that imply concerning George Eldridge's claim for an oral evidentiary hearing? It seems doubtful that such a hearing would make the process more accurate or consistent, for there is still no external standard for accuracy, and de novo, individualized, oral hearings are hardly an apt control over inconsistent decisions. But Eldridge's claim may make sense precisely because accuracy and consistency are so elusive in this system. SSA disability adjudications should perhaps be viewed as really concerned with difficult value judgments—individualized exemptions from the moral, social, and economic constraints of the work ethic, determined by a complex of medical, vocational, and environmental factors as they impinge on particular individuals. Such adjudications by their very nature elude objective verification and cannot be effectively controlled for consistency. Accordingly, they can be legitimized only by invoking either authority or consent. In a democracy consent is undoubtedly the preferable justification. Its procedural approximation would seem to be the fullest possible participation in the decisional process.

C. The Public Interest

The cost to the public of providing pretermination hearings is two-fold: (1) the direct costs of additional hearings, and (2) the costs of disability benefits paid to current, ineligible recipients pending a hearing decision. In view of the widely varying estimates in the *Mathews v. Eldridge* briefs, the Court was unwilling to hazard a guess concerning the magnitude of these costs. It was content to say that "experience with the constitutionalizing of government procedures suggests that the ultimate costs in terms of money and administrative burden would not be insubstantial." There was no indication of what "experience" the Court was relying on. Thereafter the Court lapsed into speculation about the possibility that increased costs would be paid, somehow, by the deserving recipients of the program and indulged in generalities concerning the folly of transplanting judicial-type procedures willy-nilly to administrative processes. In the end the Court fell back on judicial self-restraint.

The Court was perhaps sensible to sidestep the question of the social costs of pretermination hearings. Apparently no reliable information exists on the motivation of claimants for pursuing appeals in the Social Security system, or on the impact of *Goldberg v. Kelly* on the welfare system. Comparative statistics on requests for pretermination oral hearings under the SSI program are also unavailable. Thus no one can project the impact of a right to pretermination hearings on the rate of appeal. Moreover, the final costs would depend on how the Social Security Administration restructured the hearing process to incorporate a requirement for pretermination hearings. For example, losses from paying aid pending benefits might be minimized by speeding up the entire process; and the reconsideration level in termination cases might be discarded in favor of an oral conference at the state agency level. Whether such restructuring would offset the costs engendered by a new incentive to appeal is wholly problematic.

III. A Value-Sensitive Approach to the *Eldridge* Analysis of Due Process

The Supreme Court's analysis in *Eldridge* is not informed by systematic attention to any theory of the values underlying due process review. The approach is implicitly utilitarian but incomplete, and the Court overlooks alternative theories that might have yielded fruitful inquiry. This section attempts, first, to articulate the limits of the Court's utilitarian approach, both in *Eldridge* and as a general schema for evaluating administrative procedures, and second, to indicate the strengths and weaknesses of three alternative theories—individual dignity, equality, and tradition. These theories, at the level of abstraction here presented, required little critical justification: they are widely held, respond to strong currents in the philosophic literature concerning law, politics, and ethics, and are supported either implicitly or explicitly by the Supreme Court's due process jurisprudence.

A. Utilitarianism

Utility theory suggests that the purpose of decisional procedures—like that of social action generally—is to maximize social welfare. Indeed, the three-factor analysis enunciated in *Eldridge* appears to be a type of utilitarian, social welfare function. That function first takes into account the social value at stake in a legitimate private claim; it discounts that value by the probability that it will be preserved through the available administrative procedures, and it then subtracts from that discounted value the social cost of introducing additional procedures. When combined with the institutional posture of judicial self-restraint, utility theory can be said to yield the following plausible decision-rule: "Void procedures for lack of due process only when alternative procedures would so substantially increase social welfare that their rejection seems irrational."

The utilitarian calculus is not, however, without difficulties. The *Eldridge* Court conceives the values of procedure too narrowly: it views the sole purpose of procedural protections as enhancing accuracy, and thus limits its calculus to the benefits or costs that flow from correct to incorrect decisions. No attention is paid to "process values" that might inhere in oral proceedings or to the demoralization costs that may result from the grant-withdrawal-grant-withdrawal sequence to which claimants like Eldridge are subjected. Perhaps more important, as the Court seeks to make sense of a calculus in which accuracy is the sole goal of procedure, it tends erroneously to characterize disability hearings as concerned almost exclusively with medical impairment and thus concludes that such hearings involve only medical evidence, whose reliability would be little enhanced by oral procedure. As applied by the *Eldridge* Court the utilitarian calculus tends, as cost-benefit analyses typically do, to "dwarf soft variables" and to ignore complexities and ambiguities.

The problem with a utilitarian calculus is not merely that the Court may define the relevant costs and benefits too narrowly. However broadly conceived, the calculus asks unanswerable questions. For example, what is the social value, and the social cost, of continuing disability payments until after an oral hearing for persons initially determined to be ineligible? Answers to those questions require a technique for measuring the social value and social cost of government income transfers, but no such technique exists. Even if such formidable tasks of social accounting could be accomplished, the effectiveness of oral hearings in forestalling the losses that result from erroneous terminations would remain uncertain. In the face of these pervasive indeterminacies the *Eldridge* Court was forced to retreat to a presumption of constitutionality.

Finally, it is not clear that the utilitarian balancing analysis asks the constitutionally relevant questions. The due process clause is one of those Bill of Rights protections meant to insure individual liberty in the face of contrary collective action. Therefore, a collective legislative or administrative decision about procedure, one arguably reflecting the intensity of the contending social values and representing an optimum position from the contemporary social perspective, cannot answer the constitutional question of whether due process has been accorded. A balancing analysis that would have the Court merely redetermine the question of social utility is similarly inadequate. There is no reason to believe that the Court has superior competence or legitimacy as a utilitarian balancer except as it performs its peculiar institutional role of insuring that libertarian values are considered in the calculus of decision.

Several alternative perspectives on the values served by due process pervade the Court's jurisprudence, and may provide a principled basis for due process analysis. These perspectives can usually be incorporated into a broadly defined utilitarian formula and are therefore not necessarily antiutilitarian. But they are best treated separately because they tend to generate inquiries that are different from a strictly utilitarian approach.

B. Individual Dignity

The increasingly secular, scientific, and collectivist character of the modern American state reinforces our propensity to define fairness in the formal, and apparently neutral language of social utility. Assertions of "natural" or "inalienable" rights seem, by contrast, somewhat embarrassing. Their ancestry, and therefore their moral force, are increasingly uncertain. Moreover, their role in the history of the due process clause makes us apprehensive about their eventual reach. It takes no peculiar acuity to see that the tension in procedural due process cases is the same as that in the now discredited substantive due process jurisprudence—a tension between the efficacy of the state and the individual's right to freedom from coercion or socially imposed disadvantage.

Yet the popular moral presupposition of individual dignity, and its political counterpart, self-determination, persist. State coercion must be legitimized, not only by acceptable substantive policies, but also by political processes that respond to a democratic morality's demand for participation in decisions affecting individual and group interests. At the level of individual administrative decisions this demand appears in both the layman's and the lawyer's language as the right to a "hearing" or "to be heard," normally meaning orally and in person. To accord an individual less when his property or status is at stake requires justification, not only because he might contribute to accurate determinations, but also because a lack of personal participation causes alienation and a loss of that dignity and self-respect that society properly deems independently valuable.

The obvious difficulty with a dignitary theory of procedural due process lies in defining operational limits on the procedural claims it fosters. In its purest form the theory would suggest that decisions affecting individual interests should be made only through procedures acceptable to the person affected. This purely subjective standard of procedural due process cannot be adopted: an individual's claim to a "nonalienating" procedure is not ranked ahead of all other social values.

The available techniques for limiting the procedural claims elicited by the dignitary theory, however, either appear arbitrary or render the theory wholly inoperative. One technique is to curtail the class of substantive claims in which individuals can be said to have a right to what they consider an acceptable procedure. The "life, liberty, or property" language of the due process clause suggests such a limitation, but experience with this classification of interests has been disappointing. Any standard premised simply on preexisting legal rights renders a claimant's quest for due process, as such, either unnecessary or hopeless. Another technique for confining the dignitary theory is to define "nonalienating" procedure as any procedure that is formulated democratically. The troublesome effect of this limitation is that no procedures that are legislatively authorized can be said to encroach on individual dignity.

Notwithstanding its difficulties, the dignitary theory of due process might have contributed significantly to the *Eldridge* analysis. The questions of procedural "acceptability" which the theory poses may initially seem vacuous or at best intuitive, but they suggest a broader sensitivity than the utilitarian factor analysis to the nature of governmental decisions. Whereas the utilitarian approach seems to require an estimate of the quantitative value of the claim, the dignitary approach suggests that the Court develop a qualitative appraisal of the type of administrative decision involved. While the disability decision in *Eldridge* may be narrowly characterized as a decision about the receipt of money payments, it may also be considered from various qualitative perspectives which seem pertinent in view of the general structure of the American income-support system.

That system suggests that a disability decision is a judgment of considerable social significance, and one that the claimant should rightly perceive as having a substantial moral content. The major cash income-support programs determine eligibility, not only on the basis of simple insufficiency of income, but also, or exclusively, on the basis of a series of excuses for partial or total nonparticipation in the work force: agedness, childhood, family responsibility, injury, disability. A grant under any of these programs is an official, if sometimes grudging, stamp of approval of the claimant's status as a partially disabled worker or nonworker. It proclaims, in effect, that those who obtain it have encountered one of the politically legitimate hazards to self-sufficiency in a market economy. The recipients, therefore, are entitled to society's support. Conversely, the denial of an income-maintenance claim implies that the claim is socially illegitimate, and the claimant, however impecunious, is not excused from normal work force status.

These moral and status dimensions of the disability decision indicate that there is more at stake in disability claims than temporary loss of income. They also tend to put the disability decision in a framework that leads away from the superficial conclusion that disability decisions are a routine matter of evaluating medical evidence. Decisions with substantial "moral worth" connotations are generally expected to be highly individualized and attentive to subjective evidence. The adjudication of such issues on the basis of documents submitted largely by third parties and by adjudicators who have never confronted the claimant seems inappropriate. Instead, a court approaching an analysis of the disability claims process from the dignitary perspective might emphasize those aspects of disability decisions that focus on a particular claimant's vocational characteristics, his unique response to his medical condition, and the ultimate predictive judgment of whether the claimant should be able to work.

C. Equality

Justice in a formal philosophical sense is often defined as equality of treatment. In the realm of adjudicatory procedure, a widely recognized aspect of procedural fairness is equality of opportunity to be heard. Indeed, insofar as adjudicatory procedure is perceived to be adversarial and dispute resolving, the degree to which procedures facilitate equal opportunities for the adversaries to influence the decision may be the most important criterion by which fairness is evaluated.

Equality of opportunity is not, however, an exhaustive measure of procedural due process. While equality would seem to require an unbiased decision maker and identical opportunities to present evidence and argument, it has little to say concerning the manner in which evidence and argument are presented. A hearing participant might claim, for example, that oral proceedings, including cross-examination, would illuminate murky aspects of the case or produce a truer disclosure of facts; but if this participant's adversary or other participants are not accorded these procedural rights, he can hardly claim unequal treatment. Similarly, objection to the use of material obtained outside the record, but not from a party, is at most remotely connected with equality of access. A procedure that divested the directly affected parties of all control over the process of shaping issues and developing evidence, indeed that never informed the parties that it had begun, would be "unequal" only if institutionally biased. Yet such a procedure would widely be perceived as "unfair."

Notions of equality can nevertheless significantly inform the evaluation of any administrative process. One question we might ask is whether an investigative procedure is designed in a fashion that systematically excludes or undervalues evidence that would tend to support the position of a particular class of parties. If so, those parties might have a plausible claim that the procedure treated them unequally. Similarly, in a large-scale inquisitorial process involving many adjudicators, the question that should be posed is whether like cases receive like attention and like evidentiary development so that the influence of such arbitrary factors as location are minimized. In order to take such equality issues into account, we need only to broaden our due process horizons to include elements of procedural fairness beyond those traditionally associated with adversary proceedings. These two inquiries might have been pursued fruitfully in *Eldridge*. First, is the state agency system of decision making, which is based on documents, particularly disadvantageous for certain classes of claimants? There is some tentative evidence that it is. Cases such as *Eldridge* involving muscular or skeletal disorders, neurological problems, and multiple impairments, including psychological overlays, are widely believed to be both particularly difficult, due to the subjectivity of the evidence, and particularly prone to be reversed after oral hearing.

Second, does the inquisitorial process at the state agency level tend to treat like cases alike? If the GAO's study is indicative, the answer is decidedly no. According to that study, many, perhaps half, of the decisions are made on the basis of records that other adjudicators consider so inadequate that a decision could not be rendered. The relevance of such state agency variance to Eldridge's claim is twofold: first, it suggests that state agency determinations are unreliable and that further development at the hearings stage might substantially enhance their reliability; alternatively, it may suggest that the hierarchical or bureaucratic model of decision making, with overhead control for consistency, does not accurately describe the Social Security disability system. And if consistency is not feasible under this system, perhaps the more compelling standard for evaluating the system is the dignitary value of individualized judgment, which, as noted earlier, implies claimant participation.

D. Tradition or Evolution

Judicial reasoning, including reasoning about procedural due process, is frequently and self-consciously based on custom or precedent. In part, reliance on tradition or "authority" is a court's institutional defense against illegitimacy in a political democracy. But tradition serves other values, not the least of which are predictability and economy of effort. More importantly, the inherently conservative technique of analogy to custom and precedent seems essential to the evolutionary development and the preservation of the legal system. Traditional procedures are legitimate not only because they represent a set of continuous expectations, but because the body politic has survived their use.

The use of tradition as a guide to fundamental fairness is vulnerable, of course, to objection. Since social and economic forces are dynamic, the processes and structures that proved functional in one period will not necessarily serve effectively in the next. Indeed, evolutionary development may as often end in the extinction of a species as in adaptation and survival. For this reason alone tradition can serve only as a partial guide to judgment.

Furthermore, it may be argued that reasoning by analogy from traditional procedures does not actually provide a perspective on the values served by due process. Rather, it is a decisional technique that requires a specification of the purposes of procedural rules merely in order that the decision maker may choose from among a range of authorities or customs the particular authority or custom most analogous to the procedures being evaluated.

This objection to tradition as a theory of justification is weighty, but not devastating. What is asserted by an organic or evolutionary theory is that *the purposes of legal rules cannot be fully known.* Put more cogently, while procedural rules, like other legal rules, should presumably contribute to the maintenance of an effective social order, we cannot expect to know precisely how they do so and what the long-term effects of changes or revisions might be. Our constitutional stance should therefore be preservative and incremental, building carefully, by analogy, upon traditional modes of operation. So viewed, the justification "we have always done it that way" is not so much a retreat from reasoned and purposive decision making as a profound acknowledgment of the limits of instrumental rationality.

Viewed from a traditionalist's perspective, the Supreme Court's opinion in *Eldridge* may be said to rely on the traditional proposition that property interests may be divested temporarily without hearing, provided a subsequent opportunity for contest is afforded. *Goldberg v. Kelly* is deemed an exceptional case, from which *Eldridge* is distinguished.

Like the Court's utilitarian analysis, this general traditionalist method seems incomplete. If the premise of that method is that traditional modes of operation are to provide guidelines, then the Court should have immediately characterized the legal issue in order to select the appropriate guidelines. But given the Court's quite sensible position that administrative functions are to be evaluated individually, how was that characterization to proceed? Presumably, disability payments fall within the general domain of social welfare claims—a domain that is also treated in the *Goldberg* decision. Assuming, however, that the Court properly distinguished *Goldberg*, analogical analysis is aborted because no other Supreme Court decision pertaining to social welfare claims seems apt. Nor could it discover guiding authority in prior administrative practice, which is based on the now discredited notion that social welfare benefits are subject to discretionary divestiture. What the *Eldridge* Court needed, then, was a more general way of thinking about the termination of property interests that might apply both to traditional and to novel forms of property.

The beginnings of such an approach might be found in Justice Black's dissent in *Goldberg*, where he analogized the position of a welfare recipient to the traditional position of a creditor when his debtor refuses further performance. Normally, in that situation, the creditor is left with the inconvenience of forgoing receipt of performance while he seeks legal enforcement of an obligation that may or may not remain due. The majority opinion's implicit response to the analogy is that a welfare recipient is in a special position: he literally cannot wait because he depends upon the state's performance for survival. Given this special circumstance, the Court concludes, the traditional bearer of the risk of erroneous (or otherwise illicit) nonperformance has a constitutional right to shift that risk to the state, pending hearing. Given this reading of *Goldberg*, the *Eldridge* opinion may be interpreted as concluding simply that the special *Goldberg* circumstances did not obtain. Therefore, the traditional allocation of the risk was acceptable.

Analyzing *Goldberg* and *Eldridge* by analogy to traditional contract-default remedies is valuable because it discourages the superficial classification of welfare recipients as immediately desperate and of disability recipients as having alternative resources. A court in equity faced with an analogous issue—a request for a temporary restraining order or preliminary injunction to insure performance by an obligor—would look to the particular circumstances of the case to determine whether extraordinary remedies were justified. In so doing, the court would take into account the peculiar hardship to the plaintiff of nonperformance pending a trial, the likelihood that he might prevail on the merits, and the burden on the defendant of requiring maintenance of the status quo. The Social Security Administration, as a matter of due process of law, might sensibly be required to do the same—or at least to explain its inability to do so.

A court pursuing an analysis based on traditional contract-default remedies should also focus on the limitations of that analogy. Contract remedies presume a competitive market in which alternative obligors are available. This presumption of the availability of alternatives undergirds traditional judicial reluctance to require specific performance pending trial, or indeed after trial. The party relying on state support is in a quite different position. His market alternatives have previously been determined to be foreclosed, and his attachment to a particular income-maintenance scheme suggests that others are at best not comparable, and at worst unavailable. While this difference between contract and income-maintenance claims may not be a sufficient reason for reversing the usual allocation of the risk of error pending a full hearing in all cases, it comes close to presenting an a fortiori case for requiring that the individual income-maintenance claimant, like the contract creditor, be allowed to establish (perhaps by affidavit) that his is such a case.

Conclusion

The preceding discussion has emphasized the way that explicit attention to a range of values underlying due process of law might have led the *Eldridge* Court down analytic paths different from those that appear in Justice Powell's opinion. The discussion has largely ignored, however, arguments that would justify the result that the Court reached in terms of the alternative value theories here advanced. Those arguments are now set forth.

First, focus on the dignitary aspects of the disability decision can hardly compel the conclusion that an oral hearing is a constitutional necessity prior to the termination of benefits when a full hearing is available later. Knowledge that an oral hearing will be available at some point should certainly lessen disaffection and alienation. Indeed, Eldridge seemed secure in the knowledge that a just procedure was available. His desire to avoid taking a corrective appeal should not blind us to the support of dignitary values that the de novo appeal provides.

Second, arguments premised on equality do not necessarily carry the day for the proponent of prior hearings. The Social Security Administration's attempt to routinize and make consistent hundreds of thousands of decisions in a nationwide income-maintenance program can be criticized both for its failures in its own terms and for its tendency to ignore the way that disability decisions impinge upon perceptions of individual moral worth. On balance, however, the program that Congress enacted contains criteria that suggest a desire for both consistency and individualization. No adjudicatory process can avoid tradeoffs between the pursuit of one or the other of these goals. Thus a procedural structure incorporating (1) decisions by a single state agency based on a documentary record and subject to hierarchical quality review, followed by (2) appeal to de novo oral proceedings before independent administrative law judges, is hardly an irrational approach to the necessary compromise between consistency and individualization.

Explicit and systematic attention to the values served by a demand for due process nevertheless remains highly informative in *Eldridge* and in general. The use of analogy to traditional procedures might have helped rationalize and systematize a concern for the "desperation" of claimants that seems as impoverished in *Eldridge* as it seems profligate in *Goldberg*; and the absence in *Eldridge* of traditionalist, dignitary, or egalitarian considerations regarding the disability adjudication process permitted the Court to overlook questions of both fact and value—questions that, on reflection, seem important. The structure provided by the Court's three factors is an inadequate guide for analysis because its neutrality leaves it empty of suggestive value perspectives.

* * *

The path to a more appropriate and successful judicial role may lie in giving greater attention to the elaboration of the due process implications of the values that have been discussed. If the Court provided a structure of values within which procedures would be reviewed, it could then demand that administrators justify their processes in terms of the degree to which they support the elaborated value structure.

The Court would have to be satisfied that the administrator had carefully considered the effects of his chosen procedures on the relevant constitutional values and had made reasonable judgments concerning those effects.

A decision that an administrator had not met that standard would not result in the prescription of a particular adjudicatory technique as a constitutional, and thereafter virtually immutable necessity; but rather in a remand to the administrator. In meeting the Court's objections, the administrator (or legislature) might properly choose between specific amendment and a complete overhaul of the administrative process. Perhaps more importantly, under a due process approach that emphasized value rather than technique, neither the administrator in constructing and justifying his processes, nor the Court in reviewing them, would be limited to the increasingly sterile discussion of whether this or that particular aspect of trial-type procedure is absolutely essential to due process of law.

Cynthia R. Farina, *Conceiving Due Process*, 3 YALE J.L. & FEMINISM 189, 190-91, 197-219, 237-51, 254-72, 274-78 (1991)*

* * *

I * * * begin by exploring the problems with procedural due process jurisprudence: its schizophrenic dependence upon and rejection of the dictates of the legislature, its simultaneous overprotection and underprotection of interactions between people and their government, its contorted view of the value of process. My purpose in this first half of the article is to chronicle how a profoundly troubled doctrine has resisted twenty years of efforts to right it. * * *

Having told the story of those years in its own terms, I then consider, in the second half of the article, how we might tell a different story. I begin by suggesting that *both* the problems within procedural due process doctrine *and* our inability to solve those problems can be directly traced to the set of assumptions—about human nature, the role of law, and the relations among people and between people and their government—that have thus far engendered

---

* Reprinted with permission of the Yale Journal of Law & Feminism and Cynthia R. Farina. All rights reserved.

our thinking in this area. Where we began has led us, ineluctably, to where we have ended up. * * *

And so, finally, I will pose a very different beginning: a set of understandings, drawn from feminist theory, about what people are and need, what law might accomplish, and how we should understand the relationship between the citizenry and the state. And I will sketch (at least, preliminarily) the very different procedural due process that might be brought forth from such origins: a jurisprudence that pursues the connection between a people and their government rather than the autonomy of isolated individuals; that seeks ever-improving solutions within the particularized, living context of actual programs rather than timeless, universal answers from abstract, objective principles; and that strives to create a culture in which public power will be used with care rather than a set of weapons with which its misuse can be defended against. * * *

* * *

II. Critiques and Critiques of Critiques

* * *

No aspect of contemporary due process doctrine has escaped criticism. Without doubt, though, the lion's share of disapproval has been reserved for entitlement analysis—and with good reason. Entitlement is the linchpin of procedural due process, most immediately defining the range of protected interests, but also indirectly shaping even such ostensibly separate inquiries as what process is due. To appreciate the dilemmas of the doctrine, here is where we must start.

The troubled history of entitlement analysis can best be understood as comprising two distinct (though related) questions: *where* will we look for protected interests? and what will we require those sources to contain? * * *

A. *The Positivist Trap*

* * *

When *Goldberg v. Kelly* afforded procedural due process protection to welfare benefits, it seemed the beginning of a brave new world. Due process, Justice Brennan's opinion assured us, had at last escaped the right/privilege distinction. That assurance carried great symbolic significance. The right/privilege distinction had repeatedly thwarted the extension of due process to benefits, licenses, jobs and other advantageous relations with government. In its substantive aspect, it allowed legislatures to condition the establishment or continuance of such relationships on individual behavior that government otherwise could not compel. In its procedural aspect, it permitted officials to deny or withdraw these relationships on the basis of reasons that had been ascertained through inadequate or unreliable process or, more extreme, to act for no articulated reason at all. Catchphrase for a fairly intricate body of law, "the right/privilege distinction" stood for a fairly simple idea: The Constitution has nothing to say about how government conducts itself in relationships it is under no obligation to establish, even if those relationships are deeply important to the people involved. Unless the citizen can muster a legal basis for demanding the benefit, status or opportunity (that is, can assert a "right" to what the government offers), the only substantive or procedural constraints on official action are those which the legislature has chosen to impose.

The *Goldberg* world was new in unabashedly asserting that the Constitution mediates the intercourse between government and its people even when government is distributing the quintessential largesse, welfare. It was brave in thus opening to constitutional exploration the broad expanse of the contemporary regulatory state. When, two years later, *Roth* emphatically stated that "the Court has fully and finally rejected the wooden distinction between 'rights' and 'privileges,'" *Goldberg*'s promise seemed confirmed. * * *

But *Roth* lied, or at least was profoundly self-deluded. Determined to banish even the rhetoric of privilege, *Goldberg* had insisted that welfare "benefits are a matter of statutory entitlement for persons qualified to receive them." *Roth* took this description, which had been intended to empower citizens standing before their government, and transformed it into a burden incumbent upon the individual who would claim due process. In so doing, *Roth* turned the new doctrine irresistibly back towards right/privilege. Although the vocabulary had changed—"Is it a right?" became "Is it an entitlement?"—the methodology remained constant in two crucial respects. First, the applicability of constitutional protection depends upon a categorical assessment of the interest, rather than on the fact or effect of government interaction with the citizen. Second, this assessment hinges principally on the content of law outside the due process clause.

The commentary quickly pointed out that entitlement analysis recreates the essence of the right/privilege distinction. The objection here goes deeper than the Court's apparent unawareness that *Roth* marched us back down the hill *Goldberg* had just marched us up. If the right/privilege distinction had offered spotty and uncertain protection for citizens otherwise at the mercy of how their government chose to treat them, entitlement analysis represented a positivism that was alarming in its implications. *Roth* held, seemingly without qualification, that property interests are not created by the Constitution; "[r]ather, they are created and their dimensions are defined by existing rules or understandings that stem from an independent source such as state law. . . ." Henry Monaghan then posed a hypothetical that has since haunted the commentary:

> Suppose that a state motor vehicle statute invested automobiles with all the attributes of property as that term is generally understood, but also provided that no person who bought a car after the statute was passed would be deemed to have a "right to continued" ownership as against the state.[52]

Would an "owner" deprived of his automobile pursuant to this statute have an interest in the vehicle sufficient to trigger due process scrutiny? An earlier court, following the right/privilege distinction, surely would have thought so. Right/privilege analysis had posed no threat to traditional forms of wealth. Unself-conscious in their methodology, earlier courts knew property when they saw it. The shortcomings of right/privilege as the gate-keeper for due process were felt when courts encountered interests—such as government employment, licenses, or social welfare benefits—that possessed substantial importance to individuals but had neither traditional common law status nor statutory protection. *Goldberg*, in a great levelling, promised those newer forms of wealth the same claim to constitutional protection as traditional forms had always enjoyed. But where *Goldberg* would have levelled up, entitlement analysis now threatened to level down. If *Roth* was serious in asserting that the existence and dimensions of property interests depend upon the terms of sub-constitutional law, then traditional as well as new property is no more than whatever the legislature decides it should be. A contemporary court employing entitlement analysis would be hard-pressed to explain how automobile "owners," under Monaghan's hypothetical statute, have any interest to which due process protection could attach.

By rendering tenuous constitutional protection of interests whose protection we had always taken for granted, the unabashed positivism of entitlement analysis made manifest the worm that also lay

---

[52] [Henry Monaghan, *Of "Liberty" and "Property,"* 62 Cornell L. Rev. 405, 440 (1977).] * * *

(though perhaps better hidden) at the core of the right/privilege distinction: Due process protects people from being deprived, by their government, of only those things their government has chosen to allow them to keep. The problem is not positivism *per se*; neither is it, *per se*, the idea of a norm that binds the community only so far as the community chooses to be bound. A constitution can constitute positive law; a constitution can embody our choice to bind ourselves until we collectively choose no longer to be bound. Indeed, both of these ideas are elemental to our understanding of our Constitution. Rather, the problem is the form of positivism that looks—exclusively in the case of property, and increasingly in the case of liberty—to the provisions of sub-constitutional law. Precisely because we understand the essence of the Bill of Rights and 14th Amendment to be constraint on simple-majoritarian positive law, a doctrine that makes constitutional protection contingent upon the terms of such law is deeply disturbing if not actually, within our constitutional culture, incoherent.

Once the problem is thus identified, the remedy seems obvious. The phrase "life, liberty, or property" *must* possess intrinsic meaning that is not dependent on positive law. Entitlement analysis must be abandoned, as fundamentally misguided, in favor of a doctrine that acknowledges a robust constitutional content to those terms.

* * *

1. *Looking to Grand Theory*

However, the solution that appears so simple and sensible is revealed, almost immediately, to be fraught with difficulty. What should we understand to be the constitutional content of "property"? "[A]ny institution of property requires a justifying theory." Yet, the spectrum of possible justifications is vast, encompassing labor/natural rights theories, personality theories, and utility theories, theories in which property is constitutive of the political order and theories in which property is extra- (even anti-) political, theories that embody an egalitarian presumption and theories that embody a libertarian presumption. Even if choice among these multifarious theories were unnecessary—if, for example, history demanded that the *constitutional* meaning of property be derived from a labor/natural rights justification in the Lockean tradition—the difficulties would only have begun, for theory must then be applied to sort through the plethora of interests now seeking due process protection. A Lockean labor theory might exclude from the category of "property" most of the governmental largess of the modern regulatory state. * * *

There is little cause for optimism that any of the other "grand theories" of property would prove more tractable in identifying which of the multitude of advantageous relations with modern government are comprised in the "property" of the Fifth and Fourteenth Amendments. And, despite our first flush of natural law conviction that "liberty" will be easier, it is not. Once we get beyond the familiar terrain of the Bill of Rights, the way is largely uncharted. Immediately, there looms the great divide between "negative liberty" and "positive liberty." The choice here may not appear so difficult. In our legal tradition, negative liberty seems reassuringly familiar; indeed, in this region lie well-known landmarks: "the right of the individual to contract, to engage in any of the common occupations of life, to acquire useful knowledge, to marry, to establish a home and bring up children . . . ." Yet it takes little imagination to realize that, today, the ability to enjoy even these archetypical freedoms is not assured by merely "the right, as against the Government, to be let alone." The licenses required to marry and to enter many occupations, the permits and certificates needed to build a home, the policies and procedures constituting the public education system are but the superficial indicia of government involvement. There is, more fundamentally, the matrix of health, safety, consumer protection, environmental, and other social welfare regulations in which our personal and professional transactions are embedded, the economic programs which enable us to acquire a home or an education, the financial and social services that support our efforts to bear and raise healthy, knowledgeable, well-rounded children—all bearing witness that the liberty "generally to enjoy those privileges long recognized . . . as essential to the orderly pursuit of happiness by free men" now depends upon government's active cooperation and assistance. To live, with any appreciable degree of awareness, in our complex regulatory society is to be wary of a purely negative conception of liberty. And even this wariness would take into account only the privileged position of the healthy, able-bodied, pre-retirement age, two-parent, white family able to generate an income comfortably exceeding the poverty level. For the significant portion of our population who are poor, elderly, children, persons of color, physically or mentally challenged, or otherwise living under conditions of disadvantage and oppression, the high plain of negative liberty is not merely bleak and inhospitable, it is openly hostile and even life-threatening.

By contrast, positive liberty is a fertile land, laden with promise. From simple seeds spring richly-branched conceptions, such as Laurence Tribe's articulation of the interests entailed in freedom of speech: "One must be able to express oneself to protest the violation of other rights, but to express oneself one needs at least a decent level of nourishment, shelter, clothing, medical care, and education. To have these things, one needs either employment or income support."[76] But the very generosity of the positive theory of liberty is the genesis of problems. In a society that has evolved a plentiful standard of living through the coordination and assistance of government, positive liberty has no readily discernible stopping point.

The effort to give meaningful intrinsic content to "liberty" is thus caught in the same dilemma as the attempt to unsubstantiate "property": The available theories yield a collection of interests that is either inadequate or indeterminate. That both undertakings should end in a common quandary is not surprising. A powerful element of our political philosophical tradition has been that liberty and property are interdependent. At least for us, to identify the one may be, inescapably, to reveal the other. A sense of this interdependence may have inspired the alternative to entitlement theory proposed by Henry Monaghan and John Hart Ely. "Life, liberty, or property," they argue, should not be parsed as discrete categories, to one of which any contending interest must conform. Rather, the phrase should be understood as a unit that embraces "every interest valued by sensible persons."[79] This unitary "importance theory" has the virtue of pretermitting the exercise of classifying interests in favor of a direct focus on the meaning of the interchange with government to the individual situated in a particular cultural context. But this formulation—however promising as a new starting point—will not, without more, significantly advance the inquiry. The recognition of "value" or "importance" can take place only within some larger account of human nature and the human community, the appropriate relationship between a people and their government, and the role of law in defining and facilitating these things—in sum, the same sort of account that is central to a justification of property or a theory of liberty. The unitary "importance theory" puts us more immediately in touch with these questions, but it cannot obviate the need to make choices about how we will resolve them.

To be sure, deliberating upon and reaching a resolution of these issues would seem to be one of the most compelling tasks for a people to undertake. Whether the occasion be crafting a grand theory of "property" or "liberty," or establishing the criteria by which we will assess the "importance" of interests, it is a task of defining and realizing our society's identity. The sticking point comes when a judiciary attempts to undertake this task in the context of constitutional interpretation. As Colin Diver puts it, "the utterance of two words—*Lochner* and *Wade*—is usually enough to stop this idea in its tracks."[81] The *Lochner* objection has two distinct, though related, components.

The first challenges the legitimacy of a process in which fundamental decisions about who we are and what we value would be made by persons not elected by and unanswerable to the people. The flight from entitlement analysis—a journey begun so that the individual might not be at the mercy of the majoritarian process—is, by common reckoning, a grotesque failure if it ends in putting the majoritarian process at the mercy of the judiciary. Our anxiety that this might indeed be the outcome of attempting a robust substantive conception of "liberty" or "property" or "importance" is heightened by the disturbing propensity of those who advocate such an approach to apply their particular conception to generate results that are highly debatable. * * * Cut loose from any mooring in positive law, we suspect that due process adjudication would "be adrift in a stormy sea of 'natural' or 'fundamental' rights claims with no navigational aids beyond the imagination of the justices."[85] * * *

The second component of the *Lochner* objection represents a dilemma of comparable magnitude. One of the most troubling aspects of entitlement doctrine is its implications for takings analysis and substantive due process. Deprivation of "property" appears to

---

[76] [Laurence Tribe, American Constitutional Law 778 (2d ed. 1988).]

[79] The formulation is Monaghan's. *See* Henry Monaghan, *The Burger Court and "Our Federalism,"* 43 Law & Contemp. Probs. 39, 49 (Summer 1980). *See also* Monaghan, [*Of "Liberty" and "Property,"* 62 Cornell L. Rev. 405, 406–09 (1977)] (inter alia, "every individual 'interest' worth talking about"). Ely's version is that "the government [can't] seriously hurt you without due process of law." John Ely, Democracy and Distrust 19 (1980). To the extent that *Goldberg* can be said to embody a theory of protected interests, this appears to be it. *See* 397 U.S. at 262-63.

[81] Colin Diver, *The Wrath of Roth*, 94 Yale L.J. 1529, 1542 (1985). Lochner v. New York, 198 U.S. 45 (1905), invalidated a law prescribing maximum hours for bakery workers as an illegitimate interference with freedom of contract. Roe v. Wade, 410 U.S. 113 (1973), invalidated restrictive abortion statutes as unduly trenching on a right of privacy, which included decisions about whether to terminate pregnancy.

[85] Jerry Mashaw, *Dignitary Process: A Political Psychology of Liberal Democratic Citizenship*, 39 U. Fla. L. Rev. 433, 438 (1987).

be the constitutional trigger not only for government's responsibility to afford procedure but also for its duties to pay just compensation and to provide at least a rational justification for its actions. If property is purely the creature of positive law, Monaghan's hypothetical statute would appear to truncate not only claims for process but also these other, substantive, claims as well. Entitlement analysis thus threatens to be even more grossly underprotective of individual interests than the focus on process first suggests. And yet, giving constitutional content to liberty and property in the service of procedural due process threatens to be grossly overprotective. *Lochner* casts long shadows. No matter how often we are reassured by highly respected voices that it need not be so, we perceive behind attempts to secure property and liberty the dim outlines of a straight-jacket on progressive social change. In few areas of constitutional law do we confront as clearly the difficulty of reconciling the capacity for growth and change implicit in our commitment to self-government with the stasis entailed in our commitment to self-restraint.

2. Looking to History—And History Modified

Still, one might insist, this act of reconciliation is an inescapable part of the Bill of Rights as we understand it, and the most resonant component of the *Lochner* objection appears to be the fear that the precise content of "liberty" and "property" would be defined by the preferences of five non-elected justices. One way to minimize the danger of constitutionalizing "the judges' own notions of justice" without abandoning due process to positivism is to cleave to history: The due process clauses embody not a grand theory of liberty or property but rather a discrete, historically recoverable set of interests expressed by the framers through those terms. "Property" would include "estates in fee and . . . a motley collection of additional interests (leases, estates) that made up the bulk of private wealth," as well, presumably, as tangible personalty, to make up a group denominated "traditional" or "ordinary" or "classical" property. As these adjectives suggest, the constitutional category would track the comfortably familiar: It would legally vindicate the intuition that automobiles are property no matter what Monaghan's hypothetical statute says. Indeed, the promise of securing what we "know" to be property and liberty is felt as one of the great rewards of following in the footsteps of the framers. Proponents of a strict historical approach point out that *Goldberg's* attempt to enfold new interests in the same mantle which protected traditional ones so strained the constitutional fabric that all interests were left with only the threadbare protection of entitlement. Better to afford real protection to only certain, core interests than pseudo-protection to all.

But the protection afforded by history also proves to be thin. "Traditional property" might encompass my automobile, but what about the inspection and registration certificates and the driver's license without which I may not travel on the public highways? To resolve these questions, I might turn hopefully to "liberty," but what lies within traditional liberty is an unpleasant surprise. The original understanding appears to have encompassed merely the freedom from physical restraint. So meager does this notion of liberty appear to inhabitants of the contemporary regulatory state that only the most stout-hearted originalists can abide by it.

As an alternative, Stephen Williams has proposed that "liberty" be understood to include "the interests entitled to due process protection as of 1925."[98] Liberty thus would encompass a collection of interests recognized by the Court beginning in 1897, such as occupational liberty, the freedom of parents to control their children's education and, of course, freedom of contract. This expansion of classical liberty is justified, Williams argues, because "[t]he family resemblance between these interests and freedom from incarceration seems clear enough . . . ." Without doubt, the pressure to expand liberty beyond the classic freedom from physical restraint is great—but so is the price of surrender. The high ground of legitimacy claimed by originalism affords but little compass. To leave the sacred precinct of what the framers understood and consented to is to join the ranks of the fallen angels. By stepping off the narrow path of historically determinate meaning and judicial restraint, Williams' solution forfeited all claim to whatever justificatory power strict interpretivism possesses.

3. Looking to Analogy

Of course, this observation need not mean that no justification of Williams' proposal is possible. Indeed, his argument that restraints on the ability to contract, to pursue an occupation, and to educate one's children are *sufficiently like* restraints on one's person to be included within "liberty" represents another familiar method of determining constitutional meaning—a method that might be called analogical interpretivism. In this approach, "the job of the person interpreting the provision . . . is to identify the *sorts of evils* against which the provision was directed and to move against their contemporary

---

[98] [Stephen Williams, *Liberty and Property: The Problem of Government Benefits*, 12 J. LEGAL STUD. 1, 21 (1983).]

counterparts." As a methodology for giving constitutional content to "liberty" and "property," analogical interpretivism occupies a pragmatic middle ground between the generality of grand theory and the particularity of a historically closed set of interests. It begins with the historical set, but eludes the grasp of the dead hand by distilling from those interests some essential or common elements that can be seen to transcend the limits of history. * * *

Analogical interpretivism is no stranger to due process. It undergirds Charles Reich's early and influential article, "The New Property."[103] Property, Reich argued, has always been the secure base from which Americans assert their individuality and claim their freedom; it draws the magic circle between public and private, maintaining independence, dignity and pluralism by creating a "small but sovereign island" within the bounds of which the majority has to yield to the individual. In this way, "property" constitutes the indispensable condition of "liberty." Liberty is the preservation of the individual from the tyranny of the collective, the freedom of each to exist as an autonomous being, uncoerced (except as necessary for the maintenance of societal order) by the majority's sentiments of appropriate or reasonable behavior. Thus, taking the first critical step of analogical interpretivism—distilling that element or quality of the historical collection of interests that can then be carried forward to assess contemporary interests—Reich broadly identified "property" with individual security and "liberty" with individual independence. While this reading was not uncontroverted, it was thoroughly familiar and widely accepted. Where later analogical interpretivists such as Williams sharply part company with Reich is in the next step: applying this reading to classify interests that today claim due process protection.

Reich observed that, for many citizens, government benefits, services, jobs, contracts, and licenses have come to take the place of traditional forms of wealth. Security, independence, and individuality itself could be preserved, he argued, only by affording these beneficial relations with government the same legal protections that traditional property and liberty receive. But this reasoning, Williams pointed out, is at best hopelessly romantic and at worst positively illogical. Those who have become dependent upon government cannot be saved through the very instrument of their dependency. The only hope of preserving a vital individualism in the welfare state is to concentrate constitutional protection on those who retain some base for meaningful independence from government—that is, those who hold traditional property and thus fruitfully can exercise liberty. That due process thus fortifies only those already possessed of strength should come as no surprise: "Protection of property seems inescapably more likely to protect the propertied than the nonpropertied; protection of liberty . . . is likely to advantage primarily those with the personal capacity to use their liberty."[112]

Cast in such raw, uncompromising terms, Williams' response to Reich is easy to dismiss as a particularly offensive version of laissez-faire libertarianism. But beneath the Malthusian rhetoric lies a subtly powerful point. To call upon the state's legal regime to protect the individual from the state itself is always a delicate and chancy undertaking. Due process might accomplish this difficult feat with respect to traditional property and liberty because, although we recognize the role of law in defining and protecting these interests, we resist, on some very fundamental level, the idea that law literally *creates* them. The distance we perceive between these interests and government is what enables us to regard traditional property and liberty as bastions of individualism; it is the space on which we stand to make a credible demand that government, through its courts, protects us from itself. By contrast, many of the valuables dispensed by the regulatory state *do* seem to be the creature of government, made available to individual citizens purely because the collective will of the citizenry, expressed through its representatives, would have it so. Coincidental with the positive law that creates them, these interests offer little moral or political purchase for the sort of self-disciplining exercise due process entails, in which government responds to the individual's demands for distance between himself and the collective. A political system that recognizes simultaneously the *essentialness* and the *unlikeliness* of such demands being honored might well allow them to be made in only the strongest of cases. What first seems benighted social Darwinism may be in fact prudent constitutional economy.

Thus, Williams' analogical interpretivist theory—in which the group of protected interests extends as far as, but no further than, the freedoms of family ordering, occupation, and contract which (with traditional property and liberty) represent spheres of individual autonomy—begins to seem an astute compromise between the anachronistic spartanism of literal historical meaning and the unworkable prodigality of

---

[103] [Charles Reich, *The New Property*, 73 YALE L.J. 733, 771-74 (1964).]

[112] [Stephen Williams, *Liberty and Property: The Problem of Government Benefits*, 12 J. LEGAL STUD. 1, 27 n.86 (1983).]

Reich's vision. But at this point, Williams himself encounters two major difficulties. The first can be seen by returning to the ubiquitous automobile hypothetical. Traditional property protects my car, but even extending "liberty" to encompass the classic negative liberties will not reach the certificates and licenses I require to make meaningful use of it. Unless my access to those items is protected from government arbitrariness, any independence and security that arises from owning my car is chimerical. Williams meets this first, and most immediate, difficulty by proposing a sort of penumbra around the core protected interests: In addition to policing direct deprivations of traditional property and negative liberty, due process will intervene whenever "denial of the government benefit *burdens* traditional property or negative liberty." On the "burden" theory, at least vehicle registration and inspection certificates, and possibly even my driver's license, would be recognized as constitutionally-protected interests.

This seemingly modest, common-sensical extension of "liberty" and "property" proves, however, to possess a surprising, kudzu-like vigor. Its power springs from the elementary fact that most benefits government offers citizens are simply reincarnations of burdens on citizens' liberty and property. * * * The people who seek licenses, benefits, jobs, and other valuables from government are the same people who pay for those things by giving up substantial portions of their property and liberty. To take account of this, Williams reasoned, due process must also protect both (1) those benefits for which, if the individual tried to use a private substitute to escape government arbitrariness, he would have to, in effect, pay twice; and (2) those benefits for which there is effectively no private substitute because citizen-subsidized public intervention has substantially foreclosed private alternatives.

Here, then, is Williams' second difficulty. Despite his careful historical and analogical reasoning, the whole of the welfare state seems to be slipping into liberty and property through the back door of "burden." He attempts to stem this infiltration by narrowly applying his own pay-twice and private-preclusion tests. But the damage is done. Having begun with the meticulously pedigreed concepts of "liberty" as those interests which constitute individual independence from the collective, and "property" as those which represent individual security from government, he has arrived at two definitional standards—pay twice and private preclusion—that have only the most attenuated conceptual connection to the original categories. Consequently, the specific interests that pass even Williams' own stringent application of those tests—public education, social security benefits and welfare—bear little resemblance to the traditional property and liberty family. Indeed, they have a suspiciously Reichian, positive liberty cast. This internal instability is most clearly revealed when welfare—the epitome of individual dependence on government, the antithesis of the right to be let alone—can emerge from Williams' analysis wearing the name "property."

4. Looking to Function

It thus appears that neither grand theory, nor history, nor history-embraced-yet-transcended-through-analogy can meet all the necessary conditions of a successful attempt to give content to "property" and "liberty": a content that is rich enough (comprehending the new promises and perils of the regulatory state), but not too rich (constitutionalizing all of administrative government and resurrecting *Lochner*), attained through a methodology sufficiently principled and determinate to be regarded as a legitimate judicial exercise in constitutional interpretation. Yet the pressure to free due process from the jaws of entitlement is so strong that it impels still another strategy for escaping the positivist trap, a strategy that might broadly be called the functionalist approach.

Functionalism's central methodological metaphor is stepping back several paces, so as to see the forest rather than the trees. It encompasses a number of proposals that differ, sometimes radically, in their elements but that share a common determination to discover not the constitutional meaning of "property" or "liberty," but rather the constitutional function of due process.

* * *

Once the object of concern is seen to be the individual and the preservation of his capacity as autonomous moral and political agent (rather than categories of interests the protection of which is merely instrumental to this end), the question of what triggers due process protection becomes far less important. "[D]eprived of life, liberty, or property" is simply a synecdoche for the range of government actions that could endanger "what it means politically to be an individual or to act as an individual." To invoke due process scrutiny, all that would seem necessary is some nontrivial harm perpetrated or threatened against the individual by a government actor. The truly significant constitutional inquiry becomes: What exactly does protecting the individual from arbitrary government power entail?

Government could be said to act arbitrarily or unfairly when it harms the individual on the basis of a careless or unsound assessment of the facts of his case, or when it treats him less favorably than it treats similarly situated persons. But functionalist interpretations of due process, while not denigrating the importance of accuracy and equality, have not centered around either of these qualities—perhaps because entitlement analysis (whatever its other faults) is explicitly concerned with the correct application of decisional standards to the individual case, and equal protection analysis is the most direct vehicle for addressing disparate treatment. The principal contribution of functional approaches has been to insist that the fair, non-arbitrary exercise of government power requires more than simply correct outcomes and equal treatment. It also requires a process of interchange between government and the individual that acknowledges his existence and value, that respects and affirms his dignity.

A decisional process consonant with individual dignity implies, at a minimum, rights of what * * * have [been] called "revelation" and "participation." * * * Laurence Tribe explains, "Both the right to be heard from and the right to be told why, are analytically distinct from the right to secure a different outcome; these rights to interchange express the elementary idea that to be a *person*, rather than a *thing*, is at least to be *consulted* about what is done with one."[133] Consonant with our deepest intuitions about how the government of a free people ought to treat its citizens, the identification of an essential dignitary dimension seems finally to get at "what really bothers us" in the due process cases: Government should deal fairly and humanely with people, especially when it contemplates harming them, and it should not require something in positive law to trigger this obligation.

The intuitive appeal of a dignitary conception of due process can be analytically supported by tenets of moral and political theory, as well as by observations about the formation of individual and societal identity. Pincoffs locates the moral grounding of the rights to be told why, and to respond, in the Kantian injunction that each man be treated as an end in himself and not merely as a means.[134] To wreak harm on the individual without meaningfully consulting him because it is cheaper, or quicker, or simply less bother not to involve him, is to reduce him to an instrument in the service of efficiency or inertia. This moral imperative parallels a political imperative.

Mashaw explains, "This tradition has at its core the notion that individuals are the basic units of moral and political value."[136] "The protection of the due process clauses is the protection of individual liberty—a condition of liberal citizenship in which the significance of individual interests is individually determined." In such a political order, government must treat each citizen as an end in himself and not merely as a means for the attainment of collective ends. And, as Michelman points out, revelation and participation may be integral to the individual's sense of self and to the citizen's conception of his society. For the individual, learning why a government official is treating him unfavorably may "fill[ ] a potentially destructive gap in the individual's conception of himself."[138] If the harm descends in silence, he is left with the anxiety of uncertainty, never sure whether and in what respect he was found lacking; with knowledge may come pain, but also the opportunity for further self-awareness and growth. Similarly, to be able to respond to the decisionmaker, "to have played a part in, to have made one's apt contribution to, decisions which are about oneself may be counted important even though the decision, as it turns out, is the most unfavorable one imaginable and one's efforts have not proved influential." For the citizen, a rule securing this sort of process may be central to his normative vision of social and political arrangements, "expressing revulsion against the thought of life in a society that accepts it as normal for agents representing the society to make and act upon decisions about other members without full and frank interchange with those other members, a kind of accountability to them . . . ."

Finally, gathering together all these threads, Saphire shows how the dignitary dimension of due process "constitute[s] a necessary element of the consent which is essential to the continuing viability of a just and morally supportable constitutional government":

> [A]n individual's willingness ultimately to be subjected to deprivatory governmental action may be directly related to the extent to which the decisionmaking process generates "the feeling, so important to a popular government, that justice has been done" . . . . According the individual the opportunity to participate in the decisionmaking process—to face the deci-

---

[133] [LAURENCE TRIBE, AMERICAN CONSTITUTIONAL LAW 666 (2d ed. 1988)]

[134] [Edmund Pincoffs, *Due Process, Fraternity and a Kantian Injunction*, in NOMOS: DUE PROCESS 172, 172 (J. Roland Pennock & John Chapman eds., 1977).]

[136] [JERRY MASHAW, DUE PROCESS IN THE ADMINISTRATIVE STATE 182 (1985).]

[138] [Frank Michelman, *Formal and Associational Aims in Procedural Due Process*, in NOMOS: DUE PROCESS 127 (J. Roland Pennock & John Chapman eds., 1977).]

sionmaker, to receive explanation and revelation, and to react orally—preserves and enhances her sense of personal dignity and individual autonomy, and thereby strengthens the prospects for future obligation and consent.[142]

And so the dignitary conception of due process is revealed, not as some flimsy tissue of "feel good" constitutional interpretation, but as the fundamental pattern of our moral and political fabric, the strong warp and woof of our sense of our selves and our society. And, at this point, the dignitary conception unravels.

The fateful loose thread is consent. Consent, the manifestation of choice, is critically important to the picture of the individual as autonomous moral and political actor. The dignitary conception of due process is founded upon the proposition that a fair, moral society must safeguard the capacity for individual self-determination. Its proposed rights of revelation and participation are part of a larger emphasis on ensuring a system of social ordering that is comprehensible and responsive to those who dwell within it: a system in which the individual is not at the mercy of capricious, unknowable, uncontrollable forces but rather is able to engage in the deliberate ordering of his life, to contemplate competing visions of what is good and desirable, and purposefully to direct his actions towards the goals he has selected. But the foundational proposition has an equally basic corollary: A freely chosen fate is not an unfair fate. If individual dignity necessarily requires the opportunity to act and not simply to be acted upon, to determine one's own life and not simply to have one's life determined, it necessarily implies accepting responsibility for the actions one has taken, the decisions one has made. And, in many cases, one of those decisions is voluntarily to seek benefits, statuses or other relationships from government *in spite of the fact* that no procedural protections are offered.

Attempts to modify dignitary theory to take account of the significance and consequences of individual choice yielded a variant functional approach called monopoly theory. Monopoly theory begins at the familiar starting point: Due process aims to protect citizens from arbitrariness and unfairness in their interactions with government. It goes on, however, to add an important caveat: *when there is no other effective check on governmental power in the precise situation involved*.[143] One of the principal checks on government repression is extra-legal—the market. "Where government competes with private entities or other governments for some item, such as labor, then the individual has the weapon of *choice* available . . . ." If government will enter into a beneficial relationship only on terms that appear arbitrary or overreaching, but the individual nevertheless goes ahead to deal with it rather than seeking alternate providers, on which basis could government's position be condemned as unfair or illegitimate?

Hence, what follows from understanding the function of due process as the preservation of individual autonomy and self-determination is not ubiquitous rights to participation and revelation, but rather procedural protection tailored to those situations in which government's monopoly position forecloses the opportunity for choice. For due process to interpose a set of (inevitably costly) procedures beyond these situations would be not only grossly inefficient * * * but also deeply paternalistic, denying the individual the responsibility and capacity to order his relationships in a way that reflects the value *he* places on procedure.

Monopoly theory thus arrives, though by a different conceptual route, at a standard for triggering due process protection very similar to Stephen Williams' pay-twice and private-preclusion tests. In fact, monopoly theorists reach many of the same conclusions in specific cases. Welfare benefits and public education require due process protection because individuals have no choice but to deal with government to obtain these things. Occupational licenses would be protected on the same theory. By contrast, virtually no government employment relationships would be covered by due process; even in such classic public sector jobs as police officer, the individual has not only private analogues (*e.g.*, security guard) but also choice among levels and locations of governmental employers. Social security retirement payments and unemployment compensation would be protected because the individual has no choice about participating in these programs.

Although its aggressive market rhetoric jars ears attuned to dignitary reasoning, anyone who sees in due process a societal commitment to individual moral and political autonomy must take seriously monopoly theory's exploration of the conditions of individual choice. However, rigorously pursuing the

---

[142] [Richard Saphire, *Specifying Due Process Values: Toward a More Responsive Approach to Procedural Protection*, 127 U. PA. L. REV. 111, 190-91 (1978)] (*quoting* Joint Anti-Fascist Refugee Comm. v. McGrath, 341 U.S. 123, 172 (1951) (Frankfurter, J., concurring)).

[143] Timothy Terrell, *Causes of Action as Property*: Logan v. Zimmerman Brush Co. *and the "Government-As-Monopolist" Theory of the Due Process Clause*, 31 EMORY L.J. 491, 499 (1982).

concept of "choice" is a notoriously difficult undertaking—as illustrated by the loose application of the word by monopoly theorists themselves. Except in rare cases, it is not literally true (as the economist would be the first to insist) that the individual has "no choice" but to rely on government to educate his children or provide for his retirement, disability or unemployment. Perhaps, then, we are to understand the designation "no choice" as a capitulation to the average person's mulish tendency to perceive decisions which would require sacrifice of other valued possessions, activities or conditions as "not *really* choices," rather than as the purposeful implementation of preference ranking. But if "choice" is to be treated as a psychological phenomenon, how could employment be categorically distinguished? In many (perhaps most) cases, people do not experience jobs as fungible given appropriate adjustments for changes in working conditions, geographical location, etc. And jobs that *are* sufficiently common in most communities that they might be experienced by their holders in this way—for example, the pink collar and blue collar jobs that monopoly theory summarily excludes from due process protection—tend to present a different complication. If, as is often true with such jobs, private-sector alternatives do not include any procedural protection, in what sense could the individual's choice of position be said to evince the value *he* places on procedure? Disciples of the market might assure us that, in such cases, the market has accurately implemented the preference of this class of employees generally for wages and other substantive benefits over procedures. But if "choice" is merely acquiescence in some preexisting collectively struck balance of substance and procedure, as signalled by the individual's decision to enter or remain in a particular labor pool, then the constitutional status of occupational licenses must [need] to be reconsidered. And, having focused on the degree to which the individual should be held to have consented to the consequences that predictably follow from the way he chooses to order his life, can we automatically accept that recipients of welfare and other need-based benefits had "no choice" about dealing with government?

Thus, the difficulty with monopoly theory's effort to refine the dignitary conception to account for the significance of individual choice is that no coherent concept of choice emerges. In part, this comes from attempting to superimpose the idea of monopoly, a slippery enough notion in the private sector, onto the individual's interactions with government. More fundamentally, any serious inquiry into the extent of individual responsibility eventually recapitulates the debate between free will and determinism—a debate that becomes, if possible, even more vexed when directed at the condition of the individual situated in the economic, social and political reality of the contemporary regulatory state. It would seem that dignitary theory must, as its monopoly cousin insists, stake out some middle ground between the two extremes. It must establish some position in which the possibility of real autonomy and self-determination can be reconciled with the power and ubiquity of the welfare state, and in which vigilance in protecting the conditions of meaningful individual choice is accompanied by acknowledgement that the individual is responsible for what he has chosen. So far, however, dignitary theory has not been able to do so.

* * *

III. Origins

* * *

Due process is the constitutional mouthpiece through which we voice a multitude of anxious questions about the sort of society we are, and are becoming. When an individual complains that a government official harmed him through a process that seemed callous or unfair, he calls for an illumination of the relationship between citizens and the state in a world in which this relationship is increasingly critical to each citizen's ability to survive and prosper. When procedural due process doctrine reveals itself so incapable of generating satisfying answers to this call, we are tempted to blame the Court for stupidity, stubbornness, or shortsightedness. If only the justices would pay attention to what the critics are saying; if only they would just "fix" procedural due process. What the story of the last twenty years shows is that the conceptual and practical problems we perceive throughout the doctrine cannot be traced to some bungling that, with greater judicial attention, effort or humility, could be fixed. At every turn, the Court did choose badly—but only to avoid choices that appeared as bad or worse. Where we find ourselves is not a matter of carelessness or happenstance. Where we find ourselves, unfortunately, makes complete sense.

If we are to find our way out of this dilemma we must, paradoxically, go still more deeply into it. We must look past the apparent welter of disagreement to see that the doctrine and its various critiques are all born of a common vision. * * *

A. Images

* * *

Behind the frustrated tangle of doctrine and criticism that is procedural due process stand two powerful images: *entitlement* and *largess*. "Entitlement" is the more familiar of the two, for it is image become doctrine itself. We know it is the trigger, the test, the brass ring the plaintiff must be able to grab if he wants to stay on for the next round. Its role as *doctrine* disguises and, simultaneously, enhances its potency as *image*; like the critical clue in a mystery story, it is the commonplace object hiding in plain view. "Largess" also exercises conceptual power from hiding, although it is concealment of a different sort. The word plays no part as doctrine * * *. It is, however, the normal discourse of the commentary. Benefits, jobs, licenses, statuses, all the activities and services that are the potential objects of due process claims are known collectively as "government largess." The usage is ubiquitous and unself-conscious, a subliminal message conveyed in the accounts of commentators of all political and jurisprudential persuasions.

Strong words, "entitlement" and "largess" paint vivid pictures of the relationship between the people and their government. The image of "entitlement" is the image of the individual peremptorily asserting his claim to have rendered to him what is rightfully due and owing. He stands at the focal point, his posture one of demand, his tone one of righteous indignation. He is radiant with moral force. He seeks the restoration of the proper order of things, an order that has been disrupted by the stupidity or venality of figures (bureaucrats, one gathers) lurking in the shadows. The image of "largess" is the image of a potent magnate dispensing favors, a public Lord of the Manor moved by noble and generous condescension to do good works. Moral weight, as well as power, lies with this central figure; the people in the shadows are merely the objects of its charitable impulses. Their only appropriate response is eager gratitude; for them to thrust forward and make a claim would be a shocking display of spiritual degeneracy or social deviance.

That these should be the images that have dominated our thinking about procedural due process is remarkable in two respects. First, neither image seems to be a good representation of how we citizens actually experience the role of contemporary government. The entitlement picture is too grossly peremptory. It does not hold true across the range of activities in which government engages. We are likely, for example, to think about the category of government jobs differently than we think about the category of government benefits. Adding even greater complexity, our reactions vary within category. Access to public kindergarten feels different than access to public graduate school, just as we think differently about driver's licenses than about liquor or broadcast licenses, about administration of a public library than about a prison or mental health facility, about veterans benefits than about disaster relief or farm subsidies. We could doubtless identify certain characteristics of government-citizen relationships that affect our response across categories—importance, scarcity, voluntariness, and blameworthiness come immediately to mind—but their interaction is complicated. Rarely do we see a simple picture in which it is the rightful prerogative of the citizen to demand the good or service, and the correspondingly absolute duty of the public official to provide it.

At the same time, the largess picture is, if anything, even less true to our felt experience. We may not think of health benefits, liquor licenses, teaching jobs or parole as things that "belong" to the citizens who seek them. But neither do we think of them as things that "belong," absolutely and without qualification, to the government from which they are sought. Certainly we do not understand them as charity dispensable at the whim of public officials. Indeed, only the common currency of the largess image could desensitize us to its startling inappropriateness. To describe as "largess"—the "liberal giving to or as if to an inferior"—the array of opportunities and services our government provides its people out of public funds betrays an almost feudal mindset, a worldview that antedated the ascendence of democracy.

* * *

If the images of "entitlement" and "largess" jar with how we would instinctively describe the relationship between citizens and modern administrative government, why did they emerge as the dominant pictures? And why do we hold on to them, conjoining them in a way—"entitlement in largess"—that seems to condemn our thinking, from the very outset, to incoherence as well as inaccuracy? The explanation, I believe, is that behind the images stand a set of assumptions about people, power, government, and law; assumptions that are familiar objects hiding in plain view; assumptions that are the subliminal message in the accounts of courts and commentators.

* * *

B. Assumptions

* * *

Begin with an assumption about human nature: Man's most significant characteristics are his autonomous individuality and his rationality. Essentially separate from others, he comprises a unique constellation of needs, interests, and desires not shared (perhaps, not even knowable) by others. He experiences the fullness of his humanity when he brings to bear, upon questions of ends and of means, his capacity for reasoned decisionmaking. Hence, what he requires to flourish is the freedom to define and pursue his own vision of the good life, unsubjugated by other, competing visions. For him, independence is the desire and the requirement of full human personhood; the rational exercise of choice is the substance and the sign of full moral agency.

Which leads to an assumption about society: For this autonomous, rational individual, others are at least potentially dangerous. Each of them will be pursuing a particular conception of the good life. Even among men of good will, those conceptions will often be indifferent, if not actively hostile, to the realization of his vision—and he would be foolhardy to trust to an abundance of good will. Because each of the others' constellations of interests and desires is idiosyncratic and practically (if not fundamentally) unknowable to him, he can never be certain if, when, or from where the danger will materialize.

To mitigate this insecurity he reaches for a tenuous solution. The one common ground upon which he and others can meet is the human capacity for rationality. This quality will not be sufficient to enable them to attain a shared vision of the good life, at least beyond some fairly basic and limited point. The constellations of interests and desires are simply too mysterious, varied, and subjective. However, the others, as rational actors, should consent to a set of rules that guarantees the freedom of each to pursue his own vision of the good so long as that pursuit does not interfere with the reasonable freedom of others. One of these rules is that every individual is acknowledged as the equal of every other. This primary rule of equality generates a subsidiary rule: No individual's conception of the good may be privileged over any other's. Another and related rule is that obligations toward others which entail action contrary to the individual's own desires should be imposed only if he has consented, in some manner, to undertake those obligations.

Which leads to an assumption about the state: For the aggregate of autonomous, rational individuals, the state is both necessary and dangerous. The state must exist in order to secure the conditions within which the individual may pursue his vision of the good life. At the most basic level, government guarantees material security, policing the boundary between the individual's sphere of autonomy and others who might attempt to invade that sphere. Additionally, government guards the integrity of the framework of consensual interchange, maintaining conditions within which individuals can engage in mutually satisfying, voluntary relationships and exchanges. By thus safeguarding the freedom of each individual to pursue his own interests as he perceives them, government promotes the autonomy and self-fulfillment of each citizen and hence the good of society as a whole.

The state is dangerous because the power required to safeguard individual freedom may just as readily become an instrument of individual domination. Ceding power to another is always perilous. Power in the hands of government is a two-fold danger: It may be seized to serve the ends of individual government officials or private individuals acting in collaboration. This danger has intensified as industrial and technological advances render human existence more physically and economically interrelated. Protecting the individual against specific predatory incursions of others and maintaining the framework of voluntary interchange may no longer be sufficient to secure the conditions within which his freedom can be realized. Some individuals will lack, through no circumstances that could be attributed to their voluntary choice, the minimal resources necessary to experience autonomous personhood. Thus, the state must increasingly be prepared to supply, as well as to safeguard, the material conditions of human freedom. This will require taking resources from some individuals for redistribution to others. Official power, and hence opportunities for its misuse, proliferates. With every act of redistribution undertaken to enhance the autonomous personhood of some individuals, the state teeters precariously on the edge of thwarting other individuals' autonomous pursuit of their own conceptions of the good life.

And an assumption about law: Law is the instrument which accommodates the multifarious, potentially exploitive actions of autonomous, preference-pursuing individuals by providing forms and processes to control conflict. Through the institution of rights, law marks out zones within which the individual is free to pursue his own conception of the good, and across the boundaries of which further satisfaction of his desires is a matter of consensual arrangement with other rights-holders. The precise location of these boundaries will rarely be objectively demonstrable or self-evident. Hence the legitimacy of law's content generally depends upon the consent of affected individuals, obtained either directly through their participation in law-making or constructively through their assent to institutions of law-formation.

To fulfill its function most completely, law should possess certain formal characteristics. It should be general, impersonal, and objective to ensure equal treatment of autonomous individuals, none of whose conceptions of the good must be subordinated to any other's. It should be determinate, stable, and calculable to permit the fullest experience of liberty by allowing the individual confidence of its boundaries. It should be comprehensible and predictable to enable the individual to engage in the rational decisionmaking which is his quintessentially human characteristic. Even when law fails to forestall conflict, these formal attributes contribute to its success as a conflict-dampening device. When preference-pursuing individuals collide, their dispute (structured as competing claims of right) is most likely to be resolved acceptably if, after full opportunity for adversarial joining, winner and loser are declared by a third party not on the basis of his own values, but rather through the rational, objective application of recognizably impersonal, determinate, stable rules.

These assumptions are not unfamiliar. They closely correspond to what others have characterized as the classic premises of liberal legalism. To discover that they dominate procedural due process jurisprudence would not be at all surprising. Many would say they are the reigning assumptions of our entire legal system. Of course our thinking about due process originates in liberal-legalist assumptions. Why wouldn't we begin here? Where else would we begin?

The case against beginning here is, I hope, becoming clear. The jurisprudence we created has failed, conceptually and practically. Twenty years of trying to fix it has proven it to be incorrigible. We were quick to see the failure. We are slower to recognize the incorrigibility. We will be free to move forward only when we see the connection between this incorrigible failure and the set of assumptions from which we started and within which we have attempted reform. * * *

What is to be expected when a human subject whose nature is essentially solitary and self-contained, and whose primary motivation is the determined pursuit of his own needs and desires, interacts with another such subject? Perhaps, his interests will parallel those of the other, and cooperative action will be born of coincidental self-interest. If, however, interests do not so fortuitously coincide, then only a limited range of outcomes can be anticipated. The individual might attain a position of power, from which he is able to compel the other to yield to his wishes. Or, the individual might find himself in a position of subordination, in which he is at the mercy of the other's whim. The premise that actors are autonomous and egotistic allows us to imagine few patterns in between. In an encounter with another over a mutually-desired resource, one emerges either in control or under control, with the advantage or at a disadvantage. Now, imagine the possible patterns of interaction between citizen and government over the resources of the welfare state. Two pictures emerge: entitlement and largess.

These two pictures, entitlement (the image of control) and largess (the image of subordination), represent the *possible* dynamics in an encounter between the citizen-individual and the government-other. Which of the two is the *appropriate* dynamic—which, to put it somewhat differently, is the image towards which procedural due process doctrine ought to strive—cannot be known without consulting some normative reference point outside the pictures themselves. * * *

* * *

C. *Jurisprudence*

* * *

If law is conceived as the instrument through which autonomous selves protect themselves against the acquisitive behavior of others, then the Due Process Clauses become the promise of Ultimate Law. The pledge of "*due* process"—process that is owed or owing as a debt, as a natural or moral right—reassures the citizen-individual that he will not be relegated to the caprice of others for the treatment he receives. Here is process proclaimed as *right*, and a right is a powerful possession, a zone of noninterference, "a loaded gun that the rightholder may shoot at will in his corner of town."[258] In addition, this process is attached to "liberty" (the condition of freedom, from domination of other wills, that is the natural and desired state of the individual) and to "property" (the material circumstance that realizes this freedom, the safe base that enables you to deal, from strength, with the threat posed by individual and collective others). In one constitutional cluster, the central icons of liberal-legalist ideology come powerfully together, and the constitutional meaning seems clear and vivid.

However, when we invoke due process, thus conceived, to help us define the relationship between citizen and the modern regulatory state, all that ideological power works against us, confusing and obscuring what had appeared so clear. * * * If "property" is the bulwark of individual autonomy against the other, the desideratum of private limitation on collective power, how can it help us think about an individual's claim to a benefit, license or other share of public resources? It is like demanding from me the space that gives you room to defy me. If "liberty" is liberation from the oppression of the other, how can

---

[258] Roberto Unger, *The Critical Legal Studies Movement*, 96 HARV. L. REV. 561, 597 (1983).

it help us understand an individual's claim for employment, status, or other relationship with government? It is like demanding that I assist you in being left alone. If *"due* process," process as right, is a loaded gun that the holder may shoot at will in his corner of town, aren't you demanding that I hand you the gun with which you will then shoot me down?
* * *

For a Court trying to create a doctrine that simultaneously promotes each citizen's quest for autonomous self-fulfillment and protects each citizen from the natural tendency of all others to maximize their share of available resources, there could be, in the end, no choice but the positivist trap. The reality of redistribution could not be denied. The benefits and statuses clamoring for protection as the new property and liberty were inescapably someone else's traditional property and liberty transmuted. The Court could not find consent to the creation of these new rights/demands in the Due Process Clauses themselves—at least not through any interpretive process that met the liberal-legalist ideal of adjudication as a process of rationally noncontroversial reasoning from neutral principles. There was no place left but simple-majoritarian positive law, and the enforcement of whatever obligations have been undertaken there.

However, just as (given liberal-legalist assumptions) this solution was inevitable, so was it inevitably unacceptable. If the protection of due process depends on the content of ordinary law, the individual will find himself at the mercy of a majority of egotistic, preference-maximizing others—the very position from which the constitutional right was to secure him.

Reaction within the commentary was, accordingly, vehement and deep. Of all the proffered strategies for escaping the positivist trap, the boldest and most promising was dignitary theory. Its promise lay in its determination to supplant the "possessive, privatistic" view of process as an instrument to obtain public resources * * * with a "communal, interpersonal" vision of process as interaction between the citizen and his government. * * * But within the governing ideological framework, the transformation sought by dignitary theorists simply was not possible.

In good liberal-legalist fashion, these theorists assumed that human dignity resided in the distinctively human capacity for rational thought. From here it was but a short step to Kant for the ideal of a dignity-affirming process: "To treat anyone as a mere means is to deny the importance of his ends in life [*viz*, No citizen's conception of the good may be privileged over any other's] and, at the same time, to undermine his basis for self-respect" [*viz*, The individual experiences himself as fully human only when he can exert control over himself and his environment, not when he is directed by some external will].[266] This ideal would be realized through procedures that epitomized rational discourse: *revelation* by the decisionmaker of the grounds for action and *participation* by the individual in the form of responsive information and argument. These procedures would embody rationality, by enabling the individual to comprehend what is happening and to work at averting the threatened harm. Moreover, by preventing the decisionmaker from denying the individual's status as an autonomous, equal will, they would constitute the citizen's proof against being disposed of by his government as a less-than-human thing.

In this way, having set out to envision an alternative to process as privatistic, possessive and peremptory, dignitary theory came round full circle. All that had changed was the name of that to which the self-contained, self-centered citizen-individual lays claim. Listen to this description of how the dignitary conception of process (here called "nonformality") is thought to differ from the conception of process as an instrumentality to obtain desired things ("formality"): "It might be said that formality is the standpoint of an individual momentarily regarding others solely as means to his ends, while nonformality is the standpoint of an individual *steadfastly demanding* to be treated as an end and not solely as means."[267] For the self of liberal legalism, there can be no escape from privatism, no interchange with another that is not peremptory and possessive. Dignity means preserving self inviolate from others. Relationship means mutually acceding to the demand to be treated as an end—a fragile truce made possible not by growing trust, but by new-found modes of verifiability. The process which results is "interpersonal" only in that each confirms the other's right to egotistic separateness. * * *

And even if dignitary theorists imagined a more generous, responsive and compassionate relationship among persons and between the citizen and his government, they were forced to concede that it could never be attained through the mechanism of due process. In this world, law vindicates separation. A claim of right to dignity-affirming procedure *concedes* the absence of connection * * *. * * * Law could not change the nature of the self-sufficient,

---

[266] The language in brackets is mine; the underlying quotation is from [JERRY MASHAW, DUE PROCESS IN THE ADMINISTRATIVE STATE 195 (1985).]

[267] [Frank Michelman, *Formal and Associational Aims in Procedural Due Process, in* NOMOS: DUE PROCESS 131 (J. Roland Pennock & John Chapman eds., 1977) (emphasis added).]

egotistic combatants that come before it. Indeed, for it even to attempt to do so would be the grossest invasion of individual autonomy. Thus dignitary theorists reluctantly concluded that even if the citizen-individual could imagine desiring from his fellows something other than possessive, privatistic satisfaction, law could not assist him in achieving it.

Still, so disturbing was the danger from the collective other represented by the positivist trap that the accomplishment of freestanding, uncontingent rights of revelation and participation—limited as they concededly are—would have been no small victory for dignitary theory. But because even this theory rested upon a peremptory, proprietary rationale for process, it ultimately collapsed upon itself. Two hypothetical liberal-legalist selves might choose to accede to each other's demands for process that both constituted and verified respect for self-centered rationality. Within the mutuality of such a compact, neither could rightly claim that he was being used as mere means. In fact, however, the government official-individual whose thought processes and attention were being requisitioned had not consented to honor such a demand. Coercive revelation of his reasoning processes would simply reverse which individual was reduced to means towards another's ends. Thus dignitary theory found itself stymied by that most powerful of liberal-legalist touchstones, consent.

* * *

Note that the entire account, thus far, has proceeded on the assumption that interactions between individual and government are not fundamentally different than interactions between two "private" individuals. * * * This conflation of public and private is initially perplexing in an ideological universe that generally sets such stake on distinguishing between the two. The explanation for the apparent contradiction can be found by going back a moment to dignitary theory.

Dignitary theorists automatically and without discussion "pierced the veil" of government to regard the official engaged in public administration no differently than any individual acting in his private capacity. In this, they adhered to the liberal-legalist view of humans as separate, fully individuated beings with needs and desires not contingent, in either origin or satisfaction, upon others. Any group composed of such beings, even government, is simply an aggregation of separate selves, each retaining his essential nature unaltered by the incidental fact of affiliation. That one of two parties to a dispute over resources is a government official is significant only in that he possesses additional power in the struggle of contending wills. This understanding of the public official as simply another individual (who happens to have greater scope for self-regarding action) both set up and rendered irresolvable the "use as means" dilemma of dignitary theory. Since status as government agent is essentially irrelevant to individual identity and personhood, it cannot be the basis for any altered rights or responsibilities vis-à-vis other individuals (who happen to be seeking government resources).

* * *

IV. Different Origins and Intimations of a Different Doctrine

* * *

I have come a long way to offer a short proposition: We cannot use an ideology of autonomy, privacy and self-sufficiency to create a jurisprudence about the citizen's relationship to her community, access to public resources, and dependence upon governmental and private others. If we want a humane and satisfying account of procedural due process in modern society, we must begin with something other than the set of liberal-legalist assumptions. The new beginning I suggest here is a set of feminist understandings and methods.

Let me emphasize that it is indeed a *beginning* I speak of. I can tell you what I think are the new starting points, a series of understandings about human nature, knowledge, society, government and law. And I will suggest that they are better starting points, for they correspond in important ways to our experience of life in the contemporary regulatory state. At the same time, however, I must acknowledge these understandings as emerging rather than established, provisional rather than propositional. Feminist theory is quintessentially work-in-progress, historically still in its formative stages and also, more important, ideologically committed to remaining fluid, possibilistic and open to reassessing goals and strategies as perspective and experience grows.

* * *

* * * [T]he first step in this venture of beginning again is to resist all the old habits of mind that will ask for "feminist due process" to be delivered in a small black box neatly tied with pink ribbon. Feminist thought is a singularly promising source for a better due process jurisprudence precisely because of such elements as its commitment to theory emergent from and always transmutable by living context and its resistance to grand, olympian, acontextual solutions. If we are brave enough to grasp such resources, we can create a jurisprudence that allows us to imagine and realize a satisfying understanding of the relationship between we, the people, and our government.

And so I ask you to read this final section not as a denouement, in which all questions are answered and truth is finally revealed, but as an introduction. Consider it not a consummation but a prospectus, an invitation to join in the undertaking of conceiving procedural due process anew.

A. New Places to Begin

* * *

Begin with an insight into human nature. Personhood is a delicate and protean balance of intimacy and differentiation. What the self knows, feels and desires is shaped by interactions with others; without them, she could not be who she is. At the same time, she is an active agent in the creation of knowledge, feeling and desire; without her, others could not be who they are. Neither she, nor they, can thrive if she loses either her sense of separateness or her sense of connection. Her daily life confirms all this. The raising of children—in which she simultaneously teaches and learns, provides security and encourages independence, gives care and experiences being cared for—is perhaps the clearest manifestation, but it is only one of many. Students, neighbors, coworkers, parents and older relatives, lovers, friends, all reach out to her, asking from her and giving to her, confirming the subtle and varied ways in which she and they are materially, emotionally and intellectually interconnected.

Immersed in the reality of human interconnection, she had two profoundly different experiences of human response to dependence. One experience is the response of nurturance, the ethic of care, the acceptance of power as responsibility. She sees herself responding to need with compassion, finding fulfillment in helping others become fulfilled, making decisions by asking how others, as well as self, will be affected. The other experience is the response of exploitation, the ethic of selfishness, the use of power to dominate. She often experiences these as a victim. Embedded in her home, her job and her society is the threatened or realized violence of physical abuse, economic deprivation, psychological battering, spiritual violation. Sometimes, she experiences these as perpetrator. Uncared for herself, she may lose the capacity to care; without the material and psychological resources to help those who need her, she may close herself off to their suffering; a self battered and diminished by the indifference and predation of others, she may be able only to batter and diminish other selves.

Thus, for the feminist self, separation and connection, power and dependence are not simple phenomena. Inescapably part of the fabric of human existence and capable of representing great good and great evil, these qualities could not be sought or condemned in the abstract. Children can be, and are, destroyed both by abandonment and by smothering. Adults can be, and are, devastated both by being cast off as different and by being denied recognition as singular. The self with power over another can, and does, use it both to oppress and to save. The self reaching out to another for support can be, and is, met both with derision and with generosity. In the complex fabric of human relationships, the value of more separation or more connection, as well as the morality of power or dependence, can often be judged only within context.

Still, some basic dynamics can be recognized. When the sense of connection with the other is lost, dependence may come to evoke indifference and even ruthlessness, while power may readily degenerate into psychological and even physical violence. Similarly, when a person lacks the tangible and intangible resources and opportunities that her society generally regards as necessary for full participation in the life of the community, she becomes vulnerable, as a victim and a perpetrator, to abuse of power and exploitation of dependence.

The first of these dynamics, the relationship between the use of power and the sense of connection with others, implicates the matter of knowledge. For the feminist self, knowledge of others is not a simple phenomenon. The project of knowing is at once optimistic and deeply wary. It is optimistic in affirming that persons can achieve meaningful understanding of one another. Reflecting the experience that individuality is spun within a web of relationships, it does not conclude that selves are condemned to atomistic enigmaness. It is wary because feminism has discovered the dangerous tendency, particularly in those who possess power, to impose one's own experience as the norm and to dismiss different experiences as irrelevant or deviant, or silence their expression all together. Hence, the feminist search for knowledge is especially attuned to seeking out the voices of those who lack power.

The project of knowing is at once rational and resolutely nonrational. Because rationality is but one dimension of human awareness, rational discourse can be but one way of knowing. Empathic and intuitive ways of understanding must also be pursued, for feminism has discovered that privileging rationality—at least so long as rationality is equated with objectivity—facilitates domination by obscuring the connection with others who appear most different from the self in background, experience and power.

Finally, the project of knowing is determinedly contextual and concededly nonfinal. As before, this account of the epistemological enterprise is both descriptive, reflecting experienced qualities of human life, and normative, forswearing methods that lead to pain and oppression. Persons do not exist outside the interlacing of relations and experiences which shape identity and awareness, needs and desires; persons are not immutable bundles of static interests and uncontingent preferences. To ignore the importance of perspective and its multiplicity, or to fail to recognize that changes in circumstance can change the persons within them, is a prescription for disaster. The notion of truth as a unitary absolute that can be single-handedly wrestled to the ground and ever-after possessed has produced both arrogant colonizations and failed crusades, as those with power to effect change have mistaken the partial and provisional for the universal and timeless.

The second dynamic, the relationship between the use of power and the equitable distribution of resources and opportunities, implicates the matter of society, government and law. Because individual identity forms within personal relationships and social networks, society must be understood as both constituted from, and constitutive of, the persons within it. Its dominant forms of activity will both reflect and create their values, needs and desires. Just as a person continually shapes and is shaped by her local environment, so a people continually makes and is made by its government and its law. Given this, it would be meaningless to charge the state to avoid privileging certain conceptions of the good over others. All exercises of government power are value-laden. The greater the reliance upon government and law as forms of activity through which a society defines the physical, economic and social conditions in which citizens live, the greater is the need to acknowledge this fact. In any but the most minimalist state, the pursuit of neutrality is not only illusory but dangerous, disguising the fact that certain conceptions of the good and certain distributions of power are being favored.

* * *

For the feminist self, consent is not a simple phenomenon. On the one hand, the power of choosing is a significant experience of personhood. Growth, moral responsibility, and self-awareness all involve the exercise of choice; denial of the ability to choose is felt as a painful denigration of the self. On the other hand, because personhood develops within physical, social and historical context, what the person desires cannot be dissociated from the demands, expectations and opportunities she has experienced. Hence the very setting in which the person is asked or required to choose shapes, to some extent, the choice she makes. A failure to acknowledge the complexity of consent will end either in ideological paralysis (how could we decide that people should have, or do, something other than what they say they want?) or self-righteous callousness (why should we, who have better managed our lives, intervene to save consenting adults from themselves?).

In the feminist effort to conceive the good society, it becomes easier to acknowledge the disturbing complexity of choice because of the understanding that consent is not the sole benchmark of personal and public responsibility. That a person had once consented would not necessarily justify forcing her to bear a burden or forego a benefit. This is so even apart from the need to scrutinize carefully the conditions within which her choice arose. Because government and law are activities in which public values and identity are created as well as enforced, there will be interactions that public officials cannot orchestrate or facilitate, consistent with what we are and want to be, regardless of a particular citizen's willingness to endure them. By the same token, the absence of some act of consent would not necessarily preclude the presence of obligation. As the person experiences daily in her interactions with parents, siblings, children, neighbors or coworkers who are not necessarily people whom she would have chosen as friends, responsibility to exercise care and offer support sometimes arises from the fact of relationship itself. Hence, in understanding the obligations, of persons to one another and of government to persons, that inhere in the social and political relationship that is citizenship, consent may not be irrelevant—but it is surely not dispositive.

Given all this, it is not surprising that law in its adjudicatory dimension is not, for the feminist self, a simple phenomenon. In a culture in which citizens regularly bring into courts our most compelling social issues, adjudication represents a critical moment in which we examine the society we are and elaborate the one we aspire to become. Rights discourse offers a promising mechanism by which responsibility can be articulated and the distribution and use of power can be assessed. If, however, the language of rights can be used only to claim separation and to wrest away power, adjudication not only fails to realize its potential as a norm-discovering enterprise. It becomes an actual impediment, even a threat, to the creation of the good society. If one of the most powerful oracles of our values can speak only about the desirability of separateness and the danger of dependence, we will learn nothing about the indispensability of connection and the generous, responsible use of power. * * *

And if, having taught us that connection has no value and that predation is the norm, law then holds itself out as our protection from abuse of power, it promises most falsely. The feminist self, seeing the intricate and fragile web of interdependence between self and other, sees also the enormous devastation that the other can wreak if he repudiates those bonds. * * *

Feminist understandings recognize that law in its adjudicatory dimension cannot be a positive force in the quest for human flourishing so long as it distorts and denies important aspects of human existence. To be sure, rights as swords and shields are needed at some times and in some contexts. Sometimes, conditions of domination have so persistently and pervasively denied people the aspiration and capacity of self-determination that they will require, first and foremost, greater psychological and material independence. Sometimes, there will be no way (at least that we can presently imagine) to imbue power with the ethic of responsibility and concern, so that it can be rendered safe only by taking it away or by providing those subject to it with some defensive capability. But, at other times rights must function as bridges and channels, through which connection is established and affirmed and those with power are led to recognize responsibility and encouraged to act with compassion. Many times, a cycle of suffering can be broken only by seeking out affinity and nurturing cooperation to replace alienation and contention. Many times, power can be rendered safe only by acknowledging its reality and cultivating, in the very fact of its inevitability, a fiduciary ethic and a practice of care.

* * *

B. New Ways to Proceed

* * *

If we began from these substantive and methodological understandings, what sort of due process jurisprudence might we create?

First, we would read the text very differently. We would see in "*due* process" the promise of process appropriate, satisfying and suitable. The phrase would become an assurance of the treatment that is fitting whenever government finds it must do harm to one of its citizens, treatment in which there is acknowledgement of loss inflicted, and respect for pain incurred. That such process attaches to "life, liberty and property" bespeaks a concern with the whole of human existence, the material and psychological well-being of each that depends upon a collective commitment of respect and support. We would therefore recognize in the clauses an affirmation of the connection between the people and their government, and a pledge that government will use its tremendous power with care. The phrases would become for us an exhortation to concerned contextualization, rather than a mandate of distancing abstraction. We would understand process as "right," but understand "right" as a claim of relationship rather than a defense of separation.

The reasons why we, the people, would want such provisions in our formative document would not be hard to fathom. As persons and as citizens, we are creatures spun within a social web. Government is one of the principal institutions through which that web is shaped. Whenever the state acts as educator, employer, healer, discipliner or dispenser of needed goods and services, our individual and collective identities hang in balance. If a citizen's interaction with the state becomes an experience of frustration, self-loathing or despair, we are individually and collectively diminished. We would want our government to have always before it a reminder of this grave and special responsibility. And, at the most basic level, we would recognize that our lives depend upon the strength and vitality of this sense of connection. If the vast reservoir of public power is to be rendered safe, those who govern must never be permitted to regard citizens as alien, the other, the enemy. Hence, our aspirations and our very survival coalesce in this overarching injunction to our government (ourselves) to take care in dealing with its people (one another), an injunction that integrates and transcends all the specific exhortations to care in surrounding, more particular constitutional clauses.

Understanding the clauses in this way, we would not see the striking increase in due process litigation during this century as an unfortunate and dangerous exploitation of an accommodatingly vague phrase. Rather, we would recognize this litigation as an ongoing enterprise in self-discovery and definition, in which we seek to comprehend, humanize and render benevolent the increasingly complex, powerful and interdependent society in which we live. We would see in due process the quintessential instance of rights as "a form of communal dialogue" and realize that, of all adjudication, due process adjudication in particular could never be value-free, detached, abstract, universal, or final. We would understand that, especially at this point in our history, we *need* due process adjudication to be a consciously value-creating occasion that emphasizes the relationship between government and its people and elaborates the qualities and responsibilities of that relationship. Moreover, we would, for several reasons, perceive this enterprise as far more challenging, and far more hopeful, than we have regarded it till now.

Consider, for example, the issue of dependence. We have, until now, accepted liberal legalism's word that dependence is a dreadful thing—that it is inconsistent with full personhood (the unfettered exercise of self-determination is the essence of psychic satisfaction and moral responsibility) and fraught with peril (the other on whom one is dependent can only be expected to exploit the imbalance of power). Escaping dependence has thus been an irresistible force within procedural due process jurisprudence. And it has met the immovable object of the contemporary regulatory state. If there were ever a time when the individual could avoid dependence upon the collective, that time is gone. If it were ever possible for the citizen to aspire to a balance of power with government, it is possible no longer. The state will inevitably control access to things that we desire and require, from drivers' licenses to assistance in time of catastrophe. The state's agents will inevitably have discretion that could be used against us, no matter how rule-bound the regulatory regime. * * *

* * * Once we are freed of the burden of maintaining an impossible self-deception, we can raise our eyes to face the real question: How do we make relationships in which one person must place herself in another person's hands, relationships which do not imperil the humanity of *either* participant? Following one of the central methodological credos of feminism—learn from a thoughtful, critical examination of lived experience—we would begin to thread our way between the twin perils of despair and romanticism. We would remember that there are good parents (biological and adoptive, permanent and transitional) who raise children with love and discipline without making them feel smothered or abused, good teachers who share knowledge with students without making them feel ashamed of what they do not know, and good caretakers who lend strength to those who are in need of support without making them feel less than human for their need. From these experiences, we would know that humans can respond to even great disparities in power with compassion, responsibility and respect. And so we would have hope that human organizations could be structured to enshrine and nurture such response. At the same time, however, we would remember that families, schools and institutions have also been the sites of the most terrible violence to personhood. From this hard-won consciousness of oppression, we would know that a sentimental view of relationship can mask the cruel exploitation of imbalances in material, intellectual or psychological resources. And so we would be wary to ferret out the domination that may hide in situations of dependence. We would, in short, recognize (in yet another way) that the personal is political, as we discover that we are trying to achieve in our public life what we try to achieve in our private lives: individuation without severing connection, dependence without victimization, relationship in which selfhood is found rather than lost.

Once we reconceive *what* we are trying to do, we would have a very different understanding of *how* we should go about doing it. Due process jurisprudence has long claimed a special fluidity and sensitivity to context. Until now, however, we have been caught within the liberal-legalist drive towards determinacy, predictability and universality. Each case bore the normative responsibility of producing and conforming to abstract decisional principles capable not only of being applied, consistently and unequivocally, across the vast range of administrative contexts but also of being translated, without underprotectiveness or overintrusion, to substantive due process, takings and criminal, quasi-criminal and traditional civil adjudication. This ideological pressure to create a monolithic, self-subsistent doctrinal system left us precious little room for adaptability and innovation—and even less chance for success. * * *

Now, however, we would accept from the outset that there are no universal, multi-purpose answers. Just as the nature and needs of relationships between persons vary over time and within setting, so it must be with relationships between citizen and government. As we work to understand and perfect those relationships through invocations of due process, we will discover no philosopher's stone by which to transmute the multitude of interests implicated by government actions, no single formula for a procedural panacea. * * *

* * *

Our thinking about what interests "trigger" due process would not be caught in the positivist trap, for we would neither fear the perils nor yearn for the solutions that made the trap so fatally seductive for liberal legalism. For one thing, positive law would no longer appear the safe haven of judicial legitimacy. Once we abandon, as undesirable as well as impossible, the picture of adjudication as a value-neutral exercise in detached ratiocination, we will measure the legitimacy of judicial action not by *whether* it furthers some particular set of values, but rather by *which* values it furthers. In searching for the values that will foster human flourishing, we would understand that a positive law pedigree can provide no imprimatur. Consent is too surely contingent and too often compromised and is, in any event, not the sole touchstone of civic responsibility. In locating the meaning of government's duty of care, we would recognize that the outcome of the political processes can be but one source to consult.

In addition, the shadow of *Lochner* would recede as we accept the possibility that procedural due process implicates different interests than those which trigger substantive due process and takings analysis. Thus far, we have been confounded by the riddle of how the Constitution could intervene to mandate procedural protection for deprivation of an interest it did not require government to provide in the first place. Now, however, we would see the animating concern of procedural due process to be *how* government treats its people; *what* it is taking from them is significant only indirectly. * * * We would * * * understand that the protection of relationship is different than the protection of things. We would recognize that we do not have to think about a claim that government must take care in distributing benefits or imposing burdens as if it were a claim that government must distribute benefits or may not impose burdens.

In this sense, we would pursue the important insight of dignitary theorists that the primary focus of procedural due process should be on the quality of the interaction between government and citizen. However, because we would understand the nature and implications of that interaction very differently, we could avoid the pitfalls that condemned those theorists, within their liberal-legalist framework, to failure.

* * * Understanding personhood as a continually and necessarily interactive process rather than as a static and self-sufficient state, and viewing interchange with others as the way in which knowledge, desires and values are created rather than as a mutually exploitative confrontation, we would not regard the responsibility to communicate with another as a reduction to mere means. Indeed, affirming such a responsibility would be one of the clearest commitments to nurturing the personhood of both citizen and government official. *Each* participant in the dialogue is understood as helpful, and indeed necessary, to the fulfillment of the other. We have always assumed that the official has information which could help the citizen better order her life, presently and in the future; we would now affirm, as equally important, that the citizen has information which could help the official better do her job, presently and in the future. If knowledge is situated in context and contingent upon perspective, then a decisionmaker cannot learn to use her power wisely unless she listens to those who are affected by her decisions. Perhaps more important, in the act of interchange itself we create at least the potential for citizen and official to discover their commonality. If the responsible and careful use of power is rooted in the recognition of connection, then *both* participants have a stake in practices that facilitate this recognition. * * *

* * *

In this search for practices that foster the benign use of discretion, we would be both inspired and compelled to push our thinking beyond the narrow limits of adversary trial procedures. We would be inspired by our more hopeful view of human nature. Knowing that people are capable of using power responsibly and regardfully, we would realize that such capacity is not nurtured by encouraging official and citizen to regard each other as combatants, or by framing their interactions on the assumption that each will take advantage of the other whenever possible. For our litigation-bound legal consciousness, imagining alternative ways of proceeding that facilitate empathetic and nonadversarial decisionmaking is not easy, but there are signs that it is possible. With our rising interest in alternative dispute resolution techniques, we are slowly reaching out to other disciplines—psychology, sociology, anthropology—to broaden our conception of problem-solving methods. * * *

* * *

We frequently have been told that the goal of making public administration careful, compassionate, and courteous is utterly beyond the power of constitutional law. Until now, this was surely so. So long as human nature is modelled as fixed and the proper role of judges is prescribed as merely ending particular disputes through disinterested application of preexisting neutral rules, it is nonsensical (even threatening) to speak of the symbolic and transformative potential of constitutional adjudication. So long as courts preside over a ritualized form of combat in which truth emerges victorious from confrontation, it is ludicrous to think that the loser can be ordered to love one who has been cast, from the outset, as his enemy. If, however, we understood our individual collective identity as a constantly evolving, interactive process as much shaped by, as shaping, such culturally important activities as constitutional adjudication, then we would realize the self-fulfilling quality of predictions about what those activities can accomplish. We are a society in which judgments about the constitutionality of specific practices are frequently taken as judgments about the morality and appropriateness of those practices. For almost twenty years, due process adjudication has told administrators either that their "clients" have no right to complain about how they have been treated ("no standards, no obligations") or that they themselves can't be trusted to do their job right ("courts decide what process yields accurate decisions"). When these are the messages it has been sending, is it any wonder that contemporary procedural due process jurisprudence has not contributed to—and may indeed have undermined—the emergence of a responsible, committed and humane public administration?

How do we know what might be possible if procedural due process adjudication became a self-consciously value-generating activity in which all participants come together to discover what is right, rather than a battle in which wrongdoers are unmasked and forced to yield? Hard as it is for us to think about litigation in this way, there are even in our present world faint glimmers of hope that such an alteration is possible. Sometimes, in institutional and other complex litigation, trial judges (or their masters) find ways to refocus the adversarial, blame-inflicting tendencies of litigants and emphasize forward-looking, collaborative approaches to finding solutions. Working from a set of feminist understandings and methods, we might actually achieve the transformation of adjudication that could, in turn, transform what procedural due process jurisprudence can accomplish. From our understanding of the nature and sources of knowledge, we would recognize the importance of a judicial approach that actively seeks out the perspectives of those who live and shape the particular regulatory situation. We would not minimize the challenge of comprehending and appropriately integrating the experience of the welfare recipient or the front-line agency worker. But we would recognize that listening to these voices *in addition* to the voices of agency administrators and lawyers is not a matter of pluralism or equal time or simple courtesy. It is an epistemological and remedial imperative. We would realize that sound solutions can not be developed, let alone successfully implemented, through a process in which isolated judges formulate and deliver answers from on high.

What we would learn from this commitment to broadened participation in the discovery of due process answers might at times be difficult for us to accept. Perhaps, for example, we would be forced to acknowledge that the process patterns of revelation and participation, which have had a remarkable currency across political and philosophical camps, are the process ideals of an elite—we lawyers, scholars, and judges for whom words are powerful instruments and comfortable extensions of self. We would constantly be required to reassess our expectations not simply of what sort of process is good (is the interjection of lawyers anything other than the interjection of adversarialness?), but even of what sort of process is possible (what if a panel of welfare recipients from the community helped make continued eligibility determinations?).

And this continual reminder of the limits of our understanding of a complex world would further transform procedural due process jurisprudence, as we openly admit to the provisional, modifiable, even experimental character of the answers that emerge. The concept of solutions that depend upon context, and are modifiable with new information and circumstance, has never been completely alien to adjudication. Equity practice, particularly the injunction, has long included a self-conscious commitment to flexibility and adaptability. However, so long as liberal legalism modelled law as the marking of boundaries between opposing camps and adjudication as the public declaration of right-holder and wrongdoer, it was almost impossible for courts to avoid pronouncing absolute, timeless truth that could be altered only by a system-wrenching confession of error. Now, however, we would recognize that being "correct" in due process adjudication—as in any of the other practices by which we seek to understand and enrich our lives—is a matter of being situated in particular perspectives upon which we are obligated, always, to try to improve. And we would come to see in the continual, contextual reexamination of the practices we devise not the sign of failure, but rather the promise of success.

* * *

Additional Sources

C. Edwin Baker, *Property and Its Relation to Constitutionally Protected Liberty*, 134 U. Pa. L. Rev. 741 (1986)

Henry Friendly, *"Some Kind of Hearing,"* 123 U. Pa. L. Rev. 1267 (1975)

Sanford H. Kadish, *Methodology and Criteria in Due Process Adjudication—A Survey and Criticism*, 66 Yale L.J. 319 (1957)

Hans Linde, *Due Process of Lawmaking*, 55 Neb. L. Rev. 197 (1976)

Jerry L. Mashaw, DUE PROCESS IN THE ADMINISTRATIVE STATE (1985)

Jerry L. Mashaw, *Administrative Due Process: The Quest for a Dignitary Theory*, 61 B.U. L. Rev. 885 (1981)

Jerry L. Mashaw, *The Management Side of Due Process: Some Theoretical and Litigation Notes on the Assurance of Accuracy, Fairness and Timeliness in Adjudication of Social Welfare Claims*, 59 Cornell L. Rev. 772 (1974)

Frank Michelman, *Formal and Associational Aims in Procedural Due Process*, in NOMOS XVIII: DUE PROCESS (J. Roland Pennock & John W. Chapman eds., 1977)

Martin H. Redish & Lawrence C. Marshall, *Adjudicatory Independence and the Values of Procedural Due Process*, 95 Yale L.J. 455 (1986)

Rodney A. Smolla, *The Reemergence of the Right-Privilege Distinction in Constitutional Law: The Price of Protesting Too Much*, 35 Stan. L. Rev. 69 (1982)

Timothy Terrel, *"Property," "Due Process," and the Distinction Between Definition and Theory in Legal Analysis*, 70 Geo. L.J. 861 (1982)

John Thibaut & Laurens Walker, *A Theory of Procedure*, 66 Cal. L. Rev. 541 (1978)

Laurence Tribe, *Structural Due Process*, 10 Harv. C.R.-C.L. L. Rev. 269 (1975)

William Van Alstyne, *Cracks in "The New Property": Adjudicative Due Process in the Administrative State*, 62 Cornell L. Rev. 445 (1977)

2. The Debate About Nonlegislative Rule Exemptions to Notice-and-Comment Rulemaking Procedures

One of the major innovations in the Administrative Procedure Act is notice-and-comment rulemaking. Such rulemaking involves publication in the Federal Register of a notice of what is being proposed, a comment period during which the public can file written remarks about the proposed rule, and the agency's statement of the final rule's basis and purpose. The APA's framers intended to establish not only a reasonably efficient process but also one that involved the public.

Yet the APA's framers also wanted to assure that agencies could issue policy guidances that were nonbinding, as well as interpretations of already existing legal obligations in statutes or legislative-type rules, without having to go through notice-and-comment procedures. General statements of policy and interpretive rules—"nonlegislative" rules—allow an agency to provide information to the public without complying with notice-and-comment requirements.*

For at least two reasons, agencies in recent years have tended to make increased use of the nonlegislative rule exemptions. First, from a bureaucratic perspective, it is generally easier and less costly to issue interpretive rules and statements of policy than to go through the notice-and-comment process. Second, over the years enhanced analytical burdens on notice-and-comment rulemaking—such as those associated with presidential oversight and judicial hard-look review—have created additional incentives to develop policy through nonlegislative mechanisms.**

The excerpts in this section debate the question whether agencies should be given relatively less or more discretion to exercise power by means of nonlegislative rulemaking. In the first excerpt, Professor Robert A. Anthony criticizes the broad use of nonlegislative rule exemptions.

In the second excerpt, Professor Peter Strauss defends the use of what he calls "publication" rules, namely, interpretive rules or general statements of policy that are published but not promulgated with notice-and-comment procedures under 5 U.S.C. § 553. Professor Strauss suggests that publication rules serve important functions.

The third article by Professor Michael Asimow surveys the territory of nonlegislative rulemaking. He argues that reformers of the administrative process should give separate treatment to legislative and nonlegislative rules while recognizing that each has a role to play in a mature administrative system.

---

* There are other exemptions from notice-and-comment rulemaking procedures under 5 U.S.C. § 553. This section of the anthology focuses specifically on the "nonlegislative" rule exemptions for general statements of policy and interpretive (or interpretative) rules.

** For development of the second theme, see Thomas McGarity's article cited in the list of additional sources at the end of this section.

Robert A. Anthony, *Interpretive Rules, Policy Statements, Guidances, Manuals, and the Like—Should Federal Agencies Use Them to Bind the Public?*, 41 DUKE L.J. 1311, 1312-19, 1321-30, 1359-64, 1372-79 (1992)*

Introduction and Summary

With one exception, the answer to the question in the title is "no." To use such nonlegislative documents to bind the public violates the Administrative Procedure Act (APA) and dishonors our system of limited government. This is true whether the agency attempts to bind the public as a legal matter or as a practical matter. An agency may not make binding law except in accordance with the authorities and procedures established by Congress. To make binding law through actions in the nature of rulemaking, the agency must use legislative rules, which ordinarily must be made in accordance with the notice-and-comment procedures specified by § 553 of the APA.

The sole category of exceptions—where an agency may permissibly attempt to make a substantive nonlegislative rulemaking document binding on private parties—is for interpretive rules. These are rules that interpret statutory language which has some tangible meaning, rather than empty or vague language like "fair and equitable" or "in the public interest." An agency may nonlegislatively announce or act upon an interpretation that it intends to enforce in a binding way, so long as it stays within the fair intendment of the statute and does not add substantive content of its own. Because Congress has already acted legislatively, the agency need not exercise its own delegated legislative authority. Its attempts to enforce an interpretation can be viewed as simply implementing existing positive law previously laid down by Congress. As a practical matter, the agency in this way gives the interpretation a binding effect. The same is true where the agency interprets its own previously promulgated legislative rules.

By contrast, * * * when an agency uses rules to set forth new policies that will bind the public, it must promulgate them in the form of legislative rules. The statutory procedures for developing legislative rules serve values that have deep importance for a fair and effective administrative process and indeed for the maintenance of a democratic system of limited government.

Except to the extent that they interpret specific statutory or regulatory language, then, *nonlegislative rules like policy statements, guidances, manuals and memoranda should not be used to bind the public*. While these nonlegislative rules by definition cannot *legally* bind, agencies often inappropriately issue them with the intent or effect of imposing a *practical* binding norm upon the regulated or benefited public. Such use of nonlegislative policy documents is the capital problem addressed by this Article.

* * *

Although the subject is complex and evidence is laborious to assemble, it is manifest that nonobservance of APA rulemaking requirements is widespread. Several agencies rely in major part upon nonlegislative issuances to propagate new and changed elements in their regulatory or benefit programs.[15] This Article examines a number of agency attempts to make nonlegislative policy documents bind the public. Frequently such rules are not challenged in court, because the affected private parties cannot afford the cost or the delay of litigation, or because for other practical reasons they must accept a needed agency approval or benefit on whatever terms the agency sets.

The use of nonlegislative policy documents generally serves the important function of informing staff and the public about agency positions, and in the great majority of instances is proper and indeed very valuable. But the misuse of such documents—to bind, where legislative rules should have been used—carries great costs. Affected members of the public are likely to be confused or misled about the reach and legal quality of the standards the agency has imposed. One consequence of this uncertainty can be that affected persons are unaware that the agency intends to give its nonlegislative issuance binding effect. Probably more often, though, the private parties realize all too clearly that the agency will insist upon strict compliance, but conclude that there is little they can do to resist. In either case, the uncertainty can breed costly waste of effort among private parties trying to puzzle out how far they are bound or otherwise affected by the informal agency document.

Doubtless more costly yet is the tendency to overregulate that is nurtured when the practice of making binding law by guidances, manuals, and memoranda

---

* Reprinted with permission of Duke Law Journal and Robert A. Anthony. All rights reserved.

[15] Examples are the Health Care Financing Administration with respect to Medicare and Medicaid, the Department of Education with respect to guaranteed student loans, the Federal Energy Regulatory Commission with respect to regulation of pipelines, and the Nuclear Regulatory Commission with respect to reactor safety.

is tolerated. If such nonlegislative actions can visit upon the public the same practical effects as legislative actions do, but are far easier to accomplish, agency heads (or, more frequently, subordinate officials) will be enticed into using them. Where an agency can nonlegislatively impose standards and obligations that as a practical matter are mandatory, it eases its work greatly in several undesirable ways. It escapes the delay and the challenge of allowing public participation in the development of its rule. It probably escapes the toil and the discipline of building a strong rulemaking record. It escapes the discipline of preparing a statement of the basis and purpose justifying the rule. It may also escape APA publication requirements and Office of Management and Budget regulatory review. And if the agency can show that its informal document is not final or ripe, it will escape immediate judicial review. Indeed, for practical reasons it may escape judicial review altogether.

One can readily understand how a governmental instrument so quick, cheap, largely unchecked and low in risk, and yet so effectual, may tempt some agencies to slight the APA's mandates.

A particularly perverse phenomenon arises from some courts' emphasis upon the discretion retained by the agency as an indicator of the nonbinding character of its issuance. Under this approach, the more discretion the agency reserves in a document, the better are its chances that a court will hold that legislative rulemaking procedures were not required, even though the public was plainly meant to be bound. The theory is that the agency, by reserving discretion, has not bound itself. But the incentives work the wrong way here. The prospect of avoiding legislative procedures encourages the agency to be cagey rather than candid, and to state its rules loosely rather than precisely. A preferable test would consider whether the constraints on private persons amount to a binding of *those persons.* Otherwise, it is perfectly easy for a document to reserve plenty of discretion for the agency to act variantly, even where it makes clear that private parties will be held to strict conformity. Any tactical advantage the agency may gain will come at the expense of clarity and fairness to affected private persons.

* * *

I. A Short Taxonomical Guide to Agency Rulemaking

* * *

B. *Legislative and Nonlegislative Rules*

* * *

* * * Legislative rules *can* readily be differentiated from those that are nonlegislative. The fundamental idea is that a "legislative rule is the product of an exercise of delegated legislative power to make law through rules."

More particularly, a rule qualifies as legislative if all of the following requirements are met: 1) The agency must possess delegated statutory authority to act with respect to the subject matter of the rule. 2) Promulgation of the rule must be an intentional exercise of that delegated authority. 3) The agency must also possess delegated statutory authority to make rules with the force of law. 4) Promulgation of the rule must be an intentional exercise of the authority to make rules with the force of law. 5) Promulgation of the rule must be an effective exercise of that authority. 6) The promulgation must observe procedures mandated by the agency's organic statute and by the APA. Particularly, unless it falls within an exemption in the organic legislation or in the APA, the rule must be developed through public notice-and-comment procedures and be published in the *Federal Register.* * * *

An agency's issuance is a valid legislative rule if and only if it meets all six of these requirements. *All substantive rules that do not fit this template are nonlegislative. They are either interpretive rules (if they interpret specific statutory or regulatory language) or policy statements (if they do not).*

The APA requires the use of legislative rulemaking procedures for every rule unless the rule falls within one of the statutory exceptions. The courts have repeatedly declared that the exceptions are to be narrowly construed and reluctantly recognized, so as not to defeat the salutary purposes behind the notice-and-comment provisions of section 553. For present purposes we must lay to the side the exceptions pertaining to the subject matter of rules and to the existence of good cause to dispense with the statutory procedures. These exceptions do not relate to the rules' legal quality. And the exception for rules of agency organization, procedure or practice is also set to the side. It bears only peripherally on the present study, which is concerned with agency control or guidance of private conduct—that is, with substantive rather than procedural rules. The exceptions that are of concern here are those for interpretive rules and policy statements.

C. *Interpretive Rules and Policy Statements*

Our focus, then, is upon substantive rules, which under the APA may be 1) legislative rules, 2) interpretive rules, or 3) policy statements. This is the entire universe of substantive rules.

At this point, it is useful to envision a simple grid. Norms that interpret can be issued either legislatively or nonlegislatively. Norms that do not interpret can also be issued either legislatively or nonlegislatively. All issued legislatively under the tests stated above are legislative rules, whether they interpret or not. Those that are not legislative are either interpretive rules or policy statements, depending upon whether they interpret or not.

* * *

An interpretive rule is an agency statement that was not issued legislatively and that interprets language of a statute (or of an existing legislative rule) that has some tangible meaning.

A policy statement is an agency statement of substantive law or policy, of general or particular applicability and future effect, that was not issued legislatively and is not an interpretive rule.

* * *

All substantive nonlegislative issuances that are not interpretive rules are policy statements—whether they are captioned or issued as policy statements or manuals or guidances or memoranda or circulars or press releases or even as interpretations.

* * *

II. Nonlegislative Rules with Binding Effect

* * *

This Article deals with nonlegislative rules that have the purpose or effect of binding the public *as a practical matter*. These are nonlegislative documents that are intended to impose mandatory standards or obligations, or that as a practical matter are given that effect.

In general, a nonlegislative document is binding as a practical matter if the agency treats it the same way it treats a legislative rule—that is, as dispositive of the issues that it addresses—or leads the affected public to believe it will treat the document that way. Certain indicia that nonlegislative documents are binding in this practical sense are clearly identifiable.

Obviously, agency *enforcement action* based upon nonobservance of the nonlegislative document, or the threat of such action, bespeaks a clear intent to bind and indeed puts it into execution. Here the eating is the proof of the pudding.

Similarly, in the setting of agency actions that pass upon applications for approvals, permits, benefits, and the like, *regular application of the standards* set forth in the document evidences both the intent to bind and a practical binding effect.

A document will have practical binding effect before it is actually applied if the affected private parties are reasonably *led to believe* that failure to conform will bring adverse consequences, such as an enforcement action or denial of an application. If the document is couched in mandatory language, or in terms indicating that it will be regularly applied, a binding intent is strongly evidenced. In some circumstances, if the language of the document is such that private parties can rely on it as a norm or safe harbor by which to shape their actions, it can be binding as a practical matter.

It is possible that an agency will use mandatory or rigid language even though it does not intend the document to be regularly applied without further consideration. There is nevertheless a practical binding effect if private parties suffer or reasonably believe they will suffer by noncompliance. This phenomenon can occur especially where the document is issued at headquarters but administered in the field. Mandatory language in the document may combine with the routinized behavior of the field staff to produce a practical binding effect upon affected private parties. Although the document may not have been intended to be "finally determinative of the issues or rights to which it is addressed," its practical *effect* is to bind, and affected persons may not be able to risk noncompliance to test it. Similarly, a document that initially was intended to be nonbinding, or one as to which the intent was unclear, may harden into a fixed rule, with binding effect, by repeated application.

A further emblem of practical binding effect is the absence of an opportunity for affected private parties to be heard on proposed policy alternatives, before the policy set forth in the document is concretely applied to them, and to have their proposals considered with an open mind by the agency's policymakers. If the document is to be applied rigidly to private persons without first affording them a realistic chance to challenge its policy, its binding effect is evident. By the same token, if the agency affords such an opportunity and genuinely is open to reconsideration of the policy, the document shows neither the intent to bind nor such an effect.

All of these practical binding effects will be more severe where the affected private parties, for practical reasons, cannot invoke the aid of the courts to challenge the documents. For example, regulations may require the exhaustion of lengthy intra-agency appeals before the challenged permit can be used, even on the agency's terms.

Applying the above guides to determine when a document has practical binding force may not always be easy. As Chief Judge Patricia Wald has well observed with respect to one aspect of the problem, "[d]etermining whether a given agency action is interpretive or legislative is an extraordinarily case-specific endeavor." Similarly, Judge Kenneth Starr, having stated that a "legislative rule is recognizable by virtue of its binding effect," declared that "[t]his definitional principle, however, is hardly self-executing," and cited a number of "factors" to be examined.[99] * * *

* * *

V. The Role of Agency Discretion

As a gauge of whether an agency should have issued a policy document legislatively, the courts have made much of the discretion reserved by the agency. Certainly there is a major role for this element of the analysis. In many cases, however, it should not be determinative.

In his important *McLouth Steel [Products Corp. v. Thomas]* opinion, Judge Stephen Williams succinctly stated the test that he distilled from numerous D.C. Circuit opinions: "The question for purposes of paragraph 553 is whether a statement is a rule of present binding effect; the answer depends on whether the statement constrains the agency's discretion." The point of this approach is that, if the agency has acted *tentatively*, and reserves discretion to reconsider and to revise or vary or rescind the policy before concretely applying it, then neither the agency nor an affected private party is bound, either as a legal matter or in a practical sense. On this basis, an agency would not err in announcing its policy through a nonlegislative document.

These conclusions must rest, however, on the assumption that, *before applying the policy concretely to a private party*, the agency either will promulgate it as a legislative rule or will hold its mind open to reconsider the policy and to accord the affected party an opportunity to challenge its wisdom.

One difficulty is that this assumption is not made explicit in the cases. At bottom, however, the problem is that the assumption will be faulty in particular cases. * * * [T]he agency may well have settled firmly upon its policies, with every intent of exacting conformity from those affected. The fact that the policy is announced in a nonlegislative document—and speaks of reserved discretion to act at variance with it—does not change that intent. But under the D.C. Circuit's test, this tactic furnishes the agency with a convenient chance to have things both ways: to impose a practical binding effect upon private parties, but also plausibly to argue to the courts that the informal issuance and reserved discretion prove there was no obligation to proceed legislatively. This strategy may through bureaucratic habit be pursued in the best of faith. But in reviewing the cases one cannot avoid suspecting that the agencies consider it easy to fool the courts on these points, or at least think it is worth arguing, in the face of manifest reality, that their reservation of discretion means that they have not bound the complaining members of the public.

In fact, despite any professed reservation of discretion, a nonlegislative document as a practical matter can quite readily impose binding standards or obligations upon private parties. Their discretion is constrained even if the agency's is not. A test more consistent with the spirit of the APA than one looking to the constraints on an agency's discretion would be considered whether the intended or actual constraints on the *private persons' discretion* (that is, upon their freedom of action) amount to binding them in a practical sense. If so, the recitation that discretion is reserved should be of no moment, and the agency's circumvention of legislative rulemaking procedures should be redressed.

These points may be illustrated by the following form of disclaimer, which the EPA prepared in the summer of 1991 for inclusion in guidances and other nonlegislative issuances:

> NOTICE: The policies set out in this [document] are not final agency action, but are intended solely as guidance. They are not intended, nor can they be relied upon, to create any rights enforceable by any party in litigation with the United States. EPA officials may decide to follow the guidance provided in this [document] or to act at variance with the guidance, based on an analysis of site-specific circumstances. The Agency also reserves the right to change this guidance at any time without public notice.

It scarcely needs to be observed that this provision is wholly one-sided. * * * The quoted EPA statement preserves great discretion for the agency. But it yields no flexibility to affected persons, nor does it afford any assurance that they will have a realistic chance to challenge the substantive policy positions set forth in the document.

The literal application of the D.C. Circuit's discretion test would sanction the use of nonlegislative procedures for a document endorsed with this disclaimer. And yet if the document is binding as a practical matter—because it is framed in mandatory terms or is regularly applied or is so structured that in context affected persons cannot disregard it—it would be quite wrong to hold that such a disclaimer

---

[99] The factors * * * that reinforced the conclusion that the agency intended the action to have binding effect were: mandatory language, prior grant of "exemptions," publication in the Code of Federal Regulations, limitation upon the agency's discretion, and whether the agency could successfully prosecute persons who had complied with the document.

excuses the failure to observe notice-and-comment requirements.

To do so in such a case would leave the private party in the worst of possible worlds: The private party is bound but the agency retains full freedom to act at variance with its stated position. The reservation of discretion affords the agency scope for unpredictable behavior, without diminishing the prospective compliance burden on the private party. Alternatively, there is little to deter the agency, despite its reservation of discretion to decide variantly, from relentlessly applying the stated positions as though they had the full force of law.

Under the corollary to the D.C. Circuit's position—that the more discretion the agency reserves the less likely it is that the rule will be treated as legislative—the agency is rewarded for stating its rules with less precision and authority than might otherwise be required of it. Yet as a practical matter it still may be able to apply or threaten to apply the rule in a binding way. It is simply bad government to tolerate the notion that the more discretion an agency reserves for itself the more readily it can escape the obligation to promulgate its rules in the manner instructed by Congress.

Only if the agency makes it clear that it retains an open mind on the final terms of the policy should the fact that it retains discretion validate its use of nonlegislative guidance documents. If the agency mind is open, the affected party's opportunity at a later proceeding to contend for an alternative or modified policy, or for abandonment of the tentatively adopted one, is the functional equivalent of the opportunity to comment in a legislative rulemaking proceeding.

* * *

But if the outcome of the later proceeding is a foregone conclusion because the earlier policy statement or guidance was to be mechanically applied, there clearly has been an intent or an effect making it binding on the private parties as a practical matter, and legislative rulemaking should have been used.

* * *

VI. Administration of Policies by Agency Staff and by the States

* * *

A. *Administration of Nonlegislative Policy Documents by Agency Staff*

General knowledge of normal bureaucratic behavior permits us to postulate a basic general proposition about how nonlegislative guidance documents are administered by the agencies' own staffs, especially in the field: Staff members acting upon matters to which the guidance documents pertain will routinely and indeed automatically apply those documents, rather than considering their policy afresh before deciding whether to apply them. Staffers generally will not feel free to question the stated policies, and will not in practice do so.

Staff members, including the most conscientious, have every incentive to act in this fashion. To accept the agency guidance as conclusive is the quick and simple thing to do, and leaves staff members relatively invulnerable to criticism. By contrast, to treat the document as tentative, and therefore as subject to reconsideration upon the request of affected parties, would demand more time and effort, and would expose staff members to disapproval for departing from established positions. And treating the matter as a settled part of the operational routine is more comfortable for staff members than having to consider the policy anew each time it is to be applied.

Circumstances of course vary in our complicated government. Some nonlegislative policy documents may be framed in general language that is not capable of regularized application, and some may make it clear that the guidance is tentative only. But otherwise, I suspect that the above observations hold true in the great majority of cases. And I suspect that they hold true whether or not the agency intended its document to bind the staff. * * *

* * *

VII. Recommendations

* * *

Agencies have available to them two courses of procedural action by which to banish the vexing problems described in this Article. They may issue their new policies in binding form through the use of legislative rulemaking procedures (Recommendations A, C and D below). Or they may issue them nonlegislatively, and take care to treat them as nonbinding (Recommendation B below).

A. Accordingly, this Article recommends that agencies adhere to section 553's legislative notice-and-comment procedures for any substantive statement of general applicability (other than an interpretive rule) that (a) is intended to establish mandatory standards or to impose obligations upon private parties, or (b) is given that effect by the agency. * * *

Values served by the legislative rulemaking procedures are large ones. Fairness is furthered by giving notice to those who are to be bound both when the proposed rule is about to be considered and when the final rule is definitively published. The accuracy and thoroughness of an agency's actions are enhanced by the requirement that it invite and consider the comments of all the world, including those of directly affected persons who are able, often uniquely, to supply pertinent information and analysis. The acceptability and therefore the effectiveness of a final rule are elevated by the openness of the procedures through which it has been deliberated and by the public's sense of useful participation in a process that affects them. Its legitimacy rests upon all of these considerations, as well as upon the foundational fact that the agency has observed the procedures laid down by Congress for establishing rules with the binding force of law. The agency's accountability for its rules is deepened by the court-made requirement of a reasoned explanation based upon a substantial rulemaking record.

Beyond all of this, the APA rulemaking requirements impose a salutary discipline. That discipline deters casual and sloppy action, and thereby forestalls the confusion and needless litigation that can result from such action. And that discipline reduces tendencies toward overregulation or bureaucratic overreaching, and discourages low-profile attempts to create practically-binding norms that Congress or the Administration would not have approved.

B. Even where an agency does not plan to observe these APA procedures, but instead contemplates a nonlegislative issuance, there is a way it can preserve its fulfillment of the values just discussed. Indeed, this is the fashion in which an agency must issue any policy statement—that is, any substantive nonlegislative statement that does not interpret specific statutory or regulatory language. The agency must intend that the statement will be genuinely tentative, rather than binding, and assure that it will be so treated.

Accordingly, whenever practicable to do so, agencies should forthrightly declare in their nonlegislative policy documents that the stated policies are tentative, and that before they are applied finally to affected persons those persons will have a chance to challenge the policies * * *. Additionally, agencies should establish systems to assure that agency staff, counsel, administrative law judges, relevant state officials, and others who may apply policy statements or advise on the basis of such statements, are made aware that the policies set forth in such documents are tentative, and are subject to challenge * * * before they are applied. The agency similarly should make clear to affected private parties, by specific written advice at the time an application is made or at the commencement of enforcement or other proceedings, that the policies set forth in relevant nonlegislative documents are tentative and are subject to challenge before they are finally applied.

* * *

C. By contrast, interpretive rules—those that interpret language of a statute or of an existing legislative rule that has some tangible content—are required by law neither to be promulgated by notice-and-comment rulemaking processes (as are binding noninterpretive rules) nor to be issued tentatively while the agency maintains an open mind (as are policy statements). * * *

It would champion the worthy precepts of the APA, however, if in certain circumstances agencies would voluntarily make use of notice-and-comment rulemaking procedures to develop interpretive rules. Implicit in the doctrine that notice-and-comment procedures are not required for interpretation is a notion that affected parties are in some sense continuously on notice of any imaginable interpretations, and that it is their business (or their counsel's) to anticipate and guard against all possibilities. But when substantial interpretive changes are afoot, the values of fair notice and public participation and agency accountability demand something better.

An agency should endeavor to observe notice-and-comment procedures, I believe, whenever it contemplates the adoption of an interpretation that would 1) extend the scope of the jurisdiction the agency in fact exercises; 2) alter the obligations or liabilities of private parties; or 3) modify the terms on which the agency will grant entitlements. Of course, the rulemaking procedures need not be considered unless the change of interpretation is a substantial one that does not derive in an obvious way from established norms.

D. A final cluster of recommended practices springs from the rather obvious proposition that it should be the agency's responsibility to make the purport of its issuances clear and accessible. If the agency intends an issuance to be legislative and therefore to be legally binding, it should say so, in order that staff and affected persons will be definitively informed of the agency's intentions. It should also explain specifically how its issuance has gained legislative status. Ordinary citizens or even ordinary lawyers should not have to puzzle out the particulars of the agency's authority or its observance of procedural requirements. If the agency expects to apply its document in a binding way, it should be willing to declare that the rule is a legislative one, and to back up that claim with a showing of the specific authority and procedures it has observed. If these simple declarations were required, the public and the courts could know that documents issued without them were nonlegislative, and treat them accordingly.

Thus, this Article recommends that, in issuing any legislative rule, the agency publish as a part of the document promulgating the rule (a) a statement that the agency intends the rule to be a legislative rule, with the force of law; (b) a statement of the way in which specific statutory provisions confer upon the agency the authority to issue this particular rule in legislative form; and (c) a statement of the specific steps the agency has taken to satisfy the elements of rulemaking procedure required by 5 U.S.C. § 553 and by any other applicable statutory provisions.

Agencies will protest that the procedures called for by these recommendations will prove bothersome and will place pressures upon their time and resources. No doubt this is true. Legislative rulemaking procedures can levy upon limited agency funds, people, and other resources. It must be remembered, though, that agencies exist solely to serve the public in accordance with the law. The costs of observing the law and fair procedure are bedrock obligations that cannot legitimately be slighted simply because an agency might lack adequate resources or prefer to direct them elsewhere. At worst, they are a price to be paid for lawfulness and openness and accountability in government. The procedures here recommended are in the greatest part required by the law, which should not be dishonored in the name of a false economy. The balance of the recommendations—in the spirit of the APA—call for agencies to forswear coyness and advise the public candidly of the actions they are taking. The recommended procedures will avert the imposition of needless cost and confusion upon the public, and will foster a more uniform and punctilious process of administration within the agencies.

* * *

Peter L. Strauss, *The Rulemaking Continuum*, 41 Duke L.J. 1463, 1466-69, 1475-83 (1992)*

* * *

I.

* * * Although commonly we speak of "rulemaking" as synonymous with the notice-and-comment procedures of informal legislative rulemaking under

---

* Reprinted with permission of Peter L. Strauss. All rights reserved.

section 553, careful attention to the APA reveals four different species of activity that can produce an outcome that fits the definition of "rule" given in section 551(4): "the whole or a part of an agency statement of general or particular applicability and future effect designed to implement, interpret, or prescribe law or policy . . . ."

First, what is usually called "formal rulemaking" under section 553 consists of procedures by which rules are "made on the record after opportunity for an agency hearing [following the procedures of] sections 556 and 557 of this title . . . ." Such procedures are commonly employed for the setting of particular rates, but otherwise it is widely known that they are disfavored, and will be found mandatory only when a specific statute so requires in unmistakable terms.

Second, what is usually called "informal rulemaking" requires, in the section's *explicit* terms, a brief and rather unspecific notice warning of "*either* the terms *or* substance of the proposed rule *or* a description of the subjects and issues involved,*" followed by the affording to interested persons of "an opportunity to participate in the rulemaking through the submission of written data, views, or arguments" and concluded by an instrument of adoption that includes "a concise general statement of [the adopted rule's] basis and purpose." An agency following this procedure can create a legal instrument that, if substantively valid, has the force and effect of a statute on all those who are subject to it. It binds the agency, private parties, and the courts, and may preempt state statutes. If a statute so authorizes, its violation may form the basis for penal consequences. In formal contemplation, a valid legislative rule may be modified only by adoption of an amending rule or overruling statute. This style of rulemaking has been subject to considerable legislative and judicial elaboration in some settings, and we shall need to return to consider these developments. For the moment, one important characteristic to note about it is that this formal impact is purchased at the price of involvement at the agency's head: The adoption of legislative rules, an exercise of delegated legislative authority, is invariably an act of the particular individual or body to whom that authority has been delegated—the Secretary, the Commission, the agency Administrator.

Third, what I have elsewhere styled "publication rulemaking" is typically effected by agency staff without participation at the agency's head. For these rules, the parameters are set not by section 553, which excepts them, but by sections 552(a)(1) and (2). The latter provisions require certain agency documents either to be published in the *Federal Register* before a person can "in any manner be required to resort to, or be adversely affected by" them, or to be indexed and made available for inspection and copying or purchase before the documents "may be relied on, used, or cited as precedent by an agency against a party other than an agency" to "affect[] a member of the public." "Actual and timely notice" suffices to defend the rules' application in either case, however. Section 552(a) is explicit in identifying the documents being referred to as including "statements of general policy or interpretations of general applicability formulated and adopted by the agency," which may or may not be published in the *Federal Register* as the agency chooses, and "administrative staff manuals and instructions to staff that affect a member of the public," which are to be indexed and made available. Note that the rather elaborate language of section 552(a) contemplates that if the agency does follow the stated publication requirements it will be able to require people to resort to these instruments, and will be able to rely on them in proceedings in ways that "adversely affect" members of the public; yet more strikingly, it also strongly suggests that even if these steps are not taken, such materials may be "relied on, used, or cited as precedent" *against the agency* although they do not serve to bind the public.

Fourth, and finally, comes the body of materials that fit the APA definition of "rule" and are in some respects the product of agency process, but that meet none of the procedural specifications of the preceding three classes. Here we encounter guidance documents that might be "publication rules" if appropriately made available or if timely and actual notice were given, and also other materials of lesser dignity—press releases and the like. The public cannot be adversely affected by such rules; but, to repeat, there is at least the implication that the agency may be so affected.

II.

* * *

* * * [T]he four classes of rulemaking identified above form a natural progression in several respects.
- Of the four categories, formal rulemaking is the least frequent, the most stylized, and the most demanding of resources at the agency's head.
- Informal rulemaking is what we are accustomed to thinking of when the subject of rulemaking is raised, but a moment's reflection suggests that it, too, is in *relative* terms a rare occurrence. * * * [I]t requires agency engagement from head to toe as a public process generating formally binding results, formally determined by the agency itself.
- No such engagement or formality attends the generation of "publication rules" such as technical guidelines or staff manuals. Staff offices produce them in a profusion that overwhelms the more formal output. Here are three such comparisons that personal contacts permitted me to make with relative ease: (1) formally adopted regulations of the Internal Revenue Service occupy about a foot of library shelf space, but Revenue Rulings and other similar publications, closer to twenty feet; (2) the rules of the Federal Aviation Administration (FAA), two inches, but the corresponding technical guidance materials, well in excess of forty feet; (3) finally, Part 50 of the Nuclear Regulatory Commission's regulations on nuclear power plant safety, in the looseleaf edition, consumes three-sixteenths of an inch, while the supplemental technical guidance manuals and standard reactor plans in the same format stack up to nine and three-fourths inches. Informal conversations persuade me that these ratios are typical. Although they do not justify the practice, they do suggest that we will want to consider carefully what this extraordinary volume of standard-generating activity might be about, and what its consequences are or should be.
- No similar measure can easily be made of the unindexed materials of our fourth category, yet given the breadth of description and the substantial numbers of potential sources for such rules, we may be certain that they too are generated in vast numbers and with relative ease.

* * *

III.

* * * The pages remaining attempt to be suggestive * * * in support of the proposition that much publication rulemaking is of high value to the public, and that the public would, on balance, be harmed if it were suppressed or if agencies were signalled that such advice, once given, could easily be disregarded. * * *

In addressing these issues, the following discussion treats only publication rules that do not purport to bind private actors in a formal sense, but that a member of the public might regard as significantly limiting what an agency may lawfully do, or what that person is free to do in practice. Of course Professor Anthony [in his article excerpted above] is correct that only section 553 states the procedures by which agencies may adopt standards that in formal terms have legislative force and effect. If an agency attempts to accomplish that result by publication rulemaking, it is simply in error; but this is easily enough understood, and no data suggest that it is a significant problem. The publication rules for which problems worth discussing arise are those he describes as binding in practical effect—rules that announce to the public, for example, what Internal Revenue Service (IRS) agents will apply as their understanding of the depreciation rules of the tax laws and regulations; or indicate that the Federal Energy Regulatory Commission (FERC) will accept a given set of provisions for emergency allocation of natural gas, in the event of shortage, as complying with its regulations requiring that every rate-filing by a natural gas pipeline include provisions on that subject; or state in detail certain design parameters for nuclear power-generating facilities that the staff of the Nuclear Regulatory Commission (NRC) will accept as meeting safe-operating requirements of its regulations. These publication rules are not formally binding. A Tax Court proceeding may ultimately find that other depreciation approaches are permissible under the statutes and regulations; a pipeline or a customer disfavored by the suggested allocation scheme might well be able to persuade the FERC in a rate proceeding that some other allocation was preferable; a license applicant to NRC can seek to prove the safety of its own design. In practice, however, these options entail risks and impose costs that many will be unwilling or even unable to accept. Many if not most people will pay their taxes quietly rather than confront the IRS; the additional cost of qualifying a design for safety outside NRC's technical guidelines could easily run in the millions of dollars. Professor Anthony's analysis puts such publication rules in jeopardy; and in my judgment, that is a questionable outcome.

A.

One line of approach is suggested by the hierarchy of rulemaking procedures and activities already sketched. Informal rulemaking is both a less frequent and a more highly centralized form of rulemaking than is publication rulemaking. The relationship between these two forms of activity mirrors, within the agency, the relationship between legislation and rulemaking in the larger governmental context. One can imagine a framework of ever-increasing specificity, in which increasing detail is provided by procedures of diminishing rigorousness, adopted by actors of diminishing political responsibility. At the apex lies the Constitution, substantively the least specific yet the most directly adopted by the citizenry. Legislation is more specific, adopted not by citizens directly in any sense, but by those whom they elect as representatives for the purpose. Yet we accept that, in a complex society, the standards Congress formulates will often accomplish little more than to establish large frameworks for the resolution of issues, leaving their actual resolution in detail to agencies created for the purpose, agencies whose political accountability is secured by appointment mechanisms and the possibility of presidential and/or congressional oversight. And the agencies in turn find that complex subjects, required procedures, and the twenty-four-hour day limit the capacities of those at the very top of the agency to deal with their responsibilities; ideally, those at the head take the most important of decisions, creating an internal framework or structure of essential judgments, and then leave the inevitable further details to be worked out by their more numerous and expert staff—subject to techniques of control and oversight far more likely to be bureaucratic and procedural than directly political.

This rather conceptual scheme captures well enough a "physical" reality in which publication rules outnumber informal rules, which in turn dwarf statutes, which in turn dwarf constitutional provisions. As a general matter, we also see more and more particular focus by the decisionmaker as we descend into the details; Congress is more the generalist than EPA, and EPA's Administrator is in turn more the generalist than the team of engineers and others who may have been asked to produce technical guidelines on solid waste handling prior to incineration. * * *

Formally, we recognize, these variations are appropriately reflected in the varying dignity and force of the legal instruments each process creates. The Constitution is supreme law; validly adopted statutes control unless legislatively changed, and judicial supervision of their validity is extremely sparing insofar as questions of authority and policy judgment are concerned. Legislative rules have the force of statutes if validly adopted, and remain in force until changed by legislative rulemaking, but courts will be much more aggressive in determining the authority question respecting legislative rules than statutes. Even in the wake of *Chevron*, courts will independently determine the extent of statutory ambiguity within which an agency is privileged to formulate "reasonable" policy; and "hard look" review of an agency's policy formulations to determine, *inter alia*, whether they are indeed reasonable is appropriately more demanding than the "any rational basis" test applied to statutes. Publication rules, unlike legislative rules, are not binding on courts although they may be entitled to substantial deference; the agency may change them without formal procedure, or may decide to depart from them in the course of a proceeding—at least where its doing so would not prejudice a private party who may have relied upon them.

One possible way to imagine publication rules, then, is as a means for supplying additional detail unreasonable to expect at the level of the agency head, and in a form sufficiently flexible to permit relatively fast and easy change. If one were to take this perspective, the publication rule problem would become analogous to the delegation problem as it is conventionally expressed: Do (statutes and) legislative rules provide sufficient detail to persuade us that the agency head has done as much as it is reasonable to ask it to do, considering competing tasks, available resources, the public's interest in resolution, and the like? Seeing the issue as one of "filling in the details" responds to the same impulse as Professor Anthony's too-easy distinction between interpretive rules and general statements of policy,[44] but in my judgment his formulation improperly limits the publication rule format to interpretive activities as a lawyer might understand them. Absent that artificial limitation, the issue at root would be whether sufficient constraint embraces the decision made to permit us some comfort with the "law-full-ness" of the decision—that we could say if it were wrong, or if it were a usurpation of authority properly placed elsewhere on the political grid. It is hard to see how it could matter, in this context, whether what was being done was to give detailed content to a word, or to elaborate the physical showings that would be regarded as meeting a test stated in general terms. A publication rule could explain in detail what the Federal Reserve Board regards as a "bank," or it could lay out in some detail the physical parameters of an airplane part that will be regarded by the staff of FAA as meeting a rule's specification for resistance to metal fatigue. Calling one "interpretation" and the other "policymaking" does not change the relation of the two to the framework of statutes and regulations within which they occur.

The courts have confessed their inability to generate an administrable standard to distinguish, in general, proper from excessive delegations. Could they any better define a test for what degree of legislative rulemaking by the agency head is sufficient then to permit their staffs to "fill in the details" by publication rulemaking, subject only to such corrections as may come retrospectively through petitions for rulemaking, consideration of such issues as may eventually arise in adjudications, or the like?

Putting the issue this way draws our attention to the proposition that relief from the impact of publication rules usually *will* be after-the-fact in character—securable, if at all, only through a rather long and burdensome course of proceedings that most persons subject to such rules would prefer to avoid. Consequently, "binding in practical effect" will be an arguable characterization for a publication rule in most, if not all, cases. If I go to the Post Office to mail a package, and the clerk, after consulting his manual, concludes that it meets the publication rule explanation of the "damaged packages" that he is required by legislative rule to refuse acceptance to the mails, that will usually be the end of it. We cannot imagine that the Post Office must permit its clerk to exercise discretion in every case, treating the manual provision merely as guidance; nor do we think it must supply me with access to an adjudicatory hearing in which I can contend that my package in fact meets the requirements of the legislative rule regarding "damaged packages."[46] If I mail a lot of packages and frequently meet this inconvenience, I ought to (and do) have the opportunity to petition the agency to consider the matter, but hardly with assurance of effective future relief, and in any event with no prospect of relief for this current mailing. The question is whether legislative rules can sufficiently define "damaged packages"; or must informal rulemaking procedures, with involvement of the agency's head, also be used to "fill in the details" for the guidance of operational staff.

One could argue that little reason exists to think this issue any more tractable at the agency level than it has been for courts considering the issue of delegation. Yet the political stakes for courts in this question are not nearly what they are in the "delegation" context. Invocation of the delegation doctrine places them in confrontation with a coordinate branch of government, which they appear to be accusing of failing to do its work properly. No similar inhibitions would impede a judicial effort to encourage agencies to achieve what Colin Diver once described as "the optimal precision of administrative rules." * * *

B.

Why would we prefer having publication rules to not having them? It seems appropriate to put the

---

[44] Distinguishing between "interpretation" and "lawmaking" can have the qualities of a shell game; authorized interpretation frequently supplies judgments no one would pretend the enacting body considered * * *. Why that is not "making law" is impossible to explain. Neither § 552 nor § 553 draws the distinction Professor Anthony proposes, that permits interpretations to have a bite that policies are denied.

[46] The example just given seems useful for its accessibility; the United States Postal Service is no longer an administrative agency in the usual sense. * * *

question this way, given the relative frequency of legislative and publication rulemaking and the limits on the agency's resources at the top, where legislative rules are at least nominally made. * * * [I]t would be unreasonable to expect that any significant portion of today's publication rules would appear if notice-and-comment rulemaking were required for their adoption. * * * Apart from situations in which the agency is unable to act until it has completed some rulemaking (an unusual situation, the practical outcome of which may be that it is unable to act), costly procedural requirements may encourage or even force the agency to act without rules.

Framing the issue in this manner quickly focuses our attention on the shaping and informing character of publication rulemaking. By informing the public how the agency intends to carry out an otherwise discretionary task, publication rulemaking permits important efficiencies to those who must deal with government. Professor Anthony sees in a potential *complainant* about the policy judgments entailed in NRC's technical specifications for nuclear power plants, a party bound in practical effect by those guidelines; an applicant that wanted to strike its own course of attempted compliance with NRC's legislative regulations on safety in designing its plant, rather than follow the technical guides, would have to pay millions more to be able to convince the agency's staff of the wisdom and acceptability of its preferred alternative. But if the legislative regulations minus the technical specifications would be adequate to satisfy any obligation NRC has to "make law" on the subject of safety, should we not instead characterize the effect of the specifications as permitting most applicants to save millions they would otherwise have been required to spend in justifying the issuance of the licenses they seek? From the perspective of an applicant whose chief interest is to build a plant that will meet NRC standards, receiving such guidance from the agency where possible is strongly preferable to being left to speculate about the details of agency policies and to pay for case-by-case demonstration that it has met those policies' demands. The NRC *may* leave these issues to determination first in negotiations with uninstructed staff and then in the adjudicatory licensing proceedings in which the applicant bears the burden of showing that its design will satisfy safety requirements. Do we wish to encourage it to do so?

Permitting the discretion left open by its legislative rulemakings to be structured by publication rulemaking is valuable to the NRC (or to the FERC or to the FAA) and to the general public, as well as to the private parties most directly concerned. Case-by-case adjudication is inefficient for NRC too; it threatens not only expense but also undesirable variation in individual cases * * *. Staff instructions, manuals, and other forms of publication rules are essential tools of bureaucratic management, by which the expertise of an agency is shared throughout its structure, and staff operatives are kept under the discipline necessary to the efficient accomplishment of agency mission. These instructions need not be from the top in any formal sense, and usually are not. In any moderately complex bureaucratic structure, policy formulation of this character is made the responsibility of what may be a fair number of relatively small offices, each staffed by experts in a particular field of action. What is often a much larger body of operatives apply these policies to particular cases. Because the policies are set for them, the operatives need not aspire to expertise. If the policies were not there, and these operatives were required to act on the basis of their own knowledge and judgment, agency staffing would be a much more complex matter; even if it could be successful, substantial variation would be expected. Finally, with such policies in place, the agency head needs only to watch for signals of distress about them, not to reach an unending series of discretionary judgments; as a result, its task of control and its possibilities of effective conversation with its staff are considerably enhanced.

Putting the matter this way also suggests the high stakes for the public, including the regulated public, in encouraging the adoption of publication rules. The usual interface between a member of the public and an agency does not involve the agency head, but a relatively low-level member of staff; earlier we used the example of the postal clerk, but the welfare worker, the District Forester, the IRS examiner, the Food and Drug Administration (FDA) inspector, or the application desk officer each suggest the same result—responsibility for initial processing of the public's business. Absent, again, some basis for a judgment that the agency's * * * legislative rules are inadequate in themselves to permit the agency to function, the choice the public faces is between having the clerk apply his own interpretation of the agency's legislative rules, or having his decisions and actions further controlled by the agency's publication rules. As any reader who has faced an audit will likely attest, bureaucratic rationality is a major protection for the public having to deal with a bureaucracy, as well as an occasional annoyance. While recognizing the irritations, the affected public (especially the repeat players among them) will almost certainly prefer a state of affairs in which such instructions are publicly given and may be relied upon—that is, the lower-level bureaucrats are to follow them, and higher levels are to depart from them only with an explanation. Such instructions may not "bind" a member of the public (although like the agency caselaw they may affect or be cited against the public); binding agency staff is their very rationale.

* * *

Michael Asimow, *Nonlegislative Rulemaking and Regulatory Reform*, 1985 DUKE L.J. 381, 383-400, 402-06, 408-10, 421-25*

* * *

I. Nonlegislative Rules: Definitions and Functions

A. *Preliminary Definition of Terms.*

The theoretical difference between legislative and nonlegislative rules is clear. A legislative rule is essentially an administrative statute—an exercise of previously delegated power, new law that completes an incomplete legislative design. Legislative rules frequently prescribe, modify, or abolish duties, rights, or exemptions. In contrast, nonlegislative rules do not exercise delegated lawmaking power and thus are not administrative statutes. Instead, they provide guidance to the public and to agency staff and decisionmakers. They are not legally binding on members of the public.

Interpretive rules and policy statements serve distinct functions. An interpretive rule clarifies or explains the meaning of words used in a statute, a previous agency rule, or a judicial or agency adjudicative decision. A policy statement, on the other hand, indicates how an agency hopes or intends to exercise discretionary power in the course of performing some other administrative function. For example, a policy statement might indicate what factors will be considered and what goals will be pursued when an agency conducts investigation, prosecution, legislative rulemaking, or formal or informal adjudication.

Although the theoretical difference between the legal effect of legislative and nonlegislative rules is clear, the practical line-drawing problem has proved difficult for a number of reasons. The most important reason for the haziness of the distinction is that the practical impact of either type of rule on members of the public is the same. Most members of the public assume that all agency rules are valid, correct, and unalterable. Consequently, most people attempt to conform to them rather than to mount costly, time-consuming, and usually futile challenges. Although legislative and nonlegislative rules are conceptually distinct and although their legal effect is profoundly different, the real-world consequences are usually identical.

Another reason for the confusion surrounding the distinction is that the legal effect of agency rules is often difficult to assess. For example, both legislative and interpretive rules frequently interpret the meaning of language in a statute. Similarly, both legislative rules and policy statements often prescribe the manner in which an agency will exercise discretionary power. Moreover, an enormous variety of agency actions can be plausibly characterized as rules. Because their legal effect is difficult to determine, such actions typically resist easy placement in legislative or nonlegislative pigeonholes.

Finally, it often serves the interests of both agencies and courts to blur or manipulate the distinction between legislative and nonlegislative rules. In classifying rules, the "intention" of the agency is critical, yet courts understandably have been reluctant to accept an agency's own characterization at face value. Indeed, the courts themselves have sometimes manipulated the distinction to achieve results sought for other reasons.

B. *Role of Nonlegislative Rules in the Administrative Process.*

Nearly every agency engages constantly in the processes of legal interpretation and the structuring and narrowing of its statutory discretion. The adoption of nonlegislative rules is one way in which an agency might carry out these functions.

1. *Interpretation.* Interpretation is an indispensable part of administration, because the meaning of language in administrative materials is often obscure, ambiguous, or abstract. To conduct their business, agency heads and staff must fill the gaps, resolve ambiguities, and reduce abstractions to a practical and concrete level.

An agency might simply decide not to deal with an interpretive problem, leaving the public without guidance and allowing the staff to work things out on a case-by-case basis. However, if it seems worthwhile to arrive at an agreed-upon definition or application of language, an agency might use one of several techniques. If it has delegated power, it can

---

* Reprinted with permission of Duke Law Journal and Michael Asimow. All rights reserved.

perform the interpretive function by adopting a definitive legislative rule. It might also interpret language in the course of formal or informal adjudication or by issuing a declaratory order. It can provide interpretive guidance in answering requests for advice by individual members of the public, or it can include interpretive material in instructional manuals.

The final alternative is to adopt and publish a nonlegislative interpretive rule of general applicability. Countless interpretive rules are adopted each year by federal agencies. Revenue rulings issued by the Internal Revenue Service, advisory opinions about Hatch Act issues by the Merit Systems Protection Board, and interpretive bulletins issued by the Federal Reserve System are three prominent examples.

Interpretive material helps assure consistent day-to-day administration by agency staff and provides an invaluable resource for members of the public. Of course, an agency's legal interpretation is not legally binding on anyone; courts and members of the public are free to disagree with it. In practice, however, an agency's view of the correct resolution of legal questions usually provides the final answer. Few agency interpretations are challenged in court and almost all of those are upheld. * * *

2. *Policy Statements*. Staff members in most agencies have broad discretion whether to initiate an investigation, audit a return, grant a license, an exemption, or a dispensation, recommend prosecution, or take enforcement action. Agencies may or may not provide guidance to the staff as to how this discretion should be exercised. * * *

* * *

Policy statements are nonlegislative rules that tentatively indicate how agency decisionmakers will exercise a discretionary power. Such rules might, for example, isolate the factors that should be considered in making decisions, rank priorities, set tolerance levels, explain when dispensations should be granted, build flexibility into overly rigid rules, indicate what data are relevant, or otherwise narrow the available decisional referents that must be taken into account. Some familiar examples are the policy statements adopted by the Federal Communications Commission, the Operations Instructions of the Immigration and Naturalization Service, the Merger Guidelines and the FBI Investigative Guidelines of the Department of Justice, and the revenue procedures published by the Internal Revenue Service.

Agencies frequently consider whether a discretion-structuring rule should be adopted or made more precise. Certainly, greater precision entails significant costs, including the bureaucratic costs of formulating a rule. Formulation costs are often steep, because the staff members who have dealt with the problem may themselves be uncertain precisely why and how they do what they do. In addition, discretion-confining rules may be over- or under-inclusive, decisionmaking under the rule may be unjustifiably rigid, and the rule may highlight loopholes. Nevertheless, commentators generally agree that agencies should face and resolve the questions of how discretion will be exercised much more frequently than they do at present, a process that offers advantages to both the agency and the public.

For the agency, the very process of considering how a particular power might be structured often results in a productive process of self-criticism and the generation of alternatives and fresh points of view. * * * Moreover, an informed public is more likely to conform voluntarily to the law, thus minimizing enforcement costs.

To the public that must live with an agency's discretionary power, knowledge of how that power will be used is extremely valuable. It opens a window on an agency's decisional process and thus enables a person who is detrimentally affected to make an informed argument to the correct staff member that an exception should be made. It permits everyone who must deal with the agency equal access to vital information, thus diminishing the advantage held by experienced professionals or former agency staff members. Finally, policy statements enable the public to plan transactions with more precise knowledge of how agencies will react. As a result, a person subject to regulation or seeking a benefit is less likely to encounter difficulties with the agency. To the extent that disputes between government and regulated parties can be avoided through proper advance planning, both sides avoid the deadweight loss associated with dispute settlement and thwarted plans.

General policy statements are well calculated to control staff action and, because they must be published in the *Federal Register*, to inform the public. They provide authoritative guidance on what the staff is likely to do, yet unlike legislative rules they remain tentative, not rigid. Consequently, they leave decisionmakers room for flexible application; they do not foreclose further experimentation and learning from experience.

II. Judicial Techniques for Drawing the Legislative/Nonlegislative Distinction

* * *

A. *The Agency's Label*.

When an agency has a choice to proceed legislatively or nonlegislatively, its contemporaneous description is the most reliable test of what it actually did. * * *

Unfortunately, a court cannot always rely on labels to distinguish between legislative and nonlegislative rules. Agencies may provide vague or contradictory descriptions of their rules, or may fail to characterize their pronouncements at all. Moreover, an agency, unsure whether it has delegated power or, if it does, whether it wishes to exercise it, may try to disguise the issue by failing to describe its product clearly. In other cases, confusion may be caused by poor staff work. For example, staff members may fail to clarify whether a pronouncement that amplifies a legislative rule is intended to amend the rule or merely to interpret it. Finally, an agency might overlook the fact that a rule labelled as nonlegislative is, for some reason, legally binding on someone or some other agency, and cannot properly be treated as nonlegislative.

Thus, many courts have declared that labels are entitled to judicial deference, but cannot be dispositive of the issue of the proper characterization of a rule. Courts consistently question whether the chosen label correctly describes the legal effect of a particular rule. Otherwise, an agency might manipulate its description in order to avoid pre-enforcement judicial review, keep a low profile, or circumvent cumbersome notice and comment requirements, while achieving the desired change in staff and private party behavior.

B. *Policy Statements: The Definitiveness Test.*

* * * A difficult characterization problem is often presented when an agency with delegated legislative power chooses to adopt a policy statement without prior notice and comment. The prevailing criterion for analyzing this issue is the "definitiveness" test. If the court finds that a discretionary power has been tentatively limited, the agency's pronouncement is a policy statement; if it finds that the power is definitively limited, the pronouncement is a legislative rule.

The definitiveness rule clearly leaves much to be desired as a manageable and predictable standard for judicial decisionmaking. Because it hinges on whether a rule definitively or tentatively channels discretion, the test requires a prediction of the agency's future behavior, and the result will often turn on whether the staff used mandatory or precatory language.

On the other hand, the definitiveness test has some positive aspects. It provides a serviceable roadmap by which agencies can confine discretionary power without inviting advance public participation. An agency can be reasonably certain that notice and comment procedure will not be required if it labels a discretion-structuring rule as a policy statement, builds in assurances that the rule is tentative, and treats it in actual practice as tentative.

In addition, the definitiveness test has a certain compelling logic. If the public is denied an advance opportunity to influence a policy statement, it should have a fair chance to persuade a decisionmaker to follow a different course when the discretionary function is actually exercised in a subsequent investigation, formal or informal adjudication, or other proceeding.

Several factors are helpful in applying the definitiveness test. One is a realistic assessment of the tentativeness of a rule. Rules that seem tentative or suggestive, leaving room for decisionmakers to exercise judgment, are properly characterized as policy statements. In contrast, a rule adopted by an agency with legislative rulemaking power that appears to preclude the exercise of discretion, prescribes how it must be exercised, or leaves no administrative forum in which the exercise of discretion can be challenged, should be considered legislative.

* * *

A second factor that courts take into account when deciding whether a rule that confines a power is tentative or definitive is the precise wording used by the agency. For example, a rule that uses rebuttable presumptions, or that uses words of suggestion, like "may" or "should consider," rather than inflexible words of command, is likely to be a policy statement.

A third factor that courts may consider is actual administrative experience in applying a rule. If agency decisionmakers seem genuinely open to contrary suggestions in subsequent proceedings, a rule is likely to be a policy statement. If, however, decisionmakers appear to view themselves as bound by the rule, it may be treated as legislative.

C. *Interpretive Rules: Legal Effect Test.*

* * *

The prevailing standard for distinguishing legislative and interpretive rules can be described as the "legal effect" test. If a rule explaining the meaning of language actually makes "new law," as opposed to merely interpreting "existing law," it is legislative. Because both legislative and interpretive rules frequently explain the meaning of language, there is no obvious way to determine whether an agency with legislative rulemaking power has made "new law" or interpreted "existing law." Thus, the result often turns on whether an agency "intended" to make new law, and that determination necessarily must depend primarily on the label that the agency attached to its product.

Courts confront the characterization issue in two distinct situations—rules that explain the meaning of a statute and rules that explain the meaning of a previous legislative rule.

1. *Rules That Explain Statutes.* In considering whether a rule that explains a statute is interpretive, courts consider a number of factors in addition to the agency's label or an assessment of its intention. A rule makes "new law," as opposed to interpreting "existing law," if it fills a statutory gap by imposing a standard of conduct, creating an exemption from a standard of conduct, erecting a new regulatory structure, or otherwise implementing congressional policy by completing an incomplete statutory design. Suppose, for example, that Congress allows an agency to exempt certain transactions from the coverage of a regulatory statute. Without a rule, such transactions would not be exempt. A rule spelling out an exemption would necessarily be legislative.

As a consequence, the more vague and open-textured a statute, the more likely that a rule implementing it will be legislative rather than interpretive. On the other hand, if the statutory provision in issue is detailed, leaving relatively little room for agency implementation, a rule explaining the statute is more likely to be considered interpretive. Similarly, a rule that conforms closely to the language of the statute is likely to be considered a mere reminder and thus interpretive.

Another relevant factor in distinguishing between legislative and interpretive rules is the specificity with which an agency's delegated legislative power has been expressed. In many cases, legislative rulemaking power is conferred by a specific statutory provision. In other instances, however, a statute provides only a general rulemaking authority applicable to the entire statute; under the prevailing view, at least in the federal courts, general rulemaking provisions empower an agency to make either interpretive or legislative rules.[69] Several courts have indicated that, in doubtful cases, rules made pursuant to specific rulemaking powers are more likely to be treated as legislative than are rules made pursuant to general rulemaking powers.

2. *Rules That Explain Rules.* Many rules explain or clarify previous legislative rules. If a second rule repudiates or is irreconcilable with the prior one, the second rule must be an amendment of the first; and, of course, an amendment to a legislative rule must itself be legislative. Usually, however, the second rule is consistent with the earlier one. In such cases there is no principled way to determine whether it amends the prior rule or merely explains, clarifies, or interprets it, and courts by necessity usually defer to an agency's characterization of its intent.

On occasion, courts find second rules legislative when they deal with a matter not clearly covered by an earlier legislative rule. * * *

In many cases, a court that reviews a second rule may avoid the procedural problem entirely by merging it with the issue of substantive validity. If the court finds the second rule consistent with the first one, it follows both that the second rule is interpretive and also that it is substantively valid. If the second rule is inconsistent with the first one, it is invalid both for procedural reasons (because it was an amendment adopted without notice and comment) and substantive reasons (it could not be a valid interpretation of the earlier rule if inconsistent with it).

D. *The Substantial Impact Test.*

As we have seen, the prevailing test used to distinguish legislative and nonlegislative rules centers on the *legal effect* that an agency intended the rule to have. A conflicting line of cases holds that the critical factor in drawing the distinctions is the substantiality of the *practical impact* of a rule. Under this approach, pre-adoption procedure is required if a rule has a substantial practical impact on a significant body of regulated persons.

The substantial impact test enjoyed a considerable vogue in the early to middle 1970's. Since then, courts have cautiously but consistently rejected it in deciding whether to require notice and comment procedure before adoption of a purportedly nonlegislative rule. Nevertheless, the substantial impact test remains important for a number of related purposes. It is a factor in deciding whether the procedural or good cause exemptions apply. It is also relevant in deciding whether a procedural defect should be overlooked as a harmless error, [and] whether a nonlegislative rule must be published in the *Federal Register* * * *. Finally, the substantial impact test is useful as a guide to agencies in deciding whether voluntarily to invite public participation before adopting a particularly important nonlegislative rule.

* * *

A major shortcoming of the substantial impact test is that it has no solid foundation in the APA.

---

[69] * * * However, the general rulemaking power in the Internal Revenue Code has been interpreted to confer authority only to adopt interpretive rules. * * *

The exemption from notice and comment requirements for nonlegislative rules appears to have been written with the legal effect test, not the substantial impact test, in mind. Furthermore, the practical impact of a rule seems virtually irrelevant in determining whether an agency made new law or explained existing law. Finally, the test cannot be justified by asserting that fairness requires agencies to provide notice and comment before adopting important nonlegislative rules. After *Vermont Yankee Nuclear Power Corp. v. Natural Resources Defense Council, Inc.*, courts cannot, in the interests of fairness, improved decisionmaking, or facilitation of judicial review, require agencies to go beyond the minimum standards established in the APA when adopting rules. An agency must decide for itself whether additional procedures should be employed.

In addition to its lack of theoretical support, the substantial impact test also fails as a judicially manageable standard. Obviously, any litigated rule had a significant impact on someone; otherwise it would not be worth litigating. Whether that impact is "substantial" is a question to which no principled answer can be given, because it is impossible to quantify the variables that courts must address. As a result, judicial decisions under the substantial impact test seem ad hoc and unprincipled—considerably more so than decisions under the legal effect test.

* * *

III. Reconsidering the Statutory Exemption for Nonlegislative Rules

* * * Why not require that agencies provide notice and comment procedures before adopting most or even all nonlegislative rules? * * *

A. *Costs and Benefits of Requiring Pre-Adoption Procedures for Nonlegislative Rules.*

1. *Benefit to the Public From Pre-Adoption Procedure.* The rulemaking procedures of the APA have been widely acclaimed as a brilliant political innovation. The notice and comment procedure, together with hard-look judicial review, addresses our uneasiness with broad legislative delegations to administrative agencies and with the tenuous nature of the other legislative and judicial checks on agency behavior.

The APA notice and comment procedure infuses the rulemaking process with significant elements of openness, accountability, and legitimacy. Public participation promotes fundamental democratic values by enhancing the responsiveness of agencies to the interest groups affected by regulation. It opens the process to groups and individuals with discordant points of view who might otherwise not have been heard during an agency's routine process of consultation with the public. In short, through advance notice and comment, every constituency has an opportunity to participate in a meaningful manner in making the laws that will affect it.

The requirement that agencies invite and give consideration to public comments broadens an agency's perspective, which otherwise might not extend beyond the views of the staff or the client groups with whom the staff regularly consults. An invitation to submit comments stimulates outsiders to furnish data and other inputs, providing a source of low-cost information to agency decisionmakers. A rule is likely to be a better product if its drafters must consider seriously alternatives that they might have overlooked or take account of practical problems that otherwise would crop up only after a rule goes into effect. In addition, an agency may receive more cooperation and less obstruction from regulated interests that have had a hand in shaping the rules within which they must function. Finally, by generating a record of public comment and agency response, the notice and comment system facilitates preenforcement hard-look judicial review, an important check on factually unsupported or arbitrary regulation.

In some respects, the advantages of notice and comment rulemaking apply equally to legislative and nonlegislative rulemaking. Members of interest groups affected by nonlegislative rules would certainly utilize and probably benefit from an advance opportunity to influence an agency concerning the desirability and the content of such rules. Pre-adoption notice and comment would be a useful supplement to the channels of influence already available, such as informal consultation with the staff and post-adoption critiques and modification petitions.

Realistically, however, few nonlegislative rules have the practical significance of the great bulk of legislative rules. The vast majority of nonlegislative rules are insignificant, of primarily internal importance to the agency, or indisputably valid. An invitation to comment in such cases would produce no response or, at most, a trivial pro forma response from people paid to keep track of agency activity.

2. *Costs of Rulemaking Procedure.* Although notice and comment rulemaking procedures have a great many benefits, they are not cost-free. Indeed, the rulemaking process can be both ponderous and costly. To produce any new rule, whether legislative or nonlegislative, an agency must incur the substantial bureaucratic costs of overcoming inertia. The internal process includes research, resolution of staff conflicts, informal consultation with interested outsiders, agreement upon precise language, consensus-

building, and multilevel review. The financial and psychological costs of forging consensus within an agency on the contents of a new rule may be quite substantial.

If public participation is legally required, or if the agency chooses voluntarily to provide it, the agency must then publish a notice of its proposal in the *Federal Register* * * *. The public process continues through the receipt of comments (typically with time extensions to accommodate commentators who wish to perform studies), public hearings (which are not required but often provided), staff analysis of the comments, preparation of a reasoned statement of basis and purpose, and prepublication in the *Federal Register*. The final act takes place in the courts when the rule is subjected to pre-enforcement judicial review.

By general consensus, it usually takes between six and twelve months to push an uncontroversial rule through notice and comment procedure unless unusual steps are taken to accelerate the process. If a rule is controversial, or if an outsider or factions within the agency have an interest in delaying its adoption, a much longer delay is likely. * * *

3. *An Economic Model of Bureaucratic Choice*. Agency decisionmakers, like all rational beings, seek to function efficiently by maximizing utility—both their own and that of the regulatory program for which they are responsible. Given a fixed budget and many competing uses of available resources, efficient operation involves a constant weighing of the net marginal costs and benefits of a proposed course of action. Thus, in order to undertake a new legislative or nonlegislative rulemaking project, an agency must conclude that the net marginal benefits to the regulatory program or to the agency from adopting an incremental rule outweigh the net marginal bureaucratic costs of adopting it.

In other words, there must exist a supply curve of bureaucratic outputs; increasing the net costs of producing any particular output will usually diminish the supply of that particular output. Given an increase in cost of producing one type of product, an agency might decide to produce the same number of units and cut some other output or program. Alternatively the agency might rationally decide to use its limited resources to produce some other category of output or take advantage of some other opportunity. More typically, however, the agency would decide to produce fewer units of the more costly output while keeping the proportion of the budget allocated to it the same.

While the slope of the supply curve will vary from one agency to another, it seems likely that the supply of nonlegislative rules is quite sensitive to increases in bureaucratic production costs. Interpretive rules and policy statements are different from other bureaucratic outputs in one critical respect: a regulatory program can function without them. Legislative rules are often necessary to set a regulatory program in motion. However, the purpose of nonlegislative rules is to diminish uncertainty. For the most part, the costs of uncertainty are borne by members of the public, not by the agency. For that reason, uncertainty is an externality that agency utility-maximizers need not take into account. Thus an agency may well choose to muddle through without producing any guidance documents, or it may choose to transmit any necessary guidance to its staff through informal intra-agency memoranda, hallway conversations, or other subformal communications. It may feel little or no compulsion to issue a steady flow of publicly available nonlegislative rules.

Of course, a new interpretation or policy may improve administration or raise the level of compliance, but these are long-term considerations; in the short term, an agency can get along without them. Given a choice of how to deploy scarce internal resources, an agency might decide that it is more important to issue legislative rules, conclude pending adjudications, investigate misconduct, answer urgent requests for advice, or prepare congressional testimony. Nonlegislative rules can usually be deferred until additional resources become available. Thus they must often be losers in the unending internal struggle for resources.

Moreover, there may be staff opposition to a proposed nonlegislative rule: some will argue that it outlines possible paths of evasion, that it is over- or under-inclusive, that it will induce undue rigidity, or that it will strip staff members of their influence and power by making public the secret law they have applied. Thus, to personnel who must decide whether to adopt a new nonlegislative rule, the net regulatory benefit may seem negligible and the net costs, exclusive of the costs of public procedure, may seem substantial.

A decision to put off rulemaking is much more likely to occur if the law requires additional steps, like notice and comment procedure, to be taken before the rule can be adopted. * * *

There is some scattered empirical evidence to support the proposition that the supply of nonlegislative rules is quite sensitive to the bureaucratic costs of adopting them. * * * [T]his theme emerged again and again in the course of interviews that the author conducted in many agencies about the nonlegislative rulemaking process. Although such statements should be discounted somewhat as the predictable responses of agency staff members who do not wish to be bothered with any new controls, the author is convinced that the problem is very real.

* * *

4. *Balancing the Costs and Benefits*. Nonlegislative rules are enormously important to members of the public who must live with regulation. Any significant diminution in the flow of interpretive rules or policy statements disserves the public interest.

Interpretive rules, for example, serve a number of vital purposes. Unless an interpretation is embodied in a legislative rule, a nonlegislative interpretation is superior to other techniques. Interpretive rules are more accessible, more reliable, and, because of their generalized form, much more useful than interpretation supplied through formal or informal adjudication or advice letters.

For similar reasons, the public has an important stake in encouraging an agency to structure its discretionary powers through the adoption of nonlegislative policy statements. A published policy statement is much more useful than the same material tucked amidst the trivia in a staff manual, embedded in particularized decisions in formal or informal adjudications, or simply derived from the practices of the staff.

Given the importance of nonlegislative rules, should full-fledged notice and comment procedure be required before they are adopted? In 1946, the drafters of the APA concluded that the benefits of mandatory public procedure were outweighed by the issuance of fewer rules and by reduced effectiveness, increased cost, and undue delay.

This article concludes that their call was close but right. Mandatory pre-adoption procedure would be a significant disincentive to nonlegislative rulemaking. The public would lose more than it would gain. The loss of a large quantity of relatively unimportant nonlegislative material outweighs the benefits of providing a relatively small number of people additional opportunities to influence the content of a relatively small number of important rules.

* * *

IV. State and Federal Reform Proposals

* * *

C. *Post-adoption Notice and Comment: Administrative Conference Recommendation 76-5.*

In 1976, the Administrative Conference of the United States (ACUS) adopted Recommendation 76-5, a modest reform proposal addressed to agencies rather than to Congress or the courts. Recommendation 76-5 suggested that *voluntary* notice and comment procedures be employed when an agency anticipates that a nonlegislative rule might have a substantial impact on the public. This voluntary approach echoes admonitions in the legislative history of the APA.

In the case of generally applicable nonlegislative rules that lack a substantial impact, ACUS recommended that an agency invite members of the public to submit comments for a thirty day period *after* the rule is adopted. The agency would be required to respond to the comments within a sixty day period.

* * *

The post-adoption procedure has a number of advantages over both present law and other regulatory proposals. First, it would not delay the effective date of a rule. Because most nonlegislative rules are either trivial or clearly valid, they will elicit no comments and thus require no administrative response. Indeed, post-adoption comment does not differ significantly from the existing provision in section 553(e) of the APA, which allows interested persons to petition for the amendment or repeal of a rule. As a result, post-adoption procedure should not significantly deter agencies from adopting nonlegislative rules.

Second, a requirement of post-adoption procedure would in practice lead agencies to provide pre-adoption procedures for important rules that are expected to provoke substantial comment. In such situations, the staff may well prefer the usual and familiar pre-adoption routine instead of mandatory reconsideration of an already-adopted rule. Consequently, advance public participation in nonlegislative rule-making should increase substantially.

Third, post-adoption comment periods can be quite effective. The comments will, in many cases, identify shortcomings in the rule that can be swiftly repaired. When members of the public know that their input must be read, considered, and commented upon, they will be more likely to take the trouble to make comments.

Fourth, a record consisting of public comments and agency responses would be invaluable to a court engaged in pre-enforcement judicial review of the validity of a nonlegislative rule. The absence of a record makes review more difficult and encourages courts to hold the rules unripe for review. The availability of a more detailed record would assist a court in determining, for example, whether a nonlegislative rule is reasonable or arbitrary or whether it is consistent with the underlying statute.

Finally, post-adoption comment invites the public to share in the process of making all nonlegislative rules. In fact, because a rule that has been adopted is more visible than a proposed rule, it might attract even wider attention and comment than a pre-adoption invitation. Greater public involvement should enhance the legitimacy of the rules. At the same time, post-adoption procedure would not, in the vast majority of cases, delay the adoption of rules nor should it discourage agencies from adopting them.

Of course, there is one obvious disadvantage to post-adoption procedure—comments made after a rule is adopted may be less effective in influencing the rulemaking process. The thinking of the staff undoubtedly rigidifies after an agency has adopted and published a rule in final form. At that point, both the staff and the agency heads may be less open to alternatives, and may react defensively to critical comments. For that reason, members of the public might be less willing to take the trouble to prepare comments.

* * *

Some opponents of this proposal have complained that it will increase staff workload, because the staff will have to respond to comments, and perhaps reconsider rules, within a defined time frame. Not surprisingly, the reconsideration of nonlegislative rules is rarely a high priority task. However, it is unlikely that anyone will comment on the vast majority of all nonlegislative rules. Moreover, the public can create the same burden under existing law by petitioning for repeal or amendment of any rule.

E. *Regulatory Reform: Substance and Procedure.*

* * *

This article is a plea to regulatory reformers to treat legislative and nonlegislative rules separately. Many reasons why one might favor reforms of or controls over the legislative rulemaking process are not at all applicable to nonlegislative rules. Even if one seeks to make rulemaking more difficult so that agencies will do less of it, it does not follow that one should try to make nonlegislative rulemaking more difficult.

Given that a scheme of regulation exists, and given that an agency has adopted the legislative rules necessary to set it in motion, it serves the interests of everyone—the agency and its staff, the regulated parties, the public, staunch proponents and opponents of the regulatory scheme, seekers of efficiency, seekers of fairness—that the agency provide guidance in the form of generally applicable interpretive rules and policy statements. Costly and cumbersome procedures that would enhance the ability of a few members of the public to influence the content of a few important nonlegislative rules seriously disserve all these interests because they will necessarily decrease the flow of nonlegislative rules.

* * *

Additional Sources

Robert A. Anthony, *"Well, You Want the Permit, Don't You?": Agency Efforts to Make Nonlegislative Documents Bind the Public*, 44 Admin. L. Rev. 31 (1992)

Robert A. Anthony, *Which Agency Interpretations Should Bind Citizens and the Courts?*, 7 Yale J. on Reg. 1 (1990)

Michael Asimow, *Public Participation in the Adoption of Interpretive Rules and Policy Statements*, 75 Mich. L. Rev. 520 (1977)

Arthur E. Bonfield, *Some Tentative Thoughts on Public Participation in the Making of Interpretative Rules and General Statements of Policy Under the APA*, 23 Admin. L. Rev. 101 (1971)

Charles H. Koch, Jr., *Public Procedures for the Promulgation of Interpretative Rules and General Statements of Policy*, 64 Geo. L. J. 1047 (1976)

Ronald M. Levin, *Nonlegislative Rules and the Administrative Open Mind*, 41 Duke L.J. 1497 (1992)

Thomas O. McGarity, *Some Thoughts on "Deossifying" the Rulemaking Process*, 41 Duke L.J. 1385 (1992)

Kevin W. Saunders, *Interpretative Rules with Legislative Effect: An Analysis and a Proposal for Public Participation*, 1986 Duke L.J. 346

3. The Debate About Alternative Dispute Resolution in Administrative Procedure

The alternative dispute resolution movement, which has been an influential force in modern American law, seeks to develop alternatives to adversarial litigation for resolving conflicts in society. Although the movement emerged first in the context of general civil litigation, its influence has been felt in administrative law. There have been two principal developments. One is the emergence of negotiated rulemaking, under which affected interests and the agency sit down prior to the publication of a notice of proposed rulemaking to negotiate major aspects of a regulation. Another has been the increased use of ADR techniques in administrative adjudication.

In 1990, Congress passed statutes establishing procedures for negotiated rulemaking and the settlement of administrative disputes.* Although alternative dispute resolution techniques now have the imprimatur of legislation, they remain new to many officials and members of the affected public. The readings in this section explore ADR issues in administrative law.

The first excerpt is by attorney Philip J. Harter, a leading proponent of alternative dispute resolution in the administrative context. Mr. Harter recites basic arguments in favor of an organized negotiating process for agency rulemaking.

In the second excerpt, Professor William Funk is more critical of negotiated rulemaking. He contends that regulatory negotiation can obscure the public interest while dramatizing the selfish benefits for private interests. Moreover, he suggests that regulatory negotiation has the potential to subvert core principles of administrative law.

The next excerpt, which also is from an article by Philip Harter, provides an overview of major types of ADR techniques for resolving adjudicative disputes. As in his earlier piece, Mr. Harter exudes optimism about the potential for ADR in the administrative process.

In contrast, Professor Owen Fiss sounds an alarm with respect to ADR in general. This final excerpt, which is not limited to the administrative context, raises broad questions about the movement's emphasis on compromising disputes rather than on reaching authoritative resolutions by courts.

---

* *See* Negotiated Rulemaking Act, Pub. L. 101-648, codified at 5 U.S.C. § 561 *et seq.*, and Administrative Dispute Resolution Act, Pub. L. 101-552, codified at 5 U.S.C. §§ 556(c)(6)–(8), 571–83.

Philip J. Harter, *Negotiating Regulations: A Cure for Malaise*, 71 Geo. L.J. 1, 7, 14–18, 28–31 (1982)*

* * *

* * * Negotiations among directly affected groups conducted within both the existing policies of the statute authorizing the regulation and the existing policies of the agency, would enable the parties to participate directly in the establishment of the rule. The significant concerns of each could be considered frontally. Direct participation in rulemaking through negotiations is preferable to entrusting the decision to the wisdom and judgment of the agency, which is essential under the basic provisions of the APA, or to relying on the more formal, structured method of hybrid rulemaking in which it is difficult for anyone to make the careful trade offs necessary for an enlightened regulation. A regulation that is developed by and has the support of the respective interests would have a political legitimacy that regulations developed under any other process arguably lack.

Negotiation undoubtedly will not work for all rules. Failure to use negotiations appropriately either could lead to great abuse or could simply add another layer to the already protracted rulemaking process. Experiences in analogous areas, however, suggest instances in which negotiation could be a feasible method of setting rules, and identify the procedures that should be followed to ensure that an acceptable rule emerges from a negotiation process. * * *

* * *

* * * An agency now must review the issues involved in a proposed regulation and make an initial, tentative determination of the factual basis to support a proposed rule. During this developmental process, and certainly once the rulemaking proceeding begins, interested persons may submit factual data and policy arguments that the agency must consider in reaching its final decision on the rule. The agency, like an umpire, then assesses the competing contentions, those of the various parties and of its own staff, and weighs the relevant facts and policy in light of the criteria of the statute under which the agency operates.

---

* Copyright 1982 The Georgetown Law Journal Association. Reprinted with the permission of The Georgetown Law Journal Association, Georgetown University, and Philip J. Harter. All rights reserved.

The parties' participation is a method of ensuring that the agency has adequate information on which to base its action. Participation also has an important additional role. To the extent that the agency is "bound" by the record of the rulemaking proceeding, the parties can confine the range of discretion available to the agency through the development of the rulemaking record. The record of the rule must reflect that the agency considered the appropriate issues and must contain substantial support for factual determinations. Thus, the parties could exercise some control over an agency's discretion by participating in the hybrid process *if* all the issues could be resolved simply by conducting factual research and placing it in the record.

* * *

Although parties participate in the rulemaking process by presenting facts and arguments through procedures tailored more to develop the factual basis of rules than to reach agreement on policy, policy questions ultimately are decided largely by the agency. The agency virtually always retains a broad range of discretion, the exercise of which involves inherently political choices. For example, the agency decides which "facts" are relevant to the decision and how to reconcile such competing values as energy development versus environmental protection, or safety versus costs. The statutes usually provide little guidance. Commenting on this lack of guidance, Professor Jaffe stated that "Where in form or in substance the legislative design is incomplete, uncertain, or inchoate, a political process will take place in and around the agency, with the likely outcome a function of the usual variables which determine the product of lawmaking institutions." Professor Stewart characterized the problem similarly:

> Today, the exercise of agency discretion is inevitably seen as the essentially legislative process of adjusting the competing claims of various private interests affected by agency policy.
> . . .
> . . . [T]he application of legislative directives requires the agency to reweigh and reconcile the often nebulous or conflicting policies behind the directives in the context of a particular constellation of affected interests. The required balancing of policies is an inherently discretionary, ultimately political procedure.

The resolution of these political questions has resulted in a crisis of legitimacy that is the current malaise. Agency actions no longer gain acceptance from the presumed expertise of its staff. It is no longer viewed as legitimate simply because it fills in the gaps left by Congress, or because it is guided by widely accepted public philosophy. To the extent that rulemaking has political legitimacy, it derives from the right of affected interests to present facts and arguments to an agency under procedures designed to ensure the rationality of the agency's decision. Although this process confines and narrows agency discretion, it does not provide a forum suitable for the resolution of the political questions or for the exercise of subtle value choices.

* * *

* * * Groups affected by a regulation need the opportunity to actually participate in its development if they are to they have faith in it. A participatory process would have positive merit in and of itself because a resulting regulation would be based on the consensus of those who would be affected by it, which is, after all, the nature of political decisionmaking. Achieving the consensus of interested parties would also reduce many of the problems caused by the current adversarial process of developing regulations. * * *

* * *

Negotiating has many advantages over the adversarial process. The parties participate directly and immediately in the decision. They share in its development and concur with it, rather than "participate" by submitting information that the decisionmaker considers in reaching the decision. * * * In addition, negotiation can be a less expensive means of decisionmaking because it reduces the need to engage in defensive research in anticipation of arguments made by adversaries.

Undoubtedly the prime benefit of direct negotiations is that it enables the participants to focus squarely on their respective interests. They need not advocate and maintain extreme positions before a decisionmaker. Therefore, the parties can develop a feel for the true issues that lie within the advocated extremes and attempt to accommodate fully the competing interests. An example of this benefit occurred when a group of environmentalists opposed the construction of a dam because they feared it would lead to the development of a nearby valley. The proponents of the dam were farmers in the valley who were adversely affected by periodic floods. Negotiations between the two groups, which were begun at the behest of the governor, revealed a common interest in preserving the valley. Without the negotiations the environmentalists would have undoubtedly sued to block construction, and necessarily would have employed adversarial tactics. Negotiations, however, demonstrated the true interests of the parties and permitted them to work toward accommodation.

* * *

Negotiation enables the parties to rank their concerns and to make trades to maximize their respective interests. In a traditional proceeding an agency may be unable to anticipate the intensity with which the respective parties may view the various provisions of a proposed rule. The agency may focus on an aspect of a rule that is critical to one party, but not of particular interest to other parties. An agency simply would have to guess how to reconcile such an issue because it would not know how to rank the parties' concerns. An interested party, however, could easily decide to accommodate another party in return for concession on a critical point. An example of such a trade off process would be when a beneficiary of a proposed regulation argues that the standard should be stringent with early compliance by the regulated company. A company that must comply with the regulation might counter that the standard should be more lenient with a long lead time for compliance. An agency faced with this situation might decide to require a lax standard in response to the company's claims of excessive burdens and require a short deadline in response to the need for immediate protection. Everyone involved, however, may be more content with precisely the opposite result. A rule allowing a longer time to implement a more stringent standard might benefit both parties because the shorter time for implementation might cause disruption that would offset any savings resulting from the reduced level of regulation.

Rulemaking by negotiation can reduce the time and cost of developing regulations by emphasizing practical and empirical concerns rather than theoretical predictions. In developing a regulation under the current system, an agency must prove a factual case, at least preliminarily, and anticipate the factual information that will be submitted in the record. Because the agency lacks direct access to empirical data, the information used is often of a theoretical nature derived from models. In negotiations, the parties in interest decide together what information is necessary to make a reasonably informed decision. Therefore, the data used in negotiations may not have to be as theoretical or as extensive as it is in an adversary process. For example, one agency proposed a regulation based on highly technical, theoretical data. The parties argued that the theoretical data was unnecessary because it simply did not reflect the practical experiences of the parties and of another agency. The agency determined the validity of the assertion and modified its regulation accordingly. The lesson of this example is that the data can emphasize practical and empirical concerns rather than theoretical predictions. In turn, this emphasis on practical experience can reduce the time and cost of developing regulations by reducing the need for developing extensive theoretical data.

Negotiation also can enable the participants to focus on the details of a regulation. In the adversary process, the big points must be hit and hit hard, while the subtleties and details frequently are overlooked. Or, even if the details are not overlooked, the decisionmaker may not appreciate their consequences. In negotiations, however, interested parties can directly address all aspects of a problem in attempting to formulate workable solutions.

Overarching all the other benefits of negotiations is the added legitimacy a rule would acquire if all parties viewed the rule as reasonable and endorsed it without a fight. Affected parties would participate in the development of a rule by sharing in the decisions, ranking their own concerns and needs, and trading them with other parties. Regardless of whether the horse under design turns out to be a five-legged camel or a Kentucky Derby winner, the resulting rule would have a validity beyond those developed under the current procedures. Moreover, nothing indicates that the results would be of any lesser quality than those developed currently. Surely the *Code of Federal Regulations* stable has as many camels as derby winners.

Negotiation clearly has distinct advantages. It is therefore easy to fall into a "hot tub" view of negotiation as a method of settling disputes and establishing public policy: if only we strip off the armor of an adversarial hearing, everyone will jump into negotiations with beguiling honesty and openness to reach the optimum solution to the problem at hand. In fact, the process is far more complex than that. Negotiation must be carefully analyzed to determine not only whether it can work at all in the regulatory context, but also to identify those situations in which it is appropriate. Moreover, if a form of negotiation is to be used to develop rules issued by a government agency that determine the rights and obligations of the population at large, the process must be sensitive to methods of conducting negotiations and translating any result into a binding rule. Thus, the complex legal issues of how negotiations would relate to the APA and to the traditional political theories and values underlying rulemaking procedures must be examined.

* * *

William Funk, *When Smoke Gets in Your Eyes: Regulatory Negotiation and the Public Interest— EPA's Woodstove Standards*, 18 ENVTL. L. 55, 55-57, 78-81, 84-87, 89-97 (1987)*

* * *

I. Introduction

Regulatory negotiation is a recent development in administrative law. Philip Harter provided its first real description and justification in 1982.[1] According to Harter's analysis, informal rulemaking had become so complex and formalized that rulemakings had degenerated into adversarial proceedings with the delay, expense, and dissatisfaction characteristic of such proceedings. * * * Harter recommended that at least certain regulations should be negotiated between the interested parties, including the agency issuing the regulation. To avoid the necessity of substantial amendment of the Administrative Procedure Act as well as other statutes, Harter suggested a scheme for negotiating regulations which he believed would not run afoul of current administrative law concepts. In short, this involved the negotiation of a *proposed* rule, which the agency would then publish as its proposed rule and thereafter treat pretty much as it would any proposed rule. * * *

Since Harter's article, several agencies, including especially the Environmental Protection Agency (EPA), have experimented with negotiating proposed regulations according to Harter's formula, as reflected in the recommendations of the Administrative Conference of the United States. Assessments of those experiments have been uniformly positive, even where the regulatory negotiation failed to result in a proposed or final regulation. One of the most recent experiments resulted in an EPA proposed rule to establish emission limitations for residential woodstoves under the Clean Air Act.

---

* Reprinted with permission of Environmental Law and William Funk. All rights reserved.

[1] Harter, *Negotiating Regulations: A Cure for Malaise*, 71 GEO. L.J. 1 (1982). * * *

It is the thesis of this Article that this proposed rule is not authorized by the Clean Air Act, and that the process of developing the rule by regulatory negotiation directly contributed to this unlawful proposal. Moreover, this Article concludes that the nature of regulatory negotiation has the tendency to obscure, if not pervert, the public interest to the benefit of private interests, and that the regulatory negotiation of the woodstove emission limitation is a case study of such a perversion.

[This article proceeds to discuss in detail substantive issues relating to the woodstove rule.]

* * *

IV. The Regulatory Negotiation

The product of the regulatory negotiation [about woodstove emissions] was a draft proposed rule, which EPA agreed to publish as its proposed rule. Each of the members of the negotiating committee, including EPA, concluded a formal agreement agreeing to support and not to criticize the proposed rule. Each member, except EPA, agreed to support and not to challenge in court any final rule consistent with the proposed rule.

Pursuant to the agreement, EPA drafted a preamble for the proposed rule; that is, an explanatory statement to precede the actual proposed regulatory language upon which the committee had agreed. That preamble frankly admits that "its explanation of the reasons for particular committee decisions may not always reflect the reason why each individual committee member agreed to a particular provision of the regulation." At another point, the preamble states that, while the committee concurred with the regulation as a whole, the committee did not necessarily concur in each provision. Rather, "some parties may have made concessions in one area, in exchange for concessions from other parties in other areas." The necessary conclusion one must draw from these statements is that the preamble drafted by EPA is *not* an explanation of why or how the particular regulatory provisions were adopted. Instead, the preamble is an after-the-fact rationale attempting to justify decisions made by the negotiating committee for reasons we can never know.

In these circumstances it is entirely appropriate for readers to assess critically any explanation given by EPA for its action in light of possible alternative reasons suggested by the interests of the negotiating parties with a "stake" in the outcome, including EPA.

First, why did EPA decide to undertake this rulemaking at this time? EPA states that the rulemaking is a response to a determination that wood heaters cause air pollution which may reasonably be anticipated to endanger human health or welfare * * *. As late as 1984, however, EPA was maintaining that there was insufficient data to support a determination that airborne POM [Polycyclic Organic Matter] threatened the public health. Nor has EPA backed off from that position. Yet it was concern over POM that motivated the NRDC [National Resources Defense Council] to sue EPA, and there is ample evidence that it was that suit that motivated EPA to institute the woodstove rulemaking. Not only does the preamble to the proposed rule suggest that motivation, but earlier EPA representatives had expressly stated that the lawsuit was "spurring EPA to regulate wood stove emissions as quickly as possible." Yet, POM is not regulated by the proposed rule; only particulates are regulated, a pollutant already regulated under the national ambient air standards.

Unquestionably, woodstoves are a major source of particulates, but "unlike most other air pollutants, they are distributed almost at ground level," having only localized effects. EPA never thought to include woodstoves on its priority list of polluting stationary sources. In addition, there never was any indication that controls on woodstoves by states and localities * * * were inadequate to attain and maintain ambient air quality standards or that local concerns inhibited states and localities from adopting necessary controls. To the contrary, the evidence was overwhelming that states and localities *were* willing and able to regulate woodstove emissions where they caused significant pollution. The preamble to the proposed rule acknowledged that two states and several localities had already imposed controls, and the Regulatory Impact Analysis concluded that in the absence of a federal standard, other states and localities "almost certainly now would be adopting regulations." Rather, the ability and willingness of states and localities to take effective regulatory action with respect to woodstoves seemed to be the *problem*.

Clearly, it was the problem from the woodstove industry's perspective. The industry realistically feared numerous different and conflicting standards and test procedures, and for this reason, actively sought a nationwide emission standard "in hopes of preventing individual states from enacting their own parochial standards." The industry had already sponsored the development of a proposed national consensus standard for testing woodstove emissions under the sponsorship of the American Society of Testing and Materials. It was just a short step to link arms with the NRDC and to support EPA's promulgation of a national emission standard. * * *

In short, the evidence strongly suggests that EPA chose to regulate woodstoves at this time not because it had discovered they polluted, but because of particular pressures brought to bear on EPA by various groups with a "stake" in the outcome. Similarly, the evidence suggests that the choice of regulating under section 111 [of the Clean Air Act] was not the result of disinterested consideration, but the result of the externally imposed imperatives of a national standard and EPA's adamant refusal to recognize POM as a hazardous pollutant to be regulated under section 112. One of the primary problems with respect to section 112 regulation is that it requires emission standards for both new and existing sources of the hazardous pollutant. The regulation of the approximately twelve million existing woodstoves was viewed as not within the realm of the practicable. Consequently, if state and local regulations were out of the question, only section 111, relating to stationary sources, was left.

[There follows a discussion of legal issues with using § 111 as the basis of a woodstove rule.]

* * *

In the absence of a regulatory negotiation, it is highly likely that a number of commenters would have objected to the particular method of regulating woodstoves under section 111, if not to the basic concept of their regulation under section 111. Unable to rely on their "inside" ability to achieve a regulation that would meet their substantive objections, commenters would have an interest in raising legal objections to the rule. The negotiation process, however, not only mutes legal objections, it does bring the parties in interest "inside" the substantive rule-making process. In the case of woodstoves, for example, it meant that manufacturers and environmentalists could negotiate which woodstoves would be regulated at what level according to what timetable.

To industry, the goal was a regulation that would have the least impact on the largest number of manufacturers. This meant a standard which did not set limitations at a level unobtainable by most manufacturers or that would require major changes in their products. Moreover, whatever standard was to be adopted would have to provide enough lead time to minimize disruption of the manufacturing process. To environmentalists, the goal was a regulation that would minimize harmful pollutants as quickly as possible.

Section 111 describes the level at which emission standards under that section are to be set and also specifies when those standards are to go into effect with respect to new sources. The timing aspect is straightforward; the standard is to apply to any stationary source constructed or modified after the publication of proposed regulations (or, if there are no proposed regulations, final regulations) applicable to that source. There is no provision in the statute for changing the time when the standard will be applicable, and apparently EPA has not altered the timing before. Nevertheless, "inside" the process, the manufacturers were able to negotiate a phased compliance schedule * * *. In addition, a special one-year grace period was provided for small manufacturers, and stoves certified to meet the Oregon state standard were grandfathered * * *.

In the preamble to the proposed rule, EPA responded to the obvious legal problem in the delayed compliance dates applicable to most manufacturers; it did not bother to address the authority for either the Oregon grandfather or small manufacturer provision. EPA explained that the general requirement for new source performance standards is that they represent the use of Best Demonstrated Technology (BDT), which includes a cost consideration. With respect to woodstoves, EPA stated, there would be a substantial cost if the standard were to apply immediately. Consequently, EPA concluded, "BDT applies only to those classes of new sources that can meet the standards with a reasonable lead time."

There are at least two problems with this explanation: one legal and one practical. The practical problem is that this explanation for the delayed compliance dates first appears in the preamble to the rule. It does not appear in the Regulatory Impact Analysis, the Issue Paper dealing with compliance dates, or the minutes of negotiations relating to compliance dates. The BDT explanation is another example of EPA's preamble writers inventing an after-the-fact justification that bears no relation to the true basis for the negotiated agreement between the interested parties. As a consequence, there is nothing in the record of the proceeding to support the preamble's bald statement other than general statements that claim giving effect to the statutorily required effective date would be "disruptive to the industry."

The legal problem is that, while BDT does include a cost component, that cost component is to be considered in setting the level or stringency of the standard itself, not the time when the standard will go into effect. That is, if the need to design and produce new woodstoves will take time and, therefore, impose unacceptable costs, then those costs should be considered in deciding whether to set the standard lower, thereby reducing the need to design and produce new woodstoves. There is no authority in the law for EPA merely to delay compliance beyond the statutorily required time in order to mitigate certain manufacturers' costs of compliance with a standard which has been determined to be BDT. Such is the nature of a variance or waiver, neither of which is available to new sources under section 111, except for innovative technological systems of continuous emission reduction, which is not applicable here.

* * *

The negotiation concluded with consensus. All the parties were in agreement overall. What some had lost at one place, they had won at another. The outcome was acceptable to all. Then, to assure continued allegiance, a formal agreement between all the parties was concluded, requiring each to support the proposed rule and not to challenge the final rule, if it is consistent with the proposed rule. EPA agreed to publish as its proposed rule the proposal adopted by the consensus and to draft a preamble consistent with it. The deed was done.

V. Regulatory Negotiation and Administrative Law

The above sections of this Article have tried to demonstrate certain problems that exist in EPA's proposed woodstove emission standard and how the regulatory negotiation of this proposal caused or fostered these problems. One response to such a showing, however, is to assert that this particular regulation is idiosyncratic. The fault lies in the dynamics of this particular rule, not in the process of regulatory negotiation generally. Such a response, I believe, would be a mistake, because it is my thesis that the theory and principles of regulatory negotiation are at war with the theory and principles of American administrative law applicable to rulemaking * * *.

Modern American administrative law begins with the New Deal, and James Landis provided the best contemporary justification and explanation for the administrative state in his now classic book, The Administrative Process. According to his analysis, Congress creates administrative agencies because modern society requires governmental regulation to a degree simply beyond the resources and expertise of Congress. These agencies are empowered to make law because they are or will become expert in their fields. Not articulated, but implicit in his analysis, was a belief that these agencies faced problems capable of objective solution, that politically neutral administrators could determine finite and correct answers to the problems of modern industrial society.

Not all shared his optimistic belief in neutral bureaucrats finding objectively verifiable answers to clearly understood problems. The response, however, was not to eliminate the administrative agencies, or even to reduce their powers, but rather it was to subject their actions to procedural restraints and judicial review. The Administrative Procedure Act (APA) was the result, a compromise piece of legislation designed to constrain the discretion of agencies while legitimating their remaining discretion through procedural regularity and judicial oversight. While the APA perhaps reflects a loss of the naive faith in the natural ability of expert bureaucrats to scientifically discover objectively correct solutions to society's problems, it does not indicate a lessened determination to use agencies and rulemaking to solve politically perceived problems. In this, the APA is much like the Constitution; it does not indicate a rejection of the need for strong government for the proper functioning of modern society, but rather a healthy disrespect for the motives and abilities of men placed in power. And like much of the Constitution, the APA uses procedural mechanisms to check the power granted, while not denying the need for the power.

The continuing belief in the importance and legitimacy of agencies as regulators of private conduct, despite a distrust of the regulators, was confirmed by the great period of agency creation during the 1960's and 1970's. Now the focus was more on health and safety regulation, perhaps reflecting a once again naive belief in the existence of scientifically and objectively determinable solutions to problems, but now there was even more concern about the necessity of procedures to constrain the discretion of agencies. Both courts and Congress combined to establish procedures aimed at fostering the rationality of agency decision making. Thus, these procedures, which have come to be known as "hybrid rulemaking," focus on maximizing the information available to the agency, ensuring its critical assessment, and most importantly, requiring that the ultimate decision be objectively reasonable in light of the information obtained. Most recently, the executive branch's contribution has been to require cost/benefit analyses, again to foster rationality in agency decision making.

Today the emphasis is on deregulation, reflecting a reassessment of whether certain problems exist at all or, if they exist, are best addressed by public law solutions. Nevertheless, where a problem is still perceived to require government action, today's answer to that problem remains agency action. We have come a long way from the simple faith of James Landis, but for the most part we have not rejected his solution where there is agreement as to the need for government action. In place of his faith we have substituted procedural requirements to foster rationality, but we have not abandoned the goal of reasoned decision making to achieve the public interest.

Defining the public interest may be a different undertaking from achieving an agreed-upon public interest. In the Clean Air Act, for instance, a number of provisions, including section 111, requires the weighing of various factors, at least some of which are difficult if not impossible to quantify. The statute implies that this weighing process defines the public interest. In this realm, information and data, logic and science, are only of limited help. Here, values and philosophies may be more pertinent. Yet, here too Congress has delegated to agencies the power to make this definition. As the Supreme Court made clear in *Chevron, U.S.A. v. NRDC*, where Congress has not considered and decided the question at issue in the context of a regulatory scheme, it has implicitly delegated the authority to the agency to make that determination. Accordingly, it would be improper for the courts to second-guess the determination.

Of course, agencies are not to make their determinations in a vacuum. Procedural requirements assure input from interested parties, and recent executive orders institute a supervisory executive branch oversight of executive agencies' determinations. Moreover, this supervisory oversight can properly have a policy component; it need not be politically sterile. Nevertheless, the ultimate responsibility for the determination continues to rest with the agency. Not only is the final responsibility to be the agency's, but in the oft-quoted words of *Scenic Hudson Preservation Conference v. FPC*, an agency's role as representative of the public interest "does not permit it to act as an umpire blandly calling balls and strikes for adversaries appearing before it; the right of the public must receive active and affirmative protection at the hands of the [agency]."

The concept of regulatory negotiation stands this role on its head, first, by reducing the agency to the level of a mere participant in the formulation of the rule, and second, by essentially denying that the agency has any responsibility beyond giving effect to the consensus achieved by the group. In addition, regulatory negotiation finds its legitimacy in the agreement between the parties, rather than in the determination under law of the public interest; in other words, regulatory negotiation substitutes a private law remedy for a public law remedy.

The recommendations of the Administrative Conference of the United States, based upon Harter's study, state that an agency representative should participate in the negotiation. This is so because the agency has a stake in the outcome. Moreover, its participation should not differ in kind from that of the other parties in interest. In other words, it should bargain and trade its "interests" (the public interest) in the same way the other participants may trade their interests.

Harter recognizes the possible objection to this role as inconsistent with the concept of the agency as the sovereign decision maker. He responds by suggesting that there is no problem because the agency remains sovereign; it alone makes the final decision. Its representative to the negotiation cannot bind the agency. This response, however, is somewhat disingenuous. As Harter acknowledges, *no* party's representative to the negotiations can bind its principal. Thus, the agency remains like any other participant. The agency's representative must obtain the approval of senior officials in the agency before the agency is committed, just as other representatives must obtain the approval of their principals. However, the fact that the agency's representative is himself supposed to be a senior official makes highly probable that he will reliably be able to speak for the agency. Finally, while Harter is undoubtedly correct that the agency technically has the final decision, this power becomes theoretical at best where the agency has already agreed beforehand along with all the other participants to seek consensus in good faith, to support the consensus result, and in particular to publish as a proposed rule the rule developed by that consensus. In other words, unless an agency acts in bad faith and violates a written undertaking made at the beginning of the negotiation, it is bound to publish the consensus rule as its proposed rule.

That the agency plays no special role in the negotiation is made clear by certain other recommendations of the Administrative Conference. Thus, neutral parties should be sought as "convenors," mediators or "facilitators." Moreover, "a neutral outside individual" should be appointed, where appropriate, to receive and evaluate confidential data and to report back to the negotiating group.

This fundamental change in the role of the agency in the rulemaking process is mirrored by the fundamental change in the underlying theoretical justification for the eventual rule. As Harter admits: "Under the traditional hybrid process, the legitimacy of the rule rests on a resolution of complex factual materials and rational extrapolation from those facts, guided by the criteria of the statute. Under regulatory negotiation, however, the regulation's legitimacy would lie in the overall agreement of the parties." Stated another way, the parties to the rule are happy with it; therefore, it matters not whether the rule is rational or lawful. Discretion delegated to the agency by Congress is effectively exercised by the group of interested parties, constrained only by the need to obtain consensus. The law no longer directs or even necessarily constrains the outcome but has become merely a factor in the give-and-take necessary to achieve consensus.

To say that regulatory negotiation turns the traditional concept of administrative rulemaking on its head does not, however, compel the conclusion that it is necessarily unlawful. The Administrative Conference recommendations are carefully crafted in an attempt to comply with all the procedural requirements attendant to rulemaking. * * *

As a consequence, supporters of regulatory negotiation may suggest that "no harm, no foul." That is, if no one complains about a rule developed by regulatory negotiation, it must be deemed a success. * * *

Reliance on the absence of disagreement as evidence of legitimacy for a regulation puts a premium on assuring that the negotiating group adequately represents all affected interests. There are, however, both practical and theoretical limitations on the number of interests that may be represented and the quality of representation each interest may obtain. Where the interest is strong enough to make itself known and felt, little difficulty arises—either that interest will be represented in the negotiation or the negotiation in the end will not likely be successful. More problematic is where the interest is not well defined, organized, or strong. Reliance on the Federal Advisory Committee Act's requirement for "balanced membership" on advisory groups is not sufficient. First, unlike ordinary advisory committees, where the agency is not a member and the output is truly only a recommendation, the regulatory negotiation committees are advisory only in name. Thus, the agency's responsibility for determining the public interest, expressed in the Federal Advisory Committee Act, no longer provides the safeguard otherwise available for unrepresented interests. Second, while a general "balance" may be achievable in the committee setting, such balance is not itself sufficient to assure the representation of unrepresented persons or interests. For example, in the woodstove negotiation, the Consumer Federation of America (CFA) was supposed to represent the interests of the consumer, but consumers, as the CFA would be the first to admit, are hardly a homogenous entity. The CFA may have represented the interests associated with the mentality of a *Consumer Reports* reader, but it did not appear to lobby on behalf of poor, rural folk for whom the rule will provide little benefit and perhaps significant burden. Moreover, the fact that these people do not comment on the proposed rule or challenge a final rule in court hardly establishes that the rule is fair and wise as to them.

The tendency of alternative dispute resolution to focus on the interests of the specific parties to the dispute without regard to broader values has been noted in the literature related to alternatives to litigation. As Judge Edwards has noted, there are important differences between alternative dispute resolution where only private interests and values are at stake and where public values and interests are involved. "[I]f ADR is extended to resolve difficult issues of constitutional or public law—making use of nonlegal values to resolve important social issues or allowing those the law seeks to regulate to delimit public rights and duties—there is real reason for concern."[246] Regulatory negotiation, by reducing disputes over what is in the public interest to disputes between various private interests, and by substituting private agreement for public determinations made according to legal norms, transforms administrative rulemaking into an area of private law, and this is a fundamental alteration.

These theoretical and practical differences between regulatory negotiation and traditional rulemaking can explain how EPA's development of its proposed rule on woodstove emissions was not idiosyncratic. They suggest that the regulatory negotiation process submerged public interest values, as reflected in the terms and conditions of the statute, to the special interests of the parties involved in the negotiation. Therefore, it is hardly surprising that what emerged from that process is a proposed rule with which the parties are happy but which bears scant resemblance to what was contemplated by the statute.

VI. Conclusion

The thesis of this Article has been that the regulatory negotiation process tends to subvert the principles and values of administrative rulemaking. * * * If successful, this Article should give pause to some at least who would otherwise view regulatory negotiation as totally beneficial and benign, in light of the glowing reports of regulatory negotiation pleasing all the parties, avoiding litigation, and producing wiser and fairer regulations. However, it is not the purpose of this Article to conclude that regulatory negotiation is necessarily bad and should be shot dead in its tracks. To the contrary, the practical benefits of reg-

---

[246] [Harry Edwards, *Alternative Dispute Resolution: Panacea or Anathema?*, 99 HARV. L. REV. 668, 676 (1986).]

ulatory negotiation cannot be gainsaid, and if they have not received much attention here, it is only because there are ample other sources. It is of no small moment when the professional defenders of the environment, the affected industry, and government entities can achieve consensus on how to deal with a particular source of pollution. Rather, it is the purpose of this Article to demonstrate that regulatory negotiation, despite the fact that it can probably be accomplished without violating existing procedural requirements, fundamentally alters the dynamics of traditional administrative rulemaking from a search for the public interest, however imperfect that search may be, to a search for a consensus among private parties representing particular interests.

Only after one recognizes this fundamental change can one fully assess the advantages and disadvantages of regulatory negotiation as an alternative to traditional administrative rulemaking. Up to now, the debate over regulatory negotiation has revolved around its feasibility and methods to improve its "success" rate. Now, however, the debate should include the appropriateness of private interests determining the public values at stake in the rulemaking. In some cases the issues to be decided in the negotiation may be so bounded that any threat to public values disappears. In other cases the negotiation may claim as its subject matter issues which properly should be decided only by an agency.

* * *

Philip J. Harter, *Points on a Continuum: Dispute Resolution Procedures and the Administrative Process*, 1 ADMIN. L.J. 141, 143-51, 210-11 (1987)*

* * *

I. Introduction
A. Interest in Dispute Resolution

An extraordinary interest in alternative ways of settling disputes—alternative, that is, to the courts and formal litigation—has developed during the past decade, and particularly in the last five years. This interest has spanned the gamut of disputes, from neighborhood controversies to more serious social infractions and major corporate matters.

* * *

Interestingly, one of the major reasons for the establishment of administrative programs and the use of administrative adjudication was to provide an alternative method for resolving disputes. * * *

* * *

Today, agencies must handle increasing caseloads and are accused of exhibiting problems similar to those they were established to cure. It is not surprising, therefore, that agencies, Congress, and private organizations are anxious to find new ways to address these difficulties. Given their promise and use in the judicial setting, it is only logical that the alternative means of dispute resolution (ADR) may * * * address * * * problems in the administrative process. * * *

By using the full range of ADR techniques, ADR can provide an additional means of addressing needs within the procedures specified in the Administrative Procedure Act (APA). Indeed, the adaptation and increasingly widespread use of the ADR processes that are successful in civil litigation may offer a solution to some of the more pressing problems of the administrative process. Acceptance of these techniques will be eased by familiarity with the use of ADR procedures both within and outside of the administrative process and by an understanding of how they relate to other needs of the administrative process. * * *

B. Contested Issues

This article focuses on using non-APA procedures to resolve disputed issues, as opposed to making administrative decisions in the first instance. An agency could employ these procedures directly or through a private organization working under agency supervision. This article discusses issues that need not be so specific or narrow that they must be resolved in an adjudicatory proceeding and about which some potential disagreement has arisen that needs to be resolved. The need to resolve the matter is what is important from the perspective of this article, not the context in which the need arises.

II. Overview of the Alternatives

The major types of ADR techniques are arbitration, med-arb, factfinding, minitrial, mediation, facilitation, convening, conciliation, and negotiation.

A. Arbitration

Arbitration is closely akin to adjudication in that

---

* Reprinted with permission of the Administrative Law Journal and Philip J. Harter. All rights reserved.

a neutral party decides the matter after reviewing evidence and hearing arguments from the parties. It has been widely used for decades in labor relations and in resolving commercial disputes. It ranges in formality from very nearly that of a court to virtually without structure; the arbitrator may be called upon to apply existing law or to reach "justice under the circumstances."

B. Med-Arb

Med-arb is a hybrid of mediation and arbitration. In it, the neutral first serves as a mediator, attempting to bring about a settlement among the parties. The neutral then decides any issues remaining unresolved after the mediated negotiations. Thus, following the mediation, the neutral becomes an arbitrator. Sometimes the arbitration is binding and resolves the dispute, but in other instances the neutral prepares a report which analyzes the positions and needs of the parties and recommends a resolution.

C. Factfinding

Many controversies, particularly those that must be resolved by regulatory agencies, turn on enormously complex factual issues. In these instances, the policy or ultimate judgment on the matter cannot be decided until the facts are developed in a relatively authoritative way. Once they are, the parties may then negotiate a settlement, require further proceedings, or conduct more research. Alternatively, the facts themselves may sufficiently decide the outcome so that very little will remain to be done.

A factfinding proceeding may be appropriate for complex factual disputes. Such a proceeding generally entails the appointment of a person or group of people with technical expertise in the subject matter. The experts or factfinders assay the situation and prepare a report establishing the facts of the question entrusted. The factfinder is not asked to resolve the entire issue, only to establish the underlying facts. The matter itself will be determined in another forum, either by the parties themselves or in some other proceeding. The procedures used for making the determination range from the highly informal to near trial-like procedures. Factfinding proceedings are, of course, commonly used by administrative agencies, frequently in the form of advisory committees.

D. Minitrial

In a minitrial, the lawyers for each party are given a relatively short period—ranging from several hours to several days—to make their best case, generally following the exchange of important documents and other factual materials. The parties will sometimes call witnesses, but generally only arguments based on previously presented evidence and the legal conclusions that flow from the issues are presented. The attorneys make these presentations to representatives of the parties (executives) who have the authority to settle the controversy and usually, but not always, a neutral third party. When the arguments are concluded the representatives then meet to negotiate an agreement.

The process is designed so that the executives may view their own case in perspective, evaluating its strengths and weaknesses * * *. The neutral may be called upon to render an opinion as to how a court or jury would decide the controversy. The parties may also ask the neutral for more limited advice. The neutral is, therefore, more an agent of reality than an arbitrator. As such, his or her report would potentially change the bargaining position of the parties, thus providing an incentive to settle before the report is issued. The report may also convince a party that its case is not as strong as originally believed and hence that a settlement may be the advisable route. The function of the minitrial is to convert what could be a complex, protracted legal battle into a business decision to be made by the executives of the parties.

E. Mediation

Mediation is, simply, a negotiation involving a mediator. A mediator is a neutral third party who assists the parties in negotiating an agreement. The mediator has no independent authority and does not render a decision; the parties make the decision themselves.

The mediator, however, may be quite active in the negotiation process. He will usually help the parties frame the issues, and analyze their actual needs, as well as the needs of the other side. Another important role played by the mediator is to deflate unreasonably ambitious assertions and desires. He or she will likely offer suggestions for possible solutions for settling the issues and draft materials for the consideration of the negotiators. Some of these suggestions may, of course, come from the parties themselves, but they will be communicated in such a manner as to avoid locking a party into an idea that does not work. The mediator may also need to communicate to the parties what is likely to happen if an agreement is not reached. In the current vernacular, the mediator will help the parties define their "best alternative to a negotiated agreement" (BATNA).

The mediator may meet privately with the parties and shuttle back and forth between them. Private meetings are frequently helpful in developing a negotiation framework and sufficiently defining the issues so that the parties can address them directly in a meeting. Without prior definition, the parties may find the risk of direct discussion too great. Moreover, the shuttling can save valuable time by reducing the need for more direct, face-to-face meetings, which are always difficult to schedule among senior representatives. The mediator can also deflect attention from the negotiators by being the spokesperson to those not engaged in the discussions. More importantly, the mediator also serves as the proponent of the process itself and can help keep discussions on track and moving.

F. Facilitating

A facilitator works to help a group of individuals or parties with divergent views reach a goal or complete a task to the mutual satisfaction of the participants. The terms facilitator and mediator are often used interchangeably; but although close in meaning, the two terms are distinct. A facilitator generally runs meetings and coordinates the negotiations without becoming as involved in the substantive issues as does a mediator when working with the parties. Thus, it is common for a mediator to be a facilitator but not the reverse.

G. Convening

A convenor is a neutral who helps identify the parties with an interest in a particular issue and also identify what issues are in controversy. Thus, the convenor's task is to conduct a feasibility analysis or conflict assessment and to determine whether direct negotiations among the parties would be a recommended way to resolve the issues. If so, the convenor brings the parties together to negotiate or otherwise reach some decision.

H. Conciliation

A conciliator works to lower tensions and improve communications between the parties. Conciliation is frequently used in volatile conflicts and in disputes where the parties are unable, unwilling, or unprepared to come to the table to negotiate their differences.

I. Negotiation

Negotiation is communication between people in an effort to reach an agreement. People negotiate settlements to all sorts of large and small controversies. Negotiation is such a pervasive means of dispute resolution that it is sometimes overlooked as such. Since the vast majority of cases and issues are settled, negotiation is the lifeblood of the administrative process. Many of the procedures developed by agencies to resolve disputes are actually methods for advancing and stimulating negotiated settlements.

III. Administrative Use of Dispute Resolution Techniques

Administrative agencies utilize a broad range of ADR techniques. For example, administrative law judges and presiding officers frequently utilize hearing procedures that rival arbitration for their expedition and informality. Many types of procedures are used to induce settlement and to garner an understanding, if not agreement, on underlying scientific and technical issues. To a very real extent, the administrative process has proved to be an expeditious and innovative process.

Nevertheless, agencies could do well to study carefully the full range of dispute resolution techniques that are being developed in civil litigation and to resolve matters independent of the courts. The explicit recognition of these techniques and their adaptation to the administrative process can address some of the pressing problems faced by an encumbered administrative process.

* * *

VI. Conclusion: Where Do We Go From Here?

The administrative process itself was in large measure born as an alternative means of dispute resolution—a way other than courts for making important societal decisions. It is singularly appropriate, therefore, that it should be responsive to various forms of dispute resolution that are gaining broad acceptance in the civil sector. These processes can help administrative agencies fulfill their original potential. We are on our way in recognizing their role. That alone is a major step towards a broader, more successful use.

Owen M. Fiss, *Against Settlement*, 93 YALE L.J. 1073, 1076-78, 1082-86 (1984)*

* * *

The Imbalance of Power

By viewing the lawsuit as a quarrel between two neighbors, the dispute-resolution story that underlies

---

* Reprinted with permission of The Yale Law Journal Company, Fred B. Rothman & Company, and Owen M. Fiss. All rights reserved.

ADR implicitly asks us to assume a rough equality between the contending parties. It treats settlement as the anticipation of the outcome of trial and assumes that the terms of settlement are simply a product of the parties' predictions of that outcome. In truth, however, settlement is also a function of the resources available to each party to finance the litigation, and those resources are frequently distributed unequally. Many lawsuits do not involve a property dispute between two neighbors, or between AT&T and the government (to update the story), but rather concern a struggle between a member of a racial minority and a municipal police department over alleged brutality, or a claim by a worker against a large corporation over work-related injuries. In these cases, the distribution of financial resources, or the ability of one party to pass along its costs, will invariably infect the bargaining process, and the settlement will be at odds with a conception of justice that seeks to make the wealth of the parties irrelevant.

The disparities in resources between the parties can influence the settlement in three ways. First, the poorer party may be less able to amass and analyze the information needed to predict the outcome of the litigation, and thus be disadvantaged in the bargaining process. Second, he may need the damages he seeks immediately and thus be induced to settle as a way of accelerating payment, even though he realizes he would get less now than he might if he awaited judgment. All plaintiffs want their damages immediately, but an indigent plaintiff may be exploited by a rich defendant because his need is so great that the defendant can force him to accept a sum that is less than the ordinary present value of the judgment. Third, the poorer party might be forced to settle because he does not have the resources to finance the litigation, to cover either his own projected expenses, such as his lawyer's time, or the expenses his opponent can impose through the manipulation of procedural mechanisms such as discovery. It might seem that settlement benefits the plaintiff by allowing him to avoid the costs of litigation, but this is not so. The defendant can anticipate the plaintiff's costs if the case were to be tried fully and decrease his offer by that amount. The indigent plaintiff is a victim of the costs of litigation even if he settles.

There are exceptions. Seemingly rich defendants may sometimes be subject to financial pressures that make them as anxious to settle as indigent plaintiffs. But I doubt that these circumstances occur with any great frequency. I also doubt that institutional arrangements such as contingent fees or the provision of legal services to the poor will in fact equalize resources between contending parties: The contingent fee does not equalize resources; it only makes an indigent plaintiff vulnerable to the willingness of the private bar to invest in his case. In effect, the ability to exploit the plaintiff's lack of resources has been transferred from rich defendants to lawyers who insist upon a hefty slice of the plaintiff's recovery as their fee. These lawyers, moreover, will only work for contingent fees in certain kinds of cases, such as personal-injury suits. And the contingent fee is of no avail when the defendant is the disadvantaged party. Governmental subsidies for legal services have a broader potential, but in the civil domain the battle for these subsidies was hard-fought, and they are in fact extremely limited, especially when it comes to cases that seek systemic reform of government practices.

Of course, imbalances of power can distort judgment as well: Resources influence the quality of presentation, which in turn has an important bearing on who wins and the terms of victory. We count, however, on the guiding presence of the judge, who can employ a number of measures to lessen the impact of distributional inequalities. He can, for example, supplement the parties' presentations by asking questions, calling his own witnesses, and inviting other persons and institutions to participate as amici. These measures are likely to make only a small contribution toward moderating the influence of distributional inequalities, but should not be ignored for that reason. Not even these small steps are possible with settlement. There is, moreover, a critical difference between a process like settlement, which is based on bargaining and accepts inequalities of wealth as an integral and legitimate component of the process, and a process like judgment, which knowingly struggles against those inequalities. Judgment aspires to an autonomy from distributional inequalities, and it gathers much of its appeal from this aspiration.

* * *

The Lack of a Foundation for Continuing Judicial Involvement

The dispute-resolution story trivializes the remedial dimensions of lawsuits * * *. It supposes that the judge's duty is to declare which neighbor is right and which wrong, and that this declaration will end the judge's involvement (save in that most exceptional situation where it is also necessary * * * to issue a writ directing the sheriff to execute the declaration). Under these assumptions, settlement appears as an almost perfect substitute for judgment, for it too can declare the parties' rights. Often, however, judgment is not the end of a lawsuit but only the beginning. The involvement of the court may continue almost indefinitely. In these cases, settlement cannot provide an adequate basis for that necessary continuing involvement, and thus is no substitute for judgment.

The parties may sometimes be locked in combat with one another and view the lawsuit as only one phase in a long continuing struggle. The entry of judgment will then not end the struggle, but rather change its terms and the balance of power. One of the parties will invariably return to the court and again ask for its assistance, not so much because conditions have changed, but because the conditions that preceded the lawsuit have unfortunately not changed. This often occurs in domestic-relations cases, where the divorce decree represents only the opening salvo in an endless series of skirmishes over custody and support.

The structural reform cases that play such a prominent role on the federal docket provide another occasion for continuing judicial involvement. In these cases, courts seek to safeguard public values by restructuring large-scale bureaucratic organizations. The task is enormous, and our knowledge of how to restructure on-going bureaucratic organizations is limited. As a consequence, courts must oversee and manage the remedial process for a long time * * *.
* * *

The drive for settlement knows no bounds and can result in a consent decree even in the kinds of cases I have just mentioned, that is, even when a court finds itself embroiled in a continuing struggle between the parties or must reform a bureaucratic organization. The parties may be ignorant of the difficulties ahead or optimistic about the future, or they may simply believe that they can get more favorable terms through a bargained-for agreement. Soon, however, the inevitable happens: One party returns to court and asks the judge to modify the decree, either to make it more effective or less stringent. But the judge is at a loss: He has no basis for assessing the request. He cannot, to use Cardozo's somewhat melodramatic formula, easily decide whether the "dangers, once substantial, have become attenuated to a shadow," because, by definition, he never knew the dangers.

The allure of settlement in large part derives from the fact that it avoids the need for a trial. Settlement must thus occur before the trial is complete and the judge has entered findings of fact and conclusions of law. As a consequence, the judge confronted with a request for modification of a consent decree must retrospectively reconstruct the situation as it existed at the time the decree was entered, and decide whether conditions today have sufficiently changed to warrant a modification in that decree. In the Meat Packers litigation, for example, where a consent decree governed the industry for almost half a century, the judge confronted with a request for modification in 1960 had to reconstruct the "danger" that had existed at the time of the entry of the decree in 1920 in order to determine whether the danger had in fact become a "shadow." Such an inquiry borders on the absurd, and is likely to dissipate whatever savings in judicial resources the initial settlement may have produced.

Settlement also impedes vigorous enforcement, which sometimes requires use of the contempt power. As a formal matter, contempt is available to punish violations of a consent decree. But courts hesitate to use the power to enforce decrees that rest solely on consent, especially when enforcement is aimed at high public officials * * *. Courts do not see a mere bargain between the parties as a sufficient foundation for the exercise of their coercive powers.

Sometimes the agreement between the parties extends beyond the terms of the decree and includes stipulated "findings of fact" and "conclusions of law," but even then an adequate foundation for a strong use of the judicial power is lacking. Given the underlying purpose of settlement—to avoid trial—the so-called "findings" and "conclusions" are necessarily the products of a bargain between the parties rather than of a trial and an independent judicial judgment. Of course, a plaintiff is free to drop a lawsuit altogether (provided that the interests of certain other persons are not compromised), and a defendant can offer something in return, but that bargained-for arrangement more closely resembles a contract than an injunction. It raises a question which has already been answered whenever an injunction is issued, namely, whether the judicial power should be used to enforce it. Even assuming that the consent is freely given and authoritative, the bargain is at best contractual and does not contain the kind of enforcement commitment already embodied in a decree that is the product of a trial and the judgment of a court.

Justice Rather Than Peace

The dispute-resolution story makes settlement appear as a perfect substitute for judgment, as we just saw, by trivializing the remedial dimensions of a lawsuit, and also by reducing the social function of the lawsuit to one of resolving private disputes. In that story, settlement appears to achieve exactly the same purpose as judgment—peace between the parties—but at considerably less expense to society. The two quarreling neighbors turn to a court in order to resolve their dispute, and society makes courts available because it wants to aid in the achievement of their private ends or to secure the peace.

In my view, however, the purpose of adjudication should be understood in broader terms. Adjudication uses public resources, and employs not strangers chosen by the parties but public officials chosen by a process in which the public participates. These officials * * * possess a power that has been defined and conferred by public law, not by private agreement. Their job is not to maximize the ends of private parties, nor simply to secure the peace, but to explicate and give force to the values embodied in authoritative texts such as the Constitution and statutes: to interpret those values and to bring reality into accord with them. This duty is not discharged when the parties settle.

* * * To be against settlement is not to urge that parties be "forced" to litigate, since that would interfere with their autonomy and distort the adjudicative process * * *. To be against settlement is only to suggest that when the parties settle, society gets less than what appears, and for a price it does not know it is paying. Parties might settle while leaving justice undone. The settlement of a school suit might secure the peace, but not racial equality. Although the parties are prepared to live under the terms they bargained for, and although such peaceful coexistence may be a necessary precondition of justice, and itself a state of affairs to be valued, it is not justice itself. To settle for something means to accept less than some ideal.

* * *

Additional Sources

Harold H. Bruff, *Public Programs, Private Deciders: The Constitutionality of Arbitration in Federal Programs*, 67 Tex. L. Rev. 441 (1989)

Harry T. Edwards, *Alternative Dispute Resolution: Panacea or Anathema?*, 99 Harv. L. Rev. 668 (1986)

Jeffrey M. Gaba, *Informal Rulemaking by Settlement Agreement*, 73 Geo. L.J. 1241 (1985)

Philip J. Harter, *Dispute Resolution and Administrative Law: The History, Needs, and Future of a Complex Relationship*, 29 Vill. L. Rev. 1393 (1983-84)

Philip J. Harter, *The Role of Courts in Regulatory Negotiation—A Response to Judge Wald*, 11 Colum. J. Envtl. L. 51 (1986)

Carrie Menkel-Meadow, *Toward Another View of Legal Negotiation: The Structure of Problem Solving*, 31 UCLA L. Rev. 754 (1984)

Henry H. Perritt, Jr., *Negotiated Rulemaking Before Federal Agencies: Evaluation of Recommendations by the Administrative Conference of the United States*, 74 Geo. L.J. 1625 (1986)

Howard Raiffa, THE ART AND SCIENCE OF NEGOTIATION (1982)

Frank E.A. Sander, *Varieties of Dispute Processing*, 70 F.R.D. 111 (1976)

Lawrence Susskind & Gerard McMahon, *The Theory and Practice of Negotiated Rulemaking*, 3 Yale J. on Reg. 133 (1985)

Patricia M. Wald, *Negotiation of Environmental Disputes: A New Role for the Courts?*, 10 Colum. J. Envtl. L. 1 (1985)

Part II

Major Controversies Implicating Other Visions of Administrative Legitimacy

A. Controversies About the Instrumental Rationality of Administration in the Pursuit of Public Values

1. The Debate About Comprehensive Regulatory Analysis

In recent years, agency rulemaking increasingly has become subject to requirements of comprehensive regulatory analysis. Forms of such analysis include cost-benefit balancing. The core idea is to require an agency to make a reasonably comprehensive effort to assess the likely effects of alternative regulatory policies.

In the first excerpt, Professor Thomas McGarity discusses the basic characteristics of comprehensive regulatory analysis. Professor McGarity contrasts it with traditional "technobureaucratic rationality." Although he sees comprehensive analysis as an important tool for decisionmakers, he also underscores its constraints in practice.

Professor Steven Kelman offers a more critical perspective on cost-benefit analysis as a central technique of decisionmaking. In particular, he questions the ethical theory underlying cost-benefit balancing. Professor Kelman also raises practical objections to quantifying the consequences of governmental action in terms of a common denominator that will allow one to assess and compare costs and benefits. Professor Kelman doubts that cost-benefit analysis should guide decisionmakers to the extent that its supporters would like.

Thomas O. McGarity, *Regulatory Analysis and Regulatory Reform*, 65 TEX. L. REV. 1243, 1243-44, 1246-47, 1253-65, 1269-77, 1279-91, 1293-97, 1299-1303, 1307-08, 1310-17, 1330-31 (1987)*

I. Introduction

In the late 1960s and early 1970s, critics of federal regulation complained about the cumbersome adjudicatory procedures that agencies used to implement many regulatory actions. In response, many agencies invoked the Administrative Procedure Act's moribund informal rule-making procedures to promulgate general rules to govern private conduct. At about the same time, Congress enacted a new generation of regulatory statutes that imposed new social and environmental responsibilities on entire sectors of the economy. These "social regulation" statutes often required federal agencies to govern through informal rule making. The shift in the older agencies from the adjudicatory to the rule-making mode and the emergence of the new rule-making agencies combined in the early 1970s to produce a rule-making revolution with a potential to expand greatly the federal government's role in American society.

The rule-making revolution had been under way for less than a decade when regulated industries and unsympathetic commentators from academia began to complain about perceived abuses by overzealous agencies. Critics argued that federal agencies operated beyond the range of effective political control and were irrationally imposing burdensome requirements on regulated entities without considering the social costs of the regulations. * * *

Some critics yearned for less burdensome times when administrative agencies were more sympathetic to the regulated industries. Unconvinced of the social utility of government intervention in the marketplace, these critics argued that social regulation was an "unwarranted intrusion by the federal government into private decision making." * * *

* * *

This Article examines the rational analysis strain of regulatory reform. Its thesis is that the analytical enterprise itself warrants analysis. * * *

Like most analyses, the Article concludes on an equivocal note: although regulatory analysis unquestionably has enhanced regulatory decision making in many instances, it also has led to some poor decisions. It has sometimes reduced the role that extrinsic bureaucratic and political considerations play in regulatory decision making, but also occasionally has enhanced that role. Analysis occasionally has starkly revealed to Congress and the public the way that regulation redistributes wealth in society, and it has frequently hidden such effects in an incomprehensible sea of "cooked" numbers. When used within its considerable limitations, regulatory analysis can improve regulatory decision making, but when pressed beyond its limitations, it can distort the decision-making process. * * *

* * *

III. Regulatory Analysis as a Vehicle for Regulatory Reform

Regulatory reformers who advocate "rational agency decision making" mean to infuse the established bureaucratic culture with a new and different way of thinking. Regulatory analysis is the primary vehicle for this undertaking. Borrowing from the policy sciences, this kind of thinking may be labeled "comprehensive analytical rationality."

The term "comprehensive" describes the ideal of exploring all possible routes to the solution of a problem. The word "analytical" suggests an attempt to sort out, break down, and analyze all the relevant components of a problem and its possible solutions. Less obviously, it manifests a preference for quantitative analysis. The term "rationality" signifies the objectivity and dispassion with which it analyzes social problems without regard to whose ox is being gored. Although there is no reason in principle that comprehensive analytical rationality should rely heavily upon any particular discipline, the paradigms of neoclassical microeconomics have dominated it in the past.

This new manner of thinking contrasts sharply with the thinking that traditionally has dominated the rule-making culture, which I shall label "techno-bureaucratic rationality." I use the term "techno-bureaucratic" to distinguish the thinking that dominates highly technical and complex rule-making activities from bureaucratic thinking in general. Techno-bureaucratic thinking is a special brand of bureaucratic thinking that arises in the context of bureaucratic activities that grapple with highly complex and often unresolvable issues of science, engineering, and public policy. When OSHA regulates benzene, for example, it simply is not engaged in the same type of activity undertaken by the Postal

---

* Copyright 1987 by the Texas Law Review Association. Reprinted with permission of the Texas Law Review Association and Thomas O. McGarity. All rights reserved.

Service when it operates the post office. Although there are many similarities in the way that bureaucrats in OSHA and the Postal Service think, there are also important differences. Some models of bureaucratic thinking, such as the perceptive "muddling through" model,[82] are relevant to techno-bureaucratic rationality but do not have as much explanatory power in the technical rule-making context as they do in other bureaucratic contexts.

* * *

A. *Techno-Bureaucratic Thinking in the Traditional Rule-Making Process*

Under the traditional rule-making model, a statute, an external petition, public pressure, or the internal discovery of a problem provides the initial stimulus for rule making. A program office within the regulatory agency has the responsibility for determining the initial institutional response to the stimulus. Once assigned to the program office, the issue loses whatever visibility it once had and is submerged within the agency until the program office generates a "solution" to the problem.

* * *

Because the information available to the program office almost invariably proves inconclusive, the office faces the familiar choice between regulating in the face of substantial uncertainty or doing nothing and studying the matter further. Convinced that it is ultimately judged by the number of rules that it produces over time, the staff's natural tendency is to forge ahead. Despite uncertainties, the engineers and scientists in the program office attempt to solve the problem. The process of defining and gathering information about the problem generally will suggest at least crude solutions. After identifying a few possible solutions, the staff may roughly estimate the costs of implementing the solutions and exclude one or more as economically infeasible. The staff, however, does not devote time or resources to quantitative analyses of costs and benefits.

Most program office determinations rely heavily upon professional judgment, a kind of intuition informed by technical training and experience. The technical experts do not analyze the problem and derive an optimal solution so much as they feel their way through to an answer, accommodating affected interests along the way to reduce external resistance to their ultimate solution. The suggestion that the solution could emerge from a careful balancing of costs and benefits is fanciful to the program office staffer, who probably is inclined to regard economics as a soft science in any event. Because the program office is under constant pressure to achieve results and believes that it can realistically consider only a very limited range of options, it is naturally reluctant to expand the universe of alternatives that require study. * * *

* * *

B. *Comprehensive Analytical Thinking in Regulatory Reform*

The regulatory reformers of the mid-1970s who called for more rational regulatory decision making had comprehensive analytical rationality in mind. The ideal regulatory bureaucracy, under the comprehensive analytical model, would react to a petition for rule making, a statutory command, or public pressure by assigning the matter to a regulatory analyst—a professional with training in policy analysis or economics. The regulatory analyst would first carefully define the regulatory problem. Because comprehensive analytical thinking as currently employed depends so heavily upon the paradigms of neoclassical microeconomics, the regulatory analyst probably would define the problem in terms of market failure. * * *

After identifying a problem, the regulatory analyst next would clarify and rank the agency's goals. Congress may have done this, but very often it articulates several inconsistent goals for a particular regulatory regime. If so, the analyst would seek the guidance of upper level policy makers.

The regulatory analyst next would request that the agency's scientists and engineers identify as many technical options for addressing the problem as possible and might suggest some economic alternatives. Economists in the program office or the regulatory analysis office would be asked to "cost out" the options. This effort ideally would produce an assessment of both the primary costs of the regulation to the regulated industry and the secondary costs in terms of increased prices to consumers, lost jobs, and foreign trade deficits.

Other scientists and engineers would conduct studies, assemble data, and construct models to predict as precisely as possible the benefits of the various alternatives. If the benefits could be reduced to monetary terms, then costs and benefits would be computed for each option, and the analyst would recommend that the upper level decision makers adopt the alternative for which the benefits exceeded

---

[82] *See* Lindblom, *The Science of "Muddling Through,"* 19 PUB. ADMIN. REV. 79, 81–88 (1959).

costs by the greatest amount. If benefits could not be stated in monetary terms, then they would be stated in equivalent units so that the analyst still could assess the cost-effectiveness of different options for achieving a given benefit.

The culture of comprehensive analytical rationality is thus very different from that of techno-bureaucratic rationality. The preceding description of the characteristics of techno-bureaucratic rationality derives from the actual decision-making process in the real world, but the description of the comprehensive analytical rationality model is based upon an abstract ideal that may never be achieved.

* * *

IV. The Virtues of Regulatory Analysis

* * *

Regulatory analysis can play at least four broad roles in the regulatory process. First, its primary function is to bring comprehensive analytical rationality to bear on regulating. Second, regulatory analysis can be useful in policy management within an agency. Third, regulatory analysis can perform an informational role outside the agency's doors by informing Congress and the public of the likely effects of regulatory programs. Finally, some have viewed regulatory analysis as a vehicle for achieving regulatory relief for the regulated industry.

* * *

A. *Applying Comprehensive Analytical Rationality to Regulatory Decision Making*

* * *

1. *Options Identification.*—E.O. 12,291, the Regulatory Flexibility Act, regulatory reform proposals, and NEPA all require agencies to consider alternatives to initially favored actions. Yet agency regulatory analysts often complain of the tendency of technical staffs to adopt a conveyer-belt mind set: the staff focuses upon a single option early in a rule's germination and adheres to that option throughout the entire rule-making process. When pressed, the program office staff dutifully sandwiches its preferred option between two post hoc red herrings. In contrast, regulatory analysts, in theory, attempt to identify fresh options and pressure the program office staff to look harder for alternatives. Relying upon their training in economics, regulatory analysts search for less burdensome, market-oriented solutions to regulatory problems and explore alternative timing strategies to correspond more closely to production cycles. Incorporating regulatory analysis into the regulatory decision-making process should help expand the horizons of technical staffs in program offices.

2. *Gathering and Analyzing Information.*—Another frequently expressed virtue of regulatory analysis is its capacity to bring information about the beneficial and detrimental aspects of regulatory alternatives to the attention of the decision maker in a coherent and systematic format. The program office technical staff can, of course, provide information to decision makers and in fact is the source of much of the information that the regulatory analysts use. The regulatory analyst, however, brings a unique quantitative perspective to the information-providing task and an objective posture that seeks out a broader range of information and nuance, especially upon the detriment side of the ledger. Moreover, the regulatory analyst often has training in techniques for displaying information, such as charts, tables, and graphs, that make existing data more accessible to the harried upper level decision maker and the general public.

* * *

3. *Justification by Explicit Reference to Articulated Policies.*—Busy agency staff can lose sight of broad agency policy goals by conveniently adhering to precedent and unarticulated bureaucratic folk wisdom. Regulatory analysts resist this tendency by measuring regulatory alternatives against articulated policy goals. This procedure in turn induces decision makers to think periodically about the ultimate purposes of their rule-making efforts, thereby enhancing agency accountability and credibility.

4. *Explicit Identification of Information Gaps and Assumptions.*—Advocates of comprehensive analytical rationality acknowledge that analysts rarely have enough information to undertake purely objective analyses of every advantage and disadvantage of each regulatory option. An effective analysis, however, identifies information gaps, draws appropriate inferences from the available data, and specifies the assumptions that the analyst has relied upon in extrapolating across information gaps. The techno-bureaucratic thinker also encounters information gaps and fills them with assumptions based on his professional judgment. Although the program office staff's assumptions and inferences may be informed by experience and received professional wisdom, its predictions often are based upon an outcome-oriented policy judgment about how the world should be arranged.

Regulatory analysts believe that the technical staff too often hides this policy judgment behind a veneer of technical judgment. Advocates of regulatory analysis argue that the regulatory analyst will be more candid about the policy preferences that motivate her choice of assumptions. Moreover, the regulatory analyst can draw upon several analytical techniques to demonstrate how predictions depend upon particular assumptions. Agency decision makers and the public will thus better understand how particular assumptions affect regulatory policy choices.

5. Identifying Research Needs.—Identification of information gaps often reveals research needs. * * * When fully integrated into agency standard operating procedures, analysis can provide perspective on future research needs, as well as input on individual rules.

6. Restraint upon Inappropriate Political Considerations.—Comprehensive analytical rationality clashes with the pluralistic view that regulatory decisions should reflect the interplay among the political forces that are affected by those decisions. Insisting that decisions be based upon more than the exercise of raw political power, comprehensive analytical rationality distinguishes between politics and policy. Regulatory analysts believe that their method can lead to regulatory conclusions that are more than mere political accommodations. Moreover, regulatory analysts can shield agency decisions from parties who consider only their own narrow interests. While a regulatory analysis document may not satisfy the losers of the regulatory battle, it can reassure remote decision makers in the White House, Congress, and reviewing courts that the decision was reached in a consistent and nonpartisan fashion.

7. Identification of ''Correct'' Regulatory Results.—Many proponents of regulatory analysis believe that it can significantly aid in specifying a result that is the ''correct'' solution to the regulatory problem. The most ambitious regulatory analysts would argue that after subjecting all available alternatives to a rigorous cost-benefit analysis, the decision maker should adopt the option with the highest benefit-to-cost ratio, for only in this way can society best use its scarce resources.

B. Facilitating Policy Management

Although rarely mentioned in the policy analysis literature, regulatory analysis can be an effective management tool for ensuring bureaucratic accountability. This type of accountability is not the personnel management typically associated with public administration—ensuring that lower level officials perform their jobs well and on time. Rather, regulatory analysis can be an instrument of *policy* management by helping politically appointed upper level policy makers ensure that lower level officials are implementing the policy makers' preferences, and not their own hidden agenda.

* * *

C. Informing Congress and the Public

Although Congress is not technically a manager of the federal bureaucracy, it is intensely interested in how agencies make and implement regulatory policy. Thus, Congress also has a policy management function, and regulatory analysis can aid Congress in the same way that it aids upper level agency policy makers and OMB. Oversight committees and individual congressmen want to be aware of the impacts of important rules, and they are especially interested in any distributional effects that agency rules might have upon their important constituencies. Committees that write legislation for agencies similarly have an obligation to oversee agency policy implementation to monitor fidelity to congressional intent. Regulatory analysis documents can thus perform an important role in ensuring agency accountability to Congress.

Regulatory analysis documents also can enhance public accountability by informing affected persons and encouraging them to participate effectively in the public rule-making process. * * *

* * *

D. Providing Regulatory Relief

Another suggested virtue of regulatory analysis is its potential to induce agencies to provide relief for regulated entities. If regulatory analysis is an effective policy management tool, and policy makers in the White House and the upper reaches of the agencies desire to effectuate regulatory relief, regulatory analysis may yield that result. * * *

* * *

V. Limitations of Regulatory Analysis

The ideal view of comprehensive analytical rationality in regulatory decision making suffers considerably in the real world of conflicting values, inadequate information, and substantial uncertainties. Even its most ardent proponents acknowledge its limits, and many observers believe that comprehensive analytical rationality should be abandoned as a decision-making tool and that more realistic notions of ''bounded rationality''[147] be adopted instead. Decision makers are rarely able to do much more than muddle through the decision-making process, exploring a limited range of options, relying heavily upon intuition and back-of-the-envelope predictions, and

---

[147] *See* H. SIMON, ADMINISTRATIVE BEHAVIOR 79 (1945).

depending on rapid feedback to meet limited short-term goals. Other critics argue that bureaucratic decision making necessarily must retain an important policy component, and thus purely scientific decision making in accordance with comprehensive analytical rationality would deprive agency decisions of an important democratic dimension.

* * *

A. Impediments and Limitations in Preparing Regulatory Analysis

1. Conflicting Goals. — Many critics of policy analysis suggest that applying regulatory analysis to administrative rule making is doomed at the very first step — clarifying and ranking the goals for the regulatory process. In this pluralistic society, no single regulatory goal or ranking of goals can command a consensus. Although a broad consensus about goals may not exist, someone must decide which goals will prevail over others in the context of particular programs. Standing alone, regulatory analysis offers no criteria for ranking those goals.

The analyst nevertheless can aid upper level decision makers by measuring the available options against each of several goals. The upper level policy maker can then rank agency goals either explicitly, in explaining his action in some decision-making document, or implicitly as the agency decides similar regulatory questions over time. The analytical exercise will at least draw the decision maker's attention to agency goals and subtly encourage consistency in goal ranking over time and across agency programs.

* * *

2. Identifying Options. — One virtue of regulatory analysis is its insistence that agencies explore a wide range of options before choosing a single solution to a regulatory problem. Yet there are "inherent limitations on the capacity of a complex bureaucracy to explore alternatives."

* * * Because many regulatory analysts in the agencies do not view options identification as one of their primary roles, "the analyst is very much a processor of other people's alternatives."

Second, the options identified by the regulatory analysts are not always viable as a practical matter. An option may be beyond the agency's statutory authority, technologically infeasible, or utterly unenforceable. * * * As a result, agencies generally initiate and explore a fairly narrow range of options defined largely by precedent and agency experience. As one midlevel regulatory analyst observed, "What you can do now is very much limited by what you have done in the past."

Third, agency analysts are not immune to the tunnel vision that often afflicts program office staff. * * *

Fourth, an agency's regulatory analysts often do not become a part of the decision-making process until after the program office has already considerably limited the possible options. Suggesting innovative options late in the decision-making process would force the program office to explore the technical aspects of the new options and thus delay rule implementation. An office with responsibility for promulgating rules in a timely fashion is unlikely to view regulatory analysts' suggestions and the attendant delay with much enthusiasm.

Fifth, assuming that agency analysts do identify a broad range of realistic options, agencies will rarely have sufficient resources to explore the advantages and disadvantages of each option. The time consumed in analyzing even a limited range of options inevitably delays the issuance of many important rules. And even if regulatory analysts could analyze rapidly a large range of available options, upper level decision makers have only a limited capacity to consider them.

Despite these limitations, the analysts' efforts may still be worthwhile to some extent. Upper level decision makers are rarely sufficiently involved with the rule-making process to play a large role in seeking out innovative regulatory options. Yet when a staff recommendation contains only one realistic option, the decision maker loses much of his actual decision-making authority. * * *

* * *

3. Inadequate Information. — * * * The most frequently cited impediment to regulatory analysis is the lack of adequate information for making the projections required of good analysis. Because agency regulatory analysts rarely have sufficient time and resources to undertake original research, they must rely on existing cost studies, unvalidated health and safety information, and even anecdotal evidence. * * * Rather than conducting comprehensive research, analysts piece together snatches of information from a government statistic here, a corporate report there, and add a liberal sprinkling of anecdotal evidence derived from frequent telephone calls and perhaps a site visit or two.

Having collected the available information, agency analysts attempt to massage the data to make it more usable, but this practice principally consists of heroic attempts to gloss over glaring weaknesses in the data. The net result is an analysis laced with guesswork and plagued by uncertainties.

* * *

* * * The analytical difficulties that plague cost and economic impact assessments pale by comparison to the problems of objectively analyzing the benefits of many regulations. Regulatory benefits vary considerably with the particular regulatory effort. The following discussion thus focuses upon three different kinds of regulation: (1) economic regulation; (2) civil rights regulation; and (3) health, safety, and environmental regulation.

(i) Economic regulations. — Although economic regulation benefits are perhaps the easiest to assess, even they are often difficult to quantify. The benefit of reducing monopoly or oligopoly power is simply the value of those goods that would have been produced in a free, unimpeded market. Although relatively sophisticated models exist for calculating these benefits, many of their assumptions are controversial.

The value to consumers of accurate information about products and investment securities is even more difficult to calculate. Such a calculation requires an estimate of the amount of consumer dollars lost to fraud, unfair trade practices, and misleading advertising in the absence of regulation. Because the regulations are meant to be prophylactic in nature, their value is difficult to verify empirically.

Similarly, regulations aimed at maintaining adequate consumer services produce benefits that are difficult to calculate. For example, the benefits of obtaining a diversity of views in television programming are not easily quantifiable. And, the benefits of deregulatory initiatives that produce improved service or lower prices, which were two goals of airlines and telecommunications deregulation, are not easily reduced to precise dollar values.

(ii) Civil rights regulations. — The value of regulations aimed at providing equality of opportunity for victims of racial, religious, sex, and national origin discrimination is extremely difficult to quantify. Although literature often describes the theoretical inefficiencies of discrimination, few models, if any, predict the exact extent to which allocative efficiency would be enhanced by various antidiscrimination devices. The analytical effort is complicated because antidiscrimination rules are intended to advance unquantifiable values, such as justice, fairness, and autonomy. There are no scales, no units of measurement, and no standards of comparison. Yet these are precisely the tools that are required for comprehensive analytical standards to be useful in guiding decision makers to optimal regulatory results.

(iii) Health, safety, and environmental regulations. — The difficulties in obtaining information on the benefits of health, safety, and environmental regulations have been documented extensively in the literature. The complex interrelationships between toxic substances and health and environmental effects are currently poorly understood, and, indeed, they may never be completely comprehended. The benefits of workplace and highway safety regulations are also often difficult to predict.

Controlled studies done on human beings or in the natural environment would be the best source of direct information on the health and environmental effects of regulations of private activities. Ethical considerations, however, preclude many kinds of experiments with human beings, and experiments on disruptions of natural ecosystems are very difficult to design and conduct. Epidemiological studies can provide some direct evidence of risk, but they are notoriously inconclusive. Information on the causes of automobile accidents is similarly elusive and of varying quality. Even information on relatively straightforward benefits, such as reducing the effects of corrosive pollutants on metals, is difficult to find. Consequently, agency analysts have access to little direct evidence on the benefits of health, safety, and environmental regulation.

Although tests in surrogate systems such as animals and greenhouses are often available, they are not directly relevant to real-world experience. Often expensive to undertake, these tests raise a host of technical considerations that cloak the analytical enterprise in uncertainty. Even if such tests were directly relevant, agency analysts would encounter further uncertainties in estimating the extent of human and environmental exposure to technological risks.

Regulatory analysts face even greater uncertainties in assessing the remote and indirect benefits of regulation. For example, although the public may derive an emotional benefit from knowing that the Great Lakes and the Gulf of Mexico are being protected from destruction by water pollution, such a benefit is extremely difficult to quantify. Agencies have devoted little attention to even more easily calculated indirect benefits, such as sickness prevented, worker absenteeism avoided, and pain and suffering attributable to environment- and workplace-induced diseases averted.

* * *

4. Bias in Cost and Benefit Studies. — * * * The possibility of bias in regulatory analysis threatens its viability as a decision-making tool. Agency cost estimates may depend heavily upon information that is exclusively in the hands of the regulated industries and therefore not subject to independent verification. * * * Public interest group observers also have noted that companies may use one set of cost assessments when dealing with federal agencies and another when communicating with their shareholders. These practices undermine faith in the objectivity of regulatory analysis.

Regulatory analysts recognize this potential for bias. But because they believe that they can independently verify industry-submitted cost estimates, analysts do not consider the possibility of bias to be a great threat to the integrity of the analytical enterprise. * * *

In addition to monitoring carefully information from potentially biased sources, agencies can reduce the impact of possible bias by collecting information from multiple sources. * * *

Agencies also can reduce the possibility of bias by exposing all submitted information to intense scrutiny. * * *

* * *

5. *Inadequate Models.* —When analysts lack adequate information, they typically resort to mathematical approximations of reality. Unfortunately, the complexity of social and environmental interactions confounds attempts to mathematically approximate reality for most of the phenomena that interest the regulatory analyst. Although analysts have created sophisticated computer models of reality, stretching available knowledge to its limit, the resulting models still leave much to be desired.

The impossibility of deriving models for complex phenomena forces regulatory analysts to make significant, and frequently questionable, assumptions about reality. Because cost and benefit projections tend to be highly sensitive to these assumptions, minor changes in assumptions can significantly affect a model's predictions. Once the model's assumptions are programmed into a computer algorithm, they may be inaccessible to those who are affected by the model's predictions.

Models tend to oversimplify reality. Simplification begets inaccuracy, and inaccuracies multiply as a model's projections extrapolate from real-world data. Nevertheless, the results of the modeling effort are often stated with deceptive precision, leading decision makers to believe that they know more than they really do. Sophisticated models may be only marginally informative at best. When pressed beyond their considerable limitations, they can severely harm the decision-making process.

Regulatory analysis documents should be explicit about the assumptions of the models on which they rely. Too often, however, the regulatory analysis document merely identifies a model without explaining its critical assumptions. Close examination of the literature or original computer program may reveal those assumptions, but upper level decision makers and the public lack the time and expertise to divine modeling assumptions from primary sources. Therefore, the regulatory analysis documents themselves should identify and explain the subtle but important assumptions that undergird the model or models upon which the analysts base their predictions.

6. *Inadequate Tools for Quantification.*— * * * [S]ome essential considerations of a rational decision making are immune to quantitative analysis. An excessive preoccupation with quantification can dwarf "soft" variables, such as fairness, autonomy, and justice, as well as historic, recreational, and aesthetic values, yielding a narrow view of the world that biases decision makers against such values. Because unquantifiable effects may never appear in the regulatory analyst's quantitative predictions, quantitative analysis may disproportionately influence the policy judgment of upper level decision makers, and deceive the public as well.

Agency decision makers should insist that their regulatory analysts resist the tendency to dismiss unquantifiable variables and instead discuss them thoroughly in the text of regulatory analysis documents, even if the discussion detracts from the precision of the analyst's predictions. A comprehensive discussion of such variables necessarily will seem soft and unanalytical, but the effort must be undertaken, if only to preserve the credibility of the analytical exercise. Although a discussion of soft variables may not completely substitute for quantification, agency decision makers should not be subtly induced to ignore unquantifiable factors.

7. *Characterizing Uncertainties.*—Inadequate data, inaccurate models, and the infirmities of quantitative analysis collectively leave regulatory analysts awash in a sea of uncertainties. Adequate characterization of these uncertainties presents a significant challenge to the regulatory analyst, for if the analyst confronts the inherent uncertainties of her predictions and alerts the decision maker to her general lack of confidence, she risks rejection by decision makers who demand greater accuracy. Thus, the analyst faces almost irresistible pressures to gloss over uncertainties in making quantitative predictions. Yet if the analyst overstates her confidence in his predictions, she will mislead the decision maker, with perhaps disastrous results. Uncertainties must therefore be characterized in a way that retains the usefulness of analysis to decision makers without causing it to be misleading. Unfortunately, many of the regulatory

analysis documents prepared by agencies emphasize single value estimates of costs and benefits and do not seriously attempt to characterize uncertainties.

* * *

8. Problems of Cost-Benefit Analysis.—* * *

(a) Valuation problems.—Perhaps the most troublesome problem with cost-benefit analysis is valuing benefits. Dollar values are relatively easily assigned to the benefits of economic regulation, which are primarily dollar savings to consumers and regulated industries, but placing dollar values on health and environmental benefits is much more controversial. Although the most heated debate centers on valuing the benefits of regulations that significantly reduce mortality and morbidity risks, the same arguments apply to attempts to reduce environmental, historical, and aesthetic values to dollar amounts.

Proponents of cost-benefit analysis argue that, however distasteful it first appears, valuing lives and important amenities is unavoidable, and is done implicitly in thousands of everyday decisions. Placing an explicit monetary value on human life can prevent regulatory decision makers from inconsistently placing a high implicit value on life in one case and a low value in another. Moreover, forcing decision makers to monetize values eliminates a variable that can range from zero to infinity in cost-benefit calculations and thereby justify any regulatory decision.

Opponents of cost-benefit analysis question the morality of placing a value on human life, arguing that the process itself belittles life's intrinsic value. Other opponents, ranging across the political spectrum from the Chemical Manufacturers Institute to labor unions and environmental groups, argue that deriving a useful number for the value of a human life is simply impossible, even if it were desirable. They also argue that monetizing health and environmental benefits is, at the extreme, "incoherent" or "schizophrenic." It cannot yield a single numerical value for extremely valuable things, such as the reduction of significant mortality risks and risks to endangered species, that are not frequently traded in markets. * * *

(b) Valuing the future.—Another valuation conundrum is the rate that analysts use to discount future costs and benefits. The discount rate is an estimate of how much more a dollar in hand is worth than the promise of a dollar in the future. Most analysts agree that future costs should be discounted to present value. The correct rate of discounting benefits, however, is more controversial.

Many health and environmental regulations are intended to benefit future generations. Using a high discount rate in strict cost-benefit analysis biases the analysis against future benefits.[290] Thus, some have suggested that it may be inappropriate to discount future benefits at all, because future generations may value health and environmental amenities even more than today's population. Nevertheless, OMB has traditionally insisted that agencies use a high discount rate of ten percent in calculating the benefits of environmental regulations. Thus, the benefits of a regulation that would prevent catastrophic loss in fifty years are very low in today's dollars and are therefore likely to be outweighed by even modest costs.[293]

Although the discount rate is useful for comparing present costs and future benefits, the actual discount rate used is a policy question that should be left to upper level decision makers in the agencies. Decision makers can experiment, of course, with different discount rates, and need not establish a single discount rate for all regulatory decisions. Regulatory analysts should, however, be explicit about the discount rates used so that they do not create the impression that discount rates are being manipulated to reach predetermined regulatory results.

Regulatory analysts could help ensure against this potential misuse of discount rates by using two or more discount rates in every regulatory analysis document that addresses regulations with short-term costs and long-term benefits. * * *

(c) Distributional impacts.—Cost-benefit analysis is concerned with the efficient allocation of resources, not with the manner in which society distributes resources. So long as a policy maximizes the aggregate wealth, cost-benefit analysis does not take into account who the winners and losers are or how much wealth changes hands. A politically accountable decision maker, however, must consider distributional impacts. For economic regulation in particular, distributional considerations can be the primary

---

[290] * * * Meltsner quotes the following poem, attributed to Kenneth Boulding:

[T]he long term interest rate
Determines any project's fate.
At two percent the case is clear;
At three, some sneaking doubts appear;
At four, it draws its final breath;
While five percent is certain death.

A. MELTSNER, [POLICY ANALYSTS AND THE BUREAUCRACY 147 (1976)]; *see also* Rodgers, [*Benefits, Costs, and Risks: Oversight of Health and Environmental Decision Making*, 4 HARV. ENVTL. L. REV. 191, 198 (1980)] (noting that small adjustments in the discount rate can cause the majority of approved projects to fall below the standard requirements for approval).

[293] At a discount rate of 10%, a dollar's worth of benefits 50 years from now is worth slightly less than a penny today.

rationale for the regulatory program. Distributional concerns also motivate environmental regulators to establish stringent media quality standards to protect sensitive populations.

* * *

9. Hidden Policy Agendas.—Comprehensive analytical rationality in itself says nothing about how goals should be ranked. Many regulatory analysts, however, hold definite opinions about proper regulatory goals and their relative priorities. These opinions are partially inherent in the economic training of most regulatory analysts. Yet when regulatory analysts attempt to rank goals, they are behaving as political actors and not as objective analysts, and their input should be treated as such. When goal ranking becomes muddled in the instrumental operation of measuring alternative policies against pre-existing goals, however, the regulatory analyst's political participation may be hidden behind a veneer of objectivity.

The uncertainties that plague regulatory analysis provide ample opportunities for analysts to apply hidden policy agendas to regulatory problems. The choice between one assumption or inference and another, between a prediction at the high end or low end of a plausible range, and between liberal or conservative mathematical models is usually a policy choice. Regulatory analysts, therefore, have considerable discretion to apply policy preferences to the available data and analytical techniques to yield predictions at any point along a very large range. The possibility of political input by analysts raises important questions of accountability for the policy choices that must necessarily guide the analytical effort.

(a) Internal accountability.—Use of regulatory analysis to advance hidden policy agendas presents problems of internal accountability. By manipulating assumptions to aim predictions at the high or low end of the available range and by soft-peddling uncertainties, analysts can produce apparently objective analyses that considerably narrow the decision makers' effective range of choice. Not all regulatory analysts are Machiavellian manipulators intent upon advancing their policy preferences by deceiving unsuspecting upper level policy makers. Most regard themselves as professionals without particular goals to advance. They generally are willing to apply the policy preferences of the upper level decision makers, and actively urge upper level policy makers to communicate policy preferences. When policy preferences are accurately communicated, most analysts feel constrained to apply them, whatever their individual views or perspectives. But when policy is not well communicated, analysts are likely to advance their own policy preferences.

Upper level policy makers should understand regulatory analysis so that they can be aware of the uncertainties surrounding it. They should, for example, be suspicious of single number estimates. Requiring a range of predictions can reveal hidden agendas. The choice of models also may reveal the analysts' policy preferences. If policy considerations must govern the choice among available models, upper level policy makers should be making these choices, not regulatory analysts.

(b) External accountability.—The ability of regulatory analysts to hide policy agendas in regulatory analyses also poses problems of external accountability. Failing to reveal the policy preferences that inform predictions may persuade an unsophisticated public that facts and analysis, rather than policy, dictated a particular regulatory result. Because the decision maker's policy preferences remain hidden, he is not held publicly accountable for policy choices. The upper level decision maker can avoid accountability by subtly pressuring agency analysts to hedge predictions so that the decision appears better supported by facts and analysis than it really is.

Because of significant uncertainties, regulatory analysts may fudge data without actually misrepresenting the available information or misapplying the available analytical tools. At the extreme, the analysis may be a post hoc rationalization for decisions reached on unarticulated policy grounds.

Policy analysis is thus abused in two ways. First, there are limits to which honest analysis can be stretched to meet predetermined policy needs. In those rare cases in which the available information permits relatively confident projections, the analyst should not manipulate the analysis to suggest otherwise. Second, if the sources of policy preferences remain hidden, the policy makers themselves cannot be held accountable to Congress, the public, and other reviewing agencies.

10. Retrospective Analysis.—The accuracy of predictions can be enhanced if analysts obtain feedback from the real world. Retrospective analysis of the actual impact of regulatory requirements can provide this feedback. * * * Over time, retrospective analysis could be useful in evaluating the entire regulatory analysis enterprise. If the regulatory analyst's predictions are always inaccurate, an agency might devote fewer resources to the endeavor.

Interestingly, regulatory analysts, who analyze others' work, rarely evaluate their own work. The agencies studied in connection with this Article devoted few resources to retrospective evaluations of their regulatory analysts' previous predictions. As one EPA analyst candidly observed, "How is my career going to be advanced by doing a study that shows that three years ago the agency made a wrong prediction? It is not in my best interest." In most agencies analytical resources are strained by day-to-day work on new rule-making initiatives without adding responsibilities for retrospective analysis. Still, the few existing retrospective analyses indicate that agencies could profit from evaluating the accuracy of past analysis.

11. Deadlines and Delay.—For any decision-making body there is always a "tension between timeliness and analysis." Time-consuming regulatory analysis can delay agency rule-making managers in the program offices who complain of "paralysis by analysis." Regulatory analysis can also be used to postpone making important decisions. The need for further study and analysis can also be a convenient conflict-avoidance device. Issues that cannot be amicably resolved can be delayed pending further analysis that may eliminate the conflict.

Although regulatory efforts face time constraints, analysts should not need more time to complete their tasks than does the technical staff in the program office. Most timing problems probably occur because the services of the regulatory analysts usually are not requested until after much of the technical work on the rule is complete. Having finished the bulk of its work, the technical staff pressures the analysts to expedite their efforts. The analysts believe that they cannot do an adequate job under such time constraints and too often must make back-of-the-envelope predictions based upon little information and even less analysis. Involving regulatory analysts at an early stage of the decision-making process, when they can help set research agendas and allocate resources, would help alleviate this aspect of the timing problem.

12. Insufficient Analytical Resources.—Agency regulatory analysts frequently complain of the paucity of resources that agencies devote to analysis. Less partial observers also have identified inadequate resources as a significant impediment to regulatory analysis. But because no analysis is as thorough as it ideally could be, whether agency analysis receives adequate resources is, like most resource issues, a question of trade-offs.

* * *

Although OMB has increased the analytical burdens upon agencies, it has not recommended that they be given additional resources to perform the required analyses. Many observers suspect that OMB desires to reduce the flow of regulations by forcing agencies to shift existing resources out of regulatory programs and into analysis. If true, the status of regulatory analysis among agency employees, regulatees, and the general public is thereby reduced.

Another, probably unanticipated, consequence of imposing burdensome analytical requirements is that it provides an incentive for agencies to abandon rule making and attempt to achieve the same ends through agency adjudications. In pursuing regulatory aims agencies that can choose between rule making and adjudication may conclude that the latter is less burdensome. Adjudication almost surely would be more burdensome to the individual targets of adjudication, however, and would certainly reduce the extent of public participation in agency policy making. Nevertheless, the danger of wholesale shifts from rule making to adjudication is probably insignificant. Many agencies do not have a choice to adjudicate in lieu of rule making, and most have acquired habits and implemented procedures that are geared toward rule making.

* * *

C. Impediments to the Use of Analysis

Even after the regulatory analysts have prepared and communicated a regulatory analysis to the agency decision makers, considerable institutional impediments to its effective use in the decision-making process remain. Technical staff in the program offices and some upper level decision makers resist using analysis in regulatory decision making. Political considerations and the agency's structure also may impede severely the extent to which agency decision makers can use analysis. Finally, its use is hampered because it can be manipulated for purposes unrelated to applying comprehensive analytical rationality to regulatory problems.

1. Technical Staff Resistance to Analysis.—Many agency analysts believe that technical staff resistance is the most significant barrier to using regulatory analysis effectively in regulatory decision making. Technical personnel in the program offices often believe that analysis wastes agency time and resources. They feel both superior to and threatened by the agency analysts. They feel superior because they believe that regulatory analysis lacks rigor in the sense that an engineer or health scientist understands that concept. They believe that regulatory analysis is instead a loose amalgam of cost and benefit projections stitched together from unscientific surveys of published and unpublished literature and resting on unsupportable assumptions.

The technical staff also feels threatened by analysis because it directly challenges the status quo approaches to regulatory problem solving that the technical staff historically has dominated. An effective analyst always asks questions, challenges assumptions, and suggests new options. The analyst may even challenge the basic premises underlying the entire regulatory program. Finally, when upper level decision makers follow analysts' advice, the technical staff's traditional dominance of the decision-making process is further threatened.

* * *

2. Resistance of Upper Level Decision Makers and Political Considerations. — Agency analysts also complain of resistance from upper level decision makers. Upper level resistance to analysis, however, is not easily explained. The upper level decision maker may be unfamiliar with analytical thinking or may have adopted a techno-bureaucratic approach to decision making much like that of the program office staff. Indeed, upper level decision makers in some agencies are chosen from the program office.

Although upper level resistance to analysis may sometimes be explained by ignorance or narrow-mindedness, the more likely explanation is a concern for the political viability of agency decisions, a concern that is sometimes incompatible with comprehensive analytical rationality. Analysts frequently complain that political considerations overwhelm their analyses.

Regulatory analysis has much to do with policy, but is in many ways antithetical to politics. Analysis is unconcerned with the conflicting interests that are intensely affected by rule-making initiatives. Regulatory analysis can do little to facilitate the inevitable compromises among competing interest groups that are fundamental to successfully implementing any regulatory strategy. Agency analysts consequently believe that political considerations cause upper level decision makers to give little weight to their analyses.

* * *

3. Alternatives Beyond the Agency's Statutory Authority. — Brainstorming sessions among regulatory analysts and technical staff can yield alternatives that the agency lacks authority to implement. The agency's inability to implement these alternatives obviously impedes the use of analysis in the decision-making process.

4. Use of Analysis to Advance Substantive Goals. — One of the important themes of recent regulatory reform is the substantive goal of regulatory relief. Many regulatory reformers believe that the ability to secure regulatory relief is the primary measure of regulatory analysis' effectiveness. There are, however, several objections to this use of regulatory analysis.

First, regulatory relief can conflict with declared congressional policy. There are statutory limits to the regulatory decision maker's broad discretion. If regulatory analysis indicates that the preferred option would provide relief to the regulated industry and if that option runs counter to the agency's statute, the agency is not free to adopt it. Hence, regulatory analysis may not be used to provide regulatory relief that Congress has not authorized.

Second, promoting regulatory relief threatens the integrity of regulatory analysis. Analysis measures regulatory options against predetermined policy goals; it is incapable of defining those goals. Thorough analysis may indirectly advance regulatory relief goals, but good analysis need not necessarily yield that result. A thorough analysis may instead indicate that the regulatory response should be even more stringent. To rely upon regulatory analysis when it points toward one substantive end but deny it when it points to another is hypocritical.

Many critics believe that regulatory analysis currently is being used to provide regulatory relief by impeding or delaying the issuance of protective rules. The review process for some important rules has consumed several months or even years. Thus, although regulatory analysis has stemmed the flow of rules, it frequently has done so by brute force, rather than through the persuasiveness of its reasoning.

* * *

Using regulatory analysis to secure relief for regulated industries discredits the analytical enterprise. If regulatory beneficiaries perceive analysis as a tool for furthering regulatory relief goals, they will object to both the tool and the goals. Because they mistrust regulatory analysis, they will condemn all decisions based upon regulatory analysis as politically motivated, thereby depriving the analysis of its primary virtue—perceived objectivity.

Many program office officials strongly believe that regulatory analysis is currently used to advance particular substantive ends. This impression is almost universally shared by representatives of regulatory beneficiaries. Even many regulatory analysts in the agencies agree that regulatory analysis occasionally has been used as a weapon in a war against regulation, rather than as a tool to produce better regulation.

Regulatory analysis should be applied evenhandedly. If regulatory analysis is used to provide regulatory relief, it becomes merely another tactic in the endless conflicts over the outcome of rule-making initiatives. This is a poor use of regulatory analysis, even if for no other reason than its considerable expense to the taxpayer. If regulatory analysis is not a useful analytical tool for shaping better regulations, it should be abandoned and not cynically deployed as a barrier to further regulation. Despite the frequent identification of regulatory analysis with the regulatory relief prong of the regulatory reform movement, regulatory relief is an inappropriate use for regulatory analysis.

* * *

VII. Conclusion and Recommendations

Regulatory analysis is currently in a state of awkward adolescence. It has emerged from its infancy, but not yet matured. Often noisy and clumsy, it generally commands little respect. But despite its considerable shortcomings, regulatory analysis has important virtues. It can help decision makers and the public examine the advantages and disadvantages of regulatory options. It also can help decision makers make rational and informed decisions, although it cannot fully inform or precisely point to rational conclusions. Perhaps more importantly, it can encourage the decision maker to articulate policy preferences and demonstrate to the public how those policy preferences were applied in important rule-making initiatives. If the public and the regulatory beneficiaries are convinced that regulatory analysis is not being used cynically to reach particular substantive results, it can become an effective mechanism for enhancing public accountability.

* * *

The considerable limitations of cost-benefit analysis can be avoided by recognizing that cost-benefit analysis alone cannot dictate regulatory results in most regulatory contexts. It should be used instead to achieve more modest ends, such as setting agency priorities and structuring agency options. The less ambitious cost-effectiveness analyses may be more appropriate for rule-making initiatives that affect health, environmental, historical, artistic, and aesthetic considerations for which markets do not exist. In addition, because cost-benefit analysis does not address distributional impacts of regulations, agencies should use other tools to display such impacts for decision makers. Finally, when agencies use cost-benefit analysis in regulatory analysis documents, they should explicitly state the discount rates they use. Agencies also should use more than one discount rate to clarify the projections' sensitivity to the different discount rates and to make explicit the value the agency assigns to future benefits.

* * *

Steven Kelman, *Cost-Benefit Analysis: An Ethical Critique*, REGULATION 33, 33–40 (Jan./Feb. 1981)*

At the broadest and vaguest level, cost-benefit analysis may be regarded simply as systematic thinking about decision-making. Who can oppose, economists sometimes ask, efforts to think in a systematic way about the consequences of different courses of action? The alternative, it would appear, is unexamined decision-making. But defining cost-benefit analysis so simply leaves it with few implications for actual regulatory decision-making. Presumably, therefore, those who urge regulators to make greater use of the technique have a more extensive prescription in mind. I assume here that their prescription includes the following views:

(1) There exists a strong presumption that an act should not be undertaken unless its benefits outweigh its costs.

(2) In order to determine whether benefits outweigh costs, it is desirable to attempt to express all benefits and costs in a common scale or denominator, so that they can be compared with each other, even when some benefits and costs are not traded on markets and hence have no established dollar values.

(3) Getting decision-makers to make more use of cost-benefit techniques is important enough to warrant both the expense required to gather the data for improved cost-benefit estimation and political efforts needed to give the activity higher priority compared to other activities, also valuable in and of themselves.

My focus is on cost-benefit analysis as applied to environmental, safety, and health regulation. In that context, I examine each of the above propositions from the perspective of formal ethical theory, that is, the study of what actions it is morally right to undertake. My conclusions are:

(1) In areas of environmental, safety, and health

---

* Reprinted with the permission of The American Enterprise Institute for Public Policy Research, Washington, D.C., and Steven Kelman. All rights reserved.

regulation, there may be many instances where a certain decision might be right even though its benefits do not outweigh its costs.

(2) There are good reasons to oppose efforts to put dollar values on non-marketed benefits and costs.

(3) Given the relative frequency of occasions in the areas of environmental, safety, and health regulation where one would not wish to use a benefits-outweigh-costs test as a decision rule, and given the reasons to oppose the monetizing of non-marketed benefits or costs that is a prerequisite for cost-benefit analysis, it is not justifiable to devote major resources to the generation of data for cost-benefit calculations or to undertake efforts to "spread the gospel" of cost-benefit analysis further.

I

How do we decide whether a given action is morally right or wrong and hence, assuming the desire to act morally, why it should be undertaken or refrained from? Like the Moliere character who spoke prose without knowing it, economists who advocate use of cost-benefit analysis for public decisions are philosophers without knowing it: the answer given by cost-benefit analysis, that actions should be undertaken so as to maximize net benefits, represents one of the classic answers given by moral philosophers—that given by utilitarians. To determine whether an action is right or wrong, utilitarians tote up all the positive consequences of the action in terms of human satisfaction. The act that maximizes attainment of satisfaction under the circumstances is the right act. That the economists' answer is also the answer of one school of philosophers should not be surprising. Early on, economics was a branch of moral philosophy, and only later did it become an independent discipline.

Before proceeding further, the subtlety of the utilitarian position should be noted. The positive and negative consequences of an act for satisfaction may go beyond the act's immediate consequences. A facile version of utilitarianism would give moral sanction to a lie, for instance, if the satisfaction of an individual attained by telling the lie was greater than the suffering imposed on the lie's victim. Few utilitarians would agree. Most of them would add to the list of negative consequences the effect of the one lie on the tendency of the person who lies to tell other lies, even in instances when the lying produced less satisfaction for him than dissatisfaction for others. They would also add the negative effects of the lie on the general level of social regard for truth-telling, which has many consequences for future utility. A further consequence may be added as well. It is sometimes said that we should include in a utilitarian calculation the feeling of dissatisfaction produced in the liar (and perhaps in others) because, by telling a lie, one has "done the wrong thing." Correspondingly, in this view, among the positive consequences to be weighed into a utilitarian calculation of truth-telling is satisfaction arising from "doing the right thing." This view rests on an error, however, because it *assumes* what it is the purpose of the calculation to *determine*—that telling the truth in the instance in question is indeed the right thing to do. Economists are likely to object to this point, arguing that no feeling ought "arbitrarily" to be excluded from a complete cost-benefit calculation, including a feeling of dissatisfaction at doing the wrong thing. Indeed, the economists' cost-benefit calculations would, at least ideally, include such feelings. Note the difference between the economist's and the philosopher's cost-benefit calculations, however. The economist may choose to include feelings of dissatisfaction in his cost-benefit calculation, but what happens if somebody asks the economist, "Why is it right to evaluate an action on the basis of a cost-benefit test?" If an answer is to be given to that question (which does not normally preoccupy economists but which does concern both philosophers and the rest of us who need to be persuaded that cost-benefit analysis is right), then the circularity problem reemerges. And there is also another difficulty with counting feelings of dissatisfaction at doing the wrong thing in a cost-benefit calculation. It leads to the perverse result that under certain circumstances a lie, for example, might be morally right if the individual contemplating the lie felt no compunction about lying and morally wrong only if the individual felt such a compunction!

This error is revealing, however, because it begins to suggest a critique of utilitarianism. Utilitarianism is an important and powerful moral doctrine. But it is probably a minority position among contemporary moral philosophers. It is amazing that economists can proceed in unanimous endorsement of cost-benefit analysis as if unaware that their conceptual framework is highly controversial in the discipline from which it arose—moral philosophy.

Let us explore the critique of utilitarianism. The logical error discussed before appears to suggest that we have a notion of certain things being right or wrong that *predates* our calculation of costs and benefits. Imagine the case of an old man in Nazi Germany who is hostile to the regime. He is wondering whether he should speak out against Hitler. If he speaks out, he will lose his pension. And his action will have done nothing to increase the chances that the Nazi regime will be overthrown: he is regarded as somewhat eccentric by those around him, and nobody has ever consulted his views on political questions. Recall that one cannot add to the benefits of speaking out any satisfaction from doing "the right thing," because the purpose of the exercise is to determine whether speaking out *is* the right thing. How would the utilitarian calculation go? The benefits of the old man's speaking out would, as the example is presented, be nil, while the costs would be his loss of his pension. So the costs of action would outweigh the benefits. By the utilitarians' cost-benefit calculation, it would be *morally wrong* for the man to speak out.

Another example: two very close friends are on an Arctic expedition together. One of them falls very sick in the snow and bitter cold, and sinks quickly before anything can be done to help him. As he is dying, he asks his friend one thing, "Please, make me a solemn promise that ten years from today you will come back to this spot and place a lighted candle here to remember me." The friend solemnly promises to do so, but does not tell a soul. Now, ten years later, the friend must decide whether to keep his promise. It would be inconvenient for him to make the long trip. Since he told nobody, his failure to go will not affect the general social faith in promise-keeping. And the incident was unique enough so that it is safe to assume that his failure to go will not encourage him to break other promises. Again, the costs of the act outweigh the benefits. A utilitarian would need to believe that it would be *morally wrong* to travel to the Arctic to light the candle.

* * *

And a final example: imagine two worlds, each containing the same sum total of happiness. In the first world, this total of happiness came about from a series of acts that included a number of lies and injustices (that is, the total consisted of the immediate gross sum of happiness created by certain acts, minus any long-term unhappiness occasioned by the lies and injustices). In the second world the same amount of happiness was produced by a different series of acts, none of which involved lies or injustices. Do we have any reason to prefer the one world to the other? A utilitarian would need to believe that the choice between the two worlds is a *matter of indifference*.

To those who believe that it would not be morally wrong for the old man to speak out in Nazi Germany or for the explorer to return to the Arctic to light a candle for his deceased friend, * * * or that the choice between the two worlds is not a matter of indifference—to those of us who believe these things, utilitarianism is insufficient as a moral view. We believe that some acts whose costs are greater than their benefits may be morally right and, contrariwise, some acts whose benefits are greater than their costs may be morally wrong.

This does not mean that the question whether benefits are greater than costs is morally irrelevant. Few could claim such. Indeed, for a broad range of individual and social decisions, whether an act's benefits outweigh its costs is a sufficient question to ask. But not for all such decisions. These may involve situations where certain duties—duties not to lie, break promises, or kill, for example—make an act wrong, even if it would result in an excess of benefits over costs. Or they may involve instances where people's rights are at stake. We would not permit rape even if it could be demonstrated that the rapist derived enormous happiness from his act, while the victim experienced only minor displeasure. We do not do cost-benefit analyses of freedom of speech or trial by jury. * * * As the United Steelworkers noted in a comment on the Occupational Safety and Health Administration's economic analysis of its proposed rule to reduce worker exposure to carcinogenic coke-oven emissions, the Emancipation Proclamation was not subjected to an inflationary impact statement. The notion of human rights involves the idea that people may make certain claims to be allowed to act in certain ways or to be treated in certain ways, even if the sum of benefits achieved thereby does not outweigh the sum of costs. It is this view that underlies the statement that "workers have a right to a safe and healthy work place" and the expectation that OSHA's decisions will reflect that judgment.

In the most convincing versions of non-utilitarian ethics, various duties or rights are not absolute. But each has a *prima facie* moral validity so that, if duties or rights do not conflict, the morally right act is the act that reflects a duty or respects a right. If duties or rights do conflict, a moral judgment, based on conscious deliberation, must be made. Since one of the duties non-utilitarian philosophers enumerate is the duty of beneficence (the duty to maximize happiness), which in effect incorporates all of utilitarianism by reference, a non-utilitarian who is faced with conflicts between the results of cost-benefit analysis and non-utility-based considerations will need to undertake such deliberation. But in that deliberation, additional elements, which cannot be reduced to a question of whether benefits outweigh costs, have been introduced. Indeed, depending on the moral importance we attach to the right or duty involved, cost-benefit questions may, within wide ranges, become irrelevant to the outcome of the moral judgment.

In addition to questions involving duties and rights, there is a final sort of question where, in my view, the issue of whether benefits outweigh costs should not govern moral judgment. I noted earlier that, for the common run of questions facing individuals and societies, it is possible to begin and end our judgment simply by finding out if the benefits of the contemplated act outweigh the costs. This very fact means that one way to show the great importance, or value, attached to an area is to say that decisions involving the area should not be determined by cost-benefit calculations. This applies, I think, to the view many environmentalists have of decisions involving our natural environment. When officials are deciding what level of pollution will harm certain vulnerable people—such as asthmatics or the elderly—while not harming others, one issue involved may be the right of those people not to be sacrificed on the altar of somewhat higher living standards for the rest of us. But more broadly than this, many environmentalists fear that subjecting decisions about clean air or water to the cost-benefit tests that determine the general run of decisions remove those matters from the realm of specially valued things.

II

In order for cost-benefit calculations to be performed the way they are supposed to be, all costs and benefits must be expressed in a common measure, typically dollars, including things not normally bought and sold on markets, and to which dollar prices are therefore not attached. The most dramatic example of such things is human life itself; but many of the other benefits achieved or preserved by environmental policy—such as peace and quiet, fresh-smelling air, swimmable rivers, spectacular vistas—are not traded on markets either.

Economists who do cost-benefit analysis regard the quest after dollar values for non-market things as a difficult challenge—but one to be met with relish. They have tried to develop methods for imputing a person's "willingness to pay" for such things, their approach generally involving a search for bundled goods that *are* traded on markets and that vary as to whether they include a feature that is, *by itself*, not marketed. Thus, fresh air is not marketed, but houses in different parts of Los Angeles that are similar except for the degree of smog are. Peace and quiet is not marketed, but similar houses inside and outside airport flight paths are. The risk of death is not marketed, but similar jobs that have different levels of risk are. Economists have produced many often ingenious efforts to impute dollar prices to non-marketed things by observing the premiums accorded homes in clean air areas over similar homes in dirty areas or the premiums paid for risky jobs over similar nonrisky jobs.

These ingenious efforts are subject to criticism on a number of technical grounds. It may be difficult to control for all the dimensions of quality other than the presence or absence of the non-marketed thing. More important, in a world where people have different preferences and are subject to different constraints as they make their choices, the dollar value imputed to the non-market things that most people would wish to avoid will be lower than otherwise, because people with unusually weak aversion to those things or unusually strong constraints on their choices will be willing to take the bundled good in question at less of a discount than the average person. Thus, to use the property value discount of homes near airports as a measure of people's willingness to pay for quiet means to accept as a proxy for the rest of us the behavior of those least sensitive to noise, of airport employees (who value the convenience of a near-airport location) or of others who are susceptible to an agent's assurances that "it's not so bad." To use the wage premiums accorded hazardous work as a measure of the value of life means to accept as proxies for the rest of us the choices of people who do not have many choices or who are exceptional risk-seekers.

A second problem is that the attempts of economists to measure people's willingness to pay for non-marketed things assume that there is no difference between the price a person would require for *giving up* something to which he had a preexisting right and the price he would pay to *gain* something to which he enjoys no right. Thus, the analysis assumes no difference between how much a homeowner would need to be paid in order to give up an unobstructed mountain view that he already enjoys and how much he would be willing to pay to get an obstruction moved once it is already in place. Available evidence suggest that most people would insist on being paid far more to assent to a worsening of their situation than they would be willing to pay to improve their situation. The difference arises from such factors as being accustomed to and psychologically attached to that which one believes one enjoys by right. But this creates a circularity problem for any attempt to use cost-benefit analysis to determine *whether* to assign to, say, the homeowner the right to an unobstructed mountain view. For willingness to pay will be different depending on whether the right is assigned initially or not. The value judgment about whether to assign the right must thus be made first. (In order to set an upper bound on the value of the benefit, one might hypothetically assign the right to the person and determine how much he would need to be paid to give it up.)

Third, the efforts of economists to impute willingness to pay invariably involve bundled goods exchanged in *private* transactions. Those who use figures garnered from such analysis to provide guidance for *public* decisions assume no difference between how people value certain things in private individual transactions and how they would wish those same things to be valued in public collective decisions. In making such assumptions, economists insidiously slip into their analysis an important and controversial value judgment, growing naturally out of the highly individualistic microeconomic tradition—namely, the view that there should be no difference between private behavior and the behavior we display in public social life. An alternative view—one that enjoys, I would suggest, wide resonance among citizens—would be that public, social decisions provide an opportunity to give certain things a higher valuation than we choose, for one reason or another, to give them in our private activities.

Thus, opponents of stricter regulation of health risks often argue that we show by our daily risk-taking behavior that we do not value life infinitely, and therefore our public decisions should not reflect the high value of life that proponents of strict regulation propose. However, an alternative view is equally plausible. Precisely because we fail, for whatever reasons, to give life-saving the value in everyday personal decisions that we in some general terms believe we should give it, we may wish our social decisions to provide us the occasion to display the reverence for life that we espouse but do not always show. By this view, people do not have fixed unambiguous "preferences" to which they give expression through private activities and which therefore should be given expression in public decisions. Rather, they may have what they themselves regard as "higher" and "lower" preferences. The latter may come to the fore in private decisions, but people may want the former to come to the fore in public decisions. They may sometimes display racial prejudice, but support antidiscrimination laws. They may buy a certain product after seeing a seductive ad, but be skeptical enough of advertising to want the government to keep a close eye on it. In such cases, the use of private behavior to impute the values that should be entered for public decisions, as is done by using willingness to pay in private transactions, commits grievous offense against a view of the behavior of the citizen that is deeply ingrained in our democratic tradition. It is a view that denudes politics of any independent role in society, reducing it to a mechanistic, mimicking recalculation based on private behavior.

Finally, one may oppose the effort to place prices on a non-market thing and hence in effect incorporate it into the market system out of a fear that the very act of doing so will reduce the thing's perceived value. To place a price on the benefit may, in other words, reduce the value of that benefit. Cost-benefit analysis thus may be like the thermometer that, when placed in a liquid to be measured, itself changes the liquid's temperature.

Examples of the perceived cheapening of a thing's value by the very act of buying and selling it abound in everyday life and language. The disgust that accompanies the idea of buying and selling human beings is based on the sense that this would dramatically diminish human worth. Epithets such as "he prostituted himself," applied as linguistic analogies to people who have sold something, reflect the view that certain things should not be sold because doing so diminishes their value. * * *

The first reason that pricing something decreases its perceived value is that, in many circumstances, non-market exchange is associated with the production of certain values not associated with market exchange. These may include spontaneity and various other feelings that come from personal relationships. If a good becomes less associated with the production of positively valued feelings because of market exchange, the perceived value of the good declines to the extent that those feelings are valued. This can be seen clearly in instances where a thing may be transferred by market and by non-market mechanisms. The willingness to pay for sex bought from a prostitute is less than the perceived value of the sex consummating love. (Imagine the reaction if a practitioner of cost-benefit analysis computed the benefits of sex based on the price of prostitute services.)

Furthermore, if one values in a general sense the existence of a non-market sector because of its connection with the production of certain valued feelings, then one ascribes added value to any non-marketed good simply as a repository of values represented by the non-market sector one wishes to preserve. This seems certainly to be the case for things in nature, such as pristine streams or undisturbed forests: for many people who value them, part of their value comes from their position as repositories of values the non-market sector represents.

The second way in which placing a market price

on a thing decreases its perceived value is by removing the possibility of proclaiming that the thing is "not for sale," since things on the market by definition are for sale. The very statement that something is not for sale affirms, enhances, and protects a thing's value in a number of ways. To begin with, the statement is a way of showing that a thing is valued for its own sake, whereas selling a thing for money demonstrates that it was valued only instrumentally. Furthermore, to say that something cannot be transferred in that way places it in the exceptional category—which requires the person interested in obtaining that thing to be able to offer something else that is exceptional, rather than allowing him the easier alternative of obtaining the thing for money that could have been obtained in an infinity of ways. This enhances its value. If I am willing to say "You're a really kind person" to whoever pays me to do so, my praise loses the value that attaches to it from being exchangeable only for an act of kindness.

In addition, if we have already decided we value something highly, one way of stamping it with a cachet affirming its high value is to announce that it is "not for sale." Such an announcement does more, however, than just reflect a preexisting high valuation. It signals a thing's distinctive value to others and helps us persuade them to value the thing more highly than they otherwise might. It also expresses our resolution to safeguard that distinctive value. To state that something is not for sale is thus also a source of value for that thing, since if a thing's value is easy to affirm or protect, it will be worth more than an otherwise similar thing without such attributes.

If we proclaim that something is not for sale, we make a once-and-for-all judgment of its special value. When something is priced, the issue of its perceived value is constantly coming up, as a standing invitation to reconsider that original judgment. Were people constantly faced with questions such as "how much money could get you to give up your freedom of speech?" or "how much would you sell your vote for if you could?", the perceived value of the freedom to speak or the right to vote would soon become devastated as, in moments of weakness, people started saying "maybe it's not worth *so much* after all." Better not to be faced with the constant questioning in the first place. Something similar did in fact occur when the slogan "better red than dead" was launched by some pacifists during the Cold War. Critics pointed out that the very posing of this stark choice—in effect, "would you *really* be willing to give up your life in exchange for not living under communism?"—reduced the value people attached to freedom and thus diminished resistance to attacks on freedom.

Finally, of some things valued very highly it is stated that they are "priceless" or that they have "infinite value." Such expressions are reserved for a subset of things not for sale, such as life or health. Economists tend to scoff at talk of pricelessness. For them, saying that something is priceless is to state a willingness to trade off an infinite quantity of all other goods for one unit of the priceless good, a situation that empirically appears highly unlikely. For most people, however, the word priceless is pregnant with meaning. Its value-affirming and value-protecting functions cannot be bestowed on expressions that merely denote a determinate, albeit high, valuation. John Kennedy in his inaugural address proclaimed that the nation was ready to "pay any price [and] bear any burden . . . to assure the survival and the success of liberty." Had he said instead that we were willing to "pay a high price" or "bear a large burden" for liberty, the statement would have rung hollow.

III

An objection that advocates of cost-benefit analysis might well make to the preceding argument should be considered. I noted earlier that, in cases where various non-utility-based duties or rights conflict with the maximization of utility, it is necessary to make a deliberative judgment about what act is finally right. I also argued earlier that the search for commensurability might not always be a desirable one, that the attempt to go beyond expressing benefits in terms of (say) lives saved and costs in terms of dollars is not something devoutly to be wished.

In situations involving things that are not expressed in a common measure, advocates of cost-benefit analysis argue that people making judgments "in effect" perform cost-benefit calculations anyway. If government regulators promulgate a regulation that saves 100 lives at a cost of $1 billion, they are "in effect" valuing a life at (a minimum of) $10 million, whether or not they say that they are willing to place a dollar value on a human life. Since, in this view, cost-benefit analysis "in effect" is inevitable, it might as well be made specific.

This argument misconstrues the real difference in the reasoning processes involved. In cost-benefit analysis, equivalencies are established *in advance* as one of the raw materials for the calculation. One determines costs and benefits, one determines equivalencies (to be able to put various costs and benefits into a common measure), and then one sets to toting things up—waiting, as it were, with bated breath for the results of the calculation to come out. The outcome is determined by the arithmetic; if the outcome is a close call or if one is not good at long division, one does not know how it will turn out until the calculation is finished. In the kind of deliberative judgment that is performed without a common measure, no establishment of equivalencies occurs in advance. Equivalencies are not aids to the decision process. In fact, the decision-maker might not even be aware of what the "in effect" equivalencies were, at least before they are revealed to him afterwards by someone pointing out what he had "in effect" done. The decision-maker would see himself as simply having made a deliberative judgment; the "in effect" equivalency number did not play a causal role in the decision but at most merely reflects it. Given this, the argument against making the process explicit is the one discussed earlier in the discussion of problems with putting specific quantified values on things that are not normally quantified—that the very act of doing so may serve to reduce the value of those things.

My own judgment is that modest efforts to assess levels of benefits and costs are justified, although I do not believe that government agencies ought to sponsor efforts to put dollar prices on non-market things. I also do not believe that the cry for more cost-benefit analysis in regulation is, on the whole, justified. If regulatory officials were so insensitive about regulatory costs that they did not provide acceptable raw material for deliberative judgments (even if not of a strictly cost-benefit nature), my conclusion might be different. But a good deal of research into costs and benefits already occurs—actually, far more in the U.S. regulatory process than in that of any other industrial society. The danger now would seem to come more from the other side.

Additional Sources

Stephen Breyer, *Analyzing Regulatory Failure: Mismatches, Less Restrictive Alternatives, and Reform*, 92 Harv. L. Rev. 549 (1979)

Stephen Breyer, Breaking the Vicious Circle: Toward Effective Risk Regulation (1993)

Colin S. Diver, *Policymaking Paradigms in Administrative Law*, 95 Harv. L. Rev. 393 (1981)

Duncan Kennedy, *Cost-Benefit Analysis of Entitlement Problems: A Critique*, 33 Stan. L. Rev. 387 (1981)

Thomas O. McGarity, Reinventing Rationality: The Role of Regulatory Analysis in the Federal Bureaucracy (1991)

E.J. Mishan, Economics for Social Decisions: Elements of Cost-Benefit Analysis (1973)

Alfred S. Neely, IV, *Statutory Inhibitions to the Application of Principles of Cost/Benefit Analysis in Administrative Decision Making*, 23 Duq. L. Rev. 489 (1985)

William H. Rodgers, Jr., *Benefits, Costs, and Risks: Oversight of Health and Environmental Decisionmaking*, 4 Harv. Envtl. L. Rev. 191 (1980)

Cass R. Sunstein, *Cost-Benefit Analysis and the Separation of Powers*, 23 Ariz. L. Rev. 1267 (1981)

Laurence Tribe, *Policy Science: Analysis or Ideology?*, 2 Phil. & Pub. Aff. 66 (1972)

Project: *The Impact of Cost-Benefit Analysis on Federal Administrative Law*, 42 Admin. L. Rev. 545 (1990)

2. The Debate About Judicial Assessment of the Rationality of Agency Decisionmaking: Hard-Look Review

Another key development in modern administrative law is the emergence of hard-look review under the arbitrary and capricious standard.* Under this approach, courts ask whether an agency has taken a hard look at major alternatives to its decision, including those raised by the public and included in the record of a proceeding. In addition, courts often speak of the need for an agency to give adequate consideration to key regulatory issues in reaching a reasonable policy judgment.

In the first excerpt, Merrick Garland—an attorney who represented State Farm Mutual Automobile Insurance Co. in the Supreme Court litigation bearing that company's name—discusses the development of hard-look review. He distinguishes between what he calls "quasi-procedural review: the agencies' hard look" and "substantive review: the courts' hard look". Mr. Garland thus stresses that the hard-look doctrine has both procedural and substantive components. In general, he sees the hard-look approach as reflecting a model of administrative legitimacy that requires an agency's fidelity to the purposes of its authorizing statute.

In the next excerpt, U.S. Court of Appeals Judge Stephen Breyer presents a more cautious view of hard-look doctrine. After describing *State Farm* as representative of a fairly strict judicial attitude toward the review of substantive agency policy, he questions whether such an attitude is appropriate. In particular, Judge Breyer suggests that judges do not have the degree of expertise and the opportunity to gain specialized knowledge that may be required properly to administer the hard-look doctrine. He also suggests that aggressive judicial review of agency policy may result, however unintentionally, in conservative pressures in favor of the status quo. In conclusion, Judge Breyer states that it may be most appropriate for courts to take an aggressive attitude toward issues of law, contrary to the dictates of *Chevron*, and to assume a less aggressive attitude towards issues of policy, contrary to *State Farm*.

The final excerpt, which is by Professors Shapiro and Levy, places hard-look doctrine in a broader perspective. The authors identify three different models of judicial review. The first—which they call a structuralist model—emphasizes constitutional limits on agencies. The second—the proceduralist model—stresses procedural restraints on agencies. After identifying the strengths and limits of these models, Professors Shapiro and Levy argue that the hard-look doctrine reflects a third model, namely, that of rationalism in agency decisionmaking. They suggest that rationalism has become the primary method by which judges oversee and constrain administrative discretion. Professors Shapiro and Levy also address major concerns that have been raised about the hard-look doctrine and that apply to their model of rationalist judicial review.

---

* 5 U.S.C. § 706(2)(A).

Merrick B. Garland, *Deregulation and Judicial Review*, 98 HARV. L. REV. 505, 507, 510–13, 525–38, 541–61 (1985)*

* * *

I. Introduction

* * *

B. Deregulation and Interest Representation

In the late 1960s and early 1970s, administrative law seemed to be moving away from its traditional concern—that of protecting the autonomy of regulated parties by requiring agencies to act with fidelity to congressional purpose—and toward a model of interest representation. Courts and commentators were coming to view agencies as quasi-legislatures whose primary purpose was to balance the interests of competing societal groups. Among the more important motivations for this trend was a concern that the traditional model's focus on autonomy and fidelity was failing to protect the intended beneficiaries of regulatory programs—be they the public at large or discrete groups that Congress felt needed special protection. Both kinds of beneficiaries were perceived to be grossly underrepresented in the processes of agency decisionmaking.

This "interest representation" model had important implications for the elements of judicial review. With underrepresentation the diagnosis, increased participation in the administrative process seemed the cure. Courts liberalized standing requirements to ensure that beneficiaries had access to the agencies; they imposed hybrid rulemaking requirements to ensure that, once before the agencies, beneficiaries had a full opportunity to explain their interests; and they utilized a "quasi-procedural" scope of judicial review—known as the "hard look"—to ensure that the agencies actually considered those interests. The scope of review prescribed by the interest representation model also dictated the appropriate judicial remedy: when an agency had failed to consider all interests affected by its action, the court was to send the agency back to try again.

On the other hand, because the interest representation model conceived of agency rulemaking as an essentially political process, it did not mandate truly substantive review. Courts treated agencies with the same deference traditionally accorded legislatures: judges did not closely review agencies' findings of fact, they refused to second-guess agencies' decisions, and they declined to examine the propriety of agencies' motives. Moreover, because the model treated the administrative process as nothing more than a balancing of political interests, there was no warrant for questioning the outcome of the balancing once all interests had participated and, a fortiori, no warrant for taking affirmative remedial action to impose a particular outcome upon an unwilling agency. Not surprisingly, courts rarely invalidated agency decisions on the ground that they were arbitrary and capricious.

By the mid-1970s, the interest representation model appeared triumphant, dominating both judicial rhetoric and academic commentary. Nonetheless, from the vantage point of the 1980s, that model, although far from moribund, now appears to be on the wane. Although the quasi-procedural "hard look" doctrine remains significant, courts reviewing deregulation now engage in the kind of substantive review, and impose the kind of affirmative remedies, that cannot be justified under a model that views agencies as surrogate legislatures. And whereas in the 1970s courts were reluctant to strike down agency action as arbitrary and capricious, now decision after decision falls under that same standard.

But the decline of the interest representation model is not reflected only in the loss of its descriptive power. Rather, the deregulation cases represent a significantly different conception of the role of administrative agencies. These cases largely reject the notion that agencies should do no more than reflect shifting political balances; they insist instead that administrative action be animated by the legislative purposes underlying each agency's organic statute. By so doing, these cases have reestablished agency fidelity to congressional intent as the central concern of administrative law.

The newly evolving fidelity model does not, however, simply revert to the traditional conception of fidelity as nothing more than a regulated party's shield against the encroachment of government. While retaining the interest representation model's concern with protecting regulatory beneficiaries, the courts have recognized that merely ensuring the *participation* of all affected interests will not ensure the *protection* of those for whom Congress has expressed special solicitude. To provide such protection, the courts have turned instead to an expanded notion of fidelity, one that requires not only that the agencies not *exceed* their congressionally authorized powers, but also that they *use* those powers as Congress in-

---

* Copyright 1985 by the Harvard Law Review Association. Reprinted with permission of the Harvard Law Review Association and Merrick B. Garland. All rights reserved.

tended. In short, the courts have reached back to the oldest of administrative law values—maintaining agency constancy to congressional purpose—in order to extend protection to a new class of legislative beneficiaries.

II. Standard of Review

The appearance of challenges to deregulation in the federal courts was so sudden and novel that, as late as 1982, the D.C. Circuit could accurately state that no court had yet expressly considered what standard of review was appropriate for such cases. The principal question was whether the proper standard was the one generally applied to informal rulemaking—the "arbitrary and capricious" test—or whether a more or less deferential standard should be applied. Most lower courts settled on the arbitrary and capricious test, although few explained their choice in any detail. The Supreme Court finally resolved the matter in *Motor Vehicle Manufacturers Association of United States, Inc. v. State Farm Mutual Automobile Insurance Co.*, affirming that the arbitrary and capricious standard applies to regulation and deregulation alike.

* * *

III. Scope of Review

* * * Before the 1970s, the scope of review under the "arbitrary and capricious" standard was quite narrow, requiring only that agency action evidence a minimum of rationality. Until recently, courts rarely reversed agency decisions under that standard.

Beginning in the 1970s, however, there emerged a new, more rigorous scope of review under the arbitrary and capricious standard—a scope of review known as the "hard look." At birth, the doctrine was quasi-procedural: a set of requirements intended to ensure that the agency itself had taken a hard look at the relevant issues before reaching its decision. Courts reviewing deregulation for the first time at the start of the 1980s endorsed this approach, ratifying the hard look doctrine as an accepted weapon in the arsenal of judicial review.

But the deregulation cases did more than simply adopt the quasiprocedural elements of hard look review. By seizing upon the doctrine's nascent substantive elements, they transformed it into one that required a hard look not just by the agency, but by the court as well. This evolution culminated in the Supreme Court's decision in *State Farm*, which confirmed that hard look review was applicable to both regulation and deregulation.

* * *

A. Quasi-Procedural Review: The Agency's Hard Look

1. The Regulation Cases.—The origins of the hard look doctrine can be traced to the Supreme Court's holding in *SEC v. Chenery Corp.* that agencies must explain the bases for their decisions. Initially, this "explanation" requirement was not particularly rigorous; it demanded only enough explanation to permit the reviewing court to discern the agency's rationale. The requirement took on increased importance, however, in the context of reversals of agency policies. As Judge Leventhal explained in one of the opinions that gave the hard look doctrine its name, such reversals were "danger signals" requiring the agency to put forth a reasoned explanation sufficient to show the court that the agency had taken a "hard look" at the issues before changing direction.[108]

As the doctrine developed, the courts demanded increasingly detailed explanations of the agency's rationale; they required specification of the agency's policy premises, its reasoning, and its factual support. In time, a host of other now-familiar elements also became part of the hard look: an agency had to demonstrate that it had responded to significant points made during the public comment period, had examined all relevant factors, and had considered significant alternatives to the course of action ultimately chosen. These requirements of consideration and explanation combined to generate a kind of "paper hearing" in informal rulemaking cases, as well as a "paper record" of the agency's decisionmaking process that could serve as a basis for judicial review.

2. The Deregulation Cases.—Like the regulatory reversal cases that preceded them, the deregulation cases have been important in elaborating the nature of the hard look doctrine and establishing it as an accepted element of judicial review. Courts have set aside numerous attempts at deregulation on the ground that the agency failed to provide a detailed explanation of its reasoning process. As in the regulation context, judges have found such failures to take many forms—among them, failure to explain policy reversals and to clarify their relation to congressional intent, failure to address the objections of those adversely affected by the change, and failure to consider relevant factors, particularly those made relevant by statutory objectives.

The most significant basis for striking down agency action has been the failure to consider alterna-

---

[108] Greater Boston Television Corp. v. FCC, 444 F.2d 841, 851-52 (D.C. Cir. 1970), *cert. denied*, 403 U.S. 923 (1971) * * *.

tives to deregulation. Indeed, consideration alone has not been sufficient. Combining the consideration and explanation requirements, courts have mandated detailed explication of an agency's decision to reject regulatory alternatives, as well as of its decision to dispense with existing regulations. Even the failure to consider seeking additional information before deregulating, when insufficient information or uncertainty was a rationale for the decision to deregulate, has been the object of judicial criticism. Of particular concern in many of these cases has been an agency's failure to consider alternatives to complete deregulation when such alternatives appeared necessary to protect the intended beneficiaries of the regulatory scheme.

Finally, as in the regulation cases, the various "hard look" elements applied in the deregulation cases have combined to induce agencies to generate paper records of their decisionmaking processes. In contrast to regulation, however, in deregulation that record consists not only of the rationale and evidentiary support for the agency's current decision to deregulate, but also of the rationale for and evidence compiled in favor of the initial rule. As noted below, this dual record plays an important role in providing an evidentiary basis for the substantive review that appellate courts now conduct.

3. *The Hard Look and* Vermont Yankee.—The expanded application of hard look review did not meet with acclaim in all quarters. The sharpest critique relied upon the Supreme Court's opinion in *Vermont Yankee Nuclear Power Corp. v. Natural Resources Defense Council,* which held that the notice and comment procedures prescribed by section 4 of the APA were "the maximum procedural requirements which Congress was willing to have the courts impose upon agencies" conducting informal rulemaking. Before that 1978 decision, some courts had demanded that additional procedures be provided during informal rulemaking, including oral hearings and an opportunity for cross-examination. Although such "hybrid" procedures ensured fuller representation of all interests affected by the rulemaking, critics argued that the additional procedural hurdles destroyed informal rulemaking's salutary flexibility. In *Vermont Yankee,* a unanimous Supreme Court rebuked two appellate panels for "engrafting their own notions of proper procedures upon agencies entrusted with substantive functions by Congress," and held that the imposition of such "extra procedural devices" was beyond the power of the federal courts.

The critical question for the hard look doctrine was whether *Vermont Yankee*'s proscription of "extra procedural devices" applied to the requirements that an agency explain itself, examine objections and relevant factors, and consider alternatives. Opponents of the doctrine argued that it did. They charged that the hard look requirements contravened *Vermont Yankee*'s admonition against "dictating to the agency the methods, procedures, and time dimensions of the needed inquiry." The hard look, they said, was just one more set of procedural impediments to informal rulemaking.

There is, however, another side to this argument. Although the hard look requirements do have a procedural tinge, they may more appropriately be referred to as "quasi-procedural" because they also have a substantive aspect. At bottom, they focus not on the kind of procedure that an agency must use to generate a record, but rather on the kind of decisionmaking record the agency must produce to survive judicial review; the method of generating the record is left to the agency itself. Their concern is not with the external process by which litigants present their arguments to the agency, but with the internal thought process by which an agency decisionmaker reaches a rational decision. Thus, these requirements can be said to flow not from the APA's procedural dictates, but from its substantive command that agency decisionmaking not be "arbitrary" or "capricious."

The Supreme Court's own view regarding the validity of the quasi-procedural requirements was unclear. *Vermont Yankee* itself did not speak directly to the issue, since the case involved the imposition of purely procedural devices. Although the Court did examine whether the Atomic Energy Commission had considered alternatives to the challenged action (the licensing of a nuclear reactor), it did so under the aegis of the National Environmental Policy Act, which expressly required the consideration of alternatives. Other Supreme Court opinions requiring agencies to consider alternatives were arguably distinguishable on similar statutory grounds. Moreover, although the "explanation" requirement had a firm foundation in *Chenery* and subsequent cases, both the amount of detail demanded and the degree to which objections had to be answered were unclear, as was the amount of explanation required before an agency could legitimately reverse its course. Commentators, therefore, remained uncertain and divided over *Vermont Yankee*'s impact on the hard look.

The Supreme Court's grant of certiorari in *State Farm* promised to resolve the issue. The D.C. Circuit had vacated the Department of Transportation's rescission of its "passive restraint" rule on the ground that DOT had failed adequately both to explain its decision and to consider alternatives to rescission. The Solicitor General posed the *Vermont Yankee* issue squarely, arguing that the appellate court's judgment was "inconsistent with the teaching of *Vermont Yankee* . . . that courts may not impose additional procedural requirements on administrative agencies." Before the Supreme Court's resolution of these quasi-procedural issues can be fully appreciated, however, attention must first be paid to parallel developments on the substantive side of the hard look doctrine—developments that also came to a head with the grant of certiorari in *State Farm*.

B. Substantive Review: The Court's Hard Look

1. *The Regulation Cases.*—Until recently, substantive review of the outcome of agency decisionmaking was extremely narrow. Under the so-called "minimum rationality" or "rational basis" test also applicable to review of congressional legislation, courts accorded agencies' findings of fact great deference and upheld their policy choices as long as they were not wholly irrational. Indeed, in one of the key early cases, *Pacific States Box & Basket Co. v. White*, the Supreme Court expressly equated agencies with legislatures for purposes of judicial review. Judges reserved substantive review for instances of adjudication and formal rulemaking, to which they applied the "substantial evidence" standard—a standard purportedly distinct from, and stricter than, the arbitrary and capricious test applied to informal rulemaking. In line with the leniency of the latter test, reversal of an agency decision on the ground that it was substantively "arbitrary and capricious" remained a relatively rare event through the end of the 1970s.

The hard look doctrine was not necessarily inconsistent with the minimum rationality approach. On one view, the doctrine served to ensure only that the *agency* had taken a hard look at the facts and issues before it, not that the *court* do so. The agency had to consider the issues and alternatives, and explain its final decision, but as long as it followed those rules the court had no authority to assess the quality of the agency's consideration or the reasonableness of its explanation. An agency that failed to consider or explain might find its decision vacated and remanded, but after it considered and explained on remand, it could return to court with the same substantive result and the court would have to uphold it.

As hard look review evolved, however, some courts—particularly those reviewing regulatory reversals—appeared to be demanding something more rigorous than mere consideration and explanation. They required "adequate" consideration and "reasoned" explanation, qualifiers that were not always satisfied by proof that consideration and explanation had in fact taken place. From behind the doctrine's quasi-procedural veneer, a substantive approach was slowly emerging.

This emerging, substantive hard look had two principal elements. The first was the requirement that agencies' findings of fact have a basis in the record. Some courts began to search the rulemaking record carefully and uphold only those agency findings supported by that record. For these courts, the difference between the arbitrary and capricious standard and the substantial evidence standard was fading. Only one category of factfinding—that of the so-called "predictive facts" * * *—was carved out for gentler treatment.

Of even greater potential significance was the second element of the substantive hard look: a focus on the agency's ultimate policy choice. Some courts appeared to be infusing greater rigor into the traditional "rational basis" test. Although the semantics hardly captures the spirit of the shift, judges undertaking this kind of review were transforming the requirement of mere "minimum rationality" into one of "reasonableness." The new test plainly had more bite than the old, but its precise outlines were as yet undefined.

2. *The Deregulation Cases.*—Although some of the deregulation cases have continued to apply the old rational basis test, most have seized upon the newly substantive hard look. Moreover, while much of the rhetoric remains quasi-procedural, the tenor of the opinions suggests that on the records presented, no amount of "consideration" or "explanation" resulting in similar agency policies would have satisfied the reviewing courts. The courts' underlying substantive analysis consists of an elaboration of the twofold test emerging from the regulation cases: review of record support for agency findings and review of the "reasonableness" of decisional outcomes.

Judicial scrutiny of record support for agencies' findings of fact has been intensive in the deregulation cases and has resulted in a number of reversals for inadequate support. As in review of regulation, such rigorous scrutiny has not precluded continued deference to findings based upon "predictive facts." Courts have operated on the theory that the thoroughness of the factual support an agency can marshal for a decision depends upon the nature of the decision itself; when only prediction is possible, prediction must suffice. But to prevent the exception from swallowing the rule, courts have required agencies that rely on predictions to set forth the bases of those predictions and to demonstrate their reasonableness in light of the available evidence. In particular, the courts have looked closely to determine whether the facts provide an adequate basis for an agency's prediction that it can continue to protect the intended beneficiaries of legislation despite deregulation.

The dual nature of the record in deregulation cases—consisting of both the facts supporting the decision to deregulate and the facts originally compiled in support of the rule being repealed—has greatly facilitated substantive review. In reviewing regulation, courts face the possibility that an agency has submitted an informal record that does not reflect evidence adverse to its position. In deregulation cases, however, this problem is largely eliminated by the existence of an original record containing now-adverse views that speak with the authority of the agency itself. * * *

The deregulation cases have also given more specific content to the second element of substantive review: the requirement that the agency's policy choice be "reasonable." A number of these opinions hold that a reviewing court, after determining whether the facts relied upon by the agency have "some basis in the record," should go on to consider "whether those facts and legislative considerations by themselves could lead a reasonable person to make the judgment that the Agency has made." Beneath this rhetoric, one can discern a new analytical framework: the key issue is not whether the agency's decision is "reasonable" in some abstract sense, but whether it is reasonable in light of the facts in the record and the legislative purpose. The court's evaluation of the reasonableness of the relationship between the factual record and legislative purpose on the one hand, and the agency's decision on the other, has been the decisive factor in a substantial number of recent deregulation cases.

The new "reasonableness" test has taken on an additional dimension through its interaction with the quasi-procedural requirement that agencies consider alternatives. The agency's final decision must be reasonable not only in light of a permissible policy goal and supportable findings of fact, but also in light of the alternative choices available. Again, the courts have paid particular attention to whether an alternative can achieve the agency's lawful purposes yet still preserve at least some protection for the intended beneficiaries of the statutory scheme.

* * *

3. *Substantive Review and the Supreme Court.*—Although the Supreme Court's views on substantive review of agency action were somewhat ambiguous for most of the period under consideration here, the Court seemed to support the traditional "rational basis" inquiry rather than the "reasonableness" approach. The leading opinion was *Citizens to Preserve Overton Park v. Volpe*. Although that opinion's description of the appropriate analysis as "thorough, probing, in-depth review" could have been interpreted as an endorsement of stricter substantive scrutiny, many observers instead emphasized *Overton Park*'s characterization of the arbitrary and capricious standard as "a narrow one"—particularly in light of the Court's favorable citation of *Pacific States Box & Basket Co. v. White*. Several subsequent Supreme Court opinions seemed to buttress the conclusion that *Overton Park* required only that agencies not act "irrational[ly]." * * *

* * * [T]he *State Farm* case provided the Court with an opportunity to clarify the scope of review of informal rulemaking. The Solicitor General's brief expressly raised the question of the appropriate degree of substantive review. The arbitrary and capricious test, he argued, "performs a function akin to determining whether a statute is authorized by the Constitution." In the government's view, agencies were analogous to legislatures, and courts were bound to uphold agency decisions unless they wholly lacked a rational basis. In *State Farm*, the Court finally rejected the analogy to legislation and effectively adopted the substantive elements of the hard look.

C. *The* State Farm *Decision*

The regulation whose rescission was at issue in *State Farm* would have required automakers to install "passive restraints" in all new automobiles over a three-year period commencing on September 1, 1981. Although the use of seatbelts can drastically reduce the incidence of traffic fatalities, their rate of usage in this country is extremely low. Accordingly, in 1977 the Department of Transportation, acting pursuant to its rulemaking authority under the National Traffic and Motor Vehicle Safety Act, promulgated a regulation requiring automakers to install devices that would protect passengers without their having to take any action at all. These "passive restraints" were of two general types: airbags, which * * * inflate upon impact to protect the occupant from collision with the car's interior, and automatic seatbelts, which move into place automatically as the passenger enters the vehicle and closes the door. DOT estimated that installation of passive restraints would prevent approximately 12,000 deaths per year.

In 1981, however, a new administration announced plans to rescind the passive-restraint regulation. The automobile industry, it explained, no longer planned to comply with the regulation by providing airbags or nondetachable belts, but instead intended to install a new type of detachable automatic belt. Because these belts, once detached, require the occupant to reattach them in order to restore their automatic feature, DOT concluded that it could no longer reliably predict that regulation would induce a significant increase in usage—and therefore in occupant protection—over ordinary belts.

State Farm Mutual Automobile Insurance Company and the National Association of Independent Insurers filed petitions challenging the rescission. Upon review, the D.C. Circuit declared the rescission "arbitrary and capricious." The Supreme Court, holding the arbitrary and capricious standard equally applicable to both regulation and deregulation, reached the same conclusion.

1. Quasi-Procedural Elements.—On one level, the *State Farm* decision is a ringing endorsement of the quasi-procedural hard look. Quoting Judge Leventhal's opinion in *Greater Boston Television Corp. v. FCC*, Justice White confirmed that "an agency changing its course must supply a reasoned analysis" justifying the change. In the Court's view, DOT had failed to do so in two key respects.

First, the agency had not adequately explained its conclusion that detachable automatic belts would not substantially reduce the death toll. It is true, as the agency said, that an automatic belt, once detached, provides no protection. But, unlike ordinary belts, detachable automatic belts do provide protection unless the occupant bothers to remove them. In the Court's view, the agency had failed to consider this inertia factor adequately in assessing the value of detachable automatic belts.

The Court also thought the rescission arbitrary for a second quasi-procedural reason: the agency had rescinded the passive-restraint rule in its entirety without considering three alternatives and without explaining its reasons for rejecting them. To begin with, in view of the agency's belief that detachable belts—but not airbags—would be ineffective, "the logical response . . . would [have been] to require the installation of airbags." "At the very least," the Court said, "this alternative way of achieving the objectives of the Act should have been addressed and adequate reasons given for its abandonment." In addition, the agency had "fail[ed] to analyze" the alternative of limiting automatic belts to the nondetachable type and had failed "to articulate a basis" for rejecting that alternative. Finally, the Court observed, if the real problem were the insufficiency of evidence on the efficacy of detachable belts, the agency should at least have had "a justification for rescinding the regulation before engaging in a search for further evidence."

The Court could hardly have been more explicit in approving the judicial imposition of quasi-procedural requirements. Reciting a veritable litany of such requirements, Justice White held that an agency must "articulate a satisfactory explanation for its action," rely on its own and not appellate counsel's "*post hoc* rationalizations," "supply a reasoned analysis" justifying any reversal of course, "examine the relevant data," "'consider[] . . . the relevant factors,'" and consider "alternative way[s] of achieving . . . objectives." In response to the Solicitor General's claim that such requirements violate the spirit of *Vermont Yankee*, the Court replied with words as strong as those used in *Vermont Yankee* itself: "*Vermont Yankee*," said the Court, is not "a talisman under which any agency decision is by definition unimpeachable." The requirements of explanation and consideration of alternatives do not "impose additional procedural requirements upon an agency."

2. Substantive Elements.—Despite the Court's quasi-procedural rhetoric, it would be a mistake to interpret *State Farm* as applicable to that dimension of the hard look doctrine alone. Indeed, the Court rejected the Solicitor General's view of the scope of substantive review as firmly as it rejected his attack on quasi-procedural requirements. To his argument that the arbitrary and capricious standard mandates only that an agency exercise the minimum rationality required of a legislature by the due process clause, the Court replied, "We do not view as equivalent the presumption of constitutionality afforded legislation drafted by Congress and the presumption of regularity afforded an agency in fulfilling its statutory mandate." Rather, the Court held, an agency must articulate a "satisfactory" explanation for its actions that does not "run[] counter to the evidence before the agency" and that demonstrates a "'rational connection between the facts found and the choice made.'"

Moreover, although the Court couched its critique of DOT's actions in quasi-procedural terms—stressing the agency's failure both to explain its decision and to consider alternatives—close examination reveals that the twofold substantive test sketched in the previous Section underlay the Court's analysis. In the Court's view, the agency (1) lacked record support for its findings of fact, and (2) failed to establish a reasonable relationship between its decision on the one hand, and the relevant evidence, alternatives, and statutory purpose on the other.

(a) The Requirement of Record Support.—The first of these substantive elements appears in the Court's analysis of DOT's conclusion that detachable belts were not worth requiring. Although the majority criticized the agency for failing to explain its rationale adequately, Justice Rehnquist's separate opinion demonstrates that the agency had in fact proffered a quite detailed explanation: it was not possible to predict reliably whether occupants would make

substantial use of the new, detachable belts; without substantial usage, the safety benefits afforded by the belts were uncertain; and in light of this uncertainty, implementation of the rule did not warrant the economic costs. By any measure, the agency's explanation was not only detailed, but seemingly rational.

The Court's real concern, however, was not with the detail or logic of the agency's reasoning, but with its factual premise. Although the Court said it would "not upset the agency's view of the facts," it took pains to stress "the limitations of this record in supporting the agency's decision," noting that there was "no direct evidence in support of the agency's finding that detachable automatic belts cannot be predicted to yield a substantial increase in usage." Closely scrutinizing the record, the Court found that all prior surveys of cars equipped with automatic belts had revealed substantial increases in usage over ordinary belts. The Court noted that although the automatic belts considered in the surveys were nondetachable, inertia was on the side of protection in the case of both detachable and nondetachable belts: the occupant had to take affirmative steps in order to render the belts ineffective. Searching the record again, the Court found DOT studies establishing that such inertia was a key factor in determining usage. Accordingly, the Court concluded that "there would seem to be grounds to believe that seatbelt use by occasional users will be substantially increased by the detachable passive belts." With DOT's factual premise thus open to doubt, the Court found itself unable "to conclude that the rescission was the product of reasoned decisionmaking."

Although the Court questioned the Department's claim that it could not predict the usage rates for detachable belts, *State Farm* does not represent a retreat from the policy of permitting agencies to rely upon "predictive facts." Indeed, the Court stressed that "just as an agency may decline to issue a safety standard if it is uncertain about its efficacy, an agency may also revoke a standard on the basis of serious uncertainties *if supported by the record and reasonably explained.*" The key lies in the italicized language. If agency action is predicated upon a finding of uncertainty, the record must support the conclusion that uncertainty truly exists—just as it must support any other kind of finding upon which action is based. As the Court explained, "Recognizing that policymaking in a complex society must account for uncertainty . . . does not imply that it is sufficient for an agency to merely recite the terms 'substantial uncertainty' as a justification for its actions." In *State Farm*, the Court apparently did not believe DOT's sudden declaration—after years of contrary pronouncements—that it was now uncertain whether passive restraints would contribute to highway safety.

(b) The Requirement of a Reasonable Result.— The second element of the substantive hard look— the requirement that the agency's policy choice be reasonable in light of the evidence, alternatives, and statutory purpose—also appears in the *State Farm* opinion, particularly in the Court's analysis of the manner in which DOT dealt with alternatives to complete rescission. Again, the Court's rhetoric had a quasi-procedural flavor: Justice White complained that the agency had failed to consider the options of requiring airbags or nondetachable belts. Yet, although the agency had failed to consider an airbags-only option, it actually had not neglected to consider nondetachable belts. Recognizing this fact, the insurance companies argued not that DOT had failed to address the alternative of nondetachable belts, but that the agency had rejected it arbitrarily and capriciously. The Court ultimately agreed. After brusquely dismissing two arguments offered to explain the agency's rejection of the nondetachable-belt alternative, the Court concluded that the agency had "failed to offer the rational connection between facts and judgment required to pass muster under the arbitrary and capricious standard."

Review of the entire *State Farm* opinion reveals precisely the manner in which the agency had failed: compelling manufacturers to install nondetachable belts was an available alternative to rescinding the entire regulation; the record demonstrated that nondetachable belts consistently lead to substantial improvements in usage and thus enhance safety; and the legislative history evidenced Congress's intention that "safety . . . be the preeminent factor" in agency decisions under the National Traffic and Motor Vehicle Safety Act. The Court in effect concluded that, given the available alternatives, factual record, and congressional purpose, a reasonable administrator would not have made the choice that DOT did. One suspects that the agency could have "considered" and "explained" until it was hoarse, yet still not have changed the Court's ultimate conclusion. The substantive nature of the Court's analysis is thus readily apparent.

3. Subsequent Developments.—* * * Although some commentators have suggested that the Supreme Court's 1984 decision in *Chevron, U.S.A., Inc. v. Natural Resources Defense Council, Inc.* is inconsistent with a substantive approach, the case can in fact be harmonized with *State Farm*'s application of the hard look.

At issue in *Chevron* was the Environmental Protection Agency's interpretation of the Clean Air Act Amendments of 1977. In 1981, the EPA changed its construction of the statutory term "source" so as to ease the regulatory burdens imposed upon industry in states that had not achieved federal air quality standards. Previously, each new or modified piece of industrial equipment had been considered a separate source requiring a permit if it emitted more than a threshold amount of pollutants. Under the agency's new "plantwide" or "bubble" definition, companies were allowed to install or modify equipment without obtaining a permit as long as any resulting increase in emissions was offset by reductions in emissions from other equipment in the same plant. Reversing a decision by the D.C. Circuit, the Supreme Court held that the EPA's new definition was a "reasonable policy choice for the agency to make." "[F]ederal judges," the Court admonished, "have no constituency" and "have a duty to respect legitimate policy choices made by those who do."

The Court treated *Chevron* purely as a case of statutory construction—neither *State Farm* nor the APA was even mentioned—and arguably the two cases can be distinguished on that ground. But the line between reviewing the validity of an agency's statutory interpretations and reviewing the reasonableness of its policies is often a fine one; it is perhaps imperceptible in a case like *Chevron* where Congress had expressed no clear intention on the definitional issue in question and where the agency had actually promulgated its interpretation through the process of rulemaking. The teachings of *Chevron*, therefore, cannot be dismissed as inapplicable to the arbitrary and capricious test.

There is no need, however, to conclude that *State Farm* and *Chevron* are inconsistent. Indeed, the test of statutory construction set forth in *Chevron* parallels the description of the arbitrary and capricious test in *State Farm*: when the intent of Congress is not clear, Justice Stevens stated in *Chevron*, the court's duty is to ensure that the agency's interpretation is a "reasonable" one. Moreover, as the balance of the *Chevron* opinion suggests, "reasonableness" is to be measured—as it was in *State Farm*—against Congress's purposes in enacting the statute at issue.

Given the similarity in their analytical approaches, the difference in the cases' outcomes might be explained by the Court's differing perceptions of the quality of agency decisionmaking in the two cases. Whereas in *State Farm* the Court found that DOT had failed to "supply a reasoned analysis" for its decision, it found no such problem in *Chevron*. To the contrary, said Justice Stevens, the EPA had "considered the matter in a detailed and reasoned fashion," it had "advanced a reasonable explanation for its conclusion that the regulations [would] serve" the congressional purpose, and "its reasoning [was] supported by the public record developed in the rulemaking process." In short, the Court affirmed the agency's decision in *Chevron* only after concluding that the EPA had passed the same tests that DOT had failed in *State Farm*.

Although the analyses employed in the two cases are thus compatible, it is fair to say that the *Chevron* opinion adopts a tone considerably more deferential to agency decisionmaking than does the *State Farm* opinion. The difference in tone, however, can be explained by two factors that distinguish the cases without casting doubt upon the continued vitality of the substantive hard look.

First, the Court in *Chevron* took pains to emphasize that the case before it was not truly a deregulation case. According to Justice Stevens, the EPA itself had originally endorsed the plantwide definition of source and had changed definitions only when forced to do so by an earlier opinion of the D.C. Circuit. Thus, the EPA's most recent adoption of the plantwide definition was not a reversal warranting special judicial concern, but merely a return to the agency's own preferred position.

Second, and perhaps more important, whereas the Motor Vehicle Safety Act reflected a paramount congressional intent to advance automobile safety, the Clean Air Act Amendments in the Court's view embodied two "manifestly competing" purposes: reducing air pollution and permitting economic growth. Reconciling such conflicting policies is a particularly difficult task, the Court said, and the agency's determination thus deserves considerable deference. Because the EPA's interpretation represented a "reasonable accommodation" of the interests Congress sought to advance, the Court sustained it.

State Farm and *Chevron* can therefore be harmonized. The degree of their harmony depends on whether the Clean Air Act Amendments indeed reflect two competing congressional purposes, or whether the Court in *Chevron* exaggerated the conflict in order to permit the unrestrained exercise of agency discretion. Since the legislative history contains support for both conclusions, *Chevron* need not be read as a retreat from the commitment to hard look review expressed by the Court in *State Farm*.

D. Fidelity and the Hard Look

In view of the continuing importance of hard look review, it is worth considering why courts have made it such an integral part of the judicial repertoire. * * * As this Section suggests, the courts appear to be using hard look review to ferret out—and reject—agency actions motivated by considerations inconsistent with legislative purpose.

1. The Role of the Hard Look in Deregulation Review.—Quasi-procedural review is particularly well suited to dealing with instances of true administrative irrationality—inconsistencies generated by lack of awareness or care, or by the influence of "unconscious preference and irrelevant prejudice." The requirements that an agency consider the relevant issues and explain its rationale impose a measure of discipline. They force decisionmakers to focus on the distinctions they draw, facilitating the elimination of irrationality and carelessness from the administrative process. With these concerns alleviated, a final judicial check for "minimum rationality" of outcomes will suffice.

In reviewing deregulation, however, the courts have not been principally concerned with unconscious swerves or sudden irrationality, since most such cases have involved conscious and purposeful changes in agency policy. Rather, * * * the courts' principal concern in the deregulation cases has been that an improper motive has intruded into the decisionmaking process. The fear is that the agency is responding not to new facts, but to new policies—policies different from those the agency followed when the statute was young and its administrators possessed greater knowledge of, and perhaps fidelity to, the legislature's purpose. The oft-expressed concern, in short, is that decisions to deregulate may "constitute 'danger signals' that the will of Congress is being ignored."

In these circumstances, the explanation and consideration requirements, although helpful, are not enough. Such requirements may expose misreadings of statutory purpose, but they cannot reveal unstated motives or thwart an agency bent upon "achiev[ing] a particular result without regard to the facts at hand." As long as the court declines to examine the substance of the agency's consideration and explanation, an agency that dutifully jumps through the quasi-procedural hoops will survive review regardless of its actual motives.

Direct discovery of an agency's motives is also foreclosed. Driven by considerations of both comity and practicality, the courts have always taken a dim view of such efforts. Thus, judges need a proxy by which to gauge the agency's fidelity to statutory purpose—some method of reviewing the rationality of outcomes as a test for the legitimacy of motives. And the hard look, as it has evolved in the deregulation cases, has some power to perform that function.

The hard look first requires the agency to articulate the policies that it purports to be furthering. If the statute actually embodies such policies, the hard look then serves to expose the potential alternative means to achieve them. At this point, substantive review takes over, ensuring both that the findings of fact upon which the agency has predicated its action have support in the rulemaking record and that the agency did not simply invent them to justify a predetermined result. Finally, the hard look demands that the agency show that the course it chose was reasonable in light of the relevant policies, alternatives, and facts.

If a court finds the chosen course unreasonable, however, the problem may not necessarily—or even likely—be an administrator's sudden lapse into irrationality. Rather, it may be that the court has measured the outcome against the wrong motive. The result may be perfectly rational in light of the agency's true, but unstated, motive. The agency may have left that motive unstated, however, because it conflicts with the statute. In this way, the "reasonable relationship" test can serve as a surrogate for motivation analysis.

Evidence suggests that substantive review has in fact played this role in several of the deregulation cases. In *State Farm*, for example, the D.C. Circuit and Supreme Court both noted that when DOT initially proposed rescinding the passive-restraint requirement, it cited the "'difficulties of the automobile industry'" as a justification. Later, the appellate court noted, the White House Press Office announced the proposed rescission as part of a package of "Actions to Help the U.S. Auto Industry." When the agency finally announced the rescission itself, however, it listed the inefficacy of the detachable belt—not the plight of the automobile industry—as the reason for its decision.

If the Motor Vehicle Safety Act had empowered the agency to pursue the goal of assisting the auto industry, rescission of the passive-restraint requirement might not have been unreasonable. But as both courts stressed, although the agency could consider monetary costs, "Congress intended safety to be the preeminent factor." To be sure, the preeminence of safety considerations did not require automatic invalidation of DOT's action: the agency had not mentioned protection of the auto industry as a factor in its final decision, and direct questioning of the agency's motivations would have been improper. But when the courts measured the agency's decision to rescind against the stated goal of advancing the cause of auto safety, they found the decision unreasonable in light of the evidence and the available alternatives. The D.C. Circuit, at least, made clear its view that the agency's seemingly unreasonable result stemmed from the intrusion of an improper motive. "It is difficult to avoid the conclusion," said the court, "that [the agency's] analysis . . . has been distorted by solicitude for the economically depressed automobile industry—which is not the agency's mandate—at the expense of consideration for traffic safety, which is."

* * *

2. *The Power of the Hard Look.*—In statistical analysis, one measure of the "power" of a test is its ability to reject the hypothesis that events have occurred randomly when in fact they have not. The power of a standard of judicial review may analogously be defined as its ability to reject the usual "presumption of [agency] regularity" when an improper motive has influenced the decisionmaking process. The traditionally narrow arbitrary and capricious test has little power in this sense. When a court declines to scrutinize (or even assumes the existence of) supporting facts, ignores the presence of alternatives, and requires nothing more than a minimally rational explanation, almost any outcome can pass muster—even if it springs from an unstated, inappropriate motive. Nor does the addition of a quasi-procedural hard look provide substantial assistance. As already noted, the consideration and explanation requirements do not in themselves have much power to detect unstated motives.

By contrast, the fusing of the quasi-procedural and substantive strands of the hard look doctrine greatly enhances the power of review. By requiring not only that the agency set forth a rationale consistent with the statutory purpose and outline available alternatives, but also that the agency support its findings of fact with record evidence and choose a final outcome that is reasonable in light of the facts, alternatives, and statutory purpose, a court can substantially decrease the odds that an agency decision motivated by improper purposes will escape invalidation. This is particularly true in the case of a statute that evidences a single, discernible purpose against which the court can measure agency decisions. But it is also true in the case of a multipurpose statute when the legislature has indicated which purpose is to predominate, since the court can then discover whether the agency has pursued merely permissible policies at the expense of paramount ones. In the deregulation cases, courts have on occasion attempted to discern such a hierarchy of purposes by asking whom Congress intended the statutory scheme to protect; they have then elevated that group's protection to the status of a primary statutory goal.

Despite—or perhaps because of—its power, hard look review has two serious deficiencies. Paradoxically, it may be both too hard, and not hard enough, to ensure fidelity to congressional purpose. On the one hand, hard look review may be too hard because it may permit a court to substitute its judgment for the agency's on the pretext of determining whether a policy outcome is "reasonable." The same risk may inhere in a court's determination of which of several statutory purposes the legislature considered most important: the court may be tempted to substitute its own hierarchy of values for that of Congress.

It is hard to rebut this charge directly, beyond asserting the good faith of the judiciary. The only consolation—if it is one—is that the risk that courts will substitute their judgment for that of the legislature exists regardless of the kind of review nominally applied—whether substantive, quasi-procedural, or even purely procedural. Although the standard of review may dictate the rhetorical guise, it generally cannot eliminate the risk. Indeed, the only kind of review that does not entail that risk is no review, and that is the one "standard" clearly incompatible with the will of Congress.

On the other hand, although there is room for criticizing the hard look for being too hard, there may also be warrant for wondering whether it is hard enough. When the statute at issue does not reflect a clearly discernible purpose, but contains instead a vaguely defined "public interest" standard, there is little to assist the court in measuring the reasonableness of agency action. The same is true when the statute contains multiple goals of equal importance, as the Court found to be the case in *Chevron*. In these circumstances, the range of reasonableness is so ill-defined that almost any outcome can survive the hard look. Courts reviewing agency action under such statutory schemes may express their frustration at the absence of meaningful judicial standards, but in the end they must concede that the "weighing" of the various interests involved should be left largely to the discretion of the agency. Indeed, this goes far toward explaining the almost uniquely consistent success of the FCC—perhaps the archetypal example of an agency delegated broad powers—in defending its deregulatory initiatives.

There are, however, two important points to note about the hard look's frailty in this regard. First, the test's weakness under the circumstances described does not indicate that the test has failed to perform its function. Indeed, the hard look *should* have little power to exclude outcomes under these kinds of statutes. When Congress's purpose is vague, or when the legislature had effectively left the problem of resolving competing purposes to the agency, a number of outcomes are likely to be consistent with congressional "intent." Although such situations may reflect excessive congressional delegation, they do not raise problems of administrative fidelity. The most a court can do under such circumstances is to utilize quasi-procedural review to ensure fundamental fairness, conscientious decisionmaking, and minimum rationality.

Of course, employment of a test stiffer than the hard look—one requiring implementation of the "best" policy in any given circumstances rather than simply a "reasonable" one—would enhance the power of judicial review. Indeed, such a test would be well suited to a model of the administrative process premised on the belief that an objectively correct result can be found in any situation. But for a model designed principally to ensure fidelity to congressional intent, such a test would be counterproductive. Under most of the statutory schemes considered in this Article, Congress plainly committed to agency discretion the choice of the best means of effectuating the statutory purpose. Adoption of a "best" policy requirement would all but guarantee substitution of the court's judgment for that of the agency, and the consequent removal from the agency of the discretion Congress intended to confer.

The second point about the hard look's weakness is that its areas of greatest frailty appear to be contracting, while those of its greatest utility are expanding. Although the point can easily be overstated, we may be nearing the end of the era in which the work of agencies with sweeping legislative mandates * * * formed the grist of administrative law. * * * At the same time, a trend in favor of statutes that delegate more narrowly, and toward the use of legislative history for ranking legislative goals, will expand the field of the hard look's utility.

* * *

Stephen Breyer, *Judicial Review of Questions of Law and Policy*, 38 ADMIN. L. REV. 363, 382–85, 388–91, 393–98 (1986)*

* * *

II. Review of Agency Policy Decisions

We turn * * * to the question of when courts will hold an agency *policy* decision unlawful because it is "unreasonable." The question is difficult to answer, in part, because there is no set legal doctrine called "review of policy questions"; consequently, the case law does not purport to authoritatively gov-

---

* Reprinted with permission of Stephen Breyer. All rights reserved.

ern judicial attitude in conducting a policy review.

Nonetheless, one can focus upon two sets of legal decisions that often amount in practice to a review of the wisdom and the "reasonableness" of agency policy. First, a court sometimes will directly substitute its judgment for the agency's, on a matter of substantive policy, on the ground that the agency's decision is "arbitrary, capricious, [or] an abuse of discretion" under section 706(2)(A) of the Administrative Procedure Act. Suppose, for example, the Labor Board decides that it will permit a union business agent to buy drinks for voters before a representation election. Can a reviewing court simply find this Board policy unreasonable in light of the need for fair elections? When writing an administrative law case book in the late 1970s, the authors could find only a handful of cases that faced so directly an agency policy decision and held it "arbitrary"; by the time the second edition was published in 1985, they found many more.[66]

Second, courts more and more frequently have applied a set of procedural principles that, in effect, require the agency to take a "hard look" at relevant policy considerations before reaching a substantive decision. These principles require that the agency examine all relevant evidence, to explain its decisions in detail, to justify departures from past practices, and to consider all reasonable alternatives before reaching a final policy decision. In practice, these principles have far greater substantive impact than one might at first realize. A remand of an important agency rule (several years in the making) for more thorough consideration may well mean several years of additional proceedings, with mounting costs, and the threat of further judicial review leading to abandonment or modification of the initial project irrespective of the merits. Courts and agencies alike are aware that these "more thorough consideration" and "hard look" doctrines have substantive impact. To that extent, in examining the attitude with which the courts apply the doctrines, one is, in an important sense, examining the attitude with which they review the wisdom or reasonableness of agency substantive decisionmaking.

The important attitudinal question is how *closely* the court will examine the agency's policy decisions. To what extent will it defer to the agency's expertise? How "hard" will the court "look" at the agency's

---

[66] *Compare* S. BREYER & R. STEWART, [ADMINISTRATIVE LAW AND REGULATORY POLICY] 336 n.107 [(2d ed. 1985)] (citing cases) *with* S. BREYER & R. STEWART, ADMINISTRATIVE LAW AND REGULATORY POLICY 289 n.86 (1st ed. 1979) (citing cases).

"look"? With what state of mind is the reviewing judge to approach the question of whether the agency has inadequately thought through policy considerations, or failed to take a "hard look" at evidence or alternatives, or simply adopted an unreasonable policy?

The language in several important cases decided in the last two decades suggests an increasingly less hesitant judiciary, courts that are more ready to overturn agency policy decisions that they consider unreasonable. The D.C. Circuit speaks of the need for a "thorough, probing, in-depth review," and the need for a "substantial and searching" inquiry. The Supreme Court has vacillated linguistically, sometimes speaking of a "thorough, probing" review and sometimes speaking more traditionally about the need for courts to hesitate before substituting their judgment for that of the agency on matters of policy.

A. State Farm: An Example of "Strict Policy Review"

The "airbags" case, *Motor Vehicle Manufacturers Association of the United States v. State Farm Mutual Automobile Insurance Co.*, provides an example of a fairly strict judicial attitude toward review of substantive agency policy. * * *

* * *

The court of appeals found the agency's action was unreasonable, but only after it applied an especially *strict* standard of review, a standard it felt justified in applying because of the legislative history of the agency's authorizing statute. The Supreme Court held that the court of appeals should not have applied a *special* review standard. It wrote that the ordinary "arbitrary and capricious" standard should apply. The Court, however, found the agency's action unreasonable even under this standard. An examination of the Court's opinion in light of NHTSA's arguments suggests the Court is holding that "ordinary" reasonableness review can itself be quite strict.

* * *

B. Comparative Institutional Competence

One might ask with the "airbags" case in mind whether the judiciary is institutionally well suited for strict policy scrutiny. To what extent can a group of men and women, typically trained as lawyers rather than as administrators or regulators, operating with limited access to information and under the constraints of adversary legal process, be counted upon to supervise the vast realm of substantive agency policymaking?

First, to what extent are judges likely to sympathetically understand the problems the agency faces in setting technical standards in complex areas. In the "airbags case," for example, the Supreme Court faulted NHTSA for not having more studies or more accurate studies. But was the Court fully aware of how difficult it is for an agency seeking to set standards to obtain accurate, relevant, unbiased information? Where is the agency to look? Industry information is often "suspect," insofar as industry's economic interests are at stake. Consumer groups may be as "suspect" or biased, though perhaps in a different direction. Independent experts may not have sufficiently detailed information or may have gotten it from industry. And, it may not be practicable administratively for an agency to duplicate in-house all the expertise of others outside the federal government. Some information may, in fact, be unobtainable. For instance, was there any practical way for NHTSA to estimate the true cost of airbags or to find out what reactions drivers would likely have to the "spool-type" belt? More important perhaps, how could it "objectively" define the likely reaction of Congress to the likely reaction of drivers? Is it then forbidden to take this factor into account? Why?

The agency must also deal with a host of complex questions in deciding what *type* of standard to promulgate. Should the standard aim directly at the evil targeted (traffic deaths) or at a surrogate ("buckling-up")? How specific should the standards be? Should it try to force technological change by making the industry achieve goals beyond its present technological capabilities? Should it use a more flexible "performance standard" or a more administrable "design standard"? The agency must have an enforcement system that will test compliance with the eventual standard. But this, too, is far easier said than done. The agency must design the standard with other enforcement needs and development costs in mind. Is it unreasonable to weaken or simplify standards in order to increase the likelihood of voluntary compliance or to stretch an already tight development budget?

The agency may also have to consider various competitive concerns. How will a new standard affect industry? Will it favor some existing firms over others or will it favor all existing firms by making entry into the industry more difficult?

Industry, moreover, is only one group whose interests the agency must consider. Whenever it regulates, the agency finds before it different groups, the industry, suppliers, consumer groups, members of Congress, and its own staff, with somewhat different interests. At the very least, each group may see different aspects of the problem as important: industry may focus on costs, suppliers on competitive fairness, and consumers on safety. Each group, moreover, has a different weapon with which to threaten the agency. The staff can recommend changed standards. Industry can withhold or produce critical information or threaten legal or political action. Consumer groups can threaten to appeal to Congress or to the public through the press. A wise agency may recognize the weapons that the various parties wield and may shape its standards to minimize opposition. It can thus increase the likelihood of voluntary compliance and diminish the likelihood of court delays. The agency's final decision is likely to reflect some degree of compromise among all these interests. Such "compromise" decisions are, in a sense, "political." They may not be able to be supported through pure logic, but are they unreasonable?

Is it surprising, then, that agencies and courts often disagree about what constitutes a "reasonable" decision? The court may not appreciate the agency's need to make decisions under conditions of uncertainty. Compromises made to secure agreement among the parties may strike a court as "irrational" because the agency cannot "logically" explain them.

Second, courts work within institutional rules that deliberately disable them from seeking out information relevant to the inquiry at hand. For, while a judge, expert in the law, is permitted to scan all forms of legal authority and learning in reaching conclusions of law (and is given the resources to do so in the form of libraries, computer research tools and trained law clerks), in factual matters he is limited to review of a cold record created by those over whom he has no control and who may have strong biases.

An appellate judge cannot ask an expert to answer his technical questions or go outside the record to determine the present state of scientific or technical knowledge. But the record itself tells only part of the story, the part that the advocates have chosen to let the court see. Even if fairly complete, a cold record does not allow the judge to prove the case in great depth. A judge can spend three days reading a record of 4,000 pages and still feel somewhat unfamiliar with the facts. Docket pressures make it unusual for an appellate judge to have even three days available for record reading in an individual case. The First Circuit Court of Appeals, for example, has well over 1,000 cases per year, and each judge on the court writes fifty to sixty full published opinions each year. Even if one assumes that judges of courts that review more administrative agency cases need write only three or four, instead of five to seven, opinions per month, the judges will not have time to familiarize themselves with the enormously lengthy records. How can they analyze fully a record, for example, reflecting 10,000 comments made in response to a notice of proposed rulemaking? Can judges, when faced with such complexity and detail, do more than ask, somewhat superficially, whether the agency's result is reasonable? Can they do more than catch the grosser errors? Can they conduct the thorough, probing, in-depth review that they promise? These realities about court review provide little basis for any hope that such review will lead to significantly better policy.

Perhaps these arguments simply restate the traditional view that agencies are more "expert" on policy matters than courts, and courts should "defer" to their policy expertise. In recent years it has become fashionable to doubt agency expertise, but these considerations should lead us to ask whether these doubts offer reasons for greater reliance on judicial review or whether the substantive results of such doubts will properly deal with the substantive problem. In short, can we be confident, given the comparative institutional settings, that strong judicial review will lead to better administrative policy?

Those skeptical of the "real world" effectiveness of judicial review of agency policy decisions can find support in the long battle waged between the Court of Appeals for the District of Columbia Circuit and the Federal Communications Commission. The court, in trying to improve the quality of network broadcasting, tried to force the Commission to use intelligible "station-selection" standards. Whenever the court reversed an FCC decision, however, the FCC would typically reach the same conclusion on remand, but simply support it with a better reasoned opinion.

Similarly, a recent Brookings study argues that the effect of court review of environmental regulation, an area where case law directs strict review of policy decisions, has been random. In some instances, court-imposed requirements aimed at protecting the environment have helped, but in other instances, by distorting agency enforcement priorities, they have hurt. Further, there is reasonably strong evidence that court review of the Federal Power Commission's regulation of natural gas caused substantial economic harm. * * *

* * *

Moreover, strict judicial review creates one incentive that from a substantive perspective may be perverse. The stricter the review and the more clearly and convincingly the agency must explain the need for change, the more reluctant the agency will be to change the status quo. * * *

* * *

The reason agencies do not explore all arguments or consider all alternatives is one of practical limits of time and resources. Yet, to have to explain and to prove all this to a reviewing court risks imposing much of the very burden that not considering alternatives aims to escape. Of course, the reviewing courts may respond that only *important* alternatives and arguments must be considered. But, what counts as "important"? District courts often find that parties, having barely mentioned a legal point at the trial level, suddenly make it the heart of their case on appeal, emphasizing its (sudden but) supreme importance. Appellate courts typically consider such arguments as long as they have been at least mentioned in the district court. But district courts, unlike agencies dealing with policy change, do not face, say, 10,000 comments challenging different aspects of complex policies. And, when appellate courts "answer" an argument they write a few words or paragraphs, perhaps citing a case or two. A satisfactory answer in the agency context may mean factfinding, empirical research, detailed investigation. Accordingly, one result of strict judicial review of agency policy decisions is a strong conservative pressure in favor of the status quo.

These arguments and instances are essentially anecdotal; they do not prove that strict judicial review of policy is, from a policy perspective, unhelpful or counterproductive. But they do seem strong enough to impose a burden upon those advocating such review as a means toward better or wiser substantive policy to identify, investigate, and catalogue its successes.

C. Toward Appropriate Policy Review Reconciliation

Unfortunately, * * * no ready resolution to the problem of judicial review of *policy* is apparent, at least within the existing institutional constraints. The social imperative for control of agency power is entirely consistent with existing institutional arrangements in the context of review of law. If one believes that the more important the legal decision, the greater the need for a check outside the agency, increased judicial scrutiny automatically seems appropriate. Courts are fully capable of rigorous review of agency determinations of law, for it is the law that they are expert in, and it is in interpreting law that their legitimacy is greatest.

In reviewing the policy area, however, the pressures for control of agency power on the one hand, and for proper use of existing institutions on the other hand, are dramatically opposed. One may believe that the more important the policy decision, the greater the need for a check outside the agency. But, for reasons of "comparative expertise," increased judicial scrutiny seems *less* appropriate. It is this dilemma that makes a stable, appropriate regime for court review of policy a nearly intractable problem.

That is to say, one might conclude on the basis of the discussion that when reviewing the reasonableness of agency policy courts should apply the traditional law (the "arbitrary, capricious" standard of section 706(2)(A) of the Administrative Procedure Act) with the traditional attitude of "deference" to agency expertise. Courts would hesitate to reverse the results of a major rulemaking proceeding or to remand for what is likely to amount to several years of new proceedings. They would do so only after finding major procedural violations or very unreasonable substantive results. Judges would approach cases like *State Farm* rather like they approach jury findings in a negligence action, asking whether reasonable regulators could reasonably have come to this conclusion, given not only the evidence before them, but also the constraints of time and of the administrative environment in which the agency must work.

This type of standard, however, while coherent from a jurisprudential perspective, is not totally satisfactory * * *. For one thing, in applying it the courts effectively abdicate their role in controlling agency policymaking. Yet, the fact remains that Congress has delegated to administrators in the past fifteen years vast additional regulatory powers, often under vaguely worded, open-ended statutes. Simple "retreat" takes little account of the *growth of agency power* that gave rise to the demand for control. After all, the substantive regulatory concerns that have created pressure for outside checks upon the exercise of agency power continue to exist. One can still argue in favor of the courts by claiming that the President's efforts will be affected greatly by the politics of the day and that congressional efforts may be incoherent. Judges tend to be somewhat more neutral politically; they will try to exert the force of reason on what are basically technical rules aimed at technocratic ends; and their prestige will lead the agencies to follow their guidance.

For another thing, can one be certain about the *overall* impact of judicial scrutiny of agency policy? Does its presence act as an incentive within the agency towards more reasonable decisionmaking, arming those who would fight an overly politicized decisionmaking process with a weapon, the specter of later court reversal? Would a relaxed judicial supervisory attitude be strong enough to catch the occasional agency policy decision that is in fact highly irrational?

These nagging doubts are sufficiently serious to point, vaguely and suggestively, without endorsement, to an alternative approach that may warrant more serious study than it has had to date. One might examine the practicality of removing some of the institutional constraints that now prevent a court from conducting effective policy review. Could reviewing courts be given the tools to produce coherent, better substantive agency policy? Suggestions have been made to create a specialized administrative court. But, to make the District of Columbia Court of Appeals a genuine administrative court, capable of reviewing the wisdom of substantive policy, it would need an investigative staff. It would need the power to compel the agency to produce facts not in the record. It would have to be able to question an agency about its entire enforcement program. And it would need some understanding of how that program fits in with the work of other agencies. It would need access to appropriate substantive experts. In sum, it would need many of the powers currently given to the Office of Management and Budget, insofar as it investigates and coordinates regulatory programs.

Other nations have followed this approach. Under the French system of administrative law, for example, the power to review administrative action resides in an institutional descendant of the King's Council, now an independent, nonpolitical administrative court, called the Conseil d'Etat. Membership in the Conseil is supposed to reflect relevant expertise. Some become members after a distinguished career in the French civil service; others are recent top graduates of the highly prestigious Ecole Nationale d'Administracion (ENA), where they have studied public policy and public administration. Upon entrance into the Conseil the ENA graduate is assigned the investigation of less important cases, and is privy to its deliberations; is rotated through various operating departments of the government on special assignments, and is then eventually returned to the Conseil. The result is a collegial body, familiar with the practical problems of creating and maintaining public policy through administration.

Moreover, the Conseil is not bound by the strictures of the adversary system. It has access to information throughout the administration. Its members conduct an independent investigation of each case and present the results without being confined to a formal record. The members charged with the investigation make full use of the Conseil's internal expertise and also are expected to consult outside agencies and experts. In short, the Conseil is given a wide variety of tools which enable it to discern not only whether a given policy conforms to law (as in American courts) but also whether it is wise public policy, something that our discussion suggests may be beyond the reach of our judicial system as currently organized.

Whether one could transform an existing court of appeals into an institution more closely resembling the Conseil d'Etat is debateable. Much of the Conseil's effectiveness stems from its ability to obtain information *ex parte* from within the administration and to conduct its deliberations among investigators and judges in private, without counsel present. Yet, American judicial rules against *ex parte* communications are not all constitutional in nature; the use of amici, special masters, law clerks all suggest that investigatory powers are not inherently beyond the judiciary's reach. And, there are certain advantages to looking at the judiciary rather than say, OMB, as the nucleus for such an institution, namely greater political independence, prestige that may mean public acceptability, the ability to process individual complaints against agency behavior, and more widespread review of agency policy within the same institution.

Analysis of such a radical transformation of existing methods of policy review is well beyond the scope of this article, nor does this article endorse that approach. It only points to the existence of the possibility; and it suggests that analysis be undertaken because, given the present institutional dilemma, it may be necessary to explore quite different approaches toward making judicial review an effective check on the wisdom of substantive policymaking by agencies.

III. Conclusions

* * * First, the present law of judicial review of administrative decisionmaking, the heart of administrative law, contains an important anomaly. The law 1) requires courts to defer to agency judgments about *matters of law*, but 2) it also suggests that courts conduct independent, "in-depth" reviews of agency judgments about *matters of policy*. Is this not the exact opposite of a rational system? Would one not expect courts to conduct a stricter review of matters of law, where courts are more expert, but more lenient review of matters of policy, where agencies are more expert?

Second, in light of the anomaly, existing law is

unstable. Change of some sort seems likely. The direction that the law might take as to review of matters of law can be spelled out with clarity. But no such clarity of direction is possible in respect to review of policy. On the one hand, that change might amount to "retreat," with the courts leaving it up to the other branches of government to control agency excesses. On the other hand, change might seek to make policy review more effective. But, that change implies the need for an examination of radical transformation of existing institutions of review. An examination seems warranted to determine whether such efforts should be made.

Third, one can conclude, at a minimum, that legislative proposals that simply try to lead the courts to exercise a more "independent" judgment when reviewing agency decisions offer little promise as a direction for meaningful regulatory reform. In the area of traditional "review of agency decisions of law" such a proposal has only a limited scope for making a significant difference. In the area of judicial "review of agency decisions of policy" such a proposal would likely prove counterproductive. The problem seems more one of tailoring the courts' legal obligations in their area to their institutional capacities and strengths.

Sidney A. Shapiro and Richard E. Levy, *Heightened Scrutiny of the Fourth Branch: Separation of Powers and the Requirement of Adequate Reasons for Agency Decisions*, 1987 DUKE L.J. 387, 388, 390-98, 403-05, 407-13, 423-39*

* * *

In recent years, the requirement that administrative agencies provide adequate reasons for their decisions has come to play a central role in judicial review of agency decisions. While the increasing importance of this requirement has been recognized, no systematic study of its history and doctrinal basis has been undertaken. This article proposes that the requirement is best understood as a form of heightened scrutiny of the rationale of agency decisions and that the doctrine of separation of powers requires

---

* Reprinted with permission of the Duke Law Journal, Sidney A. Shapiro, and Richard E. Levy. All rights reserved.

such scrutiny because of the unique position of administrative agencies in terms of the constitutional structure of government. * * *

* * *

I. Political Values and Judicial Review

Over the years, the Supreme Court has struggled to accommodate the two strains of political values underlying modern American government. There is a general social consensus that government ought to adhere to such "liberal" values as representative government, separation of powers, and due process. There is less consensus about the extent to which government ought to implement "progressive" values by accepting responsibility for social and economic improvements; those values, however, retain much strength. These two strains of political values are in potential conflict, because the governmental institutions which implement progressive values do not operate in a manner that is entirely consistent with the constitutional framework designed to implement liberal values.

Judicial review of agency actions reflects this conflict because each set of political values requires a different form of judicial review.

* * *

Liberalism requires meaningful judicial review, while progressivism requires judicial review that is deferential. Thus, the problem for any theory of judicial review is how both sets of inherent American political values can be accommodated.

A. *Liberal Values in American Government.*

The principles of American democracy were influenced by the "liberal" philosophical and political movements that dominated England and Europe in the century before this country was founded. While the coercive ordering of behavior by the state restricts individual liberty, liberal thinkers agreed with Hobbes that the absence of a state is a far more devastating blow to freedom. They therefore accepted that a government was both legitimate and desirable, but that it must be a government organized by individual consent and of determinate political limits.

In the United States, the constitutional structure of government and the establishment of individual rights reflect these liberal values. Structural protections include specification of the powers of the government in the Constitution and a division of governmental authority into a legislative, executive, and judicial branch, each of which exercises certain checks over the others. Individual rights, enumerated in the Bill of Rights, include a right that deprivations of liberty and property could proceed only after the operation of due process of law.

There have always been important differences within the liberal tradition concerning the function of government. Some Liberals emphasize the Lockean view that while the existence of government is necessitated by the human condition, its only proper function is the facilitation of individual initiative. Other Liberals emphasize the republican tradition that government is responsible for promoting the general welfare. With the advent of the progressive era, those favoring governmental activism prevailed. Progressive government, however, involves activism beyond that envisioned by the Framers and is implemented in a manner that appears to threaten important liberal principles.

B. *Progressive Values in American Government.*

The progressive movement in American politics in large measure was a reaction to the social and political conditions produced by the laissez-faire political environment of the last part of the nineteenth century. The Progressives believed that government had been corrupted by the concentration of political power in large corporations, trusts and political bosses; that industry should be regulated and workers protected; that poverty and old-age hardship should be relieved; and that natural resources should be protected.

Progressive support for regulation was closely allied with a movement towards scientific rationalism, which emphasized that human and organizational behavior was the product of relationships that can rationally be deduced and described by empirical and objective inquiry. As a corollary, the Progressives believed that most social problems could be solved by expertly trained scientists or by persons familiar with the scientific disciplines. Progressive interest in scientific expertise was also the product of dissatisfaction with the corruption and inefficiency of nineteenth century government. Progressive political writers championed such expertise as a dispassionate and impartial methodology that could insulate government administration from an undesirable political environment.

Although the development of administrative government may have been a pragmatic response to the social needs of the time, its form certainly reflected progressive beliefs. The adoption of a bureaucratic form of organization and the civil service system reflected the Progressives' interest in a more efficient and less political government. The creation of the independent agency facilitated the progressive goals of specialization, efficiency and insulation from the political forces that dominated legislatures and executive branches at both the state and federal level. Finally, the expansion of state and federal regulation reflected progressive beliefs that social problems could be solved by the bureaucratic application of scientific expertise.

The adoption of progressive government threatened liberal principles. It involved the delegation of decisionmaking authority to unelected administrators, gave those administrators the authority to use legislative and judicial powers that the Constitution appears to reserve for the Congress and the federal courts, and allowed the administrators to decide matters without the constraint of legal procedures traditionally used in the judicial system. Interests antagonistic to government regulation sought to invalidate progressive programs by challenging them before the Supreme Court as inconsistent with the Constitution and the liberal values that underlie it. Through these cases, the Court began to define the place and function of the administrative process in American government. That process of definition, which continues today, requires the accommodation of liberal and progressive values.

C. *Value Conflict and the Problem of Judicial Review.*

The conflict between liberal and progressive values affects the legitimacy of administrative government. Because the authority of any institution rests ultimately on a popular belief in its legitimacy, political power must be held and exercised in accordance with a nation's laws, traditions, customs and values. Moreover, the affirmation of liberal values is all the more necessary because of growing doubts about the Progressives' assumption that social problems can be solved by the bureaucracy through application of scientific principles in a neutral fashion. In fact, administrative actions normally involve policy choices by bureaucrats who are subject to a variety of self-interested motivations and political pressures. When administrators respond to these influences, they often serve special interests of the industries they regulate rather than the purposes for which their agencies were created.

In this country, judicial review and the legitimacy of administrative government are inextricably intertwined. Among other things, judicial review serves a symbolic, or in Professor Bickel's words, a "mystic" function. The availability of judicial review suggests that the will of the majority is always subject to the limitations of the Constitution and that government therefore operates by consent inasmuch as all citizens have agreed to government action in accordance with the Constitution.

The ultimate success of judicial review, however, rests on the ability of the Supreme Court to articulate and implement principles that place administrative government within a constitutional framework. This responsibility includes both the doctrinal necessity of explaining how progressive government is consistent with liberal values and the practical necessity of articulating a version of judicial review that is an effective check and balance on administrative government. Unless both the doctrinal and practical necessities are met when individual judicial decisions are made, judicial review will be reduced to its symbolic element and the legitimation of administrative government will be more myth than reality.

* * *

II. The Evolution of Judicial Review and the Accommodation of Political Values

Over time, three different models of judicial review of administrative action have evolved.

* * *

The "structuralist" model of judicial review focused on the constitutional limits to the structure of government. This model, however, hindered the development of the regulatory state by its rigid enforcement of the doctrine of separation of powers. Eventually, popular support for progressive government forced the Court to abandon the structuralist model and instead rely on interpretation of agencies' statutory authority as the principal structural constraint on agency action.

Abandonment of the structuralist model inherently led to a deemphasis of the separation of powers doctrine. The Court compensated for the lack of structural constraints by turning to the "proceduralist" model, which placed primary emphasis on procedural fairness. While accepting the substance of agency decisions out of deference to administrative expertise and respect for popular will, the Court hoped to control agency government by stressing requirements of procedural due process.

When that compromise failed, the Court developed its current "rationalist" model, which stresses substantive review by requiring that an agency provide adequate reasons to demonstrate a rational relationship between a decision and the agency's statutory purpose. While rationalism is intended to remedy the failures of the previous models, the Court has not yet demonstrated how it preserves the liberal values reflected in the Constitution.

A. *The Structuralist Model.*

The Supreme Court initially blocked progressive programs through constitutional doctrines restricting the power or authority of Congress or the states to regulate. Once the Court abandoned these efforts, the focus shifted to whether regulation through the creation of administrative agencies was consistent with separation of powers. Despite some early indications to the contrary, the Court ultimately accepted delegation of substantial judicial and legislative authority to administrative agencies. As a consequence, structuralism now limits agencies primarily through statutory construction of the scope of agency authority.

* * *

2. *The Failure of Structuralism.* The structuralist model has effectively been reduced to its statutory interpretation component. The Supreme Court, by adopting tests requiring only minimal review of agency action, seldom applies separation of powers principles to reduce agency discretion. Even in the application of statutory interpretation to limit agency power, the Court has vacillated between accepting and restricting agency discretion and often displays considerable deference toward agencies.

The reduction of structuralism has weakened the legitimacy of administrative government. The Court has accepted agency government inconsistent with the structural scheme of executive, legislative and judicial powers established in the Constitution without ever expressly addressing the inconsistency. This failure to address the distinctive constitutional position of the administrative agencies—their status as a "fourth branch of government"—robbed structuralism of its power to legitimate administrative government. As a result, the structuralist model retained only the symbolic, "mythical" quality.

In addition * * *, structuralism failed because it could not accommodate both progressive and liberal values at a practical level. Active use of structuralism thwarted progressive government by declaring progressive programs unconstitutional. Once the constitutionality of administrative agencies was accepted, the remaining mechanism for preventing administrative error and abuse under structuralism was statutory construction. Although at times the Supreme Court has appeared to endorse this approach, albeit inconsistently, statutory interpretation cannot provide a practical means of controlling agency action.

First, a narrowing construction of statutes is not always available, especially where a statute is broadly worded for the precise purpose of giving the implementing agency considerable discretion. As a result, courts are often forced to defer to agency construction of authorizing statutes. Even where a narrowing construction is available, agencies usually retain substantial discretion. If a statute were in fact narrowed to the point that the agency is merely filling in the gaps, the progressive program would be frustrated.

Another problem with statutory interpretation is that it affects not only the individual decision being reviewed, but also the scope of the agency's authority to regulate in the future. Thus, if courts are active in construing statutes narrowly, they may undermine the regulatory framework envisioned by Congress and developed by the agency. In such cases, narrow statutory construction destroys the very advantages of efficiency, expertise and discretion which justify administrative government.

B. *The Proceduralist Model.*

With the demise of structuralism, the Court turned to proceduralist review in hopes of finding a method to legitimate agency government in terms of liberal values. This evolution was hardly surprising since liberal values are protected in the Constitution both by structural protections (largely abandoned with the reduction of the structuralist model), and by individual rights, which the proceduralist model sought to enforce in the form of due process. Proceduralism ultimately failed when it was recognized that the imposition of procedures was counterproductive and often unrelated to the substance of agency decisions.

* * *

2. *The Failure of Proceduralism.* The proceduralist orientation of administrative law reflected the "legal process" conception of judicial review advanced by scholars in the 1940s and 1950s, which focused on the relative institutional competence of courts, legislatures and agencies to make and implement social policy decisions. Administrative law scholars emphasized the comparative advantage of courts coordinating the procedural requirements by which agencies operated and the comparative disadvantage of the courts second-guessing the "expert" substantive policy decisions of those agencies. This approach, however, suffered from two fundamental flaws.

First, proceduralism failed at the theoretical level because, like structuralism, it did not acknowledge the distinct position of administrative agencies in the constitutional framework. This problem was particularly evident in the context of rulemaking. As long as the Court adhered to its holding in *Bi-Metallic Investment Co. v. State Board of Equalization* that due process requires no procedural checks upon legislative decisions by administrative agencies, the usefulness of proceduralism as a legitimating theory was substantially diluted. *Bi-Metallic* allowed Congress to determine what procedures are required when an agency engages in rulemaking. Since Congress would be free to repeal any procedural requirements used in agency rulemaking, the Constitution would impose no procedural constraints on agency rulemaking. As a result, proceduralism can not reconcile the use of rulemaking in progressive government with liberal values.

Second, judicial review under proceduralism did not provide a practical mechanism for reconciling progressive and liberal values. Proceduralism sought to preserve progressive values in the form of administrative autonomy by retaining the extremely deferential scope of review set under structuralism. This approach was premised on the assumption that while agencies are expert with regard to the substantive aspects of the regulatory scheme they administer, the courts are experts on procedure. The premise that procedural regularity will necessarily prevent error and abuse, however, is open to serious challenge.

Moreover, the proceduralist remedy for erroneous decisions—requiring additional procedures—threatened to destroy the very advantages of efficiency and expert discretion for which decisionmaking power is given to agencies. If courts can reverse erroneous decisions only by ordering additional procedures, review becomes little more than a series of agency decisions, followed by judicial remands for additional procedures. More importantly, as the court recognized in *Vermont Yankee*, agencies will be forced to use more formal procedures in run-of-the-mill cases in order to protect themselves from judicial requirements of additional procedures.

C. *The Rationalist Model.*

The decline of the proceduralist model led to a renewed interest in substantive judicial review as a means to assert liberal values. The Supreme Court has turned to the rationalist model to define the scope of substantive review by requiring agencies to provide a rational explanation for their decisions. The practical or theoretical underpinnings of this model, however, have not been fully articulated. * * *

1. *The Evolution of Rationalism.* From the beginning of progressive government, substantive review was understood to be a necessary element of agency accountability. Unless the courts make some determination as to whether an agency's decision serves the statutory purposes for which the agency was cre-

ated, agencies would be free to ignore their authorizing legislation. Nonetheless, the Court originally used an extremely deferential scope of review. It asked only whether the agency's decision had some hypothetical rational relationship to the agency's statutory mission. A decision was not reversible as long as it was "conceivably" supported by the facts in the record. Similarly, a factual determination needed only to be supported by "substantial evidence," which was evidence that a reasonable mind might accept as adequate to support a conclusion. Congress codified this standard in the APA, by allowing courts to overturn agency decisions which are "arbitrary and capricious" or without "substantial evidence."

The Court has vacillated over the degree of deference to be accorded agency decisions under the APA. In *Citizens to Preserve Overton Park, Inc. v. Volpe*, the Court described the standard for review under the arbitrary and capricious test as "searching and careful" when it reversed a decision by the Secretary of Transportation to fund a highway routed through parkland. * * * [However,] in *Baltimore Gas & Electric Co. v. Natural Resources Defense Council, Inc.*, the Court warned that the judiciary must be "most deferential" when reviewing predictions by an agency "within its area of special expertise."

In *Motor Vehicle Manufacturers Association v. State Farm Mutual Automobile Insurance Co.*, the Court apparently returned to the stricter version of review endorsed in *Overton Park*. The Court indicated that an agency must explain the "rational connection" between the facts found and the regulatory decision made, and adequately resolve the evidentiary and policy issues before it. Finally, the Court could not supply a "reasoned basis" for the agency decision if the agency failed to do so. In sum, *State Farm* signals the emergence of the Supreme Court's rationalist model of review as the basis for accommodating liberal and progressive values.

2. *The Prospects of Rationalism.* Rationalism has become the primary method of constraining administrative action. By requiring a rational explanation for their actions, the Court seeks to put administrative agencies in the same framework that legal process scholars once thought applicable only to courts. This perspective argues that political and personal motivations influencing legal decisionmaking can be checked if judges are expected to give a "reasoned elaboration" for their actions according to norms of consistent, neutral and candid decisional processes. Similarly, rationalism requires agencies to give a "reasoned elaboration" demonstrating that their decisions serve the statutory ends for which they were created.

The Court's adoption of rationalist review comes at a time when much administrative law scholarship has moved beyond a proceduralist orientation to encompass the study of substantive, political and organizational aspects of regulatory decisionmaking. This scholarship suggests that administrators often act in response to self-serving political and personal motivations. Recognition of these motivations reinforces the necessity of substantive judicial review. Without substantive judicial review, there is no check to prevent an agency from serving the purely private interests of special interest groups at the expense of the broader public interests the agency is supposed to serve.

Although the Court's adoption of the rationalist model has been widely recognized, neither the Court nor legal scholars have articulated a complete doctrinal explanation for it. The conventional assumption is that the Court requires an agency to have "adequate reasons" pursuant to its judicial review function under the APA. This explanation, however, fails to demonstrate how rationalism protects liberal values at the constitutional level, either in terms of the structure of government or in terms of due process safeguards. Until such an explanation is provided, rationalism cannot succeed as a legitimating theory for administrative agencies.

* * *

IV. Separation of Powers, Rationalism, and the Reasons Requirement

While *State Farm* marks the adoption of the rationalist model, with the requirement of adequate reasons as its central feature, the Court left the doctrinal basis of the requirement unclear. The rationalist model may best be understood as a form of heightened scrutiny of agency decisions required by separation of powers principles. * * * So articulated, the rationalist model preserves liberal values left unprotected following the demise of structuralism and the failure of proceduralism. In addition, the rationalist model accommodates progressive values better than either the structuralist or proceduralist models.

A. *Separation of Powers and the History of the Reasons Requirement.*

The reasons requirement is related to judicial review of the rationality of legislation. Such review normally is conducted under the extremely deferential "minimum rationality" test, which requires only that there be a conceivable rational basis for legislative acts. Scrutiny of the rationality of legislative purposes and means chosen to achieve them is heightened in some types of equal protection and substantive due process cases. The requirement of adequate reasons under the rationalist model entails a similar heightening of the scrutiny of agency decisions.

In an early decision, *Pacific States Box & Basket Co. v. White*, the Court equated agency and legislative action for purposes of the rational basis test, declaring that "if any state of facts reasonably can be conceived that would sustain [an order], there is a presumption of the existence of that state of facts." This is essentially identical to the rational basis test employed in judicial review of statutes that do not burden suspect classes or infringe upon fundamental rights. The subsequent evolution of the reasons requirement, however, evinces a gradual departure from minimum rationality review of agency decisions.

Minimum rationality review of agency decisions was appropriate under the structuralist model. Because agencies were perceived to be within the framework of separation of powers, *Pacific States Box & Basket*'s analogy to decisions by the legislature was understandable. By connecting agency action to a narrow statutory mandate, the requirement placed the agency within the constitutional structure of separation of powers. Once the Court accepted delegations of legislative and judicial power to administrative agencies, however, this minimum rationality form of the requirement was inappropriate.

The reasons requirement became part of the procedural safeguards required by due process when the Court moved from structuralism to proceduralism as the means of protecting liberal values. In its proceduralist form, the reasons requirement accepted only those reasons offered by the agency in support of its decisions, rather than any conceivable state of facts as it did in *Pacific States Box & Basket*. Nonetheless, under proceduralism, once an agency gave reasons for its decision, the Court continued to accord it great deference.

When the proceduralist approach failed, the next logical step was to reject *Pacific States Box & Basket* in its entirety and engage in heightened scrutiny of the adequacy of an agency's reasons. Thus, in *State Farm* the Court rejected the Department of Transportation's contention that the arbitrary and capricious standard was equivalent to the minimum rationality required of statutes, stating that "[w]e do not view as equivalent the presumption of constitutionality afforded legislation drafted by Congress and the presumption of regularity afforded an agency in fulfilling its statutory mandate." *State Farm* left unclear the basis for heightened scrutiny of administrative decisions. The Court apparently derived the requirement of adequate reasons from the arbitrary and capricious standard of review under section 706 of the APA. *State Farm* and *Pacific States Box & Basket* could therefore be reconciled by resting the heightened scrutiny approved in *State Farm* solely upon the requirements of the APA [which was adopted after *Pacific States*].

The structuralist origins of the requirement, however, suggest that this reading of *State Farm* is inappropriate and that heightened scrutiny under the reasons requirement is best understood as a product of separation of powers. In its original minimum rationality form, the requirement furthered separation of powers principles by ensuring agency fidelity to narrow statutory mandates. To implement these principles in the face of broad delegations of legislative and judicial authority to administrative agencies, heightened judicial scrutiny is necessary.

* * *

B. *Rationalism and Liberal Values*.

Understanding rationalism as a form of heightened scrutiny of administrative agencies required by separation of powers is consistent with both the history of the reasons requirement and recent Supreme Court decisions. So articulated, rationalism preserves liberal values better than either structuralism or proceduralism. First, rationalism protects liberal values on both a theoretical and a practical level through meaningful substantive scrutiny of agency actions. Second, the separation of powers basis for rationalism ensures that heightened scrutiny is available whenever an agency is delegated substantial legislative or judicial authority.

1. *Substantive Review and Liberal Values*. A successful theory of judicial review must demonstrate that liberal values have not been sacrificed to accommodate administrative government. Rationalism meets that requirement by recognizing that agency action must be subjected to heightened scrutiny to ensure that administrative decisions reflect public values. * * *

* * * [A]dministrative agencies, unlike legislatures, are not entitled to the same presumption of correctness because they are neither politically accountable nor directly subject to checks and balances. Unlike structuralism and proceduralism, rationalism protects liberal values at a theoretical level by recognizing that legislators and agency bureaucrats occupy different positions in our scheme of government and therefore must be treated differently for purposes of judicial review.

The protection of liberal values requires as a practical matter that judicial review act as a meaningful check on administrative error and abuse. Rationalism provides an effective mechanism of judicial review because it addresses the practical problem that structuralism and proceduralism could not solve. Review under the structuralist model ultimately failed because courts could not determine from a simple articulation of facts whether an agency was operating within its broad and vague statutory mandate. Proceduralism attempted to address this difficulty by requiring agencies to connect their decisions with facts in the record through a statement of reasons. This approach failed because the deferential treatment accorded to an agency's reasons enabled an agency to support virtually any decision with selective facts plucked from a large and unwieldy record. By comparison, rationalism places the burden on an agency to adequately explain its decision in terms of its statutory mandate. In order to obtain judicial approval, agencies must be able to demonstrate that they have applied their expertise in a meaningful manner and have reasonably investigated the problem they are attempting to resolve.

* * *

Whether judicial review of the reasons for an agency decision is constitutionally required depends not upon due process, but rather upon separation of powers. This conclusion has several important implications for rationalism. First, it means that the availability of review does not depend upon the existence of a liberty or property interest protected by due process. Second, unlike procedural due process protections, the requirement of review is not limited to adjudications by agencies. Thus, rationalism avoids one of the fundamental theoretical failures of proceduralism: it protects liberal values in all cases where agencies exercise powers otherwise preserved for the legislature or the judiciary. Finally, rationalism would not require federal review of decisions by *state* administrative agencies because separation of powers at the state level is a matter of state law.

C. *Rationalism and Progressive Values.*

While rationalism preserves liberal values, it also accommodates progressive values because heightened scrutiny of the rationality of agency decisions is consistent with the underlying purposes of agency government. Administrative agencies were premised upon the Progressives' belief that regulatory decisions should be the product of rational bureaucratic processes or the dispassionate application of expertise. By focusing on the reasoning used to justify an agency decision rather than the result of the decision, rationalism reinforces this progressive ideal without granting judges a license to substitute their judgment for that of the agency. Thus, unlike structuralism and proceduralism, use of the rationalist model by activist courts should not thwart progressive government.

Critics of the rationalist model can argue that it is subject to similar abuses and that it is no better equipped to find an appropriate middle ground between disruption of administrative government and abandonment of any meaningful effort to control administrative discretion. This criticism may occur at three levels. First, the use of heightened substantive scrutiny arguably invites the same sort of judicial intervention which characterized substantive due process. Second, because of the close connection between the requirement of adequate reasons and the procedures used to generate support for those reasons, employing the rationalist model could destroy administrative efficiency. Finally, substantive scrutiny of agency decisions may lead to the substitution of the policy preferences for those of agencies, in contravention of the progressive premise of administrative expertise.

1. *Substantive Due Process.* Because rationalism requires heightened scrutiny of the rationality of agency action, critics might associate it with the heightened scrutiny of legislative decisions under substantive due process. Early Supreme Court decisions striking down legislation under economic substantive due process, and more recent decisions striking down state regulation interfering with individual autonomy, have been criticized as undemocratic intervention by the Court in contravention of the will of the majority.

This criticism reflects the underlying tension between competing elements of liberal values incorporated into the Constitution. The legislature is a pluralistic institution implementing the principle of government by consent, while judicial review reflects the republican principles of limited government and separation of powers. Those who condemn judicial activism in the form of substantive due process are in effect arguing that it promotes republican values at the expense of pluralistic values, thereby upsetting the compromise envisioned by the Framers of the Constitution. * * *

While similar objections might be raised against heightened scrutiny of agency decisions under rationalism, they do not apply. Unlike substantive due process, rationalism does not place constitutional limitations on the ability of Congress to legislate. If a court reverses an agency for the failure to explain adequately how its decision serves its statutory mission, Congress is free to overrule that decision. The legislature can expressly authorize the agency's decision by amending the agency's enabling act. Moreover, rationalism assists the legislature in any necessary correction. It can foster informed political dialogue by forcing agencies to articulate the basis for their policies. Nor does heightened scrutiny of agency decisions involve the enforcement of unwritten principles and the consequent invitation to judges to impose their value preferences by invalidating agency action. The principles to be enforced under rationalism are those in the statute authorizing agency action. Thus, the proper role of statutory interpretation under rationalism is to identify the value choice embodied in a statute. Identification of values obviously must occur if judicial review is to ensure a rational relationship between agency action and the statutory objectives.

* * *

2. *Rationalism and Procedural Inefficiency.* During the period of judicial imposition of hybrid procedures, courts and commentators acknowledged that judicial decisions remanding a decision to an agency for more support might indirectly require the agency to engage in additional procedures which the *Vermont Yankee* decision had forbidden courts to impose directly. Thus, critics might argue that heightened scrutiny of the rationality of agency decisions would destroy administrative efficiency by indirectly requiring additional procedures. This criticism is, however, unpersuasive because remands for more adequate reasons allow the agency to determine whether and to what degree additional procedures will be followed.

Three possible situations may be involved when an agency decision is remanded for lack of adequate reasons. First, there may be an easily remedied flaw in the agency's logic or a gap in its reasoning process. In such a case, the agency on remand need not engage in any additional procedures to correct this flaw. Second, an agency may be required to provide additional factual support for its decision, which might lead to additional proceedings pursuant to the APA. Finally, in rare cases the agency may be unable to elicit adequate support for its reasoning without engaging in some form of hybrid procedures.

Given these divergent possibilities, a significant benefit of rationalism is that the agency determines what additional procedures, if any, are appropriate. Because on remand agencies are free to narrowly tailor any additional procedures to the inadequacies of their reasons, this form of remand ensures that any additional procedures will improve the decision of the agency. While rationalism may lead agencies to engage in more extensive reasoning in run-of-the-mill cases to avoid reversal, this change is desirable insofar as it protects liberal values and ensures that agencies apply their expertise consistently with progressive values. This reasoning need not be overly elaborate or involve formal procedures because the agency's explanation must only be "adequate." Efforts to define this standard, beginning with *State Farm*, will help to ensure that heightened scrutiny will not bog down the administrative process. Thus, rationalism avoids the problems identified in *Vermont Yankee*.

3. *Rationalism and Expertise.* The foregoing criticisms of rationalism are similar to the problems which led to the demise of structuralism and proceduralism. A third criticism, unique to rationalism, is that heightened substantive review will undercut deference to administrative expertise. Unlike structuralism and proceduralism, rationalism invites judges to scrutinize the substantive aspects of an agency's decision. This heightened scrutiny of substance, some commentators argue, will invite judges to substitute their policy preferences for those of an agency. According to these critics, judges have used and will use heightened scrutiny as a subterfuge to impose their own substantive viewpoints. We believe, however, that refinement of the rationalist model will minimize this difficulty.

Both the Supreme Court and legal commentators are currently engaged in an effort to define the requirement of adequate reasons in a comprehensive manner. At one time, particularly after *Citizens to Preserve Overton Park, Inc. v. Volpe,* the adequate reasons requirement was the subject of considerable confusion. The Court described a reviewing court's scope of review as "whether the decision was based on a consideration of the relevant factors and whether there has been a clear error of judgment." This formulation, with its open-ended phrasing concerning "relevant factors," invited judges to establish their own standards of what an agency should consider in order to produce an adequately reasoned decision. Further, the "clear error of judgment" language invited judges to consider the result reached by an agency, rather than its reasons.

In *State Farm*, the Court helped to resolve this confusion by adopting a more exact definition of the adequate reasons requirement. The Court said the requirement includes a determination of whether an agency relied on factors that Congress had not intended it to consider, whether it failed to consider "entirely" an important aspect of the problem it was resolving, and whether it offered an explanation for its decision that ran counter to the evidence or was so implausible that it could not be explained as a product of a difference in view or of agency expertise.

State Farm makes clear that the proper focus for review is not the result reached by an agency, but rather the reasons given to support that result. This distinction is important because it reminds judges that they are not to substitute their judgment for the policy choices of an agency and that the agency's reasoning may withstand scrutiny even if a judge disagrees with the result. Moreover, the focus on an agency's reasoning allows judges to acknowledge agency expertise where appropriate.

It would, of course, be naive to suppose that rationalism can completely avoid the problem of judges finding flaws in agency reasoning because they dislike the result. However, the heightened scrutiny endorsed by *State Farm* has not led to excessive reversal rates. * * * To the extent that intervention does occur under rationalism, its consequences are less severe than the consequences of intervention under the structuralist or proceduralist model. Under structuralism, judicial intervention involves either the invalidation of an agency's statute or a narrowing construction of that statute, both of which have far-reaching consequences. In contrast, intervention under the rationalist model would be case specific. Similarly, the form of remedy required by judicial intervention under proceduralism destroyed administrative efficiency. As indicated above, however, the impact of remands under rationalism is not so severe.

Although the Court's efforts to define judicial review under rationalism make review less open-ended, there will still be some variation in the scope of review. Factors such as the type of problem the agency is resolving, a court's assessment of the special expertise of an agency in a problem area, and the court's comprehension of that problem, will necessarily influence the degree of deference accorded to agency decisions. This variability, however, is not only unavoidable, it is appropriate. The type of discretion exercised in progressive government varies remarkably from agency to agency and from function to function. The accommodation of progressive and liberal values, therefore, will require different compromises in different contests.

* * *

Additional Sources

Harold Leventhal, *Environmental Decisionmaking and the Role of the Courts*, 122 U. Pa. L. Rev. 509 (1974)

Thomas O. McGarity, *Some Thoughts on "Deossifying" the Rulemaking Process*, 41 Duke L.J. 1385 (1992)

Kathleen W. Marcel, *The Role of the Courts in a Legislative and Administrative Legal System—The Use of Hard Look Review in Federal Environmental Litigation*, 62 Or. L. Rev. 403 (1983)

Peter L. Strauss, *Considering Political Alternatives to "Hard Look" Review*, 1989 Duke L.J. 538

Cass R. Sunstein, *In Defense of the Hard Look: Judicial Activism and Administrative Law*, 7 Harv. J.L. & Pub. Pol'y 51 (1984)

Cass R. Sunstein, *Deregulation and the Hard Look Doctrine*, 1983 Sup. Ct. Rev. 177

Patricia M. Wald, *Judicial Review of Complex Administrative Agency Decisions*, 462 Annals Am. Acad. Pol. & Soc. Sci. 72 (1982)

Patricia M. Wald, *Making "Informed" Decisions on the District of Columbia Circuit*, 50 Geo. Wash. L. Rev. 135 (1982)

B. Controversies About the Openness and Political Oversight of Administration in the Pursuit of a More Democratic Process

1. Debates About Openness in Government: Freedom of Information

Debate about opening up the administrative process to the public is part of a larger controversy about governmental openness. On the one hand, bureaucracies seek to make decisions in the most efficient way, which often means in a manner minimizing what bureaucracies see as extraneous political forces. This tendency leads to a penchant for secrecy, especially during the decisionmaking stage. On the other hand, the public often demands more openness on the part of the government, especially agencies. After all, learning what is happening in agencies is an important first step in developing strategies of response. Also, democratic theory requires a high degree of public knowledge about the workings of government so that the desired processes of dialogue and interaction can occur. These various themes are played out directly in the interpretation of the Freedom of Information Act.

The first excerpt, written in 1982 by Antonin Scalia, raises doubts about the Act's value. In memorable phrases, Justice Scalia calls the FOIA "the Taj Mahal of the Doctrine of Unanticipated Consequences, the Sistine Chapel of Cost-Benefit Analysis Ignored." He suggests that the FOIA has been used primarily by private interests to gain a competitive advantage by obtaining data in the government's hands about other private institutions—rather than as a means of gaining information about public policy. He also urges that the costs of the FOIA have been far out of proportion to the original estimates.

In the second excerpt, Judge Patricia M. Wald of the U.S. Court of Appeals of the District of Columbia Circuit argues that the FOIA has had significant affirmative impacts. She offers several examples of the FOIA's usefulness in permitting members of the public to gain information about official behavior. In general, she envisions the FOIA as part of a larger project of protecting citizens of the modern administrative state.

The final excerpt by Professor Robert Vaughn explores the relation between main themes in federal information policy and the theoretical structure of administrative law reflected in the ideals of administrative legitimacy that I have discussed.* In particular, Professor Vaughn shows how the rule of law ideal, the public purposes ideal, and the democratic process ideal have generated proposals for reforming information law and policy. He also shows how information proposals have reflected the strengths and limits of each of their underlying ideals, and how they have conflicted with each other in ways characteristic of the theoretical structure in which they participate. In conclusion, Professor Vaughn argues that even though information law has been seen as a somewhat isolated body of doctrine, it embodies larger theoretical controversies underlying the administrative process. He argues that this approach can enhance our understanding of the direction and limits of information law reform.

---

* See Thomas O. Sargentich, *The Reform of the American Administrative Process: The Contemporary Debate*, 1984 WISC. L. REV. 385, excerpted in Part IV.

Antonin Scalia, *The Freedom of Information Act Has No Clothes*, REGULATION 15, 15-19 (March/April 1982)*

The Freedom of Information Act (FOIA) is part of the basic weaponry of modern regulatory war, deployable against regulators and regulated alike. It differs, however, from other weaponry in the conflict, in that it is largely immune from arms limitation debate. Public discussion of the act displays a range of opinion extending from constructively-critical-but-respectful through admiring to enthralled. The media, of course, praise it lavishly, since they understandably like the "free information" it promises and provides. The Congress tends to agree with the media. The executive branch generally limits its criticism to relatively narrow or technical aspects—lest it seem to be committing the governmental equivalent of "taking the Fifth." The regulated sector also wishes to demonstrate that it has nothing to hide, and is in any case torn between aversion to those features of the act that unreasonably compromise its interests and affection for those that unreasonably compromise the government's. Through the mutually reinforcing praise of many who should know better, the act is paraded about with the veneration normally reserved for the First Amendment itself.

* * * [H]owever dim the prospect for fundamental change, the FOIA is worth examining, if only as an academic exercise. It is the Taj Mahal of the Doctrine of Unanticipated Consequences, the Sistine Chapel of Cost-Benefit Analysis Ignored.

Almost all of the Freedom of Information Act's current problems are attributable not to the original legislation enacted in 1966, but to the 1974 amendments. The 1966 version was a relatively toothless beast, sometimes kicked about shamelessly by the agencies. They delayed responses to requests for documents, replied with arbitrary denials, and overclassified documents to take advantage of the "national security" exemption. The '74 amendments were meant to remedy these defects—but they went much further. They can in fact only be understood as the product of the extraordinary era that produced them—when "public interest law," "consumerism," and "investigative journalism" were at their zenith, public trust in the government at its nadir, and the executive branch and Congress functioning more like two separate governments than two branches of the same. The amendments were drawn and debated in committee while President Nixon was in the final agony of Watergate, and were passed when President Ford was in the precarious early days of his unelected term. The executive branch managed to make a bad situation worse, by adamantly resisting virtually all changes in the act, even those that Congress was obviously bent on achieving. By the time it realized the error of its obstinacy, it was too late: the changes had been drafted and negotiated among congressmen and committees without the degree of agency participation and advice that might have made the final product—while still unpalatable—at least more realistic. The extent of the disaster may be gauged by the fact that, barely two months after taking office as a result of the Watergate coverup, President Ford felt he had to veto a bill that proclaimed "Freedom of Information" in its title. It passed easily over his veto.

When one compares what the Freedom of Information Act was in contemplation with what it has turned out to be in reality, it is apparent that something went wrong. The act and its amendments were promoted as a means of finding out about the operations of government; they have been used largely as a means of obtaining data in the government's hands concerning private institutions. They were promoted as a boon to the press, the public interest group, the little guy; they have been used most frequently by corporate lawyers. They were promoted as a minimal imposition on the operations of government; they have greatly burdened investigative agencies and the courts. The House Committee Report estimated that the 1974 amendments would cost only $100,000 a year; a single request under them has cost more than $400,000. There has grown up, since 1974, an entire industry and profession based upon the Freedom of Information Act. * * * In short, it is a far cry from John Q. Public finding out how his government works.

What happened in the 1974 amendments to the Freedom of Information Act is similar to what happened in much of the regulatory legislation and rulemaking of that era: an entirely desirable objective was pursued singlemindedly to the exclusion of equally valid competing interests. In the currently favored terminology, a lack of cost-benefit analysis; in more commonsensical terms, a loss of all sense of proportion.

Take, for example, the matter of costs. As noted above, the 1974 amendments were estimated by Congress to cost $100,000 a year. They have in fact cost many millions of dollars—no one knows precisely how much. * * *

---

* Reprinted with permission of The American Enterprise Institute for Public Policy Research, Washington, D.C., and Antonin Scalia. All rights reserved.

The question, of course, is whether this public expense is worth it, bearing in mind that the FOIA requester is not required to have any particular "need to know." The inquiry that creates this expense—perhaps for hundreds of thousands of documents—may be motivated by no more than idle curiosity. The "free lunch" aspect of the FOIA is significant not only because it takes money from the Treasury that could be better spent elsewhere, but also because it brings into the system requests that are not really important enough to be there, crowding the genuinely desirable ones to the end of the line. * * *

* * *

The preferred status of the FOIA requester in the courts is also evident in the standard of review. If a federal agency assesses a penalty against you or revokes a certificate that is necessary for your livelihood, it will do you no good to persuade a judge that the agency is probably wrong. The courts cannot reverse the agency merely because they disagree with its assessment of the facts. They can do so only when there is a lack of "substantial evidence" to support its finding. If, however, an agency denies a freedom of information request, shazam!—the full force of the Third Branch of government is summoned to the wronged party's assistance. The denial is subject to *de novo* review—which means that the court will examine the records on its own and come to its own independent decision. And whereas the general rule is that the citizen appealing to the courts must show that the agency acted improperly, in the case of an FOIA denial "the burden is on the agency to sustain its action."

The foregoing defects (and others could be added) might not be defects in the best of all possible worlds. They are foolish extravagances only because we do not have an unlimited amount of federal money to spend, an unlimited number of agency employees to assign, an unlimited number of judges to hear and decide cases. We must, alas, set some priorities—and unless the world is mad the usual Freedom of Information Act request should not be high on the list.

* * *

The defects of the Freedom of Information Act cannot be cured as long as we are dominated by the obsession that gave them birth—that the first line of defense against an arbitrary executive is do-it-yourself oversight by the public and its surrogate, the press. On that assumption, the FOIA's excesses are not defects at all, but merely the necessary price for our freedoms. It is a romantic notion, but the facts simply do not bear it out. The major exposés of recent times, from CIA mail openings to Watergate to the FBI COINTELPRO operations, owe virtually nothing to the FOIA but are primarily the product of the institutionalized checks and balances within our system of representative democracy. This is not to say that public access to government information has no useful role—only that it is not the ultimate guarantee of responsible government, justifying the sweeping aside of all other public and private interests at the mere invocation of the magical words "freedom of information."

* * *

Patricia M. Wald, *The Freedom of Information Act: A Short Case Study in the Perils and Paybacks of Legislating Democratic Values*, 33 EMORY L.J. 649, 649–71, 683 (1984)*

I. Introduction

* * *

The history of the Freedom of Information Act over nearly twenty years is a chronicle of the perils and problems of translating rhetoric into performance: a kind of morality play, if you will, about how to deal with the baggage that most significant "freedoms" carry with them, their costs in budgetary as well as human terms, and their vulnerability to shifts in political power and ideologies. It has been said that the Bill of Rights would not be approved by today's electorate. That may be unduly cynical, but the important point is that we do have the Bill of Rights firmly fixed in our Constitution.

Statutes are different; what one Congress does, another can undo. Passions of the day rage and cool in Congress as elsewhere. It is seductively easy to let go of *legislated* freedoms on the ground that they are too costly for a beleaguered Twentieth Century democracy. This is a brief history of how a very important law evolved to implement the Founders' democratic goal of open government, how its fortunes changed in the two turbulent decades just past, and how it continues to play a critical but controversial role in American life.

---

* Reprinted with permission of the Emory Law Journal and Patricia M. Wald. All rights reserved.

II. Passage of the FOIA

The Freedom of Information Act was enacted in the pre-Watergate sixties. Even then, people were concerned about unaccountable bureaucrats, public officials who, in Franklin Roosevelt's words, work "with a passion for anonymity." Leading the fight for "open government" was the press, which cited numerous instances of government agencies' random, unexplained denials of access to information about crucial decisions, denials which had covered up the mistakes or irregularities of the time. Congress had its own experience with executive refusals to disclose. For 185 years it had been fencing with the executive branch over its constitutional rights to obtain executive materials for legislation and supervision. While a freedom of information act could not settle all executive privilege questions, it would establish a legal presumption in favor of disclosure to the public and consequently compel the executive to justify any nondisclosure. * * * President Johnson signed the bill on July 4, 1966, proclaiming:

> This legislation springs from one of our most essential principles: a democracy works best when the people have all the information that the security of the Nation permits. No one should be able to pull the curtains of secrecy around decisions which can be revealed without injury to the public interest.

III. The FOIA's Historical Background

The Freedom of Information Act was enacted two centuries after the Constitution was drafted; the rights it conferred are not constitutionally protected. However, the goal it enforces—an open government accountable to the citizenry—does have solid roots in constitutional history. True, the government the Founding Fathers were familiar with was far smaller and less bureaucratic than the government of today. Elected officials, principally legislators, made decisions directly. But the fear of closed, inaccessible power was real, even then. As James Madison once warned:

> A popular Government, without popular information, or the means of acquiring it, is but a Prologue to a Farce or a Tragedy; or, perhaps both. Knowledge will forever govern ignorance; And a people who mean to be their own Governors, must arm themselves with the power which knowledge gives.

Alexander Hamilton was more sanguine:

> [An] objection . . . has been made . . . of this nature: "It is improper . . . to confer such large powers, as are proposed, upon the national government; because the seat of that government must of necessity be too remote from many of the States to admit of a proper knowledge on the part of the constituent, of the conduct of the representative body." . . . [T]he objection is in reality not well founded. . . . It ought . . . to be remembered that the citizens who inhabit the country at and near the seat of government will, in all questions that affect the general liberty and prosperity, have the same interest with those who are at a distance, and that they will stand ready to sound the alarm when necessary, and to point out the actors in any pernicious project.

To a nation spanning 5000 miles and swimming in mass information and instant communications, Hamilton's reliance on "citizens who inhabit the country at or near the seat of government" may seem a quaint relic in our national attic. Nonetheless, a direct descendant can be found in today's world. The modern American citizenry relies upon professional reporters and authors, investigators and advocates, to "sound the alarm when necessary." Perhaps professional watchdogs *must* perform that function today, when government operates from coast to coast and generates mountains of information every day.

Despite changes in the size and complexity of our society, the need for the elimination of indiscriminate secrecy in order to preserve accountability in government has remained constant. Jefferson believed that "[t]he whole of government consists in the art of being honest." While this statement is obviously an exercise in hyperbole—government must, now as in the eighteenth century, maintain some measure of secrecy—the tone and attitude toward government embodied in Jefferson's statement reflects an important aspect of American governance. If government is indeed a public trust, then information about the deeds of the trustees—those in power—must be available to the public, except when overriding concerns necessitate confidentiality. * * *

If the debacles of the last few decades have taught us anything, they have taught us that too much secrecy breeds irresponsibility. An excessive, and sometimes obsessive, passion for governmental secrecy can threaten a secure constitutional democracy. Because the match between the interests of those who exercise power and the interests of the citizens at large is far from perfect, politics cannot be left solely to the politicians. In retrospect, it seems that something like the Freedom of Information Act had to be invented to prevent a "curtain of fog and iron" from falling between the American public and its government.

IV. Application of the Act

The FOIA's concept is simple but revolutionary, like the Constitution itself. Any person, citizen or non-citizen—for whatever reason, good or ill—may file a request for an agency record, and the agency must disclose it unless the document falls within one of nine exemptions laid down in the law. If the agency refuses, the citizen can go to court on a priority basis, and the agency has to convince the court that the documents are exempt under the law. Most important, the court decides the issue afresh, without deference to the agency's call.

The nine exemptions are exclusive and are to be "narrowly construed." Yet they squeeze into a short subsection virtually every major dilemma, accommodation, and delicate balance that a modern democratic government faces: claims of national security in Exemption 1; trade secrets and confidential commercial information obtained from private companies in Exemption 4; confidential advice and recommendations underlying the formulation of public policy in Exemption 5; information that impermissibly invades personal privacy in Exemption 6 and investigative records compiled by law enforcement agencies in Exemption 7.

The FOIA grants a right which is virtually unprecedented anywhere else in the world: the right to obtain government documents just for the asking. However, no freedom is absolute; it must be balanced against other values, even other freedoms. This often excruciatingly difficult balancing ultimately determines the strength or impotence of the freedom in our national lives. So it is with the FOIA.

A critical factor in the FOIA's enforcement calculus is the power of the federal courts to determine *on their own* whether the record has to be disclosed, or whether instead it comes within one of the nine exemptions. If courts had to give traditional deference to agency interpretations of the FOIA, as they do in almost every other review of agency action, the Act might have been suffocated in infancy. At the least, the Act would not have occupied its present, major role in our national lives and governance.

Predictably, the executive branch was never enthusiastic about the Act. In the Act's first several years, agencies were recalcitrant. The journalist, Carl Stern, talked about the so-called "10th FOIA exemption": "We are not going to tell you." * * *

V. The 1974 Amendment

Watergate: in 1974, the country was suffering its shock waves. High level cover-ups, agency hit lists, covert activities, and repeated invocations of executive privilege had generated a wave of indignation against closed government. The Executive's clout and credibility in Congress were at an all-time low. Watergate created a vacuum into which the demands for FOIA reform flooded.

* * *

After 1974, the number of FOIA requests and the amount of litigation challenging agency denials increased dramatically. In 1966, the annual costs of administering FOIA requests were projected at $50,000. In 1981, the most conservative estimate of FOIA costs government-wide was $47 million; the Office of Management and Budget's figure was $250 million. As a result, courts excused the overwhelmed agencies from strict adherence to the statutory ten-day deadline for responses. In fact, requesters often had to wait months, even years on a first come, first served basis. The demand for information seemed insatiable.

For the press and public interest groups, the FOIA became the Fourth Musketeer. Exposés facilitated by the FOIA revealed:

—Ten elderly patients at a private Philadelphia nursing home died during 1964 and 1965 while they were being used as subjects in a drug experiment.

—Approximately one-third of all small corporations regularly underpaid federal income taxes in the late 1960s.

—Tests of drinking water near uranium mines in western New Mexico disclosed high levels of radioactivity and toxic wastes.

—Organizations that received federal grants to help fight alcoholism misused the taxpayers' money to influence legislation.

—Colleges' and universities' sloppy bookkeeping obscured the possible misuse of hundreds of millions of dollars of federal funds.

—A drug treatment center in Hawaii converted food stamps to make illegal cash payments to employees.

—The Consumer Product Safety Commission files contained information from a number of major manufacturers about exploding television sets.

—A Department of Energy study indicated plutonium workers might suffer from increased susceptibility to cancer.

—A Federal Trade Commission study suggested that cancer insurance was a "poor buy."

—The U.S. Public Health Service disclosed that Utah residents suffered an unusually high proportion of birth defects because of atomic bomb testing from 1950 to 1964.

In addition, Consumers Union used the Act to report on unleaded gasoline additives, hazardous denture cleaners, dangerous home car repair ramps, and other unsafe products. Ralph Nader's Health Research Group filed 300 requests with the FDA in one year and obtained 90% of them.

At least one hundred books and articles on major domestic and foreign crises were written on the basis of FOIA disclosures. Topics covered included histories of the Suez and Congo crises, U.S. policy during the Chinese Civil War in the 1940's, the Alger Hiss-Whitaker Chambers controversy, the *Rosenberg* trial and its aftermath, Vietnam, the Cuban missile crisis, the Bay of Pigs, and the Kennedy assassinations, to name only a few. The Organization of American Historians, who described its members as the smallest and least "aggressive" group of professional FOIA users, emphasized the importance of quick access to government papers for scholars working on tight schedules. They noted the "growing number of American historians [who] have turned to contemporary history" because "[w]e live in a period of such rapid change that it becomes increasingly important to continue to seriously reexamine the recent past."

From 1974 to 1981, well over 1300 FOIA cases were litigated. The subject matter of these cases reads like a tour guide to America in passage through the late 20th Century. FOIA requests relating to the environmental impact statement for the Amchitka nuclear blasts of 1970, the policies of American companies with regard to the Arab boycott of Israel, identification of Iranian officials provided with American passports during the hostage crisis, summaries of FBI files sent to the White House, senatorial questionnaires on judicial candidates, the identities of cadets dismissed for cheating at West Point, the papers and telephone logs Henry Kissinger took with him when he left the State Department, CIA information on Howard Hughes' Glomar Explorer, reports on the Martin Luther King assassination, CIA-sponsored research on behavioral control of human subjects, records of the Watergate Special Prosecutor, CIA contacts on California campuses, biographical facts about State Department employees abroad, telephone interceptions by government listening devices, DOE guidelines for construing its own regulations on emergency petroleum allocation enforcement, the Rowe Report on FBI informants working within the Ku Klux Klan, the Air Force's Agent Orange Report, BATF's "how to" investigative manuals, and FDA studies of the safety and performance of intraocular lenses have been litigated.

Often the courts have ordered disclosure over the agency's objections. But even when disclosure was not required, the government's claim of secrecy was raised to a high level of visibility. When I was in the government, it was sometimes said that government policymakers had only three choices: do it routinely and expect it to wind up in *The New York Times*, do it but don't leave a paper record, or don't do it at all. Of course, to some degree creative government officials and bureaucrats will always be able to devise ways to avoid the FOIA's disclosure requirements, and to reimpose a measure of secrecy in their decisionmaking.

Nevertheless, I have faith in the scheme created under the Act for two reasons. First, bureaucrats often have either a legal duty or a practical necessity to create paper records. Avoidance of a paper trail therefore, is not always so easy. Second, the assumption that playing it by the book will inexorably result in compelled disclosure is simply not true. If the agency can show that its record comes within one of the exemptions, it can and most often does keep the information to itself. As I have noted above, the exemptions enumerate virtually every legitimate reason an agency might have for withholding a given government record. The FOIA scheme accommodates both the valid needs for secrecy and the overarching need for government accountability.

VI. The Costs of the Act

Before he joined the court of appeals, my colleague Antonin Scalia [excerpted above] referred to the FOIA as "the Taj Mahal of the Doctrine of Unanticipated Consequences, the Sistine Chapel of Cost-Benefit Analysis Ignored."[66] Of course, like all freedoms, the FOIA turned out to have its price, financially and otherwise, and some costs proved to be more unexpected than others. The Act has been used not only to gain insight into government, but also to get an inside view into the operations of private businesses and the lives of private citizens. Businesses quickly learned how to use the FOIA to get information about their competitors. Lawyers found out that they could often extract facts more quickly through FOIA requests than through the civil discovery system. In addition, the defense and intelligence agencies have been worried that their obligations under the FOIA—or even the *perception* of their obliga-

---

[66] Scalia, *The Freedom of Information Act Has No Clothes*, REGULATION, March/April 1982 at 14, 15.

tions to disclose information—might compromise investigative and intelligence methods or, at best, dry up important confidential sources.

After 1974, the FOIA became a mini-industry. Clearinghouses sprang up for public groups, and commercial services came into being for private industry. The government spent between $50 and $200 million a year on processing and litigating the requests. One observer noted, however, that this figure must be put in context—we spend nearly $100 million annually on military bands.

One of the greatest surprises about the FOIA in action turned out to be the composition of its principal users. The press, historians, other "watchdogs," and, ultimately, the public—who would be served by their surrogates' increased ability to "sound the alarm"—had been envisioned as the chief beneficiaries of the Act. However, a General Accounting Office survey showed that only one out of every twenty FOIA requests was made by a journalist, scholar, or author. In contrast, four out of five requests were made by business executives or their lawyers, who astutely discerned the business value of the information which government obtains from industry while performing its licensing, inspecting, regulating, and contracting functions.

* * *

Lawyers also found the FOIA invaluable for litigation purposes. Information about their adversaries could often be obtained more quickly through the FOIA than through normal civil discovery channels. The Act was therefore accused of misuse as "a government subsidized discovery vehicle for the antitrust bar."

Even foreign competitors could join the game since the Act did not restrict requesters to U.S. citizens. For example, Suzuki Motor Company used the FOIA to collect Toyota submissions to the U.S. government, although Suzuki lacked comparable access to the data in Japan. * * * One major drug company reported that it sued under the FOIA to obtain copies of minutes of meetings between its own representatives and agency personnel to discover what the agency wrote down, and what information the agency was revealing about the company to others. The Act has been charged with turning agencies into information brokers between companies pursuing each other, rather than acting as a window for public assessment of how government conducts itself.

The "fear of FOIA" in turn spawned a new breed of litigation—the "reverse FOIA" suit, brought by the submitters of information who ask the courts to prohibit agencies from releasing their information to FOIA requesters. Under what conditions can an agency give assurances of confidentiality concerning information it obtains for regulatory, investigative, licensing, or procurement purposes from a business that claims it will be hurt by such disclosure? * * *

* * *

In the meantime, companies complain bitterly about agency disclosure of technical cost and management details that are contained in their bids for government contracts, while universities decry the disclosure of details contained in their research grant proposals. A chemical company representative told of a request, presumably by a competitor acting through lawyers and consulting firm intermediaries, for information which he claimed could be used to deduce production capabilities, construction cost fixtures, and critical operating data. Multinational drug manufacturers are said to prefer researching and developing innovative drugs abroad for fear that processes still undergoing testing here will be prematurely disclosed under the FOIA.

But there is another side of the story. "Public interest" groups claim that moving too precipitously to close off public disclosure of business data would invite public harm. They challenge anyone to point to actual episodes where companies have suffered economic harm from FOIA disclosures. These groups contend that industry's real aim is to hide embarrassing information such as drug company tests on humans before completing animal tests, toxic chemicals dumped into streams and rivers, inspection reports of the Department of Agriculture concerning unwholesome meat, misleading reports by a utility to its ratepayers about the costs of a new nuclear plant, and NRC reports of safety problems in nuclear plants. Tightened standards, they say, would "increase the cozy, closed door government-business dealings which were the very sort of practices the Act was designed to root out."

* * * I relate these developments at some length to make the point that freedoms—and laws implementing freedoms—are often unpredictable in whom they help and whom they hurt; they do not always distinguish between the good guys and the bad guys. These experiences under the FOIA have a ring of *deja vu* to constitutional scholars. Why should the fourth, fifth, or fourteenth amendments protect the palpably guilty as well as the hapless innocent? Why should the First amendment shield the Nazi marchers in Skokie and the Ku Klux Klan in Meridian as well as soap box socialists in Washington Square and ERA marchers on Pennsylvania Avenue?

* * *

VIII. Conclusion

My real message today is that passing a law like the FOIA is only the beginning. If the law fails, a piece of our freedom is chipped away. Times change—certain values, like open government, go in and out of favor. Other values may seem for the moment more consequential. The problems and risks of freedom change, too, in a modern, industrial, mass communication, high-tech society. The Founding Fathers, with uncanny wisdom, were able to define our most sacred freedoms, but they could not even begin to formulate the ways to make them work through three hundred years. History plays a critical role in the development of freedoms. Watergate reinvigorated a feeble FOIA and produced FOIA amendments more important in many respects than the original bill. Yet, again, history and political fortunes changed, and the FOIA came to be viewed as a kind of flower child of the irresponsible seventies, constantly threatened with defoliation. Proofs of its actual harm to law enforcement or national security were relatively meager—the perceptions of potential informers and allies, not concrete evidence of positive harm, were invoked to discredit it. And in truth, the FOIA, like all basic freedoms, sometimes hurts the worthy and sometimes helps the unworthy.

It takes constant vigilance, commitment, and common sense to make any law work. I hope we as citizens have all these qualities—in large measure—to keep the FOIA around for a long time and to make it work.

Robert G. Vaughn, *Federal Information Policy and Administrative Law*, in HANDBOOK ON REGULATION AND ADMINISTRATIVE LAW 467, 468-81 (David Rosenbloom & Richard Schwartz eds., 1994)*

The perception that federal information provisions form an isolated and perhaps idiosyncratic body of law obscures many aspects of federal information law and policy. Moreover, this perception has impeded reform of federal information law and hidden important considerations to the future of such provisions. This chapter * * * explores how federal information provisions relate to the theoretical structure of administrative law. * * * In so doing, the chapter emphasizes the Federal Freedom of Information Act [FOIA] but draws as well on examples and experience with other information provisions.

* * *

In exploring the relationship of information provisions to the theoretical structure of administrative law, this chapter relies on the ideals of administrative law used by Professor Thomas Sargentich to organize proposals for administrative reform.* Although a brief summary does not capture the detail and subtlety of his analytical scheme, a summary can provide sufficient explanation to show how information policy reflects not specialized but general debates about administrative law.

The Three Ideals of Administrative Law

Professor Sargentich articulates three competing ideals of administrative law—the rule of law ideal, the public purposes ideal and the democratic process ideal. These ideals reflect differing viewpoints regarding the appropriate character and scope of administrative law. According to Professor Sargentich, these ideals conflict with each other and constantly struggle for dominance in administrative law. Moreover, each ideal presents a core embodiment of its view but one which conflicts with the practical realities of administrative practice. Therefore, each ideal has an alternative expression more acceptable to reality but less true to the underlying ideal. Each ideal is also accompanied by a methodology of decisionmaking. A review of these three ideals, their core embodiments and alternative expressions, and methodologies permit placement of information laws in the context of administrative law theory.

This chapter discusses how federal information laws, particularly the FOIA, rely upon each of these ideals. After discussing each of these ideals, the chapter explores how the weaknesses and contradictions in each ideal have influenced the application and development of federal information policy. The inconsistencies and failures of information policy relate directly to the contradictions and weaknesses of these ideals. Although the future of federal information laws requires specific changes and modifications in those laws, that future also requires recognition of the inconsistencies in administrative theory which information policy reflects.

---

* Reprinted with permission of Marcel Dekker, Inc. and Robert G. Vaughn. All rights reserved.

* [The ideas to which Professor Vaughn is referring are elaborated in the excerpt, *The Reform of the American Administrative Process: The Contemporary Debate*, included in Part IV.]

Rule of Law Ideal

The rule of law ideal requires that administrative action rest upon positive law, preferably statutes. This ideal draws on contract theories of the state that require the consent of the governed. Therefore, the core embodiment of the rule of law ideal is formalism: that all exercises of public power must be guided by legal rules. This emphasis on legal rules is inconsistent with the immense discretion held by administrative officials and leads to the alternative expression of proceduralism. Proceduralism protects the individual from abuse of government power by requiring that administrative officials follow certain procedures before acting. Proceduralism, however, does not ultimately restrict discretion because proceduralism does not address the ability of administrative officials to act on the basis of vague, unarticulated powers that permit a number of substantive choices. The rule of law idea relies on judicial reasoning as a principal methodology. This methodology manifests the importance of restrictions on the exercise of power by the application of specific legal rules.

Information provisions, particularly the FOIA, rest in part on justifications relying on the rule of law ideal. Reliance on the rule of law ideal is reflected not only in the justifications for several information provisions but also in their specific content. For example, central to the rule of law ideal is the application of existing and known standards. One of the most common justifications for the FOIA asserted that public access was necessary in order to avoid secret law. Congress believed that agencies applied standards and procedures to the resolution of administrative disputes that were unknown to the parties. The availability of the applicable standards of decision stands as a central underpinning of the rule of law; without knowledge of the rules, it is impossible to believe that rules serve to limit administrative authority. Therefore, the FOIA requires that agencies make available to the public, without request, final opinions and orders in the adjudication of cases, statements of policy and interpretations adopted by the agency which have not been published in the *Federal Register*, and staff manuals and instructions that "affect a member of the public." The Privacy Act requires that agencies publish information regarding the character and scope of records maintained by the agency.

Open meeting provisions, such as the Sunshine in Government Act and the Federal Advisory Committee Act also relate to the rule of law ideal. These provisions generally do not permit the public to participate in agency proceedings but do require that decisions be taken in public proceedings. Although this openness helps to insure that agency standards are known to the public, the concern regarding secret law seems subsidiary to insuring that decision makers follow the applicable rules. The Federal Advisory Committee Act particularly reflects this concern because of the fear that non-governmental employees may improperly influence the application of administrative rules. The emphasis on the control of abuse contained in these provisions as well in the FOIA presuppose pre-existing and specific standards against which the behavior of governmental officials may be judged.

Congress placed enforcement of the FOIA in the courts. This placement uses the principal methodology of the rule of law ideal, judicial reasoning, as the technique for enforcement of the act. Similarly, other information provisions, including the Privacy Act, and the Sunshine in Government Act, rely on judicial enforcement. This model of enforcement, of course, assumes the applicability of the rule of law ideal.

The concept of any person access also implements the rule of law ideal. The genesis for the concept of any person access rested on the congressional desire to remove agency discretion. Agencies must treat all requesters similarly; agencies could not evaluate the purposes or motives of requesters.

As will be examined below, failures in judicial enforcement of the act reflect the weaknesses in formalism, the core embodiment of the rule of law ideal. Particularly, the substantial agency discretion that remains in the application of information laws illustrates the limits of formalism. With these information provisions, proceduralism is an inadequate substitute. Paradoxically, the reliance on formalism has actually increased agency, and judicial, discretion and thereby weakened information policy relying on the rule of law ideal.

Public Purposes Ideal

The public purposes ideal stresses the role of administrative agencies in accomplishing important public goals. The ideal draws on the importance attached to the affirmative tasks of government in policymaking and in administration. Therefore, the core embodiment is instrumentalism, "by which is meant the familiar notion that the significant worth of a policy inheres in its success as an instrument of the public good." This instrumentalism focuses on carrying out the public purposes of an agency's enabling legislation or choosing between alternatives based on agency judgments regarding the public good, as in cost-benefit analysis. By focusing on rational analysis, instrumentalism leads to ever expanding analytical schemes that inescapably become vague and devoid of substantive content. Indeed, such an approach can eventually become the guise for political manipulation. These weaknesses lead to an attempt to achieve the public good through the market and private decisionmaking rather than principally through administrative agencies. This alternative expression, however, disavows a central role for the administrative process. The public purposes ideal relies on expertise as its principal methodology. The methodology manifests the ideal's reliance on technical judgments to achieve the public good.

Information provisions, particularly the FOIA, rest also upon the public purposes ideal. Although not central to justifications for the FOIA, the improvement of agency decisionmaking procedures emerged as one of the arguments for the Act and for other open government provisions. This justification was often paired with, but differs significantly from, the argument that these provisions control abuse. Information provisions encourage better articulation of the rationale for decisions and by making these rationales available, the premises as well as the techniques of analysis can be challenged and refined by others. This argument, as does instrumentalism, sees administrative decisions as almost scientific in character.

The instrumentalist vision of agency behavior, however, conflicts in important ways with the concept of openness underlying information provisions. The exemption to the FOIA protecting agency deliberations illustrates this conflict. The deliberative process exemption rests on the need of bureaucratic organizations for secrecy. An agency needs secrecy to canvass all alternative courses of action that could be selected based on the application of rational criteria to the particular circumstances. * * *

This instrumentalist vision of agency behavior justifies considerable secrecy. In this sense, the deliberative process exemption exalts bureaucratic efficiency above the competing interest of openness and represents the incompatibility of instrumentalism with publicity that stands at the center of the rule of law ideal and with participation and oversight central to the democratic process ideal. These aspects of instrumentalism help explain why information policy turned first to the alternative expression of the public purposes ideal, use of private decisionmaking to determine the public good.

From the inception of the FOIA, Congress was aware that information acquired through the FOIA would be used for a variety of purposes other than evaluating the conduct of government officials. Critics of the act have emphasized the acquisition of much information for commercial or business purposes while proponents have noted the amount of health and safety information provided to consumers by information provisions. By 1974, Congress, at least, perceived the clearinghouse function of the FOIA as a central one. This clearinghouse function by providing information to commercial enterprises and to consumers uses the market and private decisionmaking to accomplish the public good and principally views agencies as sources of the relevant information. This perception of the FOIA represents the alternative expression of the public purposes ideal.

The FOIA did not address the management of government documents and records. The FOIA did not require that documents be created or indeed even if they be maintained. To many the failure of the FOIA to cover information management issues reduced its effectiveness. Subsequent legislation, such as the Federal Privacy Act, did resolve issues regarding the acquisition, maintenance, and use of records. More recent legislation, such as the Computer Matching Act and the Computer Security Act, address in detail the management of federal records. In the Privacy Act and these recent information provisions, federal information policy has focused much more on expertise in the management of information and records. This focus on expertise highlights the methodology of the public purposes ideal.

Commentators have noted the federal information policy lacks consistency and coherence. Information provisions contain differing often conflicting judgments regarding similar information and considerable discrepancy in the treatment of information-related issues exists among federal agencies. Implicit in these comments is the perception that unification of policy requires resolution of the issues in information policy under rational criteria. In addition, these comments contain the suggestion that more centralized administrative direction is required. These implications mirror tenets of the public purposes ideal.

Federal agencies increasingly keep documents and records in electronic form. This change in technology has generated recommendations that require modifying the role of government agencies by making these agencies responsible for developing an information policy, including dissemination of information, consistent with the regulatory goals of the agency. In some instances, an agency might wish to rely principally on the private market to accomplish its information dissemination goals. In making these judgments, the most widely known proposal offers to the agencies cost-benefit analysis. These proposals reflect instrumentalism, the core embodiment of the public purposes ideal.

* * * Partly because of the perceived isolation of public information law, discussion of the future has focused on specific proposals for change. Thus far, the discussion has generally ignored the consequences of aligning federal information policy around instrumentalism. The contradictions and weaknesses of instrumentalism permit an examination of the future from the perspective of administrative theory rather than from an analysis of specific proposals.

Democratic Process Ideal

The democratic process ideal rests on a participatory and representative decisionmaking process in which agency officials consider the views of those affected by administrative decisions. This ideal sees the administrative process as primarily a political one and as its core embodiment relies on public participation in that process. Because public participation conflicts with the bureaucratic structure of administrative decision and challenges the principle that public employees are politically neutral actors (a principle basic to the modern civil service), the ideal offers an alternative expression of oversight by politically responsive officials. This alternative expression, of course, abandons direct public participation central to the ideal. The methodology of this ideal is politics: the process of balancing and compromising affected interests. This methodology manifests the judgment that the administrative process is a political one.

The rhetoric of federal information law has been strongly anti-bureaucratic. The passage of the FOIA in 1966 followed years of hearings documenting bureaucratic abuse and arrogance in the administration of the information provision of the Administrative Procedure Act. The 1974 amendments to the FOIA expressed congressional anger at the administration of the Act. These amendments included the first provision that permitted a federal official to be held personally accountable for the arbitrary and capricious withholding of information. Likewise, the Federal Privacy Act followed extensive hearings by Senator Sam Ervin's Constitutional Rights Subcommittee regarding invasions of individual privacy by the federal bureaucracy. The Sunshine in Government Act and the Federal Advisory Committee reflected similar suspicions about the bureaucracy. The legislative history of federal information law is replete with calls to alter the practices of the bureaucracy and to return government to the people. This rhetoric shares with the democratic process ideal's core embodiment of participation a basic inconsistency with bureaucratic organization and function.

Information provisions also directly relate to the core concept of participation. Citizens must be armed with information to participate directly in the administrative process. Rights of participation such as standing to appear and the right to intervene in proceedings mean little without a right to information. The sense that citizens are the ultimate repositories of political power requiring information to be effective is aptly summarized by Madison's quote, one that often prefaces discussions of the FOIA. "A popular government without popular information or the means of acquiring it, is but a prologue to a farce or a tragedy or perhaps both."

As Professor Sargentich's analysis, however, would predict, federal information policy has not turned to the core embodiment of public participation. Information provisions do not provide persons with any right to participate in the administrative process. For example, although the Sunshine in Government Act and the Federal Advisory Committee Act require that certain meetings be open to the public, these provisions do not give members of the public any right to speak at these meetings or to otherwise participate. Document and record laws, like the FOIA, do not purport to permit public participation in agency processes or in any agency decision. One could argue that persons who obtain information either through documents and records or by observing directly an administrative proceeding could use that information to identify any rights of participation and to make those rights more meaningful. Still, it is not public information provisions that provide the right of participation.

Public information law relies more on the alternative expression of the democratic process ideal: oversight by politically responsible officials. The FOIA permits persons who obtain information about government decisions to respond to those decisions politically. When citizens are aware of the actions of the bureaucracy and understand the justifications for those actions, citizens can oppose or support those actions through the political means available to them. The right of political participation, however, requires knowledge of the need to act and information to frame arguments and objections. In this sense, the view that the FOIA is a statutory enactment of a right to information that empowers the First Amendment right of free speech captures nicely the concept of political oversight.

Federal information provisions also sought to equalize information resources. The express aim of these provisions is to give citizens and agencies a rough equality of relevant information as a basis for political conflict regarding bureaucratic actions. These provisions also contain an implicit goal as well: to equalize informational resources between interest groups who contend in political arenas. Information provisions tend to give less highly organized interests information to battle with more highly organized interests, particularly regarding administrative action affecting both groups. In this context, the disputes regarding the rights of submitters of information to the government address the ability of all groups to use the methodology of the democratic process ideal: political conflict.

As will be examined below, the practical difficulties confronting the users of public information laws, particularly the FOIA, reduce the ability of these provisions to implement even the alternative expression of the democratic process ideal. It is ironic that the strong antibureaucratic character of information provisions may have engendered a reaction beyond that justified by the effects of these provisions. Also, the conflicts emerging between categories of requesters and between requesters and submitters raise issues of "information equity" that directly concern the effectiveness of political oversight of bureaucratic action.

Application of the Three Ideals in Information Policy

Rule of Law Ideal

Despite reliance on the rule of law ideal, Congress failed to eliminate administrative discretion from the FOIA and other information laws and the courts have failed in some significant ways in structuring and controlling the exercise of this discretion. The FOIA provides some examples.

Although the FOIA adopts the principle that government records are public, the Act gives an agency considerable discretion in applying the nine exemptions that permit agencies to withhold requested documents. These exemptions incorporate interests of the government and of private parties that justify protection. The discretion of agencies is substantial in that with most of the exemptions an agency may decide to release the records even though the records are covered by one of the exemptions. It is not surprising, given the breadth of the exemptions and the discretion entailed, the bulk of litigation under the Act concerns interpretations of the exemptions.

Interpretation of the exemptions goes directly to the heart of agency discretion and tests the ability of the FOIA to rely on the specific legal rules as limitations. As Professor Sargentich's general analysis would suggest, courts have often failed to limit agency discretion. Two examples illustrate the judicial failure to structure discretion: first, the courts' interpretation of the exemption for records classified for purposes of national security; second, the courts' general approach to interpretation of the exemptions.

The first exemption, enacted as part of the FOIA in 1966, concerned national security documents and records and exempted documents "specifically required by Executive Order to be kept secret in the interest of national defense or foreign policy." The structure of the exemptions and subsequent legislative history suggest that Congress sought to limit the discretion of federal agencies in claiming this exemption. As with the Act in general, Congress relied on judicial review to implement this limitation.

In 1973, Representative Patsy Mink, among others, requested information regarding a pending underground nuclear test in Alaska. The Environmental Protection Agency refused to release the documents, claiming that as classified documents they fell under the exemption.

The United States Supreme Court ruled that courts could not examine the propriety of executive agencies' classification decisions. If appropriate government officials informed a federal court that requested documents were classified, a court must of necessity yield to that determination and conclude that the exemption applied. Therefore, in camera review of documents was impermissible and the provision of the FOIA that mandated release of non-exempt portions of documents that could be segregated did not apply.

The Supreme Court rested its ruling on interpretations of the legislative history of the exemption but emphasized the discretion granted to officials dealing with national security information. The Court also asserted that federal judges lacked the experience and expertise to evaluate the decisions of appropriate government officials and that deference was required to executive classification actions.

This ruling effectively eliminated judicial review of executive classification decisions. * * *

In the 1974 amendments to the FOIA, Congress expressly rejected the Supreme Court's interpretation of the exemption. Congress recognized that the Supreme Court's interpretation undermined the basic structure of the Act relying on judicial review. The rejection of the Supreme Court's interpretation was reflected both in the Congressional deliberations and in the text of the amendment. Several members of Congress reasserted the importance of de novo review, including in camera inspection, as a means of limiting executive discretion. The language of the exemption was altered to require that documents and records falling under the exemption must be "in fact properly classified."

In vetoing the 1974 amendments, President Ford

gave as one of the reasons, the change in the (b)(1) exemption. Congress overrode the veto, thus enacting the amendments and through the (b)(1) exemption reaffirming judicial review as a mechanism for limiting administrative discretion. Even under the revised version, however, the executive retained the authority to establish the criteria for classification.

Subsequent interpretation of the exemption reminds us of the weaknesses of formalism, the core embodiment of the rule of law ideal. Through a number of devices, federal courts have routinely refused to implement the 1974 amendment to the (b)(1) exemption. Courts have relied heavily upon agency affidavits describing withheld information as properly classified under the relevant classification order and relegated in camera inspection to a limited role in enforcing the requirement of proper classification. Moreover, agency affidavits are often viewed only by judges depriving attorneys for requesters of even a limited ability to argue regarding the propriety of the classification. The combination of these techniques has undermined the concept of de novo review and reflects continuing judicial concern about the courts' lack of experience and expertise.

* * *

Although the national security exemption concerns extremely sensitive documents regarding which broad discretion would be expected, the interpretation of the (b)(1) exemption illustrates the problem of discretion that plagues application of all of the exemptions. The approach to interpretation of the other exemptions demonstrates the commonality of the problem. In fact, interpretation of the FOIA shows that unquestioning reliance on formalism not only can be ineffective in limiting discretion but also can be harmful to information policy.

Courts early recognized that the discretion embodied in the exemptions threatened the more specific rules requiring access. Therefore, the Supreme Court articulated an approach to interpretation of the exemptions that required that the exemptions be narrowly interpreted. Commentators noted, however, that the Supreme Court often adopted the broader rather than the more narrow interpretation, while reciting the canon of narrow interpretation of the exemptions. Recently, Justice Scalia, not himself a supporter of the FOIA, expressly challenged the commitment of the Court to the canon of narrow interpretation of the exemptions. He argued that if the canon were to be meaningful, it must mean, at least, that the Court would choose the most narrow reading permitted by the language of the exemption. Justice Scalia demonstrated how, in the case before it, the Court had abandoned this canon of interpretation.

The Court's opinion reflects instead an approach in which the Court balances the governmental or private interests to be protected by the particular exemption against the policy or purpose of access to government documents. As a practical matter, the Court has articulated interests to be served by an exemption and used these interests rather than the canon of narrow construction as the primary guide to interpretation. Of course, this approach emphasizes the interests in withholding.

The attempts of Congress to limit discretion through any-person access has sharpened the focus on the interests in withholding and weakened the importance of access embodied in any-person access. In establishing the concept of any-person access, Congress sought to limit agency discretion in evaluating the reasons for access and thereby to establish the principle that government documents and records are public. In so doing, however, the law removed from inquiry the interests justifying disclosure. As a result, debate and litigation assumed the reasons for access but emphasized the reasons for withholding. This emphasis on the interests supporting withholding has given them a concreteness and detail often not given to the interests supporting disclosure. When combined with the Supreme Court's balancing approach, the unintended result of any-person access, an important aspect of formalism, has been to elevate the interests in withholding and gradually to expand the scope of administrative discretion.

It is not surprising, given the failure of the FOIA to guarantee access by limiting discretion, that a good deal of the FOIA, particularly amendments to the original Act, focus on procedures as a method of insuring access. Illustrative of this proceduralism are the 1974 and 1986 amendments to the act. A good portion, perhaps the most substantial portion, of the 1974 amendments concerned procedures including time limits for agency response, provisions for administrative appeals, and criteria for charging fees for complying with requests. Also, portions of the 1986 amendments addressed issues regarding fees and fee waivers.

These procedural rules have not been particularly effective even on their own terms. Many of the procedures, such as those regarding appeals and fees, have not been easy to apply nor to interpret. These procedures have not significantly reduced agency discretion nor insured that the rules regarding access would be clearly applied.

Perhaps a more telling indictment of proceduralism's reliance on rules lies in the lack of any serious attempt to enforce the ten-day limit on an agency response to a FOIA request. Neither the agencies nor the courts have applied this clear and unambiguous procedural rule. The principal justification for the refusal asserts that the lack of agency resources prevents agencies from complying with the rule. Good faith processing of requests has replaced the specific time limits established by Congress. This justification for failure to comply with the rule also rejects a clear congressional judgment because included in the rule must have been a congressional direction to agencies to allocate existing resources so that the directive could be satisfied. That the rule addresses the possibility of limited extensions in particular circumstances emphasizes that the justification rejects congressional judgments. Lack of compliance with a clear procedural rule challenges the underpinnings of the rule of law ideal.

The analysis above risks the conclusion that the FOIA has failed to open government documents and records to the public. This conclusion would ignore the significant accomplishments of the law, including the availability of significant amounts of important information and the alteration of agency behavior and expectations. The analysis above does demonstrate the weaknesses of formalism when confronting agency discretion and the failure of proceduralism to substitute adequately. These weaknesses suggest the limits of formalism and caution that reliance on it may lead to frustration and to damage to the goals of the FOIA. The analysis above also suggests the limitations of the rule of law ideal and directs attention to those strains of federal information policy that rely on other ideals of administrative law.

Public Purposes Ideal

Given the compromises inherent in the application of the rule of law ideal and the experience demonstrating the weaknesses of formalism and the limits of proceduralism, federal information policy has turned to aspects of the public purposes ideal. The increasing prominence of the clearinghouse function of the FOIA exemplifies this change in orientation.

Although the clearinghouse function of the FOIA was implicit in the act, the 1974 Amendments marked recognition of this function. As discussed above, this clearinghouse function represents the alternative expression of the public purposes ideal: use of the market in making decisions regarding the public good. Many experts now believe that all has been accomplished that can be with the present structure of the FOIA and that the future now requires greater use of the clearinghouse function. Indeed, these prognostications implicitly recognize the limits of the rule of law ideal and, without specifically articulating that judgment, seek salvation in another ideal.

The clearinghouse function represents the alternative expression of the public purposes ideal. Reliance on the market to establish the public good reduces the role and function of federal agencies. Two recent developments, however, point to the core embodiment of the public purposes ideal: instrumentalism. These two developments, an emphasis on information management and the electronic dissemination of information, share much with instrumentalism.

The FOIA itself did not address information management issues. As early as 1974, however, Senator Sasser commented on the lack of uniform standards, training or administration of the FOIA. He called for more centralized standards and procedures for managing information.

Subsequent legislation focused more specifically on information management issues. The Federal Privacy Act regulated how agencies could acquire, maintain and use some specific types of records. The Federal Paperwork Reduction Act, the Computer Security Act, and the Computer Matching Act also addressed issues of information management. The Computer Security Act and the Computer Matching Act directed specific management procedures. Legislation and administrative practice have increasingly perceived information policy as involving issues of management relying on agency experience and expertise in administration.

Senator Sasser's assertion of the lack of uniformity in federal information policy has become more and more obvious. The passage of a number of information-related provisions has created conflicts between these provisions, has illustrated the lack of a coherent information policy and has highlighted inconsistencies within specific information statutes.

The passage of the Federal Privacy Act generated an energetic and never completely resolved debate regarding the relationship between the Privacy Act and the FOIA. Although the courts and Congress have attempted to reconcile these conflicts, some commentators do not believe the reconciliation has been successful. In addition, more general conflicts between policies of privacy and access are in a perpetual tension that cannot be resolved simply by modifications in the Privacy Act and in the FOIA.

Other information provisions embody different, often conflicting, decisions regarding access to the same or similar information. Two examples illustrate the inconsistencies. First, the whistle-blower protection provisions permit employees, in some circumstances, to release documents that fall within one of the exemptions even if an agency has decided to withhold the documents under the FOIA. Therefore, these laws contain conflicting judgments regarding the role of agencies in determining information policy.

Second, the Consumer Product Safety Act restricts the access of certain health and safety information that would otherwise be available under the FOIA and restricts the discretion to release information that agency officials would enjoy under the FOIA. The two laws reach differing conclusions regarding the weight to be given to manufacturer interests in withholding. As a result, different federal agencies possessing similar documents regarding health and safety issues are bound by conflicting standards.

Similar inconsistencies can be found in the administration of the FOIA among federal agencies. Agencies treat similar records differently. Agency regulations can vary, agencies present differing interpretations of the law, and treat similar documents and records differently. Moreover, both Congress and the executive lack information regarding significant issues of administration of the act that makes difficult additional comparison of administration among the agencies.

The emphasis on information management and the recognition of the lack of coherent government-wide information policies suggest the need for greater centralization of administration. Many see the future of the FOIA more closely tied to agency expertise in management and administration. These suggestions implicitly require greater agency determinations of policy based on criteria developed by them.

Indeed, during the 1980s, the Office of Management and Budget's Office of Information and Regulatory Affairs used the Paperwork Reduction Act as authority for its review of agency paperwork requests and regulatory proposals. The experience with the Paperwork Reduction Act exemplifies how the desire for rational criteria in information management supports more centralized administrative direction.

Another recent development has led to more specific proposals relating federal information policy to agency management and to the agencies' determination of policy. These proposals explicitly rely on agency determination of the public good and appeal directly to instrumentalism.

Federal agencies, increasingly, store, retrieve, and disseminate information through electronic means. This change in technology required some interpretations of the FOIA including the meaning of the term "record," of when a new document is being created, and of the application of fee provisions. This change in technology also permitted a reassessment of the role of agencies in information policy.

A study conducted for the Administrative Conference of the United States by Professor Henry Perritt, leading to recommendations of the Conference, addressed both the issues of interpretation and of the role of agencies in setting information policy. The study resolved the interpretative issues in favor of application of the FOIA to electronically held records.

The study and recommendations also asserted that the change in technology for maintaining and disseminating records permitted an alteration in the ways in which agencies assessed their roles in information policy. Given the potential for dissemination of electronically held records, the Administrative Conference Recommendations identified varying levels of dissemination ranging from "access," in which agencies simply turn over electronic data for further processing; to "disclosure," in which agencies make records available electronically to persons in public reading rooms; to "dissemination," in which agencies take an active role in making electronically held records available to the public in user friendly form. Agencies could decide, based on their own assessment of their missions, to choose among the varying approaches, perhaps adopting different approaches for different types of records.

The recommendations also noted that agencies should decide whether to disseminate information themselves by creating the menus and other programming to make electronically held information widely available or by relying on private companies to accomplish the same goal. Once again, an agency was to determine which approach best served the public good.

This reliance on agency expertise in determining the public good reflects the tenets of instrumentalism. In part, agencies could determine the public good by looking to their own mission statements. The recommendations, however, commended cost-benefit analysis in determining the appropriate level of access and in deciding whether to rely on agency resources or on private enterprise.

These recent developments, pointing directly to instrumentalism, seek to alter the orientation of federal information policy. By giving agencies a greater role in policy, proponents hope to improve the administration and efficiency of information policy. These proposals also seek to identify agency interests with requester interests and to create incentives for much broader public access to government information. Proponents speak of point-of-purchase information for consumers and access to a wide range of government data bases by any person having a modem.

These proposals, although important and perhaps supportable, have failed to consider the limitations of instrumentalism. Even in these proposals that articulate the costs and benefits to be considered, cost-benefit analysis remains vague and open-ended. Professor Sargentich's analysis would predict that instrumentalism will fail to accomplish the goals of reformers because instrumentalism will permit agency determination of the public good under increasingly vague general standards. At best these will fail to guide agency decisions and which at worst will provide the justifications for political actions that may undercut the goals of the reform. These proposals also ignore the strong tension between an instrumentalist vision of agency behavior and the commitment to openness underlying public information provisions.

Democratic Process Ideal

Although federal information provisions rely on oversight, the alternative expression of the democratic process ideal—the practical difficulties confronting the users of public information laws, particularly the FOIA—reduce the ability of these provisions to provide information that permit citizens to challenge bureaucratic action politically. The FOIA provides several examples.

Users of the FOIA face delays that limit the usefulness of the FOIA. A number of studies have identified delay as a principal impediment to the proper functioning of the Act. Delay occurs at all stages in the process of seeking information, including response to the initial request and administrative and judicial review. Requesters can wait many months to receive an agency response and delays of years in completing the administrative and judicial process are not unknown. The time limits of the act have become largely irrelevant in the administration of the law, in part because the courts are unable to police these limits effectively. Courts are unwilling to act because delay will accompany judicial action particularly if an agency is processing requests in good faith. Therefore, cases appear in which requesters asked to be moved to the head of the agency queue.

Delay discourages many requesters. As important, delay makes information law less useful in providing a basis for political oversight of agency decisions. If requesters must wait months or even years for relevant information, administrative decisions and actions may have already been implemented before groups possess sufficient information to challenge them.

Delay results in part from a lack of resources. The allocation of resources, however, rests with the agencies and the administration of information laws can be seen as an irritant disconnected from more specific agency missions. Not uncommonly, FOIA officers serve part-time or are the newest attorneys in an agency counsel's office.

Delay can also reflect hostility toward requesters and toward the goals of the FOIA. For example, an examination of FOIA court decisions from 1980-1984 discovered dozens of opinions in which federal judges admonished federal officials for administration of the law. Studies of the Sunshine in Government Act and the Federal Advisory Committee Act also suggest agency noncompliance with the requirements of these laws. This hostility, in part, may represent the reaction of government officials to the anti-bureaucratic rhetoric of information provisions.

Requesters also lack sufficient knowledge to insure that provisions like the FOIA will provide the basis for political oversight of bureaucratic action. To be effective, information must be acquired when it is useful. Before requesters can seek documents, they must be aware of the existence of the records. Bureaucratic action could proceed to a point where resistance or reversal would be difficult before a potential requester would learn of the need to acquire information. Requesters lack knowledge of when to request information.

Requesters also lack knowledge of the character or description of the records that they seek. This lack of knowledge impedes requests and administrative appeals, as well as judicial review of administrative action. Requesters can often make only the most general requests and are unable to evaluate agency responses or to respond to agency arguments that documents are exempt. Although the courts have developed procedures to address the inability of requesters to address agency arguments, these procedures are not completely effective and do not apply to the administrative process. Requesters are left at a considerable disadvantage in the use of information provisions as a means to accomplish political oversight.

Many requesters are discouraged by the costs of requests. The costs of requests are more likely to screen individual requesters or requesters representing groups that lack substantial economic resources.

Congress addressed these concerns in the 1974 amendments by providing attorney fees for requesters and by permitting agencies to waive or reduce fees. In 1986 Congress modified the fee waiver provisions responding in part to restrictive interpretations of the 1974 provisions.

These congressional attempts, while useful, have not eliminated the difficulties for many requesters. The attorney fees provision does not apply to the administrative process and the grant of attorney fees is not automatic; in addition, determination of the amount of attorney fees can itself be the source of some controversy. Judicial interpretations of the 1986 changes in the fee waiver provisions do not represent a dramatic break from restrictive interpretations of the previous provisions.

The attorney fee and fee waiver provisions represent the first congressional attempts to distinguish between categories of requesters. The legislative history of the attorney fees provision distinguished public interest and media requesters from others and suggested that requesters with a commercial interest would rarely be entitled to attorney fees. The 1986 amendments to the fee waiver provision set out three categories of requesters regarding the cost of requests that could appropriately be charged against them. Once again, the most substantial charges were permitted against commercial requesters.

Although these provisions reflect many goals, they demonstrate some concern with "information equity." Commercial interests are more likely to have the resources and, in some instances, the relationship with agency personnel to acquire information. Less wealthy or well organized groups are disadvantaged. The attorney fees and fee waiver provisions help to redress the imbalance in resources.

Some recent proposals place more emphasis on distinguishing groups of requesters. For example, different categories of requesters could enjoy different procedures or perhaps different avenues for relief from denials. Experience with the fee waiver provisions suggests that this approach falters because of the difficulty of defining groups or types of requesters. For example, trade associations of large economic interests could create newsletters that might qualify as media requesters.

The debate regarding the rights of submitters of information, however, portends rules and procedures likely to impede "information equity." Much of the literature of this debate sees the principal conflict as between privacy and access, balancing the interests of submitters against the interests of those seeking the information.

This debate can also be viewed as an important one regarding "information equity," an equality of access necessary if all interests are able to use political oversight as a method of controlling bureaucratic behavior. Aside from issues of the personal privacy of individuals protected by a specific exemption, the interests of submitters are normally those of commercial interests who desire, for a variety of reasons, to protect information submitted to the government. Although requesters may themselves be large economic or commercial enterprises, many requesters are individuals or smaller, less well organized, interest groups. Particularly in areas regarding public health and safety, requesters are more likely to be individuals or representatives of more diverse groups. Therefore, the debate at one level addresses whether all groups affected by administrative action will possess the information resources necessary to seek political redress of that action.

The procedural and substantive rights granted to submitters reduce "information equity" and the effectiveness of political oversight for many interests. An executive order issued by President Reagan imposes procedural requirements that delay response to requesters and focus agency decisionmaking on the interests of submitters. Some statutory provisions, such as the Consumer Product Safety Act, elevate the interests of submitters above those of requesters.

Federal information laws, particularly the FOIA, rely on the alternative expression of the democratic process ideal. The practical difficulties confronting users of these laws have significantly reduced the effectiveness of them in permitting political oversight of bureaucratic action.

Conclusion

Although perceived as an isolated body of law, federal information provisions are firmly embedded in administrative theory. An application of Professor Sargentich's analytical model demonstrates that information provisions draw on all aspects of the three ideals for the administrative process. The reliance of information policy on each of these ideals ties information policy to administrative theory. Conflicts regarding information policy inescapably participate in major debates about theories of administrative legitimacy and decision-making.

An examination of the weaknesses of the core embodiments of two of the ideals illuminates issues in information policy in a new light and permits examination of them from a new perspective. For example, uncritical use of formalism to control administrative discretion can lead only to frustration and perhaps damage to information policy; attempts to alter the role of agencies in forming information policy by aligning information policy around instrumentalism ignore the weaknesses of instrumentalism and invite a failure easily predicted from the perspective of administrative theory. In addition, application of the alternative expression of the democratic process ideal—political oversight—provides an important basis for examining the effectiveness of information provisions.

Because the three ideals of administrative law of necessity conflict with one another, recognition of how information laws use these three ideals is crucial to the future. Recognition of the relationships between information policy and administrative theory prevents the repetition of common errors, illuminates choices previously hidden, reminds us of the limits of these approaches, and identifies the compromises and frustrations that cannot be avoided. Placement of information policy in the context of administrative theory promises significant advantages for information law and policy.

Additional Sources

Kathryn M. Braeman, *Overview of FOIA Administration in Government*, 34 Admin. L. Rev. 111 (1982)

Mary M. Cheh, *Judicial Supervision of Executive Secrecy: Rethinking Freedom of Expression for Government Employees and the Public Right of Access to Government Information*, 69 Cornell L. Rev. 690 (1984)

Michael A. Fitts, *Can Ignorance Be Bliss? Imperfect Information as a Positive Influence in Political Institutions*, 88 Mich. L. Rev. 917 (1990)

Margaret Gilhooley, *The Availability of Decisions and Precedents in Agency Adjudications: The Impact of the Freedom of Information Act Publication Requirements*, 3 Admin. L.J. Am. U. 53 (1989)

Mark H. Grunewald, *Freedom of Information Act Dispute Resolution*, 40 Admin. L. Rev. 1 (1988)

Thomas O. McGarity and Sidney A. Shapiro, *The Trade Secret Status of Health and Safety Testing Information: Reforming Agency Disclosure Policies*, 93 Harv. L. Rev. 837 (1980)

James T. O'Reilly, Federal Information Disclosure: Procedures, Forms and the Law (1990)

Leo T. Sorokin, *The Computerization of Government Information: Does It Circumvent Public Access Under the Freedom of Information Act and the Depository Library Program?*, 24 Colum. J.L. & Soc. Probs. 267 (1990)

Edward A. Tomlinson, *Use of the Freedom of Information Act for Discovery Purposes*, 43 Md. L. Rev. 119 (1984)

Robert G. Vaughn, *Administrative Alternatives and the Federal Freedom of Information Act*, 45 Ohio St. L.J. 185 (1984)

2. Debates About the Supervision of Agencies by Congress

a. The Legislative Veto of Administrative Action

In dozens of statutes over decades, Congress has asserted the power to adopt what came to be called "legislative vetoes," which are resolutions that purport to have a legally binding effect but are not adopted by means of the full legislative process.* An example of a legislative veto provision is one stating that if subsequent to the provision's passage a house of Congress adopts a resolution disapproving some administrative action, the disapproval resolution would nullify the action.

A key constitutional question was whether such a disapproval resolution should be seen as a separate article I event that needs to go through the full legislative process, or whether it could be seen as bound up in the original statutory provision that already did go through the legislative process. Over decades, the debate about the constitutionality of legislative veto resolutions raged. It came to a head in the *Chadha* litigation, which eventuated in 1983 in a broad ruling by the Supreme Court that legislative vetoes are unconstitutional.

The excerpts in this section illuminate the debate about legislative vetoes. In the first excerpt written before *Chadha*, Professors Bruff and Gellhorn contend that in policy terms legislative vetoes are flawed instruments of legislative oversight. Professors Bruff and Gellhorn argue that legislative vetoes tend to undermine the role of Congress as a whole and to maximize the power of special interests.

In the second excerpt, Professor Donald Elliott criticizes the Supreme Court's legal reasoning in *Chadha*. To Professor Elliott, a number of unsupported assumptions underlie the Court's formalistic analysis.

The final excerpt—by Judge Stephen Breyer—suggests that if Congress really wants an expedited process for reviewing administrative decisions, it could amend its rules to provide for fast-track legislation that would function in a manner similar to legislative vetoes. Judge Breyer calls his proposal a veto substitute in order to underscore that it would possess many of the attractive qualities for Congress of the legislative veto, even though it would formally comply with the constitutional requirements laid down in *Chadha*. In noting that the veto substitute would not perfectly replicate the legislative veto, Judge Breyer clarifies the ways in which *Chadha* has limited the manner in which Congress can redirect administrative behavior.

---

* The full legislative process involves (1) passage of a bill or resolution by majorities of both houses of Congress, and (2) presentment of the bill or resolution to the president for approval or veto; if the latter occurs, the item cannot become law unless it is repassed by two-thirds of both houses of Congress. *See* U.S. Constitution, Art. I, § 7, cls. 2 & 3.

Harold H. Bruff and Ernest Gellhorn, *Congressional Control of Administrative Regulation: A Study of Legislative Vetoes*, 90 HARV. L. REV. 1369, 1372-74, 1378-81, 1409-15, 1417-20, 1423-28, 1439 (1977)*

* * *

I. The Background: Constitutional, Statutory, and Policy Issues Surrounding the Legislative Veto of Rulemaking

* * *

A. *The Legislative Veto as a Substitute for the Delegation Doctrine*

Over the course of time, constitutional doctrine has developed to support administrative lawmaking. The courts have come to recognize that it is impractical for the legislature to make the innumerable policy decisions necessary to the daily operation of a large and complex government. Therefore, modern courts applying the delegation doctrine, which theoretically limits congressional grants of power to the agencies, have rejected ancient and rigid dicta that the lawmaking power vested in Congress may not be delegated elsewhere. Today the courts purport to require only that statutory delegations of congressional authority contain basic policy standards for the administrator to follow. This "standards" requirement is designed to preserve the separation of powers by placing broad policy determinations in the hands of the elected representatives rather than appointed bureaucrats and by facilitating judicial review. Yet even this minimal requirement has proved to be unworkable in practice. Almost without exception, the courts have refused to enforce constitutional constraints on congressional delegations of lawmaking authority to the agencies.
* * *

The legislative veto can be viewed as a mechanism to help fill the void left by the decline of the delegation doctrine. Its purpose is to limit agency rulemaking authority by lodging final control in Congress. But instead of controlling agency policy in advance by laying out a roadmap in the statute creating the agency, Congress now proposes to control policy * * * after the agency's expert staff and interested members of the public have had an opportunity to assist in its formation. In this way Congress can be fully informed before primary policy is decided. Still, the legislative veto is only a negative check on policies proposed by the agencies, not a means for making policy directly.

B. *Separation of Powers*

Legislative veto provisions raise a series of constitutional questions involving the separation of powers. Chief among these is whether legislative vetoes constitute an impermissible evasion of the President's veto authority or an impermissible intrusion into the powers vested in the executive or judicial branches of government (depending on whether the veto is meant for policy or legality review). Supporters of the legislative veto argue that since it is a control on administrative lawmaking similar to that which the delegation doctrine purports to impose, it is fully consistent with the separation of powers. They emphasize that the branches of government are not wholly separated but often have a limited role in one another's functions. For example, the President's veto gives him a role in legislation; the power of advice and consent gives the Senate a role in administration. If, then, the legislative veto device gives Congress an appropriately limited role in the executive function, it constitutes an appropriate counterweight to broad delegation. By returning policy making authority to Congress, it helps preserve the separation of powers. Opponents argue that legislative vetoes are functionally like legislation in that they foreclose otherwise permissible readings of statutes. To foreclose such interpretations similarly by legislation would require the approval of the President or the concurrence of two-thirds of both houses of Congress to override his veto. Thus legislative vetoes passed without presidential concurrence arguably abridge the President's role in the legislative process. Furthermore, for Congress to pass on the legality of administration rules may usurp the judicial function.

If a single house may veto regulations, the fundamental principle of bicameralism may be violated. The Constitution lodges legislative authority in a bicameral Congress, in part as an internal check against the aggrandizement of congressional power. Proposals allowing one house to veto administrative regulations appear to circumvent that check. * * *

* * *

D. *Policy Issues Surrounding Legislative Veto Provisions*

* * *

A question of central importance is whether the addition of congressional review to administration

---

* Copyright 1977 by the Harvard Law Review Association. Reprinted with permission of the Harvard Law Review Association, Harold H. Bruff, and Ernest Gellhorn. All rights reserved.

rulemaking will diminish the effectiveness of the other procedural checks which Congress and the courts have imposed on the rulemaking process. The problem is that the congressional review process may not be governed by rules as strict as those applicable to agency rulemaking. Present procedures might be replaced by a less visible or closed process of review by congressional committee members and staffs, as well as other interested Congressmen. And if interested groups can lobby Congress during the review period, their influence might render currently required public procedures for rulemaking ineffective. In any case a veto statute may reduce public participation before the agencies by shifting the focus of attention to congressional review procedures. This is not meant to suggest that Congress need adopt the same procedures it imposes upon the agencies, thereby producing a largely redundant review process. It does suggest, however, that the differences between the legislative and administrative process may make it difficult to reconcile congressional review with other aspects of rulemaking.

An overall appraisal of a legislative veto provision must examine whether it helps to assure the acceptability of agency regulations to Congress as a whole. If review authority is actually exercised by congressional committees, which are less broadly representative than the full membership of either house, the intent of Congress as a whole may not be realized. The same may be true if committee action is not visible to the other members, so that there is no attention and assent to what the committees do.

Another fundamental issue is whether the opportunity for subsequent review of agency regulations will lessen pressure in Congress for specificity in legislation delegating rulemaking power. A purpose of legislative vetoes is to allow Congress to postpone deciding policy questions until concrete resolution appears in the form of a proposed rule. Whether the effect of this approach is to increase or to decrease agency discretion will depend on the extent to which agency regulations receive actual review.

Delay is said to be a serious problem in rulemaking; Congress and the courts have often responded by imposing deadlines for promulgating rules. The legislative veto creates an additional source of delay because rules must lie before Congress for the statutory period whether or not there is serious consideration of a veto. It is difficult to estimate the costs of delay in promulgating rules that lie before Congress without awakening actual review. Such costs seem likely to vary in their visibility and their seriousness. And they would be without any corresponding benefit unless the very presence of review authority improves the drafting process by increasing agency attention to the acceptability of rules to Congress.

When review of a rule does occur, irreconcilable differences in policy between the agency and Congress may lead to long term impasses. As a result, the implementation of administrative programs may be considerably delayed or entirely thwarted. Thus, it is important to appraise whether active congressional review will tend to produce the speedy resolution of policy. This will depend on the time between rules submissions and vetoes, and on the willingness of agencies to modify vetoed rules in accordance with the will of Congress. Agencies may respond to the possibility of program interruption through legislative vetoes by using adjudication rather than rulemaking to form policy. If so, delay problems may be exacerbated by the increased use of slow adjudicative processes.

In addition to increasing delay in the administrative process, legislative veto authority may also increase Congress' already considerable workload. Much of the work of screening regulations for review must be done by hired staff, rather than committee members; consequently, already burdened staffs would have to be enlarged to implement a generally applicable veto. Furthermore, especially where proposed rules deal with complex and technical subjects, the review process itself may be difficult and time-consuming for the members of Congress. Hearings must be held and committee reports written. If a veto resolution is reported to the floor, there must be study, debate, and a vote. Whether a significant number of rules would reach this stage remains to be seen, but there is the potential for an alarming increase in the volume of Congress' business.

A final concern is that of the legislative veto's effect on judicial review. The failure of Congress to veto a rule might be construed as its ratification, and a court might feel bound to defer to Congress' implied judgment that the rule is not ultra vires or irrational. But congressional review may turn either on these legality considerations or on a rule's soundness as a matter of policy—and the nature of judicial review may depend on the nature of congressional review. Courts may be more reluctant to question the judgment of Congress where review is based on considerations of policy than where it is purportedly limited to questions of statutory intent, which are within the traditional province of the courts. Moreover, the extent of a court's scrutiny may depend on whether the rule received careful examination in Congress, at least by a committee, or was not reviewed at all. If the judiciary defers to agency rulemaking on a theory of implied ratification by Congress, there may result a net loosening of constraints on agency discretion whenever rules have received little direct examination in Congress. All of these legal questions would complicate the process of judicial review, and their resolution might entail close judicial scrutiny of the internal workings of Congress.

[There follows a discussion of five agency programs.]

* * *

III. An Appraisal of the Experience to Date

A. The Negotiation Process

Although the administration programs in the case histories were quite different, they had certain common characteristics. Each was in an area of considerable public concern, if not controversy. In all the programs except * * * [one], there was repeated major legislation during the period under study. Congress could have used such legislation to resolve issues that had emerged in rulemaking programs subject to legislative vetoes. Whether for reasons of indecision or deadlock, however, it ordinarily chose to leave these issues open in the revised statutes and to rely on the legislative veto mechanism to maintain control over agency policy initiatives. Therefore, the process of review was an active one, not one marked by congressional inattention to forthcoming rules.

Given such conditions, it is not surprising that the veto power gave rise to negotiation and compromise over the substance of rules between the agencies and the congressional oversight committees. Significant negotiations occurred in all five programs [examined in the unexcerpted article] despite their disparate natures, and it was often intense. Since the statutes generally created new programs requiring broad implementing of regulations, the initial focus of the negotiations was correspondingly broad. As the negotiations progressed, however, the issues in controversy were reduced to a small number for ultimate consideration by Congress. This narrowing process gave the committees and especially their staff substantial power to define the issues that would be likely to receive the attention of Congress as a whole.

Since the agencies demonstrated varying abilities to resist congressional demands for changes in the substance of rules, it cannot be said that the committee staffs dictated changes to the agencies. * * *

Still, the negotiation process between the committees and the agencies always resulted in some compromise, if not agreement. One reason for compromise may have been doubts concerning the constitutionality of veto provisions, which deterred Congress from issuing ultimatums to the agencies. The major determinant of the substantive effect of the veto provisions, however, seems to have been the amount of bargaining power the particular agency had with Congress. The fact that the strength of federal agencies vis-à-vis Congress varies suggests that a general veto provision might have a greater substantive impact on some agencies than on others and that this impact might depend partly on factors extrinsic to the veto process. * * *

* * *

B. Public Participation and Interest Group Influence

A vital aspect of rulemaking is the opportunity for participation by all interested parties through notice-and-comment proceedings. The presence of a legislative veto could reduce public participation before the agencies by shifting the focus of attention to congressional review. But in the case studies, public participation before the agencies continued unabated. Two reasons for this are apparent. First, the initial formulation of rules by the agency remains a critical stage in determining their substance. Public pressure at this stage may prove dispositive if the resulting rule does not awaken congressional interest. Second, even if Congress does stir, a record of considerable public interest and comment can buttress the agency in its negotiations with congressional committees, counterbalancing competing lobbying pressures. This suggests, however, that public participation before the agencies in programs subject to veto might eventually shift its emphasis from reasoned debate over policy to a showing of political strength meant to impress both the agency and Congress.

Although public comment remained a vital and effective part of the rulemaking process in the case studies, there were indications that the veto machinery may have created opportunities for circumvention of public participation. In certain subtle ways, the presence of congressional review allowed the influence of special interest groups in Congress to affect the substance of rules outside the comment process. When an agency knew of the influence and was aware of the desires of the interest groups, it sometimes attempted to avoid unfavorable review by drafting its rule to satisfy those desires. * * * Even when the agency did not try to anticipate influence in the hope of less stringent review, the influence, if real, could make itself felt in negotiations with the oversight committee. * * *

Both of the practices observed in these studies—agency speculation on the effects of pressure on Congress and the application of actual pressure on Congress during negotiations with the agency—contravene the purposes of public comment. The essence of a notice-and-comment proceeding is a public forum in which all interested parties participate openly and on equal footing. Yet an agency's internal drafting decisions and its negotiations with congressional committees are of low visibility, so that both the existence and the effort of special influence are likely to be off the record. The resultant secrecy violates two of the fundamental standards for informal rulemaking: reasoned decisionmaking based on a record and the opportunity for public participants to contest opposing presentations. Moreover, when an agency seeks support for one of its rules from an interest group, that group may later demand a quid pro quo, such as abandonment of another proposed rulemaking. Not only would such a tradeoff violate the canons of open rulemaking, but it also might escape congressional scrutiny.

In addition to destroying the openness of rulemaking, the practices observed here violate the ideal of equal access to the rulemaking process. Not all interested parties have the resources both to participate in the public comment proceedings and to lobby the committees effectively in the review process. Those groups having greater resources or prior influence with congressional committees have an additional chance to affect agency action not available to those without such resources or influence. To the extent that the negotiation phase of rulemaking subject to legislative veto authority is determinative, this additional chance constitutes an important special advantage for the few. Indeed, the dynamics of the review process may make a negotiated rule substantially harder to change through subsequent public comment. Once time and energy have been spent in negotiations between an agency and Congress, both the agency and the committee may be reluctant to revise the rules that have been thrashed out.

C. Time Constraints and Delay

Because the legislative veto involves the review of ongoing agency programs rather than the promulgation of legislation, the implementing statutes have required that review take place, if at all, within a limited period of time. While in the case studies an agency's promulgation of rules was ordinarily a slow process, including both comprehensive public comment proceedings and extended internal deliberations, consideration at the review stage was necessarily abbreviated. Congress had at most several months to review rules that may have taken the agency years to promulgate. The resulting time pressures on Congress significantly affected the quality and the thoroughness of congressional review.

* * *

Aside from time constraints, another significant restriction on the thoroughness of review was the heavy workload of members and staff of Congress. At times, work on legislation pending before the committees entirely precluded review of potentially controversial rules. More often, the work of the review process, much of which fell to the congressional staff, placed a severe burden on Congress' resources. The negotiations observed in our case studies between the staffs of the committees and the agencies imposed a greater burden on the congressional staff than much legislation. Moreover, there is some evidence that even with the present sporadic application of veto authority, an increase in staff alone would not have allowed the limited number of Congressmen to discharge their review functions effectively.

* * *

D. Political Accountability

A primary purpose of the legislative veto is to increase the political accountability of administrative regulation. In theory, the veto power insures that agency rulemaking is consistent with the intent of Congress. Experience under existing vetoes, however, reveals that political accountability is likely to be attenuated in practice. Although the veto power is meant to be exercised by one or both of the houses of Congress, floor votes of an entire house on the merits of a veto resolution were rather infrequent. Most of the effective review occurred at the committee or subcommittee level, often focusing on the concerns of a single chairman or member. Indeed, much settlement of policy occurred in behind-the-scenes negotiations between the staffs of the committees and the agencies. There were even signs that committees engaging in relatively intense negotiations with an agency tended to keep matters within the committee in order to preserve their negotiating stance, although the issues might merit floor review. Under these circumstances, the power of review was really exercised by congressional committee and their staffs, rather than by either house as a whole. By reducing the number of issues reaching Congress as a whole through negotiations, the committees and their staff could thus settle policy issues in a way in which the house as a whole might not, were it asked to decide.

Despite recent attempts in Congress to broaden the perspective and makeup of its committees, they inevitably are bodies of relatively narrow composition compared to Congress as a whole. Each member of a committee is responsible only to his or her own constituency, and the total constituency of any one committee is far from national in its scope. Moreover, the "stacking" of oversight committees with members favorable to an agency or group it regulates is not unknown: this practice can forge agency-committee alliances which reinforce the capture of agencies by the interest groups they purport to regulate. Whenever it does not report a veto resolution to the floor of a house, the committee, with its narrow constituency, wields all of Congress' review power. In such a case, the ideal of *The Federalist*—national responsibility to a national constituency—is not achieved. Furthermore, if committee negotiations receive no national publicity, as has so far been the case, those few members exercising the power of Congress may not be called to account even by their own constituencies.

This committee-based review may result in the effective amendment of statutes, whether or not those involved realize it. For a process of negotiation, once initiated, is likely to take on a life of its own. Thus, in the case studies a committee and an agency seemed sometimes to find themselves drifting over time to a position having no necessary relationship to the original statutory intent.

Although the ripening of informal negotiations into committee hearings might have been expected to increase the political accountability of the review process, in fact its effects were not striking. Hearings provided some visibility for the issues discussed, but they were not always effective in awakening the attention of members of Congress outside the oversight committee. As reactive rather than creative measures, veto resolutions both deserved and received less attention than legislation. Moreover, when a change wrought by a committee at the instance of an interest group had only a diffuse impact on the public at large, the classical logic of lobby dictated that the change would evoke little outcry.

One other factor affected the political accountability of the veto process. In all the cases studied except [one] * * *, Congressmen characterized their role as limited to reviewing the legality of the agency's rule, that is, its conformity with statutory purpose. Nevertheless, in all cases congressional review was primarily based on policy. The reason is not hard to divine: the traditional and constitutional role of Congress is the formulation and alteration of policy. Moreover, a major reason for imposition of veto authority has been the indecision of Congress on policy issues and a desire to check the agency's later resolution of them. Members of Congress are unaccustomed, and the institution is ill-equipped, to make a restrained and judicious examination of a rule's subservience to statutory purpose. Yet Congress' profession, despite these institutional realities, to review rules only for conformity with statutory intent has serious implications for the political accountability of the veto process. Review on the putative basis of legality implies that Congress is forming no new policy but is merely making sure that the conditions of the original delegation are met. The result is that veto resolutions receive less public visibility and less attention from members of Congress outside the oversight committees than, as policy decisions, they deserve.

* * *

E. The Relationship of the Agencies and Congress in the Absence of Veto Provisions

Most of the characteristics of the legislative veto process found in the case studies do not typify the current relationship between Congress and the agencies in the absence of veto authority. The principal difference is the negotiating process between congressional committee staffs and agencies, which seldom occurs in the absence of a veto provision. Indeed, the chief effect of the veto power seems to be an increase in the power of congressional committees and in the practice of negotiating over the substance of rules. It is difficult to be precise here, because many of the differences are matters of degree and the phenomena under discussion are of low visibility. Consequently much existing information is anecdotal. Nevertheless, the case studies confirm that the legislative veto power significantly alters the working relationship between Congress and the agencies.

* * *

Without the veto, a committee displeased with an agency rule has two major options. It may stage an embarrassing oversight hearing, or it may propose legislation to rectify the problem it perceives. But any legislation it proposes must obtain passage in both houses of Congress and approval by the President or a veto override. Until the proposed legislation is adopted, a controversial agency rule, if issued, remains in effect. If a committee chooses to hold a hearing, the agency may resist, testing the committee's power to obtain legislation. With the legislative veto, committee power is greatly enhanced. If a veto resolution is reported out of committee, it may need to pass in only one house * * *. Congressmen may be persuaded to support a committee recommendation for a veto as a low-cost endorsement of the oversight power of Congress without fully considering the cost to the interrupted program. Since the veto provides an easier method for altering policy, it reduces the incentive of the oversight committee to sponsor legislation. Because the veto is negative, and because it reduces pressure on committees to report legislation affirmatively resolving policy disputes with agencies, it increases substantially the chance that no policy will be formed by Congress or by the agency.

IV. The Desirability of a General Legislative Veto for Rulemaking

* * * Given the vast amount of rulemaking activity in the federal government, it seems clear that Congress has neither the time nor the inclination to extend active review under a general veto power to more than a few highly controversial rules. Even a substantial increase in congressional staff to canvass forthcoming agency rules would not necessarily lead to frequent review by Congressmen, because their number is fixed and their time is limited. Meaningful review, whether by Congressmen or their staff, seems likely to be episodic * * *.

Reflection suggests, however, that a view which minimizes the practical impact of a general veto provision is oversimplified. It does not adequately account for the nature of rulemaking and the nature of the agencies' present relations with other branches of government. Under a general legislative veto provision, agencies may be inclined to abandon rulemaking in favor of other procedures less vulnerable to congressional scrutiny for the development of policy. Moreover, if in practice Congress does not exercise the veto power assiduously, the broader delegations of authority which it fosters may result, contrary to expectations, in a net decrease in control over agency discretion. Partial duplication of the judicial function by Congress may create profound problems for the courts in their review of both congressional action and agency rules. Finally, in its use of the veto power Congress may in practice venture beyond mere supervision to improper interference in the administrative function.

A. *Effects on Agency Behavior*
* * *

The case studies suggest that a general veto provision will increase the power of interest groups to block or detect agency policy initiatives through pressure on congressional committees. * * * A committee not having the time or inclination to negotiate a given set of rules could simply report a veto resolution, which, if passed by the entire house, could lead to the kind of indefinite policy impasse found repeatedly in the case studies. Alternatively, it could attempt to deter agency submission of a rule altogether. Whenever an agency is not statutorily restricted to policymaking by rule, the threat of such pressure is likely to drive it toward greater use of adjudication. Unlike the agencies involved in the case studies, many federal agencies are free to choose adjudication. Thus, by increasing agency reliance on adjudication, a general legislative veto provision might have pervasive effects on the nature of policymaking in federal agencies.

To the extent that general veto power would increase reliance on adjudication at the expense of rulemaking, it would have the reverse of the effect intended, for it would encourage the agencies to act in ways that are even less amenable to congressional oversight than rulemaking is now. Other disadvantages of excessive adjudication would also be increased, principally delay in forming overall policy. Congress could attempt to avoid excessive resort to adjudication by requiring the agencies to engage in rulemaking for the formulation of policy. But both Congress and the courts have traditionally recognized broad discretion in the agencies to proceed by adjudication or rulemaking as their judgment dictates. Any requirement to proceed exclusively by rulemaking could sensibly be imposed only after careful study of each program involved and might be overly rigid even then.

* * *

B. *Effects on Congressional Delegations of Rulemaking Authority*
* * *

* * * [I]n practice the legislative veto may fail to define more exactly the limits of agency discretion. Existing veto provisions, particularly those in the energy statutes, often accompany broader grants of power than Congress would have made without having the veto power as a check upon their exercise. And Congress has foregone subsequent opportunities for legislative resolution of issues emerging in rulemaking programs subject to veto, preferring instead to react to the agency's policy initiatives. These facts, coupled with Congress' frequent difficulty in resolving policy by statute, indicate that a general veto provision might encourage Congress to make broader delegations than it would otherwise. If this occurs, the veto will produce a net increase in congressional control of the agencies only to the extent that there actually is close review pursuant to it. Yet under a veto statute broadly applicable to rulemaking, limits on time and resources would make it impossible for Congress to exercise continuing, close review, even with a massive increase in staff. It therefore seems likely that only a few rules would receive the careful scrutiny necessary to fulfill the assumptions underlying broad original grants of power.

Thus, this proposed technique for increasing congressional controls in delegated powers may actually result in *decreasing* those controls in practice. * * *

* * *

Since the disadvantages of the legislative veto inhere in its very nature, no combination of ameliorating techniques can eliminate them all. Congress should abandon it as a device for the oversight of agency rulemaking. There are other means by which Congress can exercise its oversight responsibility effectively without exceeding the proper bounds of its authority. * * *

* * *

E. Donald Elliott, INS v. Chadha: *The Administrative Constitution, the Constitution, and the Legislative Veto*, 1983 SUP. CT. REV. 125, 126-28, 131-47, 163-64, 166-68*

* * *

In th[e] area [of separation of powers], the Court has sought to maintain a balance between generalizations and practical accommodations. Thus, Chief Justice Burger's formalistic opinion for the Court in *Immigration and Naturalization Service v. Chadha* came as a shock. In *Chadha*, the Court held unconstitutional the legislative veto in § 244(c)(2) of the Immigration and Nationality Act, which authorized either House of Congress to disapprove by resolution the Attorney General's decision to suspend deportation of an alien. For years, distinguished legal scholars as well as officials of the Department of Justice have questioned the constitutionality of the legislative veto, arguing that it infringes on the President's veto power, and in the case of the one-house veto, that it violates the principle of bicameralism as well. What was astonishing about *Chadha* was not the result, but the scope and inflexibility of the Court's opinion.

Justice White, who alone dissented from the merits of the Court's separation of powers analysis, proclaimed *Chadha* to be of "surpassing importance" because it "sounds the death knell for nearly 200 other statutory provisions in which Congress has reserved a 'legislative veto'. . . . Today's decision strikes down in one fell swoop provisions in more laws enacted by Congress than the Court has cumulatively invalidated in its history." Justice Powell, concurring in the judgment on the "narrower ground" that the legislative veto in this particular case infringed on judicial power, seconded Justice White's assessment: "The Court's decision . . . apparently will invalidate every use of the legislative veto."

Dissenting opinions are a notoriously inaccurate source of insight into the implications of Supreme Court decisions, but in this instance, the predictions were quickly confirmed. Only days after *Chadha*, the Court affirmed summarily two decisions declaring legislative vetoes unconstitutional in circumstances arguably distinguishable from *Chadha*. * * *

Something even more fundamental than the ruling on the legislative veto was at issue in *Chadha*. According to the Court, the case turned on the plain wording of "[e]xplicit and unambiguous provisions of the Constitution [which] prescribe and define the respective functions of the Congress and of the Executive in the legislative process." Justice White denounced the majority's approach, however, as "reflect[ing] a profoundly different conception of the Constitution than that held by the Courts which sanctioned the modern administrative state." To the majority, on the other hand, Justice White seemed to be offering a mere "utilitarian argument" that the legislative veto is a "useful 'political invention'," an argument which the Court dismissed as raising policy considerations not rising to the level of constitutional significance. Thus, the difference between Justice White and the majority goes deeper than disagreement over the legislative veto. It goes to the very nature of the Constitution and to how judges are to go about relating it to the rapidly evolving structure of the "modern administrative state."

I

* * *

B. The Court's Reasoning

The Supreme Court's analysis of the legislative veto in *Chadha* turns on relatively narrow constitutional issues. The Constitution contains three "[e]xplicit and unambiguous provisions" governing lawmaking by Congress. Before a bill becomes a law, it must be "presented" to give the President an opportunity to exercise his veto. This presentment re-

---

* Copyright 1984 by The University of Chicago. Reprinted with permission of The Supreme Court Review, The University of Chicago Press, and E. Donald Elliott. All rights reserved.

quirement applies not only to "Bills," but also to "[e]very Order, Resolution, or Vote to which the Concurrence of the Senate and House of Representatives may be necessary." In addition, the Constitution vests the legislative power of the United States in a bicameral legislature composed of a Senate and a House of Representatives. Before a bill becomes a law, it must be passed by both houses of Congress. The central question presented in *Chadha* was whether the procedural requirements for passing laws—presentment and bicameral action— also apply to the legislative veto.

Chief Justice Burger's opinion for the Court in *Chadha*, which was joined by five other Justices, gives three reasons for concluding that the legislative veto is legislative action of the kind to which the Constitution's presentment and bicameralism requirements apply. None of the three is ultimately persuasive.

1. *Presumption*. The Court begins with the proposition that the Constitution divides the powers of the federal government into "three defined categories, legislative, executive and judicial." While conceding that they are not "'hermetically' sealed from one another," the Court contends that the powers of each branch are "functionally identifiable" and that "[w]hen any Branch acts, it is presumptively exercising the power the Constitution has delegated to it. * * *"

The Court's reasoning is unpersuasive for several reasons. In the first place, the Court is mistaken when it asserts that the framers "defined" the categories legislative, executive, and judicial in the Constitution. Not only is the Court incorrect—the Constitution does not define these terms—but the slip is revealing. The Court's conceptualistic approach to analyzing the issues conflicts with the more pragmatic approach which the framers actually espoused. In Federalist No. 37, for instance, Madison warns that any attempt to define the categories legislative, executive, and judicial in abstract, theoretical terms is bound to fail.[41] The most that can be said is that the Constitution uses the terms "legislative," "executive," and "judicial," but that rather than attempt to define these concepts in the abstract, the framers

left to subsequent history the working out of the relationships among them.

* * *

Even on its own terms, however, the Court's presumption sweeps in too much and proves too little. Conceding that the legislative veto is an exercise of Article I legislative power (as opposed to executive or judicial powers) does not resolve, but only poses the question before the Court. The Constitution does not require presentment to the President of all congressional actions within Article I legislative power. On the contrary, the text restricts presentment to "Bills" and to "Every Order, Resolution or Vote to which the Concurrence of the Senate and House of Representatives may be necessary. . . ." The most that can be said about the drafting history is that the Constitutional Convention wanted the presentment requirement to apply to bills and to functional equivalents of bills. Not every exercise of Article I legislative power comes within these categories, as the Court concedes. Congress has developed extensive powers to oversee the Executive's administration of the laws, for example, as an exercise of Article I legislative powers, but no one would suggest that these forms of legislative oversight by congressional committees require presentment to the President for his veto.

The question to be decided in *Chadha* was not whether the legislative veto is an exercise of Article I legislative power, but whether it is an exercise of Article I legislative power of the kind that requires presentment and bicameral action. The Court's presumption that the legislative veto is an exercise of Article I legislative power should only frame, rather than decide, the issue.

2. *Altering legal rights*. The Court does not rely on presumption alone. It goes on to argue that the House resolution vetoing the suspension of Chadha's deportation was "essentially legislative in purpose and effect." The Court's formalistic approach to the issues is disappointing, but given its source, not surprising. The Court bases its analysis on a nineteenth-century congressional report which construed the Presentment Clause as applicable to any matter which is "legislative in its character and effect." The core of the Court's reasoning is conceptual and formalistic: the legislative veto is "legislative" because it has the effect of "altering legal rights."

The legislative veto "alters legal rights," however, only because the Court chooses to characterize its effect that way. The Court's manipulation of legal categories could just as easily be turned to support

---

[41] "Experience has instructed us that no skill in the science of government has yet been able to discriminate and define with sufficient certainty its three great provinces—the legislative, executive and judiciary; or even the privileges and provinces of the different legislative branches. Questions daily occur in the course of practice, which prove the obscurity which reigns in these subjects, and which puzzle the greatest adepts in political science." *Federalist* No. 37 (Madison), *in* THE FEDERALIST PAPERS (Fairfield ed., 1961).

the opposite conclusion that the legislative veto does not alter legal rights.

The Court maintains that the legislative "purpose and effect" of the legislative veto is clear because:

> The House took action that had the purpose and effect of altering the legal rights, duties and relations of persons, including the Attorney General, Executive Branch officials and Chadha, all outside the legislative branch. . . . The one-House veto operated in this case to overrule the Attorney General and mandate Chadha's deportation; absent the House action, Chadha would remain in the United States.

The first thing to notice about the quoted passage is that the first and the last sentences are not equivalent. There is no question that "absent House action, Chadha would remain in the United States." But does that really prove that the House resolution had "the effect of altering . . . legal rights"? Not at all, any more than when a prosecutor drops charges for possession of marijuana the defendant thereby acquires the "legal right" to smoke the substance. Admittedly, prior to the House resolution Chadha was in the country legally as a result of the Attorney General's decision to suspend deportation as a matter of grace. But that does not necessarily support the conclusion that Chadha had a legal right to remain that could only be altered by statute.

Even if it could be said that Chadha had acquired "legal rights," how were those rights "altered" by the House resolution? After all, the statute authorizing the Attorney General to suspend deportation on grounds of hardship also provided that either house of Congress could veto the Attorney General's action. Why was the nature of Chadha's legal rights not defined by the statute creating them? If Chadha's only right was what the statute gave him—the right to remain in the country unless one house exercised its legislative veto—then the House's action did not alter Chadha's rights: the possibility of a legislative veto was built into them in the first place.

These questions imply, not that the Court's analysis is incorrect, but that it is arbitrary. The legislative veto "alters legal rights" only because the Court superimposes that conceptualization on the House resolution canceling the suspension of deportation. It would be equally plausible (and equally arbitrary) to manipulate the Court's abstract legal categories to say that the legislative veto did not alter legal rights.

Justice White makes precisely that argument in dissent when he describes the legislative veto as authority that Congress had "reserved" in the statute. He goes on to argue from this premise that the legislative veto does not work a "change in the legal status quo," and hence that the Constitution's procedural requirements for passing statutes do not apply to the legislative veto. * * *

* * *

The Court's opinion in *Chadha* does not turn solely on the Court's construction of Chadha's rights, however. The opinion can also be read to hold that the legislative veto is unconstitutional if it alters legal rights of any persons "including the Attorney General, Executive Branch officials *and* Chadha, all outside the legislative branch." The Court's reasoning is no less arbitrary and formalistic in discussing the "rights" of the Executive branch. The Court declares:

> Disagreement with the Attorney General's decision on Chadha's deportation . . . no less than Congress' original choice to delegate to the Attorney General the authority to make that decision, involves determination of policy that Congress can implement only one way; bicameral passage followed by presentment to the President. Congress must abide by its delegation of authority until that delegation is legislatively altered or revoked.

The first sentence merely restates the Court's conclusion in different words. The question was whether Congress could affect policy through the legislative veto without passing a statute. It is no answer to say that the legislative veto affects policy, and therefore a statute is required.

As for the second proposition—that Congress must "abide" its delegation of authority to the Attorney General—one can only ask "Why?" Again, the question is whether the legislative veto is a permissible technique for controlling exercises of delegated authority. Not a word of the Court's opinion is spent explaining why it would be contrary to the framers' principles of constitutional design or otherwise legally suspect for Congress to retain supervision over exercises of power that it has delegated.

The absence of any other explanation suggests that the Court regards its conclusion as implicit in the very concept of delegation: once power has been delegated, it is beyond recall. But there is nothing inherently implausible about some powers being delegated while others are retained.

There may be sound reasons of constitutional significance to prohibit Congress from making partial delegations of power to the Executive, but the Court does not reach that level of analysis. Instead, the opinion rests on two legal fictions, "altering legal rights'' and "delegation." The Court treats these abstractions as if they had independent and immutable existences, rather than recognizing them as constructs that serve purposes which should define their reach and measure. This approach to deciding cases by manipulating formal legal concepts is a throwback to what Llewellyn called the Formal Style of conceptualistic judicial reasoning prevalent late in the nineteenth century.

3. *Expressio unius est exclusio alterius*. Decision by presumption and legal fiction would be bad enough, but the Court makes a third argument even weaker and more palpably unreasonable than the first two: "Finally, we see that when the Framers intended to authorize either House of Congress to act alone and outside of its prescribed bicameral legislative role, they narrowly and precisely defined the procedure for such action."

The Court proceeds to list "four provisions in the Constitution, explicit and unambiguous, by which one House may act alone with the unreviewable force of law, not subject to the President's veto,"[69] and to concede in a footnote that in 1798 the Supreme Court created a fifth exception by holding that proposed constitutional amendments are not subject to the President's veto.[70] From the existence of these exceptions, the Court concludes: "Clearly, when the Draftsmen sought to confer special powers on one House, independent of the other House, or of the President, they did so in explicit, unambiguous terms."

Here the Court is engaged in another example of the style of reasoning based on mechanical legal "rules" fashionable in the late nineteenth century. The principle of construction which the Court invokes was once in common use for construing contracts and deeds to land under the maxim *expressio unius est exclusio alterius*.[72] While the maxim is occasionally still cited in cases today to buttress interpretations of contracts and certain types of statutes, it is quite a different matter juristically to rely on *expressio unius* to interpret the Constitution. The Constitution is not a mere private contract. The Constitution was intended to set in motion a process of government that would adapt to changing conditions over generations, and consequently linguistic aids to ascertaining the intent of "the Draftsmen" should carry relatively little weight in interpreting the Constitution.

Moreover, even in its native sphere of private law, *expressio unius* is subject to significant qualifications, one of which should preclude using it here. *Expressio unius* is actually a principle of evidence, not substantive law: If a writing lists some members of a class specifically, a permissive inference may be drawn that other members of the same class were meant to be excluded or else it would have been natural to list them also. The inference is only a weak one, however, and it is negated entirely if other circumstances show that the list of specifics was not intended to be exhaustive. In particular, if there is general language in addition to the enumeration of specifics, the inference suggested by *expressio unius* does not apply since the inclusion of the general language contradicts the premise that the drafters intended to include everything in the enumeration.

The Court's use of *expressio unius* in *Chadha* ignores this well-established limitation on the principle. Clearly the Constitution does not purport to specify all the ways in which Congress may exercise power, and hence the inference suggested by *expressio unius* is not applicable. Perhaps the strongest reason to conclude that the framers did not intend to include everything in the enumeration of specifics is the fact that, in John Marshall's phrase, "it is a *Constitution* we are expounding."[77] If the government established by the Constitution is to sustain itself, Congress, like the other branches, must be able to exercise not only those powers that are mentioned specifically in the text of the Constitution but also those that may be fairly implied from the overall structure that the Constitution establishes.

In the past, the Court has frequently recognized that the wording of the Constitution does not purport to enumerate Congress's powers exhaustively. Thus, even though neither power is mentioned specifically in the text of the Constitution, it has been held that Congress may approve amendments to the Constitution without presenting them to the President for veto, and that Congress may investigate and engage in other oversight activities without bicameral action or presentment. Admittedly, neither of these recognized exceptions to the requirements of presentment and bicameral action is directly analogous to the leg-

---

[69] * * * The exceptions are: the House's power to initiate impeachments, Art. I, sec. 2, cl. 6; the Senate's power to try impeachments, Art. I, sec. 3, cl. 5; the Senate's power to approve Presidential appointments, Art. II, sec. 2, cl. 2; and the Senate's power to ratify treaties, Art. II, sec. 2, cl. 2.

[70] Immigration and Naturalization Service v. Chadha, 103 S. Ct. 2764, 2786 n.20 (1983), citing Hollingsworth v. Virginia, 3 Dall. 378 (1798).

[72] ("The expression of one thing is the exclusion of the other.") * * *

[77] McCulloch v. Maryland, 4 Wheat. at 407 (1819).

islative veto, but they do illustrate that there is a category of congressional powers not mentioned in the text in addition to the power to pass statutes. Hence it is clear that the text does not enumerate Congress's powers exhaustively, and that the Court's reliance on *expressio unius* is invalid.

The doctrine that powers may be implied as well as enumerated is so fundamental that it is probably inherent in the nature of any constitution, but in the case of our Constitution the doctrine of implied powers is also codified in the Necessary and Proper Clause.[79] * * *

* * *

* * * It could be argued that the Necessary and Proper Clause is irrelevant because it only relates to the subjects on which Congress may "make laws," but it does not affect the procedures for making them. But this argument is also wide of the mark. Congress did "make laws" in accordance with the constitutional requirements of bicameral action and presentment when it passed the statutes creating legislative vetoes. As long as Congress's claim to a legislative veto is grounded on a statute, duly passed following constitutional procedures, the proper question is whether such a statute is within the range of subjects on which Congress is empowered to legislate. Any confusion on this point arises from the Court's insistence on framing the issue as whether "the Framers intended to authorize either House of Congress to act" without following proper procedures for legislating, when in fact Congress has legislated in accordance with constitutional procedures when it passed the legislative veto statutes. The proper question should be whether legislative veto statutes are within the range of subjects on which the Constitution authorizes Congress to legislate. The Necessary and Proper Clause is surely germane to that inquiry.

* * *

This is not to say, of course, that the legislative veto is constitutional. Prohibitions elsewhere in the Constitution might preclude the legislative veto even though Congress has general authority to legislate to control delegated lawmaking by the Executive. But the Court never reaches that level of analysis, nor does it identify either the source or the nature of such prohibitions. Rather, the thrust of the Court's *expressio unius* analysis is that Congress lacks power to create legislative vetoes because the legislative veto is not mentioned anywhere in the Constitution.

---

[79] Art. I, sec. 8, cl. 18.

That argument is clearly invalid. At least since *McCulloch v. Maryland*, it has been clear that powers are not necessarily denied to Congress merely because they are not enumerated specifically in the text.

It is hard to imagine why the Court deviates from a principle of our constitutional law as fundamental as the doctrine of implied powers in analyzing the legislative veto, but perhaps the explanation lies in the term "legislative veto" itself. The name associated with a legal device can carry subtle but powerful implications for the ways that we think about it. The text of the Constitution gives a veto over legislation to the President explicitly, but it makes no mention of any similar "veto" for the Congress. By calling the device at issue in *Chadha* a "legislative veto," we may unconsciously consign it to constitutionally suspect territory. The word itself creates a vague, unreasoning sense that if the framers had intended Congress to have a veto, they would have said so, just as they did for the President.

But the analogy buried inside the term legislative "veto" is an imperfect one. Unlike the President's veto, most legislative "vetoes" do not create a check on a power that the Constitution confides in another branch; instead, the legislative "veto" usually checks only powers of delegated lawmaking that are themselves conferred by statute. * * * Imagine that from the beginning the legal device at issue in *Chadha* had been called "the conditional delegation" rather than the legislative veto. Its constitutional pedigree might well be beyond question by now.

C. The Court's Dubious Jurisprudential Premises

The legislative veto may well be unconstitutional. Many thoughtful people have concluded that it is, at least in some circumstances. But if the legislative veto is unconstitutional, it is not unconstitutional for the reasons stated in *Chadha*. Whatever one's view about the merits, the *Chadha* opinion is a disappointment.

* * *

The underlying source of the problems is jurisprudential. The Court insists that the texts of the presentment clauses and the vesting of legislative power in a bicameral Congress dispose of the legislative veto *ex proprio vigore*. But constitutional texts do not apply themselves. Justice White is surely right that the Constitution is silent on the "precise question" of the legislative veto and neither "directly authorize[s]" nor "prohibit[s]" it. In order to treat the texts as dispositive, the Court must tacitly assume the postulate which should be under examination: whether the legislative veto is congressional action of the sort to which the requirements of bicameralism and presentment should apply. To answer this question necessarily requires a perspective from outside the system: "Syllogism" alone is incapable of resolving such questions.

The Court's literal approach does not really exclude policy judgments about the legislative veto, as its adherents claim; it only drives them underground, where it is more difficult to scrutinize and criticize them. It would be better if the Court were open and aboveboard about its conclusions concerning the pernicious effects of the legislative veto * * *.

The second reason that the Court's approach in *Chadha* is unsatisfactory grows out of the first. The Court's linguistic arguments and analytical approach depend on dividing government power into three stark categories—legislative, executive, and judicial—and are troublesome because they are unpersuasive on their own terms. But the Court's approach is also troubling because it excludes other considerations that should be relevant. It is as if the Court were determined to avoid acknowledging what the case is really about. Representative Levitas has charged:

> The framers of our Constitution would be most surprised to find that regulations that have the force and effect of law are today put into effect by unelected officials in the executive branch and in independent agencies rather than by the Congress. Those "laws" are not passed by either the House and Senate, nor are they signed by the President. As this practice developed over the years, Congress attempted to redress the balance with the legislative veto. The Court's opinion . . . failed to mention that it was a response to this evolving system.

Levitas has a valid point, although he overstates it. The Court does mention "lawmaking" by administrative agencies, but only in a footnote and only in the distorted context of answering a rhetorical question from one of the briefs: "Why is the Attorney General exempt from submitting his proposed changes in the law to the full bicameral process?" The answer, the Court responds in a footnote that would do Lewis Carroll proud, is that while administrative rulemaking may "resemble" lawmaking,[99] and while by statute agency rules do "prescribe law," agency rulemaking is not really "legislative" but only "quasi-legislative" "Executive action."

Besides, the Court adds, the bicameral process is "not necessary" in the case of rulemaking by agencies because the courts are available to insure that "the will of Congress has been obeyed."

The Court makes short work of the argument by assigning administrative rulemaking to a different pigeonhole. But the exercise in semantics misses the point. The growth of the bureaucracy in the Executive branch and in agencies independent of presidential control is not of constitutional significance because it raises a nice point of classification that can be laid to rest once the Court decides whether the legal category "executive" or "legislative" is more appropriate. Concern exists because of the reality that most of the federal law affecting most of the people most of the time is not made through the bicameral legislative process that the Court's opinion enshrines, but by administrative decisionmakers, who are not elected and who are not, by and large, subject to either effective presidential or judicial control.

The growth of lawmaking power in a vast administrative bureaucracy may be seen as a threat to the essence of the constitutional principle of separation of powers. Madison (not Hamilton, as the Court mistakenly states) summarized that fundamental constitutional principle in Federalist No. 51 as "contriving the interior structure of the government as that its several constituent parts may, by their mutual relations, be the means of keeping each other in their proper places." The "constant aim" of this strategy, Madison continues, "is to divide and arrange the several offices in such a manner as that each may be a check on the other." It is ironic that the Court in *Chadha*, in the name of the constitutional principles of checks and balances and separation of powers, ends up striking down one of the few existing checks on lawmaking by the bureaucracy.

* * *

III

* * *

A. Toward An Alternative Approach

A starting point for an alternative approach to the issues in *Chadha* can be found in Justice White's dissent. There are two distinct levels to the dissent. White answers the majority's formalistic, textual arguments with a conceptual argument of his own. The legislative veto is not the equivalent of a statute, White argues, because Congress has "reserv[ed]" a veto in the delegation and hence the veto does not make a change in the "legal status quo." White supports his view that a condition built into a statute is

---

[99] Immigration and Naturalization Service v. Chadha, 103 S. Ct. 2764, 2785 n.16 (1983).

not an independent exercise of legislative authority with two cases from the late 1930s which had upheld statutes giving "vetoes" to private groups. If this were all there were to White's opinion, it would be little better than the majority's equally mechanical approach.

White's dissent, however, operates on a second level as well. He sees the legislative veto in a larger perspective of evolving constitutional structure and relationships. White begins by tracing the history of the legislative veto, concluding that "it has not been a sword with which Congress has struck out to aggrandize itself at the expense of the other branches" but a "reservation of ultimate authority necessary if Congress is to fulfill its designated role under Article I as the nation's lawmaker." White then describes the growth of the "modern administrative state" in which "legislative authority is routinely delegated to the Executive branch, to the independent regulatory agencies and to private individuals and groups." Quoting Justice Jackson, White asserts that the rise of the administrative state has been "the most significant legal trend of the last century." A plethora of administrative bodies with lawmaking authority has now "become a veritable fourth branch of Government, which has deranged our three-branch legal theories."

White criticizes the majority for not "facing the reality of administrative lawmaking," but what significance White himself ascribes to administrative lawmaking is a bit murky. He suggests that the "wisdom and the constitutionality of these broad delegations [to administrative lawmakers] are matters that still have not been put to rest." White turns around, however, and argues in a key passage that "If Congress may delegate lawmaking power to independent and executive agencies, it is most difficult to understand Article I as forbidding Congress from also reserving a check on legislative powers for itself." Strictly speaking, White's point is a non sequitur: The fact that Congress may delegate legislative authority, without more, has nothing to do with whether Congress may reserve a legislative veto in the delegation. White comes back to the supposed inconsistency between the result in *Chadha* and the growth of administrative lawmaking at the conclusion of his opinion: "[The Court's holding] reflects a profoundly different conception of the Constitution than that held by the Courts which sanctioned the modern administrative state." It is clear that Justice White considers the growth of the "modern administrative state" to be relevant, but just exactly how it bears on the questions before the Court he never explains.

* * *

B. The Problem of Quasi-Constitutional Institutions

Underlying the debate between White and the majority is a problem with ramifications that go far beyond the legislative veto. In a nutshell, the problem is that the text of the Constitution creates not four branches of government, but three. White and the majority differ both conceptually and jurisprudentially over the significance of the changes in the structure of the federal government which have occurred since the New Deal. White conceives of these changes as creating the "modern administrative state." The majority, on the other hand, sees them as merely a series of delegations to the Executive, a phenomenon that goes back to the beginning of the Republic.

White's term, "the modern administrative state," is used with "increasing regularity" by contemporary political scientists, but is only beginning to achieve currency among lawyers. The concept of an "administrative state" goes well beyond the idea of delegation of lawmaking power to administrative decisionmakers. Indeed, the concept of an "administrative state" goes even further than the metaphor of a Fourth Branch. Describing administrative lawmakers as a "Fourth Branch" implies that they have achieved parity with the three original branches of government. The "administrative state," on the other hand, suggests that the growth of administrative decision-making is significant, not only in its own right, but also because administrative lawmaking has become the central lawmaking institution, and thereby that it has transformed the functions and relationships among other institutions of government. The term "the modern administrative state" implies, in short, that a qualitative change in the nature of government as a whole has resulted from the growth of administrative lawmaking.

To spell out the implications of Justice White's term is not to endorse it. Lumping a number of institutional changes together under the rubric of "the administrative state" substitutes a slogan for more precise analysis of particular institutions. In at least one crucial respect, however, White's metaphor is more perspicacious than the familiar concept of delegation which the majority employs. Delegation is a mechanistic metaphor: it implies that the thing which is delegated is the same in the hands of the recipient as it was before, and that both parties are otherwise left unchanged by the transaction. The "administrative state," on the other hand, suggests a concept of government as a holistic system. Changing one part of such a system necessarily alters the whole.

In this respect, at least, White's understanding of the significance of the rise of administrative lawmaking is superior to the majority's. The growth of a vast administrative bureaucracy with lawmaking powers is not a mere additive change to the structure of government. Inevitably it has transformed the nature and functions of existing institutions as well. The increasing importance of administrative modes of lawmaking has, for example, transformed the role of the courts in many areas of law. Rather than make common-law tort rules, for example, today federal courts are more likely to review generic rulemaking by agencies such as the National Highway Transportation Safety Administration. No longer are the courts the primary expositors of the law as they were in the nineteenth century. Instead, they review law made by others. Federal courts have become part of a composite lawmaking system, in which they function in conjunction with legislatures and administrative decisionmakers so that the law is the joint product of all three.

* * *

Justice White and the majority differ not only in how they conceive of the changes in the structure of government since the New Deal, but also in the jurisprudential significance that they ascribe to them. White senses that "the most significant legal trend of the last century" must somehow alter existing constitutional relationships. It is downright silly, White maintains, to read the language of the Constitution concerning the legislative process in isolation, without taking into account massive changes that have taken place in other lawmaking institutions. White gropes for a recognized legal doctrine that will legitimize the idea that a change in institutions of a magnitude as fundamental as the growth of the "modern administrative state" should alter the meaning and relationships among existing provisions of the Constitution. White never finds it, and perhaps no such doctrine now exists in American constitutional law. The majority dismisses White's point, characterizing it as a mere "utilitarian argument" that the legislative veto is a "useful 'political invention'." According to the majority, the growth of the administrative state and the concomitant need to control it are mere "policy arguments," which do not rise to the level of constitutional significance.

Perhaps the majority's answer suffices for a case like *Chadha*, since reasonable substitutes for the legislative veto are available. The difference between White and the majority in *Chadha* is, however, symptomatic of a deeper confusion in our law over the constitutional status and significance of lawmaking by administrative bodies, a confusion that could cause great harm if it is not resolved. * * *

* * *

Stephen Breyer, *The Legislative Veto After Chadha*, 72 GEO. L.J. 785, 792-95 (1984)*

* * *

Chadha's avoidance of consideration of the veto's functions or objectives leaves open the question of the extent to which Congress can still accomplish those functions and pursue those objectives after *Chadha*. Congress unquestionably retains a host of traditional weapons in its legislative and political arsenal that can accomplish some of the veto's objectives. These include the power to provide that legislation delegating authority to the executive expires every so often. To continue to exercise that authority, the executive would have to seek congressional approval, at which point past agency behavior that Congress disliked would become the subject of serious debate. Moreover, Congress might sometimes tailor its statutes more specifically, limiting executive power. Further, Congress can require the President, before taking action, to consult with congressional representatives whose views would carry significant political weight. Additionally, Congress can delay implementation of an executive action (as it does when the Supreme Court promulgates rules of civil procedure) until Congress has had time to consider it and to enact legislation preventing the action from taking effect. Finally, each year Congress considers the agency's budget. If a significant group of legislators strongly opposes a particular agency decision, it might well succeed in including a sentence in the appropriations bill denying the agency funds to enforce that decision.

All of these traditional alternatives, however, have obvious drawbacks or features that make them function quite differently from the legislative veto itself, and their balance of power effects are different. Building in an expiration of executive authority

---

* Reprinted with permission of Stephen Breyer. All rights reserved.

risks agency program disruption; trying carefully to tailor legislation presents the practical difficulties of greater linguistic specificity; requiring consultation does not compel obedience; delaying implementation would condition congressional control upon the eventual enactment of a law; and budget control is often random, given time pressure to enact appropriations bills. Still, these alternatives, imperfect as they are, count for something.

Moreover, if my basic view of the *Chadha* opinion is correct, it should be possible to come closer—to develop a veto substitute that satisfies the literal wording of the Constitution's bicameral and presentation clauses while it more nearly approximates the compromise functions of the legislative veto. I shall describe as a veto substitute the closest I have been able to come to doing so.

My veto substitute is a variant on the suggestion that Congress could replace veto provisions in present statutes with provisions that conditioned the legal effect of exercises of delegated authority on subsequent enactment of a confirmatory statute. * * * [T]he confirmatory law strategy would drastically and unworkably undermine executive or agency power because it is so much harder to enact a new law than to decline to exercise a veto. Thus, the confirmatory law approach is too big a gun to be of practical value.

Whether a confirmatory law is easy or difficult to enact, however, is largely a function of internal congressional procedural rules, a matter that is within the exclusive control of Congress. If those rules could be changed to make confirmatory law procedures rather like legislative veto procedures, the practical effect of the two could be made quite similar; the confirmatory law gun could be reduced to a size about equal to the legislative veto gun. Then Congress could reasonably have no more qualms about attaching the one to a delegated power than the other, and the shift of power from legislative to executive branch need not take place.

To be more specific, if the legislative procedural rules can be changed to make the enactment of a confirmatory law no more difficult than stopping the enactment of a veto resolution, then there will be no shift of power away from the executive branch. If those rules could make stopping the passage of such a law precisely as easy as the passage of a resolution of veto, then there would be no shift of power toward the executive branch. In fact, there would be no change at all in the balance of power. Because the burden of inertia is a function of internal legislative procedure, not of the Constitution, this might be done.

Take the Senate as an example. Assume that all legislative veto provisions in statutes were replaced with special confirmatory law requirements. Then suppose that the Senate rules provided a special fast track for special confirmatory laws. That fast track rule would provide: 1) when an executive branch agency enacts a regulation (or takes other action) subject to a special confirmatory law requirement, a bill embodying that special confirmatory law shall be introduced automatically (say, under the name of the Majority Leader, as sponsoring Senator); 2) the bill will be held at the desk, and not referred to committee; 3) the bill will be neither debatable nor amendable; it cannot be tabled or subjected to filibuster, etc.; and 4) the Senate will vote upon the bill, up or down, within sixty days of its introduction. The House would have a similar fast track. If the fast track is followed, the bill automatically becomes law (unless, of course, one House opposes it).

The rule could even go on to say that the bill can be derailed, that is, removed from the fast track, but only by a majority vote of the Senate. Because derailing means referral to committee, etc., it likely means defeat. In other words, the confirmatory law could be stopped, and thus the executive action at issue could be stopped, if and only if a majority of the Senate or the House votes to derail it. That *is* the one-House veto. To replicate a committee veto the rule would simply allow derailment by a majority vote of the relevant committee. If there is a need to have the executive branch action take effect immediately instead of after sixty days, the basic authorizing law would simply allow the action (say, committing troops) for sixty days, but no longer, without a confirming law.

In its main features then, the substitute fast track approach closely resembles the legislative veto. The agency is given effective authority to take an action of a specified type unless Congress disagrees. All of the compromises achieved by the veto can be largely preserved. Congress is able to delegate broad powers but retains the opportunity to review any exercises of those powers that it finds particularly objectionable, without imposing on itself the burden of reviewing each particular exercise. The method by which this is done, however, is different from that followed by the traditional legislative veto; the Constitution's language is followed as a matter of form. Thus, whatever legal questions might arise, they should not be the same as those at issue in *Chadha*.

The substitute does not replicate the veto perfectly, and the difference should be noted. First, the veto substitute imposes on Congress a degree of visible responsibility for the actions it confirms, a burden that the veto system allowed it to avoid. Under the legislative veto, the vast bulk of decisions subject to review would elicit absolutely no congressional action or consideration. Even when congressional action was initiated, a resolution of veto might be introduced into a committee only to disappear, thereby freeing the Senators from having to take a public vote on the matter. With the proposed veto substitute, however, a small group of senators could force a roll-call vote on even the most run of the mill (nondebatable, nonamendable) confirmatory law because the Constitution requires that one-fifth of the senators present retain the power to require a roll-call on any matter. Even in cases where no vote was recorded, the fact that the legislators had to admit that Congress *acted*, rather than passively failed to act, might make a difference to constituents. That in turn might make a difference to the legislator. Moreover, a future Congress or either House, hostile to the agency, might simply repeal the special procedural rules. All this might make the balance of power consequences somewhat different from those of the legislative veto.

Second, the veto substitute could affect judicial review of administrative exercises of delegated authority. The chief task of judicial review at present is to determine whether the administrative action abides by the terms of the statutory delegation that authorizes it. If, however, the agency action were promptly embodied in a new statute, there would be no opportunity for this issue to be raised because the new statute would stand independent of the original delegating statute. One can minimize this problem by making the proposal more complex. Judicial review could be preserved if the congressional rules required that each special confirmatory law include a clause rendering it ineffective unless the administrative action that initiated it would have been a valid exercise of the delegated authority, absent the requirement of a confirmatory statute. Alternative forms of language are possible, but all are complicated and Congress might be reluctant to provide them.

Third, the confirmatory law approach, unlike the legislative veto, would require the President's signature to confirm each administrative action. Where the original delegation was to the executive branch, the President might routinely be expected to back the executive agency so that the added requirement would not make much difference. Where independent agencies are involved, however, the substitute approach would, in effect, introduce an executive veto everywhere it provided for legislative review. Congress would have to choose whether to subject agency action to checks by both branches or by neither.

Fourth, it is difficult to replicate the two-House veto. One could try by having the Senate rules, for example, condition derailment on the House also voting to derail from the fast track. The fast track, however, must eventually lead to a vote, and if one House votes "no," the confirmatory law is stopped and the agency action fails.

Fifth, there is an important question of practical politics: Would Congress wish to amend its rules even if it knew that it could replicate the veto by doing so? For one thing, the overall political effects of doing so are uncertain. For another, some fine tuning, hence several consecutive amendments, would likely be needed. Finally, to open the subject of rules change is itself treacherous. Many different legislators with wide-ranging and conflicting notions of rules reform would be likely to seize the occasion to present their own ideas. Present House and Senate rules have the virtue of an uneasy compromise that has stood the test of time. Opening the subject and adopting changes that are potentially far-reaching and of uncertain outcome cannot be undertaken lightly.

In sum, the veto substitute is not a precise functional replica of the veto, but it comes close. Still, the question for Congress is whether it so strongly desires the legislative veto that it will pay the price of radical and complex change of its internal rules of procedure (a change that could bring with it a more thorough consideration of rules reform) * * *.
* * *

* * *

Additional Sources

Joseph R. Biden, *Who Needs the Legislative Veto?*, 35 Syracuse L. Rev. 685 (1984)

John R. Bolton & Kevin G. Abrams, *The Judicial and Congressional Response to the Invalidation of the Legislative Veto*, 1 J.L. & Pol. 299 (1984)

Daan Braverman, *Chadha: The Supreme Court as Umpire in Separation of Powers Disputes*, 35 Syracuse L. Rev. 735 (1984)

Barbara Hinkson Craig, Chadha: THE STORY OF AN EPIC CONSTITUTIONAL STRUGGLE (1988)

Dennis DeConcini & Robert Faucher, *The Legislative Veto: A Constitutional Amendment*, 21 Harv. J. on Legis. 29 (1984)

Robert W. Ginnane, *The Control of Federal Administration by Congressional Resolutions and Committees*, 66 Harv. L. Rev. 569 (1953)

Robert Jackson, *A Presidential Legal Opinion*, 66 Harv. L. Rev. 1353 (1953)

Frederick M. Kaiser, *Congressional Control of Executive Actions in the Aftermath of the* Chadha *Decision*, 36 Admin. L. Rev. 239 (1984)

Elliott H. Levitas & Stanley M. Brand, *Congressional Review of Executive and Agency Actions after* Chadha: *"The Son of Legislative Veto" Lives On*, 72 Geo. L.J. 801 (1984)

Robert J. Rabin, *An Overview of the* Chadha *Case*, 35 Syracuse L. Rev. 703 (1984)

Antonin Scalia, *The Legislative Veto: A False Remedy for System Overload*, Regulation, Nov./Dec. 1979 at 19

Rodney A. Smolla, *Bring Back the Legislative Veto: A Proposal for a Constitutional Amendment*, 37 Ark. L. Rev. 509 (1983)

Girardeau A. Spann, *Spinning the Legislative Veto*, 72 Geo. L.J. 813 (1984)

Peter L. Strauss, *Was There a Baby in the Bathwater? A Comment on the Supreme Court's Legislative Veto Decision*, 1983 Duke L.J. 789

b. Congressional Oversight of Administrative Action

The excerpts in this section focus on Congress' oversight role, as opposed to its authorization and appropriation functions. In the first excerpt, James Pearson, former United States Senator from Kansas, calls for greater attention to be paid to legislative oversight.

In the second excerpt, Professor Peter Shane analyzes the not uncommon situation of disagreement between the legislative and executive branches when Congress does seek information from the executive. Although Congress has broad investigatory power, the president can invoke executive privilege as a shield against disclosure. Professor Shane discusses differing approaches to the doctrine of executive privilege as well as specific cases that have involved negotiation between the two branches of government. He elaborates his understanding of the requirements of a government of laws in the context of interbranch conflicts about the sharing of information.

James B. Pearson, *Oversight: A Vital Yet Neglected Congressional Function*, 23 KAN. L. REV. 277, 277-83, 288 (1975)*

* * *

I. The Nature of Oversight

The legislative branch of government generally exercises three primary functions—investigation, legislation, and oversight. Legislation includes the basic process of drafting, evaluating, and either passing or rejecting policy proposals. Investigation, in its purest form, is primarily informational and designed to get facts and identify and publicize national problems. * * *

Oversight, while similar to investigation, is a distinct legislative function. It is, in a positive sense, "hindsight" that focuses on analysis of legislation and its administrative implementation. More specifically, oversight is comprised of two elements. The first is program review, in which Congress determines whether the programs it has created are really working. This means examining whether program administration is consistent with legislative intent. It also means, however, that Congress should check on itself. For example, Congress should inquire whether legislation is meeting the needs that existed at the time of enactment. All too often, programs once created are repeatedly extended and expanded without rectifying mistakes in the original law. Effective program evaluation should lead to correction through enactment of new legislation. The second component of oversight is more general review of an administrative agency's operations to determine if it is efficient, honest, and responsive to the needs of the people. This is a "watchdog" function, designed to assure the public that "the agencies are not only functioning, but also, more importantly, that they are functioning properly."

Congress employs numerous formal and informal mechanisms to perform oversight. Among the formal means are congressional hearings on legislation and appropriations, monitoring devices such as the General Accounting Office, and built-in legislative controls outlining reporting requirements for an agency administering a congressionally created program. The informal techniques include "case work" conducted by members' personal staffs, unwritten agreements between committee staffs and administrative agencies, and, in some instances, legislative inaction that may be viewed as tacit acceptance of an agency position.

Legislative oversight is wholly consistent with American legal traditions and precedents. John Stuart Mill, for example, contended not only that legislative control of administration is essential for liberty, but also that oversight is the task for which a legislative body is best suited. Although the Constitution does not specifically refer to oversight, the Supreme Court has generally viewed information gathering as an essential component of the legislative function. It has held that the power to legislate conferred by the Constitution also implies the power to obtain information needed for the effective exercise of the legislative function. * * *

* * *

Congress has also provided a statutory basis for oversight. Perhaps Congress' strongest statement was contained in the Legislative Reorganization Act of 1946, which assigned to each standing committee the power to "exercise continuous watchfulness of the execution by the administrative agencies concerned of any laws, the subject matter of which is within the jurisdiction of such committee." In the Legislative Reorganization Act of 1970, Congress expanded its oversight capabilities and directed standing committees to "review and study, on a continuing basis, the application, administration, and execution of those laws, or parts of laws, the subject matter of which is within the jurisdiction of that committee." * * *

II. The Need For Effective Oversight

The need for effective oversight has become more apparent in recent years as government has grown increasingly complex. Elected representatives, directly responsible to the people, should monitor program implementation to prevent government by informed but uncontrolled bureaucrats. * * *

* * *

III. The Need to Improve Oversight

Paradoxically, despite its importance, congressional oversight remains basically weak and ineffective. This may be due in no small part to the fact that overseeing the operations of the government in a comprehensive and systematic manner may be simply too large for any member of Congress or combination of members and staff to master. The problems created by the complexity of subject matter are compounded by the fragmentation of the current authority for conducting oversight. For example, the Legis-

---

* Reprinted with permission of the Kansas Law Review and James B. Pearson. All rights reserved.

lative Reorganization Act of 1946 divided responsibility for oversight among authorizing committees, appropriating committees, and general investigative committees, such as the House and Senate Government Operations Committees. As one expert has said, "Given this division, it is not surprising that oversight is episodic rather than systematic and comprehensive. Of fundamental importance is how to achieve coordination and cooperation on a systematic basis among the different committees conducting oversight so that the House and Senate can institutionally respond to [their] oversight responsibilities."

Several other institutional limits also impair Congress' ability to conduct effective oversight. The lack of adequate staff is foremost among these weaknesses. Without a staff capable of providing technical advice, Congress tends to rely upon the administrator-specialists for the shaping of public policy when those specialists have access to information with which to support their decision. * * *

Even with adequate staffing, Congress would still be stymied in its oversight efforts by an inability to gain access to independent information with which to review the executive. * * *

The shortcomings of congressional oversight might be more easily corrected if these institutional limits were the only problem. Unfortunately, the major limitation is much less tangible. The fact is that for most members of Congress oversight is not a high priority item. Oversight is less attractive politically than legislation, with which a member can achieve greater public identification, or investigations, which also have greater publicity value. Congressmen, like businessmen, lawyers, and other professionals, consider self-survival a primary concern. Thus, "when any action is perceived to contribute directly and substantially to political survival, it is likely to move towards the top of any member's priority list." In other words, when committee hearings or studies tend to have strong political payoffs, members of Congress can be counted upon to act with greater rapidity and forcefulness.

* * *

Political motivation is not the only intangible limit on oversight. For example, a committee chairman can significantly affect a committee's oversight activities. * * * Also, when a committee has a large turnover because of lack of member interest or is seen as less glamorous than other assignments, the activities calculated to provide review of the agencies under the committee's jurisdiction will probably suffer.

The lack of interest in certain subject matter is unfortunate but very natural. Conversely, there have been instances when a member of Congress had a strong personal concern that yielded positive results.
* * *
* * * On the whole, * * * it safely can be said that Congress does not possess the institutional means with which to effectively oversee the executive. When this institutional inadequacy is compounded by lack of political motivation and interest, oversight tends to suffer. Congress must address these deficiencies on both fronts by upgrading its institutional oversight mechanisms and by asserting a more positive oversight role.

* * *

IV. Conclusion

This Article began with the point that oversight is a vital yet neglected congressional function. Its effective exercise is limited by both institutional and intangible weaknesses. These limits can be attacked by revamping the committee structure, developing better independent sources of information, and designing more adequate program review standards. These changes must also be combined with a more active congressional role. Congress will probably never be able to fully perform effective oversight of all the programs it authorizes and the agencies it regulates. * * * If Congress gives oversight a status equal to that of its other functions, it will be a better representative body, more capable of meeting the needs of the people, who deserve fair, honest and efficient government operations.

Peter M. Shane, *Legal Disagreement and Negotiation in a Government of Laws: The Case of Executive Privilege Claims Against Congress*, 71 MINN. L. REV. 461, 462-66, 469-73, 476-86, 488-89, 492-97, 500-01, 508-14, 516-29, 537-40 (1987)*

Introduction

The confrontation between Congress and the first Reagan Administration over executive privilege made apparent the lack of well-ordered processes for

---

* Reprinted with permission of Peter M. Shane. All rights reserved.

resolving interbranch disputes over access to important information in the hands of the executive branch. This is troubling because the invocation of executive privilege against Congress raises obvious and important questions of government accountability. Indeed, because Congress's entitlement to such information presents serious legal questions, the lack of clear processes for resolution calls into question the customary claim that ours is a "government of laws." The more Congress's access to information about the executive branch seems subject to vagaries of politics, rather than to processes of law, the greater the apparent gap between our ideals of government accountability and the reality of government practice.

Confrontations as intense as those provoked in recent years—in particular, Anne Gorsuch's attempt to withhold Environmental Protection Agency documents and James Watt's similar attempt in the Department of the Interior—are historically exceptional, but their infrequency does not belie their importance.
* * *

* * *

One aspect of the recent confrontations that proved a particular impediment to their efficient resolution was the deep disagreement between Congress and the Executive as to applicable legal principles. Not only did the two branches take divergent negotiating positions as to what they would accept—"full disclosure to Congress" versus "no more disclosure than the President wants"—but they also took radically opposed legal positions, each branch insisting on its ultimate constitutional authority over disclosure of the information in question. The negotiations became, therefore, largely a jockeying over positions, with the legal opinions of each branch proffered to legitimate the negotiators' firmness. Given the assumption of each branch that only one branch could be constitutionally correct, each branch implied that only its position could be justified by law and on the basis of the public interest that constitutional law is supposed to embody.

The purpose of this Article is to challenge that assumption, that is, that only one branch can be "correct" on a matter of separation of powers and, consequently, that interbranch dispute resolution should vindicate that one correct version of the law. Rather, government officials should view the contending legal positions of all three branches not as divergent attempts to hypothesize the correct law for all settings, but as separate attempts to crystalize each branch's independent understanding of the law. Each branch, then, has an independent doctrine of executive privilege which is entitled to primacy within the "jurisdiction" of that branch, but which deserves only coequal status with the others in other contexts.

In so arguing, this Article does not urge that the Constitution be regarded as *not* yielding *any* answer to the problems of executive privilege. Nor should lawyers in each branch of government regard all conceivable views as equally valid. On the contrary, this Article recommends that each branch's lawyers assume a quasi-adjudicative role in determining for their respective branch the "one right answer" to any question of executive privilege. Having done so, however, they should also respect the *authority* of the other branches to arrive at different answers to the same question and to acknowledge that circumstances may at times require that the other branches' doctrines receive primacy.

Adopting this approach to executive privilege issues would have two advantages for Congress and the Executive. First, it would be conducive to a more judicious attitude toward constitutional interpretation generally within each political branch. Second, it would lend itself to a new and more constructive approach to questions of presidential prerogative that arise in the twilight zone of concurrent congressional and presidential authority.

* * *

I. The Contending Doctrines of Executive Privilege

A. The Evolution of Legal Disagreement Generally

Despite its notable commitment to legal process, the government of the United States faces inherent difficulties in achieving unitary, government-wide legal interpretation. The very distribution of power among three coequal branches of government means that each branch may evolve at least some important understandings of the law that differ from those of the other two branches. This is true even with respect to legal issues, such as the scope of the presidential war powers, that are of concern to more than one branch. In practice this means that members of one branch of government, trying assiduously to follow the law, may be following a legal theory substantially different from the theories that members of the other branches would feel obligated to follow if faced with the same legal question.

* * *

When divergences occur between the political branches on matters of constitutional interpretation, it seems natural to regard them as disagreements on what is the one correct interpretation of the law. Both may have it wrong, but both cannot have it right. This characterization of their differences of opinion, however, is not inevitable. For example, our legal system permits different states to interpret tort law differently, even under the same rubric of "negligence," unless and until Congress may decide to impose a uniform rule pursuant to its legislative powers. Different federal courts of appeals may interpret federal constitutional or statutory law differently unless and until the Supreme Court resolves the conflict. In short, there are many important situations where we regard law-interpreting institutions as having authority to disagree on the meaning of law, at least until another institution with perceived superseding jurisdiction to resolve the disagreement does so. The authority to interpret law independently extends to the boundaries of that institution's "jurisdiction."

It therefore seems plausible to ask whether each of the political branches may also have a jurisdiction within which it is permitted to interpret the Constitution independently and within which its particular interpretations are entitled to be regarded as law. * * *

* * *

B. Three Theories of Executive Privilege

1. The Judicial Doctrine of Executive Privilege

* * *

The Supreme Court has not adjudicated any executive privilege dispute with Congress, and thus no one opinion exists that purports to resolve definitively, from the judicial point of view, the principled contentions that such disputes might involve. Several Supreme Court decisions strongly imply, however, what the Court's view would be on a number of these contentions.

Of central importance is the 1974 opinion in *United States v. Nixon*, which held that the President has a constitutionally based, but defeasible, privilege to withhold information from a court based on a generalized claim of presidential confidentiality. The Court identified as the constitutional basis for the privilege "the supremacy of each branch within its own assigned area of constitutional duties," and "the valid need for protection of communications between high Government officials and those who advise and assist them in the performance of their manifold duties." The Court was untroubled that the Constitution makes no express provision for executive privilege. Instead, citing the holding of *McCulloch v. Maryland* with respect to the implied powers of Congress, the Court held that a presumptive executive branch privilege of nondisclosure could follow by analogous implication from those powers of the President that are express.

In addition to concluding that a constitutional basis exists for invoking executive privilege against courts, the *Nixon* opinion is significant for two reasons. The first is its holding that the claim of privilege in that case was overcome by the institutional need of the trial court to have the information necessary to secure "the fair administration of criminal justice." Putting aside whether the Court's balancing in *Nixon* was entirely persuasive, it is a central element of the Supreme Court's doctrine that a claim of executive privilege may be weighed against the powers of the courts to perform their assigned constitutional tasks.

The other critical point from *Nixon* is the Court's implication that different claims of privilege may be accorded different weights according to the bases of the claims. Thus, the Court distinguishes at length the generalized interest in the protection of confidential presidential communications invoked in *Nixon* from narrower claims of privilege based on military and state secrets, as to which "the courts have traditionally shown the utmost deference to Presidential responsibilities."

The Court in *Nixon* expressly reserved any questions concerning "the balance between the President's generalized interest in confidentiality . . . and congressional demands for information." It is thus not entirely certain whether the Court would recognize any constitutionally based privilege against Congress or, if it did, whether its balancing approach would be the same. On the other hand, it is hard to imagine that the Court would recognize a constitutionally based privilege of nondisclosure to the courts that would not also be relevant to a contest with Congress.

The *Nixon* case is consistent with the Court's modern balancing approach to separation of powers problems that are not squarely addressed by constitutional text. A separation of powers claim is recognized whenever the initiative of one branch substantially interferes with the power of another to accomplish its constitutional tasks. In such a case, the initiative must be justified by some overarching governmental interest. Given this general approach, the Court would surely find those executive branch responsibilities supporting the existence of privilege in *Nixon* to be no less deserving of constitutional concern when the threat to the fulfillment of those executive duties emanates from an extrajudicial source such as Congress.

* * *

The crux of the judicial doctrine of interbranch executive privilege disputes thus appears to be as follows: Congress has a constitutionally based power to demand information pursuant to investigations in aid of its legislative and oversight functions. The President, on the other hand, has a constitutionally based privilege to withhold disclosure of information, the release of which would impede the performance of executive branch responsibilities. A presumptive claim of privilege may be asserted to protect even the President's generalized interest in confidential deliberations. Executive privilege, however, is defeasible, and a claim of privilege based on a generalized interest in confidentiality may carry less force than narrower claims based on military and state secrets.

* * *

2. The Congressional Doctrine of Executive Privilege

Congress's legal understanding of executive privilege is more difficult to divine than that of the courts because relevant statutes address the issue only obliquely and because, other than statutes, conventional formats for expressing congressional legal opinion are not well established. Congress does make law predominantly by enacting statutes and it is arguable that Congress can formulate a legal doctrine only by positively legislating. Under that premise, congressional "law" respecting executive privilege would exist only to the extent that Congress has enacted a statute addressing the problem.

Congress does, however, make law other than by legislating. This is clear with respect to its internal procedures, where rules and precedents that it establishes are followed although not statutorily embodied. Congress may also make law through custom, which the Supreme Court has recognized in treating custom as a source of decisional authority in separation of powers cases.

* * *

The insight that norm prescription can occur without positive legal enactment is critically helpful in interpreting Congress's informal law respecting executive privilege and Congress. Two episodes involving James Watt and Anne Gorsuch [two Reagan Administration officials], for example, resulted in statements about the law by counsel to the clerk of the House that contained explicit policy content, were intended to be understood as authoritative, and conveyed an implicit communication of Congress's capacity to enforce its views vis-a-vis the executive branch. Their attractiveness as documents for helping to elaborate Congress's doctrine of interbranch executive privilege is enhanced by the readiness with which they can be reconciled with the prevailing interpretation of the most relevant statutes and a satisfactory "reading" of congressional custom.

With that background, the broad outlines of a congressional doctrine of executive privilege are fairly clear and unsurprising. First, Congress asserts its plenary authority to demand executive branch information in connection with any properly authorized legislative oversight hearing. For example, the Freedom of Information Act, which exempts large categories of executive branch records from mandatory public disclosure, expressly disclaims the application of those exemptions to congressional demands for information, including the exemption generally recognized as protecting documents deemed to be protected by executive privilege. The opinions of counsel assert additionally that no information generated at a staff level is properly subject to any executive privilege whatsoever. Finally, there is no limitation on the subject matter of information that Congress properly may demand; even information relating to foreign relations, including international negotiations, is within Congress's purview.

This is not to say that Congress denies the importance of withholding certain executive branch information from the public; rather, it denies the executive branch's authority to regard dissemination to Congress as public disclosure. Congress does regard itself as bound to provide for the nondisclosure of information, the dissemination of which would compromise national security. Such responsibility may obligate a congressional subcommittee, for example, to respect a good faith executive branch demand that it receive sensitive information only in "executive session." The authority to disclose information that a committee receives in executive session, however, would reside in the committee, never in the executive branch.

This rendition of Congress's doctrine vis-a-vis executive privilege may appear at odds with the various occasions on which subcommittees have acceded to executive insistence on nondisclosure. It does not appear from the history of such instances, however, that any such occasion represents an unambiguous concession to the authority of the executive branch to withhold. Even Congress's insistence that it is empowered in every instance to demand and receive executive branch information would not require Congress to stand on its asserted authority at every opportunity. It can only be said with confidence that there are many instances in which Congress's calculation of its own interests, its confidence in the President, and the asserted interests of the executive branch permit Congress to accommodate the executive branch, whatever its view of underlying principle.

3. The Executive Doctrine of Executive Privilege

As with the legislative branch, discerning the executive branch doctrine of executive privilege provokes the jurisprudential difficulties of determining the constitutional law of a branch of government that does not engage in formal constitutional adjudication. These problems are largely relieved, however, by the constitutional vesting of executive power in a single officer, the President. Unlike a congressional counsel, committee or subcommittee, whose authority may be questionable even within Congress, the President unmistakably holds the final authority within the executive branch, even as to the law. On occasions on which the President does not personally express his views, the executive legal doctrine may be espoused by the Attorney General, who is by law and tradition the chief legal representative of the executive branch. It is executive branch practice that, unless contravened by legal developments, typically Supreme Court opinions, which have greater status as law, opinions of the Attorney General are to be regarded as binding the executive branch in legal interpretation. * * *

* * * On March 24, 1969, President Nixon issued a general memorandum to the heads of executive departments and agencies concerning congressional demands for information. The Ford and Carter Administrations left this policy intact, and a 1982 redraft by President Reagan left untouched the core principle of that memorandum. That principle is that the executive branch "has an obligation to protect the confidentiality of some communications," but will invoke executive privilege against Congress only with "specific Presidential authorization," in the "most compelling circumstances," and "only after careful review demonstrates that assertion of the privilege is necessary."

The scope of the President's authority to withhold demanded information extends, under the executive view, to all information the disclosure of which would impede the responsible discharge of executive branch functions. Under the Reagan memorandum, such information may include "national security secrets, deliberative communications that form a part of the decision-making process, or other information important to the discharge of the Executive Branch's constitutional responsibilities." The last category is likely to cover the contents of investigative files assembled for law enforcement purposes, information that would disclose the identity of a government informer, or confidential, personal information about executive branch personnel. The Reagan memorandum could be used to protect such material even if it emanates originally from staff levels considerably removed from the President. In such a case, however, a claim of privilege would require presidential familiarity with and review of the materials.

Because the executive branch regards the protection of confidential information as necessary to protect the integrity of executive power generally, it cannot discharge that responsibility by divulging information to Congress under a promise that Congress will act responsibly in deciding whether to further disseminate the information. Such a delegation of control over information would be, in the executive view, an unconstitutional abdication of power analogous to an unconstitutionally overbroad congressional delegation of legislative authority in a standardless statute. Further, as attorneys general have recognized, this principled position obviates the unseemly spectacle of having the executive branch purport to decide which congressional committees are trustworthy and which are not.

A final aspect of the executive branch doctrine deserving of mention is the customary concession that the President will not invoke executive privilege to withhold information probative of official wrongdoing in the executive branch. Prior to the Nixon impeachment investigation, Presidents had repeatedly stated that the House had the right to demand executive branch evidence in connection with such inquiries. Nixon's refusal to honor Judiciary Committee subpoenas duces tecum was, therefore, reported by that Committee as an article of impeachment.

II. Legal Disagreement in a Government of Laws

The legal disagreement just described demonstrates that lawyers in each branch of government are likely to approach an executive privilege issue based on premises not shared by the other two branches. How should government lawyers respond to this fact, consistent with responsible representation of their respective client branches? In the recent executive privilege disputes, the apparent attitude of the lawyers was that one branch was right and the other was wrong, one branch was authoritative and the other branch was usurpatious. This attitude did nothing to discipline either side's tendency to assert its position in the most extreme fashion. This Part of this Article suggests that government lawyers facing separation of powers issues instead should adopt the view that each branch, within its particular jurisdiction, is entitled to interpret the Constitution for itself. Such an attitude would be conducive to more responsible intrabranch legal advice on any separation of powers question.

* * *

A. Legal Interpretation and the Government of Laws Ideal

The ideal of a "government of laws" has long embodied a popular concept of the kind of government we want, and it is a natural ideal to guide the development of a model for appropriate government lawyering. Supreme Court opinions invoke the government of laws ideal to help justify decisions. Public officials routinely invoke the government of laws ideal to explain their approval or disapproval of a wide range of government conduct. It is a reasonable prediction that, as long as judges and legal scholars continue to employ explicitly normative reasoning in the discussion of constitutional problems, the government of laws ideal will be a recurring premise in such discussions.

It is likewise reasonable to assume that the government of laws concept expresses a central aspiration for our constitutional system, widely shared by government official and citizen alike. Every past and present government official could likely offer some anecdotal support for the hypothesis that this aspiration makes a difference in official behavior. It would be surprising if the record were otherwise.

* * *

The concept of an ideal government of laws raises the question: To what sort of government does the phrase refer? Although the concept is highly general, all references to a "government of laws, and not of people" evoke at least some image of government actors guided by more than mere whim and calculation of how much whim they may indulge with impunity. It follows, therefore, that a government of laws evidences some sort of constraint on the official pursuit of individual desire.

* * *

The "government of laws" conception * * * suggests that, like drivers who stop at red lights, government actors should habitually understand their official behavior as acts of legal obligation. In deciding what it is appropriate to do in their official capacities, they should consider the applicable legal reference points in determining right and wrong, suitable and unsuitable. They should do so even when the moral certainty exists that no formal sanction will punish inattention to the applicable reference points. Conversely, they should regard legal justification as an important factor even when other, more egocentric, justifications would prompt the same behavior.

* * *

This conception of a government of laws, like a rule-based conception of accountability, obviously does not exhaust the concepts of accountability, justice, or order in society. That officials feel compelled to obey law and thus justify their acts in legal terms guarantees none of these institutional virtues. Laws themselves may be unjust. The processes of legal interpretation may be sloppy, superficial, or corrupt. Yet, if officials do feel compelled to interpret their actions in legal terms, even in cases in which no sanction threatens the failure to do so, that internalized compulsion is likely to be significant protection against arbitrariness * * *.

* * *

B. Conscientious Legal Interpretation and the Authority to Interpret Law Independently

The kind of attitude toward constitutional interpretation evidenced by both branches' lawyers in recent executive privilege confrontations does not maximize the potential for conscientious legal reasoning on which a government of laws relies. The patently adversarial cast to their opinions signified the premises underlying that attitude. First, it was assumed that only one "right" answer existed to legal issues in dispute. Further, because the answer might ultimately be sought from a court, the political branches' lawyers might legitimately articulate their respective positions as zealous advocates might prepare their briefs.

In keeping with the suggestion that a contrary view is possible—that each branch may evolve a legal interpretation which may govern within that branch's jurisdiction and which is entitled to respect from the other branches—an alternative attitude for government lawyers is likewise available to animate their legal reasoning. Government lawyers may determine separation of powers law in a manner akin in most respects to the method followed by federal courts of appeals for legal interpretation generally. That is, each branch should regard as its law those legal conclusions that appear most sound according to conventionally accepted interpretive methods applied independently by that branch.

Political branches should advert to the judicial method for determining law because achieving a government of laws requires government lawyers to attend "judiciously" to the forms and rhetoric of legal reasoning, and lawyers will be most habituated to the counsels of reason if they regard themselves as playing a quasi-adjudicative role in the elaboration of law. This suggestion may appear odd because, in many contexts, we assume that the law is best served by lawyers playing adversarial roles. The adversarial role may seem natural for political branches in inevitable competition. The obvious problem with the adversary model for the political branches' lawyers, however, is its assumption that the adversaries are regularly and legitimately accountable to dispassionate and disinterested third-party review. In separation of powers disputes, such third party review is almost always a distant prospect and, equally important, its legitimacy is far less clear to the disputants. Formal sanction and the persuasion of extraneous authority are thus such distant normative considerations to the actors involved that the adversary model becomes an insufficient behavioral prescription for dealing with politically charged areas where the practical scope of official discretion is great. What is needed is a different attitude that better tempers the salutary antagonism of the branches with the public interest in workable, responsible government.

* * *

Official understanding, explanation, and justification of government conduct is likely to be most responsible, and thus most consistent with government workability, if the officials involved regard themselves as making, not just following, constitutional law. The legal opinions of Congress or of the Department of Justice are likely to be more responsible over time if each regards itself in the role of adjudicator rather than advocate, because such an attitude is more conducive to a conscientious balancing of conflicting, legally relevant interests.

This proposition reflects common experience among lawyers. Any executive branch lawyer asked to explain the constitutional scope of executive discretion to withhold documents from Congress is going to be attentive to at least two sets of considerations: first, the institutional interests of the executive branch in the disclosure or nondisclosure of information; second, the arsenal of interpretive methods which lawyers use to reason as to the meaning of the Constitution. If such a lawyer believes her opinion must be defensible as an authoritative exposition of law, it is a plausible hope that professional pride and personal integrity will coincide to produce a legal opinion faithful to the claims of both sound legal reasoning and client interest. If the lawyer regards her opinion as only a "brief" for the executive branch side of the argument, intuition suggests that the lawyer's personal psychology will tolerate a greater indulgence of client self-interest at the expense of disinterested judgment. The difference will be one of degree, to be sure, but a difference that may be important to the habituation of government lawyers to the "counsel of reason."

* * *

It is predictable that, if animated by a judicious rather than adversarial attitude, neither of the political branches' contending doctrines of executive privilege, despite their utility to the originating branch, would be shaped entirely by short-term concern for partisan interest. Each doctrine must be formed under the pressure of the two branches' practical interdependence. Each must be formed with reference to the same kinds of interpretive methods that characterize the legal culture generally, and each will attempt to draw on the same kinds of materials, including judicial opinions, for support. Thus, even if permitting each branch to treat its own doctrine as authoritative yields only incremental benefits in the quality of official behavior, the coequal status of the branches and the degree of accountability evident in each branch's version of the law strengthens the case that those benefits can be achieved at little cost.

* * *

Some will view this argument as astonishingly naive. It rests on the premises that legal interpretation in an interbranch dispute can be something other than posturing and that the reasoning of lawyers actually affects the resolution of political disputes. Under the traditional view, only courts pronounce law; the elucidation of law by the political branches on separation of powers questions should be viewed only as part of an implementation process that is almost entirely political in two senses. First, it is primarily partisan. Second, it is attuned only to policy, not principle. What lawyers say, according to this version of reality, is no real evidence of the quality of interbranch interaction; the real action is largely behind the scenes, ad hoc, and entirely instrumental.

To ignore the political dimensions of separation of powers disputes or to try to characterize those disputes in purely legalistic terms would surely blink reality. An unrelievedly partisan account of government is, however, equally overdrawn and unpersuasive, especially without much more comprehensive evidence than is available on the actual resolution of interbranch disputes. My response to the cynical account is in part experiential because my perceptions of my own service in the Department of Justice lend subjective credibility to a more idealistic version of the reality of government, a version in which legal reasoning does matter.[116] In equal part, however, I am wary of the cynical account and committed to the argument I have advanced because the Constitution seems so strikingly to envision a government under a government of laws idea. If it is true not only that law is a form of politics, but that law for Congress and for the President is only politics in the narrowest and most partisan sense, a great part of our professed constitutionalism is an illusion and much government lawyering is merely an expensive fraud upon the public.

III. Problem-Solving Negotiation, Legal Disagreement, and Executive Privilege

The preceding Part of this Article argued that if government officials regarded each branch's views on the separation of powers as "law" for that branch—that is, as authoritative within the branch's jurisdiction—that attitude would help promote conscientious legal interpretation. The question remains whether such an attitude would be helpful or unproductive in the actual resolution of interbranch disputes. If each branch is entitled to follow its own doctrine as the law, the branches' insistence on principle might forestall efficient settlement of disputes more than if the branches regarded themselves as jointly accountable to an outside agency, such as the judicial branch.

Recent experience, however, suggests the opposite. Namely, the branches tend more to intransigent "positional" bargaining if their attitude is that only one correct version of executive privilege law exists and each branch's position is the articulation of that law. Bargaining would be more productive if the branches believed that each branch had the authority to make law within its jurisdiction and that the aim of negotiation is not to settle on one legal view as binding on both parties. The branches should perceive themselves as negotiating an immediate, concrete problem. What government needs is a theory of negotiation that steers officials, while actually bargaining, away from the vindication of doctrinal principle and toward the reconciliation of institutional interests.

* * *

A. Case Histories of Interbranch Executive Privilege Disputes

* * *

2. Anne Gorsuch: Executive Privilege and Law Enforcement

The most celebrated of recent privilege disputes involved Anne Gorsuch, President Reagan's first Administrator of the Environmental Protection Agency (EPA), who became the first head of an executive branch agency to be held in contempt of Congress while in office. The impetus for the contempt citation was Gorsuch's refusal to divulge certain documents to the Investigations and Oversight Subcommittee (Levitas subcommittee) of the House Committee on Public Works and Transportation, in connection with that subcommittee's investigation of EPA's administration of the so-called "Superfund" for the cleanup of hazardous waste dumping sites. The White House settled the dispute with the subcommittee on February 18, 1983, slightly more than two weeks after a federal district court refused to review the legality of the House contempt citation before its enforcement.

The Comprehensive Environmental Response, Compensation, and Liability Act of 1980, commonly known as the Superfund Act, created a $1.6 billion trust fund to be used for financing the cleanup of hazardous waste sites and spills of hazardous chemicals. * * * Parties responsible for hazardous waste or chemical spill sites are required to reimburse the government for cleanup costs and damages to natural resources; noncooperating parties may be fined treble damages. By executive order, President Reagan delegated his functions under the Act to the EPA Administrator, who was also designated the responsible official for enforcement of the Act.

In 1982, several House subcommittees commenced investigations of various aspects of EPA's Superfund enforcement. The Levitas subcommittee, in March 1982, commenced a general investigation of hazardous and toxic waste control, focusing on the impact of such wastes and their control on American ground and surface water resources. Of special concern were an EPA decision to suspend its prior restrictions on disposal of containerized liquid wastes in landfills that might permit the migration of such wastes to ground and surface waters and allegations that the EPA was not adequately enforcing the Su-

---

[116] The author of this Article was an OLC attorney-adviser from 1978 through 1981. Larry A. Hammond, who was Deputy Assistant Attorney General in charge of OLC during most of this period, has written:

> In many instances, . . . Jimmy Carter was not interested in playing the "lawmaker as advocate" game. . . . Carter made it known, very clearly, that if there was a legal question in a policy paper, he wanted to know whether the options were lawful or not lawful. . . . He knew that lawyers could "advocate" any position, but he wanted his Attorney General to tell him what the correct legal answer was, and he was prepared to live by it.

Letter from Larry A. Hammond to Peter M. Shane (Jan. 7, 1986). * * *

perfund provisions against parties responsible for hazardous waste sites. On September 13 and 14, 1982, subcommittee staff requested access to EPA's files on enforcement of the Superfund Act and related statutes in so-called Region II. Despite an early assurance of access, EPA subsequently informed the subcommittee that it would not make available certain materials in enforcement files connected with active cases. This dispute eventuated in the contempt citation against Administrator Gorsuch.

At almost the same time the Levitas subcommittee requested access to EPA files on Region II, the Oversight and Investigations Subcommittee (Dingell subcommittee) of the House Committee on Energy and Commerce requested documents relating to several hazardous waste sites outside Region II, on which that subcommittee's investigation of enforcement effectiveness was focusing. Although the Dingell subcommittee's investigation did not spawn any contempt citations of its own, the coexistence of different EPA oversight hearings and demands for access to enforcement files seems to have been critically important to the dynamics of the interbranch negotiation over the Levitas subpoena. The broader range of interested parties made negotiation more difficult because of the greater number of persons to satisfy, the greater likelihood that congressional access to EPA files would undermine executive control generally over the dissemination of information on Superfund investigations, and the involvement of additional strong personalities * * *.

After the Levitas subcommittee staff demanded access to EPA enforcement files in September 1982, two weeks of unsuccessful negotiations ensued at the staff level. EPA offered to permit staff access to its files, subject to prescreening by an EPA official to maintain the confidentiality of sensitive documents. The offer was declined. On September 30, 1982, the subcommittee authorized subpoenas to issue for the requested documents.

Throughout most of October 1982, service of the subpoenas was postponed under EPA assurances of cooperation. EPA continued to assert confidentiality for a limited class of litigation-related documents, but then reverted to its position of protecting all "enforcement sensitive" documents—apparently as a reaction to the issuance of a subpoena by the Dingell subcommittee for similar information. On November 22, 1982, the Levitas subcommittee served a broad subpoena on Gorsuch, demanding the documents and her testimony on December 2, 1982.

On November 30, 1982, Attorney General Smith released a letter to Representative Dingell, justifying the Administration's refusal to comply with a subpoena for "sensitive open law enforcement investigative files." Smith also forwarded the letter to Representative Levitas to explain EPA's refusal to comply fully with the latter's subpoena as well. On the same day, President Reagan issued a memorandum to Gorsuch directing that she not divulge documents from "open law enforcement files, [which] are internal deliberative materials containing enforcement strategy and statements of the Government's position on various legal issues which may be raised in enforcement actions."

The Attorney General articulated a series of justifications for the nondisclosure of open investigative files: forestalling political influence over the conduct of an investigation, preventing the disclosure of investigative sources and methods, protecting the privacy of innocent parties named in investigative files, protecting the safety of confidential informants, and maintaining the appearance of "integrity, impartiality and fairness of the law enforcement process as a whole." Smith indicated that no assurance of confidentiality from Congress would permit the President to share his responsibility to protect the information in question, but nonetheless articulated one exception to the rule of nondisclosure: "These principles will not be employed to shield documents which contain evidence of criminal or unethical conduct by agency officials from proper review."

Following the subcommittee's December 2 hearing, General Counsel Brand, on December 8, issued a legal response to the Attorney General's letter, again challenging each of his assertions as to the limitations on Congress's oversight authority. On the same day, Levitas met with Administration officials to attempt a settlement. Levitas made an offer: subcommittee staff could review and designate for copying and delivery to the subcommittee all EPA documents relative to the waste sites at issue. If EPA or the Justice Department designated any document selected for delivery as sensitive, it would remain at EPA for inspection there. If actual delivery to the subcommittee of any of these documents proved necessary, further subpoenas might issue. All information disclosed would be treated as confidential.

The following day, the Attorney General declined the settlement offer, reiterating instead EPA's original offer of access subject to EPA prescreening. The only concession was that prescreened documents would be withheld ultimately from the subcommittee only after broad-based and high-level review in the executive branch. On December 10, the full Public Works and Transportation Committee responded by recommending (in a vote along party lines) that the House hold Gorsuch in contempt.

Six days later, the House overwhelmingly approved a resolution to certify Gorsuch's "contumacious conduct" to the United States Attorney for the District of Columbia. Prior to the actual certification, the Justice Department filed an extraordinary suit in federal district court to enjoin further action to enforce the subpoena on the ground of its unconstitutionality.

The District Court on February 3, 1983 dismissed the Justice Department's suit on the ground that any constitutional issue raised by the subpoena could be resolved in a judicial proceeding brought to enforce the subpoena. With the United States Attorney's Office still insisting that it was not bound to enforce the subpoena, Levitas and Reagan reached agreement on February 18, 1983 that the subcommittee would receive edited copies of all relevant documents and a briefing on their contents and then would be permitted to review any requested unedited documents in closed session.

Although the February 18 settlement resolved the Levitas dispute, it did not end the overall imbroglio. Still pending were subpoenas from the Dingell subcommittee, which now asserted that its investigation was focusing on specific allegations of misconduct by EPA officials. Rita Lavelle, the Superfund administrator and the most prominent of these officials, was dismissed on February 7, 1983 by the President amid allegations of her perjury to Congress and improper administration of the trust fund.

Following the agreement with Levitas on February 18, further disclosures of possibly criminal conduct at EPA made prolonged resistance to the Dingell subpoenas politically impossible. On March 9, 1983, Anne Gorsuch resigned as EPA administrator and the White House agreed to deliver all subpoenaed documents to the Dingell subcommittee, subject to certain limited protections for the confidentiality of enforcement-sensitive materials.

* * *

B. The Strategy of Problem-Solving Negotiation

In the last five years, legal scholars have turned great attention to a strategy of dispute resolution that seems ideally suited to negotiating executive privilege disputes, especially in light of the branches' different legal understandings and the virtues of according them individual respect. This strategy has been variously labeled, but is perhaps easiest to understand as "problem-solving negotiation." The pioneer work popularizing this kind of approach to dispute resolution was *Getting to Yes: Negotiating Agreement Without Giving In*, coauthored by Roger Fisher and William Ury.[194] Whether one utilizes their version or some other, the key to the approach is making the parties aware of each others' underlying needs and objectives and attempting solutions that meet a great number of those needs through expanding the resources available to the parties for a resolution of the dispute. These aims stand in contrast to what Fisher and Ury decry as "positional bargaining," in which "[e]ach side takes a position, argues for it, and makes concessions to reach a compromise."

In essence, this Article argues that problem-solving negotiation provides a critical opportunity for the political branches to divorce their processes of legal argumentation from the processes of interbranch dispute resolution. The intrabranch interpretation of law, to the extent it depends on self-interest at all, should depend largely on long-term institutional interests and on the demands of internal management—and thus, on what will typically appear to each branch to be matters of principle. The respective political branches' long-term interest in dispute resolution between themselves, however, is chiefly in preventing immediate disputes from rendering government administration unworkable. It is therefore in the government's long-term interest to focus dispute resolution processes on achieving wise and efficient conclusions to short-term problems, not on the vindication of legal positions. That is precisely what problem solving should help accomplish.

According to Fisher and Ury, the success of problem-solving negotiation depends on four imperatives: separating the people negotiating and their relationship from the problem to be solved; focusing on the parties' "interests," not their "positions"; inventing options for mutual gain; and using "objective" criteria for choosing among options. They recognize that, because of various circumstances, these guidelines

---

[194]R. FISHER & W. URY, GETTING TO YES: NEGOTIATING AGREEMENT WITHOUT GIVING IN (1981). The Fisher and Ury text is sometimes criticized as superficial or unsophisticated. To some extent, such criticisms may be unfair because the work is largely prescriptive. The book does not undertake a sophisticated modeling of many currently existing negotiations examples because that is not its task. The prescriptive emphasis of Fisher and Ury, moreover, makes it a helpful tool for organizing the discussion that follows. Its ideas are readily accessible and may be presented without a degree of preliminary elaboration that might distract the reader from the specific points this Article offers on executive privilege negotiations. The discussion in this section, therefore, borrows significantly from the Fisher and Ury framework, while drawing insight as well from other works—most notably, D. LAX & J. SEBENIUS, THE MANAGER AS NEGOTIATOR: BARGAINING FOR COOPERATION AND COMPETITIVE GAIN (1986).

will not always suffice for amicable agreement. They insist, however, that some problems typically thought to call for intransigence—for example, one party's dirty tricks or initial refusal to bargain—can often be overcome through a problem-solving approach.

It is heartening to note that the most pressing objections that commentators have urged against the Fisher and Ury approach seem, whatever their general merits, to be of less than critical importance in the executive privilege context. First, it has been suggested that the problem-solving approach overlooks those aspects of bargaining that are purely distributional—that is, for which one party's gain is necessarily the other party's loss. In such a situation, there is by definition no possibility of inventing an option for mutual gain.

Although real-life negotiations almost inevitably involve distributive problems, the Fisher-Ury prescriptions nonetheless provide a useful antidote to the tendency to exaggerate any dispute's zero-sum[200] dimension. Congress and the Executive, for example, are inclined to portray informational disputes as purely distributional, pitting indivisible demands for disclosure against indivisible demands for nondisclosure. Such thinking is misleading. Just as every real-life negotiation is likely to have its distributive side, most real-life negotiations also pose opportunities for creating some joint value and some mutual gain. There are, for example, a variety of "goods" at stake in executive privilege disputes: information content, conditions for the handling of information, timing, and the viability of the branches' working relationship in general. Expanding the parties' understanding of the range of interests at stake should profoundly increase the likelihood of a non-zero-sum solution to their immediate contest.

A second objection may be that Fisher and Ury's emphasis on "reason" as an alternative to posturing in the selection among options for dispute resolution is naive. Professor James J. White has written that often resort to "objective criteria" for dispute resolution "will do no more than give the superficial appearance of reasonableness and honesty to one party's position."[203]

This observation, however, overlooks three points. First, giving a superficial appearance of reasonableness and honesty to both parties' positions at the "pie-cutting" stage of negotiations may be most effective at preserving the atmosphere of trust and genuine information sharing that are necessary elements during the "pie-enlarging" stage. Even if the endgame of any negotiation involves a final, zero-sum tradeoff, it is in the parties' interests to preserve an atmosphere up to that point that ensures that the final pool of resources is as large as possible. Second, arguing from principle may itself enlarge the pie to be divided because "[a]cting in accord with . . . a norm or principle may be of intrinsic interest to one or more of the parties." Such "an acknowledged norm need not be an absolute value in a negotiation"; it would be sufficient to help serve to expand the resources for settlement if an acknowledged norm existed to "be partly or fully traded off against other interests."

Finally, in the executive privilege context, history provides some antidote to rationalization. The genuineness of either branch's appeal to objective criteria may be measured, in part, by the role that those criteria have played in that branch's elaboration of executive privilege doctrine in the past.

This last point is an additional and especially important reason why it may actually prove helpful to negotiation if each branch is encouraged as a general matter to work out its own executive privilege doctrine independently. Each branch's doctrine would then be a source of insight, when disputes arise, as to what that branch considers its truly significant institutional interests. * * *

A third objection to problem-solving negotiation is that, for negotiations conducted in a legal environment, it is simply not possible to separate a discussion of the parties' needs—what Fisher and Ury consider the proper object of discussion—from a discussion of each party's arguments as to legal entitlement, that is, their "positions." This is precisely because the parties are likely to perceive that a vindication of their legal claims is a cognizable need. Such an objection is obviously apposite in a negotiation between private parties, each of which has a legal position that can be vindicated only by the other's acquiescence or by third-party imprimatur. It seems less apposite, however, to negotiations between Congress and the President. As long as the two political branches can reach resolutions of immediate disputes, there should be no psychological or institutional obstacle to their "agreeing to disagree" about the law. Again, their claims that they are asserting the law correctly can be psychologically vindicated through the application of each branch's doctrine to

---

[200] "Zero-sum" and "distributive" are used to denote bargaining situations where any party's realization of value implies the loss of value for another party. "Non-zero-sum" and "integrative" are used to denote bargaining situations where the possibility exists of realizing results that leave all parties better off.

[203] White, [*The Pros and Cons of "Getting to Yes,"*] 34 J. LEGAL EDUC. 115, 117 (1984).]

its own internal management. There is no practical need for either branch to acquiesce in the other's legal interpretation or to insist on judicial approval for its own.

* * *

C. Implementing the Strategy

1. Identifying the Branches' Interests

* * *

* * * [I]t is critical not to overlook the prospects that almost always exist for creating joint value between the parties to a negotiation and insuring that the pie ultimately divided represents as much joint gain as possible. An interest-based approach to executive privilege negotiations seems an especially promising suggestion because, although the negotiations are often conducted through positional bargaining, many of the branches' interests are obvious and well-known and can be used to maximize the parties' joint gains. In general, Congress is likely to be seeking information for any of three basic reasons: (1) to facilitate its regular managerial oversight, that is, its ongoing supervision of the execution of the laws; (2) to facilitate specific legislative deliberations, aimed at the possible adoption of particular legislative proposals, the possible approval of a treaty, or the like; or (3) to facilitate investigations of particular allegations of executive branch malfeasance, for example, in aid of Congress's impeachment power. * * *

To these interests may be added a congressional interest in maintaining a general atmosphere of executive cooperation with Congress. This interest is presumably present at all times, but is balanced by closely related interests in maintaining an atmosphere of mutual respect and in enabling the President to perform his job effectively.

Of course, other interests may play a role in individual disputes. For example, if an agency is politically unpopular, an executive privilege dispute may vindicate what some members of Congress or their staffs perceive as an interest in weakening the political position of the responsible administrator. This sort of interest may be reducible, of course, to the three general interests listed above, or it may have a more partisan or personal aspect. If the congressional antagonists think it in their interest to harass or discredit a cabinet member on partisan grounds, amicable negotiations may be impossible. If partisan goals are not the dominant interests, however, it is likely that Congress's needs will relate to the general categories stated above.

The executive branch's interests in controlling information will be more varied (whether or not weightier). The executive branch has a strong general interest in maintaining its decisional independence that is balanced by its needs to maintain congressional support and enable Congress to act effectively in its designated tasks. Its less overarching interests are exemplified by various grounds specified in the Freedom of Information Act for exemptions from the ordinary rule of mandatory disclosure of executive branch records:

1. Protecting national defense and foreign policy secrets;
2. Protecting trade secrets or confidential financial information;
3. Protecting the candor of intrabranch policy deliberations;
4. Preventing unwarranted invasions of personal privacy, whether of government officers, employees or private persons; or
5. Protecting the integrity of law enforcement investigations and proceedings.

As with Congress, the executive branch, in a particular dispute, may seek to vindicate a more idiosyncratic interest, such as demonstrating presidential "backbone" to an unduly officious congressional staff. Such an interest, if reducible to one of the foregoing interests, need not present an intractable problem. If, however, the executive branch wants chiefly to discredit a particular legislator with that member's constituents, good faith negotiations will obviously be more difficult.

The identification of interests, of course, is only part of successful problem solving. The task remains to motivate the negotiators to talk about their interests (legislative oversight versus presidential privacy, for example), rather than about their positions (divulge versus withhold). * * *

Executive privilege disputes thus provide a likely context in which the parties would be helped by a formal codification of each side's general interests, as well as a formal commitment to invoke those interests in highly specific terms should particular disputes arise. This should not be difficult in theory and does not require statutory enactment. Congress may state its interests in the form of a concurrent resolution, amendable at Congress's complete discretion. The President may state the executive branch's interests in an executive order, likewise amendable. If each branch stated its "case" for disclosure or nondisclosure early and specifically in these agreed-upon terms, both sides' "positions" might prove more responsible and the terms of their discussion more productive. Further, the existence prior to any discussion of general statements of the branches' interest might assist in the recognition of common ground between the branches, which itself would increase the prospects for successful problem solving.

2. Inventing Options for Mutual Gain

The next step in problem solving, once interests are well analyzed, is to reconcile those interests. * * *

Both shared and conflicting interests will likely abound in executive privilege disputes. Congress and the President have mutual interests in appearing responsible and cooperative in pursuit of the public interest. Both branches presumably have interests in the success of a government initiative that Congress has authorized and the President is implementing. In some cases, Congress may perceive a need to obtain information quickly for oversight purposes, while the executive branch interest is chiefly in preventing congressional disclosure of particular information to the public. In such an instance, it should be possible to dovetail Congress's interest in effective oversight (and full disclosure to Congress) with the executive's interest in information control (and ultimate custody of the information).

The logistical problem, of course, is how to get the branches to focus during the course of a dispute on options for mutual gain. Fisher and Ury provide a host of suggestions for avoiding four common obstacles to integrative bargaining. These obstacles are: premature judgment; thinking there is but one "right answer" to be found; assuming erroneously the existence of a zero-sum game; and having either side regard the other side's problems as "just their problems, not ours."

In the executive privilege context, however, the one suggestion that may prove most constructive is recourse to precedent and, again, the possible documentation of precedent. By this, I do not mean to suggest the normative invocation of precedent that is characteristic of adjudication and of many negotiations—that is, the use of precedent to establish one party's entitlement to favorable treatment equivalent to the treatment enjoyed by other parties in substantially similar circumstances. I mean instead that data on previous negotiations can be useful to current brainstorming by providing reminders that the branches' interests can be dovetailed and by illustrating at least some of the possibilities for doing so.

* * *

3. Separating People from the Problem

The first suggestion Fisher and Ury proffer in the elaboration of their prescribed negotiations method is to "[s]eparate the people from the problem." They point out: "Most negotiations take place in the context of an ongoing relationship where it is important to carry on each negotiation in a way that will help rather than hinder future relations and future negotiations." For this reason, Fisher and Ury strongly advise avoiding an entanglement of the parties' relationship in the dispute over substance. To this end, they argue against making the quality of the relationship depend on the outcome of the substantive negotiation. The parties to a dispute are urged, instead, to "[b]ase the relationship on accurate perceptions, clear communication, appropriate emotions, and a forward-looking, purposive outlook," independent of substance.

In applying this advice to the executive privilege context, there is an important distinction to note between the institutional relationship between the political branches and the personal relationships among the persons acting on each branch's behalf. The institutional relationship is part of the substance of executive privilege disputes, and it is therefore impossible to separate the substance of the disputes from that relationship. The advice is pointedly apt, however, with respect to the personal relationships among the individuals negotiating. People who have been involved in interbranch negotiation would surely testify that the potential for ill will and inefficiency is ever-present where committee staff and agency staff permit ego to overtake substance.

To make that point, however, is to highlight the difficulty in finding a structural solution to this particular problem. Fisher and Ury proffer a host of suggestions to help "separate the people from the problem," but all are behavioral suggestions directed at what might be called the "micro" level of negotiation, that is, the actual face-to-face encounter of bargainers. Thus, their implementation would seem to depend largely on the personalities of the individuals engaged in bargaining. If a staff person is someone who might politely be called an egomaniac, it is doubtful that negotiations will benefit much from an executive order requiring agency representatives, say, to "[m]ake emotions explicit and acknowledge them as legitimate."

Moreover, structural interbranch problems exacerbate the human tendency—distressingly evident in the halls of power—to place ego first. In particular, although the political branches have an ongoing relationship to which negotiators should be attentive, responsibility for negotiating executive privilege disputes is widely diffused on Congress's side. Fortuity alone determines the degree of sensitivity to the interbranch relationship that has been internalized by the particular member or the member's staff responsible for negotiation.

In contrast, executive privilege negotiations on the executive side are focused predominantly in the White House and in the Office of Legal Counsel of the United States Department of Justice. Other problems aside, the involvement in these disputes of a few key actors who are routinely exposed to the full breadth of issues on which Congress and the executive are interdependent should provide a strong likelihood that executive branch negotiators will have both internalized psychologically the importance of the interbranch relationship and learned the importance of subordinating their personal emotional needs to the dictates of a sound interbranch relationship.

If Congress could likewise centralize responsibility for executive privilege negotiations, at least once negotiations pass the most informal level, the routine involvement on both sides of a predictable group of actors would greatly assist in separating people from the substantive problems presented. The likeliest repositories for such responsibilities are the offices of the Speaker and Senate Majority Leader or the offices of the chairs of the respective Committees on the Judiciary. The former are preferable because, like the President (and his Attorney General), the Speaker and Majority Leader (and their staffs) should be most deeply aware of the full range of issues under consideration by the two branches and of the importance of an overall pattern of cooperation. The latter, however, have the possible advantage of deeper immersion in the relevant legal issues and the greatest day-to-day interaction with the Department of Justice on other problems.

Centralizing negotiating responsibility in some particular office in each house of Congress would greatly reduce whatever distortion is worked in negotiations by the limelight-seeking tendencies or personal idiosyncrasies of the member or staff person who happens, on a given day, to become involved in an information dispute. Unfortunately, this kind of centralization runs directly against Congress's recent centrifugal tendencies and * * * is likely to meet resistance.

4. Invoking Objective Criteria for Dispute Resolution

The final aspect of the Fisher and Ury approach involves the "distributional" aspect of bargaining, that is, where one party's gain will be the other party's concession. As noted earlier, Fisher and Ury recommend using objective criteria rather than a test of wills. They argue that "[a] constant battle for dominance threatens a relationship." It is, therefore, "far easier to deal with people when both . . . are discussing objective standards for settling a problem instead of trying to force each other to back down." As noted earlier, this suggestion does not pertain chiefly to the problem-solving aspect of a negotiation. Its aim is to constrain the parties' conduct of the distributive aspect of the negotiation in a way that does not undermine the prospects for problem solving.

As Panglossian as this may sound to the cynical, it should be easier for government institutions to approach disputes in this manner than for many private bargainers to do so. First, the branches would be aware of the incentive for principled discussion, namely, maintaining the best atmosphere for achieving whatever joint gains are possible through negotiation. Further, as noted above, precedent exists as a source of criteria outside the parties' immediate dispute, by which it becomes possible to judge the practicability of possible resolutions to the current dispute. For example, in a dispute over information that the executive branch and Congress agree can acceptably be shared with a congressional committee in executive session, the only issue for resolution is whether all copies of the material will return to the executive branch following disclosure. Discussion could turn to like disclosures in the past. The committee's counsel might then say: "We handled the Smith matter last year in the way we now propose. In what way do the two cases differ? Is this information more sensitive? Did anything subsequent to your disclosure of information last year belie the wisdom of that settlement?"

In further illustration, if Congress agrees with the executive branch that it needs only summary versions of the demanded information at the present time, the dispute concerns only the extent to which Congress may compare representative summaries with the underlying documents to ensure authenticity. The Assistant Attorney General in charge of the Office of Legal Counsel might then say: "For the Jones investigation, we allowed you to check one of every 20 summaries. Is the information we are now providing any less likely to be accurate than the Jones files? Has anything occurred to suggest the insufficiency of the sampling in Jones for your purposes?"

These examples demonstrate that the use of past executive privilege dispute resolutions as benchmarks for current reasoning can foster discussion about reasons for disclosure or nondisclosure, rather than simply assertions about what each side is entitled or willing to do.

* * *

D. Is Reform Possible?

* * *

Two good reasons exist to believe that the problem-solving approach outlined above incorporates features that would be * * * attractive to both branches * * *. First, the approach is largely adoptable, as mentioned above, by a complementary congressional resolution and presidential executive order. Such a procedure would formally preserve each branch's claim to plenary authority over executive branch information and permit each branch the formal option of backing out if the modus vivendi breaks down. Second, it eschews recourse to the courts for dispute resolution. Any such recourse bodes risks for each branch; problem solving offers promise of dispute resolution without litigative risk.

* * *

The proposal likely to meet greatest resistance is the proposal for greater centralization of Congress's negotiating "apparatus." Each Congress member's jealousy of his or her own policymaking prerogatives is a powerful disincentive against greater institutional coordination. The situation, however, is not hopeless. On one hand, the increasing entropy of Congress is an oft-noted and much lamented phenomenon. Perhaps the executive privilege area, because it is more exceptional than routine, might appear to Congress to be an attractive area for an experiment with greater institutional discipline and control.

The hardest question of incentives regarding the problem-solving approach, therefore, is whether sufficient reasons exist for the two branches to do anything at all to change their approach to these issues. Resolving all executive privilege issues on an ad hoc basis has an appeal to both branches. The executive branch may fear that a commitment to problem solving would undermine its ability to manage the outflow of information to maximum political advantage. Congress may fear lending any imprimatur, however indirect, to the legitimacy of withholding information from the legislative branch. * * *

* * *

In sum, the prospects for reform are not overwhelmingly favorable, but they do exist. * * *

* * *

Additional Sources

R. Douglas Arnold, CONGRESS AND THE BUREAUCRACY: A THEORY OF INFLUENCE (1979)

Stanley M. Brand & Sean Connelly, *Constitutional Confrontations: Preserving a Prompt and Orderly Means by Which Congress May Enforce Investigative Demands Against Executive Branch Officials*, 36 Cath. U. L. Rev. 71 (1986)

Archibald Cox, *Executive Privilege*, 122 U. Pa. L. Rev. 1383 (1974)

Louis Fisher, CONSTITUTIONAL CONFLICTS BETWEEN CONGRESS AND THE PRESIDENT (1985)

Gerald Gunther, *Judicial Hegemony and Legislative Autonomy: The* Nixon *Case and the Impeachment Process*, 22 UCLA L. Rev. 30 (1974)

Matthew D. McCubbins & Thomas Schwartz, *Congressional Oversight Overlooked: Police Patrols versus Fire Alarms*, 28 Am. J. Pol. Sci. 165 (1984)

Matthew D. McCubbins et al., *Administrative Procedures as Instruments of Political Control*, 3 J.L. Econ. & Organ. 243 (1987)

Peter M. Shane, *Negotiating for Knowledge: Administrative Responses to Congressional Demands for Information*, 44 Admin. L. Rev. 197 (1992)

Steven W. Stathis, *Executive Cooperation: Presidential Recognition of the Investigative Authority of Congress and the Courts*, 3 J.L. & Pol. 183 (1986)

Kate Stith, *Congress' Power of the Purse*, 97 Yale L.J. 1343 (1988)

William F. West & Joseph Cooper, *Legislative Influence v. Presidential Dominance: Competing Models of Bureaucratic Control*, 104 Pol. Sci. Q. 581 (1990)

3. The Debate About the Supervision of Agency Rulemaking by the President

In recent years, centralized executive oversight of agency rulemaking has become a major feature of administrative policymaking. Supporters of such oversight say it vindicates values of democratic accountability, at least to the degree that the president is seen as accountable to the public as a whole and the president's will is seen to dominate the review process. Moreover, centralized oversight is said to promote values of comprehensive rationality to the extent that executive overseers require agencies to justify their rules, within the limits of law, according to comprehensive criteria.*

In the first excerpt, Professor Harold Bruff defends presidential oversight so long as certain controls on its exercise are respected. These controls involve public disclosure of key elements of oversight decisionmaking as well as obedience to the principle that agency discretion not be displaced by centralized reviewers.

In the second excerpt, public interest lawyer Alan Morrison argues that centralized oversight frequently leads to counterproductive interference with agency rulemaking. Mr. Morrison is particularly concerned about delays caused by executive oversight, as well as what he considers the lack of expertise of persons who have been principally charged with such oversight. In Mr. Morrison's view, it is one thing for executive reviewers to ask questions about agency rules, but it is quite another—and in his mind inappropriate—for them to second-guess agency decisions. Mr. Morrison is also critical of the secrecy that surrounded executive oversight during the 1980s.

The next excerpt by Professors Strauss and Sunstein places executive oversight in the context of broadly competing views of the regulatory process. They also argue—in agreement with Professor Bruff—that centralized reviewers should not make the ultimate regulatory decision when such power is vested by statute in an agency. Although the president has the power to remove an agency head serving at his will, the removal power is not as a practical matter able to be frequently exercised. Short of removal, the authors suggest, the president's oversight authority is consultative and supervisory rather than decisional.

The fourth excerpt is by Charles Tiefer, Deputy General Counsel of the United States House of Representatives. Mr. Tiefer is a critic of the Bush Administration's program of regulatory oversight, which was carried out under the auspices of the President's Council on Competitiveness. Although Mr. Tiefer's excerpt focuses on events from 1990 to 1992, it is of more than historical importance. From the critic's perspective, one must always guard against tendencies toward secrecy and unaccountability in executive oversight—with which Mr. Tiefer charges the Council on Competitiveness.

---

* The excerpts in this section, written before President Clinton took office, raise general issues that will be relevant to any regime of executive oversight. It bears noting that President Clinton's Executive Order on the subject—E.O. No. 12,866, 58 Fed. Reg. 51,735 (Oct. 4, 1993)—was prepared in part in response to criticisms of earlier Administrations, and in particular, the Bush Administration (discussed by a congressional critic in the fourth excerpt in this section).

Harold H. Bruff, *Presidential Management of Agency Rulemaking*, 57 GEO. WASH. L. REV. 533, 533, 546-52, 554-56, 578-89 (1989)*

* * * My general conclusion is that a presidential oversight program has its place in the administrative state, but that certain controls on its exercise need to be adopted to keep it within appropriate bounds of law and policy.

* * *

III. The Evolution of Presidential Management Programs

The first executive oversight program for rulemaking was the Nixon administration's "Quality of Life" review. This program was announced as an interagency review of proposed regulations dealing with environmental quality, consumer protection, and other aspects of public health and safety. In practice the Quality of Life review program focused almost exclusively on regulations of the Environmental Protection Agency (EPA). EPA's summary of a new rule and its possible alternatives were sent to reviewing agencies (such as the Council on Wage & Price Stability), which had four weeks to comment, unless OMB extended the time. The OMB staff integrated the comments and criticisms and transmitted them to EPA. The process sometimes prolonged rulemaking for many months. Quality of Life review brought outside views of regulatory costs and alternatives to EPA, with some effects on its policymaking.

President Ford's Inflation Impact Statement program focused on the fiscal impact of regulations. By Executive Order No. 11,821, he authorized OMB to promulgate criteria for agencies to use in determining which proposals were "major" in their effects upon the overall economy. Agencies' rulemaking staffs then prepared Inflation Impact Statements outlining the costs of the rules and furnished them to OMB. It soon became clear, however, that a decentralized process that left the primary responsibility for impact assessment to the agencies would not affect policy choices as much as would external review. Charges were made that the Inflation Impact Statements were post-hoc justifications for decisions already reached rather than actual restraints on the excessive inflationary cost of rules.

In 1978, President Carter issued Executive Order No. 12,044 requiring detailed regulatory analyses of proposed agency rules and review by the Executive Office of the President. OMB subsequently issued guidance to the agencies on how to perform a regulatory analysis. President Carter then created the Regulatory Analysis Review Group (RARG), composed of representatives from the principal economic and regulatory agencies. RARG's purpose was to review a limited number of regulatory analyses having substantial economic impact. Its four-member executive committee included representatives from OMB and the Council of Economic Advisors (CEA) as permanent members; the other two memberships rotated every six months among the cabinet departments (excluding State and Defense) and EPA. RARG received staff support from the CEA and the Council on Wage and Price Stability (COWPS), and analyzed only the most important half-dozen proposed regulations each year. In the RARG review process, reports were drafted by the CEA and COWPS staff, commented on and agreed to by the permanent RARG members, and issued in final form for agency consideration.

President Carter also created the Regulatory Council, a group consisting of the heads of regulatory agencies. The Council's principal function was to develop and publish semi-annually the *Calendar of Federal Regulations*, which provided analytical synopses of 120 to 180 major regulations under development that were likely to have substantial economic or public impact. The Council also assisted regulators in developing cost-effective and consistent regulations. The Council then used the *Calendar* to help identify relationships among upcoming rules, and to develop coordinated plans for dealing with any significant interjurisdictional regulatory issues. The Council also undertook numerous studies and projects designed to improve the regulatory process.

The Ford and Carter precedents influenced the Regulatory Reform bills drafted, but never enacted, between 1978 and 1981. These bills foreshadowed OMB's subsequent role in the Reagan administration. The Office of Information and Regulatory Affairs (OIRA) within OMB was created by the Paperwork Reduction Act, a spinoff from the regulatory reform bills. The Act's more stringent requirements for agency justification of record-keeping requirements that are imposed on the public provide a statutory basis for OIRA to involve itself in the detail of new agency rules because the rules frequently require submissions, reports, and surveys. This legislation was the formal beginning of an institutional OMB structure for rulemaking oversight.

---

* Reprinted with permission of the George Washington Law Review and Harold H. Bruff. All rights reserved.

Also, all of the major bills gave key roles in oversight to OMB. The Reagan administration borrowed from the bills in the drafting of its first executive order in the first month after the change of administrations in 1981.

The Reagan administration's program for oversight of regulation is the most ambitious to date. Executive Order No. 12,291, "Federal Regulation," requires executive agencies, to the extent permitted by statute, to observe cost-benefit principles in implementing regulations. The order requires executive agencies to evaluate proposed "major rules" (those with a significant effect on the economy) according to a prescribed "regulatory impact analysis." The central innovations of Executive Order No. 12,291 are the mandatory character of its substantive requirements and its system for their enforcement by OMB.

Section 2 of the order requires agencies, to the extent permitted by law, to "adhere" to five general principles "[i]n promulgating new regulations, reviewing existing regulations, and developing legislative proposals concerning regulation." These principles require agencies to base administrative decisions on "adequate information concerning the need for and consequences of proposed government action," and to set regulatory objectives, order regulatory priorities, and undertake regulatory action in a way that will maximize the net benefits to society when costs and benefits are compared.

Section 3 of the order requires agencies to issue preliminary and final Regulatory Impact Analyses (RIAs) in connection with major rules. An RIA must include statements of the anticipated costs and benefits of the proposed rule, the anticipated incidence of those costs and benefits, the net anticipated benefits of the regulation, and other potentially more cost-effective regulatory possibilities, with an explanation, if appropriate, of the legal reasons why the most cost-effective means of achieving the anticipated benefits cannot be adopted. The cost-benefit analysis mandated by the order expressly requires the inclusion of beneficial or adverse regulatory effects that cannot be quantified in monetary terms.

On their face, these provisions do not dictate particular regulatory decisions. The terms "cost" and "benefit" are not defined by the order, and the inclusion of unquantifiable costs and benefits in the required calculus can afford agencies significant discretion. The section 2 principles are, however, expressly intended to require agencies to weigh competing values in a particular way, and to be prepared to justify regulatory decisions according to a generally prescribed form of analysis. In this sense, section 2 is not neutrally "procedural." The order is obviously meant to affect the substance of regulation.

An agency must transmit each proposed major rule, together with a preliminary RIA, to the Director of OMB sixty days prior to the publication of any notice of proposed rulemaking. OMB then has sixty days to review the submission, and may require the agency to consult concerning the preliminary RIA and notice of proposed rulemaking, and to refrain, subject to judicial or statutory deadlines, from publishing its proposal until review is concluded. The order provides, however, that these review powers shall not "be construed as displacing the agencies' responsibilities delegated by law."

Subsequently, Executive Order No. 12,498 was promulgated to establish a "regulatory planning process." This order requires the head of each executive agency to send OMB a "draft regulatory program" that describes "all significant regulatory actions" to be undertaken within one year. OMB reviews the plan for consistency with administration policy, and a final plan is published. Executive Order No. 12,498 supplements the prior order by giving agency heads and OMB more power over the early stages of the regulatory process. * * *

* * *

IV. OMB and the Agencies: Comparative Competence and Power
* * *

B. *Analysis of the Costs and Benefits of Regulation*
* * *

Executive review of regulatory analysis can promote its consistent performance in ways that judicial review cannot, for two reasons. First, although courts are decentralized, the executive can review all analyses according to a single set of criteria. Second, although courts do not attempt to require the "best" analyses, just acceptable ones, the executive can pursue both quality and consistency in the agencies' analytic techniques.

Executive Order No. 12,291 requires cost-benefit analysis, which has always been controversial for several reasons. First, the uncertainty and difficulty of the process may render it especially vulnerable to manipulation in service of predetermined outcomes. Second, it tends to be biased against regulation because the direct costs of a rule are likely to be more visible and quantifiable than are its benefits. Third, cost-benefit analysis is usually the province of economists, whose professional orientation favors private ordering and clashes with that of health scientists, who are more risk-averse to possible threats to public health.

What matters most about cost-benefit analysis is the spirit in which it is performed. One skeptic concedes that it is valuable if used by someone "committed to the underlying goals and spirit of a regulatory program," but not if used to mask anti-regulatory bias.[120] Its defenders point out that its stated purpose is to ask questions about rules that any rational observer would address.[121]

Cost-benefit analysis can reveal and counteract biases that favor excessively stringent regulation. Disputes between OMB and the agencies have persisted concerning two analytic techniques with strong implications for the desirable stringency of regulation. First, agencies have pressed for the use of multiple conservative assumptions in environmental decisions, which favors strict regulation. OMB has urged the use of discount rates for future illnesses, which implies relaxed regulation. Similarly, OMB has pursued efficiency by pressing agencies to replace traditional "command and control" regulations, such as engineering controls, with innovative market-based strategies, such as auctions of rights to pollute.

A second, less controversial, technique is cost-effectiveness analysis. It avoids direct weighing of such imponderables as the value of life by simply asking whether a given strategy is the cheapest means to a posited goal. Present regulations vary greatly by this criterion. This technique's use can help to equalize burdens of regulation, minimizing differences in costs to the economy per unit of gain, by such measures as statistical lives saved. Much of the existing disparity in approach, however, is built into the statutes due to their episodic enactment or because other values intrude, such as equalizing risks to groups of workers regardless of cost differences.

* * *

VI. *The Openness of OMB Oversight*

The extent to which OMB oversight of federal rulemaking is openly reflected in an agency's administrative record raises two legal issues. Both are clouded by uncertainty and debate. First, to what extent are unrecorded "ex parte" contacts permissible in rulemaking? Second, does the President's constitutional executive privilege extend to OIRA's discussions with agencies about their rules? Obviously, these issues are related. They have produced a wealth of analysis, if not agreement. Much of the commentary mixes law and policy, often without clearly distinguishing between them. I will try to identify the law/policy border in the following discussion.

Neither the Administrative Procedure Act (APA) nor the Due Process Clause provides a general bar to ex parte contacts in rulemaking, although some statutes limit them for particular programs. Courts reviewing rules have struggled with two rather inconsistent directives from the Supreme Court, and have consequently produced a confused body of case law. In *Vermont Yankee Nuclear Power Corp. v. Natural Resources Defense Council, Inc.*, the Court held that courts may not compel agencies to follow procedures that are not required by statute or by due process. *State Farm* emphasized, however, that an agency's administrative record must provide full substantive justification for its policy choices.

The application of these competing considerations to ex parte contacts within the executive branch was ably analyzed in *Sierra Club v. Costle*:

> The purposes of full-record review which underlie the need for disclosing ex parte conversations in some settings do not require that courts know the details of every White House contact . . . in this informal rulemaking setting. After all, any rule issued here with or without White House assistance must have the requisite *factual support* in the rulemaking record . . . . The courts will monitor all this, but they need not be omniscient to perform their role effectively. Of course, it is always possible that undisclosed Presidential prodding may direct an outcome that *is* factually based on the record, but different from the outcome that would have obtained in the absence of Presidential involvement. In such a case, it would be true that the political process did affect the outcome in a way the courts could not police. But we do not believe that Congress intended that the courts convert informal rulemaking into a rarified technocratic process, unaffected by political considerations or the presence of Presidential power.

Reflecting a similar analysis, the Administrative Conference has recommended that rulemakers "should be free to receive written or oral policy

---

[120] *National Academy of Public Administration, Presidential Management of Rulemaking in Regulatory Agencies* 44 (1987) [hereinafter NAPA Report] (providing separate views of Richard Wegman). This Report, by an able panel of the National Academy, resulted from an empirical and normative inquiry into presidential management of agency rulemaking in the Reagan administration.

[121] *See, e.g.*, Scalia, *Regulatory Review and Management*, REG., Jan./Feb. 1982, at 19, 19-20.

advice" from elsewhere in the executive branch, "without having a duty to place these intragovernmental communications in the public file of the rulemaking," unless they contain "material factual information (as distinct from indications of governmental policy)."

A. The Problem of Conduit Communications

OIRA review can provide a "conduit" by which the views of interested private persons reach an agency, without submission to the publicly available record of a rulemaking. These communications pose two kinds of problems. First, they may include new factual information or policy arguments which escape the testing process to which other material in the agency's possession is subjected by public comment. Second, due to their endorsement by OMB, they may assume special prominence in the agency's analysis, risking unfairness to those interested persons who do not enjoy the same access. These concerns for the integrity of the administrative record and for fairness to the public sound partly in law and partly in policy. They have resulted in a recommendation by the Administrative Conference that all conduit communications be revealed in the public record of a rulemaking.

Soon after issuance of Executive Order No. 12,291, the Department of Justice's Office of Legal Counsel (OLC) advised OMB regarding ex parte contacts with agencies:

> You and your staff may freely contact agencies regarding the substance of proposed regulations, and may do so by way of telephone calls, meetings, or other forms of communication unavailable to members of the public.
>
> . . .
>
> . . . [R]ulemaking agencies should disclose in the administrative file . . . substantive communications from your Office to the extent that they are (1) purely factual as opposed to deliberative in nature, or (2) received by your Office from a source outside of executive or independent agencies.
>
> . . .
>
> Notwithstanding these general recommendations, we believe that the rulemaking agency need not disclose substantive communications from your Office which form part of the agency's deliberative process.[279]

Thus, OLC's advice followed the emerging consensus among administrative lawyers regarding ex parte contacts. OMB adopted it, but not completely. In a memorandum instructing agencies on procedures under the new executive order, OMB stressed that "[b]oth the public and the agencies should understand that the primary forum for receiving factual communications concerning proposed rules is the agency." Therefore, factual materials sent to OMB were also to be sent to the agencies for inclusion in the record, and OMB promised to identify as "appropriate for the whole record of the agency rulemaking" any factual material that it developed or received and then transmitted to an agency. Omitted from this formulation was policy material received from outside the government. OMB would soon encounter substantial controversy concerning its use.

A number of health and safety rulemakings during the Reagan administration have produced complaints about conduit communications. Congressional committees overseeing the programs proved sympathetic to these complaints, and brought increasing pressure on OIRA to alter its procedures. OIRA has consistently denied that it has served as a conduit. Especially in the early years of the executive order program, however, OMB engaged in many meetings and informal contacts with interested persons, most of whom represented regulated industries. Because of OMB's heavy workload, this practice created risks that new factual material would reach agencies without identification by OMB, that policy positions of outsiders would be accepted uncritically by OMB, and that the process would display a bias toward industry. Charges arose that all three of these effects were present.

* * *

Several features of these cases probably helped to exacerbate relationships with the congressional oversight committees, whose reports developed a notably hostile tone. First, partisan politics undoubtedly played a role, as the administration and the committees squabbled over the direction regulatory policy should take. Second, in rulemaking it is often difficult to separate fact from policy, so OMB may have appeared to be violating its own rules—or, indeed, it may have done so. Third, the administration's emphasis on regulatory relief and the frequency of its contacts with industry groups opened OMB to portrayal as a special pleader for industry, instead of a critic prepared to see both the costs and benefits of regulation.

B. Conflict and Compromise: The Evolution of OMB's Disclosure Policy

By 1986, OMB was under serious pressure from

---

[279] *Contacts Between the Office of Management and Budget and Executive Branch Agencies Under Executive Order No. 12,291* (Apr. 24, 1981), *reprinted in* 5 Op. Off. Legal Counsel 107, 110-12 (1981).

both Houses of Congress. The Chairmen of three important House committees joined in an effort to deny OIRA any appropriations until limits to its powers were enacted. In the Senate, members of the Committee on Governmental Affairs pressed OMB to open its processes. OMB wanted to obtain reauthorization of the Paperwork Reduction Act and to stop the "defunding" move in the House. In June, 1986, OIRA Administrator Gramm issued a memorandum announcing new disclosure procedures. There were two antecedents for these procedures: a Senate amendment to a paperwork reauthorization bill in 1984, which failed to pass, and a special agreement OMB reached with EPA in 1985 for review of its rules.

Under the 1986 procedures, OIRA makes available copies of draft notices of proposed rulemaking and final rules that are submitted for review, along with copies of all related correspondence between OIRA and agency heads. These documents are available once the notices or final rules have been published in the Federal Register. Similarly, OIRA provides on request copies of agency submissions under Executive Order No. 12,498, following publication of the final Regulatory Program.

OIRA also agreed to stricter controls on "conduit" communications from persons outside the federal government. For these added controls OIRA referred to its earlier procedures for EPA, along with an offer to extend them to any other agency so requesting. OIRA sends these agencies copies of all written material from outsiders, advises them of all oral communications, and invites agency personnel to attend meetings concerning their rules. It also makes available in its public reading room written materials and lists of meetings and communications involving persons outside the federal government.

These procedures have removed some, but not all, of the controversy over the openness of OMB review. For review under Executive Order No. 12,291, the significant gaps in disclosure are: (1) the absence of draft notices and rules that are withdrawn by the agency and never issued; (2) the absence of correspondence between OIRA desk officers and subordinate agency personnel; and (3) the absence of summaries of oral communications between OIRA and the agencies.

C. The Scope of Executive Privilege

Analysis of the appropriate degree of openness of OMB review of rulemaking must consider the role of executive privilege, which may provide a constitutional bar to some measures. Two Supreme Court cases have shed some light on the problem. In *United States v. Nixon*, the Court recognized a constitutional executive privilege based on the President's need for confidential policy deliberations. The privilege was qualified, however, and in *Nixon* itself was overridden by the need of the courts for evidence in a criminal case.

The Court's use of a functional, balancing approach was repeated in *Nixon v. Administrator of General Services*, in which the Court upheld the power of Congress to regulate presidential papers. From a separation of powers standpoint, the Court said,

> the proper inquiry focuses on the extent to which [the Act] prevents the Executive Branch from accomplishing its constitutionally assigned functions. Only where the potential for disruption is present must we then determine whether that impact is justified by an overriding need to promote objectives within the constitutional authority of Congress.

The Court found that the activities of records archivists would cause only a limited intrusion on confidentiality, and were therefore justified by congressional needs to preserve history. It pointed out that confidentiality is a wasting asset subject to erosion by the creation of presidential libraries, the memoirs of participants, and the efforts of historians.

Congress has been of two minds about executive confidentiality. On the one hand, it has entirely exempted the President and his immediate staff from the Freedom of Information Act (FOIA), and has provided an exemption from forced disclosure for deliberative materials generated elsewhere in the executive branch. * * * On the other hand, Congress has repeatedly sought to override claims of executive privilege in order to obtain material in the hands of the executive for its own use. Courts have not announced any clear rules for these congressional-executive contests over information, and it is often difficult to litigate them at all. Consequently, informal negotiation and struggle dominate, with congressional committees obtaining most information they desire if they are persistent enough and enjoy the support of their house of Congress.

Thus, it would not reflect actual government practice to argue that the executive branch possesses a nonwaivable executive privilege for all deliberative material it generates. The executive has sometimes made such claims as a tactic in contests over information, yet it often releases such materials to congressional committees or to members of the public. Indeed, the 1986 compromise between OIRA and its oversight committees is one example of the contingent nature of executive confidentiality as it actually operates.

The executive branch has, however, two strong claims for confidentiality. First, deliberations between the President and his immediate advisers (which were involved in *Nixon* itself) implicate the President's ability to perform his constitutional functions, and deserve a strong presumption of confidentiality. Thus, if the President or his immediate advisers wish to discuss regulatory policy with an agency head, their conversations need not reach the administrative record. This privilege does not necessarily mean, however, that communications between OIRA and agencies deserve the same treatment.

Second, throughout the executive branch there is an essentially unvarying interest in protecting policy discussion while a decision is under consideration, as opposed to after the fact. This is not a matter of encouraging candid advice, which needs long-term protection to flourish. Instead, it is a matter of power over the policy decision itself. When deliberation on a pending decision is open, it is very hard to limit the lobbying of every interested person and to control the situation. With these considerations in mind, I now turn to specifics on the openness of OMB oversight.

D. Protecting the Administrative Record: A Paper Trail Or A Logging Requirement?

Regulatory oversight evolved substantially during the Reagan administration. The NAPA Report concluded that "while it appeared originally to respond to the demands of regulated industries for regulatory relief and to operate with little public and congressional scrutiny, it is now more open and restrained." NAPA called for even more openness, recommending that agencies "log, summarize, and include in the rulemaking record all communications from outside parties, OMB, or other executive or legislative branch officials concerning the merits of proposed regulations."

NAPA's approach is not the only acceptable one. Any particular disclosure feature should be judged by its marginal contribution to the values served by openness, weighed against its marginal burdens and its interference with the values served by confidentiality. I proceed by analyzing increasing levels of disclosure.

The 1986 compromise between OMB and the committees produces a "paper trail" of oversight activity. Those interested can track the written portions of OMB's activity to check its wisdom and legality. Knowing that this trail is being left, those within OIRA and the agencies can be expected to ensure that their interchange is within legal limits. Presumably, however, candor suffers somewhat. The effects are both good and bad. Pressure to ignore the administrative record or statutory limits might be less likely to occur when information must be delivered orally, and to that extent furtively. On the other hand, written advice may be crafted for the public eye, with more posturing and less incisiveness.

Less than this amount of disclosure does not seem desirable. In the early years of the Reagan administration's program, charges frequently arose that OMB was pressing an agency beyond the parameters justified by its statute or its administrative record. Under the pressure of congressional investigation, a paper trail of each controversial rulemaking emerged to allow resolution of the dispute. This pattern of inquiry and eventual disclosure, with its heavy transaction costs for all concerned, is likely to recur unless a paper trail is routinely provided. Similarly, the new controls on conduit communications seem necessary to ensure the fairness of executive oversight.

The 1986 compromise does not, however, produce a complete paper trail. One omitted category is notices and rules that are withdrawn by an agency. Adding these items would not pose much added burden for the agencies and OMB. Indeed, the availability of submissions for the Regulatory Program pursuant to Executive Order No. 12,498, whether or not the initiative matures in a notice of proposed rulemaking, shows that such an addition would be feasible.

The 1986 compromise also does not reveal correspondence among subordinate personnel, for example memoranda exchanged by desk officers and agency staff, although congressional inquiries or leaks often reveal them. The routine availability of these items would materially aid understanding of the oversight process, only a portion of which appears in formal written communications between the Administrator of OIRA and agency heads. Also, pressure to ignore an agency's statute or administrative record can occur at any level of the process. On the other hand, revealing staff dialogue might blur political accountability within both OIRA and the agencies by inviting observers to wonder who speaks for the institution, the staff or the political appointee at the top. Knowing their correspondence would be made public, staff could try to bind their superiors by taking strong positions in print. On balance, I think this material should be available, although the issue is close.

Another possible modification of the 1986 procedures would be to require agency drafts to be published in the Federal Register simultaneously with their submission to OMB. I think it better to make the drafts available only after the rulemaking notices have been published. Publicity about the pendency of review can only increase pressure on OIRA to engage in communications with interested persons. Instead, rulemaking procedure should be structured to guide persons outside the government to the agency, not to OIRA.

Whether oral communications should be "logged" (summarized and placed in the public record) presents another close question. Longstanding dispute over this procedure has made the arguments familiar. The traditional conception of rulemaking as an informal, "quasi-legislative" activity has made unrecorded ex parte contacts seem permissible. Congress has declined to amend the APA to alter that view. Moreover, an agency must defend its rules in court solely on the basis of the public record, and may not rely on facts or policy argument not reflected there.

The NAPA Report finds these considerations outweighed by improvements that disclosure will bring to the oversight dialogue. Certainly, OMB pressure to ignore the administrative record or the statute can be applied as easily by voice as by pen. Yet that pressure can occur anyway, at higher levels of the executive branch, in ways that are difficult or impossible to police. For detailed policy argument, there may be no practical alternative to writing. Moreover, agencies can request that policy advice on a particular matter be transmitted in writing whenever the content of oral advice appears to merit that check. A strict logging requirement in OIRA could simply shift oral discussion up the organization chart, or into the early rulemaking stages to which logging requirements generally do not apply.

Logging all oral communications would add a significant burden to administration. More important, it would alter the relationship between OMB and the agencies in some undesirable ways. The very presence of an executive privilege concept recognizes a positive value in informal discussion. Policy debate tends to feature negotiation and compromise, as the history of OMB oversight illustrates. Negotiation is not a flower that blooms in sunlight. Therefore, there is reason to maintain an informal, oral channel of communication between agencies and OIRA, even if more detailed, formal communication that is written down is available to the public.

The Administrative Conference has recommended that official written policy guidance to agencies from OIRA be placed in the public file of the rulemaking after the notice to which it pertains is issued. I would add other written communications between OIRA and the agencies. Written or oral policy advice from the President or his immediate advisors to agencies need not be disclosed, however, so that the constitutional executive privilege can operate. And at least for the present, a universal logging requirement seems premature.

* * *

Alan B. Morrison, *OMB Interference with Agency Rulemaking: The Wrong Way to Write a Regulation*, 99 Harv. L. Rev. 1059, 1059-60, 1062-68 (1986)*

* * *

* * * I will argue that whatever theoretical legitimacy there may be for OMB involvement in the rulemaking process, its dominance under the present system is unwarranted. Congress should eliminate OMB's involvement in the rulemaking process; and until that occurs, the President, in the interest of fairness and sensible management, should impose restrictions on OMB that eliminate the worst abuses.

I. A Little History
* * *

In one sense, Executive Order 12,291 is merely an extension of the prior system of control over agency rulemaking. In another sense, however, the Order creates a very different system, because the professed aim of this Administration is to cut back significantly, if not actually to destroy, the regulatory system established by Congress. The Administration believes that it has a mandate to do so, despite public opinion polls showing the contrary, and it has proceeded under that assumption. The difficulty with its position is that the basic laws have not been amended, and to the extent that the Administration has tried the legislative route to bring about change in the basic federal regulatory framework, it has not succeeded. It is one thing for the President to use OMB supervision of executive agencies to coordinate the issuance of agency regulations so that they are consistent with congressional statutes; but it is quite

---

* Copyright 1986 by the Harvard Law Review Association. Reprinted with permission of the Harvard Law Review Association and Alan B. Morrison. All rights reserved.

another to use the system of OMB control to frustrate or dismantle the very regulatory scheme enacted by Congress and reaffirmed over the Administration's legislative efforts.

* * *

II. The Good and the Bad

I do not dispute that OMB can perform some useful functions in the rulemaking process. Its role in coordinating related proceedings between agencies and in assuring that relevant scientific information, cost data, and alternative approaches are shared between agencies, are entirely proper. And to the extent that OMB review can help ensure that agencies give careful consideration to the principal comments submitted in a rulemaking, that is also an appropriate goal. Similarly, it is proper for OMB to insist that agencies take a hard look at the necessity for a rule, provided OMB does so in an even-handed manner.

* * *

* * * [On the other hand,] the system of OMB control imposes costly delays that are paid for through the decreased health and safety of the American public. This system also places the ultimate rulemaking decisions in the hands of OMB personnel who are neither competent in the substantive areas of regulation, nor accountable to Congress or the electorate in any meaningful sense. In addition, the entire process operates in an atmosphere of secrecy and insulation from public debate that makes a mockery of the system of open participation embodied in the Administrative Procedure Act (APA). Finally, the new Executive Order [No. 12,498] allows OMB to cut off investigations before they even begin, making it nearly impossible to attack OMB's decision that a potential rule is "unnecessary."

The Administration has principally used the system of OMB review created by the Executive Orders to implement a myopic vision of the regulatory process which places the elimination of cost to industry above all other considerations. In doing so, however, the Administration has imposed a significant price on the public resulting from the delay it causes in adoption of needed protections. While OMB ponders the validity of a proposed rule, or the agency's responses to public comments, the failure to issue health and safety rules is certain to mean deaths and injuries that could be avoided.

* * *

Although insisting on least-cost solutions for industry, the Administration's program produces greatest-cost solutions for government. In deciding whether to undertake the elaborate regulatory analyses required by the first Executive Order [No. 12,291], there is no indication that the Administration considered a cost-benefit analysis of this process—even though the costs of the documents required by the Order have been estimated at several hundred thousand dollars each. Similarly, the vast amount of additional resources spent in justifying proposed regulations to OMB, as well as in obtaining the necessary OMB clearance to undertake the studies needed to decide whether to begin work on a problem in earnest, are all burdens on the federal treasury, yet there is no indication that these costs have been balanced against the benefits to be derived from this complex labyrinth of OMB overlay.

* * * [T]he people at OMB who give "thumbs up" or "thumbs down" lack the substantive backgrounds to make intelligent judgments. Their job is not simply to ask questions and require that agencies answer them; rather, the desk officers who have principal responsibility for reviewing agency rules decide for themselves what is the "proper answer." That OMB is not simply asking questions, but demanding specific answers, is particularly troubling because the issues that OMB reviews often involve scientific determinations. * * *

It is one thing for OMB to play the role of institutional skeptic, questioning an agency in order to be sure that it has considered matters thoroughly. It is quite another for it to second-guess technical decisions made by career personnel, let alone those of Cabinet officers or other agency heads confirmed by the Senate. In addition to their lack of expertise to decide the many scientific and technical issues which arise, the group at OMB working on rules is extremely small and does not have the time or budget to review most agency decisions on any rational basis.

Supporters of OMB control of the rulemaking process argue that the concentration of decision-making power in the hands of OMB personnel is necessary to insure accountability to the electorate. Most of what OMB is doing, however, has little or nothing to do with large policy issues, except in the crudest sense that the policy of this Administration is to say no to all regulations. However, it is not the President or any other elected official, nor even anyone appointed with the advice and consent of the Senate, who is making these decisions. Therefore, if it is accountability that is the basis for increased control, a system that allows desk officers to overrule Cabinet officials cannot meet that test.

* * * [Another] fundamental difficulty with the review process is that it operates in secrecy, directly contrary to the principles of the APA. OMB provides information and misinformation to agencies and applies criteria for deciding whether to approve a rule that never appears in the public record and to which no reply is possible. While in some cases no reply is necessary, since OMB is principally recycling industry arguments that proved unsuccessful at the agency level, there are times when new reasons for opposing a proposed rule persuade OMB. In these cases the rule's supporters are handicapped by the lack of an opportunity to respond. Indeed, under the present system, OMB can simply refuse to approve a regulation without giving any reason, and an agency head is left the job of devising an acceptable explanation for refusing to proceed or for deleting a particularly offensive requirement. And, because this process operates in secret, there is no way for the public, the Congress, or the courts to know precisely what OMB has done and what the real basis is for decisions issued under the nominal signature of the agency head.

* * *

Peter L. Strauss and Cass R. Sunstein, *The Role of the President and OMB in Informal Rulemaking*, 38 ADMIN. L. REV. 181, 183–94 (1986)*

* * *

I. "Politics" vs. "Expertise": A Prefatory Note

For a long period, debates over the administrative process have been influenced by competing judgments on the respective roles of "expertise" and "politics" in regulation. James Landis' model for administration was that of neutral experts, standing above the political fray, making decisions on the basis of an objective concern with the public interest. Sometimes a different understanding prevails. Regulatory issues are often said to raise difficult questions of value on which reasonable people, or those with conflicting interests, may differ. In this view, there is no unitary public interest, and the relevant solutions must be based on "political" considerations rather than on the application of expertise. The dispute between these competing understandings helps to account for numerous more particular disagreements in administrative law.

The two understandings have important institutional implications. For believers in the value of expertise and neutral administration, it is important to insulate regulators from political processes, enabling them to inquire into issues of fact and value with some assurance that their deliberations will not be distorted by partisan concerns. For those who believe that regulatory issues present questions to be resolved "politically"—in accordance with (informed) constituent desires—decisionmaking power should be placed in the hands of those most accountable to the public. * * *

The debate between believers in regulation as application of expertise, and regulation as politics, reflects polar positions that, in our view, represent more a tension needing to be maintained than positions in themselves worthy of adoption. Technical expertise rightly plays an important role in regulatory decisions. It can, for example, set out a range of plausible options, indicating that that range is broader or narrower than might have been expected. On the other hand, judgments of value, subject uneasily or not at all to resolution on the basis of expertise, play a critical role in regulatory questions. The appropriate trade-off between risks to human life and the social and economic dislocations created by environmental regulation—to use a familiar example—is not a decision that can be made solely on the basis of immersion into technical matters. Such trade-offs are rightly placed in the hands of officials who are politically accountable; and they are rightly subject to public scrutiny and review during the regulatory process. While it is properly insisted that such judgments be made within the constraints of law, it is misleading to understand the regulatory process as if it were entirely a matter of applying technical competence.

* * *

II. Presidential Control

A. Generally

* * *

Both executive orders [Nos. 12,291 and 12,498] are directed at rulemaking undertaken pursuant to the informal procedures of the notice-and-comment provision of the Administrative Procedure Act, or particular agency statutes such as the Occupational Safety and Health Act or the Clean Air Act. Executive Order 12,291 applies to such rulemaking, exempting formal rulemaking and other on-the-record proceedings. The limited scope of the order is based

---

* Reprinted with permission of Peter L. Strauss and Cass R. Sunstein. All rights reserved.

on a perception that where matters are to be decided in on-the-record proceedings, "political" considerations have been excluded, and the views of outsiders to the proceedings must be formally conveyed. Executive Order 12,498 is applicable to "significant regulatory activities," but it is clear from context that the order is designed to control the processes of rulemaking not required to be decided on the record.

The purposes of the two orders are not difficult to identify. Both are largely a response to the widespread perception that agency decisionmaking tends to be confused and uncoordinated, that the President is well-placed to consider the whole scheme of regulation rather than discrete units of it, and that administrators are not adequately accountable to the public in general, and its political executive-designate the President, in particular. Beyond that lies the related perception that agency heads are, to an undesirable degree, the captives of their own staffs rather than politically powerful managers of agency business. Courts have created a number of techniques to attempt to respond to this problem, including review to ensure that the benefits of regulation are roughly commensurate with the costs. The value of such techniques is, however, severely diminished by institutional limits of the courts, which are not well-equipped to calculate the costs and benefits of regulatory initiatives and are incapable of imposing a hierarchical or coordinative structure. The orders represent an effort to deal with the general problem of uncoordinated and insufficiently accountable administrative decisions.

While the orders on their surface mark a major enhancement of presidential authority, a significant element of their attractiveness lies in their potential to expand the effective authority, accountability, and oversight capacity of the agency head. * * *

Finally, the orders embody a perception that the principal defect in administrative regulation is that it has been unduly intrusive and imposed substantial costs without accompanying benefits. This perception is of course highly controversial, and we venture no comment on it here.

B. The Need for a Presidential Role
* * *

It is too soon to venture a final judgment on the performance of OMB and the relevant agencies under Executive Order[s] 12,291 and * * * 12,498. * * * Moreover, experience under the two orders continues, and that experience, especially now that some of the initial difficulties have been worked out, will be of considerable importance for purposes of evaluating the program. The behavior of the executive branch is properly subject to a continuing process of academic and congressional scrutiny.

Regardless of how the process of implementation has operated thus far, there remains a powerful theoretical case * * * for the view that greater presidential control over the regulatory process is desirable. We summarize the three basic reasons for this conclusion here. * * *

First, the President is in a good position to centralize and coordinate the regulatory process. This task has become increasingly important with the proliferation of administrative agencies, whose responsibilities often overlap with one another. Over a dozen regulatory agencies, for example, are now entrusted with authority over matters relating to energy policy. The President is the only "constitutional officer charged with taking care that a 'mass of legislation' be executed." Some sort of coordinating role on the part of the President is indispensable, especially in light of the considerable discretion with which executive officials are often entrusted. * * *

Second, the President is electorally accountable. Equally important, he is the only official in government with a national constituency. These characteristics make him uniquely well-situated to design regulatory policy in a way that is responsive to the interests of the public as a whole. Agency officials, by contrast, are only indirectly accountable. They may also be subject to more parochial pressures. For these reasons, a supervisory role by the President should help ensure that discretionary decisions by regulatory agencies are responsive to the public generally.

Third, the President, by virtue of his accountability and capacity for centralization, is able to energize and direct regulatory policy in a way that would be impossible if that policy were to be set exclusively by administrative officials. These considerations are especially important when there is a national consensus that regulatory policy should be moved in particular directions.

It is a significant step from these considerations to the conclusion that presidential advisors, like those in OMB, should be given the power to supervise and coordinate the regulatory process. A principal difficulty here is that there is not an identity between the President and officials in OMB. The delegation of supervisory power to OMB over the rulemaking activities of agencies may serve, not to promote accountability, but instead to remove authority from agency heads and to confer power on staff members in OMB—thus sacrificing accountability and perhaps skewing the process against desirable government regulation. * * *

There are several responses to these concerns—responses that, in our view, justify approval of the supervisory role set forth in the two executive orders. First, the case for supervision rests largely on the need for a centralizing and coordinating role. It may be that OMB authority will not increase accountability, but at least with appropriate safeguards such authority will not diminish accountability, and it is nonetheless desirable on independent grounds. Second, the recent executive orders should, for reasons discussed above, serve to increase the authority of agency heads and to decrease the power of agency staffs. That effort should itself promote accountability, quite apart from the issue of whether OMB or the relevant agency is more subject to presidential control. Finally, the relative proximity of those in OMB—their institutional position close to the President—may justify the conclusion that they are, in a special sense, his agents for purposes of supervising the regulatory process.

OMB's role does pose substantial risks. That role will, for example, strain the capacities of OMB staff and administrators. The officials at OMB may not have the necessary technical expertise to engage in the supervisory role, and most important, their involvement may further attenuate the link between the final regulation and the rulemaking "record." But the answer to any such problem rests, we think, in a proper appreciation of these dangers by the relevant officials and in continuing efforts to obtain the information necessary to undertake supervision. In this connection, perhaps the best analogy to the role of OMB under the executive orders is the role suggested for the courts by Judge Leventhal: that of ensuring that agencies have taken a "hard look" at the relevant factors and that the decisions reflect a reasonable accommodation of the conflicting interests. In many respects, politically accountable decisionmakers have advantages over the courts in performing that task.

Moreover, the authority to make the ultimate decision rests where Congress has placed it—in the relevant agency. This understanding stems from the notion, set out in *Myers v. United States*, that the President has the authority to discharge executive officials, but at least in some cases, no power to make the ultimate decision (except insofar as the threat of discharge amounts to such power). Under this view, the President's remedy for conduct of which he disapproves is the politically costly one of removal. Short of that, his authority—and even more obviously, that of OMB—is consultative and supervisory. Recognition of the agency as the primary decisionmaker should operate as a substantial safeguard against the risks created by lack of information. And the understanding that such an allocation is lawfully required should operate as an important constraint on the operation of the supervisory process.

There is in addition the familiar danger that the supervisory role will carry with it political biases that diminish rather than increase the likelihood of sound administration, endangering the ideal of reasoned decisionmaking. The danger is perhaps made more acute by virtue of the vesting of supervisory authority in OMB, whose own institutional mission—as an agency concerned largely with costs, on the budgetary and regulatory sides—may lead to an anti-regulatory bias. * * *

While these are legitimate concerns, we do not believe that they are sufficient to justify disapproval of the current initiatives. The countervailing considerations are too strong to outweigh this risk, which, it is hoped, will be diminished by two important constraints. The first is that the supervisory role must be exercised in accordance with statute—a fact expressly recognized in the two executive orders and vindicated by judicial review. The second countervailing consideration, as noted, is that the ultimate power of decision remains vested in the relevant agency.

In light of these considerations, several measures should be undertaken to diminish the dangers and to increase the benefits of the regulatory process under the two executive orders.

First, OMB should institute a procedure to ensure public disclosure of (1) any factual materials it introduces into a rulemaking proceeding and (2) all substantive communications with persons not associated with the executive branch whenever those communications appear pointed at particular issues it is considering. Factual materials introduced by OMB stand on the same footing as factual materials introduced by the agency itself; both belong as part of the rulemaking file, at least after the notice of proposed rulemaking has been published in the Federal Register. (Before publication, no such requirements attach.) This basic principle should apply to "conduit" communications—materials received by OMB from private sources and communicated, with or without attribution, to the relevant agency. As noted above, OMB has taken steps to ensure that the process of receiving information from private organizations will be carefully controlled. But it has been sharply disputed whether those controls have been adhered to in practice. * * *

Second, agency drafts prepared under the two executive orders should, as a general rule, be made available on request to relevant congressional committees after the process of decision has run its course. During the process of decision, those drafts should be presumed confidential. But after rulemaking activity has ceased, disclosure of such drafts should allay public concerns about the role of OMB and would provide valuable information to Congress about the nature of OMB's supervisory role. There are, to be sure, the familiar dangers associated with disclosure requirements: the decisionmaking process may be chilled and candor may be less likely. In this context, however, we believe that those dangers are outweighed by the benefits of disclosure. We also believe that post-activity disclosure is a reasonable accommodation of the conflicting interests. * * * Disclosure should be understood as a matter of presidential prerogative, however, and not as an acknowledgement that the principle of executive privilege fails to protect the process of decision under the two orders. In order to reach this conclusion, it is not necessary to make any general statement about the reach of the controversial principle of executive privilege.

Third, OMB intervention should be limited to those cases in which it is called for by the rationale underlying increased presidential control. Those cases in turn involve two principal contexts. The first involves the need for coordination and centralization in the regulatory process; the second involves the need to communicate the views of the President when important regulatory issues are at stake. Intervention in the general run of cases should be undertaken subject to the understandings reflected above: it must be within the constraints of the governing statute and of the delegation of primary decisionmaking power to the agency. Limiting intervention to such cases should emphasize that OMB's role is not to duplicate the agency's work, or to act as a *de novo* decisionmaker on issues of policy, but to bring a wider perspective to bear on decisions in settings that transcend an agency's more focused responsibilities.

Finally, a procedure should be reinstituted to allow for mediation by the President in cases of disagreement between the agency and OMB. Such mediation, which existed in the early period under Executive Order 12,291, would be designed to stress that OMB acts as a surrogate for the President and that its word is not final. A procedure of this sort should be used only in unusual circumstances, however, and it should be instituted with the understanding that even the President has no authority to displace decisions statutorily delegated to subordinate officials in the executive branch.

* * *

Charles Tiefer, *The Quayle Council: "No Fingerprints" on Regulation* in THE SEMI-SOVEREIGN PRESIDENCY: THE BUSH ADMINISTRATION'S STRATEGY FOR GOVERNING WITHOUT CONGRESS 61, 64–66, 70–73, 77–87 (1994)*

Overview

In the Bush Administration's general strategy for governing without Congress, a special place goes to the president's Council on Competitiveness, known by its chair as the "Quayle Council." * * *

* * *

1989-1990: Creation, Dormancy, and Activation

Creation and Dormancy

Initially, when the Bush Administration began, it did not seek to change significantly the regulatory review system inherited from the Reagan Administration. Executive Orders 12,291 and 12,498 remained in effect, and the OIRA proceeded pursuant to them. In April 1989, President Bush did announce a Council on Competitiveness, the Quayle Council, as the successor to his own Vice Presidential Task Force. * * *

* * *

Activation in 1990

One account tells colorfully how the Quayle Council, after having neither significance nor activity in 1989 and 1990, became activated:

> Bush created the panel in 1989 but gave it new powers a year later, when he began hearing complaints from friends that his government was reregulating industries that the Reagan Administration had sought to deregulate. Not long afterward, the President appeared before aides one morning waving a newspaper clipping about reregulation and asking, "What's going on here?" Bush, who headed a task

---

* Reprinted with permission of Westview Press and Charles Tiefer. All rights reserved.

force on regulatory relief as Vice President, asked Quayle to review new regulations to make sure that costs would not outweigh benefits. Lacking a high-profile White House role at the time, Quayle jumped in with both feet.

As this account reflects, although the Quayle Council had claimed power starting in 1989, it was a year later that the president actually "asked Quayle to review new regulations."

* * *

Why does it matter that the Quayle Council had no actual activity in 1989 when it became the instrument, nominally, of executive orders 12,291 and 12,498? * * * It matters because the Quayle Council shortly began to revolutionize the authority structure behind regulation. Had the Quayle Council's role in this revolution rested on a new executive order, that executive order—an ordinary and relatively open and accountable instrument of authority—would have received intensive public, congressional, and judicial scrutiny. Instead, the Quayle Council actually drew its authority from the president's oral command as implemented by internal White House staff memoranda that did not even surface publicly for a long time.

* * *

1991: Major Interventions, Congressional Oversight

Whereas 1990 had been the year of the Quayle Council's ascendance to power, 1991 became the year of the Quayle Council massively exercising that power. Once the Quayle Council staff attained power, it took on two particular tasks that symbolized the height of President Bush's effort to weaken the environmental laws without dealing with Congress: the Clean Air Act and the Wetlands Delineation Manual. Thereafter came the season of press and congressional attention.

Clean Air Regulations

President Bush signed the Clean Air Act on November 15, 1990. During the course of Congress's consideration of the act, it had rejected numerous administration proposals for standards that would allow higher air pollution levels. In particular, when the House and Senate conferees met to strike the crucial final terms, President Bush submitted his own version. But it came too late. "[B]y the time the administration sent the conferees a counterproposal on the bill Sept. 26, it was too late to make much of a difference. . . . Congress felt free, in part, to opt for the stronger controls because of the skepticism that Bush would veto the bill * * * in the waning days of an election year session." Because Bush's own proposals and veto bargaining had initially influenced the Clean Air Act, this later loss of power over it reflected the shifting and subtle interplay of presidential-congressional interaction in a divided government.

* * *

The Quayle Council provided a mechanism for the president to propitiate and to reward his industry supporters without relying upon the president's weak support in Congress. * * *

The Quayle Council established six working groups, including the Working Group on Deregulation. In the words of the council's staff, "The Vice President has asked these working groups to make recommendations to the Council regarding particular policy and regulatory issues that arise in their respective areas." These working groups created a structure allowing delegation of power to smaller groups consisting of White House staff, the agency officials with statutory responsibility to execute the law, and other agency officials without that responsibility. The mix allowed maximum pressure by the antiregulatory officials upon the agency officials who have the responsibility while remaining within the White House framework assertedly immune from judicial review and congressional oversight. Through the Working Group on Deregulation, the president could transfer power away from the accountable head of the EPA * * * and instead confer the power on trusted White House staff lieutenants of known antiregulatory views but no public or congressional accountability.

* * *

As the Quayle Council waded into the major environmental issue of clean air, it also promulgated yet another governmentwide directive expanding its mandate. On March 2, 1991, the vice president sent a "Memorandum for Heads of Executive Departments and Agencies," entitled "Subject: Regulatory Review Process." It provided a murky recitation, with vaguely expansive overtones, of the regulatory review process within the White House and its own role in this. At its clearest point, it expanded the review beyond regulations to "include all agency policy guidance that affects the public": "Such policy guidance includes not only regulations that are published for notice and comment, but also strategy statements, guidelines, policy manuals, grant and loan procedures, Advance Notices of Proposed Rule Making, press releases and other documents announcing or implementing regulatory policy that affects the public." Like prior and subsequent governmentwide directives from the Quayle Council, the March 1991 directive asserted maximum power without providing any clarity about how it was authorized to exercise that power or what its limits were.

One of the functions of the March 1991 directive may simply have been to further shore up regulatory review during a period when the OIRA suffered a major blow to its legitimacy. As one of the signs of President Bush's need for mechanisms to govern without Congress, the Senate continued to refuse to confirm any director for the OIRA. The OIRA had not had a director since 1989. In 1990, the White House counsel's intervention had killed a compromise legislative proposal to reauthorize the OIRA. * * * Thus, the March 1991 Quayle Council directive signified a measure of support for OIRA—even without its having a legitimately confirmed head—so long as it continued to serve the Quayle Council. * * *

Besides the Clean Air Act, the other major demonstration in 1991 of the Quayle Council's power to intervene in environmental regulation concerned wetlands. Wetlands are ecologically fragile areas that are vital for wildlife, flood control, and filtering out potential contaminants of waterways. Environmental concerns mounted in the 1980s over the gradual elimination of wetlands through filling in and other actions. In a key 1988 campaign pledge repeated in the 1989 budget submission to Congress, President Bush promised "no net loss" of wetlands.

The EPA and the Army Corps of Engineers, pursuant to section 404 of the Clean Water Act, control federal permits required for developers to fill in wetlands. In 1991, the wetlands issue took shape as a controversy over impending revision of the 1989 EPA manual of guidelines for defining wetlands requiring protection. An interagency scientific team had been developing data consistent with the prior definition of wetlands. A wetland was defined, in simplified form, by the number of days per year it was saturated with water. The lower the number of days, the larger the number of acres deemed wetlands and thereby protected from elimination. The 1989 manual had used the figure of seven days of saturation per year, protecting large areas and thereby burdening President Bush's effort to fulfill his "no net loss" pledge.

Into this process came the Quayle Council, with the press describing the start of Vice President Quayle's intervention thusly:

> On his political swings around the country, Quayle said, he heard frequent complaints that the federal government was unnecessarily restricting the use of wetlands for real estate development and other business ventures. . . .
>
> Last May [1991], an official said, Quayle told the [Quayle] council's executive director, "Hubbard, we need to do something about wetlands." EPA Administrator William K. Reilly protested against the intervention . . . but Quayle received Bush's approval to become involved.

In place of seven days of saturation per year, "EPA Administrator William Reilly started negotiations on the revised manual at 10 days; the Quayle Council countered with 21." With its antiregulatory approach, the Quayle Council supplanted the agency-level technically qualified environmental teams and transformed the issue by the White House's pressuring on behalf of complaining commercial interests.

After the Quayle Council met on April 6, 1991, it issued this press release noting its new dominance of the issue:

> *OIRA and Council to review Wetlands Delineation Manual.* The Vice President announced that the proposed revisions to the Wetland Delineation Manual would be going to OIRA for review. This manual is the interagency policy that defines what land is considered to be "wetland" for government programs. The Vice President reaffirmed the President's goal of "no net loss" of wetlands as a balanced policy that both protects environmentally important wetlands and allows legitimate land use, such as farming, housing development, and the construction of roads, airports, and energy facilities.

In a famous exchange, [EPA Administrator] Reilly and Quayle almost reached a deal on the eve of a July 10 Senate subcommittee hearing, but the Quayle Council staff prevented it by an extreme antiwetlands stance. The Washington Post described the events as a "near fiasco":

> On the night before Reilly was to testify to the Senate, he, Quayle and Hubbard engaged in a round-robin series of telephone conversations trying to broker a deal. Each time Reilly thought he had Quayle's agreement, Hubbard called Reilly to say he had misunderstood. When their final agreement was presented at a White House senior staff meeting the next morning, [OMB Director] Darman and Chief of Staff John H. Sununu erupted, and a last-minute call was made to Reilly—in his car on

the way to the hearing—to tell him the deal was off.

* * *

The full Quayle Council met on July 29. Vice President Quayle "began the session by expressing astonishment that vast areas of his home state of Indiana could have been classified as wetlands under the original definition in the manual, when he knew those areas were farmland." He is quoted as suggesting, as a possible wetlands definition, "How about if we say when it's wet, it's wet?" Using the leverage gained at the meeting, the next day Quayle and Hubbard again pressured Reilly. Reilly acquiesced the next day to their figures, fifteen days of standing water and twenty-one days of surface saturation as the minimum for a wetland, an approach "which significantly narrowed the definition of wetlands in a way experts have said would halve the amount of protected acreage." On August 9, President Bush announced the outcome, which was formally published in the Federal Register as a draft regulation on August 14.

In November 1991, the White House backed down. The press linked this to other contemporaneous White House firestorms. * * *

* * *

Congressional Scrutiny

Although the Quayle Council appeared to lose the round relating to wetlands, its growing power, symbolized by its intervention into the most important of all national environmental controversies, brought it into the limelight. Congressional efforts at scrutiny had begun before with hearings of the House Subcommittee on Health and the Environment conducted in March, May, and July 1991. A spate of press coverage followed in July. In August, Vice President Quayle gained nationwide attention for his industry-supported proposals to hamper plaintiffs' lawyers in areas such as products liability, with a coating of generalized anti-lawyer rhetoric to win popular support.

Meanwhile, oversight efforts by the Senate Committee on Governmental Affairs received diversion and avoidance. Senate interrogatory letters in April and May failed to elicit a response until October, when the Quayle Council sent a letter listing the dates of the Quayle Council meetings in 1990 (three) and 1991 (six) and the names of the council's working groups (six). Otherwise, the response letter just reiterated prior statements or uttered generalities. On November 15, the Senate committee summoned the head of the OIRA to a hearing, the frustrating essence of which the Washington Post summarized in its headline "Competitiveness Council Suspected of Unduly Influencing Regulators: Secrecy Foils Senate Panel's Attempt to Probe Vice President's Group." The Senate committee followed this hearing by approving on November 22 a bill to require a public record of the OIRA's communications on rulemaking.

By the end of 1991, Quayle Council staff estimated their level of intervention as approximately fifty significant rulemakings per year. Two significant oversight controversies marked the year's end. The charges against the council's staff director, Allan B. Hubbard, that he had a conflict of interest because of his personal holdings in a chemical company began to take a serious toll. At a December 1991 hearing of the House Subcommittee on Health and the Environment on the Clean Air Act, Hubbard refused to show up. Instead, he had the White House counsel's office bless his position, based on the waiver he had received from Vice President Quayle for conflicts of interest. Eventually he simply left this post to become Quayle's campaign manager.

An even more interesting controversy in terms of the separation of powers concerned the first congressional subpoena for documents dealing with the Quayle Council. A Quayle Council working group had been developing a new set of drug approval policies for the Food and Drug Administration. These policies watered down the FDA's requirements for pharmaceutical companies to establish the efficacy of drugs. When the House Government Operations Committee's Subcommittee on Human Resources and Intergovernmental Relations, which oversees the FDA, commenced an inquiry, initially the Quayle Council staff directed the FDA to withhold documents concerning the Quayle Council.

The subcommittee responded with a subpoena to the FDA in November 1991. In a tense confrontation, the White House counsel's office threatened that the president would claim executive privilege. However, the result would have been contempt of Congress charges, for which the administration had little stomach. Moreover, the confrontation came during the same period as [the President's Chief of Staff John] Sununu's departure and the firestorm over the signing statement for the Civil Rights Act of 1991. The White House decided to give in. As the subcommittee chairman, Representative Ted Weiss (D-N.Y.) subsequently told the House during a debate on the Quayle Council:

> The White House has interfered with our investigation of the FDA and the Council on Competitiveness by ordering FDA to withhold

several hundred documents from the subcommittee. In November we issued a subpoena for these documents. Only after the subpoena was served did we receive all of the documents we requested from FDA. So do not tell us how forthcoming they are and how public their information is.

* * *

In March 1992, the subcommittee held hearings based on the documents, illuminating much about the methods used by the Quayle Council to cut back on FDA regulation of pharmaceutical safety and efficacy.

1992: Regulatory Moratorium, Power-of-Purse Battle

Regulatory Moratorium

As 1992 began and President Bush turned his full attention to reelection, he apparently decided to take an even harder stance against environmental regulations, but not to do so in an accountable way through legislative proposals or through changing the heads of the EPA and other agencies. Instead, he turned over massive new powers to the Quayle Council staff by announcing in his State of the Union Address in January 1992 an unprecedented regulatory moratorium. Although he did not hint at that time about the Quayle Council's role, it soon developed that the Quayle Council would supervise the moratorium. Moreover, the president implemented the moratorium by yet another vague governmentwide directive that further expanded the Quayle Council's powers.
* * *

On January 28, 1992, President Bush issued his memorandum entitled "Subject: Reducing the Burden of Government Regulation." It told federal agencies to stop regulatory action: "[t]o the maximum extent permitted by law, and subject to the exceptions listed below, your agency should refrain from issuing any proposed or final rule during the 90-day review period." It conferred the supervisory authority over that moratorium and over agency-reporting requirements as follows (with the emphasis added): "The 90-day review, and the preparation of [those] reports . . . will be coordinated by a working group of the Council on Competitiveness, chaired by the Chairman of the Council of Economic Advisers and the Counsel to the President." Although still occupying a position without Senate confirmation, without statutory mandate or limitations, and without appearing at congressional hearings, the White House counsel now enjoyed a new position and power as chair of the working group.

* * *

President Bush also made permanent changes, not limited to the ninety-day period, that were intended to strengthen the Quayle Council's role. The January 1992 directive installed a permanent network of officers throughout the federal government to report to the Quayle Council. It told agency heads:

> You should designate, in consultation with the Council on Competitiveness, a senior official to serve as your agency's permanent regulatory oversight official. This person will be responsible for conducting the review, for implementing the resulting proposals, and for ensuring that future regulatory actions conform to the standards set forth in this memorandum and in applicable Executive orders.

This Quayle Council network of "permanent regulatory oversight officials" throughout the government contrasted vividly with the historic system of accountable agency action. These officials in the agencies themselves would extend many of the unaccountable aspects previously limited to White House staff. They did not receive their office or authority from statute but from White House memoranda. They did not receive their appointments from Senate confirmation, or even from formal president commissioning, but from choice "in consultation with the Council on Competitiveness," meaning, in practice, by direction of the White House staff.

When the ninety-day time period for the moratorium expired, President Bush extended the moratorium in a set of widely publicized remarks. * * * The memorandum that he issued to extend the moratorium another 120 days ended with another recognition of the Quayle Council's working group headed by the White House Counsel: "In implementing your reforms and in preparing the reports described in paragraph 3, you and your agency's regulatory oversight official should continue coordinating with the Competitiveness Council's Working Group on Regulatory Reform."

Thus, the moratorium reinforced the dramatic evolution of the Quayle Council. By statute, decisions on regulations lay with the Cabinet department and agencies, accountable to law and the Congress. Step by step, White House staff had created an entire system for themselves to control regulations, established by vague presidential and vice presidential memoranda. Between 1990 and 1992, the White House staff had developed a permanent network throughout the government of officials they would choose. This network would implement criteria they would promulgate and preferences they would express, which would supplant the statutorily created and accountable system. Not even a council of accountable or elected officials but rather a mere "working group" of White House staff headed this governmentwide network.

* * *

Power of the Purse Versus Executive Prerogative

After years of attempted oversight and legislative proposals, in 1992 Congress finally confronted the executive prerogative claims of the Quayle Council by flexing its own power of the purse. In March, the House Appropriations Subcommittee that has jurisdiction over White House funds demanded and obtained from the White House a formal statement of the council's mission. This statement eschewed all mention of the various memoranda and other informal documents that had actually erected the Council's power. Apart from generalities and platitudes that were by then standard, the White House continued the fiction that power had existed all along, pursuant to the old Reagan Administration executive orders, ignoring the actual mid-1990 activation of the council * * *.

In June, the House Appropriations Committee cut from the White House appropriation bill $86,000, the salaries for two Quayle Council staffers. The Appropriations Committee's report explained: "The Council on Competitiveness acts in secret, refuses to disclose from whom it has heard, refuses to disclose all regulations in which it has intervened, and refuses to detail the actual facts and evidence upon which its decisions are based." In defunding the Quayle Council, the Appropriations Committee placed stress upon its resistance to congressional oversight: "The Committee is also very concerned about the Council's refusal to cooperate with congressional committees conducting legitimate inquiries about its activities."

Shortly thereafter, that appropriation bill came to the House floor. In a major confrontation, the House voted on July 1, 1992, to retain the funding cutoff. The sponsor of the provision, Representative David E. Skaggs (D-Colo.), emphasized the Quayle Council's resistance to oversight and contrasted it with the OMB's activity under the regulatory review executive orders:

> The heart of this problem is that the Council operates in secret, not letting the American people or Congress learn even the most basic facts about its activities. . . . The Council refuses to testify before Congress. The Council refuses to provide Congress with requested information on its activities. . . .
>
> OMB testifies before Congress on its regulatory affairs activities. The Council on Competitiveness refuses to do so, and won't even answer questions submitted to it by congressional committees. . . .

In the end, the House voted 236-183, largely on party lines, to make the cut.

Later that month OMB director Darman responded by defending the Quayle Council as "a core function of the president" and threatened a presidential veto because of the funding cutoff. When the Senate took up the White House appropriation in September, Senator John Glenn (D-Ohio), chairman of the Senate committee that had attempted oversight of the Quayle Council, offered an amendment to cut off the council's funding. However, in the face of the veto threat he withdrew the amendment. As the manager of the appropriations bill said in thanking him for withdrawing the amendment, "The White House has said that it will veto this bill if the Council's activities are restricted or defunded. Do we want to bog down this appropriations bill and the entire process . . . ?"

As the 1992 election approached, public attention on the Quayle Council issue focused on its evident role serving the political interests of the president's campaign. * * * An October study for the Wall Street Journal, on the eve of the election, explained: "[M]any of those who seek the Council's help also supply the GOP with large contributions, many of them in the form of 'soft money'—contributions for 'party-building' efforts like get-out-the-vote drives, which aren't limited by federal election laws."

* * *

Additional Sources

Harold H. Bruff, *Presidential Power and Administrative Rulemaking*, 88 Yale L.J. 451 (1979)

Lloyd N. Cutler, *The Case for Presidential Intervention in Regulatory Rulemaking by the Executive Branch*, 56 Tul. L. Rev. 830 (1982)

Lloyd N. Cutler & David R. Johnson, *Regulation and the Political Process*, 84 Yale L.J. 1395 (1975)

Christopher C. Demuth & Douglas H. Ginsburg, *White House Review of Agency Rulemaking*, 99 Harv. L. Rev. 1075 (1986)

Margaret Gilhooley, *Executive Oversight of Administrative Rulemaking: Disclosing the Impact*, 25 Ind. L. Rev. 299 (1991)

C. Boyden Gray, *Presidential Involvement in Informal Rulemaking*, 56 Tul. L. Rev. 863 (1982)

Philip J. Harter, *Executive Oversight of Rulemaking: The President Is No Stranger*, 36 Am. U. L. Rev. 557 (1987)

Oliver A. Houck, *President X and the New (Approved) Decisionmaking*, 36 Am. U. L. Rev. 535 (1987)

Thomas O. McGarity, *Presidential Control of Regulatory Agency Decisionmaking*, 36 Am. U. L. Rev. 433 (1987)

Alan B. Morrison, *Presidential Intervention in Informal Rulemaking: Striking the Proper Balance*, 56 Tul. L. Rev. 879 (1982)

James T. O'Reilly & Phyllis E. Brown, *In Search of Excellence: A Prescription for the Future of OMB Oversight of Rules*, 39 Admin. L. Rev. 421 (1987)

Morton Rosenberg, *Congress's Prerogative over Agencies and Agency Decisionmakers: The Rise and Demise of the Reagan Administration's Theory of the Unitary Executive*, 57 Geo. Wash. L. Rev. 627 (1989)

Thomas O. Sargentich, *Normative Tensions in the Theory of Presidential Oversight of Agency Rulemaking*, 7 Admin. L.J. Am. U. 325 (1993) (panel discussion)

Peter M. Shane, *Presidential Regulatory Oversight and the Separation of Powers: The Constitutionality of Executive Order No. 12,291*, 23 Ariz. L. Rev. 1235 (1981)

4. Debates About the Constitutional System of the Separation of Powers

a. The Constitutional Position of Administrative Agencies

There has been a longstanding debate about the constitutional status of independent, as opposed to executive, agencies. Executive agencies generally are headed by one person who serves at the will of the president. In contrast, independent regulatory agencies typically are headed by groups of commissioners who serve for fixed terms and cannot be removed other than for cause. The for-cause requirement generally has been understood to mean that a president seeking to remove a member of an independent agency cannot do so merely because of policy disagreements with the agency head.

In the first excerpt, Professor Geoffrey Miller argues that independent agencies are difficult to reconcile with our tripartite scheme of the separation of powers. Professor Miller rejects the pragmatic defense of independent agencies, and instead embraces a neoclassical critique of their status. In developing his argument, Professor Miller focuses on the Constitution's text, the structure of government, constitutional history, and the functions of the agencies themselves.

In contrast, Professor Peter Shane suggests that the argument against independent agencies based on the framers' original intent cannot succeed. The framers simply did not conceive of executive power in the same way in which modern critics of independent agencies do, Professor Shane argues. Moreover, Professor Shane asserts that the framers specifically contemplated that agencies would have different control relationships with the president depending upon choices made by Congress. Furthermore, he argues that a modernist attack on agency independence also fails to carry its point. He suggests that the policy advantages claimed for plenary presidential control over agencies are less clear than critics contend. Moreover, whatever the case for enhanced presidential coordination of executive policymaking, Professor Shane urges, there are countervailing values that require respect—such as the diffusion of power in our national political system and the primacy of Congress in domestic policymaking.

In the final excerpt, Professor Peter Strauss contends that we should abandon separation of powers compartmentalization of governmental functions and instead emphasize the principle of checks and balances. This approach stresses the relationship between agencies and each of the named constitutional actors: the Congress, the President, the Supreme Court and lower federal courts. Moreover, Professor Strauss argues that the values of separation of functions in agency adjudications—which are associated with due process—should be upheld along with the principle of checks and balances.

Geoffrey P. Miller, *Independent Agencies*, 1986 Sup. Ct. Rev. 41, 42–45, 50–90*

I. Introduction

* * *

* * * [T]he independent regulatory agencies have become an integral part of our national political life. The Board of Governors of the Federal Reserve System (established in 1913) regulates segments of the banking industry and controls the nation's money supply. The Federal Trade Commission (1915) polices against false and deceptive commercial practices and, in conjunction with the Department of Justice, oversees the structure of the nation's industries under the antitrust laws. The Securities and Exchange Commission (1934) regulates the issuance and subsequent resale of securities on national exchanges and over-the-counter markets. The Federal Communications Commission (1934) controls many aspects of the nation's telephone, radio, and television industries. The National Labor Relations Board (1935) oversees the relationship between organized labor and management in all but the smallest businesses. The list is long. And Congress has not lost enthusiasm for the independent agency form. In 1977 it established the Federal Energy Regulatory Commission to oversee certain aspects of energy pricing and distribution, and in 1983 it declared the independence of the Commission on Civil Rights. Proposals to establish new independent commissions, or to enhance the independence of existing agencies, are introduced in virtually every session of Congress.

Despite their undoubted integration into the national political culture, independent agencies have never quite overcome the constitutional questions that dogged the drive to establish the Interstate Commerce Commission a century ago. The notion of an agency that is neither legislature nor court, yet is independent of the executive branch, is exceedingly difficult to reconcile with a tripartite structure of government. Even fervent admirers of independent agencies have recognized this fact, conceding that they were created "[w]ithout too much political theory." And although the Supreme Court apparently endorsed the constitutionality of independent agencies in *Humphrey's Executor v. United States* and *Wiener v. United States*, these cases did not involve attempts by the President to remove agency heads on grounds of disobedience to a presidential directive.

* * *

It would be unfortunate if the debate in this controversy focused only on the general concept of agency "independence" without breaking the question down into an analysis of the specific powers at issue. Agencies throughout the federal government, even traditional "executive branch" agencies, enjoy greater or lesser amounts of independence from direct presidential control; and, conversely, even classic "independent" agencies such as the Interstate Commerce Commission are subject to a substantial amount of presidential influence. A more useful analytic approach is to undertake a detailed study of the particular form of presidential oversight and control that is being asserted. A first step toward evaluating the constitutionality of independent agencies, in other words, is to "deconstruct" the agencies into their constituent elements of independence. This article follows these analytical lines by looking specifically at the matter of removal. * * *

The thesis of this article is that Congress may not constitutionally deny the President the power to remove a policy-making official who has refused an order of the President to take an action within the officer's statutory authority. This thesis rests on a model of the President's relationship to the federal administrative state. Congress, in this model, has power to create federal agencies, to vest substantial discretion in agency heads, and to provide that action by the agency head is a necessary precondition to the effective exercise of the authority in question. The President retains the constitutional power to direct the officer to take particular actions within his or her discretion or to refrain from acting when the officer has discretion not to act. Such presidential directives can either be specific to the action in question or general programmatic instruction applicable to a range of actions or agencies. Congress may not constitutionally restrict the President's power to remove officials who fail to obey these presidential instructions, but may prohibit the President from removing officers for other reasons, such as personal animus or refusing to obey an order to do something outside the officer's statutory authority.

This thesis—that the President may not be denied the power to remove an officer who has failed to comply with a presidential directive to take an action within the scope of the officer's discretion—may sound revolutionary. In fact, the thesis could be implemented without wholesale invalidation of federal statutes. Most statutes establishing independent agen-

---

* Copyright 1987 by The University of Chicago. Reprinted with permission of The Supreme Court Review, The University of Chicago, and Geoffrey P. Miller. All rights reserved.

cies can easily be construed as including disobedience of the President's lawful instructions within the varieties of "cause" for which presidential removal is already authorized. In the relatively infrequent cases where the statutes cannot be so construed, the unconstitutionality of the removal provision would not ordinarily invalidate the agency's substantive and enforcement powers. And the President can be expected in some cases voluntarily to eschew the power to remove particular officers who now head "independent" agencies, either by means of a formal commitment or by informal policy.

This is not to deny that the proposal would have a potentially significant impact. Its effect would be to increase, in more or less important ways, the control that the President is able to exercise over the federal bureaucracy. Such a change, however, might well be a beneficial development.

* * *

III. Preliminary Considerations

A. The Removal Power

An initial problem with assessing the constitutionality of independent agencies is the lack of any set meaning to the term "independent." A wide variety of different agencies might be considered independent in some sense of the word. For example, Congress has created a substantial number of institutions as "independent agencies within the executive branch."[42] These agencies resemble traditional executive departments in that they are headed by a single administrator appointed by the President (usually with the advice and consent of the Senate) and subject to removal at the President's pleasure. They are "independent" only in the sense that they are not placed within one of the old-line executive departments, a feature that gives them a degree of administrative autonomy and a measure of direct access to the President. Second, there are legislative, or "Article I" courts of various types that perform adjudicative services but do not otherwise execute the law or engage in policy formulation through rule making.[43] These institutions are typically headed by panels of judges, appointed by the President subject to the advice and consent of the Senate, who serve for lengthy terms during which they can be removed by the President only for cause. Legislative courts operate quite free of presidential supervision (although they may be subject to review by the federal courts), and in this sense can be considered "independent" of the President. Third, there is a panoply of governmental and quasi-governmental corporations and boards that perform specialized administrative tasks. These agencies are structured in a variety of different ways, often taking a traditional corporate form[44] or operating in some type of council structure.[45] These agencies often operate with substantial freedom from presidential oversight and control, and accordingly may be termed "independent" in some sense.

These different agencies raise a variety of questions under the doctrine of separation of powers. To simplify analysis, however, this article concentrates on the traditional independent regulatory agencies, such as the SEC, ICC, FCC, Federal Reserve Board, and NLRB. This limitation raises a problem. It is not entirely clear exactly what features of the independent regulatory commissions are essential and what are merely incidental. Almost uniformly they display the following characteristics: (1) leadership by a multi-member panel; (2) political criteria for appointment, with no more than a majority allowed to come from one party; (3) broad rulemaking authority; (4) power to conduct on-the-record adjudicative hearings; (5) power to conduct investigations and to bring enforcement actions either in court or within the agency itself or both; (6) a specialized mandate directing the agency to focus either on particular industries or on specific cross-cutting problems; and (7) restrictions on the presidential removal power. In addition, most independent agencies enjoy a measure of discretionary authority over matters such as budget, relations with Congress, and positions taken in litigation.

The limits on presidential removal are distinctive. Some features—leadership by multi-member panels and specialized mandates—are significant from the standpoint of political science but do not raise constitutional issues. Other features—the broad rulemaking, adjudicatory, and prosecutional powers—do raise issues about the permissibility of combining legislative, judicial, and executive functions in a single body. These questions, however, have receded in importance over the past fifty years. And these

---

[42] *E.g.*, 12 U.S.C. § 1752a (1982) (National Credit Union Administration); 12 U.S.C. § 2241 (1982) (Farm Credit Administration); 42 U.S.C. § 1861 (1982) (National Science Foundation).

[43] *E.g.*, 26 U.S.C. § 7441 (1982) (United States Tax Court).

[44] Examples abound in the banking field, *e.g.*, the Federal National Mortgage Association, the Federal Reserve district banks, the federal home loan banks, and the federal land banks.

[45] *E.g.*, Fishery Conservation and Management Act of 1976, 16 U.S.C. §§ 1801 *et seq.* (1982) (Regional Fishery Management Councils).

features do not distinguish independent agencies from traditional executive branch agencies, at least under present conditions in which executive departments exercise broad rulemaking and adjudicatory authority. Thus, problems of combination of functions, to the extent they remain current, are not peculiar to independent agencies. The political limitations on presidential appointment raise serious separation of powers concerns under the Appointment Clause, but the executive branch has not strongly disputed these provisions. Finally, the pattern of independent agency control over budget, congressional relations, and litigation is so varied as to suggest the value of concentrating, at least initially, on the more distinctive question of removal.

B. An Approach to Separation of Powers Analysis

Before analyzing the specific problem of removal, it is useful to establish a framework for evaluating separation of powers issues generally. Here we may distinguish two general analytical approaches: the pragmatic and the neoclassical approaches. The pragmatic view, championed by Holmes and Brandeis and dominant on the Court between the 1930s and the 1970s, tends to view the separation of powers as a practical approach to government, such that the division of powers between the branches, and the system of checks and balances by which those powers are related to one another, can stand considerable stretching in order to accommodate the changing needs of a modern society. As Holmes said in a famous dissent in *Springer v. Philippine Islands*, "[w]hen we come to the fundamental distinctions it is obvious . . . that they must be received with a certain latitude or our government could not go on. . . . It does not seem to need argument to show that however we may disguise it by veiling words we do not and cannot carry out the distinction between legislative and executive action with mathematical precision and divide the branches into watertight compartments."

Contrasting with this pragmatic approach is what we might call a "neoclassical" approach, which has recently come to the fore in *Buckley v. Valeo*, *INS v. Chadha*, and other cases. The neoclassical approach, which resembles the Court's approach to these matters prior to the 1930s, takes seriously both the distinctions between the branches of government and the specific structure of checks and balances outlined in the Constitution. This approach de-emphasizes the importance of convenience and efficiency, as not being the "hallmarks . . . of democratic government," and emphasizes instead the "constitutional design for the separation of powers" and the "structure of the articles delegating and separating powers under Acts I, II, and III."

These two approaches are distinguishable principally in terms of emphasis and nuance. The pragmatic approach does not deny the importance of text and structure; it merely tends to give these factors less weight than does the neoclassical approach. The neoclassical approach, on the other hand, does not dispute that pragmatic considerations have a role to play in the constitutional analysis; it merely gives these considerations secondary, although not insignificant, importance. Nevertheless, the differences between the approaches are unmistakable, and have been noted on the Court. In the words of Justice White, the most vigorous dissenter from the new approach, the Court has recently adopted a "distressingly formalistic" view of separation of powers, resting on "rigid dogma" and "unyielding principle[s]" that are, according to White, both "misguided" and "insensitive to [the Court's] constitutional role."[58]

Justice White to the contrary notwithstanding, I believe that the neoclassical approach is the superior mode for analyzing separation of powers questions, for several reasons. First, it is congenial to the purposes of the Framers. If the history of the framing of the Constitution shows us anything, it is that the Framers viewed the separation of powers as the single greatest protection against the danger of tyranny that inheres in the process of government itself. To this end they divided the government among three branches and carefully worked out the system of checks and balances among them. The Framers were children of the Enlightenment; they took seriously the Newtonian structure of attractive and repulsive political forces that they were creating. They would have applauded the adherence to principle that Justice White finds so distressing in the Court's recent opinions.

The neoclassical approach also comports with the notion of a written Constitution. Advocates of the pragmatic approach often use a de minimis argument, observing that many of the particular mechanisms of government could be altered or abandoned without fundamentally changing our system of government or creating dangers of tyranny. It would be possible to write a constitution along the lines contemplated by this argument: such a document would set up an initial structure of legislative, executive and judicial branches, and would then allow Congress to alter this arrangement as it sees fit, pro-

---

[58] Bowsher [v. Synar], 106 S. Ct. [3181,] 3205, 3214 [(1986)] (White, J., dissenting). * * *

vided that power is not concentrated in such a manner as to create a danger of tyranny. But the Framers did not adopt such a Constitution. They set forth a detailed structure of checks and balances among the branches of government. Any one of these specific powers or immunities could perhaps be abandoned without threatening the basic structure of the system as a whole; but if all were abandoned—if the pragmatic constitution were adopted—there is little doubt that our government would evolve into something far different from what it has been for the past two centuries. The government that developed would not necessarily be a bad government; in Britain, without a written constitution, the system of separation of powers established by the Glorious Revolution evolved into a Parliamentary system that appears to govern quite adequately. But it would not be our government—a government under a written Constitution that is constrained in the degree to which it can evolve in the absence of constitutional amendment.

The neoclassical approach is consistent with the profound changes that have altered the shape of American society over the past two hundred years. The pragmatic approach sometimes invokes an argument from changed circumstances, to the effect that the rise of the administrative state has so altered the landscape of government that new roads must be cut to enable government to function according to the basic goals of the Framers: vigor and efficiency in government and the avoidance of tyranny and faction. And because administrative government vests unparalleled power and discretion in the executive branch, the balance of power among the branches that lies at the core of separation of powers requires that new governmental mechanisms be devised in order to check and limit the President's authority. At the outset, the changed circumstances argument faces the burden of showing that the world is actually different in a way that matters. It would be unwise to abandon structures of government that have proved serviceable unless the need to revise and experiment is clearly established. It is doubtful, however, that this burden can be met. The pragmatic position may well understate the degree to which the neoclassical approach is backed by real purposes that are of present concern in government as it exists today. With respect to vigor in government, it is evident that a President committed to implementing a program—whether it be a New Deal, a Fair Deal, a Great Society, or a New Federalism—can govern more energetically to the extent that he or she is not hampered by technologies of government that check and limit executive powers. As to efficiency, the centralization and coordination that a unitary executive makes possible are likely to be more conducive to efficient government than is a splintered executive branch subject to various checks and balances beyond those set forth in the text of the Constitution. As to the danger of tyranny, the analysis is ambiguous: although it could be argued that a powerful and unified executive branch poses the threat of tyranny, the system of checks and balances has proved outstandingly effective at limiting the power of Presidents when they begin to govern in an "imperial" fashion. Moreover, the benefits of splintering power are themselves ambiguous, since the abandonment of a tripartite system of government may possibly undermine the stability of the structure as a whole. As to the danger of faction, there is reason to believe that a President accountable to the entire nation is less likely to be subject to the influence of discrete interest groups than is some extraconstitutional institution established purportedly to check presidential authority. And the quid pro quo argument—that new mechanisms must be devised to check the radical increase in presidential power accompanying the rise of the administrative state—overlooks the fact that administrative government reflects an increase in the powers of *all* branches of the federal government, in particular the dramatically enhanced power of Congress under expansive interpretations of the Commerce Clause.

Finally, the neoclassical approach is desirable as a way of imposing discipline in government. The pragmatic approach too often commits the error of confusing popularity with desirability or necessity. The legislative veto is a case in point. Justice White's critique of the Court's recent decisions might have more force if they seriously impeded the processes of government or interfered with the national welfare. To date, however, there has been no indication that these decisions have resulted in anything more than minor inconveniences. Almost two hundred legislative veto provisions were cast in doubt by the *Chadha* case. The government has shown no signs of falling or being shaken. Congress has begun to find alternative, constitutionally sound methods of controlling administrative discretion under broad delegations of statutory authority. New governmental technology such as legislative vetoes is often developed, not to enhance efficiency or accountability, but to avoid having to make hard decisions or to deny accountability for the decisions that are made. The neoclassical approach to separation of powers is a useful antidote to these bad habits of governing.

For these reasons, the neoclassical approach is the preferable framework for analyzing separation of powers issues, including the question of the removal power. The neoclassical approach suggests that the starting point for analysis is the text of the Constitution, interpreted in light of the tripartite structure established by the Framers. An additional factor is the history surrounding the framing and original implementation of the system of separated powers, which may help illuminate the meaning of the Constitution as it would have been understood by the Framers. At the same time the neoclassical approach does not rule out pragmatic considerations: at some margin principles must give way to practicalities. If limitations on presidential removal have come to serve a highly valuable function in our system, the benefits of which could not reasonably be obtained by other means, then this fact would not be insignificant in the constitutional analysis. Similarly, if Presidents have acquiesced in limitations on removal, that behavior could suggest that the intrusion on executive prerogatives may be less severe than might be inferred from an analysis of text, structure, and history alone. And if limitations on removal have inserted themselves so deeply into the fabric of American public law that their invalidation would work serious disruption on government processes, then this is an argument for treading carefully in considering whether they should be struck down. Finally, the impact of prior Supreme Court decisions should be considered. Other things being equal, it would be desirable if the rule to be adopted were one that could be squared with the Court's decisions in the area. Accordingly, the relevant considerations (listed in approximate order of importance) are these: (1) text; (2) structure; (3) history; (4) function; (5) prescription; (6) remedy; and (7) case law. The following section considers each of these factors in turn.

III. Constitutionality of Limits on the Removal Power

A. Text

The starting point for textual analysis is the basic grant of authority to the President: "[t]he executive Power shall be vested in a President of the United States of America." The Constitution is crystal clear that the "executive power"—whatever that might be—was to be vested in a single individual. The concept of a unitary executive could, in principle, support theories of presidential authority far stronger than any advanced by advocates of presidential power today. It could be argued, for example, that only the President, and not Congress, has the power to establish executive agencies, on the ground that the President, as head of the executive branch, must have absolute discretion as to how that department of government is organized. This theory has never had much currency, partly because it stands in tension with the congressional authority to grant appointment power over inferior offices to courts or department heads, and partly because the first Congress established a number of executive departments by legislation without protest from President Washington. But the construction is not logically ruled out by the constitutional text. It could also be argued that the concept of a unitary executive implies that the President should at least have the power to overrule any action by department heads. Otherwise, the executive would effectively be split, contrary to the constitutional design, at least for purposes of that decision. Again, this is a road not taken, it having been accepted early on that Congress could not only create executive departments but could make action by the agency head a precondition of the effective exercise of the power. What is significant about these alternative readings is not their current viability, but rather their logical plausibility. The fact that the constitutional text can without contradiction be read to support sweeping concepts of presidential authority over administration suggests that the President's power should not fall wildly short of what the text of the Constitution could sustain. Thus the unitary executive concept provides some support for the proposition that the President should at least have the authority to issue legally binding orders to officers instructing them to take some action within their statutory discretion (or to refrain from acting where they have authority not to act). If the President has the authority to issue such instructions, it is reasonable to posit that the President should also be able to remove executive officials who for whatever reason refuse to follow these instructions, so long as the action in question is otherwise within the officer's statutory discretion.

* * *

The Constitution expressly mentions administrative departments in two principal provisions: the Appointments Clause and the Report Clause. The Appointments Clause[69] provides that the President, by and with the advice and consent of the Senate, shall appoint "Officers of the United States, whose Appointments are not herein otherwise provided for, and which shall be established by Law: but the Congress may by Law vest the Appointment of such inferior Officers, as they think proper, in the President alone, in the Courts of Law, or in the Heads of Departments." This provision rather clearly grants

---

[69] U.S. CONST., Art. II, § 2, cl. 2.

Congress the power to create executive offices "by Law," thus undermining the interpretation that only the President can organize the executive branch agencies. But it is equally clear that administrative officials who qualify as "Officers of the United States" can only be appointed by the President (with Senate approval). Members of independent regulatory commissions, as heads of departments, are clearly "Officers of the United States," and, as such, can only be appointed by the President. The fact that the President must have the power to appoint implies, albeit not unambiguously, that the President must also have broad power to remove members of regulatory agencies. Moreover, the provisions regarding appointment of inferior officers implies that the "Departments" are in the executive branch of the government, since that term is used in contradistinction to the "Courts of Law." On the other hand, the power of Congress to vest appointment of inferior officers in the heads of executive departments or the courts suggests that Congress could give some degree of autonomy to the departments.

A second reference to administrative agencies is the provision of Article II authorizing the President to "require the Opinion, in writing, of the principal Officer of each of the executive Departments, upon any Subject relating to the Duties of their respective Offices."[73] A narrow reading would suggest that the clause merely enables the President to remain informed as to the doings of the agencies, and that the fact the President was given the express power to require opinions from department heads negatives the inference * * * the President had greater inherent powers of control. But this reading, although textually consistent, may be too limited. By this clause the administrative agencies were required to report to the President. The duty to report is meaningful only if the President retains a measure of substantive authority over the doings of the agency. This conclusion is buttressed by the fact that the President can demand the "opinion" of the department head. The word suggests that the report is not simply to inform the President as to the facts of a matter, but rather to provide him or her with input leading to executive decisions. The Report Clause can easily be read to imply that the President should be able to instruct the official how to act on a matter within the official's statutory discretion, and to remove the official if he or she fails to carry out the President's directions.

Finally, the Constitution instructs the President to "take Care that the Laws be faithfully executed."[77] In terms, this is the imposition of a duty; but it necessarily carries with it the authority to perform actions necessary and proper to the accomplishment of the duty. This clause does not itself mention administrative agencies; but such agencies are implicitly alluded to by its grammatical structure. The clause does not contemplate that the President will personally execute all of the laws. The President's job is to "take care" that the laws be faithfully executed by persons unnamed—a category that no doubt includes the President but also is broad enough to encompass the heads of administrative departments as well. The President's role is one of supervision. The Take Care Clause supports the proposition that there can be some distance between the President, as supervisor, and the agency heads who actually execute the law. The President's duty to take care that the laws be faithfully executed implies the power to "supervise and guide" the actions of the administrative agencies. Without such disciplinary powers the President would be helpless to prevent the agencies from failing to execute the law as Congress intended. Thus, the clause at least implies that the President must have power to remove an agency head who the President deems to have been faithless in his execution of the law. Left open by this construction of the Take Care Clause is the situation, so common today, in which the agency is given a broad statutory mandate that permits a wide range of discretionary action. In these circumstances the agency head may act in a manner that is consistent with the broad terms of the enabling statute but which conflicts with the President's program. It is unclear whether the Take Care Clause is sufficiently broad to authorize removal simply on the ground that the officer has failed to comply with the President's instructions. When the Take Care Clause is considered in conjunction with the other clauses, however, the inference seems relatively strong that the Constitution guarantees the President the power to remove officers when they fail to follow the President's directions to take actions otherwise within their statutory discretion.

B. Structure

The Constitution establishes branches of the government and divides and allocates powers among the branches in various ways. If independent agencies are constitutional they must fit within the structure of government in some way that does not do violence to the basic architecture of the system.

1. *The "arm of Congress" theory.* One of the principal structural approaches used to justify independent agencies is what might be called the "arm of the Congress" theory. According to this view,

---

[73] U.S. CONST., Art. II, § 2, cl 1.

[77] U.S. CONST., Art. II § 3.

independent agencies function essentially as agencies of Congress and should be located within the legislative branch of government. Because they are within the legislative branch, so this argument goes, there is no violation of the tripartite principle of separation of powers. Support for this view traces back to dicta in *Humphrey's Executor* that the Federal Trade Commission is an "agency of Congress." This argument is a particular favorite of congressmen and congressional committees. Similar statements can be found in the congressional testimony of agency heads.

The "arm of Congress" theory is typically unsupported by argument. For its proponents, it suffices to label independent agencies as part of the legislative branch, without exploring the justifications for applying such a label or the implications of the categorization from the standpoint of separation of powers. The closest thing to argument is the "creation" theory: because Congress creates the independent agencies, they are "creatures" of Congress and therefore part of the legislative branch. The fallacy in the argument is too grotesque to bear elaboration. Moreover, if independent agencies are, in fact, arms of the Congress, it is evident that many of their actions must be unconstitutional. These agencies have rule making and enforcement authorities that, when exercised, "alter[ ] the legal rights, duties, and relations of persons."[84] Such actions are "essentially legislative in purpose and effect," and, as such ought to comply with the procedures for enacting legislation set out in Article I, § 8 of the Constitution. The "arm of Congress" theory has little cogency as a constitutional justification for independent agencies.

2. *The "fourth branch" theory.* The principal competing theory to justify the status of independent agencies within a tripartite structure of government is the view that these agencies are not part of any of the existing three branches. They are completely "independent" of the political and the judicial branches. Together they make up a "fourth branch" of government which has evolved by constitutional usage. This model has some vitality as a descriptive theory. And were it not for the written Constitution, it might be accurate to state that a fourth branch of government has been evolving out of the executive branch in much the same way as Parliament evolved from the status of advisor of the Crown into a separate and autonomous organ of government.

The fourth branch theory, however, cannot be reconciled with the written Constitution. The first three articles of the Constitution establish three and only three branches of the government. The overall philosophy of the Constitution is that the national government was a government of limited powers. It would be anomalous to presume that the Framers would have approved the establishment of an independent fourth branch of government. The only justification for such a theory is an extreme version of the pragmatic approach to separation of powers, under which the system of checks and balances set forth in the Constitution is taken as illustrative of a broader universe of arrangements which are permissible so long as some sort of a division and balance of governmental powers is maintained. Otherwise, there is no place for an agency exercising federal governmental powers outside the boundaries of the three branches explicitly established in the Constitution.

3. *Independent agencies as executive agencies.* What remains is the obvious and sensible view that independent agencies are part of the executive branch. It may seem somewhat odd that constitutional theory has such trouble with this approach. A partial explanation lies in the history of administrative law. Before the twentieth century, government operated without such agencies. Most federal legislation was extremely detailed, leaving the President and the department heads only the task of carrying out specifications elaborately set forth by the legislative branch. Congress was able to maintain its control of administration, despite the increasing complexity of American society during the latter part of the nineteenth century, because of the development of the system of standing committees with expertise over matters within their jurisdictions. * * *

Against this historical backdrop it may be possible to see why administrative agencies seemed at first to pose such grave constitutional problems. The typical enabling statute gave the agency a degree of authority to establish rules of conduct and to determine whether those rules had been observed in particular cases. These powers may have been so unlike the "executive" powers that Presidents and department heads had typically exercised as to seem different in kind. The rule-making authority seemed legislative, rather than executive, for the agency was not "executing" a rule but making up the standard of conduct *ab initio*. And the authority to determine whether the rules had been violated seemed not to be executive but judicial, in the sense that it involved the application of broad standards to particular actions. Hence these agencies seemed to be agents of the judicial or legislative branches rather than traditional "executive" departments.

In retrospect this difficulty appears less troubling. Today administrative agencies routinely operate un-

---

[84] [Immigration and Naturalization Service v.] Chadha, 462 U.S. [919,] 952 [(1983).]

der broad grants of delegated authority. It is not nearly as difficult to understand that their actions under these statutes can be purely executive in nature. The agencies are simply executing broad and general, rather than narrow and detailed, statutory instructions. This is not to deny the vast increase in the scope of discretionary executive power over the past fifty years. But the difference may be more one of degree than of kind. Even under the most detailed statute it will occasionally be necessary for the executive to interpret the legislative mandate and to develop formal or informal rules to guide future action. And it will be necessary to apply those rules to particular instances, with or without formal procedural protections for the affected parties. In short, the functions which in the early days of administrative law were conceptualized as "quasi-legislative" or "quasi-judicial" are for the most part nothing more than highly developed aspects of traditional executive action.

There is no indication that any of the Justices on the Supreme Court today, even those who espouse a pragmatic notion of separation of powers, would view independent agencies as located anywhere but within the executive branch of government. The structural analysis of the Constitution compels this result. And this conclusion, in turn, supports the inference that the President, as head of the executive branch, must have a considerable degree of constitutional authority to supervise and guide the activities of administrative agencies. Yet concluding that independent agencies are executive branch agencies does not definitively resolve the question of the constitutionality of limitations on the President's removal authority. There is no logical inconsistency in concluding that Congress may constitutionally limit the President's power to remove even purely executive officials. The structural analysis supports the President's constitutional authority to remove officers who have disobeyed presidential directives, but it does not logically compel this result.

C. History

Much of the history of the constitutional provisions relating to the President's removal power is exhaustively—even turgidly—documented in Chief Justice Taft's opinion in *Myers*. Taft demonstrated that the First Congress, after extensive debate in which many of the Framers participated, decided that the President alone had power to remove the head of the Department of Foreign Affairs. This fundamental decision received nearly universal acquiescence from both Congress and the Executive until the passage of the Tenure in the Office Act of 1867, which Taft characterized as an "extreme" measure adopted by a reconstruction Congress in the wake of the convulsion of the Civil War. The early history of acquiescence in the President's removal power was the principal evidence adduced by the Chief Justice to support his conclusion that Congress could not constitutionally limit the President's power to remove federal postmasters. No purpose would be served by reiterating the discussion in *Myers*, other than to note that the decision of the First Congress provides evidence for presidential removal authority, even if the case is not as powerful as Chief Justice Taft implied. There are, however, certain other elements in the historical record, left out of the *Myers* opinion, that bear on the constitutionality of independent agencies.

First, it is useful to consider the forms of administration adopted under the Continental Congress. Just as the general experience of government since 1776 informed every aspect of the Constitution of 1787, so it is highly likely that the particular experience of administrative government would inform the views of the Framers on the question of presidential control over the executive departments. The system of administration that evolved during the Revolutionary War and its aftermath was one of steadily increasing executive power. The pattern, with minor variations, was discernible across each of the important areas of administration during this formative period: war, finance, foreign affairs, the navy, and so on. Perhaps the clearest example is in the area of military affairs. The conduct of the Revolutionary War was originally entrusted to a variety of different congressional committees, each performing a specific and narrow duty * * *. In 1776, at Washington's request, Congress established a Board of War and Ordnance, consisting of five members of Congress, with overall responsibility for overseeing the war effort. This arrangement had the advantage of concentrating the task of administration in a single committee; but it too failed because of the inability or unwillingness of members other than Adams to attend to their tasks. Congress amended the system again in 1777, this time creating a Board of War comprised of five members who were not to be delegates in Congress. The removal of members of Congress from the war board was something of an improvement; but the attempt to operate the war through a multi-member board remained unsatisfactory. The obvious solution was to substitute single executive officers for the clumsy and irresponsible boards—a step that Congress did not take lightly because of its fear of vesting excessive power in a single hand. In 1781, however, Congress provided for the appointment of a Secretary of War who, although still required to report to Congress, was given a generous measure of executive powers. Among other things, Congress provided in 1785 that the Secretary of War should "appoint and remove at pleasure all persons employed under him, and [should] be responsible for their conduct in office"—a move reflecting the recognition that "the power to appoint and remove subordinates is essential to control and responsibility on the part of the real head." This arrangement apparently proved satisfactory and was maintained until the establishment of the Constitution in 1787. Thus the pattern was one of movement from congressional towards executive government. Congress, although loath to cede any of its powers to an executive, was compelled by the exigencies of war and the needs of government to do so. By the time of the Constitution, the principle of administrative management by single executive officials had been firmly established. This concept of a single executive with authority to supervise, guide, and coordinate a variety of disparate tasks and responsibilities was projected into the institution of the President of the United States, a single official with overall responsibility for all executive actions. The model of administration that developed under the Continental Congress, in other words, provided an exemplar for the Framers as they struggled to form a new government.

Additional evidence on the President's responsibility for administration can be found in the events in the Constitutional Convention. Much of the Convention's deliberations over the powers of the Presidency centered around sundry proposals to establish some kind of council to oversee and check the President's executive powers. The council idea apparently grew out of English practice, and out of the model of states in which the administrative function was exercised by a weak executive in conjunction with a council of state. Proposals to establish checks and balances within the executive branch through the establishment of a council were supported by Madison, Wilson, Ellsworth, and Franklin, among others. None of these proposals, however, succeeded. The decision not to include a council within the executive branch suggests that the President was not to be subject to internal checks over his or her responsibility to see that the laws be faithfully executed. The success of the unitary executive represents a victory for the proponents of executive power at the Convention—* * *—who believed that the President was to be the "active chief of administration." In their view, the department heads were to be completely subordinate to the chief executive, since they were to be appointable by the President alone and to hold office at his pleasure. And it was clear that this principle was to apply across the board to all executive departments regardless of function: "Nor is there any distinction made between departments on any basis of special relationship to the President."

A final piece of historical evidence not discussed in the *Myers* opinion concerns the actual administrative practice in the Washington administration. President Washington regularly consulted with the heads of the administrative departments and only infrequently overruled them. But he was not afraid to do so on matters of great public moment. None of the cabinet secretaries, not even Hamilton, settled any matter of importance without consulting the President. In Washington's administration "the power to govern was quietly but certainly taken over by the President. The heads of departments became his assistants. In the executive branch . . . the President was undisputed master." This early history of internal executive management provides some support for the inference that the President was to be in charge of the administration of the government * * *. * * * [E]xperience under the Washington Administration does cast some question on the notion of an agency operating within the executive branch and performing executive functions free of presidential supervision and control in the form of the power to remove an official who fails to comply with a presidential directive to take an action that is otherwise within the officer's statutory discretion.

D. Function

Additional evidence on the constitutionality of limitations on the President's removal authority can be obtained through an analysis of the functional justifications for those entities. Deviations from the classical model of separation of powers may be justified by sufficiently compelling considerations of policy. The burden of proof, however, should rest heavily on the proponents of new technologies of government to establish their convenience and necessity. If the goals of the agency independence themselves are questionable, or if independence is a dubious means of achieving the goals, then the argument in favor of the constitutionality of independent agencies is considerably eroded.

1. *The haphazard pattern of agency independence.* Perhaps the single most telling rebuttal to the functional justification for independent agencies is the fact that Congress has been extremely inconsistent in its use of limitations on the President's removal power. Sometimes it creates an independent agency with express limits on presidential removal; sometimes it establishes an office in the executive branch performing apparently identical functions. The Federal Trade Commission, an independent

agency, polices against violations of the antitrust laws. So does the Department of Justice, a traditional executive branch department. The Federal Reserve Board, an independent agency, the Federal Deposit Insurance Corporation, a hybrid institution with certain independent features, and the Comptroller of the Currency, a subordinate official in the Department of the Treasury, regulate different segments of the commercial banking industry; and if a bank is dissatisfied with one regulator it can simply switch to another with no essential change in function. Dangers at the workplace are regulated at the federal level by the Occupational Safety and Health Review Administration, an executive branch agency, and by an independent commission, the Occupational Safety and Health Review Commission. Nuclear safety is under the control of an independent agency, the Nuclear Regulatory Commission. There is little rhyme or reason to these different allocations of authority.

* * *

The failure of Congress to demonstrate a consistent approach to agency independence is mirrored at the theoretical level by the absence of any noncircular explanation for why independence is needed in a particular case. None of the leading proponents of independent agencies has provided any kind of a coherent theory as to when independence is desirable and when it is not. Independent agencies are sometimes justified with reference to formulae that are nothing more than descriptions of what the typical independent agency does. * * * [T]hese statements do nothing to advance understanding as to when the independent agency form is needed. Nor are matters advanced by the various justifications advanced for agency independence, such as expertise, insulation from political pressures, and the like. These justifications typically apply to any administrative agency, and accordingly suggest that the entire administrative state ought to be comprised of independent agencies. Yet no proponent of agency independence has been willing to go this far. Short of this extreme claim, however, we are left with circular justifications: the independent form should be used when it is desirable to insulate agency action from politics, when expertise is a desideratum, and so on.

The single most economical explanation for why Congress uses the independent form in some cases and not in others is that agency independence provides a useful mechanism for compromise and accommodation among competing political interest groups. Independent agencies, in this respect, are quite similar to legislative vetoes. It is often the case that there is a political consensus in favor of regulation, but that Congress is unable to adopt any particular regulation because of the existence of blocking coalitions. The obvious solution is to formulate highly general standards that veil the areas of disagreement and give the matter to an administrative agency for decision. But members of Congress, or the interest groups they serve, may not want to give up this much power to the executive branch. An obvious solution to the dilemma, prior to the *Chadha* case, was to authorize the executive action subject to legislative veto, thus breaking the legislative deadlock without granting unfettered power to the executive. Agency independence performs something of the same function. Because independent agencies are not thought subject to executive oversight, they can be given the power to decide politically controversial matters without accentuating the power of the President. And although Congress does not have the power to reverse the actions of independent agencies (short of new legislation), it probably does exercise a greater degree of influence and control over the independent agencies than over the old-line executive departments.

* * *

The political explanation for congressional decisions creating independent agencies provides scant support for the argument that such agencies are desirable because of their functional contribution to better government. If independent agencies are often established for reasons of political expediency rather than because of their clear superiority as devices for governing, the argument in favor of insulating the heads of these agencies from presidential removal is considerably undermined.

2. *The functional arguments.* The functional justification for independent agencies has tended to stress three main advantages which these agencies supposedly possess as compared with traditional executive departments: (1) focused agenda; (2) expertise; and (3) insulation from political pressures. These justifications are closely related, and in many respects are variations on the same overall theme. On analysis, each of the purported advantages turns out to be subject to serious doubt.

a). Focused agenda. One of the principal early justifications for independent agencies is that, because they operated under a specialized mandate, they would tend to have a focused regulatory agenda. In this respect the independent agencies were sharply contrasted with the great executive departments with their almost limitless range of duties. The proponents of independent agencies argued that their focused agendas would improve the efficacy and energy of government. * * *

Underlying these supposed practical advantages of focused agendas were certain deeper themes that were not always explicitly articulated. One such theme, applicable to the agencies with substantive responsibility over particular industries, was a model of administrative structure based on the organization of the regulated industry itself. This theme is explicit in the work of James Landis. Landis argued that the task of regulating large corporations is very similar to the job of managing them. And he observed that industries never organized themselves "along Montesquieu's lines" of separation of powers. Accordingly, it is only "intelligent realism" for government to "follow the industrial rather than the political analogue." When organized along industry lines, the independent agency form "vests the necessary powers with the administrative authority it creates, not too greatly concerned with the extent to which such action does violence to the traditional tripartite theory of governmental organization."

This picture of independent agencies as homologues of their subject industries reflects a vision of the role of regulation. If the function of government in the nineteenth century had been conceptualized as police power, the role of agencies in the twentieth century was to be "management." The independent agencies were to "plan" and "promote" as well as to police. * * * The agencies, in short, were to be virtual partners in the management of their subject industries; their relationship with the private sector was to have strong elements of cooperation and even boosterism—attitudes that would be difficult to engender in government officials outside the context of agencies with mandates narrowly limited to particular industrial sectors.

A second broad theme underlying the agenda-focusing rationale of independent agencies has to do with executive power. The concept of prosecutorial discretion is an aspect of the theory of separation of powers; it describes the ability of the executive branch to vary the intensity with which it enforces statutes passed by the legislative branch. In the traditional executive department, therefore, regulatory statutes will not necessarily receive effective enforcement. Much will depend on the priorities of the agency head, who must allocate scarce prosecutorial resources among competing statutory responsibilities. The single-purpose agency circumvents this problem by establishing a unified set of bureaucratic incentives on the part of agency officials. Thus, viewed through the perspective of separation of powers the function of agenda-focusing is nothing other than a form of substantive control by Congress of the discretion that the executive branch might otherwise exercise in enforcing the law.

The benefits of narrow regulatory agendas do not by themselves justify the establishment of agencies free from presidential supervision and direction. To the extent that there are benefits from this device, they can largely be obtained without the use of independent agencies. Congress may establish "independent agencies within the executive branch," which are unquestionably constitutional so long as the President retains the power to remove agency heads who do not fit in with the President's program. * * *

More fundamentally, the benefits of focused agendas are far from unambiguous. The justification for narrow agency mandates is implicitly premised on a compartmentalized view of the national economy in which particular industries operate virtually in isolation from other industries. Under this view, the operations of one independent agency in furthering the well-being of a particular industry do not create externalities affecting other industries. At most, proponents of independent agencies tend to content themselves with the simplistic view that actions that benefit a particular industry also benefit the nation as a whole. But this is obviously an error. In a highly interdependent economy regulation of any one industry necessarily affects the well-being of any number of other industries. Energy price controls affect the cost of farming; limits on particulate emissions affect the mining industry; strip mining rules affect railroads; automobile safety rules affect the demand for steel, and so on. Agencies with highly specialized agendas will tend to focus solely on matters within their jurisdiction, thus often adopting regulatory policies with perverse consequences elsewhere in the economy. Moreover, there is a dark side to the idyllic vision of the competing segments of an industry peacefully coexisting under the benign supervision of an independent agency dedicated to furthering the industry's well-being. Everyone can be made better off within an industry to the extent that the governmental body limits competition or fixes prices. Government-sponsored cartels have been far from unknown in the history of regulation; and the rosy picture of industry well-being that a government-sponsored cartel might present does not translate into net economic benefits for the society as a whole.

* * *

b). Expertise. A second functional justification for independent agencies is that they facilitate development of "expertise" in administration. The virtues of expertise are that it will lead to more efficient and effective regulations, and that it will tend to counteract the influence of politics on the regulatory process.

Proponents of independent agencies suggest that these bodies are better suited to developing administrative expertise than are traditional executive departments. The reason, in part, is the focused agenda of independent agencies, which facilitate administrative specialization. In addition, the independent agency is said to be an important stimulus in drawing highly talented men and women into government service, since their actions are not subject to review and reversal by "young bureaucrats" in some White House office. Moreover, the sustained tenure that the independent agency makes possible encourages the development of expertise through continuity in office.

The expertise rationale for agency independence has a number of problematic features. There is no evidence that the level of expertise in independent agencies is any higher than it is in executive branch agencies. The expertise that makes a difference in particular cases will be concentrated in the career staff of an agency; and for career officers it makes little difference whether their agency is independent or not. In either case the recommendations of the career officer will be reviewed by "policy-making" officials higher up in the chain of authority. And in the vast majority of cases, in both independent and executive agencies, the staff recommendations are accepted by the agency heads without change.

Moreover, the simplistic notion that "good men" (or women) will be more attracted to independent agencies is far from established even in theory. * * *

Finally, the deadening effects of lengthy job tenure and group decision making should not be disregarded. Officials who serve terms of ten or fourteen years, subject to removal only for serious malfeasance, may naturally become complacent or even lazy in their jobs. In most cases members of independent regulatory commissions can look forward to lucrative positions in private industry upon completion of their term of service. They need not distinguish themselves while in office. Indeed, because decisions are typically made by majority vote, it is rare for their personal contributions to be singled out for admiration or criticism. Members of independent regulatory commissions can get by for years doing little more than attending meetings and voting to endorse the recommendations sent up by the staff. The heads of executive departments, in contrast, typically serve for much shorter periods. Because they are individually responsible for the affairs of the agency, they have an incentive to perform their duties with vigor and attention. And the possibility of falling into disfavor with their President is an ever-present goad to their energetic performance in implementing the President's program.

c). Insulation from political pressure. A third argument for agency independence is that independent agencies are relatively insulated from political pressures. This insulation, it is said, will encourage decisions on the substantive merits of the case, thus enhancing the beneficial effects of agency expertise. More broadly, insulation from political pressures is calculated to reduce the influence of factions or interest groups, and thereby to serve the broad ideals that inspired the Framers of the Constitution.

This argument also is not a convincing justification for independent agencies. First, the optimistic ideal of nonpolitical administration is itself coming under scrutiny. The naive faith of the New Deal era administrative law theorists was that expertise alone could provide a means of deciding the fundamental questions of wealth distribution that must needs be resolved in implementating many ostensibly "neutral" statutory schemes. But today it is increasingly recognized that the broad discretionary authorities granted to administrative agencies cannot even in principle be implemented in the absence of political considerations. * * * The goal of administrative law, as perceived by many students of the subject today, is not to exclude politics altogether, but to find some means for allowing broadly political considerations to play a role in administrative decisions while at the same time protecting against undesirable forms of political influence, especially the wielding of excessive influence by special interest lobbies.

Second, these theoretical considerations to one side, it is most definitely not the case that independent agencies are insulated from political pressures. The unanimous testimony of those who have served at the highest levels of such agencies is emphatically to the contrary. * * *

Moreover, many independent agencies are subject to a particularly insidious type of faction. In agencies serving the interests of particular industries, it is all too possible for them to pass over the line of objectivity and become the advocates of their industries. The phenomenon of agency "capture" has frequently been documented. But capture by an industry is nothing else than the expression through the coercive arm of government of a particular form of faction. In this respect, the independent agencies, far from resisting the danger of faction, in fact may increase that danger as compared to the executive branch agencies. This is not to say, of course, that the President is immune from the danger of faction, or that executive branch agencies do not cater to the wishes of Congress or their regulated industries. The difference is one of degree; but to the extent it exists, it may suggest the desirability of presidential removal as a means of mitigating the force of special interests in the administration of national programs.

Finally, it is sometimes suggested that independence is necessary in order to preserve the impartiality of agency adjudications. Adjudications, however, routinely take place within "executive" agencies just as in independent agencies. And presidential interference in ongoing adjudicatory proceedings could well create the kind of bias that would invalidate the results of the adjudication under the Due Process Clause.

E. Prescription

Yet another factor bearing on the constitutionality of independent agencies is the history of acquiescence or resistance to these agencies on the part of Presidents. Essentially, this is a notion of prescription; it entails both a long and continued pattern of usage and a failure by the branch of government whose prerogatives are ostensibly infringed to protest against the custom. If a practice of government has persisted for many years without significant controversy, then this is evidence that the practice is constitutional, or has become so by prescription.

There is no doubt that independent agencies have been part of the fabric of government long enough to achieve some form of prescriptive rights. What is less clear is the status of executive acquiescence. It is evident that merely signing a bill that establishes an independent agency does not constitute acquiescence in the agency's constitutionality. The needs of government often compel Presidents to accept provisions in legislation that they consider undesirable or even unconstitutional. If merely signing a statute were tantamount to acquiescence, then the legislative veto case might have been differently decided, since the President signed most or all of the nearly two hundred federal statutes containing such provisions. Probably, what is required to prevent a conclusion that the President has acquiesced is that the President make known his opposition to a practice and do nothing affirmative to enhance it. In the context of legislative vetoes, for example, Presidents have often included their views on the constitutionality of the device in signing statements. And only in rare instances have Presidents proposed legislative vetoes or suggested that they might be acceptable across the board.

Unlike the case of legislative vetoes, the executive branch has not consistently opposed independent agencies on constitutional grounds. A survey of signing statements for legislation establishing four randomly selected independent agencies disclosed not a single instance in which the President publically noted the difficulties under the separation of powers.

Moreover, Presidents have until now backed away from direct confrontations with Congress over the status of independent agencies. And the Department of Justice has accepted the proposition that, under *Humphrey's Executor* and *Wiener*, "Congress has the authority to limit the President's power to remove quasi-judicial or quasi-legislative officers."[162]

On the other hand, Presidents and their advisors have never been partial to the independent agency form. * * * And Presidents have challenged purported limits on their removal authority in a variety of settings.[165] Moreover, a close reading of the Department of Justice opinions reveals a strong degree of antipathy toward congressional efforts to limit the President's removal power. Presidents and their lawyers have done little more than give lip service to the dicta in *Humphrey's Executor* and *Wiener* without actually taking affirmative action to enhance the position of independent agencies within the system of government. In these circumstances, the evidence of prescription is mixed, and probably is not strong enough to support the inference that the executive branch has forfeited its constitutional objections to independent agencies.

F. Remedy

It may be useful to consider the practicalities of a decision, at this point in the history of administrative government, to strike down removal limitations on constitutional grounds. This factor should not be given excessive weight. In *Chadha*, for example, the Court did not hesitate to jeopardize nearly two hundred federal statutes. On the other hand there is an obvious and substantial interest in safeguarding the orderly functioning of government. If invalidating removal limitations were to work a hardship on private parties, or massively to disrupt ongoing governmental programs, this would be a substantial argument in favor of maintaining existing limits on the President's power to remove the heads of independent agencies.

There is reason to suppose, however, that a decision consistent with the constitutional analysis set forth above might not be overly disruptive, for two reasons: (1) the organic statutes of independent agencies are often susceptible to interpretation saving

---

[162] *E.g.*, Memorandum Opinion for the Attorney General: Inspector General Legislation, 1 Op. O.L.C. 16, 18 (1977).

[165] In addition to the *Myers, Humphrey's Executor* and *Wiener* cases, see Morgan v. Tennessee Valley Authority, 115 F.2d 990, 993-94 (6th Cir. 1940), *cert. denied*, 312 U.S. 701 (1941); Ameron, Inc. v. Army Corps of Engineers, 787 F.2d 875, 885-87 (3d Cir. 1986); Martin v. Reagan, 525 F. Supp. 110 (D. Mass. 1981).

them from constitutional attack; and (2) in those relatively infrequent cases where a statute cannot be saved through interpretation, the agency's overall powers and enforcement authority can usually be preserved through the principle of severability. Moreover, even when an entire agency is invalidated, Congress could reenact the statute creating the agency free of the objectionable removal provision.

1. *Saving through interpretation*. It may often be possible to save statutes from constitutional attack through interpretation of the "cause" requirement. Many statutes creating independent agencies do not clearly set forth the kinds of actions that constitute "cause" justifying removal by the President. These statutes can rather easily be interpreted as including within the concept of cause the failure of an agency head to comply with the President's instructions to take some action otherwise within his or her statutory authority. So interpreted, they would limit the President's power to remove an officer who has either complied with the President's instructions, or who has refused to follow an instruction that would require the officer to act in a fashion plainly beyond the officer's discretion. They would also prohibit the President from removing an officer for reasons having nothing to do with the President's responsibilities of government, such as personal animus or spite. Such limitations on the President's removal authority would be constitutional under the analysis presented above.

Other statutes purportedly set forth a detailed list of the actions that justify removal. For these statutes the interpretative task is somewhat more difficult, since failure to follow a presidential directive is never stated as one of the permissible grounds. On the other hand a list can be interpreted as illustrative rather than exclusive. Thus, the failure of Congress expressly to include disobedience of a presidential order as a ground for removal does not necessarily rule it out. Moreover, it is not difficult to bring this ground of removal within the express terms of the statutes. A directive from the President requiring an officer to take an action otherwise within the officer's statutory discretion is a facially valid order. If the officer disagrees with the instruction, the proper course is resignation—a strategy that can impose considerable political costs on the President, as President Nixon discovered in the aftermath of the infamous "Saturday Night Massacre" in which the Attorney General and the Acting Attorney General resigned rather than comply with a presidential order to fire Special Prosecutor Archibald Cox. Because the President's order to an officer to take an action within the scope of the officer's discretion is a legally valid action, the officer's refusal to follow the order can easily be considered to be a form of "neglect of duty" or "malfeasance" for which removal is expressly provided under the terms of the statutes establishing purportedly "independent" agencies.

2. *Severability.* Even though the Court's power to save statutes through interpretation is very broad, there will remain cases where the text or legislative history unambiguously establishes that Congress intended to place strict limits on the President's removal authority. In such cases the constitutional analysis set forth above could mandate that the removal provision be struck down. Such a decision, however, would not necessarily disrupt ongoing agency powers, programs, or enforcement actions. Whether the other provisions of the agency's organic statute—establishing the agency, charging it with duties, and empowering it to take specified actions—would fall together with the removal provisions depends on whether these provisions are severable from the unconstitutional limitation of presidential removal. The severability inquiry, in turn, depends on whether Congress "would have enacted those provisions which are within its power, independently of that which is not." Only if it is evident that the invalid provision is a but-for condition of the remaining provisions will the entire statute be declared invalid.

In many cases the removal provision will clearly be severable from the remainder of the statute. * * *

What remains are a small number of difficult cases in which the legislative history clearly establishes that limitations on removal were an important part of the administrative scheme contemplated by Congress. It is unquestionable that there are such cases. * * * In these hard cases the question will be whether there is sufficient evidence that the independence of the agency was indeed a sine qua non of the statute. Even here, however, the courts, reflecting a natural diffidence about broad-brush constitutional decisions, have tended to find statutes to be severable unless the contrary conclusion is irresistible.

It is of course true that a decision striking down limits on the President's removal authority would allow the President greatly to increase day-to-day White House control of agency operations, an eventuality that might disrupt ongoing programs at least in the short term. The disruption resulting from such a policy, however, would not be a necessary consequence of the constitutional ruling, but rather would result from discretionary actions by the President. Moreover, it would clearly be in the President's interest not to disrupt the functioning of the executive branch through massive intrusion into traditional areas of agency discretion. In many cases the President can be expected to allow an official to remain in office until the conclusion of his or her statutory term, and even to reappoint officers initially placed in office by previous Presidents, without seeking to exert an unusual degree of influence over the officer's decisions. * * *

* * *

Peter M. Shane, *Independent Policymaking and Presidential Power: A Constitutional Analysis*, 57 GEO. WASH. L. REV. 596, 608, 613-23 (1989)*

* * *

II. Independent Agencies: Formalism and Modernism
* * *

C. Originalism and Policy Independence

The originalist argument against independent agencies cannot sustain either proposition it asserts—either that the founding generation addressed the issue of administrative policy control in a way that is reasonably analogous to our understanding of that issue, or that, insofar as they understood the problem, the "framers" and "ratifiers" vested administrative policy control in the President.

Originalists correctly insist that the organization of the presidency was one of the most important structural questions debated in connection with the framing of the Constitution. It is equally clear that the express constitutional design, relying on a "unitary president," was intended to promote accountability and "energy" in the executive. What these premises imply for administrative agencies, however, depends on the particular conception of accountability that the founding generation perceived as linked to its structural design. It is just on this point that the originalist attack on independent agencies suffers the fallacy of anachronism.

Modern originalist challengers to independent agencies assert that such agencies mitigate the President's intended accountability for the policy content of administrative decisions, that is, his *political accountability*. It is today urged that power be centralized in the President so that voters will know whom to blame if administrative policy is too "liberal," too "conservative," too "cost-insensitive," or too oblivious to nonmonetizable values. The politicized modern framework, however, is not the framework within which the founding generation conceptualized the President's accountability. To the extent that the executive was thought to enjoy discretion in carrying out congressional enactments not pertaining to military or foreign policy, the accountability that contemporaries expected pertained to what we would now categorize as *managerial accountability*. The executive was to keep within lawful bounds, spend public funds carefully, and deal with problems evenhandedly. The President's duty to take care that the laws be faithfully executed was an obligation, not a source of power. It incorporated into the Constitution the English prohibition on the executive suspension of statutes. When, for example, Publius discusses government administration, it is not in terms of its policy orientation, but rather in terms of whether administration will prove "good" or "bad." Merit, not policy, was the criterion for judging administration.

The idea that the President was to be a source of political accountability for government policy, as we currently understand it, is implicitly refuted by the original design for presidential elections. The electoral college was conceived as a repudiation, ultimately unsuccessful, of our now partisan and plebiscitory presidential politics, in favor of a meritocratic vision of the presidency. Indirect election was supposed to mitigate the degree to which politics might control the choice of Presidents. Electors were even required to cast their votes in the separate states to prevent political discussion among them from influencing their choice.

Indeed, an obvious implication of the unitary presidency is that political representativeness of the kind associated with the House of Representatives is not a goal of the executive organization. A multi-membered body would clearly have created greater opportunities for popular representation than the executive branch—for example, by geographic region—and consequently greater political accountability. Implicit in the choice of a unitary presidency was the view that the President was not to be a mirror of popular sentiment, but—as far as legislation was concerned—a defender of a unitary public interest in any case should political faction overtake public good. In this respect, his function was akin to the anticipated function of the highly undemocratic Senate. Thus, any argument that central presidential administrative authority is necessary to preserve *politi-*

---

* Reprinted with permission of the George Washington Law Review and Peter M. Shane. All rights reserved.

cal accountability is based on a democratic theory different from the original constitutional vision. The repository of the Framers' commitment to democracy, such as it was, was not the executive, but Congress—primarily, the House of Representatives.

An originalist might, of course, retreat to the argument that the Framers' commitments to centralized *managerial* accountability and energetic decisionmaking are enough to require centralized presidential authority over all administrative agencies. This argument, however, is weak for two reasons. First, it is by no means clear that Congress has today precluded the President from exercising a central *managerial* role over the agencies. Congress has provided the Office of Management and Budget—and thus the President—with a critical role in evaluating the independent agencies' budget requests and paperwork requirements. The President is typically permitted to choose the chair of each multi-member agency. "Inefficiency" and "neglect of duty" are often mentioned in the statutes authorizing independent agencies as causes sufficient to sustain the presidential removal of even an independent administrator. All of this comports with a vision of constitutionally compelled centralized management.

A careful originalist, however, should regard even these congressional decisions to be constitutionally discretionary. Whatever commitment the founding generation had to centralized management did not translate—even in the late eighteenth century—into a model of executive control over all administration at the state or federal level. We have already seen that this is true with respect to criminal prosecutors, who are, after all, administrative policymakers. Evidence regarding civil administration also supports the point.

In 1789, the first Congress created four civil administrative establishments—the departments of War, of Foreign Affairs, of the Treasury, and of the Post Office. Congress's treatment of the four agencies reflected lengthy deliberation and differing understandings as to the relation of executive power to each agency.

Two of the departments—War and Foreign Affairs—were understood to be assisting in the implementation of presidential powers vested specifically by the Constitution and were denominated "executive departments." Their organic statutes sketched their departmental organization and their duties only in broad terms. Congress anticipated a broad supervisory relationship of the President to the department.

The new Post Office establishment, however, was not called a department. The Postmaster General had a reporting relationship to the Secretary of the Treasury, and it is clear from the debates surrounding the Treasury Department that the character of Treasury was not perceived to be executive in a manner akin to the departments of War and Foreign Affairs. First, unlike the other departments, Treasury was not denominated "executive" by statute. Congress went to a great length to specify the Department's structure, creating a number of fiscal officers with reporting responsibility to the Secretary. Most tellingly, the first Congress perceived the Secretary's obligations as running to Congress as well as to the President. The most important debate in this regard centered around a proposed duty of the Secretary "to digest and prepare plans for the improvement and management of the revenue, and for the support of public credit." This wording is nearly identical to the charge to the financial officers authorized under the Articles of Confederation. Some in Congress were alarmed that this parliamentary duty would so involve the Secretary in legislation as to undermine the authority of the House; others saw the charge as undermining the President's power to propose legislation. Nonetheless, Congress conferred this duty upon the Secretary, essentially borrowing a description of the Secretary from this country's former, short-lived parliamentary system.

The implications of this analysis were borne out in practice. For several years, the Secretary of the Treasury functioned as the Committee on Ways and Means of the House of Representatives. As late as 1823, the Attorney General advised the President that, far from the President being constitutionally obligated to correct an allegedly improper settlement by the Treasury Department of an individual's claim for reimbursement, it would be legally impermissible for the President to substitute his judgment for that of the accounting officer.

The vision of an air-tight executive establishment under plenary presidential control that is conjured by originalist challengers to independent agencies thus cannot be matched by the early history of administrative practice. * * *

D. *Modernism and Policy Independence*

By now, any thoroughgoing originalist should be persuaded that the decision whether to insulate agency administrators from direct presidential policy supervision is wholly within congressional discretion. Neither the text nor the history relevant to original understanding of the separation of powers commands plenary control in the President.

Yet, originalism in this context seems almost a sleight of hand. To put it bluntly: why should we be bound, in our understanding of the President's proper role vis-a-vis a vast modern administrative bureaucracy, by the conventional conceptualization of administration in an entirely different world? An additional and perhaps more provocative level of constitutional argument is possible.

* * * [O]ne might start this argument, like the originalist argument, by observing that the Constitution clearly embodies a commitment to a unitary executive and that the fundamental purpose underlying the constitutional organization was executive accountability. It may be conceded that the terms in which the Framers discussed accountability were not the policy-laden, frankly partisan terms by which we understand the concept. They assessed administration in terms of virtues "above" politics—was administration honest or corrupt, efficient or inefficient, dedicated to the public good or overtaken by faction? But the differences in the terms by which they and we understand our very different worlds do not belie the shared concern. It is arguably as legitimate for us as it was for them to build a contemporaneous conception of accountability into our reading of the constitutional text. This is so, the modernist urges, even without a formal alteration of that text.

* * *

The modernist argument against independent agencies runs as follows. The Constitution created a unitary presidency in order to concentrate accountability in the President. Although the original constitutional vision of administration was essentially meritocratic, we have come to perceive that the administrative implementation of public policy is infused with political value judgments. The founding generation believed that House of Representatives elections would preserve political accountability, yet that is clearly not the case. An electorate unable to influence the policies that guide the exercise of administrative discretion in the executive branch is significantly disenfranchised. The way to preserve our commitments to democracy and to accountability is by reading into Article II a plenary presidential power to guide executive branch policymaking.

This argument is more compelling, it might be urged, because of thoroughly changed political, social, and economic circumstances. First, although the democratic character of the original Constitution was significantly attenuated, formal changes in the Constitution since 1789 have enlarged its commitment to popular democracy and electoral control. Because Congress now delegates such extensive policymaking authority to administrative agencies, placing ultimate policy authority in the President is the most effective mechanism for giving voters influence over the policy agenda of the agencies.

Second, the limited scope of federal activity in the late eighteenth century, especially with regard to domestic regulation, made it plausible to think Congress would keep to itself all significant discretion over federal policymaking. The scope of modern federal government activity is, by contrast, enormous, prompted by the creation of national markets and national networks of communication and transport, as well as by the reallocation of civil rights authority following the Civil War. The fact that Congress has responded by delegating important policymaking discretion with respect to virtually every aspect of our collective economic and social life creates a critical problem of coordination. The President is the only official with the current capacity to impose some coordinating discipline on a host of administrators, each of whom may otherwise fail to take account of the competing agendas of different agencies.

Finally, a core aspiration articulated by Madison for the new government structure was its utility in overcoming what Madison called the vices of "faction." To whatever extent eighteenth century social and political conditions might have rendered that hope realistic, modernists insist that our current Congress and the agencies are easy prey to narrow interests, the current analogues to factions. The President, because he has the broadest possible constituency, is least likely to fall prey to special interests. The unitary presidency thus has a potentially critical role to play in countermanding the modern influence of faction in administrative policymaking.

These are important arguments * * *. They do not rest on artificial attempts to capture what the founding generation thought, but instead urge what we should now think in applying the general concepts of accountability and coordination to our modern circumstance. If one regards constitutional argument in the modern neoclassical mode as legitimate, these arguments provide weightier ammunition than does originalism for the constitutional position advanced by the Reagan administration on the independent agency controversy.

These arguments are weightier than the originalist challenge, although, to be sure, each modernist argument is questionable on its own terms. It is by no means clear in practice that increased presidential control over agency policymaking would be truer to the electoral will than the current system. Despite President Reagan's overwhelming electoral mandates, popular opinion never swung behind key elements of his deregulatory agenda. It is plausible that public enthusiasm for the President was strengthened by the perception that he could not disturb major elements of domestic social policy that were embedded in legislation and in our bureaucratic culture before his presidency.

Likewise, coordination in the administration of statutes is a virtue only to the extent Congress wants coordination. A key anxiety underlying President Reagan's increased oversight of regulatory policymaking by non-independent agencies concerned the degree to which the Office of Management and Budget might try to enforce policy uniformity contrary to legislative intent. Although it is plausible that presidential oversight can help to "minimize duplication and conflict of regulations," this is a proposition to be tested empirically. Moreover, improvements in this regard need to be balanced against the degree to which such coordination threatens to undermine the effectiveness of individual statutory programs.

The President's precise role in resisting "faction" is likewise far from self-evident. Modern laments against "special interests" do not equate precisely with Madison's notion of faction. Madison defined faction as

> a number of citizens, whether amounting to a majority or minority of the whole, who are united and actuated by some common impulse of passion, or of interest, adverse to the rights of other citizens, or to the permanent and aggregate interests of the community.

Thus, organizations dedicated, for example, to environmental protection or civil rights enforcement—organizations that President Reagan was wont to decry as special interests—do not represent "factions" in the Madisonian sense because their ideological appeal is to the long-term common interest, not to momentary passion or self-interest. The modern "special interests" most obviously resembling Madisonian factions are the lobbyists and political action committees organized for the protection of economic interests. That these organizations might be more effectively deployed against independent agencies than non-independent agencies is an intriguing empirical proposition that must be tested, not merely assumed.

For constitutional purposes, however, the modernist arguments, whatever their empirical basis, are unpersuasive because they are incomplete. Accountability, coordination, and the obstruction of factionalism are not the only relevant general concepts that are both traceable to the Constitution and translatable for modern application. Two other constitutional principles are critically important—the diffusion of power and the primacy of Congress in domestic policymaking.

The diffusion of what we would now call regulatory power was of critical significance to late eighteenth century political thought. The Constitution thus recognizes the continuing integrity of state governments, divides the branches of the federal government, and bifurcates the federal legislative branch. Swings in popular majorities can swing the House of Representatives every two years, but not the Senate. Most regulatory power was thought to reside in the states, wherein the source of regulation most clearly analogous to our independent agencies was the common law court. The result is a deliberate impediment to coordination.

The contribution to liberty of the diffusion of power has long been treated as all but self-evident in American political thought. Our political evolution, however, has demonstrated an additional value—the profound contribution of this diffusion of power to political stability. The increased democratization of American politics has exposed deep divisions within the electorate on basic political and social questions. We have witnessed profound changes in majority sentiment on a variety of issues within even the past three decades. Because policymaking power is diffused, however, throughout different branches and among different levels of government, two things are true. Even a strong majority is likely to produce no more than incremental policy changes in short periods of time, and minority opinion, defeated in one forum, is likely to have other political forums in which to compete more effectively. This means that a political minority, when it loses an election, does not lose everything. Much less does it lose everything if its opinion was ever majority opinion and, hence, embodied in laws that would have to be repealed if another philosophy is to be implemented as law. Given how hotly the public currently contests such issues as abortion, civil rights, environmental protection, public aid to religion, and trade policy, it may be quite dangerous to raise the policy stakes in presidential elections. Empowering temporary majorities to swing quickly the whole of our policy agenda may greatly provoke electoral discontent and social strife.

This is all the more true because so much regulatory power has passed to the federal government. The development of national markets, and of national networks of communication and transport, has rendered it highly unlikely that judicially enforceable federalism principles can ever be sensibly devised to reduce the federal regulatory role. In a sense, congressional decisions to vest policy independence in administrative agencies may help to compensate for the diminished vitality of federalism. The relative lack of coordination among independent agencies may better accord with the pluralism and division that often characterizes the American electorate. From the standpoint of stability, the record of the more fully coordinated western parliamentary democracies of Europe does not seem enviable.

The salience of the diffusion of power to our decision as to whether Congress may authorize agency policy independence is even greater when considered in tandem with a second constitutional commitment—a commitment to the primacy of Congress in domestic federal policymaking. Whatever the advantages of that primacy in 1789, it might be thought to have at least two advantages two centuries later. First, the primacy of Congress, with its divided structure and staggered Senate selections, helps reinforce the bias towards incrementalism that we value as a source of stability. Second, although the diffusion of power within Congress through the proliferation of subcommittees undoubtedly diminishes the coordinating capacity of Congress, it greatly increases the likelihood that some politician will have real incentive to pay close attention to agency policy even at a microlevel. The prestige of a subcommittee chair—there were 228 subcommittees in 1987-88—is likely to be augmented by that person's success in drawing attention to issues raised by the activity of any agency within his or her subcommittee's jurisdiction.

The arguments from congressional primacy and the virtues of the diffusion of power are, of course, debatable. The actual value to the American polity of what independent agencies contribute by way of congressional primacy and the diffusion of power is as controversial as the value of what centralized executive power would contribute by way of coordination, political accountability, and the deterrence of faction. My conclusion, therefore, is that the arguments favoring agency policy independence are too weak to command that the President be denied policy supervision over agencies that are not exercising powers in areas of authority vested in the President by Article II.

I do believe, however, that the arguments are strong enough—certainly as weighty for constitutional purposes as the arguments against the policy independence of agencies * * *—that the issue as to whether policy independence is an appropriate feature of an agency is an issue within Congress's discretion to decide. There is no single argument on either side of the issue that trumps the others because it is either plainly more rooted in Constitutional values or plainly more persuasive empirically. All the arguments discussed are policy positions to be weighed in deciding as a matter of legislative judgment how it is necessary or appropriate for any individual agency to be structured. Congress is free to weigh such constitutionally rooted arguments—as well as a host of other arguments for and against independence that may not be linked rhetorically with constitutional values—because all would be within Congress's rational consideration in deciding on agency structure.

This is plainly not a defense of particular decisions Congress has made. Critics are right that no apparent principle explains why some agencies are currently "independent" and others "purely" executive. That Congress may make decisions that are difficult to rationalize or even wrong does not diminish the scope of its powers to make decisions. If the policy arguments against independence are strong enough, Congress should pay heed. My point is, however, that even the modernist Constitution favors Congress's authority to make the choice. It corroborates the likeliest inferences from a textual and historical analysis.

* * *

Peter L. Strauss, *The Place of Agencies in Government: Separation of Powers and the Fourth Branch*, 84 COLUM. L. REV. 573, 574, 578-79, 581-85, 587-92, 596-605, 609-16, 622, 625, 639-42, 667 (1984)*

Introduction

In the pages following I argue that, for any consideration of the structure given law-administration below the very apex of the governmental structure, the rigid separation-of-powers compartmentalization of governmental functions should be abandoned in favor of analysis in terms of separation of functions and checks and balances. Almost fifty years of experience has accustomed lawyers and judges to accepting the independent regulatory commissions, in the metaphor, as a "headless 'fourth branch'" of government. Although the resulting theoretical confusion has certainly been noticed, we accept the idea

---

* Reprinted with permission of the Columbia Law Review and Peter L. Strauss. All rights reserved.

of potent actors in government joining judicial, legislative and executive functions, yet falling outside the constitutionally described schemata of three named branches embracing among them the entire allocated authority of government. What would be the consequences of so viewing *all* government regulators? I believe such a shift in view would carry with it significant analytical advantages by directing our focus away from the truly insignificant structural and procedural differences between the "independent regulatory commissions" and other agencies to the relationships existing between each such agency and the three named branches. Each such agency is to some extent "independent" of each of the named branches and to some extent in relationship with each. The continued achievement of the intended balance and interaction among the three named actors at the top of government, with each continuing to have effective responsibility for its unique core function, depends on the existence of relationships between each of these actors and each agency within which that function can find voice. A shorthand way of putting the argument is that we should stop pretending that all our government (as distinct from its highest levels) can be allocated into three neat parts. The theory of separation-of-powers breaks down when attempting to locate administrative and regulatory agencies within one of the three branches; its vitality, rather, lies in the formulation and specification of the controls that Congress, the Supreme Court and the President may exercise over administration and regulation.

* * *

I. The Shape of Contemporary Administrative Government

This Part of the Article seeks to describe the ways in which contemporary federal government is structured and performs its law-administration functions. The effort proceeds from the premise that any useful legal analysis of the limits on Congress's ability to structure administrative government must, at least in large measure, accept the reality of the existing government. To no one's surprise, the description reveals a profuse variety of formal structures and a striking dispersion of governmental authorities. Both the variety and the dispersion are inconsistent with any notion that the powers of government are or can be neatly parcelled out into three piles radically separated the one from the other and each under the domination of its particular "branch." Once one descends below the level of the branch heads named in the Constitution—Congress, President, and Supreme Court—separation of powers ceases to have

descriptive power. Because agencies nonetheless exist in varying relationships with each of these paramount actors, the notion of checks and balances retains descriptive power and, hence, possible utility within the constraint of accepting the reality of the existing government.

* * *

The following four propositions identify the significant features of modern administrative government that any structural account based on the Constitution must encompass:

1. The federal agencies are placed in the structure of federal government—as cabinet agencies, independent executive agencies, or independent regulatory commissions—without apparent regard for the functions they are to perform. Their internal and public procedures do not vary with their placement. The functions they form belie simple classification as "legislative," "executive," or "judicial," but partake of all three characteristics.

2. All agencies, whether denominated executive or independent, have relationships with the President in which he is neither dominant nor powerless. They are all subject to presidential direction in significant aspects of their functioning, and able to resist presidential direction in others (generally concerning substantive decisions).

3. All agencies have oversight relationships with Congress and the federal judiciary, and these relationships generally do not vary with the type of agency used.

4. The characteristics of the oversight relations of President and Congress with "executive" and "independent" agencies owe as much (or more) to politics as to law.

* * *

A. *The Independence of Agency Function, Placement, and Structure*

Congress has employed many different forms of governmental authority in allocating the day-to-day work of government. It has created cabinet departments, cabinet-level agencies headed by individual administrators responsible to the President, independent regulatory commissions, federal corporations, independent regulatory commissions within cabinet departments, and more as means of carrying into execution the laws it enacts. And each of these bodies may itself be highly complex—an amalgam of agencies, administrations, offices, bureaus, and services, each headed by its own chief possessing statutory authority yet reporting to an assistant who reports to the agency head.

The allocation of law-administration among these forms does not follow simple functional lines. Although administrative law students and others sometimes talk uncritically as if the performance of regulation were a lodestone—as if all regulatory agencies were "independent regulatory commissions"—regulatory and policymaking responsibilities are scattered among independent and executive-branch agencies in ways that belie explanation in terms of the work agencies do. * * *

The diversity of form, however, ought not to conceal the substantial commonalities of internal structure, function, and procedure. Despite the attention often given asserted differences between single, politically responsible administrators and multimember independent commissions, these organizations are more similar than different below the highest levels. In its regulatory work each is subdivided in accordance with the same principles of bureaucratic organization, relies upon staff protected by the same civil service laws, performs the same functions, employs the same public procedures, and settles disputes using the same types of decisional personnel.

* * *

B. *Presidential Direction of Agencies*

Viewed from any perspective other than independence in policy formation, the legal regime within which agencies function is highly unified under presidential direction. Many administrative functions are centrally performed, a product of congressional recognition that all agencies share many of the administrative needs of government, for which central management under presidential supervision is highly desirable. Thus, the property of independent as well as executive-branch agencies is managed by the General Services Administration, and their contracts are entered in accordance with its procurement regulations. The Department of Justice, to varying degrees, represents their interests in court; the Office of Personnel Management and the Merit Systems Protection Board regulate their employment practices, pay scales and allocation of super-grade management posts. The protection of national secrets, with one statutory exception, occurs under an executive order, which establishes both the regime for classification and the requirements for access; and the executive branch performs the investigations that qualify persons for clearance. Government contracts contain nondiscrimination clauses, and an enforcement regime housed in an executive department has been established, again on the basis of an executive order.

Even in the arena of policy, one readily finds major respects in which agencies' work is centrally managed. The National Security Council coordinates interagency studies to develop national policy at the request of the President or a possibly affected agency, without necessary regard to the independence (or lack of it) of the agencies that may be affected. Similarly, the Office of Management and Budget coordinates agency comments on some proposed rules, promoting conferences and other collaborative efforts in order to produce a result maximally acceptable among all agencies concerned. OMB plays a coordinating role also when agencies find themselves in the jurisdictional disputes that are the inevitable consequences of the enormous number of regulatory measures Congress enacts and the many different agencies to which it assigns responsibility. Although litigation or the seeking of a formal legal opinion from the Attorney General would be possible, for example, in the face of uncertainty whether the Nuclear Regulatory Commission or the Environmental Protection Agency had primary regulatory responsibility for radioactive discharges from NRC regulated plants into EPA regulated waters, the more usual course is to put the matter before OMB, which will attempt more informally to bring the agencies to an understanding.

Other White House operations involve all agencies in the formulation or implementation of overarching national policy. Most prominent may be the OMB's annual creation of a national budget expressing the President's view of the relative priorities to be accorded the various efforts of national government. While Congress has occasionally limited the discipline of the budget process by requiring agencies simultaneously to provide the appropriate congressional committees their submissions to OMB, the President's coordinative, policy-setting function is recognized in these provisions also. Overall, presidential coordination is an activity of importance, one in which the agencies generally cooperate and from which they receive benefit as well as occasional constraint.

The independent agencies are often free, at least in a formal sense, of other relationships with the White House that characterize the executive-branch agencies. The President's influence reaches somewhat more deeply into the top layers of bureaucracy at an executive agency than at an independent commission. Where subsidiary officers in the executive agencies may be subject to presidential appointment and certainly require White House clearance, in the independent agencies only commissioners are appointed with required executive participation; staff appointments, even at the highest level, are made by the commission. The requirement that commission membership be at least nominally bipartisan does not prevent the appointment of political friends but doubtless lowers the political temperature. Typically, the independents have more authority to conduct their own litigation than executive-branch agencies do, although not exclusive authority. Executive-branch agencies have an obligation to clear legislative matters—draft statutes, budget submissions, even testimony—with the Office of Management and Budget, an obligation from which some of the independents are excused. One recent statute, the Paperwork Reduction Act of 1980, specifically empowers the independents to overrule by majority the Presidential directives respecting the collection of information to which executive branch agencies are bound. As a political matter, recent Presidents have not required the independent commissions to participate in the centralized oversight of rulemaking associated with presidentially required cost-benefit analyses of major proposals for rule-making.

Yet these differences are at best matters of degree, overstated if taken to imply rigorous control within the executive branch. Even in executive agencies, the layer over which the President enjoys direct control of personnel is very thin and political factors may make it difficult for him to exercise even those controls to the fullest. An administrator with a public constituency and mandate * * * cannot be discharged—and understands that he cannot be discharged—without substantial political cost. Also for political reasons, one may be certain that independent commission consultation with the White House about appointments often occurs, even if subdued—as in so many other matters—by the lack of obligation so to consult.

Presidential influence over the independent agencies is heightened by the special ties existing between the President and the chairmen of almost all of the independent regulatory commissions. Although all commissioners, including the chairmen, are appointed to fixed terms as commissioners, the chairman generally holds that special post at the President's pleasure. His position, moreover, gives him special influence over the agency's course, making it particularly likely that his views will find acceptance. * * *

C. *Agency Relations with Congress and the Courts*

* * * In any matter of importance, the public, the press, the intended subjects of the policy, the courts, and interested congressmen and their staffs also become involved. And one may search both the law and the literature on congressional-bureaucratic relationships or the operation of judicial review in vain for an indication that the relationships between these overseers and the agencies varies in any regular way in accordance with agency structure. The rules of judicial review distinguish between those proceedings held "on the record" and those that are not, but express no differences for such proceedings held in one type of agency or another. So also for congressional oversight relationships: budgetary controls, investigations, hearings, and all the general apparatus of congressional oversight are brought to bear across the board. As has often enough been noted, these relationships can be particularly important; congressmen and committee staffs tend to be longer-lived than Presidents and their appointees, and through hearings and budgetary actions can work much mischief.

There are, to be sure, differences of tone. The uncertainty about what "independence" means shapes the behavior of the Congress, the President and the agencies alike. Congressmen tend to talk about the independent commissions in a proprietary way—these are "our" agencies, not so much independent as independent-of-the-President. One result of this attitude—hard to measure but suggested by local belief—may be a greater intensity of congressional political oversight of the independents. Even if congressional oversight is not itself measurably more intense, it may be the more effective if not answered by counterpressures; as a former FTC Chairman recently remarked, the independent agencies "have no lifeline to the White House. [They] are naked before Congress, without protection there," because of the President's choice not to risk the political cost that assertion of his interest would entail. In any event, Congress's techniques do not vary; no particular form of dominion is asserted over "independent" agencies that is not practiced also on the agencies associated more directly with the White House. And, as already indicated, Congress generally provides for a large measure of presidential participation in the day-to-day administration, if not the policy formation, of those agencies.

* * *

II. The Limited Constitutional Instructions About the Place of Agencies in Government

* * * This Part of the essay examines * * * constitutional text, context, and interpretation to see what constraints they may impose on Congress's undoubtedly large authority to structure the inferior parts of the federal government.

From this examination will emerge three general

propositions about the three theoretical approaches to understanding the place of agencies in government identified in the introduction. The first is that, as a textual and interpretational matter, the separation-of-powers model need and probably should be taken no further than its use for understanding the interrelationships of the three named actors (Congress, President, Court) at the very pinnacle of government. Subject to definitional issues, we accept (and the Constitution is reasonably explicit) that, as among them, only Congress may legislate, only the Supreme Court may adjudicate, and only the President may see to the faithful execution of the laws; and each is to have a significant function in these respects. In this way, "separation of powers" remains vital in suggesting the forms of control each of the three may exercise over the bulk of government. Yet in the agencies, as we have seen, powers are not in fact separated and the agencies are not responsible to only one of these actors. Although agencies certainly might be assigned to one or another of the executive, legislative, or judicial branches (but not more than one, if we are rigorously to pursue the separation idea), that signifies little for the functions they perform. No compelling textual or interpretive mandate requires such a formal placement to be effected.

A second proposition emerging from the cases is that considerations of individual fairness more closely associated with the idea of separation of functions often underlie the cases in which the idea of separation of powers appears to have played a significant role. The impulses for both congressional and judicial action may arise from individuals' needs for protection from political intervention in particular cases more than any general theory about place in government; the former can be provided without necessary regard for the latter.

Finally and perhaps most importantly, the text and particularly the context suggest a series of postulates about necessary relationships between the President and administrative agencies—relationships readily understood in checks-and-balances terms. The important constraint on Congress's ability to structure the work of law-administration lies in the need to perpetuate the tensions and interactions among the three named heads of the Constitution. Whatever arrangements are made, one must remain able to characterize the President as the unitary, politically accountable head of all law-administration, sufficiently potent in his own relationships with those who actually perform it to serve as an effective counter to a feared Congress. The central inquiry is to identify those relationships that are necessary, either to conform with the constitutional text or to preserve the possibility of the President's continuing effectiveness. * * *

A. *The Text and Context of the Constitution*

The text and structure of the Constitution impose few limits on Congress's ability to structure administrative government. One scanning the Constitution for a sense of the overall structure of the federal government is immediately struck by its silences. Save for some aspects of the legislative process, it says little about how those it names as necessary elements of government—Congress, President, and Supreme Court—will perform their functions, and it says almost nothing at all about the unelected officials who, even in 1789, would necessarily perform the bulk of the government's work. Thus, article I describes in some detail the makeup of the House and Senate, the subjects on which they might act, and the manner in which they may effectively legislate; but even this relatively full description talks only to the authority and actions of elected officials. One finds no mention there of important aspects of Congress's work, or of most persons who now work on its behalf—committees and their staffs, the General Accounting Office, the Congressional Budget Office, the Library of Congress.

For articles II and III, the limitations of description are even more striking. Article II speaks directly only about elected officials, chiefly the President and his powers; it describes those powers in the most summary of terms. He is vested generally with "the executive Power," but what that is in the domestic context does not readily appear. Putting aside foreign relations and military authority—a very large part of the Presidency, but not the focus of this essay—he has the following powers and/or responsibilities:

> to appoint those "Officers of the United States . . . which shall be established by Law," subject to the requirement of senatorial confirmation and to the possibility that Congress might effectively limit this power to appointing "the Heads of Departments";

> to "require the Opinion, in writing, of the principal Officer in each of the executive Departments, upon any Subject relating to the Duties of their respective Offices";

> "from time to time give to the Congress Information of the State of the Union, and recommend to their Consideration" proposed legislation;

> to "take Care that the Laws be faithfully executed."

These provisions suggest a supervisory, perhaps

even caretaker presidential role, in relationship to shadowy "executive departments" from which opinions might be sought. One is left to infer that there would be other officers possessing legal authority to act for the government, and one simply is not told whether the President or those officers are to act on those opinions.

Article III is more direct, denying any need for inferior federal courts unless and to the extent Congress chose to create them. Only the Supreme Court is a required element of the federal judiciary, and even for that institution central issues are left unspoken—its number, its term, its authority over the work of the other named actors. In almost all significant respects, then, the job of creating and altering the shape of the federal government was left to the future—to the congressional processes suggested by Congress's authority to adopt any law "necessary and proper for carrying into Execution the foregoing Powers, and all other Powers vested by this Constitution in the Government of the United States, or in any Department or Officer thereof."

If one moves outward from the text to its structure, the context in which it was drafted, the records and debates of the constitutional convention, and its initial implementation by the first Congress, one can identify a number of fundamental underlying judgments. The text's omission to provide for the "Departments" it occasionally refers to reflects a parliamentary history in which quite detailed proposals for cabinet structure were put forward. Some decisions respecting the allocation and sharing of power within such a structure were clearly taken, but then a determination was made to eschew detailed prescription as a means of underscoring presidential responsibility and preserving congressional flexibility within the constraints of the judgments that had been made.

1. *The President is to be a Unitary, Politically Accountable Head of Government.* — Of the decisions clearly taken, perhaps none was as important as the judgment to vest the executive power in a single, elected official, the President. * * *

If the Convention was clear in its choice of a single executive—and its associated beliefs that such a person might bear focused political accountability for the work of law-execution and serve as an effective political counterweight to Congress—it was ambivalent in its expectations about the President's relations with those who would actually do the work of law-administration and desirous of the advantage of congressional flexibility in defining the structure of government within the constraints of this choice. * * * [T]he shadowy references to executive departments and, in particular, the opinions in writing clause, seem to be residues of propositions such as Governor Morris's proposal in the final days of the Convention for a council of state composed of the Chief Justice and Secretaries of Domestic Affairs, State, Foreign Affairs, War, Marine, and Commerce and Finance. The Morris proposal would have respected the central political structural judgments that had been made. Under it, each of the identified departments and their Secretaries were to have been granted specific duties—for example, the Secretary of Domestic Affairs was "to attend to matters of general policy, the state of agriculture and manufactures, the opening of roads and navigations, and the facilitating communications through the United States; and he shall, from time to time, recommend such measures and establishments as may tend to promote those objects." Yet each Secretary was distinctly under Presidential control, holding office at the President's pleasure. As a body, they were to be available to the President for the discussion of any matter he might choose to submit, and he could require from them "written opinions." Although each was to be "responsible for his opinion on the affairs relating to his particular department," the possibility of ultimate decision was placed elsewhere: the President "shall, in all cases, exercise his own judgment, and either conform to such opinion, or not, as he may think proper."

Certainly one consideration underlying rejection of the Morris proposal was the wish to leave to successive Congresses, through the medium of the necessary and proper clause, the flexibility required for shaping the government to the demands of changing circumstances. Another consideration was to enhance the accountability—and thus the power—of the President by denying him the chance to hide behind a council's approval of his acts. Indeed, the immediate working out of the constitutional scheme by the first Congress largely paralleled the Morris proposal. Cabinet departments were promptly established, with day-to-day responsibilities for administration, but reporting to the President. Following the Morris model, a practice of cabinet consultation on important issues, nonbinding but respected, quickly arose. Presidential control over the cabinet was assured by the provision in this legislation—the decision of 1789, as it came to be regarded—that the Secretaries were to serve at the President's pleasure, not for a term of years, and thus could be removed by him without cause or senatorial assent.

One ought not, however, mistake the drafters' possible ambivalence about presidential role and their willingness to trust the issue of governmental superstructure to future Congresses for a willingness to see the President assigned a role distinctly subordinate to Congress. In providing that Congress need not be convened until December of each year, the draftsmen plainly anticipated a substantial executive function. Congress's articulated functions lay in the passage of legislation to create the framework of government and then to set the standards and appropriate the funds by which the business of government would be carried on. Inevitably that legislation would be episodic—enacted without necessary care for its relationship to existing law and having to be applied to future events, not foreseen, in light of the then existing corpus of law and the exigencies of the moment. Executive authority had to provide correctives for these inherent difficulties, and it was important that the chief executive have a body of individuals, held in his confidence, with whom to consult. The responsibility of government was to be focally his; but day-to-day administration and decision, of necessity, was to be entrusted to the hands of others.

2. *The Maintenance of Tension Among the Named Bodies.*—A central, coordinating and overseeing role for the President in relation to all government "officers" is required, also, to permit that office to serve as an effective check on the otherwise to be feared authority of Congress. The framers sought both to create a more effective national government than they had previously experienced, and to make it resistant to domination by transitory majorities or those who for the moment might be the public's political representatives. To those ends, the governmental structure they created embodies both separated powers and interlocking responsibilities; the purpose was to prevent both majoritarian rashness and the governmental tyranny that could result from the conjoining of power in a single source. Maintaining conditions that would sustain the resulting tension between executive and legislature was to be the central constraint on any proposed structure for government.

The Constitutional Convention arose out of dissatisfaction with a government dominated by the legislature, a dissatisfaction on both practical and theoretical grounds. In practice, legislative government did not work; legislatures were fragmented and episodic in their attention to the affairs of state, diffusing and defeating responsibility. In theory, the joining of all government functions in one authority, unchecked by others, was an invitation to tyranny. Interpenetration of function and competition among the branches would protect liberty by preventing the irreversible accretion of ultimate power in any one. As Madison wrote in the *Federalist* papers, the essence lay in "giving to those who administer each department the necessary constitutional means and personal motives to resist encroachments of the others." Madison's strategy was given form in the veto power and in Congress's authority to create the infrastructure of executive government and to exercise plenary control over the President's expenditure of funds (and thus over the size and power of the executive establishment).

The imprecision inherent in the definition and separation of the three governmental powers contributes to the tensions among them and in that way serves the same beneficial and protective functions as were anticipated from the creation of checks and balances. In the long interludes between congressional sessions, the President would have to make as well as execute national policy; execution cannot be separated from interpretation, nor interpretation from the exercise (within whatever bounds might be statutorily defined) of a policy function. How sharp the definition of bounds had to be * * * or how far removed from the President the function of executing a given law could be placed were open questions. This imprecision invites the desired political rivalries that tend to keep the two more dangerous branches in check. At the same time it permits smoother functioning on issues of agreed importance than would a more rigid structure. * * *

Thus, while the actual text of the Constitution says little about the structure of the federal government beneath the apex, the structure and history of the Constitution make clear the framers' decisions concerning the interdependence of the three branches and the place of the agencies as subsidiary to all three. One may see the issue of balance of power among the three named branches of government as reflecting a process not an institution, with impermanence of resolution not only inevitable but desirable as an outcome. "The constitutional convention of 1787 is supposed to have created a government of 'separated powers.' It did nothing of the sort. Rather, it created a government of separated institutions sharing powers."[120] * * * [T]he checks and balances idea embodied in the Constitution creates and demands the continuance of a "tension among the branches, with each, at the margin, limiting the other," so that, in Madison's terms, "'ambition [could] be made to counteract ambition.'"

B. *Interpretations of the Constitutional Constraints*

In addition to constitutional text and context, the interpretations given the President's place in government by courts and others during the past two hundred years influence contemporary understandings of his relationship to the agencies and Congress's power

---

[120] [RICHARD NEUSTADT, PRESIDENTIAL POWER—THE POLITICS OF LEADERSHIP FROM FDR TO CARTER 26 (1980).]

to structure that relationship. Perhaps of particular importance here is the legal folklore about independent regulatory commissions, in some versions suggesting that parts of government responsible for the administration of important government programs can be put wholly beyond the President's supervisory reach. That folkloric view should seem surprising in light of the foregoing, and indeed a close look at the cases will show that that suggestion is hardly a necessary reading; the Court never had to confront so dramatic an assertion, and our understanding of its opinions can be reconstructed without much difficulty to reflect awareness of the need to maintain a tension among the named heads of government, in which all participate.

Quite different from the folklore is the proposition that Congress is free to choose between placing ultimate responsibility for decision with the President and giving that responsibility to those to whom it has initially assigned the work of administration. Even within what is undoubtedly the sphere of executive influence—for example, the conduct of law enforcement—that proposition finds support in the Constitutional Convention's failure to adopt measures such as the Morris plan. The proposition seems undebatable where Congress can find circumstances, such as a need for objective decision, that warrant placing administration beyond the sphere of its own as well as the President's political influence. Yet note that neither choice effects or is a justification for presidential *exclusion*. However unserviceable rigid separation-of-powers arguments have become beneath the very top levels of government, the checks-and-balances idea retains force: congressional arrangements that threaten the viability of an independent, unitary executive capable of opposing the Congress's own assertions of power are, for that reason, suspect.

* * *

2. The President's Removal and a Formal Approach to the Place of Administration.— The accelerating growth of national government following the Civil War brought with it the civil service laws, the first of the independent regulatory commissions, the heightened use of delegation and heightened concerns about it, and a general worrying about the relationship of the Presidency and administration. Perhaps disturbed by the consequences of relegating all this burgeoning authority to the President's political domain, and consistent with growing faith in scientific administration, leading commentators argued that "executive" and "administrative" authority were distinct—the latter belonging to professional public administrators, who could properly be placed outside the President's direction.

Understanding of the relation between the Presidency and administration was shaped by two cases of the 1920's and 30's, *Myers v. United States* and *Humphrey's Executor v. United States*. Both tested the President's claim of inherent executive authority to remove presidential appointees from office in the face of statutory limitations on removal; both appeared to use a strictly formal, separation-of-powers approach to the place of agencies in government. The seemingly opposite conclusions to which they came are usually understood in terms of that approach as denying the independent regulatory commissions any determinate place in the tripartite structure of government. Yet their conclusions can also be understood in light of the checks-and-balances approach, and so understood the opinions are both readily reconciled and consistent with the constitutional scheme.

Myers concerned a postmaster appointed to a four-year term under a statute which for fifty years had required senatorial assent to both appointment and removal of these officials. The President sought to remove him before the expiration of his term, without obtaining senatorial concurrence. The resulting litigation was difficult and portentous; special counsel was appointed in the Supreme Court, and the cause had to be argued twice there before the Court could reach its conclusions—conclusions stated in opinions of unusual length and elaborateness. A divided Court found that reserving congressional participation in the removal of an executive officer unconstitutionally invaded the President's executive function. The Court's opinion, written by a former President, suggested that the President enjoyed an inherent authority to remove every officer of government he was empowered to appoint (other than a judge protected by article III). It appeared to eradicate the executive/administrative distinction by establishing the President's disciplinary control as universally available. Congress acknowledged the apparent sweep of this decision by ceasing to provide removal protections in statutes creating new government agencies.

Humphrey's Executor resulted from President Roosevelt's effort, on the authority of *Myers*, to remove a commissioner of the Federal Trade Commission before the expiration of his seven-year statutory term. Here, a statute enacted before *Myers* required specification of cause for removal, but did not require senatorial concurrence. The President suggested no "cause" for Humphrey's removal beyond political incompatibility—a reason plainly insufficient under the statute. This challenge arose, however, at a time when presidential rather than congressional hegemony may have seemed the more palpable threat; it was decided on the same day that the Court invalidated the National Industrial Recovery Act, once the centerpiece of the New Deal, on the ground of excessive delegation to the President. Here, unlike *Myers*, decision appears to have been easy. Acting scant weeks after argument, the Court unanimously repudiated the *Myers* dicta and found that Congress could validly impose a "cause" requirement on the discharge of a Federal Trade Commissioner; given the circumstances, the Court did not have to say what cause could be.

Reading both opinions, one is struck by their emphasis on a radical separation of powers within government, with a concomitant need to place agencies *in* one or another branch, maximally free from intrusion by the others. For the *Myers* Court, "the reasonable construction of the Constitution must be that the branches should be kept separate in all cases in which they were not expressly blended, and the Constitution should be expounded to blend them no more than it affirmatively requires." From placement of the Post Office Department in the executive branch and the absence of any constitutional provision for congressional participation in removal, all else followed. For the *Humphrey's Executor* Court, "[t]he fundamental necessity of maintaining each of the three general departments of government entirely free from the control or coercive influence, direct or indirect, of either of the others, has often been stressed, and is hardly open to serious question." * * * [T]he legislative history of the Federal Trade Commission Act established a purpose that "the commission was not to be 'subject to anybody in the government but . . . only to the people of the United States;' . . . 'separate and apart from any existing department of the government—not subject to the orders of the President;'" the Court said the President could exercise no authority over its members beyond the constitutionally explicit one of appointment. Viewing both the unquestioned congressional purpose to remove the FTC from politics and the agency's particular functions, the Court described it as "an agency of the legislative or judicial department of the government," exercising in those contexts only an "executive function—as distinguished from executive power in the constitutional sense."

More than *Myers*, but perhaps in consequence of that decision, the reasoning of the *Humphrey's Executor* Court seems open to question. Remarkably, the Court did not pause to examine how a purpose to create a body "subject only to the people of the United States"—that is, apparently, beyond control of the constitutionally defined branches of government—could itself be sustained under the Constitution. Later, the opinion tells us that the agency is in *both* the legislative *and* the judicial branches, because of the functions it performs, but not how an agency can at the same moment reside in both the legislative and the judicial branches, consistent with the "fundamental necessity of maintaining each of the three general departments of government entirely free from the control or coercive influence . . . of either of the others." Nor does the Court explain its distinction between "executive function" and "executive power." Of course the commission was carrying out laws Congress had enacted; in that sense its functions could hardly have been characterized as other than executive, whatever procedures it employed to accomplish its ends. And, of course, the public procedures it employed were no different than those used by any cabinet department for similar purposes.

If the formal question where in government to place the agency is put aside, however, it is not hard to understand the Court's result. It described the FTC's functions as follows:

(1) The FTC could direct cessation of unfair methods of competition in commerce, *after* full-dress adjudicatory hearings;

(2) It could conduct investigations culminating in a report to the Congress with recommendations for legislation; and

(3) It could act 'as a master in chancery' in antitrust suits brought by the Attorney General and referred to it by a district court.

Assurance of impartiality and the absence of political controls of any character are centrally important to two parts of the statutory scheme as thus described; providing information-gathering service to Congress (not the President) characterizes the remainder. So far as the Court was educated to the Commission's functions, the FTC did little as to which unified policy direction was even arguably relevant. Thus, the need to maintain tension between the named branches was not implicated. The Court was acutely conscious, however, of the extent to which the Commission acted in circumstances calling for judicial impartiality and the removal from politics that might tend to protect it. * * *

* * * [T]hese cases can be seen as explained by the difference between * * * presidential power that implicates a struggle between the branches and one that does not. *Myers* can readily be limited to the issue presented by the provision for senatorial concurrence in removal, the Tenure of Office Act problem. * * *

Humphrey's Executor, in turn, could be understood as having turned on precisely [the] distinction between those limitations on removal where Congress has retained some role and those in which it has not. Whether or not one numbers the FTC among "the executive Departments," the purpose to make it "free from 'political domination or control'" in exercising functions for which that quality is evidently desirable establishes a justification for some tenure protection. * * * Consequently, the Court found only that Congress could legitimately insist that one holding the office of Federal Trade Commissioner serve on terms other than those of a personal adviser. It did not have to say whether the President could give the FTC Commissioners binding directives, or if so of what sort, or what might be the consequences of any failure of theirs to honor them.

So reading *Humphrey's Executor* would underscore that presidential claims to participate in the FTC's (and other independent agencies') policymaking have not been excluded by that opinion's apparently broad statement that "[t]he authority of Congress, in creating quasi-legislative or quasi-judicial agencies, to require them to act in discharge of their duties independently of executive control cannot well be doubted. . . ." "Quasi-legislative," as that Court used the phrase, referred not to policy formation but to the exercise of investigatory authority in support of reports to the Congress. Reports to the Congress, unlike rules, have no direct impact on the relationship between citizens and their government; in them, the President's claim to participate has a different character. The FTC of that era was not a rulemaker; it reached its policy conclusions through adjudications. The concern for "quasi-judicial" agencies reflects the Court's focus on the legislative requirement of impartiality, of freedom from *any* political direction to secure procedural fairness. *Humphrey's Executor* did not consider the question whether Congress constitutionally could create an administrative body free from the political direction of the President but subject to such direction from congressmen and their committees, and empower that agency to make law. Congress can be conceded the power to forbid unilateral presidential removal for "no reason at all" of an FTC Commissioner regarded as principally an adjudicator, without implying that total removal of the FTC as a policymaking organ of government from presidential oversight or control would be within its power.

* * *

C. Separation of Functions and Considerations of Individual Fairness

Much of the force apparently attached to the issue of "place" in the cases separating the President from the agencies has its source in considerations of fairness—notions more readily ascribed to the idea of separation of *functions* than separation of *powers*. Separation of powers, as a theoretical concern, has to do with the general tendency of certain governmental structures to result in (or prevent) tyrannical government—that is, a government no longer under the control of the people. Separation of functions suggests a much more atomistic inquiry, asking what combinations of functions or impacts of external influence will interfere with fair resolution of a particular proceeding. Recall the horror expressed by the *Humphrey's Executor* Court at the idea that a judge of the "legislative" Court of Claims might be subject to presidential discipline in "exercising judicial power." That the Court accepted her sitting on a *legislative* court suggests that the issue for the Court was not (or not only) one of place but one of function. Wherever she is located in government, a judge ought not to be connected with the controversy or the parties, ought not to be interested in the outcome, must learn from the parties only what they convey in the presence of each other, and—above all—ought not to be called upon to explain her decision in the political forum. External or political intervention in on-the-record decisionmaking would be regarded as inappropriate, whether done by the President or any other political figure (e.g., a legislator), whether in an independent regulatory commission or in a traditional executive department. These are judgments we reach wholly without regard to the balance of advantage between Congress and the White House in overseeing the day-to-day functioning of political government. Within agencies themselves, executive *and* independent, these judgments are reflected in the creation of officials (administrative law judges, appeal bodies, judicial officers) remarkably free of organizational responsibilities or political supervision, who perform on-the-record judging functions.

* * *

D. Conflict Between the Models or a Return to Formalism? The Work of the Past Two Terms

The preceding pages should suggest that of the three approaches commonly used to describe our government's structure, the checks-and-balances model, understood in light of the fairness aspirations of the separation-of-functions principle, best describes the complexity of contemporary government in terms that permit adherence, as well, to the framers' vision. The seeming bright-line simplicity of separation of powers, never in fact fully embraced by those who wrote the Constitution, is neither necessay as a matter of text, context or past interpretation for those parts of government not named in the Constitution itself, nor possibly successful in describing that bulk of government as it is. Courts have been able to reconcile the reality of modern administrative government and the strict separation-of-powers model, as in *Humphrey's Executor*, only by blind feats of definition—internally inconsistent while at the same time effectively negating the ability of a unitary, competent President to serve as an essential check against legislative hegemony.

* * *

The preceding review of the existing institutions of American government and of the body of textual, contextual and interpretational constraints bearing upon them should cast doubt on the idea that our Constitution *requires* that the organs of government be apportioned among one or another of three neat "branches," giving each a home in one and merely the possibility of relations with the others. President, Congress and Supreme Court are undoubtedly to be distinct in form and in function; below that level the text does not speak, sharp distinctions are frequently hard to find in fact, and the Court's occasional efforts to find them in theory have repeatedly led to embarrassments.

Thus to recognize that most of administrative government lies outside the constitutionally defined structure would not defeat the purposes either of separation of powers or of the system of checks and balances. The notions of checks and balances and (as an identifier of strong claims to attenuate political controls across the board) separation of functions are more vital in understanding the place of agencies in government. So long as separation-of-powers is maintained at the very apex of government, a checks-and-balances inquiry into the relationship of the three named bodies to the agencies and each other seems capable in itself both of explaining fully the results of past inquiries into the permissible structures of government below its apex, and of preserving the framers' vision of a government powerful enough to be efficient, yet sufficiently distracted by internal competition to avoid the threat of tyranny. * * *

* * *

III. "Checks and Balances" As a Limit on Congress's Authority to Create the Structure of Government

This Part of the essay supposes that government agencies charged with administering public law are *not* to be regarded as having been placed in one or another branch but rather exist as subordinate bodies subject to the controls of all three. Having thus put the agencies, in some sense, "out" of the executive branch, perhaps the most pressing question that remains is what if any relationship between an agency and the President might Congress (and the courts) still be required to honor. * * *

From the [Constitution's] text, three principal constraints emerge: that the President must appoint at least the head of any agency doing the work of government; that the agency in doing that work must have a relationship with the President consonant with his obligation to see to the faithful execution of all laws; and that, in particular, the President must have the authority to demand written reports of the agency prior to its action on matters within its competence, with the strong implication that consultation if not obedience will ensue. * * *

This Part argues that these constraints at a minimum require that Congress observe a principle of parity in its treatment of the possibility of political control of agency action by itself and by the President. Fairness and separation-of-*functions* considerations may often support exclusion of an agency or at least certain types of agency action from the domain of politics generally. However, Congress cannot expect to reserve political oversight for itself without recognizing corresponding oversight responsibilities in the President. Yet parity *is* a minimum; the President by virtue of his office as chief executive may be able to claim relationships beyond the constraints of parity. Recognition by the courts of a constitutionally based claim of executive privilege—that is, of private communication with agencies directly responsible for law-administration—is the most obvious example of such a claim. A more controversial claim would be for a requirement that Congress recognize presidential authority to resolve or mediate at least some types of internal policy disputes—for example, those placing separate agencies in direct confrontation with each other—or requiring judgments beyond a particular agency's ordinary responsibility and expertise.

* * * Within the range of permissible structures, the proper degree of presidential involvement was left undetermined. Nonetheless, his powers vis-a-vis government in general and Congress in particular were to be sufficient to give some assurance of maintaining a continuing tension over ultimate political authority between himself and Congress—no one branch was to become dominant. Rather than choose between the competing views of President as executor and President as overseer of execution, I want to argue that even the lesser of these views, when understood in a way that supports these structural imperatives, would imply the need for a substantial presidential relationship with any agency performing a significant governmental duty exercised pursuant to public law.

Thus, Congress's authority to create the government's structure must be constrained in a manner that will preserve essential conditions of the President's intended political responsibility for the day-to-day, law-implementing activities of government. Even the most modest notion of what constitutes executive power suggests that the President must retain substantial lines of communication and guidance. To deny the President that authority would be to deprive him and the public of that responsibility, and effectively to permit the Congress, again, to establish multiple centers of law administration primarily under its control. Similarly, the execution of not a single law but many inevitably raises questions of priority, conflict, and coordination that rarely are addressed in any of the acts concerned; particular departments, with their narrow responsibilities, may be incapable of appreciating the interplay. Attending to these conflicts seems an inevitable aspect of a chief executive's function. That a legislature creates a statute and makes its application mandatory, or perhaps dependent upon stated circumstances, does not mean that the legislature will bestow the resources necessary to achieve that end, that it ever "intended" full enforcement, or that it has carefully thought through the relationship of the new mandate to those that have preceded it and those that will follow. In addition to resolving these conflicts and setting priorities among statutes, is the practical requirement of coordinating law-administration with political program and molding both to changing circumstances. The day-to-day course of national affairs generates new issues to which a coherent response must be made and for the resolution of which the public will hold the President politically responsible.

* * *

Conclusion

The basic conclusion was asserted at the outset: given the realities of contemporary government and the inescapable constraints of constitutional text and context, we can achieve the worthy ends of those who drafted our Constitution only if we give up the notion that it embodies a neat division of all government into three separate branches, each endowed with a unique portion of governmental power and employing no other. That apportionment was made, but it was made only as to those actors occupying the very apex of government— Congress, President, and Supreme Court. The remainder of government was left undefined, in the expectation that congressional judgments about appropriate structure would serve so long as they observed the two prescriptive judgments embodied in the Constitution: that the work of law-administration be under the supervision of a unitary, politically accountable chief executive; and that the structures chosen permit, even encourage, the continuation of rivalries and tensions among the three named heads of government, in order that no one body become irreversibly dominant and thus threaten to deprive the people themselves of their voice and control.

* * *

Additional Sources

Rebecca L. Brown, *Separated Powers and Ordered Liberty*, 139 U. Pa. L. Rev. 1513 (1991)

Harold H. Bruff, *On the Constitutional Status of the Administrative Agencies*, 36 Am. U. L. Rev. 491 (1987)

Steven G. Calabresi & Kevin H. Rhodes, *The Structural Constitution: Unitary Executive, Plural Judiciary*, 105 Harv. L. Rev. 1153 (1992)

Stephen L. Carter, *The Independent Counsel Mess*, 102 Harv. L. Rev. 105 (1988)

Stephen L. Carter, *From Sick Chicken to* Synar: *The Evolution and Subsequent De-Evolution of the Separation of Powers*, 1987 B.Y.U. L. Rev. 719

Jesse H. Choper, JUDICIAL REVIEW AND THE NATIONAL POLITICAL PROCESS: A FUNCTIONAL RECONSIDERATION OF THE ROLE OF THE SUPREME COURT (1980)

David P. Currie, *The Distribution of Powers After* Bowsher, 1986 Sup. Ct. Rev. 19

E. Donald Elliott, *Why Our Separation of Powers Jurisprudence Is So Abysmal*, 57 Geo. Wash. L. Rev. 506 (1989)

Daniel J. Gifford, *The Separation of Powers Doctrine and the Regulatory Agencies after* Bowsher v. Synar, 55 Geo. Wash. L. Rev. 441 (1987)

Harold J. Krent, *Separating the Strands in Separtion of Powers Controversies*, 74 Va. L. Rev. 1253 (1988)

Geoffrey P. Miller, *The Unitary Executive in a Unified Theory of Constitutional Law: The Problem of Interpretation*, 14 Cardozo L. Rev. 201 (1993)

Richard J. Pierce, Jr., Morrison v. Olson, *Separation of Powers, and the Structure of Government*, 1988 Sup. Ct. Rev. 1

Martin H. Redish & Elizabeth J. Cisar, *"If Angels Were to Govern": The Need for Pragmatic Formalism in Separation of Powers Theory*, 41 Duke L.J. 449 (1991)

Thomas O. Sargentich, *The Contemporary Debate about Legislative-Executive Separation of Powers*, 72 Cornell L. Rev. 430 (1987)

Suzanna Sherry, *Separation of Powers: Asking a Different Question*, 30 Wm. & Mary L. Rev. 287 (1989)

Peter L. Strauss, *Formal and Functional Approaches to Separation of Powers Questions—A Foolish Inconsistency?*, 72 Cornell L. Rev. 488 (1987)

Charles Tiefer, *The Constitutionality of Independent Officers as Checks on Abuses of Executive Power*, 63 B.U. L. Rev. 59 (1983)

Paul R. Verkuil, *The Status of Independent Agencies after* Bowsher v. Synar, 1986 Duke L.J. 779

Keith Werhan, *Toward an Eclectic Approach to Separation of Powers:* Morrison v. Olson *Examined*, 16 Hastings Const. L.Q. 393 (1989)

Symposium, *The Independence of Independent Agencies*, 1988 Duke L.J. 215

b. The Parliamentary Critique of the Separation of Powers

A major criticism of our governmental institutions is the parliamentary critique of the separation of powers. From this perspective, basic weaknesses of our system—including the administrative process—could be corrected by constitutional amendments that would move the system in a parliamentary direction. The chief culprit in this literature is the Constitution's separation between the legislative and executive branches which, according to the critics, leads to an ineffective and unaccountable government.*

The first excerpt is by Lloyd Cutler, who has served as Counsel to President Carter and President Clinton and who has been a leading parliamentary critic. Mr. Cutler suggests that the government's inefficiency and unaccountability would be diminished if a newly elected president could "form a government" in the manner of parliamentary democracies.

In my article, I place the parliamentary critique in historical context in order to show that modern arguments are closely tied to longstanding claims by divergent critics frustrated with the American system. I also argue that the parliamentary critique has major empirical and normative limitations that generate serious doubts about it.

---

* Many issues in American administrative law depend on the fact that administration is carried out in the context of a constitutional scheme of separation of powers. It is thus not possible to understand the limits and potential of administration in the United States without also considering the constitutional context in which it operates.

Lloyd N. Cutler, *To Form a Government*, in SEPARATION OF POWERS: DOES IT STILL WORK? 1, 1-16 (Robert A. Goldwin & Art Kaufman eds., 1986)*

[On May 10, 1940, Winston Churchill was summoned to Buckingham Palace.] His Majesty received me most graciously and bade me sit down. He looked at me searchingly and quizzically for some moments, and then said: "I suppose you don't know why I have sent for you?" Adopting his mood, I replied: "Sir, I simply couldn't imagine why." He laughed and said: "I want to ask you to form a Government." I said I would certainly do so.

Winston S. Churchill
The Gathering Storm (1948)

Our society was one of the first to write a constitution. This reflected the confident conviction of the Enlightenment that explicit written arrangements could be devised to structure a government that would be neither tyrannical nor impotent in its time and to allow for future amendment as experience and change might require.

We are all children of this faith in a rational written arrangement for governing. Our faith should encourage us to consider changes in our Constitution—for which the framers explicitly allowed—that would assist us in adjusting to the changes in the world in which the Constitution must function. Yet we tend to resist suggestions that amendments to our existing constitutional framework are needed to govern our portion of the interdependent world society we have become and to cope with the resulting problems that all contemporary governments must resolve.

A particular shortcoming in need of a remedy is the structural inability of our government to propose, legislate, and administer a balanced program for governing. In parliamentary terms one might say that under the U.S. Constitution it is not now feasible to "form a government." The separation of powers between the legislative and executive branches, whatever its merits in 1793, has become a structure that almost guarantees stalemate today. As we wonder why we are having such a difficult time making decisions we all know must be made and projecting our power and leadership, we should reflect on whether this is one big reason.

We elect one presidential candidate over another on the basis of our judgment of the overall program he presents, his ability to carry it out, and his capacity to adapt his program to new developments as they arise. We elected President Jimmy Carter, whose program included, as one of its most important elements, the successful completion of the SALT II [Strategic Arms Limitation Treaty] negotiations that his two predecessors had been conducting since 1972. In June 1979 President Carter did complete and sign a SALT II treaty, which he and his cabinet regarded as very much in the national security interests of the United States. Notwithstanding subsequent events, the president and his cabinet continued to hold that view * * *. Because we do not form a government, however, it was not possible for President Carter to carry out this major part of his program.

Of course the constitutional requirement of Senate advice and consent to treaties presents a special situation. The case for the two-thirds rule was much stronger in 1793, when events abroad rarely affected this isolated continent and when "entangling foreign alliances" were viewed with a skeptical eye. Whether it should be maintained in an age when most treaties deal with such subjects as taxation and trade is open to question. No parliamentary regime anywhere in the world has a similar provision. But in the United States—at least for major issues like SALT—there is merit to the view that treaties should indeed require the careful bipartisan consultation essential to win a two-thirds majority. This is the principle that Woodrow Wilson fatally neglected in 1919. But it has been carefully observed by recent presidents, including President Carter for the Panama Canal treaties and the SALT II treaty. For each of these there was a clear record of support by previous Republican administrations, and there would surely have been enough votes for fairly rapid ratification if the president could have counted on the total or nearly total support of his own party—if, in short, he had truly formed a government, with a legislative majority that took the responsibility for governing.

Treaties may indeed present special cases, and I do not argue here for any change in the two-thirds requirement. But our inability to form a government able to ratify SALT II is replicated regularly over the whole range of legislation required to carry out any president's overall program, foreign and domestic. Although the enactment of legislation takes only a simple majority of both houses, that majority is very difficult to achieve. Any part of the president's

---

* Reprinted with the permission of The American Enterprise Institute for Public Policy Research, Washington, D.C., and Lloyd N. Cutler. All rights reserved.

legislative program may be defeated or amended into an entirely different measure, so that the legislative record of any presidency may bear little resemblance to the overall program the president wanted to carry out. * * * This difficulty is of course compounded when the president's party does not even hold the majority of the seats in both houses, as from 1946 to 1948, from 1954 to 1960, and from 1968 to 1976—or almost half of the duration of the seven administrations between 1946 and 1980.

In such a case the Constitution does not require or even permit the holding of a new election, in which those who oppose the president can seek office to carry out their own program. Indeed, the opponents of the various elements of the president's program usually have a different makeup from one element to another. They would probably be unable to get together on any overall program of their own or to obtain the congressional votes to carry it out. As a result the stalemate continues, and because we do not form a government, we have no overall program at all. We cannot fairly hold the president accountable for the success or failure of his program, because he lacks the constitutional power to put that program into effect.

Compare this system with the structure of parliamentary governments. A parliamentary government may have no written constitution, as in the United Kingdom. Or it may have a written constitution, as in West Germany, Japan, and Ireland, that in other respects—such as an independent judiciary and an entrenched Bill of Rights—closely resembles our own. Although it may have a ceremonial president or, as in Japan, an emperor, its executive consists of those members of the legislature chosen by the elected legislative majority. The majority elects a premier or prime minister from among its number, and he or she selects other leading members of the majority as members of the cabinet. The majority as a whole is responsible for forming and conducting the government. If any key part of its program is rejected by the legislature or if a vote of no confidence is carried, the government must resign, and either a new government must be formed out of the existing legislature, or a new legislative election must be held. If the program *is* legislated, the public can judge the result and can decide at the next regular election whether to reelect the majority or turn it out. At all times the voting public knows who is in charge and whom to hold accountable for success or failure.

* * *

Let me cite one example. In the British House of Commons, just as in our own House, some of the majority leaders are called whips. In the Commons the whips do just what their title implies. If the government cares about the pending vote, they "whip" the fellow members of the majority into compliance, under pain of party discipline if a member disobeys. On the most important votes, the leaders invoke what is called a three-line whip, which must be obeyed on pain of resignation or expulsion from the party.

In our House a Democratic majority whip can himself feel free to leave his Democratic president and the rest of the House Democratic leadership on a crucial vote if he believes it important to his constituency and his conscience to vote the other way. When he does so, he is not expected or required to resign his leadership post; indeed he is back a few hours later whipping his fellow members of the majority to vote with the president and the leadership on some other issue. All other members are equally free to vote against the president and the leadership when they feel it important to do so. The president and the leaders have a few sticks and carrots they can use to punish or reward, but nothing even approaching the power that a British government or a German government can wield against any errant member of the majority.

I am hardly the first to notice this fault. As Judge Carl McGowan has reminded us, that "young and rising academic star in the field of political science, Woodrow Wilson— happily unaware of what the future held for him in terms of successive domination of, and defeat by, the Congress—despaired in the late 19th century of the weakness of the Executive Branch vis-à-vis the Legislative, so much so that he concluded that a coalescence of the two in the style of English parliamentary government was the only hope."

As Wilson put it, "power and strict accountability for its use are the essential constituents of good Government." Our separation of executive and legislative power fractions power and prevents accountability.

In drawing this comparison, I am not blind to the proven weaknesses of parliamentary government or to the virtues that our forefathers saw in separating the executive from the legislature. In particular, the parliamentary system lacks the ability of a separate and vigilant legislature to investigate and curb the abuse of power by an arbitrary or corrupt executive. Our own recent history has underscored this virtue of separating these two branches.

Moreover, our division of executive from legislative responsibility also means that a great many more voters are represented in positions of power, rather than as mere members of a "loyal opposition." If I am a Democrat in a Republican district, my vote in the presidential election may still give me a proportional effect. If my party elects a president, I do not feel—as almost half the voters in a parliamentary constituency like Oxford must feel—wholly unrepresented. One result of this division is a sort of permanent centrism. While this means that no extreme or Thatcher-like program can be legislated, it also means fewer wild swings in statutory policy.

This is also a virtue of the constitutional division of responsibility. It is perhaps what John Adams had in mind when, at the end of his life, he wrote to his old friend and adversary Thomas Jefferson that "checks and ballances, Jefferson, . . . are our only Security, for the progress of Mind, as well as the Security of Body."

These virtues of separation are not without their costs. I believe that the costs have been mounting in the past half-century and that it is time to examine whether we can reduce the costs of separation without losing its virtues.

During this century other nations have adopted written constitutions, sometimes with our help, that blend the virtues of our system with those of the parliamentary system. The Irish constitution contains a replica of our Bill of Rights, an independent Supreme Court that can declare acts of the government unconstitutional, a figurehead president, and a parliamentary system. The postwar German and Japanese constitutions, which we helped to draft, are essentially the same. Although the Gaullist French constitution contains a Bill of Rights somewhat weaker than ours, it provides for a strong president who can dismiss the legislature and call for new elections. But it also retains the parliamentary system and its blend of executive and legislative power achieved by forming a government out of the elected legislative majority. The president, however, appoints the premier or first minister.

The Need to Govern More Effectively

We are not about to revise our own Constitution so as to incorporate a true parliamentary system. We do need to find a way, however, of coming closer to the parliamentary concept of forming a government under which the elected majority is able to carry out an overall program and is held accountable for its success or failure.

For several reasons it is far more important * * * than it was in 1940, 1900, or 1800 for our government to have the ability to formulate and carry out an overall program.

1. The first reason is that government is now constantly required to make a different kind of choice than was common in the past, a kind for which it is difficult to obtain a broad consensus. That kind of choice, which may be called allocative, has become the fundamental challenge to government today. * * *

During the second half of this century, our government has adopted a wide variety of national goals. Many of these goals—checking inflation, spurring economic growth, reducing unemployment, protecting our national security, ensuring equal opportunity, increasing social security, cleaning up the environment, improving energy efficiency—conflict with one another, and all of them compete for the same resources. There may have been a time when we could simultaneously pursue all these goals to the utmost. Even in a country as rich as this one, however, that time is now past. One of the central tasks of modern government is to make wise balancing choices among courses of action that pursue one or more of our many conflicting and competing objectives.

Furthermore, as new economic or social problems are recognized, a responsible government must *adjust* its priorities. In formulating energy policy, the need to accept realistic oil prices had to be balanced against the immediate effect of dramatic price increases on consumers and affected industries and on the overall rate of inflation. To cope with the energy crisis, earlier objectives of policy had to be accommodated along the way. Reconciling one goal with another is a continuous process. A critical regulatory goal of 1965 (automobile safety) had to be reconciled with an equally critical regulatory goal of 1970 (clean air) long before the safety goal had been achieved, just as both those critical goals had to be reconciled with 1975's key goal (closing the energy gap) long before either automobile safety or clean air had lost its importance. Reconciliation was needed because many automobile safety regulations increased vehicle size and weight and therefore increased gasoline consumption and undesirable emission and also because auto emission control devices tend to increase gasoline consumption. Moreover, throughout this fifteen-year period, we had to reconcile all three goals with another critical national objective—wage and price stability—when in pursuit of these other goals we made vehicles more costly to purchase and to operate.

In 1980 we found our automobile industry at a serious competitive disadvantage vis-à-vis Japanese and European imports, making it necessary to limit those regulatory burdens that aggravated the extent of the disadvantage. A responsible government must be able to adapt its programs to achieve the best balance among its conflicting goals as each new development arises.

For balancing choices like these, a kind of political triage, it is almost impossible to achieve a broad consensus. Every group will be against some part of the balance. If the losers on each item are given a veto on that part of the balance, a sensible balance cannot be struck.

2. The second reason is that we live in an increasingly interdependent world. What happens in distant places is now just as consequential for our security and our economy as what happens in Seattle or Miami. * * * No one would say today, as President Wilson said in 1914, that general European war could not affect us and is no concern of ours. We are now an integral part of a closely interconnected world economic and political system. We have to respond as quickly and decisively to what happens abroad as to what happens within the portion of this world system that is governed under our Constitution.

New problems requiring new adjustments come up even more frequently over the foreign horizon than over the domestic one. Consider the rapid succession of events and crises after President Carter took up the relay baton for his leg of the SALT II negotiations in 1977: [there follows a list of foreign policy crises from 1977 to 1980] * * *.

Each of these portentous events required a prompt reaction and response from our government, including in many cases a decision about how it would affect our position on the SALT II treaty. The government must be able to adapt its overall program to deal with each such event as it arises, and it must be able to execute the adapted program with reasonable dispatch. Many of these adaptations—such as changes in the levels and direction of military and economic assistance—require joint action by the president and the Congress, something that is far from automatic under our system. When Congress does act, it is prone to impose statutory conditions or prohibitions that fetter the president's discretion to negotiate an appropriate assistance package or to adapt it to fit even later developments. * * *

Indeed, the doubt that Congress will approve a presidential foreign policy initiative has seriously compromised our ability to make binding agreements with nations that form a government. Given the fate of SALT II and lesser treaties and the frequent congressional vetoes of other foreign policy actions, other nations now realize that our executive branch commitments are not as binding as theirs, that Congress may block any agreement at all, and that at the very least they must hold something back for a subsequent round of bargaining with the Congress.

3. The third reason is the change in Congress and its relations with the executive. When the Federalist and Democratic Republican parties held power, a Hamilton or a Gallatin would serve in the cabinet but continue to lead rather than report to their party colleagues in the houses of Congress. Even when the locus of congressional leadership shifted from the cabinet to the leaders of Congress itself in the early nineteenth century, it was a congressional leadership capable of collaboration with the executive. This was true until very recently. The Johnson-Rayburn collaboration with Eisenhower a generation ago is an instructive example. But now Congress itself has changed.

There have been well-intended democratic reforms of Congress and an enormous growth of the professional legislative staff. The former ability of the president to sit down with ten or fifteen leaders in each house and agree on a program those leaders could carry through Congress has virtually disappeared. The committee chairmen and the leaders no longer have the instruments of power that once enabled them to lead. A Lyndon Johnson would have a much harder time getting his way as majority leader today than when he did hold and pull those strings of power in the 1950s. When Senator Mike Mansfield became majority leader in 1961, he changed the practice of awarding committee chairmanships on the basis of seniority. He declared that all senators are created equal. He gave every Democratic senator a major committee assignment and then a subcommittee chairmanship, adding to the sharing of power by reducing the leadership's control.

In the House the seniority system was scrapped. * * * Now bills like the energy bills go to several committees, which then report conflicting versions to the floor. Now markup sessions take place in public; indeed, even the House-Senate joint conference committees, at which differing versions of the same measure are reconciled, must meet and barter in public.

* * *

Party discipline and the political party itself have also declined. Presidential candidates are no longer selected as Adlai Stevenson was, by the leaders or bosses of their party. Who are the party leaders today? There are no such people. The party is no longer the instrument that selects the candidate. Indeed, the party today, as a practical matter, is no more than a neutral open forum that holds the primary or caucus in which candidates for president and for Congress may compete for favor and be elected. The party does not dispense most of the money needed for campaigning, as European and Japanese parties do. The candidates raise most of their own money. To the extent that money influences legislative votes, it comes not from a party with a balanced program but from a variety of single-interest groups.

We now have a great many diverse and highly organized interest groups—not just broad-based agriculture, labor, business, and ethnic groups interested in a wide variety of issues affecting their members. We now have single-issue groups—environmental, consumer, abortion, right to life, pro- and anti-SALT, pro- and anti-nuclear—that stand ready to lobby for their single issue and to reward or punish legislators, both in cash and at the ballot box, according to how they respond on the single issue that is the group's raison d'être. On many specific foreign policy issues involving particular countries, exceptionally strong voting blocs in this wonderful melting pot of a nation exert a great deal of influence on individual senators and representatives.

Why the Structure Sometimes Works

It is useful to compare this modern failure of our governmental structure with its earlier classic successes. There can be no structural fault, it might be said, so long as Franklin Roosevelt could put through an entire antidepression program in 100 days or Lyndon Johnson could enact a broad program for social justice three decades later. These infrequent exceptions, however, confirm the general rule of stalemate.

If we look closely, we will find that in this century the system has succeeded only on the rare occasions when an unusual event has brought us together and created substantial consensus throughout the country on the need for a whole new program. Roosevelt had such a consensus in the early days of the New Deal and from Pearl Harbor to the end of World War II. But we tend to forget that in 1937 his court-packing plan was justifiably rejected by Congress—a good point for those who favor complete separation of the executive from the legislature—and that as late as August 1941, when Roosevelt called on Congress to pass a renewal of the Selective Service Act, passage was gained by a single vote in the House. Johnson had such a consensus for both his domestic and his Vietnam initiatives during the first three years after the shock of John Kennedy's assassination brought us together, but it was gone by 1968. Carter had it for his responses to the events in Iran and Afghanistan and to the belated realization of our need for greater energy self-sufficiency, but he did not hold it for long. * * *

When the great crisis and the resulting large consensus are not there—when the country is divided somewhere between 55-45 and 45-55 on each of a wide set of issues and the makeup of the majority is different on every issue—it has not been possible for any modern president to form a government that could legislate and carry out his overall program.

Yet modern government has to respond promptly to a wide range of new challenges. Its responses cannot be limited to those for which there is a large consensus induced by some great crisis. Modern government also has to work in every presidency, not just in one presidency out of four, when a Wilson, a Roosevelt, or a Johnson comes along. It also has to work for the president's full time in office, as it did not even for Wilson and Johnson. When they needed congressional support for the most important issue of their presidencies, they could not get it.

When the president gets only half a loaf of his overall program, it is not necessarily better than none, because it may lack the essential quality of balance. Half a loaf leaves both the president and the public in the worst of all possible worlds. The public—and the press—still expect the president to govern. But the president cannot achieve his overall program, and the public cannot fairly blame the president because he does not have the power to legislate and execute his program. Nor can the public fairly blame the individual members of Congress, because the Constitution allows them to disclaim any responsibility for forming a government and hence any accountability for its failures.

Of course the presidency always has been and will continue to be what Theodore Roosevelt called "a bully pulpit"—not a place from which to bully in the sense of intimidating the Congress and the public, but in the idiom of Roosevelt's day a marvelous place from which to exhort and lift up Congress and the public. All presidents have used the bully pulpit in this way, and this is one reason why the American people continue to revere the office and almost always revere its incumbent. Television has probably amplified the power of the bully pulpit, but it has also shortened the time span of power; few television performers can hold their audiences for four consecutive years. In any event, a bully pulpit, though a glorious thing to have and to employ, is not a government, and it has not been enough to enable any postwar president to form a government for his entire term.

Finally, the myth persists that the existing system can be made to work satisfactorily if only the president will take the trouble to consult closely with the Congress. During the period between 1947 and 1965 there were indeed remarkable cases, at least in foreign policy, where such consultation worked to great effect, even across party lines. * * * But these examples were in an era of strong leadership within the Congress and of unusual national consensus on the overall objectives of foreign policy and the measures needed to carry them out.

* * *

* * * Except on the rare issues where there is such a consensus, the structural problems usually prove too difficult to overcome. In each administration it becomes more difficult to make the present system work effectively on the range of issues, both domestic and foreign, that the United States must now manage even though there is no large consensus.

Changing the Structure through Constitutional Amendment

If we decide we want the ability to form a government, the only way to get it is to amend the Constitution. That, of course, is extremely difficult. Since 1793, when the Bill of Rights was added, we have amended the Constitution only sixteen times. Some of these amendments were structural, such as the direct election of senators, votes for women and eighteen-year-olds, the two-term limit for presidents, and the selection of a successor vice president. But none has touched the basic separation of executive and legislative powers.

The most we can hope for is a set of modest changes that would make our structure work somewhat more in the manner of a parliamentary system, with somewhat less separation between the executive and the legislature than now exists. There are several proposals. Here are some of the more interesting ideas.

1. We now vote for a presidential candidate and a vice-presidential candidate as an inseparable team. We could require that in presidential election years voters in each congressional district vote for a trio of candidates, as a team, for president, vice president, and member of Congress. This would tie the political fortunes of the party's presidential and congressional candidates to one another and give them some incentive for sticking together after they are elected. Such a proposal could be combined with a four-year term for members of the House of Representatives. This would tie the presidential and congressional candidates even more closely and has the added virtue of giving members greater protection against the pressures of single-issue political groups.
* * *

* * *

2. Another idea is to permit or require the president to select 50 percent of his cabinet from among the members of his party in the Senate and the House, who would retain their seats while serving in the cabinet. This would be only a minor infringement on the constitutional principle of separation of powers, but it would require a change in Article I, section 6, which provides that "no person holding any office under the United States shall be a member of either house during his continuance in office." It would tend to increase the intimacy between the executive and the legislature and add to their sense of collective responsibility. The 50 percent test would leave the president adequate room to bring other qualified persons into his cabinet, even though they did not hold elective office.

3. A third intriguing suggestion is to provide the president with the power, to be exercised not more than once in his term, to dissolve Congress and call for new congressional elections. This is the power now vested in the president under the French constitution. It would provide the opportunity that does not now exist to break an executive-legislative impasse and to let the public decide whether it wishes to elect senators and representatives who *will* legislate the president's overall program.

For obvious reasons, the president would invoke such a power only as a last resort, but his ability to do so could have a powerful influence on congressional responses to his initiatives. This would of course be a radical and highly controversial proposal, and it raises a number of technical difficulties relating to the timing and conduct of the new election, the staggering of senatorial terms, and similar matters. But it would significantly enhance the president's power to form a government.

The experience of presidents—such as Nixon in 1970—who sought to use the midterm election as a referendum on their programs suggests that any such dissolution and new election would be as likely to continue the impasse as to break it. Perhaps any exercise of the power to dissolve Congress should automatically require a new presidential election as well. Even then, the American public might be perverse enough to reelect all the incumbents to office.

4. Another variant on the same idea is that in addition to empowering the president to call for new congressional elections, we might empower a majority or two-thirds of both houses to call for new presidential elections. * * *

5. Another proposal that deserves consideration is a single six-year presidential term, an idea with

many supporters, among them Presidents Eisenhower, Johnson, and Carter, to say nothing of a great many political scientists. (The French constitution provides a seven-year term for the president but permits reelection.) Of course, presidents would like to be elected and then forget about politics and get to the high ground of saving the world. But if first-term presidents did not have the leverage of reelection, we might institutionalize for every presidency the lame duck impotence we now see when a president is not running for reelection.

6. It may be that one combination of elements of the third, fourth, and fifth proposals would be worthy of further study. It would be roughly as follows:

- The president, vice president, senators, and representatives would all be elected for simultaneous six-year terms.
- On one occasion each term the president could dissolve Congress and call for new congressional elections for the remainder of the term. If he did so, Congress, by majority vote of both houses within thirty days of his action, could call for simultaneous new elections for president and vice president for the remainder of the term.
- All state primaries and state conventions for any required midterm elections would be held 60 days after the first call for new elections. Any required national presidential nominating conventions would be held 30 days later. The national elections would be held 60 days after the state primary elections and state conventions. The entire cycle would take 120 days. The dissolved Congress would be free to remain in session for part or all of this period.
- Presidents would be allowed to serve only one full six-year term. If a midterm presidential election were called, the incumbent would be eligible to run and, if reelected, to serve the balance of his six-year term.

Limiting each president to one six-year term would enhance the objectivity and public acceptance of the measures he urges in the national interest. He would not be regarded as a lame duck, because of his continuing power to dissolve Congress. Our capacity to form a government would be enhanced if the president could break an impasse by calling for a new congressional election and by the power of Congress to respond by calling for a new presidential election.

Six-year terms for senators and representatives would diminish the power of single-interest groups to veto balanced programs for governing. Because any midterm elections would have to be held promptly, a single national primary, a shorter campaign cycle, and public financing of congressional campaigns—three reforms with independent virtues of their own—would become a necessity for the midterm election. Once tried in a midterm election, they might well be adopted for regular elections as well.

7. One final proposal may be mentioned. It would be possible, through constitutional amendment, to revise the legislative process in the following way. Congress would first enact broad mandates, declaring general policies and directions and leaving the precise allocative choices, within a congressionally approved budget, to the president. All agencies would be responsible to the president. By dividing tasks among them and making the difficult choices of fulfilling some congressional directions at the expense of others, the president would fill in the exact choices, the allocative decisions. Then any presidential action would be returned to Congress, where it would await a two-house legislative veto. If not so vetoed within a specified period, the action would become law.

If the legislative veto could be overturned by a presidential veto—subject in turn to a two-thirds override—this proposal would go a long way toward enhancing the president's ability to form a government. In any event, it should enable the elected president to carry out the program he ran on, subject to congressional oversight, and end the stalemate over whether to legislate the president's program in the first instance. It would let Congress and the president each do what they have shown they now do best.

Such a resequencing, of course, would turn the present process on its head. But it would bring much closer to reality the persisting myth that it is up to the president to govern—something he now lacks the constitutional power to do.

Conclusion

* * *

The point of this article is not to persuade the reader of the virtue of any particular amendment. I am far from persuaded myself. But I am convinced of these propositions:

- We need to do better than we have in forming a government for this country, and the need is becoming more acute.
- The structure of our Constitution prevents us from doing significantly better.
- It is time to start thinking and debating about whether and how to correct this structural fault.

* * *

Thomas O. Sargentich, *The Limits of the Parliamentary Critique of the Separation of Powers*, 34 WM. & MARY L. REV. 679, 679–704, 707–39 (1993)*

I. Introduction

* * *

The parliamentary critics with whom I will deal tend to admire the strength of the British Prime Minister as compared with what they see as the relative weakness of the United States President. In particular, the British chief executive does not face an independent legislative branch that regularly pursues its own agenda. To be sure, the British Parliament can vote no confidence in the Prime Minister and thereby can force a resignation or a new election. Yet in Britain this is hardly a common occurrence. Moreover, a parliamentary system can be an extremely weak form of government if a prime minister's power depends on a shaky coalition of divergent parties. In modern Britain, however, there has been a rather strong two-party system along with a winner-take-all electoral arrangement that has tended to guarantee that one of the two leading parties—Labour or the Conservatives—will dominate Parliament.

Critics often contrast the separation of powers with what they describe as the unity, effectiveness and accountability of the parliamentary system. On these grounds they propose amendments to the U.S. Constitution embodying the spirit of parliamentary-style arrangements. * * *

* * *

My discussion will begin with a historical overview of key precursors of modern parliamentary criticism. I will start with the views of British journalist Walter Bagehot, whose work centrally influenced his American admirer, Woodrow Wilson. During the twentieth century, parliamentary arguments have been repeatedly repackaged in widely differing contexts. Each successive wave of argument has shown a large intellectual debt to Bagehot and Wilson.

Understanding the history of parliamentary reformism helps to bring into focus the critique's empirical and normative limitations. For decades, critics have asserted that catastrophe will overwhelm our system if it continues to operate under the Constitution's structure. Yet the sky has not fallen. The empirical case for major change in the separation of powers, although dramatically asserted, has simply not been established.

In addition, I will suggest, the idea that the nation would be able to manage its way out of its political difficulties if its constitutional structure were changed is remarkably reductionist. It disregards key cultural, historical and political variables that provide the vital context of the British—or for that matter any other—governmental model.

Moreover, the argument for parliamentary reform does not pay sufficient attention to the principle of promoting broad public dialogue in order to secure the legitimacy of constitutional government. In particular, the parliamentary critics dealt with here embrace an extremely constrained view of the relationship between the President and Congress. The critics' push for a stronger and more unified governmental structure supports a managerial vision of the Constitution that fails to appreciate the virtues of checks and balances. At bottom, the parliamentary critique * * * tends to build up the executive's power at the direct expense of the national legislature. These tendencies need to be clearly borne in mind to the extent that the heritage of parliamentary reformism continues to inform serious proposals for change.

II. The Historical Development of the Parliamentary Critique

The parliamentary critique's intellectual lineage can be traced to the mid-nineteenth century in England, the classical parliamentary age. A leading journalist and political commentator during the mid-Victorian period, Walter Bagehot, especially influenced the most prominent nineteenth-century expositor of parliamentary ideas, Woodrow Wilson. Because Wilson has been more influential in American debate, I will discuss his ideas first, and then I will show the linkages between them and Bagehot's views.

A. Nineteenth Century Origins

1. Woodrow Wilson

* * * In the late 1870s, Woodrow Wilson published a paper criticizing Congress for what he considered to be irresponsible government. He elaborated his views in an article in 1884 and a book—perhaps his most famous academic work—in 1885.

Wilson's 1884 article called for amending Article I, section 6, of the Constitution in order to permit members of Congress to serve in the President's cabinet. In addition, Wilson supported coordinating the

---

* Reprinted with permission of the William and Mary Law Review and Thomas O. Sargentich. All rights reserved.

terms of office of members of Congress and the President. Both of these suggestions are classic, often repeated parliamentary proposals designed to limit the independence of Congress from the executive.

* * *

Wilson's 1885 book, *Congressional Government*, expanded on the argument for such proposals. * * *

Wilson contrasted his picture of an unresponsive U.S. government with his rather idealized vision of the British system. To Wilson, the House of Commons was an especially accountable forum for vigorous debates about the day's great issues. "The whole conduct of the government," he opined admiringly, "turns upon what is said in the Commons. . . ." He pointedly distinguished debates in Parliament from debates in Congress, which "have no tithe of this interest, because they have no tithe of such significance and importance." The significance of the House of Commons' debates inhered in the fact that Parliament could vote no confidence in the government and thereby could force it to resign. When legislative debates involve such high stakes, Wilson argued, they are more likely to be conducted seriously.

Wilson's enthusiasm for the British parliamentary system was the flip side of his critique of the separation of powers, which he saw as a prescription for "paralysis in moments of emergency" and stalemate in ordinary times. He noted that under the separation of powers, few if any significant measures could be undertaken by one branch of government without the "consent or cooperation" of another branch. This meant that no single governmental authority in the United States—neither the President nor Congress—is the "supreme, ultimate head" and therefore that "[p]olicy cannot be either prompt or straightforward."

Wilson was aware that his analysis struck at the heart of the framers' design, which he frankly criticized for resting on a "grievous mistake" of parceling out powers and responsibilities to different branches of government. He imagined that if the framers were to reassemble in the early 1880s, "they would be the first to admit that the only fruit of dividing power had been to make it irresponsible." He considered that the constitutional structure lacked strength, promptness, and efficiency. He complained that "[n]obody stands sponsor for the policy of the government."

Wilson's writing in the 1880s thus reflected a two-part critique. First, he contended that when governmental power is divided under a system of separation of powers, it necessarily becomes ineffective. This presupposed that unified power is required for effective government. The agent of unity in the British parliamentary system is the Prime Minister's cabinet, which consists of department heads who also are leaders of the majority party in Parliament. Second, he argued that when power is divided, it becomes irresponsible. This view depended on the notion that the possibility of "turning out" a government can permit the people to express their views on major issues, which in turn can keep the government more responsible to the people. These arguments about effectiveness and accountability, so central to Wilson's analysis, have remained at the heart of all subsequent parliamentary criticisms of the separation of powers.

2. Walter Bagehot

Wilson's critique in the 1880s was directly influenced by Bagehot's study of the English constitution, which was published in England in 1867 and in the United States in 1877. Indeed, Wilson specifically noted his intellectual debt to Bagehot.

* * *

As Wilson was to do later, Bagehot praised the accountable character of executive leadership chosen from the membership of the legislature. Bagehot also took pains to praise the House of Commons, which he saw as the "great scene of debate, the great engine of popular instruction and political controversy." For Bagehot, as for Wilson subsequently, what gave parliamentary debate such importance was the potential for the legislature to "turn out" a government.

In addition, Bagehot prefigured Wilson's attack on the separation of powers as an essentially weak form of government. Under "presidential government"—Bagehot's term for the system in the United States—the executive can easily be "hampered" by Congress. In contrast, "a strong Cabinet can obtain the concurrence of the legislature in all acts which facilitate its administration." The oneness of the two branches in England meant that the executive "is itself, so to say, the legislature."

Bagehot also attacked the fixed terms of office for officials under the U.S. Constitution. The existence of fixed terms meant that "whether [the government] works well or works ill . . . by law you must keep it." Unlike the situation in a parliamentary system, in the United States there is no option of calling a new election—and that fact was seen by Bagehot to signal a key structural weakness.

Bagehot's assault on the separation of powers included the broad claim that it undermined sovereignty itself: "The splitting of sovereignty into many parts amounts to there being no sovereign.'' Above all, Bagehot believed that it was necessary to maintain "singleness and unity" in government. The English constitution was seen to obey a "principle of choosing a single sovereign authority," whereas the U.S. government was seen to follow a "principle of having many sovereign authorities" and to rest on a hope "that their multitude may atone for their inferiority." Bagehot offered the opinion that only American "genius," "moderation," and "regard for the law" had averted what otherwise would "long ago" have been "a bad end" for the presidential system.

3. Wilson's and Bagehot's Arguments in Historical Context

The nineteenth-century proponents of the parliamentary critique need to be viewed in their historical contexts. After all, Wilson and Bagehot geared their appraisals to political conditions in their own times. Accordingly, the widespread reliance on their authority by parliamentary critics in the modern period must be questioned as fundamentally ahistorical.

In particular, Wilson wrote in the wake of the Civil War and a succession of relatively weak Presidents. Moreover, Wilson's work did not focus on the experiences of earlier strong Presidents, such as Thomas Jefferson or Andrew Jackson. Furthermore, Wilson wrote during a period in which Congress was dominant and in which there was a lack of centralizing institutions within Congress itself.

Conditions changed on many levels. By the early 1900s, there had been stronger Presidents who provided a larger measure of national leadership under our constitutional system—such as Grover Cleveland, William McKinley, and especially Theodore Roosevelt. In addition, there had emerged powerful legislative leaders in the House of Representatives as well as the Senate.

In the wake of such developments, Wilson himself fundamentally shifted orientation. In 1908, he published another book that took for granted the existence of a powerful President and did not rhapsodize, as did his earlier work, about parliamentary institutions. Wilson in 1908 stressed that "we have grown more and more inclined . . . to look to the President as the unifying force in our complex system." Having moved away from the British cabinet and toward the President as the source of unity in government, Wilson returned to the fold of commentators preoccupied above all with U.S. institutions. Wilson's early-twentieth century appreciation for the special role of the office of the presidency stayed with him as he shifted from being an academic to being Governor of New Jersey and, finally, President himself.

Bagehot, for his part, has been described by a modern historian of the Victorian age as "the intelligent voice" of the mid-nineteenth century. The mid-century conditions in which he wrote were rapidly overtaken by events. Specifically, Bagehot observed English institutions in 1865 and 1866, which was before the major reforms of 1867 that expanded the electorate to include males in the urban working class. These reforms, in the words of one commentator, "ended the classic age of parliamentary government" that furnished the immediate context of Bagehot's study.

In addition, Bagehot's vision of parliamentary government cannot properly be seen in isolation from a set of social attitudes closely associated with his era, class and educational level. In particular, he enunciated a relatively common Victorian conception of the marginality of the uneducated lower classes. He wrote: "the working classes contribute almost nothing to our corporate public opinion. . . ." Bagehot considered that "their want of influence in Parliament does not impair the coincidence of Parliament with public opinion." For Bagehot, "public opinion" consisted of the views of the educated middle and the upper classes: "Certain persons are by common consent agreed to be wiser than others, and their opinion is, by consent, to rank for much more than its numerical value."

In these attitudes, Bagehot embraced the system of deference by the lower to the higher social orders that was central to mid-Victorian culture. A deferential society, "even though its lowest classes are not intelligent," was in Bagehot's mind "far more suited to a Cabinet government than any kind of democratic country." That was seen as true because cabinet government allowed the "highest classes" to rule and thereby permitted "political excellence" to flourish.

Furthermore, Bagehot wrote in a period of relatively weak political parties, especially as compared with the situation in his country in the late twentieth century. He specifically assumed that parties were "not composed of warm partisans." Indeed, if that had not been so, the result for Bagehot would have been dire: "Parliamentary government would become the worst of governments—a sectarian government." His image of Members of Parliament presupposed their ability to distance themselves from party positions in determining the best course for the nation. In this sense, party government for Bagehot was necessarily "mild."

Bagehot's vision of the relatively independent Member of Parliament plainly predated many changes in the British political system, including the extension of the suffrage, the growing role of government in society, and the emergence of coordinated party machines. * * *

Bagehot's world differed in other fundamental ways from that which later evolved in Britain. He could not and did not foresee the extent to which debate in Parliament would become, in many contexts, a sheer formality. Nor did he anticipate the rising power of the civil service and the Prime Minister. He also did not envision the changing role of the cabinet. In modern commentary, Bagehot's conception of the cabinet itself has been seen as a "dignified" form masking the real power of the parties, the bureaucracy and the Prime Minister.

Accordingly, as one reviews Wilson's and Bagehot's parliamentary critiques, one should simultaneously underscore their historical constraints. In this as in so many instances, observations geared originally to particular times and places should be used cautiously by succeeding generations to make claims about new and different realities.

B. Twentieth Century Critics

During the twentieth century, the role of the United States in domestic and international affairs has expanded greatly, and the President has become increasingly powerful. Despite these well-known developments, there has been striking continuity in parliamentary-style arguments against the separation of powers.

Constitutional proposals during the twentieth century have ranged across a wide front. In 1921, William MacDonald proposed having the President choose a premier from among leading members of Congress. The Premier would lead the cabinet, and the cabinet, consisting of legislators, would resign office upon a congressional vote signalling no confidence. In 1935, William Yandell Elliott recommended that the President be empowered to dissolve Congress and to call a new election on one occasion during his term. He also urged that the Senate's powers be considerably reduced so that legislative power could be concentrated in the House of Representatives. In 1942, Henry Hazlitt supported a system in which the legislature would choose a premier, who would be the head of government and would select a cabinet. Like Elliott, Hazlitt wanted the Senate's powers to be severely curtailed. In 1945, Thomas Finletter urged the creation of a joint executive-legislative cabinet. He also proposed empowering the President to call a new election to resolve conflicts between the cabinet and Congress. Moreover, he wanted the President and members of Congress to be elected to simultaneous six-year terms.

The basic aims of such proposals should be familiar to readers of Bagehot and Wilson: they seek to make government more effective and more accountable by altering the system of separation of powers. In this part, I will elaborate on these views with reference to three main sources of parliamentary argumentation: Henry Hazlitt, who embraced large-scale parliamentary changes during World War II; Charles Hardin, who advanced parliamentary ideas in response to the Watergate crisis of the early 1970s; and critics during the 1980s, who expressed particular concern about national budget deficits. After reviewing these arguments, I will discuss major empirical and normative limits of the parliamentary critique.

1. Henry Hazlitt and World War II

In 1942, journalist Henry Hazlitt called for sweeping parliamentary reform. In so doing, he specifically emphasized his debt to Bagehot and the early Wilson. In Bagehot, Hazlitt saw "the most penetrating analyst of political constitutions in modern times." In the early Wilson, he found an insightful forebear whose diagnosis of American government he approvingly recounted.

Hazlitt believed with Bagehot and Wilson that the separation of powers was unworkable because it promoted deadlock between the legislative and executive branches. He also believed that it should be possible for an issue to be taken to the country by means of a special election. An example of when this process would have been useful, according to Hazlitt, was the conflict between President Wilson and the Senate on whether to join the League of Nations and the World Court after World War I. Moreover, he suggested that America's decision not to join the League contributed directly to Hitler's rise and thus to World War II. Hazlitt further indicated that America's success in World War II depended on whether there would be wholesale parliamentary reform.

Hazlitt defended his ideas on traditional effectiveness and accountability grounds. When speaking in the former mode, he drew on military analogies. Suppose, he wrote, that "our troops were led by three different generals, any one of whom could countermand the orders of the other." The reference to three generals was meant, of course, to evoke a picture of three quarreling branches of government. For Hazlitt, disabling confusion was inherent in a system of separation of powers. Hazlitt also pointedly contrasted our constitutional system with the unification of power in corporate life.

Hazlitt's accountability argument similarly drew on longstanding premises of the parliamentary critique. He insisted that when power is shared among different actors and when things go wrong or problems fester, it is difficult to assign blame. As a result, in Hazlitt's view, people tend to become frustrated with the political process. Hazlitt adopted a tone of urgency in rejecting what he referred to as the "procrastinator's argument" for less than sweeping constitutional change.

2. Charles Hardin and the Watergate Crisis

In * * * 1974 * * *, political scientist Charles Hardin strongly embraced parliamentary proposals in response to problems of the early 1970s. He was particularly concerned about the Watergate affair. This affair involved not only a break-in during June 1972 at the Democratic Party headquarters in the Watergate office complex in Washington, D.C., but also efforts by highly placed administration officials to cover up the incident's scope. The Watergate episode—described by Charles Hardin as America's "gravest political crisis since the Civil War"—involved senior members of the executive branch, including the Attorney General, key aides to the President, and ultimately President Nixon himself. A prolonged process of congressional and criminal investigations culminated in the House Judiciary Committee's vote for articles of impeachment and constitutional litigation about an independent prosecutor's subpoena of certain tapes of presidential conversations. After the Supreme Court ruled in *United States v. Nixon* that the prosecutor's subpoena was not defeated by principles of executive privilege, President Nixon turned over materials containing highly incriminating evidence. This evidence was considered to include a "smoking gun" that directly implicated the President in a cover-up. Shortly thereafter, Nixon became the first U.S. President to resign from office.

To Charles Hardin, these events revealed a major weakness of the separation of powers. To be sure, one might well reach the opposite conclusion if one were to see Watergate as having demonstrated the system's ability to survive a crisis. Hardin believed, however, that a parliamentary system could have handled Watergate better. Under a parliamentary model, there could have been a vote of no confidence in the head of government. This possibility, he believed, could have allowed the nation to avoid the painful prolongation of the crisis. In our system, by contrast, the President can be removed only by impeachment.

Since Hardin wanted the executive's survival to depend on majority support from Congress, he argued that the President should resign whenever such support disappeared. He also proposed that the President, Senators and members of the House of Representatives be elected to concurrent four-year terms. In a special twist, he argued that approximately 150 at-large members should be added to the present 435 members of the House. These 150 members would be divided among the two major parties after a presidential election in order to assure that the party electing the President would have a working majority in the House.

Hardin also sought to foster the institution of an opposition party. To achieve this end, he proposed giving a seat in the House to the defeated presidential candidate of the two major parties. The defeated candidate would be awarded membership on House committees, access to the House floor for debate, funds for an office, and an official residence. At the same time, Hardin proposed reducing the Senate's power by eliminating its ability to hold up treaties or presidential appointments. Also, under Hardin's scheme, if the Senate rejected a bill and it was adopted twice by the House, it would be deemed to have been passed by Congress and would go to the President as proposed legislation.

Hardin maintained that there was no need for a constitutional amendment spelling out the President's power to dissolve Congress or Congress' power to throw out the administration. He expected that the practice of legislative votes of confidence would "naturally evolve" in a setting reformed along the lines he otherwise urged. If a President ever lost majority support, "he will be incapacitated and," Hardin asserted, "it would be logical for him to resign." Ultimately, Hardin believed, no confidence votes could be expected to become "the normal way that one government ends and another is chosen."

3. Parliamentary Critics of the 1980s

In recent years, parliamentary proponents have proliferated. They include former executive branch officials, scholars, and many others. Although they differ in their particular arguments, they continue to advance key aspects of the basic critique advanced by their forebears. A leading source of contemporary ideas has been the privately organized Committee on the Constitutional System, which received wide attention for a 1987 report urging a package of parliamentary reforms.

Contemporary critics take aim both at the separation of powers *and* at what they regard as an unduly incohesive party system. They deplore what is commonly called "divided government," namely, the control by one major party of Congress or at least one House and the simultaneous control of the presidency by the other major party. In six of ten presidential elections from 1956 to 1992—in 1956, 1968, 1972, 1980, 1984 and 1988—voters "divided" the government in this way by electing a Republican President and, at the same time, a Democratic Congress or at least House of Representatives.

It is important to underscore that concerns about divided government and the party system are not confined to partisans of the parliamentary critique. Moreover, concerns about divided government deserve and have received attention in their own right. My emphasis here is on the way in which such concerns have been used to buttress the basic program of parliamentary reformism. At bottom, the would-be reformers argue that the stalemate said to attend divided government is made vastly worse by the separation of powers.

For example, Douglas Dillon, co-chair of the Committee on the Constitutional System, argued that divided government in a system of separated powers leads to a condition of "stalemate whenever important and difficult issues are involved." Lloyd Cutler, another Committee co-chair, stressed that the President faces difficulties in making agreements with foreign nations because of the possibility of serious congressional opposition. More generally, he decried the lack of ability in the United States to "form a government" that will promote unity between the legislative and executive branches in the manner of parliamentary systems. James Sundquist, a member of the Committee's Board of Directors, also embraced the basic parliamentary critique of the separation of powers. He argued that the problem of the federal budget deficit has been exacerbated by a structural tendency toward endless bickering between the President and Congress. For these various critics, such bickering has been a regular feature of modern presidencies, including those of Presidents Ford, Carter, Reagan, and Bush. To be sure, critics have acknowledged that President Reagan achieved striking changes in national policy during his early years in office. They have insisted, however, that this was a short-lived period and that the customary pattern is one of institutional deadlock.

* * *

III. The Empirical and Normative Premises of the Parliamentary Critique

* * *

In this part, I will turn from the task of describing and clarifying key commitments of the parliamentary critique to the task of assessing the reform program's general premises. These premises are found in the critique's broad arguments for constitutional change, and they are not to be confused with specific claims at lower levels of generality that attend specific proposals. * * *

My focus will remain on the critique's general premises because if they raise serious questions, as I suggest they do, then the nature of the debate that has been carried on should change. * * *

* * *

A. *The Empirical Foundation of the Parliamentary Critique*

The key empirical premise of the parliamentary critique is that the U.S. constitutional system is inevitably prone to prolonged and debilitating stalemate. There are substantial reasons for questioning this broad-scale assertion.

To begin, the critique's empirical argument assumes that whenever there is conflict between the legislative and executive branches, such conflict is a symptom of constitutional tendencies toward stalemate. The possibilities that controversy could be constructive or that fruitful negotiation could occur after some degree of impasse lie outside the parliamentarians' frame of reference. Moreover, the idea that different approaches might usefully be joined together after a process of negotiation between the branches seems to remain beyond their purview. Instead of constructive possibilities, what parliamentary critics regularly see is confusion, paralysis and weakness.

Such a simplifying vision has considerable difficulty dealing with the subtleties of particular political conflicts. Take Henry Hazlitt: he expressed his concerns about the course of World War II in terms of a fear of deadlock between the executive and legislative branches. Take Charles Hardin: he conveyed his alarm about Watergate in terms of a critique of structural tensions in our system of government. Take contemporary critics: they often express their intense frustration with national budget deficits in terms of their laments about the separation of powers. Yet we know that World War II, Watergate and contemporary budget realities are very different topics. Is it not evident that a critique that treats them so similarly risks overlooking important complexities and alternative explanations lying outside a preconceived frame of reference?

To elaborate, consider the World War II, Watergate, and deficit examples along with two others prominently noted in the parliamentary literature: the Senate's failure to approve the League of Nations treaty after World War I and Franklin Roosevelt's 1937 Court-packing plan.

Let us start with the League of Nations experience. Assuredly, it was an instance in which the

President's policy was thwarted by the Senate. Does that show structural "stalemate" in some general sense, as Hazlitt claimed it did? Of course, the defeat would not have occurred if the Senate did not have the power to stop a treaty by refusing to give it a two-thirds vote of support. What does that prove? One needs to ask about the range of factors that actually prompted the treaty's disapproval. Consider, for example, the personalities of key political actors, public concern after World War I about continuing foreign obligations of the United States, and President Wilson's overall strategy for dealing with the Senate. Ultimately, President Wilson lost the treaty when he refused to negotiate with the Senate about the reservations it proposed for the treaty. By contrast, to cite a modern example, President Carter succeeded in obtaining ratification of the controversial Panama Canal treaties through compromises on reservations.

In view of the complex texture of the political processes involved in the Versailles treaty debate, it seems remarkably overstated to claim that failure to approve the agreement resulted from our governmental structure. The structure was a necessary but by no means a sufficient condition for the outcome. Moreover, to focus on the result of a particular treaty process is to overlook the larger value of having the Senate participate, whatever the consequence in a specific case.

Consider also Hazlitt's point about World War II. Hazlitt suggested that the failure of the United States to ratify the League of Nations treaty led directly to Hitler's rise to power and eventually to war. What about the role played by Germany in the causation of World War II? Surely, multiple factors led to serious destabilization in that country after World War I. These observations seem so plain that one has to wonder whether Hazlitt's concern about World War II should be viewed primarily as an argumentative device for focusing attention on his structural argument. In any event, the United States helped to win World War II with the constitutional structure that Hazlitt so vehemently attacked.

Now consider Franklin Roosevelt's Supreme Court-packing plan, in which he proposed expanding the size of the Supreme Court in order to allow for the appointment of new Justices who could be expected to approve New Deal policies. This plan's failure was seen by Hazlitt as another confirmation of structural weakness in the U.S. government. His notion was that the President advanced a relatively extreme proposal, Congress balked, and the President carried on in other areas while dropping the Court-packing package. Hazlitt asserted that in a parliamentary system, the Court proposal would "almost certainly" not have been made. If it had been made and if a majority in Congress had been against it—as ultimately was the case in 1937—the President would have had to resign and face a special election.

As interesting as this speculation is, the Court-packing plan seems to reveal the opposite of Hazlitt's suggestion: it appears to illustrate the potential *dangers* of a parliamentary arrangement. The plan is precisely the sort of extreme administration program that could well not be stopped in a system such as Britain's. The reason is that Parliament generally rubberstamps the administration's policies, assuming that the government has a majority in the legislature. Arthur Schlesinger, Jr., has made this argument in claiming that the lesson of 1937 was not that the Court-packing plan's unpopularity should have sent the President packing, but rather that defeat of such a plan in the first place would be unlikely in a parliamentary system. So viewed, the example pointedly confirms the importance of separation of powers and checks and balances.

The example of Watergate has been cited by Hardin as another instance of the inherent weakness of the separation of powers. The idea was that the extended period of investigation and oversight by the Senate, the House of Representatives, and the judiciary seriously weakened the governmental system. Parliamentary reformers like Hardin would have preferred the option of a vote of no confidence and a special election to save the nation from the prolonged agonies of a burdened chief executive.

A key difficulty with Hardin's story is its presupposition that, in Britain for instance, a special election would have been called. Although that is theoretically possible, the notion takes for granted that Watergate-like events would come to light in the first instance. That is problematical, however, given the British system's tendency to shy away from the kind of intense and independent investigations of government that were critical in uncovering the Watergate affair. At a minimum, a majority in Parliament would have strong incentives not to embarrass the executive unduly. After all, a new election could lead to loss of the majority's control of Parliament and the government. Moreover, a new election would require Members of Parliament to defend against electoral challenges. The members could be expected to suppose that they have better things to do with their time. Ultimately, one has to ask whether Watergate shows that the U.S. constitutional system failed or, in the alternative, that the system worked by allowing disclosure of wrongdoing at the top of government.

Finally, consider the often-cited example of continuing national budget deficits. For contemporary parliamentary critics, the separation of powers and divided government have worked together to create what might be called a situation of hyper-stalemate in addressing the deficits. The underlying empirical assessment is traditional: it is that the U.S. constitutional system is prone to deadlock and weakness.

Yet numerous factors appear to account for the nation's budgetary situation that have little to do as such with the legislative-executive separation of powers. Of clear importance in the creation of large deficits were numerous policy decisions during the 1980s that simultaneously reduced income taxes, funded social programs, and supported a large defense build-up. *Conscious policymaking*, not structural inevitabilities, generated massive deficits.

One might respond by urging that the persistence of the deficits requires a separate explanation and that the best one is structural stalemate between the legislative and executive branches. This explanation also is extremely problematical. The fact is that national policymakers have vigorously disagreed about what to do about the deficits. Some have argued that the issue in general has been overblown. Others have supported a variety of steps without coming to common ground about which ones to take. Substantive policy controversies of such magnitude cannot be explained away in terms of constitutional structure.

When one backs away from the various specific examples that have been said to illustrate the failure of the separation of powers, the simplistic character of a singleminded structural explanation comes into sharp focus. History and politics are more complex than any unicausal constitutional explanation will admit. In particular, deep disagreements about the substance of policy—what people are attempting to do—are at the core of periods of confusion or conflict. It bears mention in this regard that the United States is not alone today in the manifest frustration of its people with its political process. Indeed, a number of established democracies in the contemporary period—notably including parliamentary democracies—show signs of tension between their leaders and their citizens and evidence of political disengagement, division, and doubt.

Furthermore, significant and controversial policies have continued to be adopted in modern legislation in the United States. The 1970s, a period of divided government, was a time of major growth in domestic programs through legislation. The 1980s also saw much dramatic legislative activity. These facts directly undercut the stalemate thesis. They may even suggest that the existence of power in competing branches of government could promote the proliferation of policymaking, for each institution may be able to initiate action that the other might not have initiated. However that may be, as an empirical matter the case against the separation of powers must be strenuously questioned.

One is left with the thought that the parliamentarians' claims may be less descriptive than normative in character. After all, the ultimate idea is that our government *should* be less divided and less conflict-ridden. I will now turn to the critique's normative underpinnings.

B. The Normative Foundation of the Parliamentary Critique

The normative foundation of the parliamentary critique has three main aspects: a set of general standards for assessing the separation of powers; a particular picture of parliamentary institutions; and a certain view of constitutional values in the United States. I will discuss each of these matters in turn.

1. General Standards for Assessing the Separation of Powers

At the outset, one needs directly to confront the parliamentary critique's key arguments about the alleged ineffectiveness and unaccountability of the separation of powers. Both contentions, I will suggest, are plagued by a striking degree of vagueness and, in the end, emptiness.

a. The Effectiveness Argument

Everyone wants the government to be effective. Yet eventually one has to confront the fundamental question evaded by the parliamentary critique: effective for what ends? Effectiveness, after all, is concerned with the efficacy by which given goals are advanced. If I said that I was "effective" today in writing a letter, I would mean that I accomplished my letter writing. To state that I was "effective," however, is to declare nothing about whether writing a letter was the best use of my time. It also does not establish a substantive basis on which to judge the finished product. Such an evasion of substance is magnified when one speaks of an entire institution or set of institutions—indeed, an entire government—as being "effective" or "ineffective." Again, the real question is: effective for what ends?

The parliamentary critique's tendency to avoid specific substantive baselines is deep-seated. The critique asserts that *whatever* one wants the U.S. government to do, it cannot do it effectively. This approach may well have been chosen to appeal to a wide range of frustrated citizens. As one parliamentary proponent has noted with frankness: "To support constitutional reform, one must be prepared to gamble." Notably, one must gamble that the policies one deems acceptable will be implemented within the constitutional structure so earnestly sought.

Something terribly important is missing in a critique that regularly avoids the substance of political debate. From the viewpoint of people who, for example, opposed President Reagan's regulatory policies, there were significant virtues in the system of checks and balances that gave Congress the power to slow down or redirect the administration's efforts. Moreover, this virtue of checks and balances is not limited to one partisan perspective, for the basic point also applies to those who have opposed the policies of Democratic Presidents.

The existence of two different approaches to the sequence of implementing parliamentary ideas highlights the effectiveness argument's emptiness. The first approach would simultaneously pursue constitutional *and* party-related reforms. The second would advance party-related reforms first and only thereafter would pursue constitutional change. On the former view, the constitutional system needs to be altered immediately. On the latter view, the nature of political debate in the United States as carried out by the two major parties needs to be transformed first, and thereafter one should consider readjusting the major institutions of government.

The latter view has been described by James MacGregor Burns, who has called for revitalizing the major parties as the initial step in strengthening the government as a whole. In particular, he has sought a reinvigorated Democratic party that would capture the energies of the left in domestic politics in order to match the Republican party that has moved to the right in recent years. From this perspective, the existence of definite and discrete party programs is an important precondition to effective governmental reform.

The key point here is that the effectiveness argument, cast as it is at such a high level of generality, does not address or resolve the basic choice that Burns notes. Once again, the argument reveals itself as a remarkably empty vessel that is ready to be given highly divergent meanings in particular contexts.

b. The Accountability Argument

The second major argument of the parliamentary critique—that the separation of powers is an unaccountable system of government—also confronts serious problems. The contention rests on the premise that accountability requires unity in government so that the people will know whom to hold responsible for success or failure. Yet is the public so simpleminded as to be unable to assign responsibility for policy when *both* the executive and the legislative branches have an active hand in shaping policy? Joint responsibility is still responsibility. To assume that one branch needs to have overriding influence on policy in order for officials to be accountable is to bootstrap a premise about cohesive government onto the separate notion of political accountability.

Moreover, it is doubtful whether the substitution of a major check on government resulting from a special election, in place of the multiple and ongoing checks now asserted by different power centers on each other, would actually result in a net gain for accountability. After all, ongoing checks and balances between the legislative and executive branches are themselves a source of political accountability.

* * *

In addition, one must question the notion that accountability will be especially enhanced by providing for the possibility of a special election. In general, elections do provide a mechanism for holding officials accountable to the people. Yet parliamentary critics have something more specific in mind when they assail the separation of powers for being relatively less accountable than a parliamentary system. For the critics, a system that creates the possibility of a special election will allow an issue to be taken to the country so that a new, specifically tailored mandate can guide a new administration, thereby rendering it more accountable to the people.

As a practical matter, the idea of taking an issue to the country to overcome governmental deadlock raises serious questions. If there is governmental conflict, why is it not also likely for there to be deep division in the country? Moreover, can one expect an election campaign to stay focused on a particular issue or cluster of issues? In a heterogeneous society such as the United States, debate in a campaign leading up to a special election could quickly include discussion of many divergent issues. The underlying image of a great national forum for resolving some particular question in a special election might or might not turn out to bear any resemblance to reality.

Even assuming the existence of an unproblematical mandate resulting from a special election, how does the parliamentary critique deal with the likelihood of changing attitudes and conditions after such an election? On the logic of the parliamentary position, an electoral mandate apparently lasts in undiminished form until the next election. What if the political climate significantly changes and some different matters come to the fore, yet another special or a regular election is not held?

Furthermore, the parliamentary critique's emphasis on the use of a special election to seek a national mandate to which the government is to be held accountable depends on the idea of a relatively unitary perspective adopted by the nation's voting majority. How comfortably does the notion of a sweeping national mandate on some overriding issue fit with the normative concerns of modern pluralistic politics?

* * *

In fact, it seems admirable to have a governmental structure that fosters an ongoing struggle among diverse views and does not promote the lasting domination of one particular orientation. A different approach might initially lead to stronger government. If so, it would purchase strength at the expense of democratic debate. Moreover, in the long run a supposedly "strong" government as imagined by parliamentary critics might well be weakened by a tendency to disregard the diversity of Americans' views.

In important ways, the accountability argument is closely related to the effectiveness argument. Both call for a more centralized governmental structure able to pursue policies with less need for negotiation between Congress and the executive. Unsurprisingly, the problems with the two arguments are closely related. Both speak in vague generalities, and both evade substantive differences and choices in our political community.

2. A Picture of Parliamentary Institutions

A parliamentary critic might respond by suggesting that since we are talking about alternative constitutional systems, it is necessary only to establish that another structure has salient advantages over our own. Let us present a general picture of the British system, a proponent might urge, to understand its comparative superiority.

A key problem with this response is that it tends to rely on a caricatured version of the parliamentary system. In the first place, the parliamentary critique often overlooks that the British example is only one of innumerable modern parliamentary systems and that others differ in basic respects. It may be unsurprising that parliamentary proponents of constitutional change in the United States do not dwell on the intricacies of comparative constitutionalism, but the burden of their argument should lead them to consider main variations on parliamentary themes.

Moreover, in concentrating on the British experience, parliamentary critics often fail to take account of the important ways in which that nation's political system depends upon its unique history and culture.

British commentators are not hesitant to point out such relationships. As H.R.G. Greaves noted * * *, the British constitution cannot be understood "without reference to the chief characteristics of society." Such factors as the British class system and the relative ethnic homogeneity of much of the country's people—without denying the significance of nationality differences among England, Scotland, Wales, and Northern Ireland—should be contrasted to conditions in the United States.

In response, parliamentary proponents might well protest that they do not wish to transplant British institutions wholesale into this country. Yet even limited borrowing of basic ideas of another country's political structure risks overlooking that those ideas emerged in a distinct habitat. The British parliamentary system functions as it does not just because it is parliamentary but because it is British.

Furthermore, admiration for British institutions should not blind us to the fact that they have been sharply criticized in that country. Many critics have argued that such institutions give unwarranted power to the administration of the moment. * * *

The source of contemporary concerns about the British executive's dominance is the same as the British system's singular strength: a majority in Parliament basically guarantees passage of the Prime Minister's program. As Sir Ivor Jennings observed * * *, "the Opposition will, almost certainly, be defeated in the House of Commons because it is a minority."

These points have not received sufficient recognition by parliamentary proponents in the United States. The justification for characterizing parliamentary government as accountable is that, in theory, the executive in a parliamentary system can be voted out of office by the legislature. A key problem with this image is that, at least in modern Britain, the legislature generally does not use the vote of no confidence as a serious or active check on the executive.

In fact, one of the most important trends in British political institutions during the present century has been the sharp growth of prime ministerial power. This development has been associated with a marked drop in the cabinet's power and the rise of a powerful civil service with a penchant for secrecy. Notably absent from this picture is a legislature with incentives closely to review or openly to question governmental policy. This absence is not surprising. In the parliamentary system, if there is a loss of confidence in the executive, the government will resign and new elections will be held. An election obviously generates doubt about the future of each Member of Parliament. Such a prospect does create strong pressures—

apart from those of the party system itself—for the majority to support the Prime Minister.

* * *

3. A View of Constitutional Values in the United States

Parliamentary critics might respond that the separation of powers might have been well-suited for an agrarian and isolated nation, but it is not suitable today. This view conjures up an image of a constitutional straightjacket that unduly confines a world power as it seeks to address serious issues domestically and internationally. From this perspective, the constitutional framework is said to need a transfusion of energy from another model.

The central assumption underlying the straightjacket and transfusion images is that Americans are stuck with a rigid and unbending system. That assumption is wide of the mark. The institutions of United States government have evolved dramatically since the nation's founding, as shown by the tremendous growth in the power of the President and the emergence of so-called "independent" agencies. In other, not entirely consistent ways, the constitutional structure has hardly been static. However superficially appealing it may be to blame present problems on the decisions of our forbears, a thesis about the dead hand of 1787 is unduly strained.

In any event, one must consider the broader implications of a frontal assault on the separation of powers as outdated, ineffective, and unaccountable. The assault calls into question core aspects of the Constitution, and it offers in their place a vision of firm and unified governmental management. What does this approach sacrifice?

Ultimately, a number of fundamental values are threatened. At the most basic level, the argument overlooks the importance of deliberation, dialogue, and debate involving the institutions of U.S. government and the public. I will develop this theme in two parts: first, by elaborating what I will call the parliamentary critique's managerial ethos; and second, by contrasting that ethos with the principle of dialogue underlying checks and balances.

a. The Parliamentary Critique's Managerial Ethos

The parliamentary critique's leading image of government is of an efficient machine of centralized decisionmaking that sets its goals clearly, accomplishes them smoothly, and does not engage in wrangling about ends or means. This is a highly abstract vision of the job of government as one of instrumental management.

Given the parliamentary literature's tendency to focus on management values, it is unsurprising that often it explicitly or implicitly idealizes corporate structures of governance. In fact, the literature reflects admiration for hierarchical forms of decisionmaking in general. After all, if decisions are seen to move up a chain of command with someone at the top able to say, "This is it," there should be less room for the difficulties that attend a process of broader debate about proposed policy.

This managerial ethos inevitably highlights the executive virtues at the expense of open deliberation and ongoing participation in the political process. It also directly attacks checks and balances. Even though bargaining can be expected to continue within the executive branch, the critique would have it tamed in the relations between the executive and the legislature.

Take, for instance, Lloyd Cutler's summation* of the relative efficiency of our system of separation of powers as compared with that of parliamentary systems. He has contrasted the "success rates" of the two forms of government. He defined success as the executive's ability to get its program through the legislature. Under this definition, he has stated, the constitutional system in the United States "is only four-fifths as efficient" as parliamentary government when both the presidency and Congress are controlled by the same party. When there is "divided government," he has written, the United States system is "only two-thirds as efficient" as parliamentary regimes. He has proclaimed that parliamentary regimes are "very close to one hundred percent" efficient. The reason for parliamentary success in this comparison is that the executive generally can count on the legislature's support for whatever it proposes, assuming that the executive's party has a working legislative majority.

Cutler's characterization of the relative success of the two systems is striking for a number of reasons. To speak of success without considering the content of governmental policy is to confirm the parliamentary critique's basic tendency to avoid substantive discussion of concrete public issues. Note also that in the end *the President's success* becomes the definition of success in general. It matters not at all what the Congress proposes. The underlying notion is that the government's manager—the President in our system, the Prime Minister in the British system—needs to be able to manage. This view removes from consideration the possibility that another branch

---

* [Lloyd N. Cutler, *Party Government Under the American Constitution*, 134 U. PA. L. REV. 25 (1985).]

of government might have something usefully different to say about public policy.

To be sure, managerialism is not a foreign set of ideas in the context of American policymaking. Its image of "getting the job done" efficiently is central to modern debates about the legitimacy of the administrative process. Managerialism also is at the root of a number of important developments in administrative law, especially including the evolution of centralized executive oversight of agency rulemaking. Yet managerialism is only an aspect of a number of competing visions of public administration, and it captures only a few of the broader normative ideas associated with contemporary ideals of administration. Moreover, it is one thing to speak of administration in managerial terms, but it is quite another to speak of the interactions between the executive *and* the legislative branches in terms of such a vision. Managerialists may be frustrated because Congress does not speak their language, but that is precisely the point: Congress speaks the language not of managers but of the democratic process, messy though it is.

The parliamentary critique's managerial ethos has profound implications in the modern age of expanded presidential power. Since the New Deal and World War II, it has been widely recognized that the President has become the initiating institution of U.S. government. The presidency's centrality has reached such a level that the holder of that office is often seen in popular terms as the embodiment of national unity. In this context, a critique that further exalts the President by calling for the dominance of managerial values risks seriously unbalancing the relations between the two political branches.

One therefore should not be misled into thinking that parliamentary critics seek to advance the interests of the parliament or the legislature. This misunderstanding might be understandable given the literature's rhetoric praising Bagehot's model of government, under which independent Members of Parliament thoughtfully voted their consciences on the great issues of the day. The modern critique in the United States, however, is a managerially-oriented, presidentially-focused approach that exalts hierarchical control of policymaking by the executive. Again, this set of commitments may have a good deal of force when one is considering the executive branch by itself. When used as the prism through which to view the interaction of the executive and legislative branches, however, the vision seriously undermines the role of checks and balances in general and Congress in particular.

b. The Principle of Dialogue Underlying the Constitution's Structure

* * *

In recent years, there has been a revival of interest among courts, lawyers and legal scholars in the doctrine and theory of the separation of powers and checks and balances. * * * Such discussions often have emphasized the singular importance of the political dialogue and interaction fostered by the Constitution's structure.

The fundamental idea is that through the separation of powers and checks and balances, different voices—those of the President, the Senate, and the House of Representatives—can be expected to contribute to public debate about the ends and means of national policy. The notions are familiar: the President speaks as the nationally-elected voice of the people generally; the Senate represents the states; and the House represents particular constituencies that often have highly local concerns. More generally, the President speaks for the nation, and members of Congress—while being concerned with matters of national import—speak especially for different constituent parts of the nation. This constitutional structure guarantees that diverse perspectives will contribute to dialogue about public policy. Such a system is in direct tension with the top-down imperatives of the managerial ethos of parliamentarism.

Certain *caveats* are important here. First, the Constitution's structure cannot be assumed to guarantee an optimally broad dialogue among different groups in the polity. To the contrary, there are major constraints on the scope of political debate, especially including the relative powerlessness of certain groups. Much more should be done in my view to broaden political dialogue in order to include unrepresented voices. Second, separation of powers and checks and balances are designed to moderate the tendencies of a full-blown democratic regime, which could be swayed by momentary impulses of an aroused public. To that extent, the idea of dialogue in the context of the Constitution's structure needs to be distinguished from pure democratic rule. Third, other countries have evolved their own systems for achieving dialogue; my comments are directed specifically at the system in the United States.

Nevertheless, fundamental values are at stake. Foremost among them are the ideas of expanded access to power and broad dialogue in the context of our constitutional and political system. The possibilities of expanded access and dialogue follow directly from the fact that the constitutional structure is more decentralized, less unified, and thus less managerially neat than many parliamentarians would prefer. Because different institutions share power, individuals and groups may have a greater chance of winning the ear of some powerful official in their efforts to achieve representation. The significance of this fact is highlighted by taking the perspective of those who might not otherwise gain a political hearing, for instance because they do not have majority support and are not likely to achieve it in the future.

Expansion of political access and dialogue is an intelligent response to the social diversity of the United States. Having multiple pathways to power can assist in channelling social conflict in an internally riven social context. Indeed, since our nation is so diversified, it is unsurprising that people are often reluctant to embrace the idea of unity in government.

The Constitution's structure also is reassuring on the level of day-to-day partisanship * * *. For those who oppose the policies of a given administration, the value of checks on the executive is obvious. Vigorous dialogue about policymaking fostered by checks and balances also serves a number of affirmative purposes. In particular, it can promote better decisions by encouraging fuller consideration of significant alternatives.

In addition, separation of powers and checks and balances can help to prevent the dominance of particular factions or special interests. A major theme of discussions of the U.S. government has been that factions frequently gain more power than their numbers warrant. The overriding question has been how to control or limit the negative effects of special interests. Increasingly, commentators have noted that a healthy system of checks and balances, fostering debate about the impacts of governmental action as well as about competing public values, can help to ameliorate the problem of faction. This notion does not have to be cast only in terms of having certain selfish interests check other selfish interests. More generally, the contest among competing public visions, resting on larger commitments to the general good, can play out openly in a scheme of active checks and balances. To be sure, a focus on the amelioration of factional dominance should not lead one to a romanticized image of American political debate. Yet the point remains that the program of promoting checks and balances can have a moderating impact on factional control of government.

One might say in response that the broader the dialogue, the harder it will be to make any decision that sticks. One can understand the impulses for clarity that inform such a response. A system of separation of powers and checks and balances does carry with it a considerable potential for messiness and untidiness. Whatever else one might say about the Supreme Court's opinion in *INS v. Chadha*, the Court put well the basic point relevant here: "Convenience and efficiency are not the primary objectives—or the hallmarks—of democratic government" as envisioned in the United States Constitution.

Without meaning at all to suggest that the Constitution's system is ideal, one can say that it advances significant values and that these values are not sufficiently acknowledged by the parliamentary critique. After all, unity and effectiveness can exist in an autocratic system that is hostile to the norms of open dialogue. If we see broadened political debate in the United States as an important public aim, then we should expect—and embrace—some trade-offs in terms of managerial neatness.

IV. Conclusion

For decades parliamentary critics of the separation of powers have reproduced the same basic analysis of the structure of government in the United States. In the 1880s, Woodrow Wilson argued that the division between the legislature and the executive was a guarantee of ineffectual government. In the early 1920s, William McDonald expressed similar concerns when claiming, rather inconsistently, that our governmental structure was the source of the public's "feeling of indifference" toward political affairs as well as of "the thinly disguised talk of revolution." During World War II, Henry Hazlitt worried about the nation's ability to win the war given the constraints of the separation of powers. At the end of World War II, Thomas Finletter feared that the United States could not lead the western alliance during peace time unless "radical improvements" were made in the federal constitutional structure. During the Watergate period, Charles Hardin expressed grave concerns about the future of our government in the absence of parliamentary-style changes. During the 1980s, other parliamentary critics attributed growing national budget deficits to weaknesses in our constitutional structure.

No doubt, tomorrow will bring other issues to prominence along with renewed attacks on the separation of powers. Yet it seems clear that no single answer can be an all-purpose response to each major challenge to our government. A one-size-fits-all approach is inappropriate given the complexity of modern society and politics.

In the end, when one looks beyond the details of parliamentary proposals to their underlying premises, one finds serious empirical and normative limits. As an empirical matter, notwithstanding predictions to the contrary, the constitutional system has neither collapsed nor proven unable to adopt innovative policies. Moreover, periods of supposed political stalemate in our history can be accounted for by a number of explanations other than one solely dealing with structural features of our constitutional arrangement. Furthermore, the managerial ethos of parliamentary reformism is in direct tension with important values associated with the dialogue that attends our system of checks and balances. The term "parliamentary reform" should not be allowed to cloud the fact that the critics advance a highly pro-executive position that would seek a strong government primarily by undercutting the independence of Congress.

The main limits of the parliamentary critique should be kept in mind as we continue to examine ways to make our government more responsive to the needs of individuals and the community. On the one hand, we should be quite wary of calls for change in the direction of a parliamentary system. On the other hand, we should be alert to the importance of a relatively open and deliberative politics that not only upholds the ideals of separation of powers and checks and balances, but also pursues reasonably efficacious responses to particular problems. It has been said that "we live in the description of a place and not in the place itself." This is as true of our vision of political possibilities as of anything else. We ultimately are responsible for developing and defending the images—the descriptions—that resonate with public values we embrace.

Additional Sources

Philip C. Bobbitt, *The Committee on the Constitutional System Proposals: Coherence and Dominance*, 30 Wm. & Mary L. Rev. 403 (1989)

James W. Ceaser, *In Defense of Separation of Powers*, in SEPARATION OF POWERS—DOES IT STILL WORK? (Robert A. Goldwin & Art Kaufman eds., 1986)

Erwin Chemerinsky, *The Question's Not Clear, But Party Government Is Not the Answer*, 30 Wm. & Mary L. Rev. 411 (1989)

Lloyd N. Cutler, *Some Reflections About Divided Government*, 18 Pres. Stud. Q. 485 (1988)

Charles M. Hardin, CONSTITUTIONAL REFORM IN AMERICA: ESSAYS ON THE SEPARATION OF POWERS (1989)

Charles M. Hardin, PRESIDENTIAL POWER AND ACCOUNTABILITY: TOWARD A NEW CONSTITUTION (1974)

Mark P. Petracca et. al., *Proposals for Constitutional Reform: An Evaluation of the Committee on the Constitutional System*, 20 Pres. Stud. Q. 503 (1990)

Don K. Price, *Words of Caution About Structural Change*, in REFORMING AMERICAN GOVERNMENT: THE BICENTENNIAL PAPERS OF THE COMMITTEE ON THE CONSTITUTIONAL SYSTEM (Donald Robinson ed., 1985)

Arthur M. Schlesinger, Jr., *Leave the Constitution Alone*, in REFORMING AMERICAN GOVERNMENT: THE BICENTENNIAL PAPERS OF THE COMMITTEE ON THE CONSTITUTIONAL SYSTEM (Donald Robinson ed., 1985)

James L. Sundquist, CONSTITUTIONAL REFORM AND EFFECTIVE GOVERNMENT (rev. ed. 1992)

James L. Sundquist, *Response to the Petracca-Bailey-Smith Evaluation of the Committee on the Constitutional System*, 20 Pres. Stud. Q. 533 (1990)

James L. Sundquist, *Needed: A Political Theory for the New Era of Coalition Government in the United States*, 103 Pol. Sci. Q. 613 (1988-89)

James Q. Wilson, *Political Parties and the Separation of Powers*, in SEPARATION OF POWERS: DOES IT STILL WORK? (Robert A. Goldwin & Art Kaufman eds., 1986)

Committee on the Constitutional System, A BICENTENNIAL ANALYSIS OF THE AMERICAN POLITICAL STRUCTURE: REPORT AND RECOMMENDATIONS OF THE COMMITTEE ON THE CONSTITUTIONAL SYSTEM (1987)

Part III

Other Major Controversies About the Role of Courts Implicating Competing Visions of Administrative Legitimacy

A. The Controversy About the Reviewability of Agency Decisionmaking

This section deals with the reviewability of issues raised in administrative litigation. Under the Administrative Procedure Act, there are two types of nonreviewability: the first involves situations in which judicial review is precluded by statute, and the second involves cases in which the action in question is "committed to agency discretion by law."*

The excerpt by Professor Ronald M. Levin deals with the second strand of reviewability doctrine. Professor Levin examines the Supreme Court's discussion in two leading cases: *Overton Park* and *Heckler v. Chaney*. *Overton Park* is remembered for its language suggesting that whether an issue is committed to agency discretion will turn on whether there is "law to apply." Professor Levin criticizes this "law to apply" standard.

When turning to *Heckler v. Chaney*, Professor Levin suggests that although the opinion appears to rely upon the "law to apply" standard, a more careful analysis indicates that more is going on in the Court's analysis—for the Court's reasoning can be seen to reflect pragmatic concerns. Professor Levin elaborates a pragmatic approach to nonreviewability, and he defends it against those who might suggest that it is too open-ended. In so doing, Professor Levin provides a helpful backdrop against which to consider "committed to agency discretion" issues in general.

---

* 5 U.S.C. §§ 701(a)(1) & (2). The first branch of reviewability doctrine turns on an interpretation of the statutory provision that purportedly bars judicial review. Courts frequently read such provisions narrowly in order to give voice to a general presumption of the availability of judicial review.

Ronald M. Levin, *Understanding Unreviewability in Administrative Law*, 74 MINN. L. REV. 689, 690-94, 702, 704-20, 734, 740-50, 779 (1990)*

* * *

Introduction

One of the more intriguing developments in recent administrative law scholarship has been a changed attitude toward the role of judicial review in controlling administrative action. A generation ago, scholars could assume without much soul-searching that judicial review was fundamental to the sound governance of the regulatory system. Today, some of the most respected commentators in the field offer pointed and often biting criticisms of the courts' place in the administrative process. Naturally, this new intellectual climate has affected the timeless debate over the proper *intensity* of judicial review. Sharing the stage, however, are increasingly prevalent questions about *whether* the judiciary should review certain agency actions, or at least some of the determinations that underlie them.

In part, the debate over reviewability focuses on statutes that directly prohibit courts from examining some or all aspects of certain agency conduct: this debate looks at the proper ground rules for interpreting preclusion statutes and also at whether new ones should be enacted. On another level, the debate focuses on actions that are, in the language of the Administrative Procedure Act (APA), "committed to agency discretion by law." This somewhat awkward phrase refers to actions that are exempt from review because of judicial self-restraint rather than because of perceived congressional command.

This Article deals with the "committed to agency discretion" category of unreviewable administrative action. The category always has been considered quite small; some theorists have refused to acknowledge that it even exists in a meaningful sense. Nevertheless, the "committed to agency discretion" clause of the APA, section 701(a)(2), has shown surprising life during the past several years. In *Heckler v. Chaney*, the Supreme Court relied squarely on that clause to hold that agency refusals to initiate proceedings are presumptively unreviewable. * * * [I]n *Webster v. Doe*, the Court held under section 701(a)(2) that a dismissed employee of the Central Intelligence Agency could not challenge his termination in the federal courts, except on constitutional grounds.

The Court's revival of section 701(a)(2) makes scholarly analysis of its scope a pressing priority, because existing understandings of its meaning are surprisingly underdeveloped. Since 1971 the primary guideline used to determine whether an agency action is "committed to agency discretion" has been whether there is "law to apply" to the administrative decision. * * * Yet the test, first announced in *Citizens to Preserve Overton Park, Inc. v. Volpe*, is simplistic, historically unfounded, and needlessly rigid in its implications. It ignores so many of the considerations that undoubtedly should influence decisions about unreviewability that the lower courts have tortured and evaded the formula in as many ways as they can contrive. * * *

The "law to apply" formula, then, may be on the verge of losing its influence; but if it passes from the administrative law scene, what will replace it? This Article suggests a clearer way of framing the issues posed by the "committed to agency discretion" doctrine. The key lies in a new solution to what might be called the Supreme Court's "judicial restraint dilemma." On the one hand, the Court is committed to preventing excessive judicial intervention in executive branch activities; on the other it prefers to shun the exercise of federal common lawmaking power. These priorities come into conflict in the unreviewability context. The Court has pretended that the responsibility for curtailing excessive judicial review lies with Congress—a premise that is becoming progressively harder to sustain. The only way the Court will be able to tame the unruly law of unreviewability is to become less timid about utilizing its common law powers toward that end.

* * *

I. The Problem of Unreviewability

The APA's judicial review chapter provides that agency action is normally subject to review, but also states in section 701(a) that the chapter "does not apply to the extent that (1) statutes preclude judicial review; or (2) agency action is committed to agency discretion by law." The first of the two numbered clauses does not create interpretation difficulties (although there may be uncertainty as to whether a given statute actually precludes review). The cryptic language of the second clause, however, has generated tremendous confusion.

The most fundamental point in controversy has been whether this "committed to agency discretion" clause renders any administrative action unreviewable. As used in this Article, the term "unreviewabil-

---

* Reprinted with permission of the Minnesota Law Review and Ronald M. Levin. All rights reserved.

ity" refers to a situation in which the courts deliberately refrain from reviewing an agency action, or at least some of the findings and conclusions underlying it. An agency's action is *totally* unreviewable if all of its premises escape the court's examination; it is *partially* unreviewable if only some of them do. Thus, unreviewability is a threshold defense, like standing or ripeness. When the government prevails on this defense, a particular administrative action or finding receives no scrutiny—not even deferential scrutiny—on judicial review. * * *

* * *

II. Unreviewability in the Supreme Court

A. Background

Although courts have not enjoyed much success in defining which administrative actions to treat as unreviewable, one premise about the substantive scope of section 701(a)(2) is uncontroversial: the clause applies to only a small fraction of all agency actions. * * *

* * *

B. *Overton Park*

The Supreme Court advanced its first general explanation of the meaning of section 701(a)(2) in *Citizens to Preserve Overton Park, Inc. v. Volpe*. The plaintiffs, a citizen group, challenged a decision of the Secretary of Transportation approving a proposed highway route that would bisect a public park. The citizen group relied on two identically worded highway funding statutes that forbade the use of public park land for road construction unless there was "no feasible and prudent alternative." Ultimately, the Court remanded the case so the lower courts could decide whether the Secretary had properly applied the statutory criterion. Before reaching the merits, however, the Court considered whether plaintiffs were entitled to any judicial review. After finding that review was not precluded by statute, the Court continued:

> Similarly, the Secretary's decision here does not fall within the exception for action "committed to agency discretion." This is a very narrow exception. . . . The legislative history of the Administrative Procedure Act indicates that it is applicable in those rare instances where "statutes are drawn in such broad terms that in a given case there is no law to apply."

The Court then construed the words "no feasible and prudent alternative" in the highway funding statutes as requiring the Secretary to give "paramount importance" to protection of park land, unless there were "extraordinary" levels of cost or community disruption, or other "truly unusual" factors. On this premise, the Supreme Court had no trouble disposing of the section 701(a)(2) argument: "Plainly, there is 'law to apply' and thus the exemption for action 'committed to agency discretion' is inapplicable."

The four sentences quoted above constituted the Court's only analysis of section 701(a)(2). Indeed, under the circumstances, the brevity of the Court's discussion was not surprising. The *Overton Park* case was decided on an expedited timetable: only three months elapsed from the day the Supreme Court granted review until the day when the decision came down. Technical errors pervading the Court's opinion on a variety of issues suggest that this hurried pace was not without its costs. Moreover, the Secretary had not even argued that the agency action was unreviewable, and therefore the briefing on section 701(a)(2) had been almost negligible. These background circumstances may help explain some of the serious flaws in the Court's apparent holding that the applicability of section 701(a)(2) turns solely on whether there is "law to apply" to the agency decision.

The most fundamental flaw in this position was that the Court seemed to obscure the distinction between the issue of reviewability and the issue of legality. The Court drew its "no law to apply" test from the language of the Senate Judiciary Committee report on the APA. Under the theory of that report, * * * an agency action is "committed to agency discretion" only when there are no grounds on which the action could possibly be set aside. When this condition is met, however, the agency action obviously would survive judicial review in any event. Consequently, this view would make section 701(a)(2) mere surplusage, because the APA would generate exactly the same results without the clause as with it. Indeed, the report's theory renders the idea of unreviewability meaningless. Before declaring that a particular type of agency action could not conceivably be reversed, a conscientious court surely will examine the challenger's contentions to see if any of them has arguable merit. Yet this is essentially the same inquiry that the court would conduct if it were examining the agency action on the merits. Under the Senate report's theory, therefore, only by actually *reviewing* an agency action can a court declare that the action is unreviewable!

To the extent that the "law to apply" formula *restricted* the scope of section 701(a)(2), the Court's position was somewhat understandable, despite the weakness of its analytical underpinnings. Justice Marshall's professed desire to treat the clause as a "very narrow" exception was well served by a rule that meant, in effect, that no agency action would be deemed "committed to agency discretion" in the face of a colorable claim that the agency had exceeded its statutory mandate. * * *

What was more puzzling about the *Overton Park* test was the kind of unreviewability that it *preserved*. Consider a case in which the relevant statutes have granted the agency sweeping discretion, but the challenger claims the agency has exercised its discretion improperly. The challenger probably would assert this claim under section 706(2)(A) of the APA, which states that an agency action shall be set aside if found to be "arbitrary, capricious, [or] an abuse of discretion." Under *Overton Park*, this type of scrutiny—known as arbitrariness review or abuse of discretion review—is simply unavailable if there is no "law to apply."

Presumably, if the Court gave any thought to this implication of the "law to apply" test, it assumed that a reviewing court simply could not conduct abuse of discretion review without "law to apply." I call this line of analysis the "futility" theory: an action should be deemed "committed to agency discretion" if judicial review would be infeasible and therefore futile. The futility theory is superficially plausible to the extent one equates abuse of discretion review with an inquiry into whether the agency used legally relevant factors in exercising its discretion. If there are no legally relevant factors, the argument goes, a court obviously cannot conduct this inquiry.

This reasoning, however, completely ignores certain additional theories that today's courts routinely use in reviewing agency actions for abuse of discretion. A plaintiff might claim, for example, that the agency misunderstood the facts, that it departed from its precedents without a good reason, that it did not reason in a minimally plausible fashion, or that it made an unconscionable value judgment. These arguments can be called "pure" abuse of discretion theories, because they do not rest on an assertion that the agency misunderstood its governing statute or any other source of legal constraints. Although these theories were only beginning to emerge at the time of *Overton Park*, each of them is now a well established component of substantive judicial review doctrine. * * *

When these aspects of scope-of-review doctrine are considered, the futility theory's weakness immediately becomes evident. Pure abuse of discretion inquiries do not depend on the contents of the statute under which an agency acts; therefore, it is illogical to suppose that the lack of "law to apply" makes these inquiries unworkable. If judicial review of the agency's factual perceptions, logic, and consistency is acceptable when the agency operates under significant statutory restrictions, it should be no less acceptable when the agency is not doing so.[92]

* * *

The Supreme Court's cursory analysis of section 701(a)(2) in *Overton Park*, then, left the law of unreviewability in a decidedly unstable state. * * *

C. Heckler v. Chaney

* * *

* * * [*Heckler v. Chaney*] began when eight death row prisoners wrote to the Food and Drug Administration (FDA), contending that state governments' use of lethal drug injections as a means of capital punishment violated the Food, Drug, and Cosmetic Act, because the drugs were not "safe and effective" for human execution. They asked the FDA Commissioner to proceed against state authorities who were using the drugs for such "unauthorized" purposes. When the Commissioner refused, the prisoners sought judicial review.

The district court dismissed the complaint, but the District of Columbia Circuit reversed, holding that the FDA's rejection of the prisoner's request was reviewable and had been arbitrary and capricious. Then-Judge Scalia dissented, asserting that the FDA's decision should be considered unreviewable as an exercise of traditional prosecutorial discretion. In a follow-up opinion, he also protested the D.C. Circuit's frequent resort to pragmatic considerations, rather than the *Overton Park* "law to apply" test, in deciding questions of reviewability.

* * * [I]n an opinion written by Justice Rehnquist and joined by seven other Justices, the Court held

---

[92] The analysis in the text is similar, but not identical, to that of Professor Davis. He argues that, even in the absence of "law to apply," a reviewing court can always test an agency's exercise of discretion against "such omnipresent standards as justice, fairness, and reasonableness." Davis, *"No Law to Apply"*, 25 SAN DIEGO L. REV. 1, 6 (1988). Many administrative lawyers (and more than a few judges) would likely believe, however, that Davis's open-ended phrasing risks the very dangers of judicial usurpation that a doctrine of unreviewability is supposed to prevent. In my view, the present case law on abuse of discretion review identifies a number of relatively conservative theories by which a court may consider reversing agencies on grounds that are independent of "law." One can, therefore, demonstrate the inadequacy of the futility theory without any need to bless judicial discretion as unequivocally as Davis seems to contemplate.

broadly that an agency refusal to institute investigative or enforcement proceedings was "presumptively unreviewable." This presumption could be rebutted when Congress furnished "law to apply" in the form of substantive guidelines circumscribing an agency's enforcement discretion. Congress had not, however, placed relevant limits on the FDA's freedom to decline to use its enforcement authority, and therefore the court of appeals' decision had to be reversed. Only Justice Marshall rejected the Court's analysis. He argued, in a lengthy opinion concurring in the result, that the FDA's decision was reviewable, but should be upheld on the merits.

On the surface, *Chaney* appeared to be a strong vindication of the *Overton Park* test of unreviewability; most commentators have read it that way. When the Court's reasoning is scrutinized, however, *Chaney* proves to be just the opposite. The Court subtly undermined the "law to apply" formalism, substituting a decidedly functional approach. This conclusion emerges from an examination of three aspects of the Court's reasoning: 1) its general exegesis of the meaning of section 701(a)(2); 2) its explanation of why exercises of enforcement discretion "presumptively" fall within that provision; and 3) its suggestions about the circumstances in which such agency discretion might nevertheless be reviewable.

1. *Chaney* and the "law to apply" test

Before turning to the specific question of enforcement discretion, Justice Rehnquist presented what appeared to be a general theoretical framework for analysis of section 701(a)(2). He quoted at length from *Overton Park*, explaining its construction of the clause in light of what I call the "futility" theory. That is, he read section 701(a)(2) to mean that

> review is not to be had if the statute is drawn so that a court would have no meaningful standard against which to judge the agency's exercise of discretion. . . . This construction avoids conflict with the "abuse of discretion" standard of review in § 706—if no judicially manageable standards are available for judging how and when an agency should exercise its discretion, then it is impossible to evaluate agency action for "abuse of discretion."

Unfortunately, this explanation did not come to grips with the problems in the *Overton Park* analysis. If the only agency actions that fall within section 701(a)(2) are actions that could not, in any "meaningful" or "judicially manageable" sense, be deemed abuses of discretion, the concept of unreviewability serves no purpose. Such agency actions would survive "merits" scrutiny under section 706 in any event. Thus, the Court's explanation of the "law to apply" test did not solve the problem of devising a rationale for section 701(a)(2) under which the clause would not be superfluous. Moreover, even if one accepts the premise that unreviewability should depend on the availability of "meaningful standards," the "law to apply" analysis falsely assumes that a broad statute makes judicial review unworkable. The truth is that, regardless of how broadly "the statute is drawn," courts typically have some "judicially manageable standards" available for abuse of discretion review.

The peculiar facts of *Chaney* provide a good illustration of the latter point, for one can easily conceive of ways in which the Commissioner could have abused his discretion in responding to the prisoners' petition, even if we assume that the Food, Drug, and Cosmetic Act did not limit the FDA's enforcement discretion. Suppose, for example, the FDA had declined to proceed against execution drugs on the ground that they were not dangerous at all. If the record contained strong contrary evidence, a court might regard this decision as arbitrary, because a regulatory decision that rests on unjustifiable factual assumptions is an abuse of discretion. Alternatively, suppose that the Commissioner had denied the prisoners' petition on the ground that anyone who is sentenced to capital punishment should die an agonizing, lingering death. Quite apart from the question of whether anything in the statute bears on this rationale, one can easily picture a judge holding that deliberate cruelty is an unconscionable basis for decision, and therefore an abuse of discretion—a "clear error of judgment," in the words of *Overton Park*. Finally, suppose the Commissioner had announced that the FDA would not act on the petition because the agency wished to leave the issue to state-level health officers. This rationale would be completely illogical, because such officers could not override state *statutes* requiring execution by injection. As such, the rationale for the FDA's refusal to proceed against execution drugs could be challenged as lacking the "reasoned analysis" required under abuse of discretion case law.

Other examples can be imagined, but these sufficiently demonstrate why the futility theory, standing alone, could not have logically supported the Court's finding of unreviewability in *Chaney*. In each of the hypothetical cases, the basis for reversal would be unrelated to the dictates of the Food, Drug, and Cosmetic Act. In short, what the *Chaney* Court did not acknowledge is that, even if the Act did not contain "manageable standards" delineating how the Commissioner *must* use his discretion, general administrative law doctrine on abuse of discretion identifies certain ways in which he *must not* use it. * * *

2. *Chaney* and the pragmatic calculus

On some level, the Court evidently was aware that *Overton Park* alone could not persuasively support a holding that the FDA Commissioner's decision was unreviewable. For, after expounding the above elaboration of the "law to apply" test, the Court abruptly laid the test aside and began to discuss various practical considerations that demonstrated the "general unsuitability for judicial review of agency decisions to refuse enforcement."

At least some of these practical arguments were persuasive. Perhaps the strongest argument was that, when an agency decides which alleged law violators it will pursue, it must take into account such variables as its chances of prevailing in the action, its overall regulatory priorities, and competing uses for its limited budget and personnel. Judicial supervision of these choices might not be impossible, but it would at least be unusually difficult. Even many observers who favor a narrow application of *Chaney* concede that the managerial nature of agencies' decisions about how they can best deploy scarce resources warrants considerable solicitude from the courts during judicial review. Moreover, there was force to the Court's comment that "when an agency *does* act to enforce, that action itself provides a focus for judicial review, inasmuch as the agency must have exercised its power in some manner." The Court apparently meant that judicial review of agency inaction may be "unfocused" because the court cannot know what measures the agency ultimately would have adopted if it had commenced a proceeding.

Justice Rehnquist's other arguments for the presumptive unreviewability of agencies' nonenforcement decisions were weaker and might even be considered makeweights. First, the Court argued that "when an agency refuses to act it generally does not exercise its *coercive power* over an individual's liberty or property rights." Even if one were to accept the dubious premise that persons coerced by agency action deserve review more than persons who hope to benefit from such action, the Court's argument was strikingly overbroad. Numerous agency decisions that courts routinely review are also noncoercive: for instance, appeals from denials of Social Security disability benefits make up a large fraction of the federal courts' caseload. The Court also drew an analogy between agency inaction and a prosecutor's decision not to seek a criminal indictment—ignoring substantial differences between the two factual contexts.[128]

* * * What is important is the role of functional arguments in the structure of the *Chaney* Court's analysis. The opinion's pointed reliance on those arguments demonstrated that the Court was not interested in a straightforward application of its earlier futility analysis. Had the Court been prepared to adhere strictly to the *Overton Park* "law to apply" test, such policy considerations would have been irrelevant, and the case would have been over almost immediately. Thus, although Justice Rehnquist did not offer a precise concept of how the two parts of his analysis fit together, the Court evidently was groping toward a more complex approach to section 701(a)(2), in which the absence of "law to apply" would be an important factor militating against reviewability, but not necessarily a dispositive factor.

Part of the reason that *Chaney* has been mistakenly interpreted as a simple reaffirmation of *Overton Park* is that, in addressing the circumstances in which the *Chaney* presumption against review of nonenforcement decisions could be rebutted, the Court focused on what it termed a "law to apply" issue. A plaintiff could overcome the presumption by showing that a statute prescribed substantive priorities or other limits on an agency's enforcement discretion. As an example, the Court referred to its 1975 decision in *Dunlop v. Bachowski*, which had permitted judicial review of the Secretary of Labor's decision not to challenge a union election under the Labor-Management Reporting and Disclosure Act (LMRDA). The key to the *Dunlop* holding, Justice Rehnquist explained, was that the language of the LMRDA had constrained the Secretary's enforcement discretion, directing him to file suit "if he finds probable cause to believe that a violation . . . has occurred." The statutory directive, therefore, had provided "law" that a reviewing court could properly enforce.

In this portion of the *Chaney* opinion, however, the phrase "law to apply" served a function that was entirely different from its role in *Overton Park*. The Court did not treat the absence of law to apply as a self-sufficient *reason* for the rule of unreviewability; rather, it regarded the availability of law to apply as

---

[128] *See Chaney*, 470 U.S. at 847-50 (Marshall, J., dissenting) (beneficiaries of regulatory schemes have a direct and tangible stake in enforcement, transcending society's generalized interest in criminal law enforcement; and the overall trend in administrative law has been away from unconstrained discretion); Note, *Judicial Review of Administrative Inaction*, 83 COLUM. L. REV. 627, 657-61 (1983).

a *limitation* on a rule of unreviewability that was largely rooted in practical considerations. The distinction is subtle but significant. The Court's position implied that examination of a wide range of functional considerations would not necessarily be foreclosed when courts faced novel reviewability issues in later cases. Such courts might decide, as *Chaney* had, that a given agency determination should be reviewed only on the basis of "law," but that outcome would not be a foregone conclusion.

3. *Chaney*'s caveats

A final bit of evidence that the Court was not strictly wedded to the futility theory was Justice Rehnquist's readiness to mention situations in which the *Chaney* rule might not come into play. The *Dunlop* type of case did not appear to be the only one in which a plaintiff could overcome the *Chaney* "presumption." In asides and footnotes scattered throughout the opinion, the Court hinted that agency inaction might be reviewable: 1) where the agency refused to commence rulemaking proceedings; 2) where the plaintiff alleged that the agency's nonenforcement decision contravened the Constitution or the agency's rules; 3) where the agency's inaction was "based solely on the belief that it lacks jurisdiction"; or 4) where "the agency has 'consciously and expressly adopted a general policy' that is so extreme as to amount to an abdication of its statutory responsibilities." Moreover, the tenor of the *Chaney* opinion did not indicate that these escape routes were the only ones that the Court would consider upholding. Indeed, Justice Brennan suggested in his concurring opinion that the *Chaney* holding would not prevent a court from reviewing allegations that an agency's nonenforcement decision had resulted from bribery, although he assumed that the Court had not explicitly reserved this possibility.[142]

Neither Justice Rehnquist nor Justice Brennan seriously attempted to explain how these qualifications could be reconciled with the "law to apply" analysis that the Court's opinion purported to endorse. Collectively, however, these reserved issues reinforced the impression that the Court was prepared to embrace a far more complex conception of section 701(a)(2) than the *Overton Park* reasoning alone could sustain. Or, at the very least, these qualifications suggested that Justice Rehnquist had been able to attract near-unanimous support for his opinion only by conspicuously leaving room for such complexity.

In summary, the *Chaney* opinion suffered from a deep theoretical inconsistency. Although Justice Rehnquist initially attempted to make sense of *Overton Park*, he then effectively acknowledged the inadequacy of the "law to apply" reasoning by resting the *Chaney* rule of presumptive unreviewability largely on pragmatic grounds. The Court therefore deserves credit for shifting unreviewability analysis in *Chaney* to a more credible footing than the formalist approach of *Overton Park*. Perhaps the Court would have deserved even more credit if the transformation had not been so poorly articulated as to have escaped the notice of so many readers.

* * *

III. Beyond "Law to Apply"

* * * The Court could clarify its analysis by explicitly acknowledging what it is already doing implicitly: it should cease treating the "law to apply" test as the exclusive standard for identifying actions that are "committed to agency discretion." Instead, the Court should candidly approach section 701(a)(2) as a source of authority for elaborating a "common law of unreviewability."

* * *

B. A Common Law of Unreviewability

* * * The Supreme Court should acknowledge the common law role that it, in any event, obviously feels impelled to play. It could do so by replacing the formalistic *Overton Park* analysis with a pragmatic approach to section 701(a)(2).

Under such an analysis, a court could legitimately consider a wide variety of historical, utilitarian, and prudential arguments in deciding whether to refrain from judicial review in a given case. Of course, individual judges should not have unfettered discretion to accept or reject any administrative case presented to the courts. The Supreme Court, and to a lesser extent lower courts, could establish case law rules declaring a broad class of agency actions unreviewable. Or, at times, the courts might prefer to resort, as the Supreme Court did in *Chaney*, to the weaker device of a "presumption," which implies that courts in subsequent cases may sometimes make reasoned departures from the general rule. At still other times, a court might find the accepted rules and presumptions unhelpful and, therefore, embark on a fresh examination of competing policy issues. Over

---

[142] [*Chaney*, 470 U.S.] at 839 (Brennan, J., concurring). Although Justice Brennan did not elaborate, probably the simplest way to justify review in such a case would be to argue that the federal criminal bribery statute, 18 U.S.C. § 201(b)–(c) (1988), furnishes "law to apply" to the agency's decision. * * *

time, various aspects of the law of unreviewability probably would fluctuate between rule and ad hoc decisions, as often occurs in subject areas governed by the common law.

It would be unrealistic to suppose that we could predict with any specificity where the pragmatic approach would lead. Based on the existing case law under section 701(a)(2), however, one may expect that this approach to the "committed to agency discretion" doctrine would: 1) remain narrow in its scope; 2) usually be invoked in certain peripheral areas of administrative action; and 3) shield legal issues from judicial scrutiny less often than factual and discretionary issues.

1. Narrow Application

In the unreviewability law of the future, the scope of the "committed to agency discretion" doctrine is likely to remain very limited. * * * A standard account of the contributions of judicial review would read something like this: Scrutiny of administrative action by an independent judiciary is an integral part of the American checks and balances system—a powerful deterrent to abuses of power and an effective remedy when abuses occur. By helping maintain public confidence that government officials remain subject to the rule of law, judicial review also bolsters the legitimacy of agency action. The courts' supervision of agency action complements the oversight activities of political actors, who often have parochial interests at heart or are inaccessible, as a practical matter, to some victims of regulatory action or inaction. Finally, judicial review can enhance the quality of administrative action by exposing partiality, carelessness, and perverseness in agencies' reasoning.

* * * [U]nder the pragmatic approach to section 701(a)(2), the presumption [of the availability of judicial review] likely will give way where the courts find sufficiently strong practical reasons to exercise self-restraint.

2. Kinds of Unreviewable Actions

Predicting the circumstances that would trigger application of section 701(a)(2) under a pragmatic approach is a highly speculative undertaking. The scholarly literature on the subject is exceedingly sparse. There is, of course, a burgeoning literature on the shortcomings of judicial review. In general, however, these critiques, even if accepted at face value, do not seem readily adaptable to the effort to define the scope of the "committed to agency discretion" doctrine. * * *

Next let us consider whether the case law provides more direction. Some courts have tried to resolve reviewability questions with balancing tests. Under the best known formula, originated by the First Circuit in *Hahn v. Gottlieb* and used by other courts up until the time of *Chaney*, availability of judicial review should depend on three factors: "first, the appropriateness of the issues raised for review by the courts; second, the need for judicial supervision to safeguard the interests of the plaintiffs; and third, the impact of review on the effectiveness of the agency in carrying out its assigned role." The *Hahn* formula is roughly consistent with the pragmatic analysis under discussion here. Such a formula, however, is obviously too general and all-embracing to offer courts very much meaningful direction. * * * *Hahn* furnishes a starting point for analysis, not a self-sufficient guideline.

Cases with a narrower focus may also be illuminating. Possibly the most reliable way to project the future of the common law of unreviewability is to examine several categories of agency actions that have been held unreviewable under section 701(a)(2) in the recent past. One group of cases involves agency actions arising from unusually sensitive subject areas. Actions relating to foreign policy, military, and national security affairs are among the strongest candidates for being considered "committed to agency discretion." Courts simply do not give these matters the same kind of "hard look" that domestic policy decisions routinely receive. This self-restraint rests on policies similar to those underlying the political question doctrine: the courts' lack of information about foreign affairs, the confidentiality of much of that information, and the need to minimize the incoherence that results when American foreign policy is articulated by multiple voices. The desire to curtail judicial involvement in delicate subject areas also extends to certain corners of the domestic realm. For example, the Federal Reserve Board's regulation of the nation's money supply has long been regarded as a function that courts could not possibly supervise effectively; therefore, they decline to attempt review.

Another group of cases concerns informal, unstructured agency operations that are closely related to the agency's management of its workload and may not reflect conclusions on the merits of the petitioner's substantive claims. Such agency decisions frequently are made on grounds that courts cannot easily evaluate in a constructive way. * * * In adopting a limited bar to review of administrative prosecutorial discretion, *Chaney* relied on the abstract quality of the issues presented and on the problems inherent in judicial attempts to supervise agencies' resource allocation decisions. * * *

Finally, courts likely will hold unreviewability appropriate when the petitioner challenges a phase of administrative activity that does not directly affect private interests. An instructive case in this category is *Natural Resources Defense Council, Inc. v. Hodel*. There, a statute required the Secretary of Interior to submit a report to Congress explaining "in detail" why he had rejected certain proposals concerning offshore oil and gas leasing. The state of California asked the District of Columbia Circuit to review whether the Secretary's response had been sufficiently "detailed." The court refused, observing that the "agency action" at issue was entirely unlike the rulemaking and adjudicative functions that courts normally review, and that the presumption of reviewability was "woefully inapposite" in this context.

3. Partial Unreviewability

Another likely element of a pragmatic approach to section 701(a)(2) would be liberal use of the concept of partial unreviewability. Thus, much as they have done in statutory preclusion cases, courts applying section 701(a)(2) probably would treat many agency actions as reviewable on some grounds but not on others. Judges already tend to assume that agency actions that are to some extent "committed to agency discretion" remain reviewable for compliance with the Constitution. A similar but broader principle would be that certain agency actions may be challenged on legal grounds, but not on abuse of discretion grounds. The cases show some support for this proposition * * *.

There can be several justifications for such a rule of partial unreviewability. First, courts traditionally have been regarded as the "final authorities" in interpreting statutory commands and other legal mandates; their competence and legitimacy in that realm is widely accepted. When courts review factual and discretionary determinations, however, they confront issues on which the agency often has superior expertise and experience. Indeed, even when unreviewability is not involved, a reviewing court generally examines an agency's factual and discretionary conclusions only to determine whether they are rational, not whether they are correct. Accordingly, a decision not to exercise this judicial function has less tendency to subvert the principle of checks and balances than a refusal to review an agency's legal interpretations.

Second, when a court resolves a legal issue, it characteristically writes an opinion interpreting the relevant statute or regulations; that decision provides lasting guidance to the agency and the public. A judicial opinion deciding whether an agency acted arbitrarily, when no explicit legal issues are raised, has more limited precedential value. In an era when docket pressures weigh heavily on the federal judiciary, the desire to make efficient use of judicial resources bolsters the case for foreclosing appeals that add to the courts' workload without contributing proportionately to the growth of the substantive law.

Third, review of factual and discretionary issues imposes certain tangible costs on agencies that review of legal issues does not. When the reasoning underlying an agency's exercise of discretion is subject to judicial review, the agency has to furnish a written opinion; when factual premises are subject to review, the agency has to compile a record. Thus, the threat of judicial review encourages greater formality in administrative decisionmaking. Administrative decisions that for policy reasons should remain extremely informal might, therefore, be exempted from the full power of "hard look" review. Such logic, however, allows for judicial review that does not indirectly shape the agency's procedures—for example, review to determine whether the action on its face exceeds the agency's statutory authority.

Besides providing a rationale for one type of partial unreviewability, these practical distinctions between legal and factual issues suggest an attractive way to reconcile the formalist and pragmatic approaches to section 701(a)(2). Many authorities speak as though the "law to apply" test and a pragmatic approach are mutually exclusive, but this is not necessarily so. A better view is the one that prevailed before *Overton Park*: the presence or absence of "law to apply" is *one relevant factor* that courts should weigh along with others in the pragmatic calculus. * * *

Specifically, the *presence* of law against which the court can judge the plaintiff's claims should *usually* be a sufficient reason to permit judicial review of those claims; thus, the *Overton Park* analysis should control most cases. Nevertheless, courts should recognize the possibility that, in a relatively small number of cases, countervailing considerations will dictate that a claim of legal error should remain unadjudicated. On the other hand, the *absence* of "law to apply" should militate to some degree against judicial review. Because abuse of discretion review remains feasible in such a case, however, the court should continue to weigh arguments for and against review before it decides how far, if at all, the action is "committed to agency discretion."

* * *

Conclusion: The Future of Unreviewability
* * *

The law of unreviewability cannot become intellectually respectable * * * without a major overhaul. Sooner or later, the Court will have to face up to the flaws in the *Overton Park* analysis of unreviewability—its shaky historical foundations, its circularity, and its dubious assumptions about the potential sweep of modern scope-of-review doctrine. In recent years the Court has been giving the "law to apply" test little more than lip service, but before long even lip service will cease to be credible. The "pragmatic approach" advocated in this Article would allow issues arising under section 701(a)(2) to be debated with far greater clarity and candor.

* * *

Additional Sources

Ruth Colker, *Administrative Prosecutorial Indiscretion*, 63 Tul. L. Rev. 877 (1989)

Kenneth Culp Davis, *"No Law to Apply,"* 25 San Diego L. Rev. 1 (1988)

Charles H. Koch, Jr., *Judicial Review of Administrative Discretion*, 54 Geo. Wash. L. Rev. 469 (1986)

Sandra Day O'Connor, *Reflections on Preclusion of Judicial Review in England and the United States*, 27 Wm. & Mary L. Rev. 643 (1986)

Robert K. Rasmussen, *Coalition Formation and the Presumption of Reviewability: A Response to Rodriguez*, 45 Vand. L. Rev. 779 (1992)

Daniel B. Rodriguez, *The Presumption of Reviewability: A Study in Canonical Construction and Its Consequences*, 45 Vand. L. Rev. 743 (1992)

John M. Rogers, *A Fresh Look at Agency "Discretion,"* 57 Tul. L. Rev. 776 (1983)

Harvey Saferstein, *Nonreviewability: A Functional Analysis of "Committed to Agency Discretion,"* 82 Harv. L. Rev. 367 (1968)

Marianne K. Smythe, *Judicial Review of Rule Rescissions*, 84 Colum. L. Rev. 1928 (1984)

Richard B. Stewart and Cass R. Sunstein, *Public Programs and Private Rights*, 95 Harv. L. Rev. 1193 (1982)

Cass R. Sunstein, *Reviewing Agency Inaction After* Heckler v. Chaney, 52 U. Chi. L. Rev. 653 (1985)

Paul R. Verkuil, *Congressional Limitations on Judicial Review of Rules*, 57 Tul. L. Rev. 733 (1983)

B. The Controversy About the Plaintiff's Standing to Sue an Agency

Perhaps the most important of the threshold issues is that of the plaintiff's standing to sue. Modern standing doctrine in administrative law traces to the 1970 decision, *Association of Data Processing Service Organizations v. Camp*. This case established that a plaintiff must allege injury in fact and that the interest sought to be vindicated must be arguably within the zone of interests protected by the statute or constitutional provision in question. Since 1970, the doctrine has evolved considerably. During the 1980s, the Supreme Court made it clear that a plaintiff must establish causation, that is, that the defendant's behavior is likely to have caused the alleged injury, as well as redressability, that is, that the relief sought would likely redress the injury asserted. The development of these requirements has stirred a wide-ranging debate.

The excerpts in this section by Antonin Scalia and Cass Sunstein reflect deeply opposing views of standing. In his 1983 article, Antonin Scalia argues that the object of a regulation—i.e., the party actually being regulated—generally has standing, but that the beneficiary of a regulation or law who wishes a court to order an agency to do something to vindicate a statute's purposes must be viewed in a different light. The object of regulatory power is seen as a "minority" being singled out by the government for adverse treatment and therefore as a proper subject for judicial attention. However, the beneficiary of a law or regulation is seen as a member of the community's majority who must establish a highly specific interest in order to invoke the power of a federal court. Although Justice Scalia acknowledges that a strict limitation on the ability of beneficiaries to sue may well lead to broader underenforcement of the law, he does not see this as a problem. In closing comments, Justice Scalia indicates that standing doctrine could develop along the lines suggested in his piece. His comments have proven prescient, as he has himself contributed as a Justice to modern debates about tightening up the requirements of standing.

Professor Sunstein responds to Justice Scalia's 1983 article and his 1992 opinion in *Lujan v. Defenders of Wildlife*, which embodies some of the ideas of the earlier article. Professor Sunstein critiques the main elements of *Lujan*. In particular, he discusses what he calls *Lujan*'s most important and novel holding—namely, that Congress cannot grant standing to citizens. In Professor Sunstein's eyes, Congress should have a vigorous but not unlimited role in the creation of citizen suits. Moreover, he criticizes *Lujan*'s reliance on article II, the article of the U.S. Constitution residing power in the president as chief executive, in analyzing standing issues under article III. For Professor Sunstein, the standing of beneficiaries should raise no serious article II issue. Moreover, he specifically criticizes the minority-majority distinction and other themes that Scalia enunciated in his 1983 article.

The third and fourth excerpts criticize the foundational concept of the plaintiff's injury in fact. Professor William Fletcher argues that the injury in fact requirement is seriously flawed. He suggests that it presumes one can make a non-normative judgment of fact at the threshold of litigation by assessing the plaintiff's injury and determining whether it is sufficiently concrete and particularistic. Professor Fletcher argues that the attempt to rest standing on a non-normative basis ultimately fails. He contends that behind an assessment of injury in fact lie unanalyzed normative judgments about the nature of a claim in given litigation.

In the final excerpt, Professor Gene Nichol further critiques the injury in fact concept by arguing that it is highly manipulable. He makes this point especially in the context of redressability doctrine. Professor Nichol discusses cases involving situations in which the plaintiffs sought an opportunity to participate in certain processes without the intrusion of some governmental act they consider illegal. If one were to frame the issue in terms of injury to an opportunity, then the question of redressability would be whether the relief sought will lead to plaintiff's achievement of such opportunity. On the other hand, if one were to read the injury more narrowly, the question of redressability could become whether or not a specific result actually would be achieved by the plaintiff. In short, redressability analysis can lead to different consequences depending on whether one adopts a relatively broader or narrower conception of injury in fact.

Antonin Scalia, *The Doctrine of Standing as an Essential Element of the Separation of Powers*, 17 SUFFOLK U. L. REV. 881, 881-82, 885-86, 890, 892-97 (1983)*

* * *

My thesis is that the judicial doctrine of standing is a crucial and inseparable element of that principle [of the separation of powers], whose disregard will inevitably produce—as it has during the past few decades—an overjudicialization of the processes of self-governance. More specifically, I suggest that courts need to accord greater weight than they have in recent times to the traditional requirement that the plaintiff's alleged injury be a particularized one, which sets him apart from the citizenry at large.

* * *

II. Recent Changes in the Doctrine

* * * As I would prefer to view the matter, the Court must always hear the case of a litigant who asserts the violation of a legal right. In some cases, the existence of such a right is, on the basis of our common-law traditions, entirely clear—as is the case, for example, when a statutory provision requires an agent of the executive to provide a particular benefit directly to a particular individual. (That was the sort of right asserted in *Marbury v. Madison*.) In other cases, however, the legislative intent to create a legal right is much more problematic—for example, when Congress requires the executive to implement a general program (such as environmental protection) which will enhance the welfare of many individuals. In such cases, as I view the matter, the courts apply the various "prudential" factors, not by virtue of their own inherent authority to expand or constrict standing, but rather as a set of presumptions derived from common-law tradition designed to determine whether a legal right exists. Thus, when the legislature explicitly *says* that a private right exists, this so-called "prudential" inquiry is displaced. Ultimately, however (as I shall discuss in more detail shortly), there is a limit upon even the power of Congress to convert generalized benefits into legal rights—and that is the limitation imposed by the so-called "core" requirement of standing. It is a limitation, I would assert, only upon the *congressional* power to confer standing, and not

upon the courts, since the courts *have* no such power to begin with.

* * *

III. Standing and the Separation of Powers

* * *

* * * The great change that has occurred in the role of the courts in recent years results in part from their ability to address issues that were previously considered beyond their ken. But in at least equal measure, in my opinion, it results from the courts' ability to address both new and old issues promptly at the behest of almost anyone who has an interest in the outcome. It is of no use to draw the courts into a public policy dispute after the battle is over, or after the enthusiasm that produced it has waned. The *sine qua non* for emergence of the courts as an equal partner with the executive and legislative branches in the formulation of public policy was the assurance of prompt access to the courts by those interested in conducting the debate. The full-time public interest law firm, as permanently in place as the full-time congressional lobby, became a widespread phenomenon only in the last few decades not because prior to that time the courts could not reach issues profoundly affecting public policy; but rather because prior to that time the ability to present those issues at will * * * was drastically circumscribed. The change has been effected by a number of means, including * * * alteration in the doctrine of ripeness (so that suits once thought premature may now be brought at once), and—to return to the point—alteration in the doctrine of standing.

IV. The Separation of Powers and the Rights of Individuals

* * * Is standing functionally related to the distinctive role that we expect the courts to perform? The question is not of purely academic interest, because if there is a functional relationship it may have some bearing upon how issues of standing are decided in particular cases.

There is, I think, a functional relationship, which can best be described by saying that the law of standing roughly restricts courts to their traditional undemocratic role of protecting individuals and minorities against impositions of the majority, and excludes them from the even more undemocratic role of prescribing how the other two branches should function in order to serve the interest *of the majority itself*. Thus, when an individual who is the very *object* of a law's requirement or prohibition seeks to challenge it, he always has standing. This is the classic case of the law bearing down upon the individual himself, and the court will not pause to inquire whether the grievance is a "generalized" one.

---

* Reprinted with permission of the Suffolk University Law Review and Antonin Scalia. All rights reserved.

Contrast that classic form of court challenge with the increasingly frequent administrative law cases in which the plaintiff is complaining of an agency's unlawful *failure* to impose a requirement or prohibition upon *someone else*. Such a failure harms the plaintiff, by depriving him, as a citizen, of governmental acts which the Constitution and laws require. But that harm alone is, so to speak, a *majoritarian* one. The plaintiff may *care* more about it; he may be a more ardent proponent of constitutional regularity or of the necessity of the governmental act that has been wrongfully omitted. But that does not establish that he has been harmed distinctively—only that he assesses the harm as more grave, which is a fair subject for democratic debate in which he may persuade the rest of us. Since our readiness to be persuaded is no less than his own (we are harmed just as much) there is no reason to remove the matter from the political process and place it in the courts. Unless the plaintiff can show some respect in which he is harmed *more* than the rest of us (for example, he is a worker in the particular plant where the Occupational Safety and Health Administration has wrongfully waived legal safety requirements) he has not established any basis for concern that the majority is suppressing or ignoring the rights of a minority that wants protection, and thus has not established the prerequisite for judicial intervention.

That explains, I think, why "concrete injury"—an injury apart from the mere breach of the social contract, so to speak, effected by the very fact of unlawful government action—is the indispensable prerequisite of standing. Only that can separate the plaintiff from all the rest of us who also claim benefit of the social contract, and can thus entitle him to some special protection from the democratic manner in which we ordinarily run our social-contractual affairs. Of course concrete injury is a necessary but not necessarily sufficient condition. The plaintiff must establish not merely minority status, but minority status relevant to the particular governmental transgression that he seeks to correct. If the concrete harm that he will suffer as a consequence of the government's failure to observe the law is purely fortuitous—in the sense that the law was not specifically designed to avoid that harm, but rather for some other (usually more general) purpose—then the majority's failure to require observance of the law cannot be said to be directed *against him*, and his entitlement to the special protection of the courts disappears. That is the essential inquiry conducted under the heading of whether the plaintiff who claims standing has suffered any "legal wrong"; or whether he comes within the definition of "adversely affected" or "aggrieved" party under the various substantive statutes that employ such terms; or whether he is within a substantive statute's protected "zone of interests" * * *.

If I am correct that the doctrine of standing, as applied to challenges to governmental action, is an essential means of restricting the courts to their assigned role of protecting minority rather than majority interests, several consequences follow. First of all, a consequence of some theoretical interest but relatively small practical effect: it would follow that not *all* "concrete injury" indirectly following from governmental action or inaction would be capable of supporting a congressional conferral of standing. One can conceive of such a concrete injury so widely shared that a congressional specification that the statute at issue was meant to preclude precisely that injury would nevertheless not suffice to mark out a subgroup of the body politic requiring judicial protection. For example, allegedly wrongful governmental action that affects "all who breathe." There is surely no reason to believe that an alleged governmental default of such general impact would not receive fair consideration in the normal political process.

A more practical consequence pertains not to congressional power to confer standing, but to judicial interpretation of congressional intent in that regard. If the doctrine does serve the separation-of-powers function I have suggested, then in the process of answering the abstruse question whether a "legal wrong" has been committed, or whether a person is "adversely affected or aggrieved," so that standing does exist, the courts should bear in mind the *object* of the exercise, and should not be inclined to assume congressional designation of a "minority group" so broad that it embraces virtually the entire population. * * *

* * * Even if the doctrine of standing was once meant to restrict judges "solely, to decide on the rights of individuals," what is wrong with having them protect the rights of the majority as well? They've done so well at the one, why not promote them to the other? The answer is that there is no reason to believe they will be any good at it. In fact, they have in a way been specifically *designed* to be bad at it—selected from the aristocracy of the highly educated, instructed to be governed by a body of knowledge that values abstract principle above concrete result, and (just in case any connection with the man in the street might subsist) removed from all accountability to the electorate. That is just perfect for a body that is supposed to protect the individual against the people; it is just terrible (unless you are a monarchist) for a group that is supposed to decide what is good for the people. Where the courts,

in the supposed interest of all the people, do enforce upon the executive branch adherence to legislative policies that the political process itself would not enforce, they are likely (despite the best of intentions) to be enforcing the political prejudices of their own class. * * * It may well be, of course, that the judges know what is good for the people better than the people themselves; or that democracy simply does not permit the *genuine* desires of the people to be given effect; but those are not the premises under which our system operates.

Does what I have said mean that, so long as no minority interests are affected, "important legislative purposes, heralded in the halls of Congress, [can be] lost or misdirected in the vast hallways of the federal bureaucracy?" Of *course* it does—and a good thing, too. Where no peculiar harm to particular individuals or minorities is in question, lots of once-heralded programs ought to get lost or misdirected, in vast hallways or elsewhere. Yesterday's herald is today's bore—although we judges, in the seclusion of our chambers, may not be *au courant* enough to realize it. The ability to lose or misdirect laws can be said to be one of the prime engines of social change, and the prohibition against such carelessness is (believe it or not) profoundly conservative. Sunday blue laws, for example, were widely unenforced long before they were widely repealed—and had the first not been possible the second might never have occurred.

V. Return to the Original Understanding

In the early 1970's * * * the subject addressed by the present paper would have been of merely historical interest. It might have been retitled "Former Relevance of Standing to the Separation of Powers." Since that time, however, the Supreme Court's theory has returned to earlier traditions, and there may be reason to believe that its practice will as well. * * *

* * *

Cass R. Sunstein, *What's Standing After* Lujan? *Of Citizen Suits, "Injuries," and Article III*, 91 MICH. L. REV. 163, 164-66, 197-209, 211-20, 223-31 (1992)*

Introduction

In 1983, Judge Antonin Scalia, of the U.S. Court of Appeals for the District of Columbia Circuit, published a dramatic and provocative essay on the law of standing. The thesis can be found in the title: *The Doctrine of Standing as an Essential Element of the Separation of Powers* [excerpted above]. Only recently named a judge, and having taught administrative and constitutional law for many years, Judge Scalia called for a significant shift in the law of standing.

Judge Scalia's argument hinged on a distinction between two kinds of cases. "[W]hen an individual who is the very *object* of a law's requirement or prohibition seeks to challenge it, he always has standing." But standing should frequently be unavailable when "the plaintiff is complaining of an agency's unlawful *failure* to impose a requirement or prohibition upon *someone else*." In the latter case, Judge Scalia contended that there was a serious interference with executive power. Judge Scalia concluded that in cases of the latter sort, courts should hold that Article III imposes "a limit upon even the power of Congress to convert generalized benefits into legal rights. . . ." * * *

In 1992, Justice Antonin Scalia wrote the dramatic opinion for the Supreme Court in *Lujan v. Defenders of Wildlife*, which significantly shifts the law of standing. The opinion hinges on a distinction between two kinds of cases. "When . . . the plaintiff is himself an object of the action (or forgone action) at issue . . . there is ordinarily little question" that he has standing. "When, however, . . . a plaintiff's asserted injury arises from the government's allegedly unlawful regulation (or lack of regulation) of *someone else*, much more is needed." In the latter case, there is the risk of serious interference with executive power, in the form of a "transfer from the President to the courts" of "the Chief Executive's most important constitutional duty, to 'take Care that the Laws be faithfully executed.'" Through Justice Scalia's opinion, the Court held that Article III required invalidation of an explicit congressional grant of standing to "citizens." The Court had not answered this question before.

Lujan may well be one of the most important standing cases since World War II. Read for all it is worth, the decision invalidates the large number of statutes in which Congress has attempted to use the "citizen-suit" device as a mechanism for controlling unlawfully inadequate enforcement of the law. Indeed, the decision ranks among the most important in history in terms of the sheer number of federal statutes that it apparently has invalidated. The citizen suit has become a staple of federal environmental law in particular: nearly every major environmental

---

* Reprinted with permission of the Michigan Law Review and Cass R. Sunstein. All rights reserved.

statute provides for citizen standing. The place of the citizen in environmental and regulatory law has now been drawn into sharp question.

But the importance of *Lujan* does not lie only in the invalidation of the citizen suit. The decision revises the law of standing in several other ways as well. And it raises a host of new puzzles for later cases to solve.

* * *

II. *Lujan*: Description and Appraisal

* * *

A. *What the Court Said*

The *Lujan* case arose under the Endangered Species Act of 1973 (ESA). The ESA is an aggressive set of protections for endangered species. Its key provision says that "Each Federal agency shall, in consultation with and with the assistance of the Secretary [of the Interior], insure that any action authorized, funded, or carried out by such agency . . . is not likely to jeopardize the continued existence of any endangered species . . . ."

For many years it has been uncertain whether the obligations of the ESA apply to actions of the U.S. government that are taken in foreign countries. In 1978, the relevant authorities agreed that the ESA did indeed apply outside the United States. But in 1983, the Interior Department initiated a change in its position. An important new regulation, ultimately issued in 1986, announced that the ESA would apply only to actions within the United States or on the high seas.

The regulation had a number of important consequences. American agencies funding foreign projects were no longer required to consult with the Secretary of the Interior if their projects would jeopardize the existence of endangered species. The ESA would provide no obstacle to the expenditure of American taxpayer dollars to projects that would threaten to eliminate endangered species outside U.S. borders.

Environmental organizations, including Defenders of Wildlife, brought suit, claiming that the new regulation violated the statute. To establish standing, two members of Defenders of Wildlife claimed that they suffered an injury in fact. Joyce Kelly swore in an affidavit that she had traveled to Egypt in 1986 and viewed the habitat of the endangered Nile crocodile. She claimed that she "intended to do so again, and hoped to observe the crocodile directly." Amy Skilbred claimed that she had traveled to Sri Lanka in 1981 and observed the habitat of "endangered species such as the Asian elephant and the leopard." She also claimed that she intended to return to Sri Lanka to see members of these species. In a deposition, she acknowledged that she did not have a certain date for return.

The Court's opinion, devoted entirely to the issue of standing, is quite straightforward. It falls into four parts: a general statement about standing; a discussion of injury in fact; an assessment of redressability; and a treatment of the citizen suit.

The general statement begins with a description of the function of standing in a system of separation of powers. According to the Court, Article III requires an "irreducible constitutional minimum of standing," with three elements: (1) an injury in fact that is both (a) concrete and particularized and (b) actual or imminent rather than conjectural or hypothetical; (2) a demonstration that the injury is fairly traceable to the acts of the defendant, rather than of some third party; and (3) a showing that it is likely that the injury will be redressed by a decision favorable to the plaintiff.

This opening statement breaks little new ground. But the Court added that the standing issue will often be affected by "whether the plaintiff is himself an object of the action (or forgone action) at issue." If the plaintiff is an object, the three requirements will ordinarily be met. But when an "injury arises from the government's allegedly unlawful regulation (or lack of regulation) of *someone else*, much more is needed." In such cases, there is the problem that "causation and redressability ordinarily hinge on the response of the regulated (or regulable) third party to the government action or inaction—and perhaps on the response of others as well." The Court suggested that in such cases standing "is ordinarily 'substantially more difficult' to establish." * * *

So much for the preliminaries. The Court's first specific holding was that an injury in fact had not been established. The intention to visit the places harboring endangered species was not enough. The plaintiffs had set out no particular plans. They specified no time when their indefinite plans would materialize. Thus they had shown no "actual or imminent" injury. Nor could plaintiffs show injuries in fact by demonstrating a nexus linking the affected habitats with all the world's ecosystems, or linking their own "professional" interests in observing endangered species with the interests of all persons so engaged. The fact that ecosystems are generally interrelated was not enough, because the plaintiffs could not show that they used portions of an ecosystem "perceptibly affected by the unlawful action in question." Standing was similarly not available to anyone having an interest in studying or seeing endangered species, because of a professional commitment or otherwise. There must be "a factual showing of perceptible harm." This, then, was the Court's reasoning on injury in fact.

The second conclusion in Justice Scalia's opinion, accepted by only a plurality of the Court, was that the plaintiffs could not show redressability. * * * There were two problems, suggesting that the plaintiffs might not benefit from a decree in their favor.

First, suppose that the district court awarded relief against the Secretary; suppose that it required the Secretary to issue a regulation mandating consultation with him for foreign projects threatening an endangered species. It would remain unclear that the funding agencies would be bound by this regulation. They might simply ignore it; they might not consult at all. For this reason, there would be no clear benefits to the plaintiffs from a favorable ruling.

Second, the American agencies provide only part of the funding for the relevant foreign projects. Most of the money comes from elsewhere. "AID, for example, has provided less than 10% of the funding" for one of the projects at issue in the case. Justice Scalia found it unclear whether the elimination of that partial fraction would affect the projects or the species in question. "[I]t is entirely conjectural whether the nonagency activity that affects respondents will be altered or affected by the agency action they seek to achieve." The plaintiffs could not show redressability, because a decree on their behalf might not yield their desired result.

The Court's third conclusion was its most important. The court of appeals had relied on the citizen-suit provision of the ESA, permitting "any person [to] commence a civil suit on his own behalf * * * to enjoin any person, including the United States and any other governmental instrumentality or agency . . . who is alleged to be in violation of any provision of this chapter." In a discussion with large consequences, the Court held in effect that this provision was unconstitutional as applied.

The Court emphasized that Article III requires something more than "a generally available grievance about government—claiming only harm to his and every citizen's interest in proper application of the Constitution and laws, and seeking relief that no more directly and tangibly benefits him than it does the public at large." To support this contention, the Court cited cases from the 1920s and 1930s rejecting suits by citizens complaining about government action on constitutional grounds. It also pointed to a number of post-1970 cases appearing to suggest that Article III in fact required a particularized injury.

The Court acknowledged that in none of these cases had Congress explicitly granted citizens a right to bring suit. But in the Court's view, this difference did not matter. The Court emphasized that "[v]indicating the *public* interest (including the public interest in government observance of the Constitution and laws) is the function of Congress and the Chief Executive." In particular, the Court said that if Congress could turn "the undifferentiated public interest in executive officers' compliance with the law into an 'individual right' vindicable in the courts," it would be transferring "from the President to the courts the Chief Executive's most important constitutional duty," that is, "to 'take Care that the Laws be faithfully executed.'" Thus, the Court's decision rested on the fear that, if Congress could grant standing here, it would turn the judges into overseers, and usurpers, of the President himself. Here Article II helped give context to Article III.

* * *

B. *Evaluation*

* * *

1. *Injury*

* * *

If we accept the Court's definition of injury, its conclusion was perhaps an innovation, but not an entirely implausible one. Its chief importance lay in the insistence that the injury must be "imminent." It is true that none of the plaintiffs could prove that they would revisit the relevant sites. So long as injury in fact is required, perhaps this point is decisive. * * *

An argument to the contrary would suggest that one of the original purposes of the injury-in-fact test, made explicit in [*Association of Data Processing Service Organization, Inc. v. Camp*], was to ensure that standing could be a simple, threshold determination, without an elaborate process of assessing the pleadings. In any case, it would be strange and unfortunate if jurisdictional issues turned out to rest on complex factual inquiries. In this light, it might seem to make little sense to require plaintiffs to purchase an airline ticket. Perhaps this is unnecessary formalism. But the Court's point is at least one on which reasonable people can differ. * * *

A trickier issue, not dealt with in any of the opinions, involves the appropriate characterization of the injury. To understand the point, we need to look at a famous case that is seemingly far afield. *Regents of the University of California v. Bakke* presented an often-overlooked problem of standing. Bakke himself could not show that without the affirmative action program he challenged, he would have been admitted to the medical school of the University of California at Davis. It was therefore argued that he could not meet the Article III requirement of injury in fact.

The Court responded in a way that has potentially major implications:

> [E]ven if Bakke had been unable to prove that he would have been admitted in the absence of the special program, it would not follow that he lacked standing. . . . The trial court found such an injury, apart from failure to be admitted, in the University's decision not to permit Bakke to compete for all 100 places in the class, simply because of his race.

What happened here was that the *Bakke* Court found injury, causation, and redressability by the simple doctrinal device of *recharacterizing the injury*. In *Bakke*, the Court described the injury as involving not admission to medical school but the opportunity to compete on equal terms. The Court has not explicitly used this technique in any other case, but it might easily have done so. In *Simon v. Eastern Kentucky Welfare Rights Organization* [*EKWRO*], for example, the Court might have said that the injury consisted not of a refusal of admission to a hospital, but instead of a decision not to permit the plaintiffs to have an opportunity to be admitted on the terms specified by law, simply because of unlawful incentives created by the IRS. In this way, *Bakke* and *EKWRO* were structurally similar. Likewise, in *Allen v. Wright*, the Court might have recharacterized the injury as an opportunity not to have the desegregation process distorted by the incentives created through the grant of unlawful tax deductions to private schools.

Suppose that, in *Lujan* itself, the plaintiffs had claimed that their injury consisted not of an inability to see certain species but of a diminished opportunity to do so. This diminished opportunity allegedly resulted from unlawful government action. On this view, the ESA was designed to ensure not that no species would become extinct—that was not an adequate description of the injury at issue—but more precisely that endangered species would not be subject to increased threats of extinction because of federal governmental action. The injury of which the plaintiffs complained was the harm to their professional and tourist opportunities created by those increased risks.

On this view, the injury in *Lujan* would therefore run parallel to that created by violations of the Equal Protection Clause, which is designed not to ensure that certain people get into medical school, but instead that they are not subject to increased risks of exclusion because of racial factors. Structurally, a plausible conception of the harm in *Lujan* would accord with that in *Bakke*—a harm to an opportunity, here the opportunity to observe certain species.

If *Bakke* is right on the standing question, it is not so easy to explain why the same approach would have been wrong in *Lujan*. If there is a difference between the relevant injuries, it may stem from the fact that the Equal Protection Clause conspicuously protects the right to compete on an equal basis; this is not a contestable interpretation (however much we may dispute what "equal" means). The clause does not confer the right to a certain set of favorable outcomes. The ESA is far more ambiguous on this score. Perhaps the injury against which it guards is the actual loss of an endangered species because of U.S. government action, rather than the diminished opportunity to view such a species in its natural habitat.

But this interpretation is far from clear. Why could we not view the ESA as protecting the right to have the opportunity to see endangered species unaffected by adverse action by government agencies? Surely Congress has the constitutional power to create such a right. But courts may wish to avoid this interpretation in the absence of an especially clear congressional statement. The recharacterization of injuries to include less particularized, "opportunity" harms does expand the category of people entitled to bring suit. At some point the recharacterization will mean that all, or almost all, citizens are harmed in the same way. Prudential considerations might well counsel against this step.

This point suggests that, when Congress has not spoken clearly, courts should not allow injuries to be characterized in such broad terms that the plaintiff is not particularly affected. But in *Lujan*, there was no such problem. The plaintiffs had a fully plausible professional and educational interest in the species at issue. If the plaintiffs had tried to characterize their injury as the diminished opportunity to promote their interests, they should have been permitted to do so. There is little law on this issue, but perhaps inventive plaintiffs will be permitted to make efforts in this direction in the future.

* * *

The third problem involves the notion of injury in fact. I have suggested that whether there is such an injury turns not merely on facts but also on whether the law has recognized certain harms as legal ones. This principle means, for example, that a person in New York has no standing to challenge racial discrimination in Iowa, as no law treats distant discrimination as an injury. The same result would occur with a *Lujan*-style action brought before enactment of the ESA. But now suppose that Congress has given to all Americans a kind of beneficial legal interest in the survival of the Nile crocodile, at least in the sense that it has granted each of us a jointly held property right, operating against acts of the U.S. government that threaten to destroy the species. Suppose too that Congress has granted every American the right to sue to vindicate that property right. What in the Constitution forbids this action? Surely not the Due Process Clause; surely not Article II; and surely not Article III.

I suggest that this is very much what happened in the ESA itself. By creating citizen standing, Congress in essence created the relevant property interest and allowed citizens to vindicate it. To this extent, Congress did indeed create the requisite injury in fact, and the Court should have recognized it as such. If a problem remains, perhaps it lies in Congress' failure to be explicit on the point. This may ultimately be the meaning of Justice Kennedy's concurring opinion, and if so it remains possible for Congress to solve the problem through more careful drafting. * * *

2. *Redressability*

On the question of redressability, there was no majority for the Court. Three [J]ustices saw no problem with redressability; two Justices refused to speak to the issue; four Justices found a constitutional defect. Because no majority spoke, the *Lujan* case has little precedential value on this question.

To evaluate the issue of redressability in the recent cases, it is important to understand why courts require redressability at all. The basic reason is akin to that underlying the prohibition on advisory opinions. Let us suppose that an injury in fact is required. If a decree in the plaintiff's favor will not remedy that injury, is not such a decree an advisory opinion, at least with respect to the plaintiff? If the harm to the plaintiff will persist after the decree, why should the court become involved at all? For this reason, the redressability requirement seems to be a reasonable inference from the requirement of injury in fact. In the abstract, it makes perfect sense.

The difficulty arises in cases in which Congress has attempted to restructure administrative and private incentives so as to bring about structural or systemic change, but in a way that will not necessarily yield the particular outcomes sought in particular cases. Assume, for example, that Congress expressly forbids the grant of federal funds to international projects that threaten endangered species. If the agency withholds the funds, no particular project will necessarily be stopped, nor will any particular species necessarily be saved. The project may go forward without American participation, or the species may not survive even without the project. Or suppose that Congress forbids universities receiving federal funds from discriminating on the basis of race. If the funds are withheld, discrimination may continue. No prediction on this score can avoid being "speculative."

In cases of this kind, the relevant harm consists of a grant of funds that makes certain harms more likely as a result of the contribution of American tax dollars—the loss of a species or the incidence of discrimination. The examples illustrate what Congress frequently attempts to do in the areas of funding requirements, environmental protection, and risk regulation in general: it attempts to change incentives in a way that should produce aggregate changes without necessarily affecting outcomes in particular cases. * * *

In such cases, *whether an injury is redressable depends on how it is characterized*. If the injury is described in sharply particularistic, common law-like terms, it will not be redressable, since the consequences of victory for any particular plaintiff cannot be ascertained in advance. But if it is characterized as an increased risk of harm—if that is the relevant injury—it will certainly be redressed by a decree in the plaintiff's favor. A decision to require compliance with national ambient air quality standards will make the air cleaner, and that will decrease the risk of harm to people in the relevant territory. Cases of this sort are a staple of modern administrative law. * * *

The point casts light on Justice Kennedy's suggestion that courts "must be sensitive to the articulation of new rights of action that do not have clear analogs in our common-law tradition." Indeed, in these sorts of cases it makes little sense to ask if a decree in the plaintiff's favor will remedy a common law-like injury. The question is: What is the harm that Congress sought to prevent? To answer this question, a court has to engage in statutory interpretation. In the end, the issue of redressability, like that of injury in fact, turns on what Congress has provided. Redressability might even be understood as a crude proxy for an inquiry into legislative instructions about who is entitled to bring suit.

In *Lujan*, the harm Congress sought to prevent would indeed have been redressed by the decree. The alleged violation was a procedural one—that is, a failure to require consultation with the Secretary of the Interior on the fact that the project threatened an endangered species. If we suppose that the injury-in-fact requirement is met, the redressability issue poses no further obstacle. If plaintiffs were injured by the failure to consult, then a decree ordering consultation would have redressed the harm. Of course, survival of the endangered species is not a necessary consequence of the requirement to consult. Perhaps the agencies would refuse to consult; perhaps removal of funding would not affect any species. But none of this is relevant. For purposes of redressability, a requirement of consultation must merely affect incentives in the statutorily required way.

On this point, *Lujan* is self-contradictory, and the internal contradiction helps show why redressability should have presented no problem. The Court acknowledged (without any real explanation) that in some cases involving procedural violations, plaintiffs need not show redressability. The Court stated that "[t]his is not a case where plaintiffs are seeking to enforce a procedural requirement the disregard of which could impair a separate concrete interest of theirs . . ." and added in a crucial footnote: "The person who has been accorded a procedural right to protect his concrete interests can assert that right without meeting all the normal standards for redressability and immediacy."

As noted, the Court did not explain this conclusion * * *. But if plaintiffs need not meet the normal standards for redressability for procedural violations, it follows that plaintiffs in *Lujan* itself need not have met the normal standards for redressability. Indeed, under this reasoning, redressability need not be shown in a wide range of cases in which a plaintiff contends that the executive branch has failed to comply with a procedural requirement imposed by law.

A contrary conclusion would produce surprising results. It would mean that Article III imposed a constitutional obstacle to most ordinary administrative law cases. In the usual case, a litigant contends that an agency has failed to follow some procedural requirement—by holding inadequate hearings, failing to give notice, meeting with private people, or attending to a statutorily irrelevant factor. In all such cases, it might well be said, under the apparent standard in *Lujan*, that the redressability requirement has not been met. In such cases, it is entirely "speculative" whether a decree in the defendant's favor will remedy the alleged injury. *Lujan* cannot be understood to say that these conventional cases have all of a sudden become nonjusticiable.

* * *

3. Citizen Suits

By far the most important and novel holding in *Lujan* was that Congress cannot grant standing to citizens. The largest conclusion, also set out in Justice Scalia's 1983 *Suffolk Law Review* article, is that Article III requires a concrete, particularized, actual, or imminent injury in fact that also satisfies the causation and redressability requirements. * * *

* * *

b. Article II and the Take Care Clause. The Court's * * * argument is that standing limitations for citizens are necessary in order to protect against intrusions on the President's power under the Take Care Clause. This is an extremely important claim. It links Justice Scalia's *Lujan* opinion with his insistence elsewhere on a "unitary executive," one that is free from interference by others.[225] * * * But what is the precise relationship between standing limitations and the President's power to take care that the laws be faithfully executed?

From its text and history, it seems clear that the Take Care Clause confers both a duty and a power and that it does indeed impose limits on what courts can do to the bureaucracy. The Take Care Clause confers a power insofar as it grants to the President, and no one else, the authority to oversee the execution of federal law. The provision therefore carries implications for the perennial question of the President's power over the administration. It also suggests that oversight of bureaucratic implementation falls to the President, not to Congress or the courts.

But the Take Care Clause confers a duty insofar as it imposes on the President both a responsibility to be faithful to law and an obligation to enforce the law as it has been enacted, rather than as he would have wished it to be. It is for this reason that the standard administrative law case raises no issue under the Take Care Clause. If an object of regulation establishes that an agency has enforced the law in an unlawful way, the President has violated his duty under the Take Care Clause. A judicial decree to this effect raises no problem under that clause; it merely enforces the constitutional obligation in the constitutionally authorized way.

This point is not limited to cases involving regulated objects. If a regulatory beneficiary with standing persuades a court that the President is violating the law, and the court so holds, there is no constitutional difficulty. Imagine, for example, that the plaintiffs in *Lujan* had purchased their plane tickets and made plans to leave for the relevant countries on a certain date. The *Lujan* Court acknowledged that such circumstances would give rise to standing.

---

[225] *See* Morrison v. Olson, 487 U.S. 654, 727 (1988) (Scalia, J., dissenting).

If the plaintiffs proceeded to win on the merits, no problem would arise under the Take Care Clause. A judicial decision for the plaintiffs would signal that the President had violated his constitutional command to respect and enforce the ESA as enacted.

We can thus conclude that the Take Care Clause poses no problems in suits by regulated objects, and also no problem in suits by regulatory beneficiaries, even if they are requiring the executive to enforce certain laws against his will. All of this suggests that the relationship between standing limits and the Take Care Clause is at best ambiguous—and in the end, I believe, nonexistent. If a court could set aside executive action at the behest of plaintiffs with a plane ticket, why does the Take Care Clause forbid it from doing so at the behest of plaintiffs without a ticket? Why do courts become "virtually continuing monitors of the wisdom and soundness of Executive action" if they hear claims of official illegality in the second class of cases?

These questions do not establish that there are no limits on standing. But they do raise doubts about the relevance of the Take Care Clause. In fact they suggest that the clause, however relevant it may be to many issues on administrative law, is irrelevant to the question of standing.

Lujan seems to be built in key part on the idea that citizen standing—like other legislative interference with the President's power to execute the law—is unacceptable under Article II. Indeed, many of the recent standing cases might be thought to be Article II cases masquerading under the guise of Article III; we may even say that the Article II tail is wagging the Article III dog. But the conflation of Article II and Article III concerns has led to serious confusion. If a plaintiff with a plane ticket can sue under the ESA without offense to Article II, then it makes no sense to say that Article II is violated if a plaintiff lacking such a ticket initiates a proceeding. Beneficiary standing poses no Article II issue. The two articles raise quite different concerns; they should be analyzed separately.

The Court's answer, set out in a brief passage, appears to take the following form. It is one thing for judges to protect "individual rights." Courts can properly engage in this task, which is uniquely theirs. But it is another thing to protect "public rights that have been legislatively pronounced to belong to each individual who forms part of the public." In the end, however, this argument seems to have little to do with the Take Care Clause. Instead, it must rest on the understanding that Article III places a substantive limitation on what sorts of harms can count as legally cognizable injuries.

* * *

c. Article III. In the end the best defense of *Lujan* must be that Article III allows federal courts to assume jurisdiction only when the plaintiff has a certain sort of interest. The core of the argument appears in Justice Scalia's 1983 article: Cases involving the requisite interests comport with "an accurate description of the sort of business courts had traditionally entertained, and hence of the distinctive business to which they were presumably to be limited under the Constitution." The statement is surprisingly casual. No historical argument is offered for the claim about the traditional "sort of business." Moreover, the word "presumably" takes the place of a complex historical argument.

As a matter of history, * * * Scalia's claim is not sound; in fact, it is baseless. * * * [C]ourts had "traditionally entertained" a wide variety of suits instituted by strangers. Neither English nor American practice supports the view that stranger suits are constitutionally impermissible. There is no evidence that Article III was designed to forbid Congress from entertaining such suits. On the contrary, the practice of the early Congress * * * suggests that there were no limits on congressional creation of standing.

The absence of a firm basis for *Lujan* in constitutional text or history should probably be decisive against the Court's reasoning. If the text and history are compatible with what Congress has done in creating citizen suits, courts have no warrant to intervene. To reach this conclusion, it is not necessary to linger over Justice Scalia's more abstract and speculative argument about the appropriate role of the courts in a democracy, an argument that stems from political theory. But because that argument is obviously influencing the development of standing principles in the Supreme Court and elsewhere, it is worthwhile to address the argument here.

C. Detour I: Justice Scalia's Conception of Standing

In his 1983 essay, Justice Scalia argued that "courts need to accord greater weight than they have in recent times to the traditional requirement that the plaintiff's alleged injury be a particularized one, which sets him apart from the citizenry at large." Scalia acknowledged that this was "not a linguistically inevitable conclusion." The text of Article III does not suggest that a personal injury is necessary. But in his key statement, discussed above, Scalia defended the limitation on grounds of tradition.

Scalia explicitly claimed that "there is a limit upon even the power of Congress to convert generalized benefits into legal rights—and that is the limitation imposed by the so-called 'core' requirement of standing." A central concern is what Scalia describes as the recent rise of the courts as "equal partners" with the legislative and executive branches. In his view, this unfortunate development is related to the law of standing. Thus Scalia suggests that "[t]he *sine qua non* for emergence of the courts as an equal partner with the executive and legislative branches in the formulation of public policy was the assurance of prompt access to the courts by those interested in conducting the debate." Unlimited standing gave people this prompt access, thus impairing the system of separation of powers in two ways: first, by providing more occasions for judicial review of executive action; second, by changing the timing of that review.

The core of Scalia's argument, however, lies elsewhere.

[T]he law of standing roughly restricts courts to their traditional undemocratic role of protecting individuals and minorities against impositions of the majority, and excludes them from the even more undemocratic role of prescribing how the other two branches should function in order to serve the interest of the majority itself.

It is through this lens that Scalia offers the distinction with which I began this article. In the first class of cases, "an individual who is the very *object* of a law's requirement or prohibition seeks to challenge it"; here, standing is simple. In the second class, "the plaintiff is complaining of an agency's unlawful *failure* to impose a requirement or prohibition upon *someone else*"; here the harm is "a *majoritarian* one."

The central point in the analysis is that

[u]nless the plaintiff can show some respect in which he is harmed *more* than the rest of us . . . he has not established any basis for concern that the majority is suppressing or ignoring the rights of a minority that wants protection, and thus has not established the prerequisite for judicial intervention.

Thus, the "doctrine of standing . . . is an essential means of restricting the courts to their assigned role of protecting minority rather than majority interests." Scalia urged that judges had been assigned this role by the Constitution, and also that the other role—the protection of majority interests—would be poorly executed by judges.

* * *

Scalia was alert to the concern that, without broad standing for beneficiaries, legislative enactments would be unlawfully underenforced within the bureaucracy. Indeed, he noted that statutes might get "lost or misdirected" in the executive branch; furthermore, he admitted that this was indeed the consequence of his proposal. But—and this is the article's striking conclusion—this is "a good thing." Executive nonimplementation of statutes is part of a well-functioning democratic process, keeping law current with existing views. "Yesterday's herald is today's bore."

This is a provocative and arresting argument, made in short compass. But it faces several difficulties. One problem is that the argument is strikingly ahistorical. The article does not address the question whether the Framers actually had this conception of Article III. * * * There is considerable evidence to the contrary.

A second problem is that the approach seems inconsistent with some of the most prominent aspects of Justice Scalia's own jurisprudence. Justice Scalia usually insists that judges should read constitutional provisions at a low level of generality and avoid infusing them with broad "values" of their own. In his view, such impositions increase the occasions for judicial invalidation of legislation. In this case, however, Scalia reads Article III broadly, invests it with general, controversial values, and ultimately recommends judicial invalidation of the outcomes of democratic processes. The theory of "minority rights" is after all a controversial theory of democracy, counselling courts to act in some cases but not in others. Let us assume that the argument is plausible, as it indeed appears to be. Should even a plausible theory of this kind be invoked in order to invalidate a law that is not inconsistent with the text and history of the Constitution?

There is a further problem. In a case of beneficiary or citizen standing, courts are not enforcing "executive branch adherence to legislative policies that the political process itself would not enforce." Instead, they are requiring the executive branch to adhere to the law, that is, to outcomes that the political process has endorsed. In *Lujan*, for example, the plaintiffs would have won only if they could have shown an unambiguous legislative judgment in their favor. Standing would produce "legislative policies that the political process itself would not enforce" only if courts systematically misinterpreted statutes. But this seems to be an unsupportable assumption.

In addition, it is hardly a good thing if agency implementation defeats legislative judgments. Suppose, for example, that the EPA decided that statutes calling for a form of cost-benefit balancing should be construed not to allow consideration of costs, and thus to require a kind of environmental absolutism. Would it be plausible to say that this is "a good thing," so long as the agency, supervised as it is by the President, had so concluded? Surely not. Agency rejection of congressional enactments, even if motivated by the President himself, is inconsistent with the system of separation of powers.

* * *

To bring this problem closer to the standing issue, suppose that an agency decides that the ESA should not be applied to American activities in foreign nations, when in fact Congress plainly intended that the ESA should apply abroad. Is this a good thing? On the contrary, it is a violation of democratic aspirations and (more relevant still) of the system for national lawmaking set up by Articles I and II of the Constitution. If agency enforcement beyond that intended by Congress is not "a good thing," even where the agency responds to political pressures, it is not "a good thing" where an agency undertakes a pattern of enforcement that violates congressional will through abdication or failure to act. Asymmetry on this point would simply translate judicial antipathy to regulation into administrative law. The foreclosure of standing cannot plausibly be defended as a means of allowing the bureaucracy to implement the law in a manner that conflicts with the governing statute.

Let us turn, finally, to Justice Scalia's argument from democratic theory, referred to briefly in *Lujan* itself. That argument rests on a distinction between minority and majority interests. The distinction between regulatory objects and regulatory beneficiaries, for purposes of standing, is said to rest on this prior distinction, which is itself said to be well adapted to the special role of courts in the American legal system. "Objects" represent a minority whose interests require judicial protection; "beneficiaries" represent a majority who can protect their concerns through the political process. But there are two problems with this argument. The first is that it does not justify a distinction between the objects and beneficiaries of regulation. The second is that it turns on an inadequate conception of the workings of American democracy.

Suppose we agreed that courts should not protect majority interests through administrative law. The result would be to jeopardize standing for many objects of regulation, not merely for beneficiaries. Often the objects of regulation are indeed majority interests. A regulation might, for example, affect a large number of companies at once, and in the process impose costs principally on consumers, which is to say on nearly all of us. Majorities are affected even when "objects" are at risk. But objects are not therefore to be deprived of standing, at least not without wreaking havoc on traditional administrative law. Indeed, the objects of regulation are not systematically more likely to be "majorities" than the beneficiaries. If we were to build our theory of standing on majority status, we must rethink standing in important ways—but not in the ways recommended by Justice Scalia. The majority-minority distinction is too crude a basis for distinguishing beneficiaries from objects.

Now let us turn to the workings of American democracy. Justice Scalia's argument seems to be that courts are well-suited to protecting minorities, which cannot protect themselves through the democratic process, whereas they are in a poor position to protect majorities, whose natural forum is the democratic process. The politically responsive institution is in turn the executive branch.

But this argument is too simple. Some minorities are especially well-organized and do indeed have access to the political process, including the executive branch. The point is well documented. At least sometimes, regulated industries are a prominent example. But they are not therefore to be deprived of standing.

Moreover, some majorities are so diffuse and ill-organized that they face systematic transaction costs barriers to the exercise of ongoing political influence. This point is well documented in the area of environmental protection and elsewhere. The citizen suit is designed as a corrective. Essentially, this cause of action reflects the congressional judgment that some interests, including those of majorities, are so diffuse and unorganized that they require judicial protection in the implementation process. Congress' judgment to this effect receives distinguished support from a significant body of empirical and analytic literature. Even if judges do not agree with that judgment, they should not foreclose the cause of action in the name of the Constitution.

I conclude that Justice Scalia's essay does not justify the view that Article III forbids the citizen suit. If Congress has chosen to rely on the citizen suit, courts should not foreclose that choice.

* * *

III. The Future

Lujan settled some important questions. But it left many issues open, and it raised at least as many new ones. * * *

* * *

A. Easy Cases: What Lujan Permits

The *Lujan* opinion does not reject a number of cases in which courts have given standing to environmental plaintiffs. On the contrary, it expressly endorses many such cases, even when the plaintiff is complaining that the executive has taken inadequate action to enforce the law. To this extent, the invalidation of the citizen suit allows a good deal of room for private litigants—regulatory beneficiaries—to initiate proceedings against the executive branch. The case therefore introduces some uncertainty into the law, but it probably does not work any fundamental shift in the environmental area.

The Court thus makes clear that, if an environmental plaintiff can show that its members use the particular environmental resource that is at risk, standing is available. It follows, for example, that a citizen in New York could, post-*Lujan*, complain about the failure to enforce clean air or clean water requirements in New York. * * *

It also remains clear that some procedural injuries can produce standing under Article III. The Court writes:

> This is not a case where plaintiffs are seeking to enforce a procedural requirement the disregard of which could impair a separate concrete interest of theirs (e.g., the procedural requirement for a hearing prior to denial of their license application, or the procedural requirement for an environmental impact statement before a federal facility is constructed next door to them).

A citizen can thus complain about a failure to prepare an environmental impact statement (EIS) even though it is "speculative" whether the statement will cause the project to be abandoned.

Standing remains available in all cases under the National Environmental Policy Act (NEPA) whenever plaintiffs can show that the project, if completed, would adversely affect their interests. A concrete injury of this kind is sufficient even if ordinary redressability cannot be shown. "The person who has been accorded a procedural right to protect his concrete interests can assert that right without meeting all the normal standards for redressability and immediacy."

It is clear that the Court believes this; but, as noted above, it is not clear why the Court does so. If Article III requires redressability, most NEPA suits indeed seem unconstitutional. In the typical NEPA action, there is no assurance that completion of an adequate EIS would have any consequence at all for the plaintiffs. One might well think, as the government urged in *Lujan*, that NEPA suits frequently violate Article III.

But as the *Lujan* Court appears to acknowledge, this would be an odd and far-reaching conclusion. It is almost always the case that procedural rights have only speculative consequences for a litigant. If a judge is found to have ruled in favor of party A after taking a bribe from party A, it remains speculative whether an unbiased judge would have ruled for party B. Does party B therefore lack standing? Or suppose that an administrator is found to have violated the Administrative Procedure Act by promulgating a regulation without first publishing it for comment in the Federal Register. It is entirely speculative whether compliance would make any difference to the complainants. The *Lujan* Court, however, does not want the redressability requirement to bar standing in such cases.

Perhaps the Court is endorsing Justice Kennedy's suggestion that "Congress has the power to define injuries and articulate chains of causation that will give rise to a case or controversy where none existed before." More deeply, however, I think that the Court's conclusion on this point exemplifies several of the problems associated with the whole notion of redressability. A procedural right is created, not because it necessarily yields particular outcomes, but because it structures incentives and creates pressures that Congress has deemed important to effective regulation. The same is true for the sorts of interests at stake in the ESA and in many other environmental statutes. Congress is attempting not to dictate outcomes but to create procedural guarantees that will produce certain regulatory incentives. * * *

This point might well have arisen in *Lujan* itself. Even though it did not, the opinion makes clear that procedural harms remain cognizable when ordinary injuries are involved, despite the absence of redressability.

B. Easy Cases: What Lujan Forecloses

Thus far I have explained the types of suits *Lujan* has left untouched. But it is equally clear that *Lujan* forecloses "pure" citizen suits. In these suits, a stranger with an ideological or law-enforcement interest initiates a proceeding against the government, seeking to require an agency to undertake action of the sort required by law. Many environmental statutes now allow such actions, and plaintiffs have brought many suits of this kind. Under *Lujan*, these suits are unacceptable. Congress must at a minimum "identify the injury it seeks to vindicate and relate the injury to the class of persons entitled to bring suit." If Congress has simply given standing to citizens, this requirement has not been met. The plaintiff must point to a concrete injury, not merely to a congressional grant of standing.

C. *Injury in Fact?*

The discussion thus far has focused to a large extent on changes in the law of injury in fact. *Lujan* extends this change, placing a renewed emphasis on the notion that the harm must be imminent and nonspeculative. This requirement will likely carry more weight than it has in the past. Before *Lujan*, requiring people to obtain a plane ticket or to make firm plans to visit the habitat of endangered species might well have been unnecessarily formalistic. Now such actions are apparently required. But this is not a fundamental revision of previous law. * * *

Harder questions could arise in consumer cases, which play a large role in contemporary administrative law. Suppose, for example, that the government imposes on automobile manufacturers fuel economy requirements that are less stringent than the law requires. Typically, plaintiffs will argue that their injury consists of a diminished opportunity to purchase the products in question. After *Lujan*, standing becomes a difficult issue in such cases. A court might find that the plaintiffs lack a concrete or particularized interest. They are perhaps not readily distinguished from the public at large. There is an issue about speculativeness as well: perhaps the relationship between a consumer and a product that he allegedly wants is the same as the relationship between the *Lujan* plaintiffs and an endangered species, in the sense that in neither case is it clear that the injury will occur as a result of the complained-of government acts.

A consumer case of this sort may differ from *Lujan*, however, in the important sense that a consumer who complains of a diminished opportunity to purchase a product can very plausibly claim that he will in fact purchase that product. This claim is probably less speculative than that in *Lujan*. It is possible to discount an "intention" to undertake difficult foreign travel at an unspecified time; the intention may not show sufficient likelihood of harm. But it is harder to discount an intention to purchase a specified product, which usually applies to a single, simple transaction. The distinction suggests that, at least as *Lujan* stands, it does not significantly affect the standard consumers' action. In the automobile case, the key point is that a more-or-less sharply defined category of consumers is distinctly affected in a relatively nonspeculative way, and this is probably enough for standing.

The same would be true in the standard broadcasting case, in which listeners or viewers in a defined area, or of defined programming, challenge an FCC decision that bears on their programming choices. If the FCC refuses to license a classical music station, there is a concrete injury, and it is sufficiently particularized under *Lujan*. The intention to listen to a station is not as conjectural as the travel intention at issue in *Lujan*.

Greater difficulties may arise in some similar actions, as when, for example, consumers challenge an FDA or EPA regulation allowing carcinogens to be added to food. There may be serious standing problems in such cases. A person complaining about such a regulation might be said to be suffering an injury that is speculative or generalized. This is especially likely insofar as the injury is characterized as an actual incidence of cancer. It is extremely speculative to suggest that the introduction of carcinogenic substances into food additives will produce cancer in particular human beings.

The issue becomes harder if the injury is characterized as a greater risk of cancer. In that event, the injury is less speculative; but it is unclear that it is sufficiently particularized. On Justice Kennedy's view, there is probably enough for standing, for he insisted that standing can exist even if the injury is very widely shared. This is indeed the correct view, because it is the most plausible conception of the injury that Congress sought to prevent. But the issue is now open.

D. *Redressability*

Because only four justices concluded that the redressability requirement had not been met in *Lujan*, the case probably offers no real lessons on that issue. After *Lujan*, the law of redressability thus remains as it was before: Extremely fuzzy and highly manipulable. It is manipulable, first, because there is no clear metric by which to decide whether it is "speculative" to say that a decree will remedy the plaintiff's injury. It is manipulable, second, because, as we have seen, whether an injury is redressable depends on how it is defined. If the injury in the *Bakke* case was defined as the right to attend law school, the redressability requirement was violated. If the injury in a standard environmental case is defined as the right not to suffer concrete personal health damage as a result of environmental harm, many environmental plaintiffs will be unable to show redressability. If, however, the injury is defined as freedom from a certain risk of health damage, there is no problem of redressability. This indeed appears to be the way courts conventionally treat the issue.

* * *

If we were to start afresh, the best way to handle the issue would be to say that the question of standing depends on whether Congress has authorized the plaintiff to bring suit. We should be asking whether the injury that Congress sought to prevent would likely be redressed by a favorable judgment. The redressability requirement might be understood as a crude way of asking that very question under the general rubric of "injury in fact." We might therefore try to answer the redressability question by characterizing the injury in the way desired by Congress, and then seeing if that injury would be removed by a decree in the plaintiff's favor. Through this route, the question of characterization could be resolved through legislative judgments, not judicial ones. And while the resulting issues of statutory interpretation will not always be simple, they raise the right questions.

E. *What Role Remains for the Citizen Suit?*

The status of the citizen suit is somewhat obscure after *Lujan*. At a minimum, we know that Congress cannot grant standing to people who have no personal stake in the outcome of an agency action. But Justice Kennedy, joined by Justice Souter, said that Congress "has the power to define injuries and articulate chains of causation that will give rise to a case or controversy where none existed before." This is a potentially crucial phrase. What does it mean? At a minimum, it means that Congress can create rights foreign to the common law. These include the right to be free from discrimination, the right to occupational safety, indeed, the vast panoply of statutory rights going beyond common law understandings. It must also mean that Congress has the power to find causation, perhaps deploying its factfinding power, where courts would not do so. Justice Kennedy thus suggests that Congress can find causation and redressability even where courts would disagree. Perhaps courts will review such findings under a deferential standard.

This view would not change the outcome in *Lujan*. In that case, there was no injury in fact. But it might well make a difference in the several cases in which the Court has previously rejected standing on grounds of causation and redressability. Congress might well have the power to alter those outcomes.

Suppose, for example, that Congress found that efforts to produce desegregation were adversely affected by a grant of tax deductions to schools that discriminated on the basis of race. This finding might well call for a reversal of the outcome in *Allen v. Wright*. Or suppose that Congress found that failure to attain national ambient air quality standards in New York had adverse health effects on the citizens of New York, New Jersey, Connecticut, and Pennsylvania. Perhaps courts would have to respect this finding.

The more difficult question involves constraints on Congress' "power to define injuries." Can Congress say that opportunity-type injuries are legally cognizable? Might Congress follow the *Bakke* strategy and conclude that standing exists in many cases involving increases in risks or attempts to alter incentives? *Lujan* provides no authoritative answer. But Justice Kennedy's concurrence suggests that Congress does possess power to define these events as injuries for purposes of standing. Justice Kennedy emphasized that standing need not be based solely on common law-like injuries; his concern was that, in creating the citizen suit, Congress had not even identified the injury it was attempting to redress. Congress can meet this concern by identifying injuries, building on the common law framework to recognize probabilistic, systemic, or regulatory harms. The decreased probability of injury, the grant of opportunities, and the provision of appropriate incentives are key goals of the regulatory state. It should not be difficult for Congress to connect these goals to the injuries it seeks to prevent. Nothing in Article III forbids this course, even after *Lujan*.

* * *

William A. Fletcher, *The Structure of Standing*, 98 YALE L.J. 221, 221, 223–34 (1988)*

Introduction
* * *

As currently constructed, standing is a preliminary jurisdictional requirement, formulated at a high level of generality and applied across the entire domain of law. In individual cases, the generality of the doctrine often forces us to leave unarticulated important considerations that bear on the question of whether standing should be granted or denied. This consequence is obvious in the apparent lawlessness of many standing cases when the wildly vacillating results in those cases are explained in the analytic

---

* Reprinted with permission of The Yale Law Journal Company, Fred B. Rothman & Company, and William A. Fletcher. All rights reserved.

terms made available by current doctrine. But we mistake the nature of the problem if we condemn the results in standing cases. The problem lies, rather, in the structure of the doctrine.

* * *

I. Origins of Modern Standing Law

* * * It is * * * clear that current standing law is a relatively recent creation. In the late nineteenth and early twentieth centuries, a plaintiff's right to bring suit was determined by reference to a particular common law, statutory, or constitutional right, or sometimes to a mixture of statutory or constitutional prohibitions and common law remedial principles. * * * [N]o general doctrine of standing existed. Nor, indeed, was the term "standing" used as the doctrinal heading under which a person's right to sue was determined. As late as 1923, in *Frothingham v. Mellon*, the Supreme Court denied a federal taxpayer the right to challenge the federal Maternity Act on the ground that the taxpayer's interest was "minute and indeterminable" without ever employing the word "standing."

The creation of a separately articulated and self-conscious law of standing can be traced to two overlapping developments in the last half-century: the growth of the administrative state and an increase in litigation to articulate and enforce public, primarily constitutional, values. As private entities increasingly came to be controlled by statutory and regulatory duties, as government increasingly came to be controlled by statutory and constitutional commands, and as individuals sought to control the greatly augmented power of the government through the judicial process, many kinds of plaintiffs and would-be plaintiffs sought the articulation and enforcement of new and existing rights in the federal courts. Beginning in earnest in the 1930's, the Supreme Court began to develop a new doctrine, or perhaps more accurately, a new set of loosely linked proto-doctrines, to replace the relatively stable formulations that had previously been used to decide who could sue to enforce various rights.

Among the difficult questions posed by the enormous growth of administrative agencies in the 1930's, one of the most prominent was how to determine who could sue to enforce the legal duties of an agency. It was not feasible to infer simply from the existence of an agency's duty that any plaintiff who might benefit from the performance of the duty should have the right to enforce it. In some circumstances, the most desirable scheme might be to permit standing broadly, conferring the right to sue on "private attorneys general" who, for reasons of public policy, should be permitted to sue as appropriate guardians of the public interest. In other circumstances, the most desirable scheme might be to grant standing narrowly, refusing to give it even to some of those directly affected by the actions of the agency * * *.

Both before and after the enactment of the Administrative Procedure Act, standing determinations were based on an amalgam of statutory interpretation and common law assumptions. In some cases, the substantive statute clearly denied standing. For example, the act providing for veterans' benefits prohibited judicial review of the agency's denial of such benefits, even when sought by the veteran whose claim was at stake. In other cases, the statute explicitly conferred standing. For example, the Communications Act of 1934 conferred standing on "any . . . person . . . aggrieved or whose interests [are] adversely affected by any decision of the [Federal Communications] Commission complained of," whether or not that person alleged an interest that the Commission was legally required to consider in making its decision. In still others, where the statute was silent, the Court looked to see if the right was analogous to a recognized common law right of property, contract, or tort. The Administrative Procedure Act, enacted in 1946, provided judicial review of agency actions to a "person . . . adversely affected or aggrieved by [agency] action within the meaning of [a] relevant statute," but it is fairly clear that the reference to "relevant statute" was intended not only to continue the flexibility and variation in response to particular statutory grants and purposes, but also to continue the reliance on common law analogies and assumptions to provide texture and meaning to the statutes.

The increase in litigation over public values is more difficult to pinpoint in time because litigation in this country has always been used to articulate and enforce public values. But, generally speaking, federal litigation in the 1960's and 1970's increasingly involved attempts to establish and enforce public, often constitutional, values by litigants who were not individually affected by the conduct of which they complained in any way markedly different from most of the population. * * *

* * *

II. The Essential Nature of the Standing Question

* * *

A true standing decision determines whether a plaintiff has a right to judicial relief in any federal court, not just the Supreme Court. The essence of a true standing question is the following: Does the plaintiff have a legal right to judicial enforcement of an asserted legal duty? This question should be seen as a question of substantive law, answerable by reference to the statutory or constitutional provision whose protection is invoked. * * *

A. Injury in Fact

Properly understood, standing doctrine should not require that a plaintiff have suffered "injury in fact." I shall elaborate on this view, using as my point of departure a case that specifically disavows it. In *Association of Data Processing Service Organizations v. Camp*, an association of data processors sued to invalidate a rule promulgated by the Comptroller of the Currency permitting national banks to provide data processing services to other banks and to bank customers. More damage to the intellectual structure of the law of standing can be traced to *Data Processing* than to any other single decision. The issue was whether the association was entitled to judicial review under section 10(a) of the Administrative Procedure Act and two substantive statutes, the Bank Service Corporation Act and the National Bank Act. Justice Douglas, writing for the Court, set forth a two-fold test requiring that plaintiffs allege "injury in fact" and that "the interest sought to be protected by the complainant [be] arguably within the zone of interests to be protected or regulated by the statute or constitutional guarantee in question." * * *

It has become part of the received wisdom since *Data Processing* that a plaintiff must show "injury in fact" in order for an Article III federal court to hear the dispute. Even the *Data Processing* dissenters, who rejected the "arguably within the zone of interests" part of the test, agreed that "injury in fact" was a constitutional requirement. * * * *Data Processing* was the first case to state that "injury in fact" was required, and to formulate the issue of plaintiff's standing as a factual (and therefore an ostensibly non-normative) matter.

Since *Data Processing*, the Court has treated the "injury in fact" requirement as part of the basic conceptual scheme of Article III, both inside and outside the administrative law setting in which the term had its origin. * * * Despite the Court's uncritical acceptance of the "injury in fact" requirement, it is a singularly unhelpful, even incoherent, addition to the law of standing.

Professor Jaffe argued in the 1960's that the federal courts were not, as a historical matter, constitutionally forbidden to entertain "public actions." I am inclined to agree with him as a historical matter, but I will not argue against the "injury in fact" test on that ground here. Rather, I wish to show that the "injury in fact" requirement cannot be applied in a non-normative way. There cannot be a merely factual determination whether a plaintiff has been injured except in the relatively trivial sense of determining whether plaintiff is telling the truth about her sense of injury.

If we put to one side people who lie about their states of mind, we should concede that anyone who claims to be injured is, in fact, injured if she can prove the allegations of her complaint. If this is so, there can be no practical significance to the Court's "injury in fact" test because all people sincerely claiming injury automatically satisfy it. This should be so because to impose additional requirements under the guise of requiring an allegation of "injury in fact" is not to require a neutral, "factual" showing, but rather to impose standards of injury derived from some external normative source. There is nothing wrong with a legal system imposing such external standards of injury; indeed, that is what a legal system must do when it decides which causes of action to recognize as valid legal claims. However, in employing such standards, we measure something that is ascertainable only by reference to a normative structure.

A homely example can be used to illustrate the point. Imagine two siblings who compare, as children will, the treatment they receive from their parents. If one child receives a new bicycle, the other child may complain if he does not also receive a new bicycle or some equivalent. A parent who has just bought a bicycle for one child is likely to say (or at least I have found myself saying) to the complaining child, "It doesn't hurt you that I got a bicycle for your sister." Of course, I am wrong if I say that. The child *is* feeling hurt. What I really mean, or should mean if I think about it, is that the child should not feel hurt; or that the child has no "right" to feel hurt; or that I do not wish to recognize the feeling as a hurt (perhaps because if I so recognized it, I would feel some obligation to avoid doing what has caused it). The complaining child is invoking a sort of familial equal protection clause: What the parents give to one child, they must give to the other. The parent, in denying that injury exists, is not denying the sense of injury but is, rather, denying the existence of such a family norm.

Another example can be used, this time from law. Imagine someone who is seriously concerned about federal government cutbacks in welfare payments, but who is not himself a welfare recipient. He feels so strongly about the matter that he occasionally loses sleep after walking past homeless people sleeping in the streets, and he spends money he would not otherwise spend to support a private charity providing aid to the homeless. If such a person brings suit challenging the cutback as contrary to the governing statute, we might be inclined to say that he is not "injured in fact." We are wrong here, too. The person *is* injured "in fact." We may be led to see this if we imagine a case in which my neighbor's dog is chained in his back yard, close to my bedroom window, and barks all night. I lose sleep, and I spend money on earplugs and a double glazed window. In other words, my injuries are comparable to those of the person in the homeless example, for I lose sleep and spend money. In this context, we say quite readily that I have been injured "in fact." Indeed, the law agrees with the assessment of injury and protects me with a cause of action for nuisance.

The case of my neighbor's dog should force us to rethink the conclusion in the homeless example that there was no "injury in fact." A statement that a plaintiff in such a case suffered no "injury in fact" was based on some normative judgment about what ought to constitute a judicially cognizable injury in the particular context, not whether an actual injury occurred. What we mean, or should mean if we think about it, is that he is not hurt in a way that we wish the courts to recognize—perhaps because it is obvious that other people (the homeless) are hurt in what we conceive to be a more direct and serious way, because we may not wish to help the homeless when the claim of injury comes from someone whom we consider to be a bystander, or even because we simply do not wish to help the homeless.

I am not suggesting that the nature and degree of a person's injury should be irrelevant to a determination of whether that person should have a cause of action to protect the asserted right. Quite the contrary, for the nature and degree of injury are critical issues in deciding whether to provide legal protection. But it cannot be seen as a merely "factual" question. Rather, it must be seen as part of the question of the nature and scope of the substantive legal right on which plaintiff relies.

If this is so, it impedes rather than assists analysis to insist that "case or controversy" under Article III requires as a minimum threshold an "injury in fact," in the words of *Data Processing*, or a "distinct and palpable injury," in the words of *Warth v. Seldin*. If such a requirement of injury is a constitutional minimum that Congress cannot remove by statute, the Court is either insisting on something that can have no meaning beyond a requirement that plaintiff be truthful about the injury she is claiming to suffer, or the Court is *sub silentio* inserting into its ostensibly factual requirement of injury a normative structure of what constitutes judicially cognizable injury that Congress is forbidden to change.

Although the Court is not accustomed to thinking of its Article III standing doctrine this way—indeed, those who have insisted most strongly on the "injury in fact" requirement are accustomed to thinking of the proper judicial role in quite the opposite way—superimposing an "injury in fact" test upon an inquiry into the meaning of a statute is a way for the Court to enlarge its powers at the expense of Congress. To use a phrase that is particular anathema to those members of the Court most anxious to tell us that there are Article III limitations on statutory grants of standing, one may even say that the "injury in fact" test is a form of substantive due process. For the Court to limit the power of Congress to create statutory rights enforceable by certain groups of people—to limit, in other words, the power of Congress to create standing—is to limit the power of Congress to define and protect against certain kinds of injury that the Court thinks it improper to protect against.

Where standing to enforce statutorily established duties is at issue, an "injury in fact" requirement operates as a limitation on the power normally exercised by a legislative body. One may couch the limitation in relatively old-fashioned terms and say that it restricts the power of the legislature to create causes of action. Or one may couch it in more modern language and say that it limits the power of the legislature to articulate public values and choose the manner in which they may be enforced. In significant part, a debate over what constitutes "injury in fact" sufficient for Article III is thus a debate about separation of powers and the respective responsibilities of Congress and the Court. Behind the Court's insistence on "injury in fact" as a constitutional test lies a desire to avoid "an overjudicialization of the processes of self-governance." Yet, as I have just suggested, the "injury in fact" requirement, if seriously insisted on, may have quite the opposite consequence. If there is a problem of excessive "judicialization," the solution lies elsewhere. * * *

Gene R. Nichol, Jr., *Rethinking Standing*, 72 CAL. L. REV. 68, 73-75, 78-82 (1984)*

* * *

* * * [T]he law of standing has become so disjointed that the danger now exists that the Court will come to accept it as a manipulable doctrine whose primary value lies in its ability to serve nonjurisdic-

---

* Copyright 1984 by California Law Review Inc. Reprinted with permission of California Law Review Inc. and Gene R. Nichol. All rights reserved.

tional ends. Standing law is unsatisfactory in part, of course, because of unprincipled decisionmaking. More importantly, however, its shortcomings can also be traced to the weakness of its claimed foundation—injury in fact.

A. Tracking Injury

The entire body of modern standing law has its roots in the concept of injury in fact. When the Supreme Court adopted the injury-in-fact test in the 1970 decision *Association of Data Processing Service Organizations, Inc. v. Camp*, it apparently sought to accomplish two important objectives. First, it sought to liberalize access to the federal courts. Second, the Court attempted to give content to the Administrative Procedure Act's grant of standing to a person "aggrieved by agency action within the meaning of a relevant statute."

More important for analytical purposes, however, is the Court's search in *Data Processing* for an overriding principle, removed from the likelihood of ultimate recovery, the desirability of the claim on the merits, or principles of separation of powers, to instruct the threshold standing inquiry. In theory, therefore, the injury-in-fact principle seeks to establish a minimum quantum of constitutionally required harm—hopefully to be measured in something akin to an objective fashion—necessary to invoke the federal judicial power. The injury-in-fact standard sought to broaden judicial access by diverting attention from the legal interests asserted—which, under pre-*Data Processing* standards, easily folded the standing inquiry into a decision on the merits—to objective, concrete harm. Consider the appellation itself—injury *in fact*—as distinguished, one supposes, from injury protected by law. The monetary loss that arises from the competition of national banks, for example, is objective and indisputable without regard for any "legal" interest. Thus, as a standing principle, injury in fact seemed ideal since it ensured a personal stake by hinging itself to harm and separating itself from the claim on the merits because it was not dependent upon interests created or protected by law.

This concept of standing performed well initially. In the years immediately following *Data Processing*, the Court interpreted its liberalized standard to encompass various forms of economic loss, the threat of criminal prosecution, and even esthetic or environmental injuries. Each of these harms, quite distinct from any interest established by statute or constitutional provision, created standing where it would have been questionable before.

The injury-in-fact test, however, soon began to break away from its moorings. The Court, in giving standing to environmental claims, relied on injuries that were not only intangible, but also subjective in the sense that they necessarily depended upon the psychological makeup of the plaintiff. In its prior decisions concerning legislative reapportionment and the establishment clause, the Court found sufficient injuries such as vote dilution and the degradation resulting from the "union of government and religion." Such harms could not be separated from legal interests as easily as the Court might have hoped when it created the *Data Processing* standard. As a final complication, Congress began to grant statutory standing even when the interests to be asserted were relatively abstract and widely shared.

The Burger Court responded to this recognition of intangible, subjective, shared, or legally related injuries by attempting to tighten the injury-in-fact standard. Article III now requires "distinct" and "palpable" injury. No judicial definition of the new term has been offered, but I assume it requires that a litigant suffer tangible injury that distinguishes him from the populace at large. The cases reveal, however, that despite valiant attempts the Court has been unable to maintain such a line. The difficulty has arisen because the injury standard is being asked to do much more than it was designed to accomplish, and much more than it can reasonably be expected to achieve.

* * *

The distinct and palpable injury standard has failed to provide a neutral and objectively ascertainable method of measuring access to the federal courts. As standing jurisprudence began to embrace subjective and intangible interests, the term "injury in fact" offered little guidance in measuring the scope of the case or controversy requirement. At the same time, when faced with shared constitutional claims, the Court began to sense that liberal standing rules posed a threat to the appropriate separation of powers. The Court's response, rather than tying constitutional harm to comprehensible standards, has been to taint its analysis of harm by including extraneous considerations. If the particularized injury standard was designed to supply an overarching measurement of judicial authority, removed from the merits of the claim or concern for separation of powers, it no longer performs that task.

B. Injury and Redressability

The injury concept has suffered from judicial manipulation by its use in redressability analysis as well. For more than a decade, standing doctrine has required that the injury asserted by the plaintiff be likely to be redressed by a favorable decision. The nature of the interplay between redressability and injury, however, has apparently escaped the Burger Court.

Consider a few examples. In *Linda R.S. v. Richard D.* the mother of an illegitimate child challenged the discriminatory enforcement of a Texas child support statute. The statute had been construed to apply to married parents only. The Court ruled that the plaintiff failed to meet the redressability hurdle since the requested relief—nondiscriminatory enforcement—would not ensure the payment of support. Two years later, in *Warth v. Seldin*, the Court held that plaintiffs seeking to challenge the exclusionary zoning practices of Penfield, New York failed to satisfy the redressability standard because they could not prove that they would actually be able to obtain housing if the ordinance were invalidated. Finally, in *Simon v. Eastern Kentucky Welfare Rights Organization*, several indigents attempted to challenge a revenue ruling that allowed hospitals to qualify for favorable tax treatment even if they reduced service to indigents. The plaintiffs claimed that the allegedly illegal ruling resulted in the denial of hospital access to the poor. Concluding that even if the challengers prevailed, it was just as plausible that hospitals would elect to forgo favorable tax treatment rather than shoulder the costs of expanded treatment of indigents, the Court ruled that the redressability requirement had not been met.

Such cases demonstrate the ease with which the Court, by toying with the scope of the injury at issue, can raise or lower the redressability hurdle. In *Linda R.S.*, *Warth*, and *Simon*, the Court overstated the injuries that the plaintiffs sought to have redressed. In *Linda R.S.*, the Court refused jurisdiction because even a decree requiring nondiscriminatory enforcement would not ensure support. But why was obtaining the payment of child support considered the relevant injury? The mother in *Linda R.S.* sought to be treated on an equal basis with married mothers. Her injury—denial of equal treatment—would undoubtedly have been redressed by an affirmative decree requiring enforcement of child support obligations against unmarried fathers. Similarly, the *Warth* plaintiffs sought not only to obtain housing in Penfield. They also asserted their interest in equal participation in a housing market not distorted by unconstitutional zoning practices. The denial of a meaningful opportunity to persuade others to construct low cost housing in Penfield, for example, would have been redressed by a determination that the ordinance was unconstitutional. The indigents in *Simon* had no objection to receiving hospital access, but the interest they asserted would more appropriately be described as having hospital decisions concerning the services offered to indigents accurately reflect an earlier incentive structure implicitly approved by the Congress. Again, that injury would have been redressed by the claim presented.

* * *

Equal protection cases provide the clearest examples of the Court's inability to maintain a principled line. In the *Regents of the University of California v. Bakke*, a substantial question arose concerning Alan Bakke's ability to prove that he would have been admitted to medical school absent the contested affirmative action program. The Court skirted the standing issue, however, by declaring that the university's "decision not to permit Bakke to compete for all 100 places" was the relevant injury. That harm would, of course, be redressed by a favorable ruling. If, however, the *Warth* plaintiffs could redress their injuries only by showing that they would actually obtain housing, and if the mother in *Linda R.S.* was required to show that she would actually receive support payments, Bakke should have been made to prove that he would have gotten into medical school. The interest in equal opportunity was insufficient to provide standing in *Linda R.S.* and *Warth*, but it eventually got Alan Bakke into medical school.

A hypothetical brings the issue into better focus. Suppose that an exclusive suburb, separately incorporated, passed a statute prohibiting blacks from purchasing housing in the locale. Assume further that the suburb is composed entirely of ten-acre privately owned parcels, each valued in excess of $500,000. The facts, as developed, indicate that no one in the suburb has present plans to sell. How would plaintiffs achieve standing in such a case? Must they not only be black, but also be able to prove capacity and willingness to buy a $500,000 home? Even if the plaintiffs make that showing, is their injury nonredressable without proof of a willing seller? Under *Warth*, standing would be denied unless the plaintiffs were black, rich, and had a seller in tow. Under *Bakke* they could obtain standing merely by showing that the statute denied them the opportunity to seek housing at that locale. My guess is that if such a case arose, the Court would be even more lenient, and ask no more of a plaintiff than that he be black. That, however, is because of the attractiveness of the claim on the merits.

Which injury *should* be the focus of the inquiry? Under the Court's standing jargon, an apparent dilemma exists. If * * * redressability of the governmental discrimination is sufficient and it is unnecessary for the plaintiffs to show that they will achieve the "ultimate" goal of their efforts—the purchase of a $500,000 home—do not the litigants assert mere generalized claims to good government? Does not the concrete harm, sought so eagerly by the particularized injury standard, become constitutionally irrelevant? But if *Warth* and *Simon* state the correct principle, will not the Court be forced to say that black plaintiffs who have less than $500,000 have no standing because even if the suburb discriminates, that in no way changes the plaintiffs' lives?

* * *

Additional Sources

Evan Caminker, *The Constitutionality of Qui Tam Actions*, 99 Yale L.J. 341 (1989)

David P. Currie, *Misunderstanding Standing*, 1981 Sup. Ct. Rev. 41

David A. Logan, *Standing to Sue: A Proposed Separation of Powers Analysis*, 1984 Wis. L. Rev. 37

Henry P. Monaghan, *Third Party Standing*, 84 Colum. L. Rev. 277 (1984)

Gene R. Nichol, Jr., *Justice Scalia, Standing, and Public Law Litigation*, 42 Duke L.J. 1141 (1993)

Richard J. Pierce, Jr., Lujan v. Defenders of Wildlife: *Standing as a Judicially Imposed Limit on Legislative Power*, 42 Duke L.J. 1170 (1993)

Robert A. Sedler, *Standing and the Burger Court: An Analysis and Some Proposals for Legislative Reform*, 30 Rutgers L. Rev. 863 (1977)

Richard B. Stewart, *The Reformation of American Administrative Law*, 88 Harv. L. Rev. 1669 (1975)

Richard B. Stewart & Cass R. Sunstein, *Public Programs and Private Rights*, 95 Harv. L. Rev. 1193 (1982)

Cass R. Sunstein, *Standing and the Privatization of Public Law*, 88 Colum. L. Rev. 1432 (1988)

Mark V. Tushnet, *The Sociology of Article III: A Response to Prof. Brilmayer*, 93 Harv. L. Rev. 1698 (1980)

Mark V. Tushnet, *The New Law of Standing: A Plea for Abandonment*, 62 Cornell L. Rev. 663 (1977)

Joseph Vining, LEGAL IDENTITY: THE COMING OF AGE OF PUBLIC LAW (1978)

Steven L. Winter, *The Metaphor of Standing and the Problem of Self-Governance*, 40 Stan. L. Rev. 1371 (1988)

C. The Controversy About Agency Nonacquiescence to Judicial Rulings

The selective refusal to abide by adverse decisions of courts—called agency nonacquiescence—is not an uncommon behavior by administrative agencies. The practice pits two sets of values against each other. On the one hand, a stringent notion of the rule of law could require agencies to comply with the adverse rulings of courts. On the other hand, agency nonacquiescence can promote nationally uniform policymaking and generate conflicts among the circuits so that there can be ongoing debate in our judicial system.

The excerpts in this section illuminate the opposing sides in the debate about agency nonacquiescence. Professors Samuel Estreicher and Richard Revesz defend nonacquiescence in certain circumstances. In response, Professors Matthew Diller and Nancy Morawetz argue that Professors Estreicher and Revesz overstate their case and inappropriately downplay important objections to nonacquiescence.

Samuel Estreicher and Richard L. Revesz, *Nonacquiescence by Federal Administrative Agencies*, 98 YALE L.J. 679, 681–83, 687–88, 718–20, 723–31, 735–37, 741–53, 771–72 (1989)*

* * *

Introduction

The selective refusal of administrative agencies to conduct their internal proceedings consistently with adverse rulings of the courts of appeals—a practice commonly termed agency nonacquiescence—is not new in American law. Over the past sixty years, many agencies have insisted, in varying degrees, on the authority to pursue their policies, despite conflicting court decisions, until the Supreme Court is prepared to issue a nationally binding resolution. For example, the National Labor Relations Board (NLRB) asserted this prerogative as early as the 1940's, and has invoked it intermittently since then. Similarly, since the 1920's, the Internal Revenue Service (IRS) has periodically engaged in nonacquiescence. * * * [D]espite occasional judicial criticism, nonacquiescence persisted without either legitimation or interdiction by Congress or the Supreme Court. The overall response of the legal system was one of tolerance mixed with disquiet.

In the late 1970's, however, the courts of appeals began to express the view that the practice borders on lawlessness and should not be tolerated. The criticism of the Social Security Administration's (SSA's) aggressive nonacquiescence during the first half of the Reagan Administration was particularly scathing. In an effort to reduce the number of recipients of Social Security disability benefits in the face of circuit court rulings requiring proof of a change in medical condition before benefits could be terminated, SSA directed its personnel to follow agency policy and disregard contrary directions of the court of appeals. The result was a series of agency-court conflicts that culminated in the Ninth Circuit's entry of a circuit-wide injunction against continued nonacquiescence in the *Lopez v. Heckler* litigation and in Congress's serious consideration of legislation to bar SSA's nonacquiescence practice.

The SSA practice achieved particular notoriety because each of SSA's decisions is normally reviewed, on appeal, in a single identifiable court of appeals—the circuit in which the claimant resides. From the perspective of the reviewing court, SSA's nonacquiescence appears to embody a claim that the agency is entirely free to disregard binding law in the circuit. In contrast, agencies such as the NLRB administer statutes with considerably broader venue provisions; thus, a particular order may be reviewed by a number of courts of appeals. While nonacquiescence by these agencies has been criticized, the indictment is necessarily tempered by the fact that the venue provisions make it difficult for any particular court of appeals to insist on exclusive superintendence over the particular agency order.

The status of agency nonacquiescence in our legal system remains uncertain. Despite considerable writings on the subject, there has been no systematic evaluation of the practice's costs and benefits. Neither has there been a serious proposal for reducing, in a manner consistent with the respective institutional responsibilities of an agency and its reviewing court, the debilitating tensions between these two institutions that nonacquiescence engenders. Our study principally addresses these issues.

* * *

I. Defining the Problem
* * *

B. Categories of Nonacquiescence

The term "nonacquiescence" is often used loosely to include three distinct types of agency behavior. To evaluate properly the arguments for and against the practice, we must examine each of these categories separately.

First, an agency engages in *inter*circuit nonacquiescence when it refuses to follow, in its administrative proceedings, the case law of a court of appeals other than the one that will review the agency's decision. Second, an agency engages in *intra*circuit nonacquiescence when the relevant venue provisions establish that review will be to a particular court of appeals and the agency nonetheless refuses to follow, in its administrative proceedings, the case law of that court.

The third category is defined by reference to venue choice. Here, the agency refuses to follow the case law of a court of appeals that has rejected its position, but review may be had either in that court or in one that has not rejected the agency's position. Broad venue choice is fairly common * * *. * * *

Normally, under conditions of venue choice, the identity of the reviewing court will be uncertain at

---

* Reprinted with permission of The Yale Law Journal Company, Fred B. Rothman & Company, Samuel Estreicher, and Richard L. Revesz. All rights reserved.

the time the agency makes its decision. Such uncertainty is not eliminated simply because the agency has a basis for predicting which circuit will hear the case. Only where all uncertainty is removed—for example, because all courts of proper venue have adopted positions contrary to the agency's policy—does an agency's continued nonadherence to circuit law become intracircuit nonacquiescence.

None of these three categories is implicated when an agency attempts in good faith, and with reasonable basis in fact and law, to distinguish an adverse decision of a court of appeals. Nonacquiescence arises only where the agency, unable to invoke such a distinction, nevertheless declines to be bound by the adverse circuit rule.

All three categories are agency-centered. They each look to the posture of the case at the time of the administrative decision, rather than at the time of the judicial decision. Such a focus is particularly important in the venue choice category. There will be times when the agency's action will be reviewed in a circuit that previously had rejected the agency's position. From the perspective of that court, the case will look like one of intracircuit nonacquiescence, since the court will be reviewing an administrative decision that was inconsistent, even at the time it was made, with circuit law. But when the agency decided the case, by definition, the range of possible venues precluded certain prediction that the case would be reviewed in that court, rather than in a court that had not rejected the agency's position. Because the purpose of our study is to devise standards for agency conduct, only an *ex ante* perspective, specifying what conduct may be realistically expected of the agency at the time of its decision, is appropriate.

* * *

III. The Constitutionality of Agency Nonacquiescence

Several courts and commentators have concluded, often without detailed elaboration, that an administrative agency's refusal to acquiesce in contrary circuit court rulings is unconstitutional, or, at the very least, comes close to transgressing constitutional limitations. Such critics of nonacquiescence have excoriated the practice in broad strokes, seemingly excluding the possibility of justification in particular circumstances. If this view—the per se unconstitutionality of agency nonacquiescence—is correct, our inquiry should move directly to the question of remediation: how best to ensure that agencies are suitably deterred from straying beyond constitutional limits. On the other hand, if there is no per se bar, and the validity of a nonacquiescence policy depends on what justification an agency can present in a particular case, we should proceed to analyze the competing interests implicated by nonacquiescence.

* * *

A. *Specifying the Argument*

It is important to define with specificity the contours of our consideration of the constitutional argument. First, we deal explicitly only with intracircuit nonacquiescence—with cases in which the agency, at the time of its administrative proceedings, knows, by virtue of the venue rules, which court of appeals will review its action, and yet proceeds contrary to a ruling of that court. If the per se argument fails here, it follows *a fortiori* that it will also fail for the two other categories of nonacquiescence that we have defined. Indeed, in pursuing a policy of intercircuit nonacquiescence, by definition the agency is not acting inconsistently with the case law of the court of appeals that will review its action, and that court is under no obligation to follow the ruling of the circuit that previously rejected the agency's position. The disregard of judicial authority, which undergirds the charge of unconstitutionality, is therefore less direct, and the claim of obedience less compelling. For the same reason, the claim of unconstitutionality is also stronger in the intracircuit context than where, because of venue choice, the agency does not know with absolute certainty, at the time of its administrative proceedings, whether its action will be reviewed in a court of appeals that rejected its position rather than in a court that either has not addressed the legality of the agency's position or has upheld that position.

Second, our discussion addresses only cases in which the organic statute under which the agency operates does not, of its own force, command the agency to conform its administrative proceedings to the law of the circuit that will review its action. Where such a bar is present, an agency acts *ultra vires* if it refuses to adhere to circuit law, and the legality of the agency's action can be decisively resolved as a matter of statutory construction. * * *

* * *

B. *The Separation of Powers Objection*

* * * Our approach assumes that the Supreme Court's pronouncements on federal law must be obeyed not only by the particular parties to the dispute, but also by all within the regulatory reach of federal law. * * * The question here is whether our constitutional system requires that federal administrative agencies acting within the jurisdictional reach of a court of appeals must accord the same measure of obedience to a ruling of that court.

In addressing this question, we first reject two competing views of the relationship between an administrative agency and its reviewing courts, conceptions that have figured prominently in the judicial and secondary writings on the subject: first, that the status of an agency, particularly that of an adjudicatory agency, is analogous to that of a district court in the circuit; and, second, that an agency is part of a co-equal branch of government with independent responsibility for the interpretation of federal law.

The first characterization argues strongly against intracircuit nonacquiescence, for a district court is bound in all instances to follow the rulings of its supervising court of appeals. This view, however, fails to account for the congressional delegation of substantive policymaking authority to the administrative agencies and the resulting constraints on the review role of the federal courts under basic administrative law principles as articulated in *SEC v. Chenery Corp.* Administrative agencies, unlike district courts, are responsible for a nationally uniform administration of the statutes entrusted to them, and are typically the principal decisionmakers under these statutes. The court's role is the reactive one of checking for abuse of discretion or other transgressions of statutory limitations. Indeed, even on questions of statutory interpretation, a strong rule of deference to agency views operates in lieu of the *de novo* review characteristic of appellate consideration of trial court determinations of questions of law.

* * *

Unlike the district court analogy, the co-equal branch analogy, at least in its strong form, argues sweepingly for the constitutionality of nonacquiescence because it does not recognize for any federal court a superior role in the interpretation of federal statutory law to that exercised by administrative agencies, except with respect to the adjudication of the rights of the parties before the court. The co-equal branch analogy significantly overstates the autonomy of administrative agencies. Like the district court analogy, the co-equal branch analogy is inconsistent with our constitutional scheme. * * *

* * *

In thinking about whether the courts of appeals should be treated like the Supreme Court, it is important to bear in mind that the *Cooper v. Aaron* principle assumes that the law forming the basis for the obligation to acquiesce is no longer in flux. The southern governors were embarking on a fundamentally illegitimate campaign of resistance precisely because the Supreme Court in *Brown* [*v. Board of Education*] and its progeny made clear that all public schools had to desegregate. The desegregation principle was established and reaffirmed by the Court at a level of generality that precluded any effort at common law modification or narrowing through the drawing of factual or legal distinctions. The duty of generalized compliance in the *Cooper v. Aaron* sense emerges, however, only when the process of federal law development has been completed in this manner. Any continued resistance to a ruling of the Supreme Court after that point must be confined to the arena of public opinion and, ultimately, to the Article V amendment process.

The rulings of the courts of appeals, by contrast, are in a sense only intermediate points of decision in this process of federal law development. This conclusion follows most directly from the absence of intercircuit stare decisis and from other features of the federal system's commitment to the process of intercircuit percolation. The fact that the circuits are free to disagree with each other, that the government is insulated under *United States v. Mendoza* from the constraints of nonmutual collateral estoppel in order to ensure the possibility of multiple circuit consideration of a rule of law, and that the Supreme Court itself relies on intercircuit conflicts as an important signaling device for case selection and as a source of doctrinal materials for decisionmaking, makes clear that the law remains in a state of flux even well after a particular court of appeals has announced its rule on a subject.

It might be argued, of course, that even if the law is in flux nationally, the process of legal development has ended in the particular circuit, hence rendering illegitimate an agency's policy of intracircuit nonacquiescence. A court of appeals, however, does not enjoy sovereign responsibility over its territory akin to that enjoyed by a state court on questions of state law; it is still engaged in the process of interpreting a *unitary* national law and remains a part of that process even after it has ruled on the subject. Thus, a court of appeals is expected to be open to reconsidering prior rulings in the light of developments in other circuits; the role of the circuits in harmonizing federal law in this manner is an important adjunct to the Supreme Court's role as conflict-resolver.

* * *

These arguments are less persuasive for courts of appeals of national jurisdiction, such as the Federal Circuit in patent cases, and for the regional circuits themselves where they have been given nationally exclusive responsibility over particular subject matter, such as the D.C. Circuit has over various types of administrative appeals. In those cases, of course, the law is much more resistant to change because, at least for certain issues, there will be no intercircuit dialogue and percolation. But it would nonetheless be a mistake, in considering the per se constitutionality of nonacquiescence, mechanically to equate these courts with the Supreme Court.

The fact that circuit law is typically made by panels of three judges (some of whom may not be active members of the court of appeals) renders a single decision on a particular issue more open to reexamination by a subsequent panel than is true of the Supreme Court's pronouncements. This result is reinforced by the fact that a court of appeals generally acts on the basis of mandatory jurisdiction, and therefore almost certainly considers a particular issue more frequently and in more diverse factual contexts than does the Supreme Court, with its largely discretionary docket.

We do not mean to place too much emphasis, however, on the panel/en banc distinction. Indeed, to the extent that the courts of appeals have provided, as most have, that a decision of a panel is binding on all subsequent panels and can be overruled only by the en banc court, the distinction cannot be made to carry too much weight. At the same time, however, in part because of the practical barriers to frequent resort to en banc consideration, a subsequent panel, without formally overruling a decision, might be receptive to finding ways of distinguishing a prior precedent of a different panel. Whether a particular litigation posture constitutes nonacquiescence must depend on whether legally plausible arguments can be made to distinguish the agency's policy from the ruling of the court of appeals. Thus, aggressive positions that would be considered nonacquiescence in the face of a Supreme Court decision, or of an en banc decision by a court of appeals, might not be considered nonacquiescence when they follow an initial panel decision on the subject.

* * *

The foregoing would suggest that, to the extent that intracircuit nonacquiescence has a claim to legitimacy, this claim flows from the *intermediate* and *nonuniform* character of the ruling of the regional circuit court. The relevant question, therefore, is how an agency with national jurisdiction over a particular problem must react to the rulings of a court of limited geographic jurisdiction, which can render neither final nor nationally uniform rules of decision.

In considering whether (and how) the Constitution speaks to this question, it is useful to ask whether the following hypothetical statute would be unconstitutional. Assume that Congress passes a generic cross-agency statute akin to the APA, providing that, in the absence of contrary direction in the agency's organic statute, the following rules apply: (1) any decision by a regional court of appeals in an appeal from agency action will be binding on the parties (unless overturned by the Supreme Court); (2) agencies are not subject to nonmutual collateral estoppel; (3) the ruling of a court of appeals will be given the usual stare decisis effect in its own circuit; (4) courts are free to sanction an agency for continued unjustified nonacquiescence through the EAJA, injunctive process, or other legally available means; and (5) absent an injunction, the agency need not conform its internal proceedings to the rulings of a regional court of appeals, if it can invoke justification, sufficient under APA standards, for such nonacquiescence.

The first four elements of this hypothetical statute reflect the status quo; the fifth authorizes nonacquiescence subject to review for justification. We believe that this hypothetical statute reflects Congress's implicit understanding in constructing our administrative lawmaking system and that it is consistent with principles of separation of powers.

Two serious objections can be raised to our reliance on this hypothetical statute. The first is that Congress has not explicitly enacted such a statute, but at best has been silent on the subject of intracircuit nonacquiescence. This objection fails to account, however, for the fact that agencies act pursuant to broad delegations of authority and normally do not have to demonstrate explicit authorization. Moreover, an implicit authorization of nonacquiescence is embedded in the congressional choice in favor of administrative government. One of the goals that Congress sought to promote was uniformity in the administration of federal law. At first glance, uniformity appears to fit uncomfortably with percolation and with the lack of intercircuit stare decisis. After all, if the different regional circuits were precluded from taking different approaches, uniformity would be achieved far more easily and without the need to tolerate agency/court conflict. But there is no reason why our federal system cannot express a preference for the uniform administration of federal law at the agency level, and still desire a scheme of judicial review that improves the quality of legal rules through dialogue and percolation. Intracircuit nonacquiescence permits an agency to preserve uniform administration while the state of the law in the circuits is still in flux. We believe that this dual objective is the best account of the congressional objectives in enacting statutes providing for administrative policymaking and enforcement subject to judicial review. Thus, for the purposes of assessing the constitutionality of nonacquiescence, we are prepared to treat the current administrative landscape as if the hypothetical statute permitting nonacquiescence by the courts of appeals had in fact been enacted.

The second objection is that such a statute, if enacted, would contravene constitutional limits. We do not believe this to be the case, however, because of the wide-ranging power that Congress enjoys over the jurisdiction of the lower federal courts. To reach this conclusion, we focus on two distinct arguments.

First, unlike the Supreme Court, the lower federal courts are creatures of Congress. The Constitution merely authorizes Congress to establish them; it does not mandate their establishment. As a result, it is certainly not inconceivable that Congress might have the constitutional authority to make administrative action reviewable only by the Supreme Court on writ of certiorari. If Congress need not establish the lower federal courts, it can entrust them with jurisdiction over certain subject matters but not others. We may feel uneasy, it is true, about limiting Article III review in this manner, given the Supreme Court's inability to review more than a small percentage of the cases on its certiorari docket, but it is far from clear whether this problem is one of constitutional significance. If Congress can pursue uniformity at the administrative level to the extent of abolishing circuit court review of agency action altogether, then in what sense can it be said to be acting unconstitutionally by taking the less extreme step of providing for review in the courts of appeals while authorizing intracircuit nonacquiescence, subject to court review and, where appropriate, sanctions and injunctions?

This line of argument might be criticized on the grounds that the "greater" power of eliminating circuit court review altogether does not necessarily carry with it the "lesser" power of preserving circuit court superintendence yet authorizing intracircuit nonacquiescence. There are many instances in our legal system in which the government makes itself subject to constitutional limitations by undertaking activities that it is under no constitutional obligation to undertake. For example, if the government creates a public park system it may not discriminatorily deny access to speakers of disfavored views; more to the point, the fact that a right to an intermediate appeal is not constitutionally mandated does not mean that litigants can be denied due process rights on appeal.

But in many other contexts, "greater includes the lesser" arguments, as they might be called, are a perfectly acceptable mode of legal analysis. It is quite possible that such an argument holds for our hypothetical statute as well. But while the existence of a plausible "greater with the lesser" argument informs the constitutional inquiry, we do not rely exclusively on such an argument, because we believe that the "lesser" power can stand on its own * * *.

* * *

IV. An Evaluation of the Costs and Benefits of Nonacquiescence

In this section, we evaluate the policy considerations implicated by the three different categories of nonacquiescence. We conclude that intracircuit nonacquiescence can be justified only as an interim measure that allows the agency to maintain a uniform administration of its governing statute following an adverse decision by a court of appeals while the agency seeks in the courts a national validation of its position. For the other two categories, we do not believe that limitations would advance the proper functioning of the administrative lawmaking system.

A. *Intercircuit Nonacquiescence*

Given the lack of intercircuit stare decisis, and the reasons underlying our system of intercircuit dialogue, an agency's ability to engage in intercircuit nonacquiescence should not be constrained. The costs and benefits of intercircuit nonacquiescence must be evaluated in light of our legal system's rejection of intercircuit stare decisis, which, in turn, can be justified only by reference to the benefits of intercircuit dialogue. * * *

The benefits of dialogue can be grouped into four categories. First, doctrinal dialogue takes place when one court of appeals addresses the legal reasoning of another and reaches a different conclusion. Such dialogue is likely to result in better decisions, as it will produce a more careful and focused consideration of the issues.

Second, experiential dialogue occurs when courts of appeals are able to observe and compare the consequences of different legal rules. This empirical evidence is relevant both to circuits that have not yet considered an issue as well as to ones that may wish to reconsider their position.

Third, the conflicts produced by intercircuit dialogue play a useful role in signalling to the Supreme Court the difficulty of particular legal issues, and thereby help the Court make better case selection decisions. Difficult issues are likely to have been decided incorrectly in the first instance and are also likely to result in intercircuit conflicts. Under a regime of intercircuit stare decisis, the Supreme Court is hampered in two ways: (1) without the signalling role of intercircuit conflicts, the Court has to expend more of its resources to identify difficult issues that may have been resolved incorrectly by the first court of appeals to address them, and (2) to the extent that the Court fails to identify such cases, it may let stand erroneous decisions below.

Fourth, doctrinal and experiential dialogue on the part of the circuits aids the Supreme Court in deciding cases on the merits. Doctrinal dialogue isolates the issues on which the courts of appeals are divided and presents the competing positions on those issues, probably stated in their most compelling terms. As to experiential dialogue, the Supreme Court, like the circuits, benefits from the existence of a store of accumulated experience.

* * *

B. *Nonacquiescence in the Face of Venue Choice*

As we have indicated, nonacquiescence in the presence of venue choice arises where an agency refuses, in its administrative proceedings, to follow a ruling of a court of appeals, where the other courts to which an appeal may lie either have upheld the agency's position or have not yet addressed the legality of that position. For the most part, this category raises the same issues as intercircuit nonacquiescence.

Consider an example in which, because of the breadth of the venue provisions, the agency's proceedings could be reviewed in any of the regional circuits. If the agency is to avoid nonacquiescence, it will have to conform its administrative proceeding to the ruling of the circuit that had previously rejected its position. * * *

* * *

* * * [A] bar against nonacquiescence under conditions of venue choice is undesirable for the same reasons as is a bar against intercircuit nonacquiescence. Moreover, venue choice makes it exceedingly difficult, in some situations practically impossible, for an agency to continue to press its preferred policy in circuits that have not rejected it, without thereby having that policy repeatedly challenged in circuits that have previously rejected it. To remove the friction between agency and court that is thereby caused, we recommend the elimination, or at least the substantial reduction, of venue choice. * * *

C. *Intracircuit Nonacquiescence*

Given our conclusion that, even though a court of appeals has rejected an agency's policy, the agency should be allowed to continue to press that policy in other circuits, what rules should apply to cases that are reviewable only in the circuit that has rejected the agency's policy? Consistent with the proper role of agencies and courts in our legal system, we believe that there should not be an absolute bar against intracircuit nonacquiescence. However, such nonacquiescence can be justified only as an interim measure that allows the agency to maintain a uniform administration of its governing statute while it makes reasonable attempts to persuade the courts to validate its position.

1. *Intercircuit Dialogue*

It is true that even if an agency must conform its administrative proceedings to the case law of the court of appeals to which review would lie, where this case law is inconsistent with the agency's policy, the agency can continue to press that policy in other circuits if it chooses to do so. Thus, a bar against intracircuit nonacquiescence would not truncate the development of the law. Other circuits would have the opportunity to uphold the agency's position. If the Supreme Court eventually grants certiorari to resolve the conflict among the circuits, it will benefit from being able to observe the effects of the different legal regimes.

Nonetheless, an inflexible bar against intracircuit nonacquiescence constrains the dialogue among the circuits. * * * [Using an] example of EPA's use of independent contractors, consider a scenario in which that question comes first before the Second Circuit, which strikes down the use of such contractors, and then before the Seventh and Ninth Circuits, which uphold it. It would be desirable for the agency to be able to go back before the Second Circuit and reargue its position in light of its subsequent victories. The Second Circuit might be persuaded by the arguments of the two other circuits, and the conflicting positions might be harmonized without the need for review by the Supreme Court.

But the Second Circuit will be unable to reconsider this issue unless EPA can use independent contractors in cases subject to review in that circuit. To do so, however, entails acting contrary to the case law of the court of appeals to which review lies—that is, engaging in intracircuit nonacquiescence. Similarly, intracircuit nonacquiescence is a prerequisite to judicial reconsideration of a regulatory agency's substantive policy under schemes in which the agency's failure to bring enforcement actions is unreviewable. Thus, a total bar against intracircuit nonacquiescence would make it impossible for a circuit that at one time ruled against the agency to continue a dialogue with circuits that subsequently ruled for the agency. Resolution of the conflict among the circuits would require Supreme Court intervention, thereby adding unnecessarily to the Court's workload. Moreover, the resulting asymmetry again fits uncomfortably with the concept of administrative deference. If intracircuit nonacquiescence is barred, only the circuit that ruled for the agency would be open to possible reconsideration of its position; rulings against the agency would be immune to such reconsideration. Here, too, the one-way ratchet moves exclusively in the direction of disapproval of the agency's action.

A bar against intracircuit nonacquiescence also delays the harmonization of federal law. Were such a bar in place, conflicts could be harmonized without intervention by the Supreme Court only if the courts of appeals that ruled *for* the agency reconsidered their position. The courts that ruled against it would ordinarily not have an occasion to reexamine their prior rulings, even where they might have found persuasive the views of the other circuits.

It is true, of course, that the Supreme Court and Congress can always intervene. But * * * both of these institutions have limited decisional capacity, and Congress may be unwilling for other reasons to reopen consideration of the statute in question. Moreover, the Supreme Court may be reluctant to intervene every time a conflict arises. Either because of perceived benefits of further intercircuit dialogue, or in order to avoid committing its docket excessively to the administrative law area, the Court may wish to defer its intervention until it is clear that the circuits that ruled against the agency will not depart from that position, particularly where the adverse rulings preceded those supporting the agency's views. It is quite likely, therefore, that the conflict may persist for a longer period of time than if the circuits that ruled against the agency had been able to take a new look at the agency's policy following its acceptance in other circuits.

Critics of nonacquiescence urge that agencies have the means to prod intercircuit dialogue without disregarding the law of the reviewing court of appeals. For example, our colleague, Burt Neuborne, has suggested that, while agencies would have to conform their internal administrative proceedings to circuit law, they might seek a declaratory judgment when they were ready to seek reconsideration of the adverse circuit rule.

There are at least four serious problems with this suggestion. The first, fatal from a practical standpoint, is the likely unavailability of such a procedure under current law for many agencies. The typical statute requires the agency to have made some concrete decision, whether the promulgation of a rule or regulation, or the issuance of an order affecting particular parties, before judicial review may be had. Second, if current law were revised to authorize such a procedure, there are serious questions whether Article III courts could be employed to rule on abstract questions of statutory interpretation in the absence of concrete controversies. Third, even if these constitutional doubts were overcome, the envisioned procedure would only address one of the reasons for allowing interim nonacquiescence—the generation of case vehicles for seeking reconsideration of disfavored circuit precedent. The other costs of compelling agencies to revamp their policies and procedures while the law is in flux would remain. Fourth, a declaratory judgment procedure would require some alteration of fundamental premises of our administrative lawmaking system, which presently assigns to agencies the principal policymaking role and to courts a reactive, monitoring function. For courts to intervene, and law to be made, in a manner divorced from the agency's exercise of discretion would reverse this allocation of responsibility. It is questionable whether concern over nonacquiescence should drive such a radical change in institutional arrangements.

Neither are we persuaded by approaches that would authorize intracircuit nonacquiescence only after at least one circuit has ruled in the agency's favor, or only in a small number of "test" cases. Reconsideration may be appropriate not only when a conflict has arisen, but also when the court's rule may have undesirable consequences not fully considered by the first panel which, if brought to the circuit's attention in another case, might lead to a suitable narrowing or, in some cases, abandonment of the rule. * * *

* * *

2. *Uniform Outcomes*

We have shown that a bar against intracircuit nonacquiescence, even where it contemplates limited exceptions, may delay the development of uniform rules. In addition, it undermines important goals of uniformity that underlie the administrative law system. The problems of uniformity can be divided into three major categories: externalities, interstate competition, and fairness.

Externalities—in the sense of cross-circuit effects—are present when economic activity that takes place in one region produces adverse effects in another region. Air pollution, for example, can travel long distances and will not respect the geographic boundaries of states or of the regional courts of appeals. Under the Clean Air Act, EPA regulates air quality by means of ambient standards, which limit the permissible concentrations of particular pollutants in the air. In order to achieve these ambient standards, the agency also regulates the emissions from new sources—sources constructed after the promulgation of the applicable regulations. The emission standards are uniform nationwide and are set by reference to categories of polluters (for example, coal-fired electric plants). If one circuit were to strike down regulations limiting the permissible emissions of a particular pollutant, the effects would be felt not only in that circuit, but in downwind circuits as well. For the ambient standards to be met in those circuits, the agency would have to define more stringent circuit-specific emission standards for those downwind states. Thus, the actions of the court of appeals that struck down the administrative policy will have important effects even outside the geographic jurisdiction of that circuit, forcing the agency to take suboptimal measures in the downwind circuits to counteract the impact of the court's action.

Another central goal of federal regulation is to prevent regions from competing for industry by offering a more favorable economic climate at the expense of other societal goals. For example, federal regulation in the labor field can be justified, in part, as an attempt to prevent interstate competition for industry at the expense of worker protection. If one circuit takes a more restrictive view than does the NLRB of what constitutes a mandatory subject for collective bargaining, employers in that circuit have more entrepreneurial flexibility, and perhaps lower labor costs, than their counterparts in other circuits, creating incentives for new industry to establish itself in that circuit and for existing industry to move there from other circuits. As long as the conflict among the circuits persists, there will be undesirable regional competition.

Finally, uniformity promotes some fairness values. Whether the agency acts as regulator of private sector activity or administers a benefit program, Congress intended by enacting federal law to promote horizontal uniformity—equal treatment of regulatees or claimants regardless of where in this country the dispute or claim arose. To the extent the agency is required to alter its policy to conform to adverse circuit rulings, the federal interest in horizontal uniformity is undermined.

3. *Differential Administration*

If an agency cannot engage in intracircuit nonacquiescence, it will have to administer its statute differently in various parts of the country, if, after its policy is rejected in one circuit, it wants to continue pressing that policy in other circuits. Differential administration can impose significant costs on an agency. * * *

* * *

4. *Distributional Effects*

* * * [I]ntracircuit nonacquiescence produces undesirable distributional consequences. A litigant's ability to obtain the benefit of the case law of the reviewing court of appeals will depend on whether he has sufficient resources to pursue an appeal to the federal courts. The result is analogous to one in which a litigant before a court is told that he can purchase the rule of law which will govern the disposition of his case and that more favorable rules of law are progressively more expensive. This distributional unfairness is the central cost of intracircuit nonacquiescence.

A by-product of these distributional effects is the lack of uniformity in the output of the administrative lawmaking system. When lack of resources prevents a litigant's challenge to the agency's nonacquiescence in court, the result will be vertical disuniformity—disuniformity in outcome between those who pursue their case into the courts and those who do not. Like horizontal disuniformity, which is present when different circuits adjudicate under different legal standards, vertical disuniformity also undermines the goals of uniform administration of federal law. Vertical disuniformity is especially troublesome because the negative impact of the differential policy will probably fall disproportionately on those parties least able to bear it.

5. *Workload of the Federal Courts*

Nonacquiescence is likely to increase the volume of cases reaching the federal courts. Indeed, it is logical to expect that, when the relevant court of appeals has rejected the policy underlying agency action, a relatively large number of litigants would seek review.

In the case of intracircuit nonacquiescence, the link is quite direct. Because a litigant will probably prevail simply through the application of stare decisis, there will be a strong incentive to seek review, since, in balancing the costs and benefits of challenging the agency action, the discount for the risk of not prevailing before the court will be very small. In contrast, if the agency had acquiesced, the litigant would have been satisfied with the agency's decision and the case would never have entered the federal courts.

The explosion in the workload of the federal

courts has been well documented. Strong arguments have also been made about how the problem cannot be addressed simply by appointing more judges because, at some point, an increase in the number of judges would lead to a deterioration in the quality of the courts. The contribution that nonacquiescence makes to burgeoning federal caseloads is a cost that must be considered.

6. *Assessing the Competing Factors*

The presence of weighty factors on both sides of the scale suggests that either a per se prohibition or an unqualified endorsement of intracircuit nonacquiescence would be undesirable, and that striking a proper balance between the competing values will be exceedingly difficult. It is a useful starting point to consider situations at the extreme where continued intracircuit nonacquiescence should not be tolerated.

One such situation is where all of the circuits have ruled against the agency and the Supreme Court has repeatedly declined to grant certiorari. Continued nonacquiescence under such a scenario would raise the specter of unconstitutionality. In this setting, our reasons for concluding that the *Cooper v. Aaron* principle does not carry over to the circuit courts would lose much of their force: Federal law would not be in flux, and the judicial rejection of the agency's position could not be attributed to the isolated decision of a single circuit panel.

Neither could nonacquiescence under these circumstances be defended by a cost-benefit calculus. The relevant comparison is between the effects of two uniform policies: the agency's original policy as against a new policy that would be consistent with the rulings of the courts of appeals. From the perspective of the goal of uniformity, the latter outcome is clearly preferable since the former produces vertical disuniformity. Similarly, from the perspective of distributional effects, the latter outcome is also clearly preferable, as the governing rule of law will not depend on access to litigation resources. Moreover, neither outcome introduces costs of differential administration, as they both contemplate that the agency would be implementing a uniform policy.

The only argument that the agency could muster in favor of maintaining its original policy would be based on the cost of the change to a new policy. But that argument would simply be a restatement of the co-equal branch analogy: that the agency's responsibility for the interpretation of federal law is of equal stature in the legal hierarchy as that of the courts. We thus reject intracircuit nonacquiescence under these circumstances.

A second scenario would have the agency continuing to engage in intracircuit nonacquiescence after all of the courts of appeals have addressed the validity of the agency's policy and have split on that question, the circuits have had an opportunity, which they have declined, to reconsider their original rulings, and neither the Supreme Court nor Congress has been willing to resolve the conflict. We think it highly unlikely that both the Supreme Court and Congress would let stand persisting conflict among the circuits on issues of any real importance. The Court's repeated refusal to intervene in the face of an intercircuit conflict therefore might be read as a signal to the agency to fashion a policy that is consistent with the rulings of the circuits.

The critical factor here, too, is that the law is no longer flux: The circuits have proven unwilling to reconcile their views, and Congress and the Court, by their inaction, have chosen to tolerate horizontal disuniformity in the administration of the particular statute. In such circumstances, intracircuit nonacquiescence is undesirable on policy grounds because it produces distributional unfairness without the compensating benefits of prodding intercircuit harmonization or Supreme Court intervention.

We turn next to a situation in which the law at the circuit court level is in flux—it is still conceivable that some courts will reconsider their original decisions adverse to the agency and that the agency's policy will ultimately be uniformly validated. Assume, for example, that the agency loses before one circuit and then wins before the next two considering its policy. Certainly, at that point one would not say that a uniform outcome in the agency's favor is foreclosed, or even improbable. In such circumstances, nonacquiescence may lead to a quicker resolution of intercircuit conflicts, with consequent benefits in terms of the goals of uniform administration. Moreover, there are cost savings from obviating the need for differential administration during the period in which the agency has a reasonable basis to believe that its policy might yet prevail. On the other side of the equation are the distributional concerns. While sympathetic to such concerns, we believe that they should not be an automatic trump, except where Congress has spoken on the question in the governing statute.

In light of the preceding discussion, we conclude that intracircuit nonacquiescence is justified only where it is an adjunct to litigation designed to yield a uniform rule in favor of the agency's preferred policy. It follows, as a corollary, that once it becomes unlikely that relitigation will lead to judicial acceptance of the agency's policy, intracircuit nonacquiescence loses its justification; the agency must then fashion an approach consistent with the law of the circuit, even though it remains free to continue to press its preferred policy in circuits that have not yet rejected it. * * *

* * *

Conclusion

* * *

Our Article takes a middle course between the co-equal branch and district court metaphors * * *. Our approach recognizes a role for the courts in policing agency practices in this area, but also acknowledges the legitimacy of an agency's desire to maintain a uniform administration of its governing statute while it reasonably seeks the national validation of its preferred position. The virtue of this approach is not that it travels an intermediate course. Rather, it flows from a theory of the proper functions of courts and agencies in the administrative state. It attempts to do justice to the respective responsibilities of, and the delicate interaction between, these key institutions in our administrative lawmaking system.

Matthew Diller and Nancy Morawetz,
Intracircuit Nonacquiescence and the Breakdown of the Rule of Law: A Response to Estreicher and Revesz, 99 YALE L.J. 801, 801-05, 807-17, 821-23 (1990)*

Over the past decade, administrative agency nonacquiescence—the refusal of an administrative agency to apply the law of the reviewing court—has been roundly condemned by the courts. In requiring agencies to comply with circuit precedent, the courts have drawn a sharp line between authority of the government to pursue litigation in circuits that have not yet ruled on an issue and its obligation to accept the settled law of circuits that have ruled against the government. * * *

In their recent article, *Nonacquiescence by Federal Administrative Agencies*, Professors Samuel Estreicher and Richard Revesz argue that nonacquiescence within a circuit may be legitimate, even when the law of circuit is clearly settled. They argue that nonacquiescence in a circuit's case law is permissible so long as the agency is reasonably seeking to vindicate its position in the courts and is forwarding a position that is not "so bereft of support in available legal materials that it is unlikely to be accepted by any other court of appeals." * * *

* * *

This Comment critiques Estreicher and Revesz' underlying assumption about our legal system and their proposed standard for permissible nonacquiescence. We argue that their proposal upsets the balance between agencies and courts by rendering the judiciary essentially powerless to enforce congressional limitations on agency conduct for long periods of time. * * *

* * *

I. The Role of Circuit Court Precedent in Achieving Stability and Consistency in the Application of Federal Laws

An essential function of a judicial system is to maintain the rule of law. Continuity between legal standards as expressed in judicial decisions and legal standards as observed outside the courts is a central aspect of the rule of law. This continuity protects the judiciary from being overwhelmed by individual cases, provides for equality of treatment that is not dependent on access to the courts, and enables parties to order their affairs. Absent an ability to establish a rule of law, a judicial system becomes solely a resolver of individual disputes for those who pursue litigations, rather than an expositor of norms.

The central premise of Estreicher and Revesz' article is that our judicial system should be treated as incapable of establishing a rule of law in cases involving Federal agencies unless and until there is percolation of issues throughout the courts of appeals and resolution by the Supreme Court or Congress. Prior to such a nationwide resolution of an issue, they treat the law as established by the circuit courts as merely tentative statements by courts that lack authority to maintain a rule of law within their jurisdictions. They therefore allow agencies to continue to apply rules as though there were no judicial declaration of invalidity, so long as there is a possibility that the agency will eventually convince another circuit of the correctness of the agency's position. * * *

* * *

Estreicher and Revesz' view of circuit court precedent is inconsistent with the central role assigned to these courts in the Federal judicial system. Although they correctly note that one function of circuit courts is to participate in the process of national law

---

* Reprinted with permission of The Yale Law Journal, Fred B. Rothman & Company, Matthew Diller, and Nancy Morawetz. All rights reserved.

development, they would have this role triumph over the circuit court's essential function of providing a measure of judicial repose within each regional circuit. * * *

The judicial branch is structured to ensure uniformity and stability of legal standards within each regional circuit while permitting disuniformity among the circuits. The circuit system serves to allocate the judicial power among manageable units that can preserve the rule of law within their jurisdiction through adherence to stare decisis. Intercircuit stare decisis, however, is not necessary to the maintenance of the rule of law. As long as parties can discern which circuit law applies to any given conduct, the parties can shape their action to conform to legal standards. Furthermore, permitting circuits to independently examine issues contributes to resolution of important legal questions on a national basis. Accordingly, each circuit remains completely free to accept or reject the reasoning of other courts of appeals. This mixture of uniformity and diversity strikes a balance that permits legal issues to receive independent examination by a number of courts, while at the same time maintaining a unitary rule of law in any given geographic location.

* * *

The value of maintaining stability in circuit court precedent flows directly from the nature of a hierarchical legal system. To control the volume of cases requiring adjudication, the circuit courts are designed to hear a limited number of cases, with more routine matters decided by the district courts and administrative agencies, and with parties conforming their conduct to the rule of law. If the decision of the circuits were not accorded precedential weight, but were constantly open to question, these courts could be easily overwhelmed by parties raising issues addressed in earlier rulings by the same court. The system simply could not function if precedent were so unstable.

Because of the size of the Federal agency docket subject to review, the stability and consistency created by these rules for achieving judicial repose within each circuit are essential to orderly judicial review of agency action. Federal agencies process many times the number of cases that are reviewed in Federal court. When agencies apply rules differently from the courts, agency adjudication becomes simply a hurdle to overcome before obtaining judicial review. The potential for overwhelming the courts with challenges to agency determinations is staggering. This burden would be even greater if the courts were expected constantly to reconsider their precedents either by abandoning prior panel rulings or through the en banc process.

* * *

Apart from these structural reasons why circuit court decisions serve as definitive statements of law within their jurisdictions, there are many practical reasons why Estreicher and Revesz' vision of the role of circuit law is unrealistic. They essentially view case law as setting forth distinct issues that are developed in a large number of circuits and ultimately resolved by a conflict resolver, such as the Supreme Court. Although this view of the law may make sense from the perspective of issues the Supreme Court has actually decided, it mischaracterizes the nature of the judicial landscape on statutory issues. Many statutory issues are too short lived to be passed on by all circuits and to warrant Supreme Court review. Other issues may arise too infrequently to be passed on by a large number of circuits. Some issues are not significant enough to lead to higher review. With respect to many issues, the circuits will ultimately agree with each other.

Of course, when a significant conflict develops, the Supreme Court will sometimes intervene. Estreicher and Revesz, however, significantly overstate the role of Supreme Court review in resolving statutory issues. They view the potential for intercircuit conflict followed by Supreme Court resolution to be so great as to render decisions by the courts of appeals mere points along the path to the high court. While the Supreme Court remains, along with Congress, the arbiter of last resort on statutory issues, its decisional capacity is small compared to the large number of statutory matters addressed by the courts of appeals.

Even if the Supreme Court eventually resolves an issue decided by the court of appeals, there are numerous reasons to treat the declarations of the courts of appeals as authoritative, pending a determination by the Supreme Court. The Supreme Court frequently addresses narrowly framed questions that leave many matters unresolved. By issuing narrowly tailored rulings, the Supreme Court can alter the debate on statutory issues rather than finally resolving the matters in dispute. Furthermore, the Supreme Court may sustain the courts of appeals that ruled against an agency. Lastly, the interval between a court of appeals decision and a subsequent Supreme Court decision on the same issue is often measured in years. During this period, the court of appeals decision remains the last word within the circuit in which it was rendered.

Altogether, because of the likelihood that the Federal courts will agree as to matters of statutory interpretation, the rules curtailing revision of precedent, and limitations on Supreme Court review, our legal system treats the law of the circuit as authoritative until it is overturned. By modeling their analysis on three contingencies—that the courts of appeals might come into conflict whenever the agency's position is not "bereft of support," that any such conflict could lead to reconsideration by the first court or to Supreme Court review, and that such reconsideration or review will overturn a circuit court decision adverse to the agency—Estreicher and Revesz treat the exceptional situation as the norm and vastly understate the degree to which our judicial system depends on the circuit courts to provide order and stability in the administration of the law.

II. The Cost and Benefits of Nonacquiescence

In light of structural limitations on circuit reconsideration of past precedent, Estreicher and Revesz have greatly overstated the systemic benefits of nonacquiescence while underestimating the devastating costs nonacquiescence may have in practice. Each of the benefits they associate with nonacquiescence is premised on a strong likelihood that circuits will depart from the rules of stare decisis. In fact, only three cost-benefit factors play a significant role: the hardship for those who are denied the benefit of the circuit rule at the administrative level and are unable to seek the judicial review necessary to gain the benefit of the court rule; the financial cost and hardship due to delay imposed on those who manage to appeal to court; and the burden of repetitive litigation, borne by the judiciary. Because the hardship to parties affected by nonacquiescence can only be mitigated through massive litigation, the overall costs of nonacquiescence can be shifted but will always remain significant.

* * *

As Estreicher and Revesz recognize, agency compliance with circuit law within a circuit does not inhibit the primary form of intercircuit dialogue where circuits consider issues that have been ruled on by other circuits. But they propose that proper "percolation" of issues in the courts of appeals requires that circuit courts reconsider issues that they previously resolved. The marginal benefits to intercircuit dialogue that Estreicher and Revesz attribute to nonacquiescence depend on such circuit reconsideration being common, if not the norm. Given the circuit court rules designed to achieve stability of precedent, however, it will be the rare case in which nonacquiescence leads to any additional intercircuit dialogue.

The stability of circuit law also provides strong reason to doubt that nonacquiescence enhances uniform application of Federal law. Estreicher and Revesz suggest that requiring administrative adherence to decisions of the courts of appeals within their jurisdiction promotes disuniformity among regions of the country, and in some situations, may even lead to decisions in one jurisdiction having effects in other jurisdictions. Thus, they suggest an air pollution standard applied in one state will affect a downwind state's air and will affect the relative competitiveness of industry in two states. At a more general level, they suggest that treating people differently depending on where they live is inherently unfair.

The difficulty with this analysis is that it presumes that nonacquiescence somehow enhances national uniformity. Problems caused by differing regional rules are irrelevant to an analysis of nonacquiescence unless nonacquiescence contributes to uniformity across regions. Only in exceptional circumstances where the circuit will depart from its past precedent is there any possibility that intracircuit nonacquiescence will advance intercircuit uniformity. Nonacquiescence by itself does not lead to uniform application of the law, because in regions where the judicial precedent sets forth standards or procedures that differ from the policy applied by an agency, parties that lose before the agency need only seek judicial review to obtain the benefit of circuit court precedent. Absent barriers to judicial review (such as lack of legal counsel, lack of knowledge that the standards applied by the judiciary differ from those of the agency, or a judgment that the amount at issue does not justify the cost of litigation), all disappointed parties affected by nonacquiescence can be expected to vindicate their rights in court. So long as the circuit court's rule continues to be available to those who live in its regions, nonacquiescence only serves to cause gross disuniformity between those who can pursue their appeals and those who cannot.

The third benefit Estreicher and Revesz attribute to nonacquiescence is that it saves the agency the costs of differential administration associated with applying different sets of rules in different parts of the country. Here Estreicher and Revesz focus solely on the costs of following circuit law, while ignoring administrative saving from adherence to the law that, in all likelihood, would be applied by the reviewing court. Courts are likely to find error in agency decisions that are not made in accordance with circuit law. Because of the deference granted to agencies as fact finders, the outcome on appeal will often be a remand to the agency for application of judicial standards to the case. This is especially likely when the court concludes that there has been an error of law, or that some required procedural rule has not been followed. As a result, any accurate measure of the administrative costs of nonacquiescence must account for both the cost of differential administration and the cost of conducting additional administrative proceedings to apply the law of the circuit. In many cases, nonacquiescence causes two rounds of administrative proceedings where only one would have been necessary if circuit rules had been applied by the agency in the first instance. * * *

While Estreicher and Revesz inflate the benefits of nonacquiescence, they vastly understate its costs. They identify two costs: distributional consequences for those who do not appeal and increased judicial workload. Each of these repercussions is far more severe than they suggest.

Estreicher and Revesz recognize that nonacquiescence frequently imposes costs on parties who lack the resources or the sophistication to commence litigation to obtain the benefit of judicial precedent. These parties are unable to obtain the benefit of circuit court rules and may suffer serious harms, such as the termination of subsistence benefits or deportation, which would be avoided by application of circuit court precedent. Indeed, even for those who have the resources to obtain judicial review, Estreicher and Revesz recognize that the costs of litigation may result in affected parties deciding not to pursue their right to application of circuit precedent. As a result, nonacquiescence creates its own disuniformities by making a different set of rules available to those who can litigate and those who cannot. The availability of one set of legal standards for those who seek review and another set for those who are unable to vindicate their rights in court undermines the integrity of administrative government. Such a dual standard of law is particularly offensive because it is not an incidental by-product of nonacquiescence. Rather, from an agency's standpoint, many benefits of nonacquiescence are directly related to the inability of affected parties to challenge its decisions in court.

The disparate treatment of the rich and the poor engendered by nonacquiescence is not the only distributional consequence of such a policy. An additional and potentially devastating consequence of nonacquiescence is that those parties before the agency that can and do appeal to court must wait until they have exhausted administrative and judicial proceedings before they can receive the benefit of the circuit's law. The Estreicher and Revesz analysis missed this crucial time dimension.

The hardship caused by having to wait for judicial rules to be applied is perhaps clearest in the Social Security context. A recent study by the General Accounting Office shows that the average length of time between an initial application for Social Security benefits and completion of proceedings following remand is close to four years. During this time period, many disabled persons are forced to subsist on state public assistance programs. Others are left with no means of subsistence. The benefits these claimants receive after years of administrative and judicial proceedings can hardly compensate for the loss of the benefits when they were most needed. While waiting for the application of circuit law to their cases, claimants may be deprived of basic necessities such as food, shelter, and necessary medical care. They literally may not survive until the day when benefits are finally granted.

Outside the Social Security context, delay creates cognizable costs, although not as dire. For example, Estreicher and Revesz suggest that the Merit Systems Protection Board engages in some degrees of intracircuit nonacquiescence. In these cases, significant delays in grade increases and reinstatement may affect an individual's career path and ability to obtain a full remedy. Although these hardships are less dramatic, they remain a cost to be factored into any cost-benefit analysis of nonacquiescence.

The final factor Estreicher and Revesz consider is the impact that nonacquiescence has on the workload of the Federal courts. Although they recognize that it is "logical to expect" that the workload will increase with nonacquiescence, they do not discuss the magnitude of the burden their proposal places on the courts. If all disappointed parties before the agencies pursued their rights, the court would be crushed by the burden of adjudicating repetitive identical cases. In the Social Security context, for example, the rate of judicial filings soared following the agency's adoption of a policy of nonacquiescence, leading to a significant impact on the judicial docket.
* * *

A fair consideration of the costs and supposed benefits of nonacquiescence requires rejection of Estreicher and Revesz' proposed standard. Each benefit they identify is based on a view of the judicial system that does not square with the rules applied by the circuit courts. In contrast to the illusory benefits of nonacquiescence, its costs are undeniable.

* * *

IV. The Constitutionality of Nonacquiescence Under the Existing Structure for Judicial Review of Agency Action

Estreicher and Revesz analyze the constitutionality of nonacquiescence by postulating the existence of a statute explicitly authorizing such conduct by Federal agencies. They conclude that this hypothetical statute would pass constitutional muster. Regardless of whether one accepts the legality of such a statute, this analysis sheds little light on the constitutionality of nonacquiescence in the absence of such express congressional authorization. * * * [B]ecause nonacquiescence implicates the scope and efficacy of judicial review, it cannot be assumed that Congress has delegated the matter to agencies through general grants of rulemaking or other quasi-legislative authority. Accordingly, the fact that Congress may be able to fashion a scheme of judicial review that permits nonacquiescence does not further the analysis of whether agencies can nonacquiesce given the existing structure of judicial review.

Without the benefit of express congressional guidance on the issue, assessment of the constitutionality of nonacquiescence calls for closer examination of the role of Article III courts in resolving disputes and declaring the law. Esteicher and Revesz accept the premise that the highest Article III court, the Supreme Court, issues declarations of law binding on the executive department through precedential effect. *Marbury v. Madison* settled the proposition that the judiciary can issue statements of law that bind officials of the other branches. In *Cooper v. Aaron*, the Court held that its declarations of law are binding on governmental officials sworn to uphold the law, even though they may not have been formal parties to the case and were not bound by the terms of a court order. Read together, *Marbury* and *Cooper* articulate a system of judicial review under which the judiciary does not simply issue narrowly framed orders which bind the parties to a case, but also announces declarations of law binding on the executive branch through precedential effect.

* * *

In contrast, Estreicher and Revesz' proposal renders the decision of a circuit court little more than a vote to be counted in a later determination of what the law should be. While their proposal would minimize the possibility that agencies would act in reliance on declarations that are subject to change, it would greatly reduce the power of the judicial branch to issue binding statements of law. It would also create an anomalous situation where the accepted rules of agency conduct would conflict with the rules available to parties in court. The judiciary's role as resolver of individual disputes would be severed from its function as declarer of the law, thereby undermining the system of voluntary compliance that society relies on to resolve most disputes without resort to the judiciary. Above all, the system they propose is not the model that Congress and the courts have adopted.

* * *

Additional Sources

William Wade Buzbee, *Administrative Agency Intracircuit Nonacquiescence*, 85 Colum. L. Rev. 582 (1985)

Dan T. Coenen, *The Constitutional Case Against Intracircuit Nonacquiescence*, 75 Minn. L. Rev. 1339 (1991)

Samuel Estreicher & Richard L. Revesz, *The Uneasy Case Against Intracircuit Nonacquiescence: A Reply*, 99 Yale L.J. 831 (1990)

Carolyn A. Kubitschek, *Social Security Administration Nonacquiescence: The Need for Legislative Curbs on Agency Discretion*, 50 U. Pitt. L. Rev. 399 (1989)

Deborah Maranville, *Nonacquiescence: Outlaw Agencies, Imperial Courts, and the Perils of Pluralism*, 39 Vand. L. Rev. 471 (1986)

Burt Neuborne, *The Binding Quality of Supreme Court Precedent*, 61 Tul. L. Rev. 991 (1987)

Gary L. Rodgers, *The Commissioner "Does Not Acquiesce,"* 59 Neb. L. Rev. 1001 (1980)

Joshua I. Schwartz, *Nonacquiescence,* Crowell v. Benson, *and Administrative Adjudication*, 77 Geo. L.J. 1815 (1989)

Joseph F. Weis, Jr., *Agency Non-Acquiescence—Respectful Lawlessness or Legitimate Disagreement?*, 48 U. Pitt. L. Rev. 845 (1987)

James Roy Williams, *The Social Security Administration's Policy of Non-Acquiescence*, 12 N. Ky. L. Rev. 253 (1985)

D. The General Controversy About the Role of Courts in Administrative Law

Inevitably, contemporary debates about administrative law include major controversies about the general role of courts. In the first excerpt, Professor Keith Werhan defends the idea that courts should actively check agency power. He sets forth this traditional understanding as well as what he calls the neoclassical model of administrative law, which he sees as a reaction against the traditional understanding. The neoclassical model is exemplified by *Chevron*, which ostensibly seeks to cut back the judicial role by limiting the domain of "law" as opposed to "policy" in administrative controversies. This "classical" distinction between law and policy is melded with a "neoclassical" skepticism about the competence and integrity of courts as reviewers of agency policymaking. While tracing these ideas in a number of doctrines, Professor Werhan criticizes the neoclassical model.

In the second excerpt, Professor Shep Melnick, a political scientist, questions the role of courts as active reviewers of agency decisionmaking. He suggests, for instance, that judicial intervention can lead directly to delays in rulemaking. Moreover, judicial review can create serious uncertainties for agencies, which may respond by adding additional procedures and developing larger rulemaking files, thereby making rulemaking more inefficient. Furthermore, Professor Melnick suggests that aggressive judicial review shifts power from agency policymakers to agency lawyers, and that such a result undercuts the goal of coherent and sensible agency policy.

Keith Werhan, *The Neoclassical Revival in Administrative Law*, 44 ADMIN. L. REV. 567, 567-69, 583-91, 594-602, 604, 606-15, 618-20, 626-27 (1992)*

I. Introduction

Federal administrative law has entered a period of transition. On the surface, the change is clear. It has been dominated by the Supreme Court's retrenchment into a policy of acquiescence with respect to an expanding array of decisionmaking by federal agencies. The Supreme Court's decision several years ago in *Chevron v. NRDC* has assumed instrumental and symbolic importance in charting this new deference. * * *

For all of this attention by scholars, courts, and litigants, as well as the decision's undeniable impact, the ultimate meaning and implications of *Chevron* remain unsettled. This uncertainty is due less to any ambiguity in the *Chevron* opinion than to the decision's implications for the traditional understanding of administrative law, which are profound. This article examines those implications by placing *Chevron* in the context of a broad range of recent Supreme Court decisions that have redrawn the lines of authority between agencies and reviewing courts. I argue that the *Chevron* decision's primary importance lies in its leading role in the Supreme Court's recent rejection of the traditional model of administrative law and its ongoing experiment to fashion a replacement paradigm.

I label this new paradigm the "neoclassical model," in order to suggest its apparent appeal to the Court. The neoclassical model seeks to unite the classical distinction between law and policy with a postmodern skepticism about the competence and integrity of courts to oversee agency decisionmaking. The distinguishing trademark, and bite, of the model is its rigid definition of "law," one which limits the concept to the clearly expressed intent of an authoritative lawmaker, such as Congress, and which thereby denies reviewing courts an active role in the administrative process. The model thus offers the simplicity of a central organizing principle for administrative law that minimizes reliance on the courts to control the system.

Another source of the neoclassical model's appeal is its timing. The model surfaced in the late 1970s and gained momentum during the 1980s. This followed a period of intense judicial activism, roughly from the mid-1960s to mid-1970s, when courts assumed a major responsibility for ensuring the openness of agency decisionmaking processes and the soundness of the decisionmaking itself. The neoclassical model represents not only a reaction to the excesses of that activism, but also a severe overreaction that aims to overturn and replace the traditional model of administrative law as well.

* * *

II. The Evolution of the Traditional Model of Administrative Law

The core components of the traditional model of administrative law are deceptively simple. At the outset, the model posits that agencies owe their creation to, and are empowered by, Congress. According to the model, Congress creates an agency by enacting a statute (usually called an "enabling act" or an "organic statute" interchangeably), which provides rules that control and limit the agency's exercise of its authority. As a corollary, the traditional model requires agencies to follow procedures which ensure that their decisions comply with statutory authority. The ultimate assurance of agency compliance, however, is the availability of judicial review, which the model generally requires.

* * *

III. Disenchantment with the Traditional Model: The Concern with Interest Representation

The postwar dominance of the traditional model of administrative law masked its vulnerability. The major source of unease has been in the set of legal process assumptions of institutional competence which provides the model its apparent coherence. The weakest link, ironically, proved to be the agency. Observers increasingly questioned the optimistic assumptions of agency behavior that the traditional model had absorbed from Progressive and New Deal ideology. The crucial shift was one of perception. Administrative decisionmaking came to be seen as less technocratic and more political in nature.

As this revision eventually took hold, the mystique of the administrator began to dim. When an agency decision is viewed as political, the desirability of agency discretion is brought into question. The claim for autonomy of agency decisionmakers, as well as for their insulation from political actors, becomes increasingly doubtful. Agency claims of technical expertise lose power if the nature of their work is at least as political as it is "scientific."

---

* Reprinted with permission of Keith Werhan. All rights reserved.

* * *

Because agency decisionmakers could no longer be trusted to exercise their considerable discretion quite so freely, courts felt the need to increase their responsibility to ensure that agencies act reasonably. To accommodate the new judicial role, administrative law underwent another evolution. * * * Inevitably, in light of the prevailing skepticism of administrative expertise and corresponding disenchantment with agency autonomy, reformers no longer treated agencies as uniquely situated to engage in policy formation. Instead, drawing on pluralist theory, they analogized agency decisionmaking processes to those of the legislature, whose function is to reconcile the claims of competing interest groups affected by the ultimate decision.

To implement the revised theory, reformers proposed an interrelated series of changes in government administration which, when taken together, have been labeled the "interest representation" model of administrative law. The unifying theme of interest-representation reforms was the perceived need to open up administrative processes so that the full array of interests affected by an agency's action could be represented in the decisionmaking. This revision of the traditional model essentially prescribes more democracy to cure agency failure. By doing so, reformers expected to improve the substance and fairness of agency decisions.

This ambition is reflected by the changes in administrative law doctrine effected during the interest-representation era. To lower barriers to public participation in the administrative process, the courts relaxed standards governing party initiation of agency proceedings and intervention in ongoing agency proceedings. The Supreme Court reinforced the democratization of agency processes by lowering traditional barriers to judicial review. Emphasizing interest-representation goals, the Court manifested a newfound willingness to review agency action whenever the interests of a challenger had been harmed. Thus, the Court would find litigant standing to sue an agency if the plaintiff alleged "injury in fact." The Court welcomed preenforcement legal challenges to agency rulemaking that carried a "direct and immediate" effect to the challenger. The Court also endorsed a presumption of judicial review of final agency action, reading narrowly the APA exceptions to the availability of review. The activist judicial posture, as well as the distrust of agencies, that characterized the interest-representation model was also reflected by the Court's willingness to infer private rights of action to enforce statutory and constitutional rights. Such private actions allowed courts an additional check on agencies that had ignored their mission.

The Court's transformation of the rules governing access to the courts by those who challenge agency action presumed a more active review function than that contemplated by the traditional model. Agencies, no longer protected by assumptions that they simply executed congressional authority by applying their expertise to solve public problems in the public interest, now were required to account more fully for their decisionmaking. Courts substantially intensified their procedural and substantive review of agency action. Both dimensions of the Court's newly energized approach to judicial review stretched the traditional model and have remained controversial.

* * *

* * * With the rise of interest-representation concerns, courts began to take a "hard look" at agency decisionmaking before legitimating administrative action. * * * [H]ard-look judicial review focuses on the soundness of the agency's decisionmaking, rather than on the correctness of the ultimate decision itself. As Judge Leventhal explained in his influential exposition of hard-look doctrine:

> [The court's] supervisory function calls on [it] to intervene . . . if [it] becomes aware, especially from a combination of danger signals, that the agency has not really taken a "hard look" at the salient problems, and has not genuinely engaged in reasoned decision-making. If the agency has not shirked this fundamental task, however, the court exercises restraint and affirms the agency's action even though the court would on its own account have made different findings or adopted different standards.[146]

For Judge Leventhal, the hard-look approach, if administered properly, achieves two legal process ideals: it insists that agencies engage in "reasoned decision-making," while observing the "salutary principle of judicial restraint."

The paradigmatic, as well as generative, decision of the hard-look era was by the Supreme Court in *Citizens to Preserve Overton Park, Inc. v. Volpe*. In *Overton Park*, the Court considered a lawsuit by private citizens and conservation organizations challenging the decision by the Secretary of Transporta-

---

[146] *Greater Boston Television Corp.*, 444 F.2d at 851 (footnote omitted).

tion to authorize funding of a major highway through a city park. They claimed the Secretary's decision violated federal enabling statutes that limited the funding of such projects through public parks. The Court began its analysis * * * by independently interpreting the enabling statutes to define the boundaries of the Secretary's funding authority. * * * [T]he Court found itself in disagreement with the agency, allowing for considerably less discretion than that which the Secretary had found when he read the statute. The Court did not hesitate to trump the agency's reading with its own * * *.

The cleanest break * * * occurred when the Court moved from its interpretation of the enabling act to inquire whether the Secretary's decision abused the discretion vested by the statute. * * * [I]n *Overton Park*, the Court did not * * * back off, establishing instead the subtle position of hard-look review:

> [T]he court must consider whether the decision was based on a consideration of the relevant factors and whether there has been a clear error of judgment. Although this inquiry into the facts is to be searching and careful, the ultimate standard of review is a narrow one. The court is not empowered to substitute its judgment for that of the agency.

* * * [T]he Court in *Overton Park* made clear that its review would be vigorous. In a powerful signal to lower courts, agencies, and private litigants, the Court in *Overton Park* returned the case to the district court because, it found, there was "an inadequate basis" for it to engage in the newly decreed style of judicial review. * * * The primary importance of *Overton Park* was its manifestation of a new judicial mood, one that discounted claims of agency expertise and that required convincing justifications before upholding agency decisions.

Whereas the traditional model had difficulty withstanding the doubts created by its reliance on the presumed institutional competence of administrative agencies, the hard-look judicial review of the interest-representation era created its own doubts about the competence of courts to walk the *Overton Park* tightrope. Many observers increasingly doubted the capacity of a court to engage in a "searching and careful" review of the factual basis of agency decisionmaking, yet avoid substituting its policy judgment for the agency's. Those doubts were fueled by the extraordinary detail of many hard-look opinions.
* * *

* * *

IV. The Neoclassical Revival

Beginning in the late 1970s, and accelerating during the 1980s, the Supreme Court turned away from the interest-representation model, adopting yet another approach to administrative law. This new approach, which I label the "neoclassical model" has, as its focal point, a revival of the classical distinction between law and policy. The law-policy distinction, while important to the traditional model of administrative law, had become increasingly obscured during the interest-representation era. Yet, the neoclassical model's reemphasis of the law-policy distinction does not signal a return to a "classical" or a "traditional" understanding of administrative law. Because of the distinctive understanding of the law-policy distinction reflected in the neoclassical model, the Court's approach is new, and troubling.

Rather than attempt at the outset to develop the neoclassical model abstractly, I will have the Court present its new approach in the context of recently decided cases across a broad spectrum of agency-court relations. * * *

A. The *Chevron* Decision
* * *

The central rationale for the *Chevron* transformation of judicial role is the law-policy distinction associated with classical legal theory. This theme, and the distinctive uses to which *Chevron* puts it, comes through most prominently in the final paragraphs of Justice Stevens's opinion. On this account, the reviewing court's duty is restricted to the application of law, which Justice Stevens apparently restricts to enforcing "the unambiguously expressed intent of Congress." If there is ambiguity, the question is one of policy, not law, and the primary decisionmaking responsibility is the agency's, not the court's. "Judges are not experts in the field," Justice Stevens explained, "and are not part of either political branch of the Government." The agencies, by contrast, are part of a "political branch," and it is "entirely appropriate" for them "to make such policy choices—resolving the competing interests which Congress itself either inadvertently did not resolve, or intentionally left to be resolved by the agency charged with the administration of the statute in light of everyday realities."

The *Chevron* decision reflects an obvious break with the "hard-look" attitude of the interest-representation model that dominated the preceding decade. The Court's opinion in *Chevron* reads as if it had been written with a determination to reverse the tendency of interest-representation practitioners to blur the distinction between law and policy. This feature of *Chevron* is not in conflict with the traditional model, which was never itself comfortable with the more ambitious leanings of interest representation. Yet, more subtly, *Chevron* departs from the traditional model of administrative law as well. The key signal of that departure are the harsh words directed at the court of appeals for engaging in purposeful statutory interpretation, the centerpiece of * * * the traditional model. After *Chevron*, the traditional approach to judicial review of agency action was tainted as judicial policymaking, a "basic legal error" that judges must avoid. The Court now doubted judicial competence to interpret all enabling statutes that are not, in effect, self-interpreting. Thus, *Chevron*'s revival of the law-policy distinction carried a conception of the distinction far removed from that of legal process thinking and of the traditional model. Clarity, after *Chevron*, became the line of demarcation between law and policy, and accordingly, between the authority of courts and agencies.

B. *Chevron* in Context

The Court's opinion in *Chevron*, which is so jarring in its potential, calls for a more careful critique than the sketch in the preceding section. It is a mistake, however, to focus on the decision in isolation. *Chevron*, for all the boldness of its rhetoric, is hardly an aberration. The sharp distinction between law and policy reflected in that opinion has been a recurring theme in recent Supreme Court decisions that have recast virtually all aspects of judicial review of agency action. * * *

1. *The Rejection of Judicially Imposed Hybrid Rulemaking*

In retrospect, it seems clear that the neoclassical revival began in 1978 with the Supreme Court's well-known decision in *Vermont Yankee Nuclear Power Corp. v. NRDC*. *Vermont Yankee*'s status as a pivotal case has been clear from the date of its announcement. The Court used *Vermont Yankee* to halt the growing practice among the courts of appeals during the interest-representation era to require hybrid rulemaking procedures which had not been specified by positive law. The D.C. Circuit had invalidated a regulation because the procedures the agency followed, albeit in compliance with the notice-and-comment requirements of the APA, were not "sufficient to ventilate the issues." The Supreme Court responded with a scolding tone similar to that in *Chevron*, reprimanding the court of appeals for having "seriously misread" its role on judicial review. The corrective, in the neoclassical style, was to return the reviewing court to its proper role of enforcing positive law. * * *

The Court's primary justification for denying courts the power to require hybrid rulemaking procedures was a strict enforcement of the law-policy distinction. Absent constitutional requirements or extremely compelling circumstances, courts are without power to overturn rulemaking proceedings on the basis of procedural devices that go beyond the "statutory *minima.*" The Court's rationale was firmly anchored in neoclassical assumptions. Judges, the Court explained, "should . . . not stray beyond the judicial province to explore the procedural format or to impose upon the agency its own notion of which procedures are 'best' or most likely to further some vague, undefined public good." Gone are the legal process assumptions of judicial competence to fashion fair and effective procedures. After *Vermont Yankee*, procedural decisionmaking has largely been brought within the policymaking discretion of the agency itself, insulated from judicial review. * * *

2. *Restricting the Availability of Judicial Review*

The neoclassical project of formalizing, and thereby limiting, judicial review of administrative decisionmaking has been pronounced in the Supreme Court's recently revised approach to the availability of judicial review of agency action. Change has occurred across the board. The law-policy distinction, strictly applied, informs the Court's negation of the presumption of reviewability of agency action, its increasingly restrictive approach to allowing litigants standing to challenge governmental activities, and its hesitancy to imply private rights of action to enforce statutory responsibilities placed on governmental actors.

a. Negating the Presumption of Reviewability

The proposition that judicial review will generally be available to secure the legitimacy of agency action is a central component of the traditional model of administrative law. During the interest-representation era, the Supreme Court energized that idea in *Abbott Laboratories v. Gardner*, finding a "basic presumption" that final agency action will be subject to judicial review in suits filed by anyone adversely affected by the action. In 1985, less than one year after *Chevron*, the Court decided *Heckler v. Chaney*, which reversed that presumption in lawsuits challenging an agency's alleged failure to take enforcement action pursuant to its enabling statute. The Court decided that agency inaction presumptively falls within the APA's provision that exempts from judicial review "agency action [which] is committed to agency discretion by law." * * *

The theme of the Court's opinion in *Chaney*, once again, was the need to limit the power of reviewing courts. The Supreme Court criticized the approach taken by the court of appeals, which had looked at "pragmatic considerations" to determine "whether the interests at stake are important enough to justify intervention in the agencies' decisionmaking." Such an approach, the Court feared, would lead courts into considerations of policy, which are beyond the limited competence of reviewing courts to evaluate. Invoking a central theme of neoclassical thinking, the Court emphasized that agencies are "far better equipped than the courts" to balance "the many variables" that inform enforcement decisions. Moreover, the Court in *Chaney* revealed doubts about the role of judicial review that went to the heart of the traditional model. "The danger that agencies may not carry out their delegated powers with sufficient vigor," the Court explained, "does not necessarily lead to the conclusion that courts are the most appropriate body to police this aspect of their performance."

True to a neoclassical orientation, the Court addressed its concerns that courts reviewing agency inaction would become overly involved in policymaking by insisting that courts limit themselves to the application of clearly expressed legal constraints on agency discretion. * * *

The Court's approach in *Chaney* to the reviewability of agency inaction is consistent with that of *Vermont Yankee* and *Chevron*. In all three cases, the Court reasserted the law-policy distinction to separate cleanly the roles of reviewing court and agency. In no case does a judge's sense of the need for judicial review trigger the review power; only the existence of "law" to apply as against the agency suffices.

* * *

b. Restrictions on Standing

While on the threshold of the interest-representation era, the Supreme Court relaxed the standing requirements necessary for litigants to challenge administrative actors in federal court. In *Association of Data Processing Service Organizations v. Camp*, the Court, writing just one year before *Overton Park*, held that a litigant need not show that agency action violated one's legal rights in order to challenge the action. Instead, the Court focused on whether the litigant alleged that the agency's action caused him or her "injury in fact, economic or otherwise." The *Data Processing* approach fit the interest-representation, hard-look mood. By shifting the focus from rights to interests, courts could serve the interest-representation ideal of allowing those who are affected by agency decisionmaking to challenge the decision. Indeed, the Court in *Data Processing* explicitly noted that its lowering of standard barriers fit the "trend . . . toward enlargement of the class of people who may protest administrative action."

In the neoclassical era, that trend has been reversed. Although this reversal is reflected in a number of recent Supreme Court decisions, the restrictiveness and formality of the current approach to standing is well represented by *Allen v. Wright*, which the Court issued several days after *Chevron*. In *Allen*, the Court denied standing to the parents of black public school children who claimed that the Internal Revenue Service (IRS) had not enforced its statutory responsibility to deny tax-exempt status to racially discriminatory private schools. The Court distilled two claims of injury from the parents' complaint. First, the parents claimed harm by "the mere fact" that the federal government, because of the allegedly inadequate administration by IRS, provided financial aid to racially discriminatory schools. Second, the parents claimed that tax exemptions to racially discriminatory private schools undercut their efforts to desegregate public schools in their communities. The Court found neither claim sufficient to secure standing.

The Court held that the first claim of injury was too abstract to be "judicially cognizable." Plaintiffs have "no standing to complain simply that their Government is violating the law." Nor could they claim the funding had stigmatized them as members of the racial group subjected to the alleged discrimination. Such a stigmatic injury, the Court held, is available only to those who have been denied equal treatment by the challenged discriminatory activity.

The plaintiffs' second claim of injury was inadequate for a different reason. Indeed, the Court acknowledged that any governmental constriction of their children's ability to receive an education in a racially integrated school is "one of the most serious injuries recognized in our legal system." The Court held, however, that any such injury suffered by the plaintiffs was not traceable to IRS. The causal link between IRS's grant of tax exemptions to some racially discriminatory schools and desegregation of the public schools in the plaintiffs' communities, the Court found, was "attenuated at best." Plaintiffs' injuries, if any, were more directly traceable to actions of "third parties," such as parents who send their children to racially discriminatory private schools and the operators of those schools.

Neoclassical formalism drives the *Allen* rejection of these claims. Throughout its analysis, the Court voiced concern over the need to limit judges' power to involve themselves in policy disputes. To accept standing, the Court worried, "would pave the way generally for suits challenging, not specifically identifiable Government violations of *law*, but the particular programs agencies establish to carry out their legal obligations." The Justices would not allow the transformation of federal courts into "'a vehicle for the vindication of the value *interests* of concerned bystanders.'" Thus, the Court's recent restriction of standing doctrine, as reflected in *Allen*, reinforces the neoclassical repudiation of interest-representation values, while reaffirming the idea that courts should avoid involvement in agency policymaking by narrowing their focus to "specifically identifiable Government violations of law."

c. Reluctance to Imply Private Rights of Action

In recent years, the Court has been increasingly reluctant to imply causes of action by program beneficiaries against federal agencies to enforce statutory protections and responsibilities. This posture is a reversal from the Court's approach to implied rights of action when interest-representation values held more sway. * * *

* * *

4. *The Persistence of Substantive, Hard-Look Review*

There is always counterpoint in administrative law. Against the broad-based retreat into neoclassical formality I have described stands the Court's recent embrace of substantive, hard-look judicial review of agency action in *Motor Vehicle Manufacturers Association v. State Farm Mutual Automobile Insurance Co.* There is irony here. It was dissatisfaction with the judicial activism reflected by hard-look review that largely contributed to the neoclassical revival. Yet it is here, just one year before *Chevron*, that the Court refused the invitation to break with the hard-look approach it had generated in *Overton Park*.

* * *

There is * * * obvious tension between *State Farm* and *Chevron* yet, at least on one level, the decisions can be reconciled. The Court's standard of review in both cases is the same; it measures the reasonableness of agency action. * * *

Although the outcomes in the two cases are different, that can be explained on substantive grounds: EPA's adoption of the bubble regulation was reasonable, while NHTSA's rescission of the passive restraint requirement was not. In this view, EPA was able to ground an adequate justification of its decision on the rulemaking record, whereas NHTSA was not. Moreover, in *State Farm* the Court seemed convinced that rescinding the passive restraint rule would cost lives, while in *Chevron*, the Court was willing to accept that the bubble rule would not necessarily dirty the air. In sum, the differing judicial responses to agency action exhibited in *State Farm* and *Chevron* simply may reflect the differing quality of agency decisionmaking under review.

This reconciliation, although it has some validity, is ultimately unsatisfying. In spirit, tone, and approach, *Chevron* could hardly be farther from *State Farm*. The Court in *Chevron* not only failed to exhibit the in-depth judicial probing apparent in *State Farm*, but also seemed oddly indifferent in its acceptance of the agency rationale. The Court in *Chevron* seemed far closer to Justice (now Chief Justice) Rehnquist's approach in *State Farm* than to that of the majority. Chief Justice Rehnquist, who wrote for four Justices in *State Farm*, agreed that NHTSA needed to explain why it had not simply abandoned the detachable belt option and required installation of airbags or nondetachable belts. Chief Justice Rehnquist, however, would have upheld the agency's decision to rescind the detachable belt requirement. He criticized the majority for ignoring an overtly political rationale for NHTSA's rescission of that requirement:

A change in administration brought about by the people casting their votes is a perfectly reasonable basis for an executive agency's reappraisal of the costs and benefits of its programs and regulations. As long as the agency remains within the bounds established by Congress, it is entitled to assess administrative records and evaluate priorities in light of the philosophy of the administration.

If one adds to Chief Justice Rehnquist's approach that the "bounds established by Congress" must be clear in order to limit the play of agency politics, one has a faithful account of *Chevron*.

The movement between *State Farm* and *Chevron* is best captured by reconciling Chief Justice Rehnquist's minority opinion in *State Farm* with the Court's approach in *Chevron*. The Court's justification in *Chevron* for transferring power to control the meaning of ambiguous statutes from the courts to agencies, in effect, adopted Chief Justice Rehnquist's position in *State Farm*. The Court made this clear when it observed that "an agency to which Congress has delegated policymaking responsibilities may, within the limits of that delegation, properly rely upon the incumbent administration's views of the wise policy to inform its judgments.''

V. A Critique of the Neoclassical Model

The most immediate impact of the neoclassical model has been to reverse, at least for the most part, the expansionist tendencies of the interest-representation model. The constitutive decisions of the two models are mirror images of each other. For almost every interest-representation decision that increased some dimension of the power of reviewing courts, there now exists a neoclassical decision that reduces that power. Yet, the neoclassical model does not merely provide a counterbalance to the excesses of judicial activism. It promises as well to replace the traditional model of administrative law.

The neoclassical reconceptualization of the law-policy distinction significantly changes the nature and role of the legislative, administrative, and judicial actors in the governing system. * * * [T]he neoclassical model largely rejects, rather than builds upon, New Deal assumptions. The neoclassical approach draws its power by reaching beyond the New Deal to the Golden Age of the American founding generation, when in the first years of the nineteenth century, the Court introduced the law-policy distinction to organize decisionmaking responsibility in the fledgling government. In bringing that classical distinction up to date, the model largely ignores New Deal theory and rejects legal process assumptions, relying instead on post-legal process skepticism of the legislative and judicial functions to generate a narrow conception of what counts as "law." It is this curious joinder of a desire to return to classical order with a knowing, postmodern skepticism that accounts for much of the neoclassical model's appeal.

* * *

A. The Neoclassical Model and *Marbury*

The neoclassical model, which is organized according to the distinction between law and policy, draws much of its power from *Marbury v. Madison*, the fountainhead of American public law. In *Marbury*, the Court, speaking through Chief Justice Marshall, asserted the power to review, and if appropriate, to set aside, the acts of the legislative and executive branches of the national government. The Court grounded both assertions of power on the law-policy distinction. Indeed, the *Marbury* opinion is chiefly remembered for Chief Justice Marshall's claim, "It is emphatically the province and duty of the judicial department to say what the law is." As a less noticed corollary, however, *Marbury* places matters of policy outside the "province and duty" of the courts to be handled by the political branches.

* * *

The neoclassical model seeks to secure its legitimacy on this understanding of *Marbury*. The all-or-nothing quality of the law-policy distinction in *Chevron* fits Chief Justice Marshall's rhetoric. The *Chevron* insistence that reviewing courts limit themselves to enforcing unambiguous statutory commands recalls the *Marbury* assertion that a court's reviewing power is triggered "where a specific duty is assigned by law. . . ." Correspondingly, the *Marbury* injunction that discretionary acts by the executive "are only politically examinable" supports the *Chevron* position that, in the absence of clear statutory directives, courts must "respect legitimate policy choices" of government actors who are answerable to a political constituency.

In separating law from policy, however, Marshall did not mean to exclude the Court from political decisions. In truth, Marshall's aims were utterly inconsistent with the neoclassical project. Marshall separated law from policy in order to ensure that the Court would play a meaningful role in the governing structure. Marshall did not want to flee from, or make the Court subservient to, majoritarian politics. He sought to remove the Court from the withering partisan politics of the time, so that he could position the Court to limit political authority from threatening the core values of American society. Viewed in its historical perspective, *Marbury* is a shaky foundation for the neoclassical revival.

The innovation of *Chevron*, of course, is the equation of the interpretation of ambiguous statutes with the making of policy. In the neoclassical reformulation of *Marbury*, the reviewing court's role is limited to the enforcement of *clear* statutory commands because only with clarity does an agency have a *duty* to take a particular course of action. A judicial role is appropriate because, in such a situation, there is only one lawful option for the agency—to do what the law requires. If the statute is unclear, however, the neoclassical reading of *Marbury* frees the administrator from legal constraints because he or she has discretion to choose among more than one lawful option. It is the existence of interpretive discretion that converts statutory reading into a political act, that is, one guided by policy choice rather than by law. For *Chevron*, it is the clarity of a law, not merely the existence of a law, which separates law and policy.

It is on the equation of statutory ambiguity with policy discretion that *Chevron* and the neoclassical model depart from *Marbury*. For Chief Justice Marshall, statutory interpretation, even of an ambiguous statute, was ultimately for the Court. The essence of the judicial power, in Marshall's view, was the interpretation of laws as they apply to individuals. In claiming that judges would be limited to enforcing the law, Marshall did not suggest that courts should interpret the law mechanically. He fully understood that the Court's duty to interpret and apply law would involve discretion. His strategy was to cabin and justify that discretion by tying it to the task of discerning the "course prescribed by law," rather than of implementing the "will of the Judge." In discerning "the course prescribed by law," Marshall gave no indication that he would defer to the statutory reading of political actors.

* * *

The law-policy distinction of *Marbury*, properly understood, supports the traditional model of administrative law, not the neoclassical model. Both models follow Marshall's injunction that reviewing courts focus on law and limit themselves to enforcement of that law. The excesses of the interest-representation era, which strayed from that teaching, were thus in considerable tension with *Marbury*. But Marshall's focus on law did not deny the court's power, indeed its "province and duty," to interpret the law, even in the face of congressional ambiguity or silence. The neoclassical denial of a court's power to impose its interpretation of an ambiguous statute on administrative actors cannot be tied to the classical understanding of the law-policy distinction established in *Marbury*.

B. The Neoclassical Model and Postlegal Process Statutory Interpretation

Although the neoclassical model gains much from its rhetorical connection to the classical distinction between law and policy, its guiding spirit comes from a rejection of the legal process theory of statutory interpretation, the cementing agent of the traditional model of administrative law. The central feature of the legal process approach holds that a court should "[i]nterpret the words of the statute immediately in question so as to carry out the purpose as best it can. . . ." Neoclassicism's rejection of this tenet is seen clearest in *Chevron*, but it serves as a central premise of the other neoclassical decisions as well.

The neoclassical retreat from the legal process approach proceeds from the insight that ambiguous enabling statutes create discretion in courts or agencies, or both, to supply meaning. This observation is hardly new. As was developed in the preceding section, Marshall himself acknowledged that statutory interpretation provided "discretion" to judges, but he argued that it was a legitimate "legal discretion" by which courts would follow "the will of the Legislature," not the "will of the Judge." But beginning with the legal realist movement earlier in this century, and increasingly in recent years, many have become deeply skeptical of the court's ability to discern the actual will of the legislature underlying an ambiguous statute. This doubt about the possibility of an intentionalist approach has also surfaced with respect to the traditional sources of legislative history, with critics questioning whether they can provide accurate guides to the legislative mind. More fundamentally, skeptics, again joining the legal realists, question whether there is a legislative mind for any interpreter to discover. Although individual legislators may have an intent, it is fictional, according to this critique, to say that the legislature, as an entity, itself is of one collective mind when it enacts a statute.

* * * To the extent that statutory purpose is grounded on legislative intent, of course, it is subject to all of the challenges to an intentionalist approach to statutory interpretation. Even when the purposive approach to statutory interpretation looks beyond intentionalism and directs courts to interpret the statute so that it serves a "reasonable" purpose, it remains vulnerable. In the postmodern world, many interpreters have become far less confident than were those of the postwar generation that one can examine the context of a legislative action and ascertain which purposes are reasonable, and which are not. As a result, there is increased fear that, in practice, the judges' "reasoned elaboration" of statutory purpose prescribed by legal process theory degenerates into their simply giving effect to their policy preferences.
* * *

Neoclassical critics of an active judicial role in the enforcement of statutory restraints on agencies have internalized this realist critique of intentionalist and purposive approaches to statutory interpretation. Thus, they conclude that, at least with respect to ambiguous statutes, there is no reason to prefer judicial interpretation over agency interpretation. The result is a call for judicial acquiescence to agency interpretations quite unlike the judicial deference of the traditional model. Courts are not told to give due consideration to the interpretations by agencies, as under the traditional model, but to cede interpretive authority to them. This instruction does not reflect the Progressive or New Deal confidence in the independence or expertise of administrators, but rather an utter lack of confidence in the competence of judges. * * *

The legal process advocacy of purposive statutory interpretation has been undermined in recent years not only by a skepticism of judicial interpretive competence, but also by increasing doubts about the legislative process. Legal process theory deems all law, including statutes, to serve intelligible, rational, public-regarding purposes. Public choice scholarship, which has gained increased acceptance among legal theorists in recent years, profoundly challenges that assumption.

* * *

In truth, the public choice approach to statutory interpretation manifested in *Chevron* reflects a normative choice, not an empirical imperative, to read statutes in so limited a manner. There is considerable irony here. The neoclassical model presents reviewing courts as largely passive participants in the administrative process. According to the model, courts should routinely defer, even acquiesce, to administrative interpretation of legislative design. But that acquiescence is grounded on a controversial conception of statutory interpretation and of the legislative process, a conception that the legislature itself does not necessarily share. Seen in this light, *Chevron* and the neoclassical canon reflect the type of judicial activism they purport to displace, with the Court, in effect, privileging its conception of the legislative process over that of Congress.

There are two objections, each consistent with public choice theory, that argue against the normative choice reflected in *Chevron*. First, the effect of the * * * [*Chevron*] approach to interpreting enabling statutes is to transfer interpretive power from reviewing courts to agencies. This, of course, is by design. It reflects the neoclassical skepticism of judicial interpretive competence and the desire to achieve greater political accountability. Public choice theory, however, should make one hesitate to transfer such power to agency actors. The theory would predict that administrators, no less than legislators, will act in their own self-interest, responding to interest-group bidding or to other political actors who are themselves responding to the pressure of interest groups. Public choice theory provides no basis to expect that agency interpretations of statutory ambiguity would serve the public interest better than judicial interpretations, or indeed, would pursue public purposes at all.

The second, more profound objection to the * * * [*Chevron*] approach to statutory interpretation is that it may make matters worse. Although an important justification of *Chevron* has been the perception that it serves majoritarianism, the neoclassical model's languid approach to statutory interpretation exacerbates the defects in the majoritarian process exposed by public choice scholarship. Paradoxically, public choice theory provides stronger support for the type of purposive statutory interpretation endorsed by the traditional model of administrative law than it does for the * * * [*Chevron*] approach. Because of constitutional (and public) expectations, legislators typically provide public-regarding purposes to justify and explain statutory enactments. When resolving ambiguities in the statute, the traditional model urges judges to hold the legislators to those public-regarding purposes. This task does not necessarily require judges to ascertain the legislative intent. If that intent is unclear, indeed even if the legislators were in fact motivated by self-interested dealmaking, the traditional model requires the judge to interpret enabling statutes *as if* the regulatory programs they create are designed to achieve public-regarding purposes. By making this normative choice, judges counteract, rather than exacerbate, the flaws in the legislative and administrative processes exposed by public choice scholarship. They also serve the crucial majoritarian function *Chevron* would have them avoid, that of aligning the exercise of public power with the public interest.

C. The Neoclassical Model and the Balance of Power

The question * * * ultimately whether to replace the traditional model of administrative law with the neoclassical model, requires a decision as to the appropriate allocation of power in the administrative state. From this perspective, the neoclassical model is best understood as a reaction against the excesses of activist judicial review during the interest-representation era of the mid-1960s to mid-1970s. As one canvasses the neoclassical decisions, it becomes clear that the Supreme Court has retrenched in virtually all the areas of the judicial review of agency action that it had expanded during the interest-representation period. * * *

The central failing of the neoclassical model, viewed in this light, is that it overreacts to the excesses produced by the interest-representation revision of the traditional mode. It redresses the transfer of agency authority to courts by skewing the allocation of power in the opposite direction. Because of this, the neoclassical model suffers from the same debilitating defect that brought down interest-representation: it creates an imbalance of governing power that destabilizes the administrative system. As a result, the neoclassical model is in significant, and irreconcilable, tension with the ideas of separation of powers and checks and balances that permeate the American structure of government.

* * *

VI. Conclusion: One Tentative Cheer for the Traditional Model

The neoclassical model is a deeply flawed replacement of the traditional model. Its formality, as well as its profound skepticism of the integrity of governance, make it too unattractive and unstable to qualify as a fitting successor. The model attempts to deny courts the ambit of judgment and sensitivity that our jurisprudence has traditionally thought necessary to interpret law. It creates an imbalance of governmental power based primarily on doubts about one set of government actors (legislators and judges) rather than any special confidence in another (administrators). It creates a formalistic arrangement of profound emptiness, essentially expecting one mediating principle—the law-policy distinction—to order administrative law. Although no single approach could accomplish such a feat, resort to an all-or-nothing construct such as the neoclassical model is especially unavailing.

It is in the light of these criticisms of the neoclassical model that the virtue of the traditional model of administrative law is best seen. The traditional model allows reviewing courts to employ a contextual approach to fix their responsibility of reviewing agency decisionmaking. It is impossible to imagine a meaningful approach to the courts' role in the administrative state that would deny a place for judicial discretion and value choices. No plausible rule for reviewing courts could "avoid the process of judgment." The virtue of the traditional model is its flexibility and its balance, its embrace of judicial as well as administrative discretion.

This is not to say that the traditional model is without flaws of its own. The legal process assumptions that underlie the model are inadequate. Post-legal process developments in theories of legislative, administrative, and judicial behavior must be absorbed to refine the institutional understandings on which the model rests. Over the years, however, the traditional model of administrative law has exhibited considerable adaptive powers, which have facilitated accommodations to changed expectations, while maintaining a rough balance among governmental actors. * * *

R. Shep Melnick, *Administrative Law and Bureaucratic Reality*, 44 ADMIN. L. REV. 245, 246-50, 255-58 (1992)*

* * *

In recent years a small group of scholars have taken a closer look at how court decisions have reshaped administrative agencies and their policies. The purpose of this article is to acquaint students of administrative law with some of these findings.[4] As will soon become clear, most of these studies show that judicial intervention has had an unfortunate effect on policymaking. Judicial review has subjected agencies to debilitating delay and uncertainty. Courts have heaped new tasks on agencies while decreasing their ability to perform any of them. They have forced agencies to substitute trivial pursuits for important ones. And they have discouraged administrators from taking responsibility for their actions and for educating the public.

To those who suspect that these findings reflect either the biases of the author or the peculiarities of the cases chosen for close analysis, I offer the following challenge: provide us with detailed studies of cases in which the courts have improved policymaking. There surely must be some. Unsupported assertions about the malevolence of bureaucrats and the good will of judges do not constitute a convincing reply to these empirical studies.

Rulemaking

Let me start with the most obvious problem, rulemaking delay. In the late 1970s William H. Rodgers, Jr. summed up the conventional wisdom about aggressive judicial review of agency rulemaking by saying, "The hard look doctrine plays no favorites; it is advanced as enthusiastically by industry as it is

---

* Reprinted with permission of R. Shep Melnick. All rights reserved.

[4] I will focus primarily on the following books: ROBERT A. KATZMANN, INSTITUTIONAL DISABILITY: THE SAGA OF TRANSPORTATION POLICY FOR THE DISABLED (1986); JERRY L. MASHAW & DAVID L. HARFST, THE STRUGGLE FOR AUTO SAFETY (1990); R. SHEP MELNICK, REGULATION AND THE COURTS: THE CASE OF THE CLEAN AIR ACT (1983); JEREMY RABKIN, JUDICIAL COMPULSIONS: HOW PUBLIC LAW DISTORTS PUBLIC POLICY (1989); and MARTIN M. SHAPIRO, WHO GUARDS THE GUARDIANS? JUDICIAL CONTROL OF ADMINISTRATION (1988). A recent article by Robert Kagan combines a brief case study with an insightful analysis of what he calls "adversarial legalism." Robert A. Kagan, *Adversarial Legalism and American Government*, 10 J. POL'Y ANALYSIS & MGMT. 369 (1991).

by environmentalists. Its acceptance is deep."[6] Ten years later many people are having second thoughts.

In retrospect, what happened is quite clear. The courts said, consider all the "relevant" evidence, respond to all "significant" comments, and weigh all "reasonable" alternatives. Who could object to that? The problem was that judges failed to explain what they meant by "relevant," "significant," and "reasonable." Like pornography, they knew it only after they saw it. Since agencies do not like losing big court cases, they reacted defensively, accumulating more and more information, responding to all comments, and covering all their bets. The rulemaking record grew enormously, far beyond any judge's ability to review it. As a result, it took longer and longer to complete the rulemaking process. Richard Pierce reports that "the time required to make policy through rulemaking has been stretched to nearly a decade."[8] In some instances the final rules appeared just as the underlying problem had disappeared or changed fundamentally.

Thus began a vicious cycle: the more effort agencies put into rulemaking, the more they feared losing, and the more defensive rulemaking became. Even then, they lost a significant number of cases—it was just too hard to predict what a randomly selected panel of judges would do. Draw two Reagan appointees on a three-judge panel and you might well lose because you regulated too much; draw two Carter appointees, you might lose because you regulated too little. Little wonder that many agencies looked for ways to avoid the rulemaking quagmire. Some agencies decided it would be easier to use adjudication to establish agency policy. Others set policy through interpretive rulings or internal enforcement policies. So instead of more rules, we have more discretion; instead of uniformity, we have particularism. Just as water runs downhill, agencies run away from uncertainty, which is what the judicial review often represented.

Jerry Mashaw and David Harfst's recent book presents a particularly graphic example of how a federal agency has responded to "hard look" judicial review by virtually abandoning rulemaking. After the courts rejected its first set of safety rules, the National Highway Traffic Safety Administration replaced rulemaking with a recall strategy. Decisions of other federal courts made this strategy easy to pursue. The only problem was that recalls do little to improve auto safety.[11] * * *

This does not mean that agencies never engage in rulemaking or win in court. What do we know about the effects of judicial review for the substance of the rules that are issued? In the area of health and safety standards both my research and the work of John Mendeloff indicate that judicial review has decreased the *number* of standards but increased their *stringency*. Why? Because at the same time that industry is challenging an agency's evidence, public interest groups are charging that the agency has not sufficiently protected the public health.

Judges on key courts have often insisted that EPA and some other agencies take a "health only" approach to standard-setting, especially when a carcinogen is involved. In *Lead Industries Assn'n. v. EPA*, for example, Judge Skelly Wright announced that the legislative history of the Clean Air Act "shows [that] the Administrator may not consider economic or technological feasibility in setting air quality standards." In another decision involving standards for airborne lead, Judge Wright hearkened back to Judge Bazelon's famous claim about the "special judicial interest in favor of protection of the health and welfare of the people."[15]

The courts have hardly been consistent on this. The Supreme Court's rulings on OSHA's statutory mandate are far from doctrinaire—in fact they are incoherent. For many years the Supreme Court's inability to speak clearly on such matters left the lower courts—especially the D.C. Circuit—in control. The D.C. Circuit now appears to be pulling back from its previous absolutist position, but in the 1970s and 1980s the message EPA and other agencies often got was this: If you want a standard to survive, collect lots of information, make the rule very stringent, and then use enforcement discretion to avoid the politically dangerous consequences of this stringency. With so few standards being set, environmentalists insisted that the ones that survived were really tough. Seeing these stringent regulations coming down the pike, business fought them tooth and nail, adding to the delay.

Mendeloff convincingly argues that this peculiar combination of underregulation and overregulation

---

[6] William H. Rodgers, Jr., *A Hard Look at* Vermont Yankee: *Environmental Law Under Close Scrutiny*, 67 GEO. L.J. 699, 706 (1979) (footnote omitted).

[8] Richard J. Pierce, Jr., *Two Problems in Administrative Law: Political Polarity on the District of Columbia Circuit and Judicial Deterrence of Agency Rulemaking*, 1988 DUKE L.J. 300, 302.

[11] [JERRY L. MASHAW & DAVID L. HARFST, THE STRUGGLE FOR AUTO SAFETY, ch. 5, 8 (1990).]

[15] Ethyl Corp. v. EPA, 541 F.2d 1, 24 (D.C. Cir. 1976) (echoing the opinion of Bazelon in EDF v. Ruckelshaus, 439 F.2d 584, 598 (D.C. Cir 1971)).

leads us to get far less safety bang for the buck than European nations, which set more standards, but make them individually more lenient. The courts do not bear sole responsibility for this costly adversarial system, but they surely add to the problem. How is it possible to arrange a grand compromise—more standards for less stringency—if any trade association or environmental group can challenge it in court and have a shot at winning? How is it possible to encourage open horse-trading when the courts are insisting upon "rational" decisionmaking based on the accumulation of enormous amounts of technical information?

Action-Forcing Litigation

Many of the statutes passed by Congress in the 1970s and 1980s were filled with so-called nondiscretionary duties: deadlines, "hammers," and the like. A 1985 study co-authored by the Environmental Law Institute and the Environmental and Energy Study Institute reports that EPA alone was subject to 328 statutory deadlines. Among the other findings of this study were the following:

1. "Very few statutory deadlines (14 percent) have been met."

2. "Congress imposes more deadlines on EPA than it can possibly meet."

3. "Court-ordered deadlines almost always command top management attention at EPA. Top management takes the threat of contempt quite seriously and personally, even though the threat is not real."

4. "The multiplicity of deadlines reduces EPA's ability to assign priority to anything not subject to a deadline."

What this means is that scores of deadlines and other statutory requirements are lying around, usually unused, but still potential weapons in lawsuits—or threatened lawsuits. Do nondiscretionary duties and court enforcement produce "the rule of law"? Of course not; they produce the rule of those who decide which lawsuits to bring. Or, to put it another way, it transfers responsibility for setting agency priority from top administrators to interest groups, some of which use attorneys' fees won in these relatively easy cases to cross-subsidize other activities. It is hard to imagine a worse way to apportion agency resources.

* * *

National Uniformity

In some policy areas judicial review has substantially reduced the uniformity of federal law. There is no little irony in this. Ever since the days of John Marshall, federal courts have tried (and often succeeded) to strengthen the Union by reining in the states. Now that we have created a large number of federal agencies charged with carrying out nationally uniform programs, extensive court intervention all too often creates different rules for different circuits. As Peter Strauss has pointed out, "[T]he infrequency of Supreme Court review combines with the formal independence of each circuit's law from that of the other circuits to permit a gradual balkanization of federal law."[52] He notes that the legal profession has "yet to come to grips with the problem."

Although the problem has arisen in a variety of areas—tax law, labor law, education of the handicapped, and welfare, to name a few—it became most apparent in the heated confrontation between the courts and the executive branch over disability benefits. The agency charged with carrying out disability reviews, the Social Security Administration (SSA), is the very embodiment of the New Deal's commitment to national uniformity. The SSA's willingness to engage in "non-acquiescence" in order to preserve this uniformity predated the Reagan Administration's attempt to purge the disability rolls in the early 1980s. The heavy-handedness of the Reagan Administration's policies should not blind us to the larger issue. In her recent book on the SSA, Martha Derthick has this to say about the agency's much-maligned nonacquiescence policy:

> The underlying premise—that policy must be nationally uniform—was not in the least contrived for the occasion. It was contained in law, Congress having stipulated in 1980 that administration of the disability insurance program be "uniform . . . throughout the United States." Just as important, it had long been at the core of the agency's operating code. . . . [T]his code had been reinforced in the SSA's case by the particular historical circumstance that its programs and administrative style were a reaction against the features of American federalism. For the SSA's programs to develop regional differences would be more than a monumental inconvenience to the agency; it would constitute a humiliating retrogression to the time when state governments dominated

---

[52] Peter L. Strauss, *One Hundred Fifty Cases Per Year: Some Implications of the Supreme Court's Limited Resources for Judicial Review of Agency Action*, 87 COLUM. L. REV. 1093, 1105 (1987).

domestic functions and citizens were treated differently depending on where they happened to live. The SSA's very existence rested on the belief that such differences were unfair.[56]

Compared with agencies like the SSA, the IRS, or even EPA, the federal judiciary is a highly decentralized institution. Constant intervention by the decentralized judiciary can lead to confusion and unfairness. It can also have a corrosive effect on the sense of mission of an agency like the Social Security Administration—a commitment to national uniformity and to prompt determinations, which has served us well since 1935.

Power within the Agency

Aggressive judicial review creates winners and losers within administrative agencies. Clearly the biggest losers are political executives, who are less able to set priorities or to resist demands from congressional committees and interest groups. The biggest winners are lawyers with the agency's Office of General Counsel. Many studies of courts and agencies have come to this conclusion. OGC attorneys are the ones who explain what the courts are likely to accept and reject. Frequently—especially on remand—they end up writing substantial portions of the regulations. At the risk of offending my readers, let me suggest two difficulties with this transfer of power to their "brother" and "sister" attorneys.

First, many of these lawyers work in the agency for a relatively short period of time; they are bright, aggressive young men and women who yearn to "cast a shadow" before moving on to a more lucrative career elsewhere. In that sense they are no different from congressional staffers, law clerks, or many lower-echelon people in the White House. More cocky neophytes with short time horizons is hardly what Washington needs.

Second, few of these lawyers have ever run anything. They seldom have a sense of how hard it is to manage a program at the regional or state level. As Martin Shapiro has put it, the judicial demand for rationality

> tends to shift power within the agencies from those who are really concerned about making policies that work to those concerned with defending them in court . . . from real administrators responsible for the actual operations of programs to lawyers. And it will often lead to

a choice of the alternative that can most easily be made to appear synoptic rather than the one that seems best.[58]

* * *

Get Real, Administrative Law

This article has suggested both that courts often make a mess of policy because they have a poor understanding of administrative agencies and that administrative law has done little to correct judicial misperceptions. What understanding of bureaucracy might be more accurate? Let me propose the following generalization about public bureaucracies in the United States: They are almost always given huge, even utopian, goals and are then saddled with a large number of constraints that prevent them from achieving these goals efficiently—or even at all. We tell EPA, for example, to protect the public health with an adequate margin of safety, but advise it not to spend too much money or put anyone out of work. We tell them to use the best scientific evidence, but refuse to let them pay enough to recruit top-flight scientists, and then we tell them, "By the way, do it within 90 days." We expect bureaucrats to account for every penny of public money, to record every conversation with a member of an interest group, to show that they have treated everyone equally, and to consider all the relevant information and alternatives—but to stop producing all that red tape and being so damn slow.

Courts are particularly likely to make these conflicting demands because they are so decentralized, their exposure to policymaking is so episodic, and the opportunities for forum-shopping are so apparent to interest groups. Courts are good at responding to complaints, and people have lots of complaints about bureaucracy. The problem is that these complaints often require incompatible responses. Today the D.C. Circuit hears a case brought by environmental groups complaining about unconscionable delay. In two years the Sixth Circuit will hear industry complain about shoddy evidence and exorbitant costs. And two years after that a district court judge in Cleveland will be asked to balance the "equities" in order to keep a particular local factory in operation. Who considers the connection among all these decisions? The Supreme Court? Simply to ask this question is to answer it—no one does.

What is to be done? Most obviously, judges

---

[56] Martha Derthick, Agency Under Stress: The Social Security Administration in American Government 141 (1990) (quoting Social Security Act of 1980 . . .).

[58] [Martin N. Shapiro, Who Guards the Guardians? Judicial Control of Administration 152 (1988).]

should remember a key part of the Hippocratic oath: First, do no harm. In administrative law that translates into the command, defer! defer! Just as importantly, administrative law needs to become less self-absorbed and more concerned about how public bureaucracies work. * * *

* * *

Additional Sources

Stephen Breyer, *Judicial Review of Questions of Law and Policy*, 38 Admin. L. Rev. 363 (1986)

Christopher F. Edley, Jr., ADMINISTRATIVE LAW: RETHINKING JUDICIAL CONTROL OF BUREAUCRACY (1990)

Donald L. Horowitz, THE COURTS AND SOCIAL POLICY (1977)

Ronald M. Levin, *Administrative Discretion, Judicial Review, and the Gloomy World of Judge Smith*, 1986 Duke L.J. 258 (1986)

Ronald M. Levin, *Federal Scope-of-Review Standards: A Preliminary Restatement*, 37 Admin. L. Rev. 95 (1985)

Jerry L. Mashaw & David L. Harfst, *Regulation and Legal Culture: The Case of Motor Vehicle Safety*, 4 Yale J. on Reg. 257 (1987)

Abner J. Mikva, *The Changing Role of Judicial Review*, 38 Admin. L. Rev. 115 (1986)

William F. Pedersen, Jr., *Formal Records and Informal Rulemaking*, 85 Yale L.J. 38 (1975)

Richard J. Pierce, Jr., *The Role of the Judiciary in Implementing an Agency Theory of Government*, 64 N.Y.U. L. Rev. 1239 (1989)

Richard J. Pierce, Jr., *Two Problems in Administrative Law: Political Polarity on the District of Columbia Circuit and Judicial Deterrence of Agency Rulemaking*, 1988 Duke L.J. 300

Judith Resnick, *Managerial Judges*, 96 Harv. L. Rev. 374 (1982)

Thomas O. Sargentich, *The Future of Administrative Law*, 104 Harv. L. Rev. 769 (1991) (reviewing Christopher F. Edley, Jr., ADMINISTRATIVE LAW: RETHINKING JUDICIAL CONTROL OF BUREAUCRACY (1990))

Thomas O. Sargentich, *The Supreme Court's Administrative Law Jurisprudence*, 7 Admin. L.J. Am. U. 273 (1993) (panel discussion)

Loren A. Smith, *Judicialization: The Twilight of Administrative Law*, 1985 Duke L.J. 427

Richard B. Stewart & Cass R. Sunstein, *Public Programs and Private Rights*, 95 Harv. L. Rev. 1193 (1982)

Cass R. Sunstein, *On the Costs and Benefits of Aggressive Judicial Review of Agency Action*, 1989 Duke L.J. 522

Patricia M. Wald, *The Contribution of the D.C. Circuit to Administrative Law*, 40 Admin. L. Rev. 507 (1988)

Patricia M. Wald, *The "New Administrative Law"—With the Same Old Judges in It?*, 1991 Duke L.J. 647

Part IV

Competing Theoretical Perspectives on the Administrative Process

A characteristic feature of modern administrative law is the depth of theoretical debates underlying the field as a whole. A variety of general perspectives on the administrative process yield divergent suggestions for reform as well as competing pictures of agency legitimacy.

In this section, several contrasting points of view are represented. The first excerpt, by economist George Stigler, highlights a number of themes that have become central to public choice literature about American politics and administration. Underlying George Stigler's article is a hard-headed sense that economic regulation is acquired by economic interests to serve their preexisting agendas. Not only are economic actors seen as rational maximizers of their self-interest, but also politicians are seen as rational maximizers of their ends, particularly their receipt of votes and money for campaigns. Statutes that establish regulatory programs are thus viewed through a lens that stresses bargaining to maximize self-interest.

This law-and-economics vision has had considerable influence in modern debates about administrative law. In opposition, there are many critics who consider it too narrow to the extent that it does not take account of the moral or ideological motives of actors in the political or administrative system. Others claim that it does not adequately acknowledge that law not only reflects preexisting self-interest but also can change a person's vision of his or her self-interest. One body of theory rejecting the hard-headed, pluralistic premises of law-and-economics analysis is civic republican thought. Such thought informs the excerpt by Professor Mark Seidenfeld.

Professor Seidenfeld explicitly distinguishes civic republicanism from the pluralistic law-and-economics vision. He argues that administrative reform should foster enhanced deliberation about the public good. He suggests that administrative agencies may actually be the best institution of government in which to realize the values of civic republicanism, as agencies are removed from the overt political bargaining that swirls around legislatures, and administrative officials are more attuned to political life than are isolated federal judges.

The third and fourth excerpts present different pictures of alternative models of the legitimacy of administration. Professor Gerald Frug identifies a number of historically significant images of administration that, he contends, have been used to reassure the public about the power of public bureaucracies. After discussing each of his models, he argues they are in many ways fundamentally contradictory and problematic.

In my excerpt, I argue that three ideals—the rule of law, the public purposes, and the democratic process models—embody major competing visions of how to justify and control modern administrative power. I also suggest that there are core and alternative expressions of each ideal, that each version has its own difficulties, and that elements of the different ideals frequently are combined in reform proposals. Because the ideals are fundamentally in competition with each other, particular reform proposals can be expected to call forth typical defenses and critiques drawing upon the competing visions.*

---

* The three competing ideals—pursuit of the substantive and procedural values of the rule of law; pursuit of instrumentally rational means toward the achievement of public purposes; and pursuit of a more open and accountable administrative process in the name of the values of the democratic process—inform the general structure of this anthology. Part I focuses on—but is not limited to—rule of law issues. Part II concentrates on public purposes and democratic process issues. Part III deals with the role of courts in matters that involve competition among ideals of administration. Part IV reflects theoretical debates that include but are not limited to the image of competing ideals.

George J. Stigler, *The Theory of Economic Regulation*, 2 BELL J. OF ECON. & MGMT. SCI. 3, 3-7, 10-14, 17-18 (1971)*

* * *

The state—the machinery and power of the state—is a potential resource or threat to every industry in the society. With its power to prohibit or compel, to take or give money, the state can and does selectively help or hurt a vast number of industries. * * * The central tasks of the theory of economic regulation are to explain who will receive the benefits or burdens of regulation, what form regulation will take, and the effects of regulation upon the allocation of resources.

Regulation may be actively sought by an industry, or it may be thrust upon it. A central thesis of this paper is that, as a rule, regulation is acquired by the industry and is designed and operated primarily for its benefit. There are regulations whose net effects upon the regulated industry are undeniably onerous; a simple example is the differentially heavy taxation of the industry's product (whiskey, playing cards). These onerous regulations, however, are exceptional and can be explained by the same theory that explains beneficial (we may call it "acquired") regulation.

Two main alternative views of the regulation of industry are widely held. The first is that regulation is instituted primarily for the protection and benefit of the public at large or some large subclass of the public. In this view, the regulations which injure the public—as when the oil import quotas increase the cost of petroleum products to America by $5 billion or more a year—are costs of some social goal (here, national defense) or, occasionally, perversions of the regulatory philosophy. The second view is essentially that the political process defies rational explanation: "politics" is an imponderable, a constantly and unpredictably shifting mixture of forces of the most diverse nature, comprehending acts of great moral virtue (the emancipation of slaves) and of the most vulgar venality (the congressman feathering his own nest).

Let us consider a problem posed by the oil import quota system: why does not the powerful industry which obtained this expensive program instead choose direct cash subsidies from the public treasury? The "protection of the public" theory of regulation must say that the choice of import quotas is dictated by the concern of the federal government for an adequate domestic supply of petroleum in the event of war—a remark calculated to elicit uproarious laughter at the Petroleum Club. Such laughter aside, if national defense were the goal of the quotas, a tariff would be a more economical instrument of policy: it would retain the profits of exclusion for the treasury. The non-rationalist view would explain the policy by the inability of consumers to measure the cost to them of the import quotas, and hence their willingness to pay $5 billion in higher prices rather than the $2.5 billion in cash that would be equally attractive to the industry. Our profit-maximizing theory says that the explanation lies in a different direction: the present members of the refining industries would have to share a cash subsidy with all new entrants into the refining industry. Only when the elasticity of supply of an industry is small will the industry prefer cash to controls over entry or output.

This question, why does an industry solicit the coercive powers of the state rather than its cash, is offered only to illustrate the approach of the present paper. We assume that political systems are rationally devised and rationally employed, which is to say that they are appropriate instruments for the fulfillment of desires of members of the society. This is not to say that the state will serve any person's concept of the public interest: indeed the problem of regulation is the problem of discovering when and why an industry (or other group of like-minded people) is able to use the state for its purposes, or is singled out by the state to be used for alien purposes.

1. What benefits can a state provide to an industry?

The state has one basic resource which in pure principle is not shared with even the mightiest of its citizens: the power to coerce. The state can seize money by the only method which is permitted by the laws of a civilized society, by taxation. The state can ordain the physical movements of resources and the economic decisions of household and firms without their consent. These powers provide the possibilities for the utilization of the state by an industry to increase its profitability. The main policies which an industry (or occupation) may seek of the state are four.

The most obvious contribution that a group may seek of the government is a direct subsidy of money. The domestic airlines received "air mail" subsidies (even if they did not carry mail) of $1.5 billion through 1968. The merchant marine has received construction and operation subsidies reaching almost

---

* Copyright 1971. Reprinted with permission of RAND and Bell Journal. All rights reserved.

$3 billion since World War II. The education industry has long shown a masterful skill in obtaining public funds: for example, universities and colleges have received federal funds exceeding $3 billion annually in recent years, as well as subsidized loans for dormitories and other construction. The veterans of wars have often received direct cash bonuses.

We have already sketched the main explanation for the fact that an industry with power to obtain governmental favors usually does not use this power to get money: unless the list of beneficiaries can be limited by an acceptable device, whatever amount of subsidies the industry can obtain will be dissipated among a growing number of rivals. The airlines quickly moved away from competitive bidding for air mail contracts to avoid this problem. On the other hand, the premier universities have not devised a method of excluding other claimants for research funds, and in the long run they will receive much-reduced shares of federal research monies.

The second major public resource commonly sought by an industry is control over entry by new rivals. There is considerable, not to say excessive, discussion in economic literature of the rise of peculiar price policies (limit prices), vertical integration, and similar devices to retard the rate of entry of new firms into oligopolistic industries. Such devices are vastly less efficacious (economical) than the certificate of convenience and necessity (which includes, of course, the import and production quotas of the oil and tobacco industries).

* * *

We propose the general hypothesis: every industry or occupation that has enough political power to utilize the state will seek to control entry. In addition, the regulatory policy will often be so fashioned as to retard the rate of growth of new firms. * * *

One variant of the control of entry is the protective tariff (and the corresponding barriers which have been raised to interstate movements of goods and people). The benefits of protection to an industry, one might think, will usually be dissipated by the entry of new domestic producers, and the question naturally arises: Why does the industry not also seek domestic entry controls? In a few industries (petroleum) the domestic controls have been obtained, but not in most. The tariff will be effective if there is a specialized domestic resource necessary to the industry; oil-producing lands is an example. Even if an industry has only durable specialized resources, it will gain if its contraction is slowed by a tariff.

A third general set of powers of the state which will be sought by the industry are those which affect substitutes and complements. Crudely put, the butter producers wish to suppress margarine and encourage the production of bread. The airline industry actively supports the federal subsidies to airports; the building trade unions have opposed labor-saving materials through building codes. We shall examine shortly a specific case of inter-industry competition in transportation.

The fourth class of public policies sought by an industry is directed to price-fixing. Even the industry that has achieved entry control will often want price controls administered by a body with coercive powers. If the number of firms in the regulated industry is even moderately large, price discrimination will be difficult to maintain in the absence of public support. The prohibition of interest on demand deposits, which is probably effective in preventing interest payments to most non-business depositors, is a case in point. Where there are no diseconomies of large scale for the individual firm (e.g., a motor trucking firm can add trucks under a given license as common carrier), price control is essential to achieve more than competitive rates of return.

Limitations upon political benefits

These various political boons are not obtained by the industry in a pure profit-maximizing form. The political process erects certain limitations upon the exercise of cartel policies by an industry. These limitations are of three sorts.

First, the distribution of control of the industry among the firms in the industry is changed. In an unregulated industry each firm's influence upon price and output is proportional to its share of industry output (at least in a simple arithmetic sense of direct capacity to change output). The political decisions take account also of the political strength of the various firms, so small firms have a larger influence than they would possess in an unregulated industry. Thus, when quotas are given to firms, the small firms will almost always receive larger quotas than cost-minimizing practices would allow. * * *

Second, the procedural safeguards required of public processes are costly. The delays which are dictated by both law and bureaucratic thoughts of self-survival can be large: Robert Gerwig found the price of gas sold in interstate commerce to be 5 to 6 percent higher than in intrastate commerce because of the administrative costs (including delay) of Federal Power Commission reviews.

Finally, the political process automatically admits powerful outsiders to the industry's councils. It is well known that the allocation of television channels among communities does not maximize industry revenue but reflects pressures to serve many smaller communities. The abandonment of an unprofitable rail line is an even more notorious area of outsider participation.

These limitations are predictable, and they must all enter into the calculus of the profitability of regulation of an industry.

* * *

2. The costs of obtaining legislation

When an industry receives a grant of power from the state, the benefit to the industry will fall short of the damage to the rest of the community. Even if there were no deadweight losses from acquired regulation, however, one might expect a democratic society to reject such industry requests unless the industry controlled a majority of the votes. A direct and informed vote on oil import quotas would reject the scheme. (If it did not, our theory of rational political processes would be contradicted.) To explain why many industries are able to employ the political machinery to their own ends, we must examine the nature of the political process in a democracy.

A consumer chooses between rail and air travel, for example, by voting with his pocketbook: he patronizes on a given day that mode of transportation he prefers. A similar form of economic voting occurs with decisions on where to work or where to invest one's capital. The market accumulates these economic votes, predicts their future course, and invests accordingly.

Because the political decision is coercive, the decision process is fundamentally different from that of the market. If the public is asked to make a decision between two transportation media comparable to the individual's decision on how to travel—say, whether airlines or railroads should receive a federal subsidy—the decision must be abided by everyone, travellers and non-travellers, travellers this year and travellers next year. This compelled universality of political decisions makes for two differences between democratic political decision processes and market processes.

(1) The decisions must be made simultaneously by a large number of persons (or their representatives): the political process demands simultaneity of decision. If A were to vote on the referendum today, B tomorrow, C the day after, and so on, the accumulation of a majority decision would be both expensive and suspect. (A might wish to cast a different vote now than last month.)

The condition of simultaneity imposes a major burden upon the political decision process. It makes voting on specific issues prohibitively expensive: it is a significant cost even to engage in the transaction of buying a plane ticket when I wish to travel; it would be stupendously expensive to me to engage in the physically similar transaction of voting (i.e., patronizing a polling place) whenever a number of my fellow citizens desired to register their views on railroads versus airplanes. To cope with this condition of simultaneity, the voters must employ representatives with wide discretion and must eschew direct expressions of marginal changes in preferences. This characteristic also implies that the political decision does not predict voter desires and make preparations to fulfill them in advance of their realization.

(2) The democratic decision process must involve "all" the community, not simply those who are directly concerned with a decision. In a private market, the non-traveller never votes on rail versus plane travel, while the huge shipper casts many votes each day. The political decision process cannot exclude the uninterested voter: the abuses of any exclusion except self-exclusion are obvious. Hence, the political process does not allow participation in proportion to interest and knowledge. In a measure, this difficulty is moderated by other political activities besides voting which do allow a more effective vote to interested parties: persuasion, employment of skilled legislative representatives, etc. Nevertheless, the political system does not offer good incentives like those in private markets to the acquisition of knowledge. If I consume ten times as much of public service A (streets) as of B (schools), I do not have incentives to acquire corresponding amounts of knowledge about the public provision of these services.

These characteristics of the political process can be modified by having numerous levels of government (so I have somewhat more incentive to learn about local schools than about the whole state school system) and by selective use of direct decision (bond referenda). The chief method of coping with the characteristics, however, is to employ more or less full-time representatives organized in (disciplined by) firms which are called political parties or machines.

The representative and his party are rewarded for their discovery and fulfillment of the political desires of their constituency by success in election and the perquisites of office. If the representative could confidently await reelection whenever he voted against an economic policy that injured the society, he would assuredly do so. Unfortunately virtue does not always command so high a price. If the representative denies ten large industries their special subsidies of money or governmental power, they will dedicate themselves to the election of a more complaisant successor: the stakes are that important. This does not mean that every large industry can get what it wants or all that it wants: it does mean that the representative and his party must find a coalition of voter interests more durable than the anti-industry side of every industry policy proposal. A representative cannot win or keep office with the support of the sum of those who are opposed to: oil import quotas, farm subsidies, airport subsidies, hospital subsidies, unnecessary navy shipyards, an inequitable public housing program, and rural electrification subsidies.

The political decision process has as its dominant characteristic infrequent, universal (in principle) participation, as we have noted: political decisions must be infrequent and they must be global. The voter's expenditure to learn the merits of individual policy proposals and to express his preferences (by individual and group representation as well as by voting) are determined by expected costs and returns, just as they are in the private marketplace. The costs of comprehensive information are higher in the political arena because information must be sought on many issues of little or no direct concern to the individual, and accordingly he will know little about most matters before the legislature. The expressions of preferences in voting will be less precise than the expressions of preferences in the marketplace because many uninformed people will be voting and affecting the decision.

The channels of political decision-making can thus be described as gross or filtered or noisy. If everyone has a negligible preference for policy A over B, the preference will not be discovered or acted upon. If voter group X wants a policy that injures non-X by a small amount, it will not pay non-X to discover this and act against the policy. The system is calculated to implement all strongly felt preferences of majorities and many strongly felt preferences of minorities but to disregard the lesser preferences of majorities and minorities. The filtering or grossness will be reduced by any reduction in the cost to the citizen of acquiring information and expressing desires and by any increase in the probability that his vote will influence policy.

The industry which seeks political power must go to the appropriate seller, the political party. The political party has costs of operation, costs of maintaining an organization and competing in elections. These costs of the political process are viewed excessively narrowly in the literature on the financing of elections: elections are to the political process what merchandizing is to the process of producing a commodity, only an essential final step. The party maintains its organization and electoral appeal by the performance of costly services to the voter at all times, not just before elections. Part of the costs of services and organization are borne by putting a part of the party's workers on the public payroll. An opposition party, however, is usually essential insurance for the voters to discipline the party in power, and the opposition party's costs are not fully met by public funds.

The industry which seeks regulation must be prepared to pay with the two things a party needs: votes and resources. The resources may be provided by campaign contributions, contributed services (the businessman heads a fund-raising committee), and more indirect methods such as the employment of party workers. The votes in support of the measure are rallied, and the votes in opposition are dispersed, by expensive programs to educate (or uneducate) members of the industry and of other concerned industries.

These costs of legislation probably increase with the size of the industry seeking the legislation. Larger industries seek programs which cost the society more and arouse more opposition from substantially affected groups. The tasks of persuasion, both within and without the industry, also increase with its size. The fixed size of the political "market," however, probably makes the cost of obtaining legislation increase less rapidly than industry size. The smallest industries are therefore effectively precluded from the political process unless they have some special advantage such as geographical concentration in a sparsely settled political subdivision.

If a political party has in effect a monopoly control over the governmental machine, one might expect that it could collect most of the benefits of regulation for itself. Political parties, however, are perhaps an ideal illustration of Demsetz' theory of natural monopoly. If one party becomes extortionate (or badly mistaken in its reading of effective desires), it is possible to elect another party which will provide the governmental services at a price more closely proportioned to costs of the party. If entry into politics is effectively controlled, we should expect one-party dominance to lead that party to solicit requests for protective legislation but to exact a higher price for the legislation.

The internal structure of the political party, and the manner in which the perquisites of office are distributed among its members, offer fascinating areas for study in this context. The elective officials are at the pinnacle of the political system—there is no substitute for the ability to hold the public offices. I conjecture that much of the compensation to the legislative leaders takes the form of extra-political payments. Why are so many politicians lawyers?—because everyone employs lawyers, so the congressman's firm is a suitable avenue of compensation, whereas a physician would have to be given bribes rather than patronage. Most enterprises patronize insurance companies and banks, so we may expect that legislators commonly have financial affiliations with such enterprises.

The financing of industry-wide activities such as the pursuit of legislation raises the usual problem of the free rider. We do not possess a satisfactory theory of group behavior—indeed this theory is the theory of oligopoly with one addition: in the very large number industry (e.g., agriculture) the political party itself will undertake the entrepreneurial role in providing favorable legislation. We can go no further than the infirmities of oligopoly theory allow, which is to say, we can make only plausible conjectures such as that the more concentrated the industry, the more resources it can invest in the campaign for legislation.

Occupational licensing

The licensing of occupations is a possible use of the political process to improve the economic circumstances of a group. The license is an effective barrier to entry because occupational practice without the license is a criminal offense. Since much occupational licensing is performed at the state level, the area provides an opportunity to search for the characteristics of an occupation which give it political power.

Although there are serious data limitations, we may investigate several characteristics of an occupation which should influence its ability to secure political power:

(1) *The size of the occupation.* Quite simply, the larger the occupation, the more votes it has. (Under some circumstances, therefore, one would wish to exclude non-citizens from the measure of size.)

(2) *The per capita income of the occupation.* The income of the occupation is the product of its number and average income, so this variable and the preceding will reflect the total income of the occupation. The income of the occupation is presumably an index of the probable rewards of successful political action: in the absence of specific knowledge of supply and demand functions, we expect licensing to increase each occupation's equilibrium income by roughly the same proportion. In a more sophisticated version, one would predict that the less the elasticity of demand for the occupation's services, the more profitable licensing would be. * * *

The average income of occupational members is an appropriate variable in comparisons among occupations, but it is inappropriate to comparisons of one occupation in various states because real income will be approximately equal (in the absence of regulation) in each state.

(3) *The concentration of the occupation in large cities.* When the occupation organizes a campaign to obtain favorable legislation, it incurs expenses in the solicitation of support, and these are higher for a diffused occupation than a concentrated one. The solicitation of support is complicated by the free-rider problem in that individual members cannot be excluded from the benefits of legislation even if they have not shared the costs of receiving it. If most of the occupation is concentrated in a few large centers, these problems (we suspect) are much reduced in intensity: regulation may even begin at the local governmental level. * * *

(4) *The presence of a cohesive opposition to licensing.* If an occupation deals with the public at large, the costs which licensing imposes upon any one customer or industry will be small and it will not be economic for that customer or industry to combat the drive for licensure. If the injured group finds it feasible and profitable to act jointly, however, it will oppose the effort to get licensure, and (by increasing its cost) weaken, delay, or prevent the legislation. The same attributes—numbers of voters, wealth, and ease of organization—which favor an occupation in the political arena, of course, favor also any adversary group. Thus, a small occupation employed by only one industry which has few employers will have difficulty in getting licensure; whereas a large occupation serving everyone will encounter no organized opposition.

* * *

3. Conclusion

The idealistic view of public regulation is deeply imbedded in professional economic thought. So many economists, for example, have denounced the ICC for its pro-railroad policies that this has become a cliché of the literature. This criticism seems to me exactly as appropriate as a criticism of the Great Atlantic and Pacific Tea Company for selling groceries, or as a criticism of a politician for currying popular support. The fundamental vice of such criticism is that it misdirects attention: it suggests that the way to get an ICC which is not subservient to the carriers is to preach to the commissioners or to the people who appoint the commissioners. The only way to get a different commission would be to change the political support for the Commission, and reward commissioners on a basis unrelated to their services to the carriers.

Until the basic logic of political life is developed, reformers will be ill-equipped to use the state for their reforms, and victims of the pervasive use of the state's support of special groups will be helpless to protect themselves. Economists should quickly establish the license to practice on the rational theory of political behavior.

* * *

Mark Seidenfeld, *A Civic Republican Justification for the Bureaucratic State*, 105 HARV. L. REV. 1511, 1514-16, 1528-34, 1536-38, 1541-45, 1548-54, 1559-67, 1570-73 (1992)*

* * *

* * * Modern civic republicans view the Constitution as an attempt to ensure that government decisions are a product of deliberation that respects and reflects the values of all members of society. Civic republicanism promises democratic government that does not exclude or coerce citizens whose backgrounds and values differ from those of mainstream society. The civic republican model rejects the pluralistic assertion that government can, at best, implement deals that divide political spoils according to the pre-political preferences of interest groups. Instead, government's primary responsibility is to enable the citizenry to deliberate about altering preferences and to reach consensus on the common good.

* * *

* * * I contend that, on the whole, civic republicanism is consistent with broad delegations of political decisionmaking authority to officials with greater expertise and fewer immediate political pressures than directly elected officials or legislators. Moreover, given the current ethic that approves of the private pursuit of self-interest as a means of making social policy, reliance on a more politically isolated administrative state may be necessary to implement something approaching the civic republican ideal.

---

* Copyright 1992 by the Harvard Law Review Association. Reprinted with permission of the Harvard Law Review Association and Mark Seidenfeld. All rights reserved.

* * *

This thesis has several implications for public policy. First, it suggests that congressional and judicial efforts to limit agency discretion and thereby eliminate perceived problems with the legitimacy of agency policymaking are often misguided. Second, if administrative policy-setting is to achieve the civic republican ideal, agency decisionmaking processes must proceed in a manner consistent with civic republican theory. Hence, my thesis suggests the need for numerous changes in administrative law. For example, Congress should amend the Administrative Procedure Act to require public involvement in the early stages of agency policy formulation. Congress should also require that its members and the White House staff reveal all of their interactions with agency personnel. Courts should abandon the rigid dichotomy that they draw between agency decisions of law and decisions of policy, and should review both for persuasiveness in light of pragmatic limitations.

* * *

II. Civic Republicanism—Its Promises and Its Pitfalls

A. Civic Republicanism Defined

Civic republicanism has evolved as a concurrence of liberal and republican theory that simultaneously seeks to foster individual freedom from government-imposed values and freedom collectively to define the values of the relevant political community. According to civic republicanism, the state acts legitimately only if it furthers the "common good" of the political community. Unlike more traditional republican theories, civic republicanism neither posits some external conception of the common good nor relies on some elite body to define it. Instead, civic republicanism embraces an ongoing deliberative process, inclusive of all cultures, values, needs, and interests, to arrive at the public good. Civic republicans see the development of a conception of the common good as a fundamental purpose of democracy—a purpose necessary for individual self-identity and self-fulfillment.

Civic republicanism also posits that no individual acting in her political capacity should be subservient to other political actors. Hence, the theory does not equate the public good that legitimates government action with majority rule. Social consensus about what is best for the community *as a community*, not as the aggregation of individuals' private interests, is the defining feature of the common good. Government's political decisions—that is, the law—must embody this consensus of the common good.

Civic republicanism does not ignore individuals' private interests or the culturally and historically defined values from which these interests derive. It does, however, encourage people to understand and empathize with others whose values reflect different experiences with cultural backgrounds. It assumes that the deliberative process, if properly structured, will transform these values and ultimately reveal commonalities shared by different citizens. It is this transformative power of politics that enables the polity to reach consensus about the common good. Through the transformative power of politics, citizens are able to define the community norms that restrict the behavior of all community members, yet that all accept as just.

The ideals of civic republican theory translate into general operative criteria that good government must satisfy. First and foremost, the demand for deliberative government means that before the government acts, it must engage in public discourse about whether the action will further the common good. Public debate and discussion foster widespread awareness of other citizens' views of the public interest and thereby facilitate consensus. Deliberative government also requires that the decisionmaker, be it the President, legislature, judge, or agency, explain how its decisions further the common good. This requirement guards against political "deals" that advance the private interests of particular factions within society. Explanation by the decisionmaker also promotes understanding of how government action relates to the common good and thus encourages acceptance of that action.

* * *

The civic republican condition that political participants not be subservient to one another mandates that government decisionmakers have equal regard for all interests. No private preference is a priori illegitimate; a private interest may be deemed illegitimate only if the deliberative process reveals it to be inconsistent with universally shared norms of ethics or justice. Decisionmakers should evaluate the positions of participants in the political process by the persuasiveness of their arguments and not by the identity, status, or number of individuals supporting each position. It is not enough that a decision garners popular support or reflects a political bargain that furthers the private interests of a majority of citizens; to be legitimate, a decision must respect the positions of all interest groups and respond to their arguments in terms of the good of the community.

* * *

B. *The Promise of Civic Republicanism*

The appeal of civic republicanism derives both from the richness of the role it defines for citizens—to determine the identity of their political community—and from its explicit attempt to counter factional competition. Pluralism accepts factionalism as a given and defines the public interest as an aggregation of private values. By doing so, pluralism denies the importance of community and thereby precludes many regulatory outcomes that might prove fulfilling to the entire populace in the long run. In fact, pluralistic democracy reveres the pursuit of private interest, for to enhance individual private interest is to enhance the aggregate of such interests. * * * In contrast, by insisting that government actions reflect social consensus about the common good, civic republicanism facilitates the adoption of law that respects the interests of minorities and other groups historically excluded from political power and that simultaneously comports with the polity's general sense of justice. This facilitation, however, can occur only if the decisionmaking process includes representatives of groups normally excluded from the political process or so frustrated by it that they have become apathetic or even alienated.

* * *

C. *The Potential Pitfalls of Civic Republicanism*

Because civic republican theory envisions a broader array of government activity than a theory that credits only the pursuit of private wants, the theory also creates a potential for abuse that some fear may be worse than the factionalism that it tries to alleviate. First, civic republicanism may facilitate the pursuit of private ends by the politically powerful. Second, it may grant the state substantial latitude to impose on the populace what is in fact an inaccurate conception of the common good.

Fears that civic republicanism may increase enforcement of private-interest deals stem from the belief that there is no common good apart from the aggregate of individuals' private preferences. The civic republican response draws upon the intuition that if one asks individuals what is good for society and what is good for them personally, one will usually get different answers. Individuals arrive at conceptions of the public interest in part by imagining what it would be like to be in the shoes of others—by empathizing with the problems and aspirations of citizens from different backgrounds who have different needs and wants. Each individual has some subjective notion of the common good—a notion that embodies public values shared with others in the community. Civic republicanism requires that the government base its actions on these public values rather than on the private desires that citizens bring into political discourse.

Another criticism that raises the specter of private dealmaking asserts that even if a common good does exist, individuals will inevitably pursue their self-interest. This inevitability suggests that the operative elements of civic republicanism—discussion and debate, access, and substantive checks by independent institutions against the pursuit of self-interest—will not preclude politically powerful groups from cutting deals to serve their separate interests. The current failure of checks and balances in the federal government to constrain factional politics gives credence to this concern. Deliberation, however, should not simply be dismissed as an ineffective moderating influence on factional conduct.

In many instances, people do not recognize that their political positions stem from personal experiences and values. They may not be aware of other conceptions of the public interest or understand how their conception would affect those who differ from them. They may also "delude" themselves into thinking that the values that guide their self-interested behavior accord with the public interest. By informing citizens about others' conceptions of the public interest and by revealing to them how their own conceptions might harm others, the deliberative process can help educate citizens and unmask self-delusions. In addition, requiring explanation of government decisions will sometimes prevent decisionmakers from crediting raw political power. Some political deals simply cannot be justified persuasively in principled terms. At least at the margin, the prospect of an independent review to ensure reasoned decisionmaking will deter interest groups from striking deals. Finally, if courts seriously required an agency to explain why a change in policy better serves the public interest than does the status quo, regulators would hesitate to give post hoc rationalizations for unprincipled political decisions. The agency's past explanations of its policies would frame the debate about present controversies; the whole vocabulary for the discussion of a policy choice would depend on principles announced in previous decisions. An agency that provided reasons truly unrelated to the actual basis for a decision might find itself hamstrung by a policy that it never wanted to adopt.

In short, the human propensity to pursue self-interest is not fatal to civic republican theory. Civic republicanism explicitly recognizes this propensity and responds by demanding institutional constraints that discourage such pursuits. Instead of undermining the call for a civic republican political norm, the strong tendency to act in one's self-interest highlights the need for such a norm. The suggested alternative—constraining government to limit the influence of humanity's evil tendencies—provides no answer to those without the means to compete in a society of purely private transactions or to those who see their identity as bound with that of their community.

* * *

III. The Administrative State As a Means of Fulfilling the Civic Republican Promise

Administrative agencies—the so-called fourth branch of government—may be the only institutions capable of fulfilling the civic republican ideal of deliberative decisionmaking. Congress adheres primarily to pluralistic norms and responds most directly to factional influence. Although one proponent of civic republicanism, Cass Sunstein, has sought to revitalize Congress's deliberative processes through more active judicial review[150] the size, structure, and historically-rooted decisionmaking procedures of Congress render the prospect of revitalization unlikely. Perhaps for this reason, another proponent of civic republicanism, Frank Michelman, has called upon the judiciary to define directly the values that underlie governmental policy and are embodied in law.[151] Courts, however, are too far removed from the voice of the citizenry, and judges' backgrounds are too homogenous and distinct from those of many Americans to ensure that judicially-defined policy will accord with the public values of the polity.

Administrative agencies, however, fall between the extremes of the politically over-responsive Congress and the over-insulated courts. Agencies are therefore prime candidates to institute a civic republican model of policymaking. Some recent administrative resolutions of tough policy choices illustrate the role that agencies can play. For example, although the American public, experts, and government officials all agreed that the United States should close some military bases, Congress was unable to close any, or even set the criteria for deciding which bases should be closed. Too many representatives found the prospect of a base closing in their district politically unacceptable. A special commission, however,

---

[150] *See* [CASS R. SUNSTEIN, AFTER THE RIGHTS REVOLUTION 164 (1990); Cass R. Sunstein, *Interest Groups in American Public Law*, 38 STAN. L. REV. 29, 72 (1985).]

[151] *See* [Frank I. Michelman, *The Supreme Court, 1985 Term—Foreword: Traces Of Self-Government*, 100 HARV. L. REV. 4, 66-73 (1986); Frank I. Michelman, *Law's Republic*, 97 YALE L.J. 1493, 1537 (1988).]

was able to order base closings and do so in a fashion that took into account efficiency concerns, the need for national defense, and the economic dislocations in areas where bases will close.

I believe that the success achieved by the Defense Base Closure and Realignment Commission was not an anomaly. The place of administrative agencies in government—subordinate and responsible to Congress, the courts, and the President—allows for the checks on agency decisionmaking that ensure politically informed discourse and prevent purely politically-driven outcomes. The bureaucratic structure of administrative agencies and the processes by which they frequently decide questions of policy also foster deliberative government. * * *

A. The Place of Administrative Agencies in American Government

1. Availability of Judicial Review to Ensure Deliberative Decisionmaking. —Although the legitimacy of the judiciary stems from its use of reasoned decisionmaking, the courts are ill-equipped to delineate the public values that flow from political deliberation. Federal judges are not politically accountable. Although political independence frees them from the pressures that encourage interest group accommodation, it also accords them great latitude to impose their subjective conceptions of the public interest on the nation. Courts have neither the motivation nor the means to obtain information about the values of the general polity, on which civic republicanism's common good depends. The federal courts are also necessarily reactive—they can legitimately decide only the issues brought before them by litigants and therefore cannot establish a policy-setting agenda. Courts might provide, at best, only a partial delineation of the public values and policies necessary to implement civic republican theory.

Furthermore, the courtroom is not a forum designed to develop a consensus about the public good. Procedural formality makes participation in the judicial process expensive. Judicial proceedings are adversarial; participants focus on claiming legal entitlements and furthering their private interests. In the course of zealously advocating their individual interests, litigants lead the judicial process away from achieving true understanding and finding common ground for consensus. Parties to litigation ordinarily do not adequately represent many potentially affected interest groups. They also do not tend to modify their positions in response to discourse with their adversaries. Contrary to the lessons of basic civics, the adversarial system is neither good at revealing the truth nor facilitating the discovery of public values.

* * *

The structure and decisionmaking processes of Congress are not conducive to deliberation. Although legislative hearings nominally allow various interest groups to present and explain their positions, Congress, as a body, does not spend much time mulling over the issues and arguments raised. Rather, it entrusts the clarification of issues and drafting of proposed legislation to committees. Major committees control the legislative agenda and thereby greatly influence and constrain the outcomes reached by the full body. The members of these committees must consider their own constituencies and special interest supporters; they cannot realistically be expected to perform their screening function primarily with the public interest in mind. Instead, committee members typically engage in agenda control, vote trading, and log-rolling in order to obtain votes for the regulatory legislation that they support.

By the time a bill reaches the floor of the House or Senate, it reflects a myriad of political bargains and compromises. Thus, even if one could characterize the floor debates as deliberative, the influence of private interest groups would still taint the legislative process. Moreover, much congressional debate reflects efforts by factions to get their preferred readings of bills on the record in the hope that a court or agency will interpret the statute in their favor. Often, a majority of members are absent from the floor during the so-called floor debate. Except perhaps when Congress debates legislation on highly publicized issues of broad public concern, the legislative process facilitates coalition building and is antagonistic to the deliberative development of consensus about the public good.

* * *

My civic republican model explicitly provides that the reviewing court's proper function is to ensure that the agency interpreted the statute in a deliberative manner. The court should not interfere with the agency's use of its expertise and political awareness to reach a decision that the agency truly believes is good policy. Nonetheless, the court must make sure that the agency responded to all significant comments regarding the wisdom of its interpretation. The court must also make sure that the agency explained persuasively how its decision furthers the public interest. In other words, a court reviewing an agency interpretation must not measure the agency's action against the court's own reading of the statute, but instead must ensure that the agency followed the civic republican model of deliberative decisionmaking.

* * *

2. *Availability of Review by Politically Accountable Branches.* —Because courts are more insulated from the political pulse of the people than are agencies, judicial review alone is insufficient to ensure that agency policies remain true to the polity's consensus values. The place of administrative agencies in American constitutional government, however, also permits Congress and the President to review agency policies with an eye toward popularly held values. Although review by Congress and the President by no means ensures the fidelity of agency policy to a consensus of the common good, such review cabins agency decisionmaking so that it cannot stray too far from that consensus.

Congress's most direct reaction to an agency policy with which it disagrees is an explicit statutory override of an agency decision. Legislators typically override agency action, however, only when they realize that the agency decision poses a political problem, and when they are also able to agree on a solution that their constituencies support. Because overrides entail significant transaction costs, they occur infrequently. In addition, overrides make legislators vulnerable to attack by interest groups whose immediate private interests the legislation threatens. Finally, such legislation must first pass through the subcommittees and committees responsible for the particular area of regulation. Of late, party influence and seniority have become less significant to the workings of the committee system. In the absence of these organizing forces, committees often cannot forge the coalitions necessary for legislative action. These factors contribute to an institutional inertia that undercuts the effectiveness of direct legislative reaction as a regular means of checking agency policymaking. Nevertheless, on several occasions, Congress has modified agency determinations that it found too extreme.

More often, Congress uses its power of the purse to keep agencies from adopting policies that stray from the desires of affected interest groups. In the scramble for legislative appropriations, an agency needs an advocate on Capitol Hill—especially one on the appropriations subcommittee that oversees the agency's regulatory program. Appropriations subcommittees frequently specify which programs are to receive funds. They also engage in non-statutory control over agency programs, for example, by requiring the agency to give the subcommittee advance notice of changes from the mutually understood allocation of appropriated funds. Although the White House's role in reviewing and coordinating budget requests from the various agencies complicates the influence of appropriations committees, evidence suggests that agency policies do respond to changes in the make-up and prevailing ideology of the agencies' appropriations committees.

Presidential review of agency policy is another means that brings the values of the electorate to bear on agency decisions. White House review, when properly structured, encourages deliberation and public interest oriented policymaking. The President answers to the entire electorate and thus has an incentive to oppose policies that hurt the general public more than they help particular interest groups. Three factors, however, temper the desirability of relying on presidential oversight of agency policy. First, the Office of Management and Budget, the White House arm for agency review, does not have the expertise to make ultimate regulatory decisions and may itself have an anti-regulatory bias. Second, even in national elections, the electoral process biases outcomes toward the status quo and the interests of powerful groups. Third, allowing any centralized institution under the direct control of one individual to dictate policy invites decisionmakers to rely on backroom discussions and, more generally, to subvert deliberative processes, even if that individual is electorally accountable.

* * *

The President's appointment power can also profoundly affect regulatory policy. The President should appoint agency members who share her perspective on matters that the agency will address. Assuming that this perspective was a factor in the President's election, the result would be an agency decisionmaker who harbored many of the relevant basic values and public aspirations of the national electorate.

None of the mechanisms for judicial and political oversight of agency action, taken alone, ensures that agencies will not pursue their own goals and agendas. Nonetheless, the mechanisms reinforce one another as means of limiting agency discretion. This intricate interplay seems to suggest that meaningful political constraints do exist, at least against agencies pursuing goals far afield from those desired by the interest groups affected.

B. *The Structure of the Bureaucracy*

In addition to administrative agencies' place in government, their internal structure also encourages deliberative decisionmaking aimed at furthering public rather than private values. At the core of almost every agency is a professional staff, chosen for its knowledge rather than for its political views or affiliations. The staff forms the base of a pyramid that has the ultimate decisionmakers, who are generally political appointees, at the apex. Although these appointees generate the agency's policy agenda, they depend on the bureaucrats below to evaluate the various alternatives for implementing broad policies. Career staff members derive their power primarily from their professional training and their relationships with interest group representatives who frequently control important information—in other words, from job-specific expertise. This expertise allows bureaucrats to exert significant influence on public policy even when their role is merely advisory. Although career staff rarely initiate consideration of general policies, the debate over policy alternatives often starts at lower levels and travels up the pyramid. This process has the potential to focus the debate on a professional understanding of the public interest rather than on accommodation of private interests.

* * *

C. Agency Policymaking Procedures

The availability of agency procedures that facilitate access and public interest oriented discourse provides a third basis for my optimism about the ability of the administrative state to implement a civic republican model of policymaking. In particular, the paradigmatic process for agency formulation of policy—informal rulemaking—is specifically geared to advance the requirements of civic republican theory. Informal rulemaking requires public notice sufficient to inform interest groups that the agency is considering a policy that might affect them. Any group that keeps abreast of developments at a particular agency or regularly reviews the *Federal Register* learns of the agency's commencement of an informal rulemaking proceeding. Comment procedures provide relatively easy access to the discourse among interest groups and the dialogue between those groups and decisionmakers.

The availability of rulemaking procedures, however, fuels my optimism only to a limited extent. The actual procedures that agencies use may discourage them from taking advantage of the discourse that notice and comment rulemaking can produce. The most pervasive problem with informal rulemaking is that an agency usually investigates the issues and has its staff perform preliminary analyses of regulatory options before it initiates a rulemaking proceeding. Because this preliminary work is done without organized public input, the interest groups not informed in the preliminary stages may feel excluded from the rulemaking process and assume an antagonistic attitude upon a rule's proposal. Moreover, if only "insider" interest groups have input into the preliminary stages of a rule's development, the rule itself is apt to favor their private interests. An agency can exacerbate these problems by withholding data and staff analyses that may have prompted it to initiate the rulemaking proceeding or to formulate the proposed rule as it did. Furthermore, informal rulemaking proceedings do not mandate that parties have an opportunity to respond to comments filed by other groups. The only chance to respond may be through a petition for reconsideration or for judicial review, and by that time, the agency and "insider" groups are likely to have crystallized their positions and hence to view other parties as adversaries. As a result, informal rulemaking often does not generate true discourse but rather encourages participants to pursue their private interest single-mindedly.

Despite the flaws in current rulemaking practices, Congress and the courts can act to overcome the institutional problems outlined above. In several cases, courts have struck down regulations promulgated when the agency did not first disclose the scientific data upon which it relied, because the regulations ignored meaningful industry comments. In other cases, judges have added an opportunity for additional rounds of comments after the agency has changed its position. Both types of court action help ensure that rulemaking proceedings fulfill their potential as vehicles for civic republican deliberation. Requirements that agencies reveal the value choices inherent in the selection of one rule over an alternative and that they encourage representatives of various interests to discuss fundamental issues would also further civic republican aims.

* * *

IV. Avoiding the Pitfalls of Civic Republicanism
* * *

A. Regulation that Promotes Decisionmakers' Private Interests

Unless other government institutions or private interest groups impose constraints, regulators will often pursue their own private interests. This pursuit partially explains the failure of the New Deal agency model, which naively assumed that regulators would diligently implement statutory goals. History has shown that all too often regulators shirk their responsibilities; they prefer the leisure and security that accompanies the continuation of what is routine.

Hence, civic republican theory must address the phenomenon of agency lethargy. Two interrelated approaches can help solve the problem of agency shirking. First, requiring agencies to state and justify their agendas would focus attention on agencies that do not take sufficient steps to meet their statutory mandates. At present, agencies tend to set their agendas in political rather than in more deliberative forums. Media coverage of announced agendas could generate political pressure on Congress and the President to remedy extreme cases of shirking. If the history of the administrative state teaches us anything, however, it is that private interest groups are more dedicated and probably more efficient monitors of agency actions than are government officials. Legislators and the President may prefer the relative stability and lack of controversy that often accompany agency inaction. Hence, the formal involvement of the public in setting an agency's agenda might be needed to goad agency officials into explicitly considering long-term regulatory goals. * * *

In addition to shirking, officials' self-interest also creates incentives for them to augment their regulatory authority. Greater power allows regulators to increase monopoly rents, which they can then trade to interest groups in return for personal benefits such as future jobs or freedom from criticism. Regulators may also derive a direct psychic benefit from the power they exercise. Thus, the potential for regulators to pursue their self-interest suggests that Congress should limit agencies' discretion to expand their regulatory power; likewise, reviewing courts should not defer to an agency's statutory interpretation that increases the bounds of the agency's jurisdiction.

B. Agency Capture by Private Interest Groups

The second potential pitfall of civic republicanism stems from the ability of an ostensibly regulated industry to influence government policy. According to the capture hypothesis, instead of providing meaningful input into deliberation about the public interest, industry representatives co-opt governmental regulatory power in order to satisfy their private desires. * * *

Traditional theory posits that interest groups face a much easier task if they set out to capture an agency than if they try to capture Congress. Often agency staff members have worked in the regulated industry and thus share the industry's perspective and values. Many agency staff members expect to work eventually for some regulated entity, at which time they will cash in on the inside knowledge and experience gained in relatively low paying government positions. Not wanting to jeopardize this opportunity, they hesitate to criticize harshly industry proposals and arguments. In addition, well-organized and well-funded regulated entities can also affect the immediate interests of agency staff members and heads; if these individuals do not accede to the demands of the regulated entity, they may find themselves embroiled in numerous adversarial proceedings, which reduce their ability to address other regulatory matters. Finally, it is easier to influence the few agency members who are responsible for making ultimate decisions than the hundreds of legislators needed to pass regulatory bills.

This accepted learning, however, may grossly overstate the susceptibility of agencies to capture relative to the susceptibility of Congress. An agency organized into distinct offices, each filled by professionals from different backgrounds who communicate with a different clientele, can avoid decisions that reflect a single industry's perspective. Consideration and discussion of regulatory policy by various departments make that policy less likely to reflect the views of one group of agency staff members who may be imbued with a particular industry's values. Staff members' understanding that their goal should be to implement the public interest may further enhance their tendency to try to reach a universal accord on policy. This understanding may even encourage selection of public servants predisposed to the use of persuasive discourse.

The perception that employment opportunities within a regulated industry may depend on favoritism by career staff members does create some potential for agency capture, but this potential is unlikely to be significant. First, because conflict of interest statutes outlaw exchanges of influence for future jobs, staff members cannot solicit promises of future employment in exchange for favorable industry treatment. To provide favorable treatment without a guarantee of future employment is a risky strategy; the staff member may jeopardize her career in the agency. Second, although some staff members perceive that pro-industry bias helps secure a subsequent industry job, many staff members do not perceive this. Frequently, the regulated entity hires individuals who will best promote its interests after they are hired. Thus, it will prefer a staff member who knows how the agency operates even if she has previously worked to the entity's detriment. Third, structuring agencies to involve various interest groups and staff offices in the policy debate and requiring agencies to support their decisions with persuasive reasons would minimize the likelihood that capture of some staff members will cause the agency to adopt (and to defend successfully on review) a pro-industry policy.

Finally, focusing on the difference between the number of members of Congress who vote on legislation and the number of agency members who vote on regulation creates misperceptions about the relative ability of special interest groups to capture agencies. Although all members of Congress have a vote, their choices are dictated to a large extent by the actions of smaller subcommittees and powerful committee chairs. Furthermore, committee staffs play an important role in legislative decisionmaking, and inducements to favor industry can be just as great for congressional staff members as for agency personnel. In fact, legislative staff may be more prone to capture because their work generally occurs behind closed doors, unlike all but the most informal aspects of agency decisionmaking. Finally, special interest groups might enjoy greater influence over legislators than agency members because legislators are directly elected and hence more vulnerable to public sentiments that funded interest groups can generate.

* * *

Civic republicanism suggests three requirements that courts might impose an agency to guard against capture. Courts should require an agency to grant meaningful access to all affected groups, honestly justify its decisions by appeal to the public welfare, and act deliberatively in reaching its conclusion about which policy best serves that welfare. To implement these requirements, courts should remand agency decisions for further consideration when the agency does not actively encourage full participation by groups representing diffuse interests. Courts should also expand the "hard look" approach to judicial review of agency action to apply to all agency exercises of discretion (including statutory interpretation). In addition, the judiciary should demand that the agency explain how it conceives of the public interest, how that conception comports with the agency's authorizing statute, how the particular policy advances that conception, and why the arguments opposing that policy are less persuasive. Although this type of review provides no guarantee against policy decisions driven by agency capture, it sharply decreases the likelihood that an agency will adopt such decisions without public scrutiny and publicity.

C. Regulators' Pursuit of Their Own Conception of the Public Interest

A third potential pitfall of civic republican government is that decisionmakers will implement their idiosyncratic conceptions of the public interest rather than society's consensus about that interest. Pursuit of a personal notion of the public interest may plague congressional as well as agency decisionmaking, at least to the extent that influential members of Congress enjoy sufficient "slack" from electoral oversight. Nonetheless, the potential may be greater for agency members to impose their own conception of the public interest on the rest of society because they are fewer in number and feel no direct electoral constraints.

As in the case of capture, monitoring by private interest groups may identify when an agency has gone awry, but it will not cure the problem in a suitable manner. Along with the concern that private interests group monitoring encourages agencies to seek a pluralistic equilibrium, there is the added problem that public-interest-minded decisionmakers are unlikely to be swayed by private interest group inducements.

Judicial review may help to check despotic regulators, but may not suffice on its own to avoid this pitfall. Judicial mandates of participation by all facets of society, deliberation prior to agency decisionmaking, and justification of the decision in terms of the public interest (including explanations of deviations from past conceptions) encourage regulators to think hard about their own conceptions of the public interest. Review will thus help well-meaning but misinformed regulators make better decisions. The danger still exists, however, that a justification of an agency decision, cloaked in the language of public interest, may in fact be based only on a regulator's idiosyncratic conception of that interest. It may be difficult for courts to determine whether a regulatory goal couched as advancing some general interest of the populace is in fact a goal shared generally by the polity or instead is a community oriented goal imposed by the agency.

The requirement that potentially affected groups participate in the deliberative process may help courts make this determination, but only to a limited extent. The record may indicate that many of the participants in the proceeding opposed a policy for sound reasons to which the agency decision did not respond. Yet the record often does not clearly reveal whether an agency policy truly comports with some shared principle of the common good; full deliberative proceedings may instead generate obfuscating arguments. A requirement of consistency is also not likely to constrain an agency: presumably the agency would be happy to impose its view of the public good on a consistent basis. * * *

Civic republicanism thus must also look to the politically accountable branches to constrain well-meaning but despotic agencies. In doing so, however, it must not constrain agencies in a manner that increases the power of individuals within those branches to override and control agency policymaking or else it merely invites the replacement of one despot by another. Despite this limitation, the political branches can meaningfully check runaway regulators in two ways.

First, Congress as a whole can and should directly review agency policy to ensure that it comports with the polity's conception of the public good. Congress,

although not perfectly deliberative in its legislative process, is accountable to the various factions in society. Although legislative procedures favor factional influence, the bicameral structure of Congress, the presidential veto, and the fact that the committee system can more easily block legislation than generate it all make it unlikely that a congressional override will replace an agency policy that serves the public interest with one that explicitly caters to private interests. Congress thus should play an important monitoring role, *at the end of the deliberative policy-setting process,* to ensure that the agency does not adopt a policy that conflicts with popular values.
* * *

Second, the President can use her appointment power to guard against regulators who are likely to entertain idiosyncratic views of the public interest. The President's ability to choose an appointee who shares her broad conception of the public interest, which presumably comports with the consensus of those who elected her, provides the most important means of keeping the bureaucracy accountable to the polity. Because appointments of agency members occur relatively infrequently, they attract media attention, which helps ensure that the entire electorate holds the President accountable for the quality and ideology of the appointee. Thus, the President's appointment power can provide another check against despotic agencies without unduly empowering the President.

* * *

Gerald E. Frug, *The Ideology of Bureaucracy in American Law*, 97 Harv. L. Rev. 1276, 1279–84, 1295–1304, 1312–13, 1315–23, 1326–28, 1330–43, 1351–56, 1359–60, 1368–71, 1373–87 (1984)*

* * *

I. The Argument
A. The Stories that Justify Bureaucracy

From the time of their introduction into American life, large-scale business corporations and the administrative state that regulates them have raised profound questions about the kind of nation we are creating and the kind of people we are becoming. One way to understand the nature of these questions is to examine the ways dissident political movements have contested the foundation, growth, and predominance of bureaucratic entities. From the republicans of the Revolutionary period through the Jacksonians, populists, and labor organizers of the nineteenth century, to modern writers on economic and political democracy, dissidents have charged that public and private power has become vested in the hands of the few. This concentration of power, they have argued, threatens fundamental ideals of liberty and equality, whether these ideals are understood in terms of an economy founded on widespread individual entrepreneurship, a polity based on democratically controlled decisionmaking, or a theory of the self that emphasizes the ability of individuals to control the nature of their work and their essential life choices. * * *

Dissidents have also charged that the emergence of large-scale bureaucratic enterprise has transformed day-to-day life experience. Sometimes this criticism refers to the alienation that has invaded ordinary human activity: the lack of fulfillment people derive from their work, the sense of dealing with organizations seemingly beyond their own, even anyone's, control. At other times, this criticism is directed at the increasing sameness and conformity within everyday life. People act by reference to their roles in life, and these roles are reproduced endlessly: McDonald's, McDonald's everywhere. Whether they emphasize the problems of human estrangement or those of conformity, critics charge that the bureaucratization of life has diminished the possibility of an authentic experience of the self.

Dissidents' complaints about the growth of large-scale public and private enterprise, however, have been simply a subtheme in American political discourse, one that has been overwhelmed by the growth of these enterprises and the voices of their defenders. The defenders of bureaucracy have allied its emergence with the idea of progress, the advances of the technological age, and the realities of a modern, complex society. Bureaucracy, we are told, is a necessary, inevitable feature of modern life. Only a foolish romantic—a reactionary who idealizes a past that never really existed and could not conceivably exist—could hope to dismantle or radically to alter current public or private bureaucratic organizations. Once they establish this argument of necessity, defenders of bureaucracy then typically demonstrate why these organizations constitute desirable forms of human association. Here, more than in mass meetings or even in the family, personal domination is subject to checks and balances. Moreover, far from

---

* Copyright 1984 by the Harvard Law Review Association. Reprinted with permission of the Harvard Law Review Association and Gerald E. Frug. All rights reserved.

creating a diminished sense of self, modern large-scale organizations have made possible an unparalleled expansion of people's opportunity to choose their own life-style. * * *

The history of the conflict over bureaucratic organization in America is important because it affects our current stance toward these institutions. Subordinate dissident concerns about the exercise of managerial power and about the dangers of bureaucracy to personal freedom have influenced both the growth and the defense of large-scale organizations. Indeed, one can understand the changing forms of justification offered for bureaucratic organization in terms of an historical progression fueled by a dialectic of critique and response. But one can also view our relationship to the historical controversy over bureaucracy in less causal terms. From this perspective, the historical debate simply replicates our own ambivalent feelings about the desirability and the danger of bureaucratic institutions: the debate between bureaucracy's defenders and dissidents is one we still carry on—within ourselves.

* * * In this Article, I identify four different attempts to understand and defend corporations and administrative agencies. These four approaches represent responses to the critique of both managerial domination and the erosion of the space for personal self-expression. Taken together, they not only encapsulate all the principal themes of corporate and administrative law but also dominate organizational theory as a whole.

* * *

The first of these models, which I call the formalist model, can be associated with the work of late nineteenth and early twentieth century bureaucratic theorists such as Max Weber, Frederick Taylor, and Ernst Freund. These theorists portrayed bureaucracy as a rationalized, disciplined mechanism for implementing the wishes of its creators, whether stockholders or legislators. They saw bureaucratic power as unthreatening because they understood bureaucratic organizations to be objective instruments under the control of those who delegated power to them. Indeed, constituent control not only prevented abuse of managerial power but also preserved a sphere for the full expression of subjective experience in the activity of those outside the bureaucracy whose wishes the bureaucracy carried out.

The second form of bureaucratic legitimation, which I call the expertise model, developed in response to the critique of the formalist model. Progressives and certain New Dealers—including organization theorists like Philip Selznick, corporate managerialists like Chester Barnard, Elton Mayo, Peter Drucker, and Douglas McGregor, and administrative law scholars like Woodrow Wilson and James Landis—agreed with the charge that bureaucracies were not in fact controlled by commands issued from outside. They recognized the enormous range of discretion exercised by bureaucratic managers; indeed, they argued that this discretion was not only an unavoidable ingredient of bureaucratic life but also its very raison d'etre. Instead of fearing bureaucratic discretion, these thinkers welcomed it because they perceived the managers and employees who exercised it to be "experts" whose professionalism simultaneously limited the scope of their power, prevented personal domination, and made possible the creativity and flexibility necessary to the effectiveness of the bureaucratic form.

The third theory of bureaucratic legitimacy, which I call the judicial review model, was a reaction against the "excesses" of the expertise model. Those who articulated this point of view, including such legal scholars as Felix Frankfurter, Lon Fuller, Louis Jaffe, and Kenneth Culp Davis, expressed doubts that either constituent control or managerial expertise could limit the exercise of bureaucratic power. That limit had to be located instead in the ability of the courts to review and, when necessary, to overturn the actions of bureaucratic organizations. Bureaucracy could be rendered nonthreatening, in their view, only if adequately subject to the rule of law. Because the intrusion of the courts would be limited, however, managers and constituents would retain primary control over bureaucratic activities.

Finally, in the 1960's and 1970's, liberal democrats, whose ideas about administrative law have been analyzed by Richard Stewart, and conservative representatives of the "Chicago School," whose work has become a mainstay of current writing about corporate law, criticized the effectiveness and credibility of the judicial review model. These theorists, who espouse what I call the market/pluralist model, ground the legitimacy of administrative and corporate structures on the operation of either political or market mechanisms within bureaucratic structures. As they see it, either interest-group politics or market forces intervene to discipline bureaucratic management; in addition, these mechanisms allow people to express themselves about how bureaucracies should operate.

* * *

Each model of bureaucratic legitimacy is a story designed to tell its listeners: "Don't worry, bureaucratic organizations are under control." All of administrative and corporate law can, in my view, be understood as an expression of one of these stories or of a combination of them. These bodies of law comprise, in other words, a series of assurances that the legal system can overcome the perennial concerns about bureaucratic organizations. The most prominent concern that these areas of legal doctrine address is the fear that bureaucratic managers—whether public or private—can control bureaucratic power in a manner adverse to the interests of the shareholders or citizens whom they purport to serve. * * *

* * *

E. The Choice Between Bureaucracy and Democracy

* * * Bureaucracy is the primary form of organized power in America today, and it is therefore a primary target for those who seek liberation from modern forms of human domination. The ideology that reassures us that bureaucracy is legitimate is demobilizing because it conceals the need to reorder American society to bring to life better versions of the ideal of human freedom. Critical theory seeks to undermine this ideology by exposing the false consciousness through which people understand the world. Such an exposure is itself an act of liberation.

Of course, this sort of liberation cannot alone ensure human freedom. New forms of human association designed to take the place of bureaucracy must themselves be subject to the same critique. But this critique has its limits—there is a stopping place. This would be reached when people abandoned abstract arguments that seek to defend some form of life as a structure that can protect human individuality—when people jointly recognize that no structure can protect us from each other given the variable, intersubjective, interdependent nature of human relationships. The forms of organization that would then be created would not be understood as an answer to the human predicament. They would be transparently open to transformation (no form of organization is necessary) and always in need of transformation (all forms of organization create forms of domination that need to be combatted).

I use the ideal of participatory democracy to represent this different kind of social organization. Of course, some proponents of participatory democracy reduce it to a concrete structure that "solves" the problems of social life. These proponents should be subjected to the same critique that I lodge here against the proponents of bureaucracy. But other advocates of reinvigorating the notion of democracy are not vulnerable to the critique advanced here. They understand the term "democracy" to refer to the process by which people create for themselves the form of organized existence within which they live. Only by creating these forms together can people confront the intersubjective nature of social life. Moreover, unless people do so *themselves,* the artificial structures through which they operate will threaten to function beyond their control. In this view, the term "participatory democracy" does not describe a fixed series of limited possibilities of human organization but the ideal under which the possibilities of joint transformation of social life are collected. This essay is an attempted contribution to the effort of many others to make the creation of such new forms of organization possible.

II. An Analysis of Administrative and Corporate Law Doctrines

* * *

A. The Formalist Model

1. The Model Described.—Captivated by theories of instrumental rationality and notions of technocratic efficiency, formalist thinkers have attempted to understand bureaucracy by likening it to a machine. This machine imagery evokes a number of different ideas. First, a machine is a means employed to achieve others' ends. These ends may be controversial, but the machine itself takes no part in resolving the controversy. The machine is a neutral device; all value judgments take place outside of its operation. The machine itself does not exercise "discretion" in any sense. The machine is also a highly technical and complex device, one that would be damaged by a mere layman's tinkering. It works because each part has a specified function that is properly integrated with the specified functions of the other parts. Machines work because they are well designed; all intellectual effort concerning the machine goes into its design. Once the machine is functioning in accordance with an adequate blueprint, all problems relating to its operation can safely be entrusted to a technician. If the machine fails to work properly, one calls the person who designed it (or another expert) to fix it. There is no reason to think that the operation of a machine will pose threats that should be checked by an outside force like "judicial review," the "discipline of the market," or "democratic control." Finally, machines are so powerful and efficient that life without them is inconceivable. Only a fool would suggest that a return to handmade products would be desirable or even possible. The remedy for any problem generated by machines is to improve them, not to replace them with romantic notions of a more human form of production.

These three aspects of the machine—its instrumental relationship to predetermined ends, its technical design, and its symbolic association with modern efficiency—are the central elements in the formalist vision of bureaucracy. Bureaucracy, we are told, is simply a means to effectuate the ends of its constituents—the citizens or shareholders whose interests it serves. Bureaucratic organization is based on the categories of instrumental rationality: it sharply distinguishes values and facts, ends and means, desire and performance. Values, ends, and desires—the subjective part of the human personality—are the attributes of the constituents who control the bureaucracy rather than of the bureaucracy itself. The bureaucracy is "objective": it cannot exercise threatening discretion because it merely responds to constituents' commands. If the shareholders say, "Maximize profits" or the legislators say, "Eliminate dangerous health hazards," it does so. These directions are "formally realizable"—they impel the bureaucratic official to respond to a multitude of fact situations in a way determined by the directive itself. In legal theory terms, the reasoning from the rules issued by those who control the bureaucracy is formalistic: the mere invocation of the rules, together with the conclusions they imply, determines the outcome of any concrete bureaucratic decision.

* * *

* * * Bureaucracy [on this view] operates in accordance with a familiar definition of freedom: to be free, one must be independent of the personal or subjective will of others and subservient only to general, impersonal laws. Furthermore, because technical competence defines each person's position within the organization, everyone has the opportunity to rise to the level of her/his abilities. The formalist vision thus embodies both a norm of equal opportunity and the democratic ideal of eliminating the relevance of social hierarchies in the selection of those who exercise power.

2. Formalism in Administrative Law: The Nondelegation Doctrine.—The doctrine of administrative law that best reflects the attempt to effectuate "subjective" constituent goals through an "objective" bureaucracy is the "nondelegation doctrine." This doctrine grounds the legitimacy of government bureaucracies on legislative authorization and control of their actions. According to the doctrine, the legislature must retain primary decisionmaking authority for governmental activity because it represents the subjective desires of the democratic electorate. Bureaucrats must carry out the wishes of the people (as expressed by their chosen representatives), not their own personal conceptions of the good. Subjectivity— or at least the important aspects of subjectivity—is thus located outside the bureaucracy. The nondelegation doctrine seeks to enforce bureaucratic objectivity by preventing the legislature from shifting any critical aspects of subjective decisionmaking to the bureaucratic agency. If such a delegation of power is attempted, it will be declared unconstitutional.

The nondelegation doctrine, however, has never asserted a simple and rigid demarcation between subjective legislative decisionmaking and objective bureaucratic implementation. The doctrine also inserts subjectivity into the bureaucratic role and objectivity into the legislative one. Administrative agencies have never been restricted to purely objective functions; some room for discretionary activity within the command-implementing bureaucracy has always seemed indispensable. * * *

In addition to admitting, as a dangerous supplement, some subjectivity into bureaucratic objectivity, the nondelegation doctrine embodies an objective restraint on legislative subjectivity. The nondelegation doctrine is designed to put some objective limits on the legislature's desire to avoid decisionmaking by passing the buck to the bureaucracy. This objective restraint on the legislature's power to delegate authority supplements the doctrine's general effort to locate policymaking authority in the hands of the legislature. Yet courts that have interpreted the nondelegation doctrine have recognized that one of the critical ingredients of policymaking authority is the ability to decide how much to decide oneself and how much to let others decide as problems develop. Too rigorous a restriction on delegation would render it "impossible to exercise . . . power at all." The legislature must be "free . . . to choose . . . the flexibility attainable by the use of less restrictive standards." Accordingly, the nondelegation doctrine must specify when the legislature can refuse to decide public policy issues in order to preserve flexibility and when it needs to decide them in order to control excessive bureaucratic discretion.

We now have the conflicting structure of the nondelegation doctrine before us. With respect to the relationship between the legislature and the bureaucracy, the critical task of the doctrine is to confine the bureaucracy within the objective limits charted by the legislature's subjective policy judgments. Viewed from the standpoint of the legislature alone, the doctrine seeks to impose objective constraints on the legislature's subjective desire to shirk its responsibilities. From the point of view of the bureaucracy alone, the doctrine must permit agencies adequate subjective discretion: they must have enough room to maneuver or the "wheels of government" will "stop." The nondelegation doctrine is thus crucially dependent on the lines it seeks to draw between the appropriate functions of the legislature and those of the bureaucracy, between legitimate and illegitimate legislative decisions to delegate power, and between the proper kind of bureaucratic subjectivity and its needed objectivity.

In an attempt to draw these lines, the courts have articulated a series of "tests" that a delegation of power must meet in order to be constitutional: the legislature must lay down an "intelligible principle," decide the "fundamental policy questions," exercise the "essentials" of the legislative function. These tests appear harmoniously to combine subjectivity and objectivity—they comfort us by suggesting that, if they are met, there will be adequate legislative decisionmaking to ensure meaningful bureaucratic objectivity, yet not so much legislative decisionmaking as to prevent needed bureaucratic discretion. * * * But while their strength lies in their ability to suggest that, if they are properly applied, everything will be all right, their weakness lies in their inability to generate any consistent application. Legal argument about nondelegation consists of applying these tests to specific delegations of power, applications that generate contradictory conclusions: any delegation both does and does not satisfy the relevant tests.

One form this legal argument takes is to treat the key words of these tests as abstractions, but one can deduce from these abstractions opposite results. Consider, for example, a specific delegation of authority: the Federal Price Administrator's power to fix prices of commodities if the prices "in his judgment will be fair and equitable and will effectuate the purposes of the Act." Legal arguments about whether this delegation meets the test of the nondelegation doctrine—the goal of laying down an "intelligible principle"—consist in treating some aspect of the subjective-objective combination that the test unites as if it were the test's only meaning. It might be argued, for example, that the delegation meets the test because the test requires only limited detail. ("The legislature needs to provide only an intelligible principle, not a blueprint.") This argument emphasizes the need for subjectivity on both sides of the legislature/bureaucracy boundary—the importance of legislative flexibility and the necessity of bureaucratic discretion. Alternatively, it might be argued that the delegation fails the test because the test requires adequate detail. ("The legislature must provide an intelligible principle, not empty words.") This argument emphasizes the need for objectivity on both sides of the boundary—the importance of restraining legislative abdication of responsibility and of curbing uncontrolled bureaucratic discretion. Because the word "intelligible" is designed to combine two contradictory notions—one enabling the legislature to delegate and one restraining it—both arguments correctly apply the test. The dual nature of the goal generates the two-sided character of legal argument, as well as its ultimate indeterminacy. The test merely restates the question of the appropriate extent of delegation; it cannot inform a decision that requires resolution of the delegation issue.

* * *

4. An Overview of the Critique of the Model.— Discretion appears within the bureaucracy as a supplement to its essentially objective functioning; discretion is added to the operation of bureaucracy in order to make its objectivity possible. To be objective, the bureaucracy has to carry out the wishes of its constituents, but to do so it must refer to their general intentions ("maximize profits") or their specific commands ("fix prices"). Either reference requires the bureaucratic actors to use their discretion.
* * *
As we learned from the analysis of the nondelegation doctrine, the need for bureaucratic discretion is not diminished if specific commands are given to the bureaucracy by its constituents. Any application of the commands to specific situations requires the exercise of bureaucratic subjectivity—deciding what the words mean, what their purpose is, or how their meaning and their purpose can be made consistent with each other. Implementers cannot grasp other people's wishes in a way unmediated by their own consciousness. Any application of others' desires combines "implication" (the implementers' efforts to arrive at the constituents' hypothetical meaning) and "construction" (the implementers' pursuit of what they think ought to be the meaning when there is no clear evidence one way or the other). Yet contract law scholars have shown that the processes of locating meaning in the speaker, the document, or the facts (implication) and of locating it in the interpreters themselves (construction) merge into each other. The processes cannot be subdivided into objective and subjective components. Nor can they be disentangled here.

The formalist model, then, envisions that the bureaucracy will objectively implement constituents' desires and includes, as a necessary supplement, the demand that the bureaucracy exercise its discretion in order to perform this task. Of course, this supplement is dangerous: the formalist model provides no mechanism for limiting this discretion once it exists.
* * *

* * *

* * * For me, the dangerous supplement analysis is a useful way to understand the force of the different kinds of criticism that can be lodged against the formalist vision of bureaucratic organizations (and other visions as well). For example, the most familiar political attack on the formalist model of bureaucracy has been the attempt to demonstrate that the model fails to present a convincing scheme for protecting and enhancing human freedom. To the extent that people have built bureaucracies, as Michael Crozier suggested in his classic study of *The Bureaucratic Phenomenon*, "to evade face-to-face relationships and situations of personal dependency whose authoritarian tone they cannot bear," formalist theorists have not realized their objective. The formalist model suggests no way to prevent the subjectivity that is an inextricable attribute of bureaucracy from becoming the exercise of personal domination. Indeed, the model assumes that subjectivity is arbitrary and uncontrollable and should therefore have no place in the bureaucracy. Moreover, to the extent that the objectification of constituents' desires permits the bureaucracy to deny constituents what they want, it transforms the bureaucracy into a threat to the constituents' security rather than an expression of their will. Bureaucratic organization loses its machinelike character and becomes one of the decisionmakers—a decisionmaker whose discretion the formalist model cannot defend.

* * *

The dangerous supplement analysis can be useful in another way as well: it can help us to be self-critical about our own assimilation of the formalist version of bureaucratic life. The formalist model still retains considerable power to provide us with ways of adjusting to, even feeling good about, a life dominated by bureaucratic organization. We can, for example, associate ourselves with the objective side of the model and project important aspects of subjective discretion onto others. As managers or employees, we can perform our daily tasks at work without having to agonize over the decisions we are making or the actions we are taking. Responsibility for them can be displaced onto those—legislators, shareholders, bosses—whose mandate we are following. Even as legislators, shareholders, or bosses, we can displace responsibility further: we can claim that the demands of the Constitution or of the profit system or the competitive struggle require us to do what we are doing. Alternatively, we can displace responsibility onto our agents; after all, we never decided that our decision should be carried out *that* way. In this manner, all of us can feel that it is really someone else who has the power, and thus the moral duty, to modify the kind of world we are putting into place.

* * *

These stances represent ways to define ourselves in terms of the formalist vision. But these forms of self-definition, like the model itself, are tolerable only as long as there is some space (at home, in the voting booth) where we can express our subjectivity—our sense of self—without its being infected by the bureaucracies we have created. The dangerous supplement analysis should help us see how such a protection of the self is unattainable. Because the experience of subjectivity cannot be disentangled from the structures in which people live, no realm of subjectivity can be protected from the attempt to objectify bureaucratic life. There are no "shareholders" or "citizens" in the world who are not simultaneously subordinates within bureaucratic structures. The attempt to objectify human life within bureaucracies threatens to affect people in their lives as a whole—it shapes their way of dealing with the world even in their "free" activities as citizens or shareholders. Thus, the inability to divide people into components means that bureaucratic objectivity invades and transforms the subjective experience of the few people who are supposed to control—and take responsibility for—bureaucratic objectivity. Everyone is in danger of becoming "One Dimensional Man," a human being who has lost the ability to sense the rich possibilities of human existence by reducing life to the terms of instrumental rationality. Because all human existence is affected by bureaucratic structures, the formalist model's attempt to rob some aspects of life of "personal" qualities threatens the life experience itself. * * *

B. The Expertise Model

1. The Model Described.—The expertise model takes as its premise one element of the critique of formalism. The model not only concedes but even celebrates the ineradicable role of subjectivity and discretion in bureaucratic operation. Bureaucratic institutions depend for their success on these ingredients. Bureaucracy, in this model, is not an impersonal machine but a social system, a way of mobilizing all aspects of the human personality in order to transform individuals into a functioning group. Indeed, writers on bureaucratic theory often refer to this view of bureaucracy as "organic," to contrast it with the "mechanical" nature of the formalist model. This metaphor is designed to capture bureaucracy's dependence on the nonrational, subjective, human-relations side of life, as well as its holistic method of integrating its specialized components.

Expertise theorists picture a bureaucracy as a "natural community" organized to pursue a common purpose. Because this community is built on loyalty rather than on discipline, its effective organization depends more on the psychology of its members than on the formal realizability of its rules. To be effective, the organization must internalize as part of its collective consciousness the common purpose that unites its members; this purpose will then both define and be defined by the members' daily activities. Expertise theorists have thus focused on the sociological issue of how organizations can foster the cooperative pursuit of a common goal. In such an effort, it would obviously be a mistake to overlook any aspect of human personality, just as it would be wrong to emphasize formal organization-chart relationships among employees. People function within the bureaucracy with their whole personality and not just their rational, objective side. Indeed, organizations themselves function—and must be understood—as if they were human beings, entities not reducible to the combination of their separable elements. As a consequence, organizational success depends on the creation of a successfully integrated organizational personality, not on rationalist schemes to rid the organization of subjective discretion.

Within the organization, the role of the executive is crucial. His function is "leadership," and his qualifications derive from his expert knowledge of how to exercise leadership. He serves as the catalyst or "indispensable fulminator" who gives concrete definition to the goals of the organization and mobilizes it to achieve them. According to one expertise theorist, "the essential task of management is to arrange organizational conditions and methods of operation so that people can achieve their own goals best by directing their own efforts toward organizational objectives." The successful executive excels in such a task not because of his technical knowledge (technicians work for him) or his ability to enforce clear rules (he may dispense with them) but because of his expertise as a "generalist." This expertise depends on his personal qualities: judgment, character, ingenuity, energy, enthusiasm, imagination, creativity. Just as the organization is successful when it melds diverse individuals into an organizational personality, the executive is successful when he embodies that personality.

The executive's organizational personality not only defines his character but also sets limits on his behavior. The executive is constrained by his organizational role to act in accordance with the organization's needs; the office, in this sense, makes the man. To function effectively, he must adopt a "professionalism of spirit." "Judgment," therefore, is not just an indispensable executive ability; it also restrains the executive's discretion. A failure of judgment—a failure to grasp the organization's needs—will destroy the organization and the executive along with it. Similarly, "competence" functions both as an executive quality and as a restraint; the executive must be careful not to let his work extend beyond his field of competence. The virtues and the restraints of these qualities of judgment and competence constitute the executive's expertise. * * *

* * *

The expertise model can be summarized by envisioning it as the mirror image of the formalist model. The formalist model posits a "hard" inside (a machinelike, objective bureaucracy) controlled by a "soft" outside (the arbitrary, subjective desires of the bureaucracy's constituents). The expertise model, by contrast, depicts a "soft" inside (the flexible creation of an organizational purpose energized by a flexible, creative executive) controlled by a "hard" outside (the limits of professionalism, expertise, and competence that constrain organizational flexibility within appropriate bounds). Stated differently, the formalist model seeks to organize subjectivity and objectivity by relegating subjectivity to the constituents outside the bureaucracy and locating objectivity inside the bureaucracy, while the expertise model seeks to locate subjectivity in the internal functioning of the bureaucracy and to relegate objectivity to the role of limiting this internal functioning.

An ability to distinguish and render compatible subjectivity and objectivity, however, is as important to the expertise model as it is to the formalist model. In the expertise model, the successful operation of the bureaucracy depends on its flexibility and its responsiveness to the personalized judgments of those who function within it. If the organization is not functioning properly, the solution is to find the "right people" to make it work, not to constrain the organization with rationalist organizational devices. Only those inside the bureaucracy have the appropriate intuitions about how it works and how best to effectuate its purpose. Objective constraints threaten all these ingredients of organizational success: flexibility, responsiveness, the right people, intuition. An attempt to impose generalized rules or structured behavior on the organization would rob it of its unique "personality." Thus, the subjectivity of the organization requires that objectivity have only a narrowly circumscribed role within the organization's internal structure.

Yet objectivity is crucial to the task of keeping the organization within appropriate limits. These limits—the professional expertise of the employees, the hard facts that they must grapple with, or the political or competitive realities of the environment in which the organization operates—are genuine constraints only if they are not subject to the will of the employees whose actions they seek to limit. It would be a contradiction to suggest that the employees could be constrained by factors subject to their own will. Thus, the objective constraints must be kept distinct from the subjective qualities of bureaucratic decisionmaking.

2. *The Business Judgment Rule and Administrative Expertise.*—* * * The concept of administrative expertise, while not itself a "doctrine," is part of the rhetoric of administrative law opinions that invokes the same kind of deference to bureaucratic decisions, with the same qualifications, when made by administrative agencies. * * *

* * * [T]he idea of expertise contains two elements: the decisionmaker must exercise "judgment" and he must act "impersonally." The judgment requirement is called the "duty of care" in corporate law; in administrative law it is embodied in the requirement that the agency's decision not be "arbitrary" or "capricious." In both fields, the judgment required is largely subjective. Its soundness derives from the personal knowledge and experience of the decisionmaker—his "insight" or "intuition." But the concept of judgment also includes an important objective feature: a judgment must be "rational" and "informed," not just the result of a throw of the dice. The problem in both corporate and administrative law is to prevent this supplementary objective constraint from supplanting the creativity upon which expert judgment must be founded.

By contrast, the requirement of impersonality is largely objective: the decisionmaker must reject his self-interest and act instead in the interest of the corporation or the public at large. * * * Theorists in both fields recognize, however, that even the most impersonal decisionmaking must contain subjective elements. The decisionmaker must rely on his own personal qualities—his own expertise—in making his decision. Thus, the task of legal doctrine is to prevent these subjective elements from overriding the disinterest on which the professional judgment must be based.

* * *

(b) The Requirement of Impersonality.—* * * Neither taking the impersonality requirement seriously nor refusing to take it seriously seems to work. The impersonality requirement seeks to remove bias because bias is too personal and too subjective to be allowed in bureaucratic decisionmaking. On the other hand, the requirement permits expert discretion: expert judgment remains personal (no two experts are alike), but it is safely objectified. A restraint on expertise would take objectivity too seriously because it would intrude on the flexibility needed for creative decisionmaking. The difficulty of distinguishing expertise from bias is, however, well known. * * *

Courts commonly deal with the problematic distinction between expertise and bias by emphasizing deference to management discretion at the expense of restraining it. For example, in *Association of National Advertisers v. FTC*, the court held that a decisionmaker who had previously expressed his opinion on the issue before him would not be disqualified for bias absent "a clear and convincing showing that the agency member has an unalterably closed mind on matters critical to the disposition of the proceeding." As the dissent pointed out, this standard imposes "a practically impossible impediment in a great many cases to a showing of bias, even when the decisionmaker has in fact made up his mind in advance of the hearing." * * *

3. *The Vision of Super-Expert.*—Some writers admit that the decisions of ordinary corporate and government officials do not conform with meaningful standards of professional judgment or impartiality. They concede that bureaucratic decisionmakers exercise subjective discretion without the necessary objective limits. Their solution to the problem of bureaucratic legitimacy, however, is not to abandon the expertise model but to redouble their efforts to realize it. To do so, they seek to place bureaucratic pseudo-experts under the supervision of "real" experts. Into the chaos of the world of the expertise model, they insert a figure truly worthy of comic-book adventure stories: Super-Expert.

Fans of Super-Expert attribute the current difficulties of the expertise model to its failure to take the objective side of the concept of expertise seriously enough. The role they would assign to Super-Expert is buttressing this needed objectivity. He could do so in a variety of ways. In administrative law, he might sit on a reviewing board designed to check the veracity of the agency's technocratic analysis or serve as an advisor to, or even become, a judge. In any of these roles his expertise will enable him effectively to review agency decisionmaking. * * *

* * *

* * * [T]he conflict between the need for Super-

Expert to be independent and the need for him to be informed merely reproduces the discussion of the expertise/bias distinction presented in the Section on the requirement of impersonality. The knowledge necessary to qualify Super-Expert as an independent director, like the knowledge qualifying a government official as an expert, simultaneously threatens to make him biased. Furthermore, the contradictory aspects of Super-Expert's role present the same dilemma as the one discussed in the "judgment" section: taking the requirements of objectivity seriously enough to make them effective would lead to the elimination not only of the bad elements of discretion but of the desirable elements as well. All these issues are similar because they all are based on the idea that expertise requires impersonality *and* judgment. Both ingredients are necessary to legitimate an expert's power. A judgment infected with personal bias is no more satisfactory than is an impersonal decision uninformed by an adequate grasp of the issue to be decided. But these requirements conflict with each other. The qualities necessary to make a judgment are the same qualities that lead to personal predispositions or bias. To put the matter in the opposite way, genuine absence of personal involvement in an issue precludes the making of a judgment: "the participation of the speaker . . . [is part of] any sincere statement of fact." In short, impersonal judgment is a contradiction in terms, and every attempt to split the difference—to allow some personal involvement but not too much—simply creates a structure of manipulation. Such a structure, as we have seen, underlies legal argument about * * * the meaning of administrative expertise. The same manipulable structure can be found in the proposals to find a role in bureaucratic life for Super-Expert. No human candidate for the job could possibly exist. Only in our imagination can a superhero be sufficiently outside the world to remain unprejudiced by contacts with it yet still be able to intervene effectively in the world to prevent might from making right.

4. An Overview of the Critique of the Model. — This discussion of the concept of impersonal judgment should indicate to the reader how the concept of expertise can be understood in terms of the dangerous supplement. Expertise theorists, unlike formalist thinkers, clearly see bureaucratic power as an expression of the will of bureaucratic officials themselves. Indeed this subjectivity is, as we have noted, the feature of bureaucratic officials that expertise theorists most seek to nurture and defend. Yet some objective limits on official discretion have always been an indispensable supplement to bureaucratic subjectivity: experts are people whose subjective decisions are confined within appropriate objective boundaries. These boundaries, of course, endanger the ability to exercise the necessary discretion. Thus, the boundaries must not assume the place of the rulelike, mechanistic restraints that made formalist bureaucracy undesirable and unworkable. The only way to limit these objective constraints is to establish them "correctly" by perfecting the discipline of professionalism and ensuring the exercise of the "right" kinds of judgment. The meaning of an expert's discretion therefore includes, as an ineradicable but threatening component, the needed objective restraints.

The converse is also true. Although expertise theorists perceive the "objective" qualities of professionalism and judgment as something outside the individual to which he must adapt, they are also qualities that the professional himself helps to define. This ability to be self-policing is one of the features that makes him a professional. Of course, this feature of professionalism is one of its dangers as well as one of its virtues. The limits can work only if the right people define them; outsiders—"laymen"—certainly cannot perform this function. * * * In short, the objectivity of the expertise model can be defined only by its purported antithesis, subjectivity.

But if subjectivity is defined in terms of objectivity and objectivity in terms of subjectivity, the task of "drawing a line" between the two can have no meaning. Nor can there be meaning to the task of dividing subjectivity into its good and bad parts (discretion and arbitrariness) and objectivity into its good and bad parts (sensible and excessive restraint). These subdivisions restate the problems of defining the subjective/objective dichotomy itself. There is no standpoint, immune from arbitrariness, from which one can make the discretion/arbitrariness or sensible/excessive distinctions, nor is there a standpoint, subject to only the right restraints, that enables one to make these distinctions either. Without a coherent subjective/objective distinction, there is no way to make sense of the legitimating pretense of the expertise model at all.

The expertise model's inability to separate subjectivity and objectivity does not, however, prevent it from helping us reassure ourselves about the legitimacy of living a bureaucratic life. We can win deference from others by asserting our expertise in our own narrow specialty ("I'm the one around here who knows tax law") and then feel comfortable about leaving the basic decisions that structure our workplace to those in charge ("That's up to the Dean"). We can even become convinced that we are getting what we want from the bureaucratic organization by accepting the reasonableness of the bureaucratic leadership's suggestions about what we should want. After all, it's their job to know about organizational needs. * * *

* * *

* * * By deferring to expertise and asserting it ourselves, *we* help create a world organized around the pretense that some people, armed and limited by their special knowledge, can be trusted to be in charge. Once in charge, these experts must carry on the pretense of proclaiming how essential it is that others rely on their "inside" judgment; otherwise, the emptiness of their claims to leadership might be discovered. The more loudly they proclaim, the more credible the pretense becomes and the more it reinforces people's deference to and assertion of expert knowledge. As Alasdair MacIntyre suggests, "Bureaucratic Man" can thrive only if all of us invent a fiction of expertise that assigns to the character of the "broad-gauged" leader a role that justifies our own powerlessness:

> Belief in managerial expertise is * * * one more illusion and a peculiarly modern one, the illusion of a power not ourselves that claims to make for righteousness. Hence the manager as *character* . . . depends for its sustained existence on the systematic perpetuation of misunderstanding and of belief in fictions. The fetishism of commodities has been supplemented by another just as important fetishism, that of bureaucratic skills. . . . [I]n the social world * * * private preferences are advanced under the cover of identifying the presence or absence of the findings of experts. . . . The effects . . . have been to produce *not* scientifically managed social control, but a skillful dramatic imitation of such control. It is histrionic success which gives power and authority to our culture.[190]

C. The Judicial Review Model

1. The Model Described.—Unlike both the formalist and the expertise models, which seek to justify bureaucracy by properly organizing its subjective and objective components, the judicial review and market/pluralist models seek outside help to legitimate the bureaucratic structure. The judicial review and market/pluralist models take as their premise that

---

[190] A. MACINTYRE, [AFTER VIRTUE 101-02 (1981).] * * *

no form of bureaucratic organization can be self-policing. The judicial review model assigns the role of police officer to the courts, and the model's ability to legitimate bureaucracy rests on this judicial role. Bureaucratic legitimacy is derived from the courts' own legitimacy: it is because we can trust the courts that we can trust the bureaucracy.

The courts' function under the judicial review model is to prevent any serious abuse of power that a bureaucracy organized in accordance with the formalist or expertise models might otherwise generate. One way to describe this task is to say that the judiciary subjects the bureaucracy to the rule of law. This description emphasizes the limitations on the judicial role: as long as the bureaucracy operates within the limits of the law, its constituents and employees are free to function as they see fit. The description also underscores why judicial review is essential to bureaucratic legitimacy: self-policing is no more credible when practiced by bureaucratic managers than it is when practiced by anyone else in society. Objective limits on bureaucracy, whether understood in formalist or expertise terms, are meaningful only if they are legally enforceable.

An alternative way of describing the judicial role stresses the importance of having a decisionmaker independent of the bureaucracy ensure that it actually carries out the constituents' will (the formalist idea) or that it actually operates within its expertise (the expertise idea). In this view, it is not essential sharply to distinguish law (the function of the courts) and policymaking (the function of the bureaucracy). Even if courts exercise "a large and messy admixture of powers," outside review is still necessary to keep organizational insiders honest. Judges seem uniquely qualified to perform this function because a judge's "professional tradition insulates him from narrow political pressures . . . . [H]e is governed by a professional ideal of reflective and dispassionate analysis. . . ." Moreover, when the facts demand their intervention, judges are able to act in an appropriately ad hoc and nonbureaucratic way and to invite wide participation by representatives of competing interests. Of course, in any particular case the bureaucracy's greater political accountability or technical expertise may make judicial intervention undesirable. But some role for the conscientious exercise of judicial oversight seems indispensable.

Whichever description of the judicial function one adopts, the critical task for the judicial review model is drawing the proper line between the role of the bureaucracy and the role of the courts. Too little judicial intervention would render the bureaucracy uncontrolled and allow it to exercise arbitrary power.

But too much intervention would prevent the bureaucracy from adequately performing its functions and would jeopardize its important role in society. The boundary between courts and bureaucracy must therefore enable the judiciary to deter bureaucratic abuse while permitting the bureaucracy to exercise necessary freedom of action.

Judicial review theorists have traditionally sought to draw this line by defining and separating the institutional competence of the courts and the bureaucracy. * * * Professor Jaffe suggests that the function of the courts is to serve as "a constant reminder to the administration and a constant source of assurance and security to the citizen."[194] Given such a responsibility, "the line between the two [courts and bureaucracy] cannot be drawn with a ruler." A good deal of "corruption, favoritism, inefficiency, and irresponsibility" will occur regardless of judicial review. Judges cannot redress every administrative failure, but only those that, in their careful judgment, demand intervention * * *. * * *

Although Professor Jaffe is but one of the vast array of legal scholars who have addressed the court/bureaucracy boundary, he is representative of their general approach. These legal scholars do not seek to expound any general theory of bureaucracy; instead, they see the bureaucratic organization in formalist and expertise terms. Indeed their fundamental assumption is that the courts must normally treat bureaucratic operation as legitimate. Judicial intervention must be exceptional to ensure that the courts do not jeopardize their own institutional capacities and legitimacy. * * * If the role of the courts is to remain circumscribed, judicially imposed limits on the bureaucracy cannot go "too far" in questioning the legitimacy of the bureaucratic form. Yet there must be enough judicial review to make the existence of a judicial check on the bureaucracy convincing. * * *

As this description of the judicial role indicates, judicial review theorists have sought to distinguish and render compatible the subjective and objective aspects of life on both sides of the court/bureaucracy boundary. First and foremost, they have tried to describe the judicial role as both subjective and objective. They have generally rejected rigid attempts to circumscribe the court's role; judicial discretion about when and how to intervene is essential. But if judicial intervention were too subjective, it would belie the assertion that the courts are applying legal—not personal—judgment in restraining the bureaucracy. Thus, the courts must act professionally and rationally while exercising their flexibility and discretion. To be effective, these objective restraints must not be invaded by the exercise of judicial subjectivity.

The need to separate yet combine the subjective and objective elements exists on the bureaucracy side of the boundary as well. Judicial review theorists recognize that no model of bureaucracy can eliminate the exercise of bureaucratic discretion, and they also understand that each model imposes some objective limits on that discretion. Accordingly, courts must respect "appropriate" bureaucratic subjectivity and eliminate only "improper" subjectivity. Similarly, they need to be able to tell when objective constraints on the bureaucracy are working properly and when they are not. In short, courts need to ensure that the bureaucracy properly melds its subjective and objective elements.

One way to understand this complex subjective/objective structure is to examine the judicial review model's relationship to its two predecessors. The judicial review model might simply be viewed as an extension of the expertise model. If so, both sides of the court/bureaucracy boundary would be understandable through the category of expertise: the courts would be one set of experts and the bureaucracy another. After all, the language of expertise is frequently applied to judges—scholars speak of their "professional tradition" and "the limits of their role"—as well as to bureaucratic officials. Under this view, the task of the judicial review model would be to keep each set of experts within its own field of competence. If the judicial review model were merely a bifurcated version of the expertise model, however, the critique of the judicial review model would simply consist of a double application of the critique of the expertise model—once to the courts and once to the bureaucracy. The failure of the expertise model to establish a coherent role for either set of experts would make it impossible to draw a boundary between courts and bureaucracy.

One could also see the judicial review model as an extension of the formalist model. The judiciary could be understood as applying the rule of law, rather than its expertise, in its review of bureaucratic action. We might say that judges, like formalist bureaucracies, respond only to the will of the legislature or to that of the framers. The bureaucracy could also be seen as objectively carrying out constituent will. This reformulation of the judicial review model, however, would simply make the judicial review model susceptible to a double application of the critique of the formalist model. Under either the formalist or expertise version of the judicial role, the clash

---

[194] L. Jaffe, [Judicial Control of Administrative Action 325 (1965).]

of subjectivity and objectivity on both sides of the court/bureaucracy boundary would frustrate the judicial review theorists' attempt to specify the proper functions of the courts and the bureaucracy.

In my view, the judicial review model attempts to embrace these formalist and expertise versions simultaneously. It envisions both the courts and the bureaucracy in mixed formalist-expertise terms, seeking in each case some middle ground between the formalist and expertise poles. Yet the attempt to combine formalism and expertise subjects the judicial review model to the critique of *both* predecessor models on *both* sides of the court/bureaucracy boundary. The coincidence of subjectivity and objectivity—and the consequent need to divide them—is increased geometrically. Everywhere one turns, there is a problem that requires an objective/subjective distinction. As a result, the judicial review model enunciates thousands of "tests" and judicial techniques that restate over and over again the attempt to combine yet separate subjectivity and objectivity.

2. Substantive Definitions of the Court/Bureaucracy Boundary. —The mixed expertise-formalist structure of the judicial review model can be illustrated by examining the substantive tests that define the kinds of bureaucratic malfunctioning that will provoke judicial intervention. * * *

* * * In *Universal Camera Corp. v. NLRB,* a paradigmatic instance of the judicial review model in administrative law, Justice Frankfurter addressed an important test setting the court/bureaucracy boundary: an administrative factfinding shall be conclusive if supported by substantial evidence on the record considered as a whole. Describing how the courts should apply this standard, Justice Frankfurter recognized that the substantial evidence test did not furnish a "calculus of value by which a reviewing court can assess the evidence" underlying a bureaucratic factfinding. "[W]e cannot escape," he said, "the use of undefined defining terms." But if the words of the test do not help, what will? Justice Frankfurter answered first with the language of expertise:

> Enforcement of such broad standards implies subtlety of mind and solidity of judgment. . . . It cannot be too often repeated that judges are not automata. The ultimate reliance for the fair operation of any standard is a judiciary of high competence and character and the constant play of an informed professional critique upon its work.

But this reference to the character of the judiciary relied too heavily on judicial discretion; he therefore immediately supplemented it with an appeal to the will of the legislature, the language of formalism:

> But a standard leaving an unavoidable margin for individual judgment does not leave the judicial judgment at large even though the phrasing of the standard does not wholly fence it in. The legislative history of these Acts demonstrates a purpose to impose on courts a responsibility which has not always been recognized. . . . We should fail in our duty to effectuate the will of Congress if we denied recognition to expressed Congressional disapproval of the finality accorded to [agency] findings by some decisions of this and lower courts, or even of the atmosphere which may have favored those decisions.

Justice Frankfurter thus defined and circumscribed the court's role by understanding it in joint formalist-expertise terms. He envisioned the courts as organizations that could successfully combine the features of apparently antithetical models of bureaucratic legitimacy.

In doing so, Justice Frankfurter had to avoid transparently contradictory combinations of the two models. Contradictory pairings are certainly possible: a formalist-objective message (restrain yourself—obey the legislative will) can be combined with an expertise-subjective message (intervene—use your expertise), or a formalist-subjective message (intervene—obey the legislative will) can be combined with an expertise-objective message (restrain yourself—be limited by your expertise). Justice Frankfurter could avoid these undesirable expertise-formalism combinations because of the manipulability of the formalist and expertise structures. Formalist and expertise rhetoric can be combined to appear consistent with each other because any specific bureaucratic or judicial action can be justified separately by using either rhetoric. A legislative attempt to deny jurisdiction to the courts can routinely be "narrowly construed" to allow the intervention demanded by expertise, just as a broad legislative authorization of intervention can be construed to require no more than the courts are competent to handle. It is this malleability that enables the courts to make the combination of formalism and expertise appear convincing.

Even so, the formalism-expertise combination can be interpreted in two antithetical ways: legislation and judicial expertise can either impose a double constraint on judicial intervention or provide a double authorization for judges to employ their discretion in reviewing the bureaucracy's actions. The possibility of both readings means that the judicial review model gives the courts a divided message: be limited by your expertise and by the will of the legislature (objectivity) and be empowered by your expertise and the will of the legislature, as you interpret it, to prevent bureaucratic abuse (subjectivity). * * * Yet neither reading could conceivably be the "right" one. The judicial review model adopts both interpretations of the judicial role simultaneously. The "objective" reading can only be understood by incorporating within its definition of objectivity a subjective supplement, and the subjective reading has no meaning without an objective supplement.

This subjective/objective structure undermines the courts' ability to give a single, coherent meaning to the key terms of the substantive tests that fix the court/bureaucracy boundary. Whenever the court seeks to define "intelligible principle," "fair and reasonable," or "substantial evidence," its own divided sense of mission splits those terms into two possible meanings. The words assume contradictory meanings for the courts because they invoke two opposing views of what the court is supposed to do: restrain itself and intervene. It is in this sense that the contradictions within formalism and expertise, rather than being resolved by the judicial review model, are instead absorbed into the model's theory of the judicial role.

* * *

The combined subjective/objective nature of both the court's role and the "facts" of bureaucratic activity generates an almost limitless variety of contradictory arguments within the judicial review model. Arguments can focus either on characteristics of the courts or on those of the bureaucracy. Moreover, whichever side of the court/bureaucracy boundary is being discussed, the proper role of the institution can be envisioned in either expertise or formalist terms. Even this expertise or formalist rhetoric can itself be subdivided: one can emphasize either the subjective or objective aspect of the model in question. Thus, if one limits oneself only to the three kinds of categorization just mentioned—court/bureaucracy, expertise/formalism, and subjective/objective—eight possible arguments become available. I list below examples of these arguments, all of which are taken from the section of the Breyer and Stewart administrative law casebook[216] dealing with the proper role of the courts in interpreting the law that governs administrative decisionmaking. The first four of these examples focus on the courts; the second four focus on the bureaucracy. Within each group of four, two arguments are phrased in expertise terms and two in formalist terms. Finally, every expertise and formalist argument is stated in a subjective and an objective form.

(1) *Court-Expertise-Subjective.* The court should intervene: We are "deciding the naked question of law."

(2) *Court-Expertise-Objective.* The court should restrain itself: "Nothing prevents the administrator from drawing the lines as he thinks best. . . . The courts have no business to tell him where to put them."

(3) *Court-Formalist-Subjective.* The court should intervene: "Congress did not delegate to the [agency] the function of defining the purpose of the statute. The question . . . is a judicial and not an administrative question."

(4) *Court-Formalist-Objective.* The court should restrain itself: "It is not the province of a court to absorb the administrative functions to such an extent that the executive or legislative agencies become mere fact-finding bodies deprived of the advantages of prompt and definitive action."

(5) *Bureaucracy-Expertise-Subjective.* The agency's discretion must be limited: "If we were obliged to depend upon administrative interpretation for light in finding the meaning of the statute, the inconsistency of the Board's decision would leave us in the dark. But there are difficult questions of policy . . . which, together with changes in Board membership, account for the contradictory views [taken by the Board]."

(6) *Bureaucracy-Expertise-Objective.* The agency has exercised its discretion appropriately: "Everyday experience in administration of the statute gives it [the agency] familiarity with the circumstances and backgrounds. . . . Resolving [the] question . . . 'belongs to the usual administrative routine' of the Board."

(7) *Bureaucracy-Formalism-Subjective.* The agency's discretion must be limited: "The determination of the extent of authority given to a delegated agency by Congress is not left for the decision of him in whom authority is vested."

(8) *Bureaucracy-Formalism-Objective.* The agency has exercised its discretion appropriately: "[W]here reasonable minds may differ as to which of several remedial measures should be chosen, courts should defer to the informed experience and judgment of the agency to whom Congress delegated appropriate authority."

---

[216] *See* S. BREYER AND R. STEWART, [ADMINISTRATIVE LAW AND REGULATORY POLICY 227-49 (1979).]

* * * This oscillation illustrates the failure of substantive tests to instruct the court when to intervene in bureaucratic decisionmaking. Courts divide bureaucratic actions into categories of "acceptable" and "unacceptable" by shifting their vision of the appropriate judicial role or of the effectiveness of internal constraints on bureaucratic activity—shifts that themselves re-create the subjective/objective contradictions of the judicial review model.

* * *

4. An Overview of the Model. — * * * The judicial review model is so closely tied to its formalist and expertise counterparts that a repetition of this dangerous supplement analysis would be otiose. From my point of view, it seems more worthwhile to speculate on how anyone might have come to believe in the judicial review model—to give some sense of the context within which this truly extraordinary structure can be understood. I would therefore like to suggest two possible ways of contextualizing the judicial review model.

First, one might think of the judicial review model as a stage in an Hegelian version of historical development. To do so, one needs to understand the emergence of judicial review as a reaction to the inadequacies of the expertise and formalist models that preceded it. These two models represented opposed ways of organizing bureaucracy: formalism limited bureaucratic discretion in order to reinforce outsiders' control of the bureaucracy, while expertise encouraged bureaucratic discretion by limiting outsiders' intervention into the bureaucratic process. At the same time, however, the ideas of expertise and formalism could be employed together to correct the defects of each model taken separately. Expertise could justify the bureaucratic discretion that formalism could not prevent, and formalism could provide the limits on bureaucratic discretion that expertise seemed unable to impose upon itself. Thus it might have appeared to judicial review theorists that they could escape the clash of contradictory visions of bureaucratic organization by, paradoxically, combining them. * * *

This process of historical development through contradiction could not, however, stop with the emergence of the judicial review model. The model itself would have to be negated, affirmed, and transcended. Indeed, there is some indication that this process is taking place. The judiciary's effort to ensure that bureaucratic decisions are "rational" has led the bureaucracy to respond by shifting the basis of its decisions to the language of technical expertise. As the bureaucracy has increasingly supported its decisions with policy analyses, economic projections, and other technical support, the judiciary has lost its ability to engage in meaningful substantive review of bureaucratic decisions. This process has become particularly striking in administrative law in recent years. The judiciary's attempt to justify the substance of bureaucratic decisionmaking has altered the forms of policymaking to such an extent that courts have found themselves incompetent to engage in effective review. The effort to create substantive judicial review has, in short, resulted in its own undoing.

* * *

This description of the emergence and decline of the judicial review model suggests two different versions of the next historical stage. One is a revised form of the expertise model, in which greater technical support for administrative factfinding and an increased role for super-experts and disinterested directors in corporate decisionmaking replace the courts as the basis of bureaucratic legitimacy. The role of the courts as the source of independent oversight over the bureaucracy would thus be affirmed, negated, and transcended by the emergence of true experts who would assume the courts' role. * * * The second version focuses on the emergence of widespread participation in the bureaucratic process through political participation or market mechanisms; once these participatory processes are fully in place, the implied consent of these participants would form the basis of bureaucratic legitimacy. In this view, the courts' role in affixing the legitimating imprimatur on bureaucratic decisionmaking would be assumed by the constituents themselves. This is the market/pluralist model * * *.

* * *

It is important to recognize that the attempt to legitimate bureaucratic organization through judicial review was the product of the generation of legal thinkers who sought to reconstruct a theory of law in the wake of legal realism. Although these legal scholars thought the legal realists "went too far," they could not retreat to the mechanical jurisprudence that realism had so decisively destroyed. If a viable theory of law existed—and it had to exist—it would have to contain the insights of the realists within the limits of a reconstructed legal formalism. The solution these legal scholars adopted was to combine realism and formalism into a "third way" by allocating institutional competence among the courts, the legislature, and the bureaucracy * * *.

* * *

Yet another ingredient in the creation of a judicial review theory was the theorists' attitude toward democracy. Although they assumed that democracy was desirable, they sought to define the democratic process narrowly. Democracy was not a way of actually operating social organizations. It was instead a means of choosing among competing elites for leadership, a process that supported extant bureaucratic forms by legitimating them through an image of consensus. The maintenance of this consensus required that any judicial intervention in corporate or governmental affairs be exceptional. Of course, a theory of democratic consent could validate every action taken by a bureaucratic organization; the courts therefore had to ensure that some limits were placed upon bureaucracy. But the courts were themselves limited by democratic consensus; to maintain their own legitimacy, they had to respect democratic limits and defer to the support conferred by democracy on the bureaucracies they policed.

* * *

* * * Refinement of the judicial review theory seems a Sisyphean task, given the relentlessness of the restatements of the subjective/objective structure that the refinements generate. The middle positions, instead of resolving the problems they address, seem merely to sweep them aside in an effort to protect the status quo through incremental change. The emptiness of the phrases endlessly combined and recombined to form "tests" appears as an evasion of thought rather than an exercise of subtlety. That is why, from the outside, those who seek to perfect the model emerge as priests of a lost religion who "brazenly . . . [advertise] their own failure as the triumph of worldly wisdom over intellectual and political enthusiasm."

D. The Market/Pluralist Model

1. The Model Described. —Theorists of the market/pluralist model, like those of the judicial review model, despair of finding a way in which bureaucracy by itself can combine its subjective and objective components harmoniously. They too turn outside the bureaucracy to find some mechanism to control its power. For market/pluralist theorists, the policing function is performed not through judicial surveillance but through the interjection of another form of social organization into the operation of the bureaucracy. Many aspects of social life are possible candidates for this role, but I will analyze here only the two that are the most prominent in legal thought—the market and the political process.

Market/pluralist theorists contend that the "discipline of the market" or the "demands of the political process" can (or do) protect the constituents of the bureaucracy from domination by bureaucratic officials. They also suggest that these processes enable individuals to express their own subjective preferences about how the bureaucracy should function. * * *

* * *

Pluralist thinkers have * * * suggested that injecting political conflict into the public bureaucracy's decisionmaking processes would make government more responsive to the public interest. Although the government is already representative of the people from one point of view, these theorists contend that controlling bureaucratic decisionmaking requires more than elections or legislative commands to the bureaucracy. Even with these controls, bureaucratic decisionmaking remains biased in favor of special interests instead of being representative of the people as a whole. This danger of bureaucratic favoritism can be solved, they contend, only by ensuring that all relevant interest groups participate in the decisionmaking process. If bureaucratic decisionmakers must adequately take into account the views of all relevant groups, the decisions they make will resemble those that would be made by the people themselves. The bureaucracy's decisions will then reflect its constituents' wishes because the same process—interest-group conflict—will occur both inside and outside the bureaucracy.

Despite their important differences, the market and pluralist visions of bureaucratic operation share the same basic structure. Both visions fear excessive management discretion, and both therefore attempt to bring this discretion under constituent control through some nonbureaucratic process. Both also rely on this process to express the subjective desires of the bureaucracy's constituents. Under each theory, in short, the nonbureaucratic process provides the subjective and objective ingredients needed to legitimate bureaucracy. The pluralist vision, moreover, is itself a "market theory" of politics: it relies on the balance of competing interest groups, as the market relies on the balance of economic forces, to legitimate the outcome of social conflict. Finally, neither version seeks to alter the essential role of management within the bureaucratic structure; on the contrary, each seeks to perpetuate this role as long as it is kept within its proper bounds.

* * *

3. The Disciplining Mechanism of Interest-Group Pluralism. —Pluralist thinkers seek to police the bureaucracy by injecting a democratic political process into its method of decisionmaking. To do so, they need to construct as complex a disciplining mechanism as that advocated by market theorists. First, they must identify all relevant interests and allow representatives of each to participate in the bureaucratic decisionmaking process; otherwise, the model's claim that it inserts "the will of the people" into the process will be undermined. Second, they have to decide what kind of participation by these interest-group representatives is appropriate. In administrative law, this means that pluralist theorists have to determine the extent to which the government officials charged with the statutory duty to implement the law should be influenced by the views of interest-group representatives. * * * Finally, once the appropriate interest-group representatives are selected and the extent of their influence in bureaucratic decisionmaking has been determined, pluralist thinkers must decide how the representatives of the various groups should resolve the conflicts among their views on organizational policy. This decision requires the establishment of rules for structuring the interest-group conflict. Each of these three ingredients of the model creates a subjective/objective combination that renders the model subject to a critique already advanced.

First of all, like expertise theorists, pluralist thinkers need to determine the content of the constraints they would place on managerial discretion. In the expertise model, these constraints were described in terms of professionalism, impartial judgment, or expertise; here, they are described in terms of a popular mandate produced by the interaction of relevant interest groups. Both expertise and the popular mandate, however, must be defined by the right people: not everyone can participate in the decisions about what expertise or the popular mandate is. Thus, for the pluralist, some way of ascertaining the popular mandate short of asking every individual for her or his personal views is essential. To begin with, only the views of groups can be counted; moreover, of these groups, only a limited number can actually participate in bureaucratic decisionmaking. * * * Of course, if there is insufficient representation, the claim that all appropriate interests are being heard will sound hollow, but too much participation is out of the question. The resulting subjective delineation of the "relevant" groups—or, to put it in the opposite way, the proper objectification of people's subjective desires necessary to make communication of their views possible—creates a familiar, manipulable subjective/objective structure.

The best known doctrine reflecting this structure is the law of standing in administrative law. This body of law, as numerous scholars have shown, oscillates between reliance on arguments that favor expansion of participation in bureaucratic decisionmaking and on those that oppose it. Advocates of expansion emphasize both the unfairness of excluding some people affected by a decision from the decisionmaking process and the value that their additional information would contribute to an informed administrative decision. The other side stresses the costs of allowing too much participation, the danger of rendering the bureaucratic process unworkable, and the possibility that allowing participation by people with only a trivial interest in the outcome could jeopardize the chance of a fair settlement. * * *

The apparent impossibility of allowing everyone affected by a bureaucratic decision to participate in the decisionmaking process generates the second requirement of the pluralist version of the model—the insistence that the interest groups that do participate should have a voice in, but should not determine, the results of bureaucratic decisionmaking. This limited role is understandable because the participating interest groups are characterized in two alternative ways. At times, interest groups are seen as representatives of selfishly narrow points of view, "factions" whose limited agendas conflict with the more general corporate or public interest. At other times, they appear, collectively, to be as close an approximation of the bureaucracy's constituency as it is possible to create. These two characterizations alternatively describe interest groups as representatives of subjective desire and representatives of objective neutrality.

Instead of choosing between these characterizations, interest-group pluralists embrace both sides of the subjective/objective picture. In administrative law, the view that interest groups are selfish suggests that the government should itself actively advance the welfare of "unorganized" interests not represented in decisionmaking proceedings; otherwise, government decisionmaking would simply advance the partisan desires of the few who participate in agency hearings. The view that interest groups are representative, on the other hand, suggests that government officials should be responsive to the wishes of the groups that appear before them. To resolve this conflict, administrative law doctrine suggests that the interest groups' views be "adequately considered" or "seriously weighed" by the officials charged with implementing the law. These phrases nicely combine both sides of the dilemma.

* * *

4. An Overview of the Model.—The characteristic

feature of the market/pluralist model is that its advocates shift the focus of bureaucratic legitimation away from the bureaucracy itself to other ideas about the organization of society; almost their entire discussion focuses on the "market" or the "political process." It is not hard to understand why setting up these processes in the right way becomes an overriding obsession for these theorists. Without a properly functioning market or political process, they cannot justify the operation of the bureaucratic process. In other words, the market or the political process is an indispensable supplement—although no more than a supplement—to the legitimate operation of bureaucratic organizations.

Characterizing the market and the political process as supplements, in a way that should by now be familiar, does not indicate that they are dangerous supplements. Is there a reason for market/pluralist theorists to fear these supplements? I think there is. Unlike their predecessors, market/pluralist theorists attempt to legitimate bureaucracy by appealing to the desirability of a nonbureaucratic, nonhierarchical vision of social life. Indeed, both the market and democracy have been characterized as the antithesis of the bureaucratic form of organization. Market/pluralist theorists, then, seek to capitalize on the attractiveness of these forms of life while, at the same time, limiting the scope of their operation. They seem to trust the market or the political process rather than bureaucracy itself, yet they seem anxious to use egalitarian ideals only as a way to advance the cause of bureaucratic organization.

As a result, market/pluralist theorists need to draw a line between the role of egalitarian economic and political processes and the role of bureaucracy. They can do so only by envisioning the market and politics in a way that circumscribes their more radical possibilities. This effort is evident in the theorists' relentless attempts to fashion rules for the market and the political process that make them consistent with bureaucratic forms of life. For example, rather than questioning the general allocation of entitlements in bureaucratic organizations, market theorists simply modify them to generate what they claim will be an "efficient allocation" of what people with purchasing power want produced. Similarly, pluralist theorists, instead of elaborating on the classical idea of democracy as a process of active, popular participation in social decisionmaking, reduce the idea of democracy to the result of conflict among competing interest groups. This view interprets democracy to be consistent with the perpetuation of the rule of elites; democracy becomes no more than "that institutional arrangement for arriving at political decisions in which individuals acquire the power to decide by means of a competitive struggle for the people's vote."

These circumscribed definitions of the market and democracy also help *us* accommodate ourselves to the everyday world of bureaucratic organizations. Like market theorists, we often focus our attention not on the bureaucracies themselves but on our dreams of how the market can make bureaucracies serve our own ends. Thus, we can treat our work lives within these organizations as instrumental; we can see our jobs simply as ways of providing the means we need to enjoy our lives as market participants. * * * Everyday life becomes a menu from which we can select what we want; we tend not to notice that we did not participate in the decisions about what should be on the menu. Indeed, the market offers us more than just a way to obtain subjective satisfaction from bureaucratic organizations; it also serves as the objective explanation for our inability to make fundamental changes in the nature of these organizations. Nonbureaucratic forms of enterprise simply can't compete; the market—if not the local version, then surely the "world market"—forces us to operate in the bureaucratic form. We know this to be true because we are motivated and unnerved in our life at work by the "demands of competition"; even when we observe it as outsiders, the relentless rise and fall of institutions proves that survival depends on bureaucratic efficiency. The market thus serves both as a way of expressing ourselves and as a way of feeling constrained; it convinces us that freedom and necessity take the same form.

The same can be said of democracy. Because we live in a democracy, we can express our subjective choices about bureaucratic organizations by fighting for what we want. If we dislike something about our workplace, we can organize with people similarly inclined and, through political infighting, try to get those in charge to make the necessary changes. In the public arena, we can assert our views in administrative or legislative hearings. If we do nothing, we have only ourselves to blame. Because we normally do nothing, the emotion we generally express concerning this kind of political participation is regret: we might be able to do something about the world if only we had the time and energy. Indeed, our ideas about interest-group conflict not only help us explain how we might get more of what we want from bureaucracies if we tried harder but also provide the reason why we must accept the fundamentals of bureaucratic life even if we do not like them. Current bureaucratic structures, after all, seem powerfully influenced by those who have the time, energy, and money to engage in political conflict. Their ability to achieve something through group struggle limits our chances of achieving our own goals. Even if we tried to advance our ideas, chances are we wouldn't get very far. When we do try to get our views accepted, we are often outnumbered, outargued, or outspent. That's what democracy means: you can't win every time. Thus, although interest-group conflict seems to be the way to make our goals a reality, it simultaneously limits our ability to put our own ideas into practice.

By internalizing these market and pluralist accommodations to bureaucratic life, we convince ourselves that, notwithstanding the existence of modern bureaucracies, we are currently experiencing the kind of freedom promised by the ideals of the market and democracy. This is a most insidious form of accommodation to bureaucracy, because through it we lose the sense of hope, the sense of alternatives to the bureaucratic form, that these ideals inspire. If we freed ourselves from these truncated definitions of the market and democracy, however, we could imagine ways to overcome the very form of organized life that market/pluralist theorists (and we) now seek to defend. As market theorists, we could see our goal as rethinking, redividing, and reallocating the entitlements that make up the current structure of large-scale organization. By establishing alternative definitions of the market, we could transform both the hierarchic structure of bureaucratic organizations and the separation of employees from the people whose interests they purport to serve. Similarly, the institutionalization of democracy could build upon the ultimate appeal of the democratic way of life—that "people can and should govern themselves." * * *

III. Some Concluding Thoughts

The argument I have advanced in this Article might engender three types of response from readers disinclined to criticize the role of bureaucratic organizations in American society. First, one might ask, even if the models of bureaucratic legitimation are self-contradictory, why can't they all be combined to make sense out of * * * administrative law? After all, no single model can describe current legal doctrine concerning bureaucratic organization; in fact, each model seems to function best in a particular legal or organizational context. Combining the models might therefore correct the defects of each one considered separately. Second, what does this Article suggest that bureaucratic theorists actually *do*, given the impossibility of drawing a line between subjectivity and objectivity? As far as one can tell, the theorists described and criticized in this Article are simply struggling the best they can to deal with a complex and contradictory world. Unless this Article can suggest some better way for these theorists to engage in this struggle, criticizing their efforts seems pointless. Finally, even if these models and the legal discourse built around them are nothing more than deceptive reassurances about bureaucratic organization, what practical difference could it possibly make? Surely bureaucracy is an inevitable feature of modern society; we may not like it, but there is nothing we can do about it. My concluding thoughts address these three responses in turn.

First, there is the matter of combining the different models or contextualizing them. This indeed is what many modern theorists do. * * *

How does combining them help? If you push hard on any one ingredient of the combination, it will be exposed as a restatement, not a resolution, of the problem of bureaucratic power. But perhaps the combination allows all of the models together to cure the defects of each one considered separately; together, that is, they might add up to something. This idea, however, has already been subjected to criticism in my discussion of the judicial review model. Combining the different models only shifts the problem of making a subjective/objective distinction away from any particular model and locates it instead in the boundaries between different models. * * *

Combining the models also provides theorists with a new kind of mechanism for deception. Theorists can reassure themselves about the existence of objectivity or subjectivity by deferring the needed element to some model not then under examination. When they find that the concept of expertise is too manipulable to ensure objectivity, they can assume that the objectivity necessary to curb managerial power can be found elsewhere—in the intervention of judicial review, for example. Of course, once they turn their attention to judicial review, they see how unreliable it is as a source of objectivity. Yet their normal reaction to this insight is simply to assume that objective constraints exist somewhere else—back in expertise, perhaps * * *. The same sort of deferral pervades the attempt to locate subjectivity somewhere: if it doesn't seem to be where one is looking, one can act as if it is safely lodged in another part of the system. Adding the ingredients together, then, allows people to believe that although the device they are considering at any particular moment is empty, one of the others surely is better. This ability to move the necessary subjectivity or objectivity around endlessly helps theorists convince themselves (and us) that the internal difficulties of each particular story of bureaucratic legitimacy are unimportant. But this reassurance is comforting only as long as the process of deferral is itself hidden from view.

* * *

This brings me to the second response to my argument: what does this Article suggest that bureaucratic theorists do, given the impossibility of drawing a line between subjectivity and objectivity? What alternative is there to seeking, the best one can, a basis for building some objective limits on power and for allowing needed subjective discretion? My answer to this line of questioning must start with isolating the fundamental project undertaken by bureaucratic theorists. Their effort can be characterized as an attempt to defend a controversial feature of social life—bureaucracy—by giving it to a more basic aspect of social life that is itself noncontroversial. Such an effort to ground social institutions on some unchallengeable foundation is not new; one need only think of the attempts to derive the appropriate organization of society from the will of God. Moreover, it is not surprising that the bureaucratic theorists' foundation embraces some notion of objectivity: how can people trust these concentrations of power unless they can be shown to be objective in some way? Nor is it surprising that the foundation must include subjectivity as well: why should anyone want bureaucracies unless they are responsive in some way to individual desires? Thus, bureaucratic theorists base their models of bureaucracy on aspects of social life that seem to promise an appropriate mix of objectivity and subjectivity * * *.

This Article suggests that such a search for a foundation for social life is a futile and empty project. If subjectivity can be understood only as the dangerous supplement of objectivity and objectivity only as the dangerous supplement of subjectivity, each of these concepts is based on the other. If so, neither concept can possibly be the "foundation" of the other. No foundation can support an item it rests on. And if law and society relate to each other as dangerous supplements, neither of them can provide a stable basis on which to construct the other. * * * There is no such "thing" as "subjectivity" divorced from "objectivity," "law" independent of "society," "facts" isolated from "theory," a theory of "judicial review" defined separately from a theory of "bureaucracy." All of these concepts can be understood only in terms of their relationships to each other; each takes on meaning only through those relationships. Moreover, the tactic of combining the models of bureaucratic legitimation into a complex intermixture constitutes yet another deceptive attempt to find a legitimating foundation for bureaucratic organization * * *.

* * *

Why have these theorists been so wedded to a search for a foundation for bureaucratic organizations? Perhaps they fear that, without such a foundation, all organized forms of social life—including bureaucratic forms—would constantly be open to reimagination and reconstruction. But another explanation seems more plausible to me. I referred to it earlier when I quoted Michael Crozier: "Why do they build bureaucracies? . . . [W]e should like to suggest that they are trying to evade face-to-face relationships and situations of personal dependency whose authoritarian tone they cannot bear." This view suggests that all four models of bureaucracy are attempts to escape from the problems of face-to-face human relationships; all of them promise us that human relationships—even relationships built on hierarchy and separation—can be made unthreatening through some organizational arrangement. Within each bureaucratic vision, theorists seek to mediate human interactions with a device that transcends ordinary human qualities; they would protect us from each other through formal rules, the impersonality of expertise, or the intervention of the courts, the market, or the political process. I have argued in this Article, however, that all of these mediations are forms of deception. Each of them conceals the exercise of personalized, human domination in the organizations within which we work and live.

These days, a critique of bureaucratic institutions as a form of domination does not automatically engender a drive for organizational change. Many people concede that no theory (or combination of theories) can justify the arbitrary power exercised by and within bureaucratic institutions, yet they nonetheless accept and defend these organizations. These people—I shall call them "modest realists"—treat the failure of bureaucratic theory as unimportant. They believe that bureaucracy rests on a foundation more secure than any theory: to them, accepting the existence of bureaucratic organizations simply means adjusting to the real world as it is. Bureaucracy may be imperfect or even self-contradictory they say, but so what? So is everything else. Abandoning any attempt to articulate a justification for these organizations, modest realists ground their defense of bureaucracy on the lack of viable alternatives to the status quo. It is not that modest realists are against change altogether; indeed, they admit that present organizations have lots of imperfections, and they generally have suggestions themselves about improvements that can be made. But they react to suggestions for change (even their own) by shifting the burden of persuasion: existing organizations must be accepted, albeit reluctantly and with reservations, until something else is proved to be better. This procedural move allows modest realists to defend themselves from criticism about their own lack of ideas justifying bureaucracy; rather than defend their own position, they simply ask their critics to defend theirs.

Moreover, modest realists tend to respond to their critics' concrete suggestions for change in the manner of a sober grown-up addressing a naive child. If the suggestion is "in the ballpark," they treat it as one more factor that needs to be "weighed" against a host of other competing factors, and the likelihood that they will accept the suggestion is low. Chances are that it has already been weighed and found overridden by other factors, or has already been taken into account to the extent that it has merit, or has yet to develop a sufficient track record to be seriously considered, or is simply too trivial a revision of the status quo to be worth pursuing. If, on the other hand, the suggestion proposes some radical change, the modest realist dismisses it out of hand as utopian. "Things are complicated and difficult," one almost hears the modest realist saying. "Of course we have a long way to go. But everything is a tough policy choice, and every decision we make will have its faults. All we can do is the best we can."

In my view, modest realists have not rejected bureaucratic theory in favor of sophisticated reflection about the real world as it is. They have instead absorbed the various bureaucratic theories into their view of the world—indeed, into their very definition of themselves. * * *

Like judicial review theorists, modest realists accept bureaucracy as a fact of life, although they are willing to limit its excesses. They too apply a deferential standard when they inquire into bureaucratic institutions because they fear that excessive attempts to change things will just make matters worse. When asked to decide something, they act like judges: they "balance," they "weigh," they shift burdens of proof. Like judges, they leave the person whose ideas they are evaluating in the dark about how their ultimate decision is being made. Finally, like interest-group pluralists, modest realists think that any proposals for changing bureaucratic institutions should be framed in terms of legislative action. Whether or not they seek change through interest-group politics themselves, they are careful not to let their political views influence the way they act in their other roles in life. * * *

Modest realists have so internalized the bureaucratic moves—moves that, as we have seen, enable them to argue for and against everything—that it is hard to know what form of argument might convince them to rethink their approach. They are not likely to pay much attention to the theoretical critique of their position advanced in this Article; they want to put theory aside and engage in instrumental decisionmaking. They feel they can handle the subjective/objective structure of their position simply by making the tough choices as best they can. Indeed, if I were to conclude this Article with some specific suggestion for nonbureaucratic structures * * * they would immediately disregard the rest of the Article and focus their attention solely on the proposed alternative. ("Now," they might say, "here's something *real* to discuss.") In doing so, they would simply substitute their perspective for my own. Once the argument is cast in their preferred form, they would evaluate the suggestion with their fine-tuned skepticism, no doubt discarding it as "outweighed" by other, more sophisticated factors. That's the way they approach ideas; that's the way they think.

This Article is designed to criticize this way of thinking. I am suggesting that the modest realist approach to the world, like those more closely associated with the particular models themselves, is a way people accommodate themselves to bureaucracy in thought as well as in action. Modest realists substitute for the subjective/objective structure of theory the equally flexible, equally manipulable subjective/objective structure of "modifying" the "status quo." They treat some aspects of the world as objectively necessary and other aspects as open to our joint reconstruction. Like any other subjective/objective structure, however, this is a form of self-deception—perhaps its most pervasive modern form. My critique will mean something to modest realists only if they try to get outside this way of thinking, only if they criticize it as a whole. A suggestion for change won't cause them to do so; merely reading this Article will probably not cause them to do so either. Instead, they will have to experience the manipulability of their way of thinking themselves—perhaps when they try to teach * * * administrative law—or actually engage in action with others in a way that makes the possibility of different ways of approaching the world seem real to them.

Modest realists could abandon their effort to treat some aspects of the world as fixed and others as subject to human modification; they could, in other words, abandon their own characteristic attempt to secure a foundation for social life. If they (and other defenders of the bureaucratic form) thought of the world in terms of human, interpersonal contact, the idea of creating separate spheres of permanence and mobility—of creating separate spheres of subjectivity and objectivity of any kind—would seem bizarre. In our daily encounters with others, we recognize that we help create each other through our interactions. It is because these interactions are both necessary and threatening that all of them must continuously be open to reconstruction and revision. In the everyday world of human interdependence, there can be no such thing as a "foundation" that could render (even part of) social life noncontroversial.

It may be hard, however, for modest realists, as well as other readers, to think it worthwhile to give up the search for a foundation that would render human relationships unthreatening. They may, for example, believe that we risk tyranny without such a foundation. It is certainly true that, without foundations, there is no guarantee against tyranny; its likelihood will depend on what people do. But foundations have never protected us against tyranny either; there are no such things. Even the fabrication of foundations hasn't helped; we have never been able to "deduce" from some ultimate foundation the things that are worth fighting for and worth fighting against. Without a (mythical) foundation for our views, we admittedly are (still) unable to say what our choices are based on. But social choices are certainly not arbitrary: choices about how to live and what kind of world to create are neither "objective" nor "subjective," neither certain nor meaningless. They cannot be characterized either way once we recognize how crucially the nature of human relationships and institutions affect who we are. The alternative to "foundations" is not "chaos" but the joint reconstruction of social life, the prospect I referred to at the outset as the quest of participatory democracy. Acting together, we could begin to dismantle the structure of bureaucratic organizations—not all at once, but piece by piece. In their place we could substitute forms of human relationship that better reflect our aspirations for human development and equality. * * *

But surely, one might object, all of this is utopian and farfetched. After all, bureaucracy is a necessary, indispensable part of modern life. Given the realities of the modern world, what is the point of criticizing the ideology of bureaucracy? One point, certainly, is to suggest that the appeal to the necessity of bureaucracy is built on the same foundations as the other arguments analyzed in this Article. After all, what exactly is the necessary modern form of social life? Some have suggested that an organization built on a rationalized structure of preestablished rules is the necessary (and efficient) form of organization, while others have suggested instead that it is necessary to create a structure of loyalty within the organization. The reader should recognize shades of the formalist and the expertise models of organization in these statements. Indeed, of the claims for the necessity of bureaucracy, the two most important have been based on the indispensability of formalism * * * and of expertise * * *. Each of these claims has also been made in a less absolutist way, suggesting that the particular form is necessary only in a specific "context." Indeed, a review of the literature of organizational necessity reveals that bureaucratic theorists have offered a bewildering variety of contradictory notions of what is necessary in the modern world. But all of these different appeals to the "inevitable consequences of social life in an industrial civilization" have one thing in common: they are all ways in which people themselves manufacture the necessity that renders them powerless to change the world. * * *

* * *

Thomas O. Sargentich, *The Reform of the American Administrative Process: The Contemporary Debate*, 1984 WIS. L. REV. 385, 386, 391-413, 415-442*

I. Introduction

In recent years, the broad-scale reform of the American administrative process has attracted notable attention. Politicians, administrators, other participants in the administrative process, and scholars have generated a large literature recommending a diverse spectrum of proposals designed to improve the basic institutional relationships and methods of administrative decisionmaking.

* * *

One who would analyze the contemporary debate might proceed from a number of perspectives. It is not uncommon to discuss a specific effort or proposal in terms of its discrete rationale, application, and limitations. One also could concentrate on an empirical study of the activities of certain agencies in particular areas of public policy. Furthermore, one could undertake a historical survey of the debate, seeking for instance to compare the most recent proposals with earlier ones or to link the emergence of contemporary concerns with broader trends in Amer-

---

* Reprinted with permission of the Wisconsin Law Review and Thomas O. Sargentich. All rights reserved.

ican society. The approach of this Article differs from all of these, for it seeks primarily to understand the basic conceptual underpinnings of the major types of reformist argument reflected in key proposals for change * * *. No claim is advanced here that all of the strains and nuances in the debate may be reduced to a level of general conceptual controversy. It is suggested, however, that the central themes of the main reform proposals may be usefully illuminated in terms of such controversy.

It appears true that the daily practice of administration, both by those in government and by others seeking to achieve a result through government, seldom focuses for long on broad theory about the nature and legitimacy of the administrative process. Although administrative reformers employ arguments borrowing premises from deeper normative positions, their concentration is likely to center on the concrete ends in view, not on basic concepts. Nonetheless, it remains relevant to ask whether the contemporary debate about administrative reform has any underlying intellectual structure, or whether it simply reflects an accretion of disparate, largely ad hoc proposals without broader organization or pattern. If the debate may be seen to have such a structure, then one will be better able to grasp the central constraints of key proposals, the chief relationships among different reformist positions, and the major terms and limits of the debate itself.

II. A Conceptual Framework for Understanding Administrative Reform

This Article's thesis is that the contemporary debate does have an underlying intellectual structure that revolves around the complex interrelationships among three mutually contradictory ideals of the administrative process. The three ideals address the fundamental questions of the ultimate source of the legitimacy of the administrative process and the character of the decisionmaking engaged in by administrative actors. The ideals, for the sake of shorthand reference, will be called the rule of law ideal, the public purposes ideal, and the democratic process ideal.

By their very nature, these ideals embody their own governing pictures of how a well-regulated, legitimate, and rationally-functioning administrative process should operate. The pictures incorporate at their core a conception of administrative reality, or at least, administrative possibility within the limits of reality. If one were to infuse an ideal with personality, one might say that each one is steadily seeking its fuller realization in practice. The incessantly critical strain of each ideal is by no means accidental; each is a ready reservoir of premises and positions that may be used to support change of existing structures in order to lessen the always present distance between the actual process and the ideal itself. To this extent, the competing ideals are well-suited to reformist discourse: they stand, if you will, with one foot resting on the present administrative process, with certain understandings about its basic character and possibilities, and with another foot directed at the future.

Although their particular answers differ, the three ideals respond to the same fundamental questions. On what general normative principles may the use of often substantial public power by unelected agency officials in our political system be justified and, at least for the system as a whole, legitimated? Moreover, what is the characteristic mode of decisionmaking that principal actors in the administrative process, especially agency officials but also including judges or members of Congress, attempt to realize and ought to perfect? By resolving these fundamental issues in strikingly different ways, the rule of law, public purposes, and democratic process ideals stake out demonstrably distinct conceptual ground for subsequent defense and development. The distinctions among these three positions provide the basic pattern underlying the contemporary debate.

In addition, there is a central movement within the constellation of ideas giving body to the contemporary debate. This movement occurs within each ideal itself. Each ideal may be seen as having what will be referred to as a "core" embodiment as well as an "alternative" expression. The core embodiment represents the set of institutional commitments, predictions about the future, and normative premises that proponents of the ideal believe to be necessary for its full realization directly through the mechanisms of a reformed administrative process. * * *

But the main point to note here is that the very force that animates the core embodiment of each ideal—namely, single-minded devotion to a pristine, overarching vision of the legitimacy and character of administrative decisionmaking—risks the ideal's own undoing. * * * [C]ritical visions need to be rooted in some picture of reality that itself seems capable of being achieved, or approximately so, in the reasonably near future. If an ideal begins to appear wildly improbable in its assumptions about the actual process and its capacities for change, it gradually will cease to be a generative source of reformist criticism and will recede into the background as a construct of sheer imagination.

In the contemporary debate, the core embodiments of each of the three ideals seem caught in this basic difficulty. On the one hand, each core is committed to the most direct realization of the full promise of a powerful and central ideal within the context of a reformed administrative process. On the other hand, each core, if fully realized, would dramatically reorder the existing administrative process beyond the limits of mere reform. Ultimately, each core embodiment, taken in the fullness of its critical power, would require substantial and deep-seated alteration in that process in order to be fully realized. Since there is an abiding gap between the core embodiments and the existing administrative process, the direct realization of each core in the name of reform appears as deeply problematical as it does radically transformative of that process.

Furthermore, in some respects the core of each ideal, to be completely realized, requires reforms that undermine the fundamental ideal itself. To that degree, regardless of its normative power, each core is self-defeating.

Despite these difficulties, the three ideals are of central and continuing importance in understanding and restructuring the American administrative process within the terms of debate reflected in contemporary reformist criticism. Therefore, critics are driven to reformulate the basic ideals in order to preserve them. This reformulation is seen in the movement from a core embodiment to an alternative expression of each ideal.

Each alternative expression retains the underlying ideal's commitment to a particular conception of the legitimacy of the administrative process. At the same time, the alternative expression embraces an indirect method for realizing the values reflected in the ideal. Each alternative in effect trades a less direct means of realizing the fundamental ideal for a tighter fit between the expression itself and the existing administrative process. Thus, by its terms or implications, each ideal's alternative expression, as opposed to its core embodiment, is much less radically transformative of the administrative process. To that extent, the alternative expression is a more successful reformist vision because it provides a better account of the existing process and imposes on it less strenuous requirements for change. At the same time, the alternative expression is a less powerful normative vision precisely because it accepts an indirect method of vindicating its underlying legitimating principles.

This movement from a core embodiment to an alternative expression may be identified with respect to each of the three competing ideals in the contemporary debate. The following chart schematically identifies the three competing ideals, their core embodiments, and their alternative expressions:

Three Competing Ideals	Core Embodiments	Alternative Expressions
I. Rule of Law Ideal	A. Formalism	B. Proceduralism
II. Public Purposes Ideal	A. Instrumentalism	B. The Market
III. Democratic Process Ideal	A. Participation	B. Oversight

As will be discussed, each of the competing ideals, viewed in general terms and in relation to both core embodiment and alternative expression, has significant power in the contemporary debate. At the same time, each one has its own intrinsic weaknesses and limitations.

Given the wide array of arguments advanced to criticize the administrative process, it would be odd if different organizations of ideas in the contemporary debate could not exist. This Article does not contend that the foregoing conceptual framework is the only possible one. The chief claims for this framework are threefold.

First, this framework shows that the contemporary debate has a deep structure of basic oppositions among three distinct ideals of the administrative process. No one of these ideals may be abandoned within the terms of this debate, and each is at war with the others.

Second, this framework reveals an underlying dynamic within each ideal. This is the movement within each ideal from a core embodiment to an alternative expression, which occurs, it appears, in response to the central difficulties of realizing the core embodiment itself.

Third, despite the surface complexity and variety of the contemporary debate, this framework underscores that the reform debate is more self-contained and limited in scope than it may initially appear. Much of the debate's richness may be explained in terms of the efforts to work out the deep, competing normative commitments in the context of specific proposals.

* * *

III. The First Major Ideal of the Administrative Process Reflected in the Contemporary Debate: The Rule of Law Ideal

A. The Nature of the Rule of Law Ideal

The first central ideal reflected in the contemporary debate is the rule of law ideal. The ideal of the rule of law, as is often noted, commands the participants in the administrative process, notably including administrators but also including reviewing courts, to adhere to the dictates of public laws laid down in advance by the sovereign legislature. This ideal permeates administrative law in general, furnishing the foundational notion that agency action lacks legitimacy unless grounded in law, normally a statute. Nor surprisingly, it also is central to the contemporary debate about administrative reform.

* * *

The jurisprudential conception most directly connected with the rule of law ideal is that of legal formalism. This much used term does not refer to a narrow view of legal rationality holding that every result in specific cases can and should be deduced as a matter of conceptual analysis from prior legal rules. Indeed, the usage here is not confined to any particular theory of the nature of rules or principles that furnish the basis of legal decisionmaking. Rather, legal formalism is used in a more generalized way to refer to a range of possible theories emphasizing the role of specifically legal constraints on public power, especially as it affects individuals' entitlements. The dominant theme of a formalist perspective on the administrative process is that decisions about the use of public power are to be governed by legal norms—which for our purposes may include principles in Ronald Dworkin's sense or rules in H.L.A. Hart's sense[32]—that are presumed to be relatively autonomous from the sphere of frankly political decisions. On this persistently debated view, the sphere of politics is seen to generate value choices and to articulate them in legal norms. The legal realm is conceived to involve the use of such norms and the evolution of legal doctrine in concrete cases without any direct intrusion into politics.

The rule of law ideal's division of the world of public authority into presumptively distinct spheres of political and legal decisionmaking enables the ideal to provide within its own terms a ready explanation of and justification for legislative and judicial action. However, it is less able easily to account for administrative behavior. Under the ideal's premises, lawmaking by the sovereign legislature involves the enunciation of legal norms necessary for private freedom, and adjudication involves the application of legal norms in individual cases. Administration, by contrast, has no easily conceived central function in this bifurcated view of decisionmaking about law. On the one hand, to the extent that administrators themselves enunciate legal norms, as they assuredly do in rulemaking proceedings, their action partakes of the essential role of the legislature. But on the other hand, to the extent that administrators decide cases, as in adjudicatory proceedings, they share the fundamental task of courts.

The rule of law ideal seeks to overcome this potential instability regarding the place of administrative decisionmaking by pragmatically acknowledging that administrative behavior may reflect either a rule-giving or a rule-applying mode. Whatever function is being performed, the key characteristic of any given administrative action on this view is that it must be authorized by and grounded in some prior public law. * * *

This complex of notions furnishes the major premises of certain suggestions for reforming the existing administrative process. One example of a traditional notion put forward by some as a promising basis for significant reform, if it were more seriously applied, is the nondelegation doctrine. This doctrine bars Congress from abrogating its constitutional responsibility by delegating its legislative function to agencies. The basic premises underlying the nondelegation doctrine may be seen as little more than somewhat narrowed restatements of those of the rule of law ideal itself. Like the ideal, the nondelegation doctrine holds, first, that legitimate agency action is necessarily governed by preexisting laws derived from the sovereign lawgiver and, second, that the process of legal decisionmaking engaged in by an agency must be traced specifically to the elaboration of legal norms, rather than to frankly political choice.

Different approaches in judicial decisions applying the nondelegation doctrine may be explained in large measure in terms of the degree of specificity required of the authorizing statutes. Decisions rendered during the doctrine's heyday, notably *Schechter Poultry* and *Panama Refining*, emphasized the need for rather specific and determinate authorizations of actions undertaken by agencies. In later opinions, such as *Yakus* and *Amalgamated Meat Cutters*, which are considered to represent the doctrine's demise, courts have been much more willing to uphold extraordinarily broad authorizations by the legislature, so long as the tasks of administration have been marked out with some identifiable degree of definiteness, if not clarity, by intelligible principles in the authorizing statutes. Even though judicial decisions thus differ in their emphasis on the supposed rigors implicit in the nondelegation doctrine, in general their analysis proceeds on the basis of the rule of law ideal's main premises.

Just as the strengths of the nondelegation doctrine derive from its embrace of the powerful vision under-

---

[32] *See* R. Dworkin, Taking Rights Seriously (1977); H.L.A. Hart, The Concept of Law (1961).

lying the rule of law ideal, so, too, its ultimate instabilities as a doctrine by means of which to reform the administrative process can be traced to its embodiment of that ideal. As noted earlier, a key element of the ideal is the familiar * * * vision * * * [that the function of courts] is to employ legal norms in particular cases in accordance with the dictates of legal formalism. When courts invalidate administrative action as unauthorized because there has been an undue delegation of power to an agency, courts also are invalidating in a given case the statutory provision that purportedly governed the action in the first place. Such constitutionally-based nullification of legislative enactments in the administrative context presents the same conundra * * * that are raised so often in discussions of judicial review in general. For present purposes, the chief difficulties are that when courts so invalidate statutes, they may appear to step beyond the role assigned to them under the rule of law ideal as mere expositors of legal norms, and in any event, in such circumstances they come into direct conflict with the premises of the vision of political legitimacy at the ideal's core. For these reasons, the rule of law ideal itself exerts a continuing pressure against the active application by courts of the nondelegation doctrine, even though the doctrine itself basically reflects that very ideal.

From this vantage point, one can grasp with greater sympathy the considerable challenge confronting those who, in the name of administrative reform, seek to "revive" the nondelegation doctrine. On the one hand, reformist proponents of the doctrine are able to borrow central aspects of a leading ideal of the administrative process * * *. On the other hand, these proponents inevitably confront the internal restraint embodied in the rule of law ideal itself regarding the proper role of courts as expositors of the law. Of course, constitutional norms take precedence over statutory ones, but in practice there remains persistent pressure against outright invalidation of a legislative judgment. Accordingly, to the extent that the rule of law ideal remains dominant, it seems likely that one may expect to observe continued bows in the direction of the nondelegation doctrine in criticisms of administrative action, as well as a prudent reliance on less drastic alternatives to the doctrine itself—such as a greater willingness simply to interpret statutes narrowly in order to avoid potential questions about undue delegations.

B. The Limitations of the Core Formalist Embodiment of the Rule of Law Ideal

The core formalist embodiment of the rule of law ideal achieves its normative force by purporting to distinguish between blatantly political and more strictly legal decisionmaking, and by confining the administrative process to the latter. This fundamental aspiration depends upon the existence of relatively determinate and autonomous norms of public law, which ideally are to structure and guide specific agency decisionmaking.

In reality, however, the norms of public law often are remarkably indeterminate and sweeping in their scope. One sees this immediately by reviewing statutes that, for instance, authorize action in the "public interest, convenience and necessity." Such a statutory standard plainly is designed to afford substantial room for the play of administrative discretion. In fact, one of the most familiar justifications for creating many administrative agencies and programs is that there must exist an institutional context for the exercise of executive discretion guided chiefly by specialized expertise about public problems. The rule of law ideal's own premises simply do not provide an adequate account of the primary place of such discretion and expertise in the operation and development of the administrative process.

Given that highly open-ended legal norms are at the center, not the periphery, of administrative life, it often would be strained indeed to describe agency actions as truly grounded in law as distinguished from policy analysis, political choices, or bureaucratic patterns having at most an attenuated link with the law as such. The problem here is not that formalism can account for no open-ended legal norms, but rather that in administrative law such norms are dominant, not exceptional, and the premises of the formalist model do not acknowledge such a phenomenon. Examples of multifactored, open-ended agency decisionmaking that are difficult to account for under the formalist approach are not hard to identify. They range from adjudicative processes, such as licensing by the Federal Communications Commission, to complex rulemaking, such as that by the Environmental Protection Agency or the Occupational Safety and Health Administration. * * *

Several explanations, based largely on the asserted necessities or practical constraints of modern government, have been advanced to account for the predominance of such open-ended norms. In part, Congress may lack the time, staff, or other resources needed to delineate with precision the legal limits on agency action. Moreover, agency discretion often has been perceived as an independent value because it allows for experimentation, flexibility, and change without recourse to statutory amendment. Also, as a political matter, it appears to be expedient for Congress to legislate in highly general terms. The less specific the proposed legislation, the more likely may be the achievement of the necessary consensus for enactment, which is difficult to accomplish even in the most propitious of circumstances. By such an approach, Congress may avoid the necessity of making certain controversial decisions about matters of public debate that may be expected to generate considerable clamor. At least, it assuredly is more convenient to assign such difficult tasks to agencies, from which Congress readily may seek to distance itself should the clamor become sufficiently widespread.

Even more fundamentally, the very character of statutory norms designed to criticize existing institutions—for instance, antidiscrimination norms, such as in legislation broadly prohibiting discrimination against the handicapped—may require that they embody rather general and open-ended principles. If the critical norms were highly specific and thus strictly confined in their reference or implications, their force as catalysts of social change inevitably would be blunted. Thus, if the rule of law ideal is to allow for serious criticism of existing social institutions, it appears that it must be seen to permit open-ended principles in public law. To this extent, however, the ideal fosters the very condition that precipitates the frustration of its formalist aspirations.

These several factors, taken together, render highly problematical the full achievement of the formalist model of the rule of law ideal. They also may help to explain why, despite the ideal's continuing centrality in the theory of administrative law, its core embodiment has been the progenitor of relatively few contemporary proposals for reform.[48]

C. The Proceduralist Alternative to the Core Formalist Embodiment of the Rule of Law Ideal

A primary response by those embracing the basic vision underlying the rule of law ideal to the difficulties of realizing its formalist core is to place less concentration on substantive legal constraints on agency action and more emphasis on procedural limitations. Proceduralism continues to reflect the rule of law's commitment to legal norms as necessary restraints on potentially overweening and arbitrary public power. However, proceduralism tends to de-emphasize the place of determinate and autonomous legal norms as the guides of agency decisionmaking, while stressing in their place the need for broadly applicable procedural safeguards as the guarantors of a regularized and fair process.

The animating image underlying the proceduralist critique of administration involves the application of the state's considerable powers in matters affecting discrete individuals. In such situations, the proceduralist's concern, not unexpectedly, is with fostering the autonomy and private rights of the person in a reasonably nonarbitrary process. The guiding idea is that of fairness toward the individual. Under this conception it is critical to afford each person a "day in court" when the state proposes to act against one's interests. It is essential from this perspective to provide a person the opportunity to understand and respond to any accusations or assertions that could lead to agency action against him or her. In particular cases, the full panoply of formalities associated with a judicial, trial-type process may be employed in the name of proceduralism. Whatever the formalities employed, their rationale on these premises is to uphold a highly individualistic conception of fairness and regularity in administrative processes.

Of course, in an administrative context in which decisions affect large numbers of persons and groups in society, the image of a one-on-one encounter between the state and an individual often is somewhat amiss. Nonetheless, the basic project of assuring a nonarbitrary, fair, and regularized process with basic due process guarantees still is widely pursued, even if the means are modified to fit the realities of broad-scale policymaking, such as, for example, through agency rulemaking.

Proceduralism has exerted a powerful influence on the development of administrative law, much of which consists, after all, of the procedural norms structuring adjudicatory and rulemaking proceedings. To find other instances of proceduralism, one need look no farther than cases dealing with due process hearing rights or cases involving the review of agency action for possible arbitrariness or capriciousness. In the last context, some courts have adopted a relatively assertive attitude toward administrative behavior that has required agencies, if not to follow specific procedures as such, at least to provide a reasonably full explanation of the basis for any given decision. This, in turn, requires agencies to undertake a relatively careful decisional process in order to survive judicial review. * * *

Although the proceduralist model has exerted considerable practical influence in the development

---

[48] The rule of law ideal's core is perhaps most consistent with efforts by Congress carefully to review and redraft as necessary the underlying substantive authorities of different agencies in order to be certain that statutory delegations are as clear and determinate as possible. Yet the center of gravity in the contemporary reform debate has been in the area of government-wide reform, not agency-by-agency statutory review. *But see* Federal Trade Commission Improvements Act of 1980, Pub. L. No. 96-252, 94 Stat. 374 (1980).

of administrative law, its conceptual status is less secure. To a substantial degree, it represents an inherently unstable compromise. On the one hand, proceduralism does not specifically advance the rule of law ideal's commitment to substantive legal norms that govern legal decisionmaking and constrain agency action. On the other hand, proceduralism essentially maintains the rule of law ideal's vision of political legitimacy * * *. In particular, proceduralism retains the ideas that administrative action lacks legitimacy unless it is authorized by law * * *.

This combination of commitments leads to an incompleteness within proceduralism itself. By embracing the rule of law ideal's vision of political legitimacy, proceduralism embodies the ideal's conception of a demarcation between the spheres of public action and private autonomy. In particular, proceduralism accepts—or at the very least never rejects—the rule of law ideal's vision of law as a constraint on public power that marks the boundaries of a realm of private rights. However, by abandoning the rule of law ideal's emphasis on substantive formalism and by stressing in its place the importance of proceduralism—or, if you will, procedural formalism—as a check on agency discretion, proceduralism fails to satisfy the conditions ultimately needed to realize its own political ideal. This is so because purely proceduralist restraints on agency action do not, and indeed they cannot, substantively delimit the sphere of public power, as distinct from the realm of private rights. If one wishes to accomplish such a task, one will need a substantive explanation of the basis for such a demarcation, which proceduralism lacks.

Such conceptual incompleteness plagues contemporary proceduralist proposals for administrative reform. Take, for instance, the so-called Bumpers Amendment, which for several years has been proposed by Senator Dale Bumpers. Although not enacted, this amendment in 1982 was adopted in one version by the Senate by a vote of 94 to 0 and, in a somewhat different version, by the House Committee on the Judiciary. The amendment essentially would broaden the scope of judicial review of agency action such as by requiring courts not to "presume" that challenged agency action is valid and by requiring courts to review issues of fact in informal rulemaking under a somewhat more stringent standard. Putting aside the amendment's details, * * * the proposal is grounded on a conviction that agencies tend to be too activist in their use of their broad delegations and, as a result, tend to trench excessively upon the private realm of social life. This basic rationale represents a straightforward restatement of the rule of law ideal's commitments to establishing and enforcing a substantive demarcation between the public and private spheres.

However, the Bumpers Amendment does not even purport to accomplish such objectives. To the contrary, its major proponent has expressed serious doubt whether Congress ever could do much at all to narrow broad delegations * * *. True to its proceduralist underpinnings, the amendment essentially would call upon the judiciary to "take a closer look" at challenged agency action.

The ultimate defense of the amendment is that agencies, by having to satisfy stricter standards of judicial review, may be expected in general to compile more complete records and, partly as a result, to engage in more cautious and self-restrictive deliberations under existing authorizations before reaching final positions. Whatever else may be observed about such an approach to administrative reform, in terms of the rule of law ideal itself, it is at best a partial solution to the problem it seeks to address. The underlying problem—assuring that agencies remain within the bounds of substantive law—can be addressed under the rule of law ideal by clarifying the limits of the law and by relying on courts to police them. To adopt the second step without even attempting the first one is to expand the judicial role without providing determinate guides that judges or administrators may follow. Such an approach borrows the rule of law rhetoric about the place of courts as the guardians of legal constraints on administration without providing the normative underpinnings necessary to give content to such an ideal.

IV. The Second Major Ideal Reflected in the Contemporary Debate: The Public Purposes Ideal

A. The Nature of the Public Purposes Ideal

The second of the three competing ideals of the administrative process reflected in the contemporary debate may be called the public purposes ideal. Stated broadly, this ideal's central emphasis is to foster the realization of valued public ends. At bottom, the ideal necessarily starts with a conception—and there are various ones—of the nature of the ends or purposes to be advanced by administrative action. The ideal's chief premise is that the primary standard for criticizing the administrative process lies in its ability to promote, and at all costs not to impede, the achievement of such a conception. Unlike the rule of law ideal, the public purposes ideal does not place primary emphasis on legal norms as necessary constraints on public power. Rather, it mainly stresses the affirmative tasks of governmental policymaking in general and administrative action in particular.

The ideal's most direct embodiment may be referred to as instrumentalism, by which is meant the familiar notion that the significant worth of a policy inheres in its success as an instrument of the public good—that is, as a means whereby something valued may be achieved or furthered. In the context of administrative reform, the instrumentalist critique holds that the legitimacy of the administrative process turns on its ability to realize valued public ends in an effective and efficient manner.

Plainly, the crucial variables that determine the nature of different instrumentalist conceptions of reform depend on the theories of the purposes to be rationally promoted and the allowable means of pursuing them. For present purposes, two main types of instrumentalist approaches that lie roughly toward opposite poles of a continuum of possible perspectives are of particular interest.

On one instrumentalist view, reflected in its essentials in the enduring New Deal conception of the expert agency put forward for instance by James Landis,[67] the public purposes to be achieved are those identified in an agency's authorizing legislation. The ultimate basis for this commitment is the notion that legislative enactments are the legitimate repositories of the sovereign will and, therefore, their guidance of and limitations on the expert agency must be taken quite seriously in identifying the goals to be promoted. Furthermore, on this view the allowable range of means for achieving given ends is presumed to be significantly contained, even if still capacious. This range includes the direct and necessary methods of promoting statutory ends so long as the methods may be fairly said to be consistent with an agency's central tasks under its authorizing legislation.

A second instrumentalist approach expands the range of desired ends along with the allowable means of reaching them, not by expressly countenancing the violation of statutes to be sure, but by assuming that broad delegations are consistent with a sweeping consideration of alternative goals and the widest possible variety of means for achieving them. This view is reflected, for instance, in various contemporary proposals for conducting agency rulemaking in accordance with the dictates of comprehensive cost-benefit analysis. In general terms, the well-recognized principle underlying cost-benefit analysis is that the right, or rational, course of action is one which, within the general limits of law, maximizes social benefits while minimizing social costs, as conceived within the context of various possible theories of benefits and costs. Like classical utilitarianism, whose intellectual heritage cost-benefit analysis in part borrows, such an expanded instrumentalist conception exudes notable confidence about the power of human reason to predict and calculate the consequences of agency decisions and to select a course of conduct that will maximize desired ends and minimize undesired results.

Whether approached from the perspective of Landis or of modern proponents of plenary cost-benefit analysis, the vision of bureaucratic instrumentalism in general furnishes valuable tools for justifying and criticizing administrative decisionmaking. In contrast with the rule of law ideal, instrumentalism does not emphasize an antinomy between law-making by the legislature and law-applying by the courts. Rather, instrumentalism seeks to establish a unified conception of rational administrative policymaking distinct from both the law-promulgating function of the legislature and the law-applying mode of the courts. This attempt may be seen in the writings of the New Deal's defenders who emphasized the special role of agency expertise in realizing given policy ends and in more recent discussions by those who embrace the perspective of "policy science" as a foundation for understanding administrative behavior.

In the contemporary debate, instrumentalism's core is reflected most prominently in legislative proposals to require agencies to conduct rulemaking in accordance with some version of a cost-benefit or similar analysis of alternative courses of action. The major claim for cost-benefit analysis itself is essentially the argument in favor of instrumentalism: it is designed to foster formally rational, instrumental decisionmaking by agencies. From this perspective, regulatory reform bills have been proposed that would, among other things, impose a cost-benefit analysis or similar requirement in order to make more "rational" the rulemaking process. * * *

B. *The Limitations of the Core Instrumentalist Embodiment of the Public Purposes Ideal*

The core instrumentalist embodiment of the public purposes ideal, like the core of the rule of law ideal, provides a powerful and central normative perspective from which to criticize the contemporary administrative process. However, also like the core of the rule of law ideal, instrumentalism ultimately does not offer an adequate understanding or justification of the modern administrative process, which appears inevitably to operate in ways that lie beyond the purview of a fully instrumentalist vision.

In particular, instrumentalism focuses on the need for expert, rational analysis as the foundation of ad-

---

[67] *See* J. Landis [The Administrative Process (1938).]

ministrative decisionmaking. This image stands in sharp contrast to a system imbued with custom, habit, inertia, and "irrational" political intervention. * * * [I]t would be difficult indeed to contend that such elements are not critical in various administrative contexts. The premises of the instrumentalist core of the public purposes ideal do not provide an adequate account of the undeniable importance of such forces in the administrative process. To that extent, instrumentalism's premises, taken on their own terms and despite their continuing importance, furnish a limited and ultimately problematical basis for a program of administrative reform.

Moreover, the instrumentalist core has an inherently self-defeating tendency to encourage broader and broader analytical undertakings in which the scope of contemplated ends and means is ever expanding. The tendency seems to be reflected historically in the shift in the center of gravity in instrumentalist critiques during recent decades from the "expertise" conception of Landis to the plenary cost-benefit balancing proposals prominent in the contemporary reform debate. The apparent trend toward broadening the scope of instrumentalist analysis is consistent with the underlying goal of achieving a truly rational result. On instrumentalist terms, what would be more rational than the "most" optimal solution to a public policy problem that takes into account all reasonable ends and means? Although such a progression toward greater breadth of analysis seems inescapable, it leads ultimately to a perspective on the administrative process that lacks any firm normative moorings. To the extent that nearly everything is to be taken into account and virtually all factors must be balanced against all others, an expanded instrumentalist conception becomes increasingly empty, difficult to apply, and indeterminate in its results.

However much one may criticize the vagueness of the instrumentalist critique, such a view of administration can be especially useful in a regime in which political authorities seek a general cover for manipulating the process. Thus, the official justification of decisions may be cast, at least in part, in formally instrumentalist terms, but actual decisions in fact may be generated by essentially political factors—such as influence by dominant societal interests and ad hoc intervention in agency rulemaking by the Executive Office of the President. Such a possibility is more than a speculative concern, given the contemporary emphasis on Executive Office oversight of cost-benefit analysis conducted initially by agencies. * * *

Furthermore, to the extent that expanded instrumentalism as an analytical approach becomes linked with Executive Office oversight of administration, the role of individual agencies as expert decisionmakers is likely to be substantially eroded. This is likely, at least, so long as actual power over the administrative process is wielded by Executive Office staff, whose perspectives frequently may differ from those of agency officials. On the one hand, such a result may be applauded by critics who decry the supposed narrowness of particular agencies and their asserted tendency to be dominated by regulated industries (and congressional committees and subcommittees), and who perceive a need for greater centralized direction by the President and those directly responsible to him. On the other hand, the basically instrumentalist view of agencies as valuable centers of managerial and substantive expertise is itself put at serious risk by such a program.

Aside from sharing these general problems of instrumentalism, cost-benefit analysis generates a number of more specific doubts. As is often asked, is it really possible to determine in advance all of the material consequences of all possible alternative means to all reasonable intermediate goals that would further some given ultimate end, and to assess these various consequences in terms of some common standards of "costs" and "benefits"? The theory of cost-benefit analysis, taken to its extreme, would require such a herculean undertaking in order to arrive at a truly rational result. However, it commonly is noted that, at least as a practical matter, cost-benefit analysis must take for granted some reasonably limited set of preconceived ends and means, and their selection will depend on choices that themselves are not founded on any cost-benefit analysis.

Moreover, assuming a limited range of preconceived ends and means, will it actually be possible to measure with accuracy the benefits as well as the costs of the consequences of different possible agency actions? One must establish some common denominator in terms of which to assess or assign weights to various outcomes. However, the outcomes may have significantly differing characteristics and thus may not be readily susceptible to reduction to a common standard of measurement. Also, it frequently is observed that cost-benefit analysis may be systematically skewed by the particular difficulties of predicting and assigning values to the benefits, as opposed to the costs, of rules. Benefits, such as cleaner air or water, may be more difficult to predict and measure simply because of limits in our scientific understanding, for instance of the effects on human health and the environment of varying degrees of improvement in air or water quality. Also, benefits are especially difficult to state in quantifiable terms since they commonly are diffuse and long-term.

More generally, cost-benefit analysis appears heedless of the view that there are certain values in society—moral, political, aesthetic, whatever—that many may consider worthy of pursuit even if they do not fully satisfy rigorous cost-benefit criteria. Clean air, clean water, and healthful working environments may be viewed as such fundamental values of nature and life itself that it would deny their basic worth to subject them to a cost-benefit standard of decision. Whatever may be said in this regard about any particular value, cost-benefit analysis is subject to serious question because it denies that any values or combinations of values may be morally worthy of vindication on their own terms. This objection is a version of the broader point that a utilitarian ethics, by merging all particular goods into one general conception of the good, tends not to acknowledge the power of plural conceptions of values having distinct and independent claims of moral force.

A frequent response to such various criticisms of cost-benefit analysis is that at least it forces regulators to become consciously aware of trade-offs that are inevitably made, and thus it requires regulators explicitly to weigh factors they might otherwise ignore or devalue. The technique is said to direct decisionmaking toward relatively objective matters and away from momentary, irrational, and often broadly political considerations.

* * * [However,] there is a considerable difference between choosing an outcome because of its presumed cost-benefit ratio, on the one hand, and selecting an outcome on other grounds and then observing that it might be "translated" into cost-benefit terms if one were so inclined, on the other hand.

Moreover, even * * * [accepting] the above noted defense of cost-benefit methodology * * *, it represents a retreat from many of the central claims made for such analysis. As an expression of instrumentalist reasoning, cost-benefit analysis purports to provide a technique for determining the right result in an administrative context, or at least, the right range of results. It thus is put forward by its strongest proponents, to borrow a phrase, as a rule of decision. However, the foregoing response moves from this position to the defense of a multifactored balancing approach that essentially requires decisionmakers to focus on various conceivable alternatives, weigh their respective consequences, and otherwise hone analytical skills. This is a use of cost-benefit balancing as a tool—not a rule—of decision.

When a shift has occurred to a defense of a multifactored balancing technique, proponents to cost-benefit analysis have moved to what may be considered a basically process-oriented perspective. Although balancing analysis is supposed to be conducted carefully, it leaves the substantive grounds for decision essentially open to administrative discretion. In this way, the perspective bears a certain resemblance to the method of courts that send back to agencies for further elaboration decisions reviewed and remanded under the so called hard look approach. It would be error to confuse a process-oriented technique that basically requires more explanation of administrative action with cost-benefit analysis in its most fundamental form.

C. The Market-Based Alternative to the Core Instrumentalist Embodiment of the Public Purposes Ideal

The primary alternative expression of the public purposes ideal takes seriously the manifest difficulties of realizing the instrumentalist core through direct action by administrative agencies. Instead, it seeks to achieve the public good through the indirect means of the market. The market, as is well known, is conceived as a set of economic institutions and relationships in which relevant actors are presumed to be capable of making, and to be routinely motivated to make, rational decisions in various situations of choice about the most efficient ways of achieving their own ends. Taken as a whole, these decisions are assumed to embody the public interest, which thus is an aggregative conception defined in terms of the total of private wants and aversions expressed in the market. On this view, the major function of the administrative process is to avoid interference with and, when necessary, to foster the conduct of largely nongovernmental decisionmaking.

To be sure, there are substantial differences between an instrumentalist commitment to bureaucratic action and a market-based critique of administration. The effort to view them here as aspects of a single, more encompassing ideal should not * * * obscure those differences. Basically, the former places direct faith in, while the latter tends to disavow, the administrative process as the primary arena in which public ends are to be pursued. At the same time, market theory retains the larger objective of the public good, while redefining it as the sum of private economic choices. Thus, both perspectives share the more general picture of a well-regulated administrative process as an effective and efficient promoter of valued public purposes. This broadly managerialist vision is retained by the market-based model even when, in some contexts, it claims that there should be no regulation or other type of administrative intervention in the market. In such contexts, the administrative process is essentially viewed as most effective when it is least active.

The market-based alternative is reflected, for example, in recent writings about the administrative process by now-Judge Stephen Breyer, who has undertaken a broad-ranging critique of regulation within the terms of this model.[88] One of its major premises is that the market alone has certain imperfections that do not permit it to operate, as pure theory would have it, as a fully efficient allocator of values. Accordingly, there is room for intervention by the administrative process in order to correct such imperfections to the greatest extent possible. For instance, the lack of adequate consumer information may be "corrected" by disclosure regulation in given cases, and the existence of certain externalities of productive processes, such as pollution, may be adjusted for by regulatory requirements. However, the central notion underlying such a critique remains: any administrative imposition should be geared primarily toward restoring the conditions required for a more perfect operation of market forces. At all costs, regulatory requirements should not be allowed to supplant or deeply to interfere with the market, for such results are viewed as leading inexorably to a fundamental misallocation of society's resources.

These ideas are reflected in the contemporary debate in various contexts, particularly including that of economic regulation. For example, it has been urged that power over matters of entry, pricing, and conditions of service in certain regulated industries should be returned generally to the market. Such proposals have been buttressed by empirical studies that have been interpreted to support the view that prices would be lower, service would be improved, and competition would be more energetic if administrative interventions would be halted or at least relaxed. * * *

Related proposals for administrative reform rest on the notion that if a regulated industry should not be deregulated, then the remaining regulation itself should be rooted in the theory of the market. This conviction rests on the premise that regulation should exist when, but only when, it is necessary to correct market imperfections. Any regulation that satisfies this condition also must be tailored to be as consistent as possible with existing economic realities. Such a perspective provides the tools for criticizing standard regulatory controls, which often tend basically to compel or prohibit certain activities. For the economic critic, these regulatory edicts, or "command-and-control" regulatory requirements as they have been called, frequently are seen as rather ham-fisted and ineffective because they restrict considerably the options of the industry being regulated. Greater flexibility, for instance in being able to choose among different pollution control technologies or devices, is said to be necessary for an administrative regime to coexist with the market. * * *

In recent years, market-based arguments that manifest a basic hostility to regulatory activities have assumed striking prominence. In part, this may reflect the apparent vitality of an emphasis on economics in various fields of law. It also seems to reflect contemporary political pressures to shrink the scope of federal regulation.

One of the chief constraints of the market-based conception is that it, like proceduralism, is ultimately an indirect and partial embodiment of its most general underlying ideal. The public purposes ideal holds that the role of administration is to advance valued ends in society. The market-based approach rejects the effort primarily to realize such an ideal directly through the operation of the administrative process. Instead, it relies mainly on the presumed efficiencies of the market, supplemented only to the extent necessary. This position requires fundamental faith in the market as an efficient mechanism for achieving the social good. However, the market-based theory itself, in many of its formulations, seems to call this faith into serious question.

For instance, many proponents of the market model themselves recognize a broad range of rationales for administrative intervention. These include the following: the existence of monopoly power that is capable of overcoming legitimate competition; the existence of natural monopolies in certain industries, such as utilities, where economies of scale are considerable; the lack of adequate consumer information; the existence of externalities, which involve costs imposed on society by productive processes that are not borne directly by the enterprises in question; the potential for unfair windfall profits resulting from the elimination of price ceilings when some suppliers have substantial inventories of a deregulated commodity; and the perceived need to eliminate "excessive" competition or to moderate distributional inequities that may result from a sudden or severe scarcity of a valued good.

One is left with the unmistakable impression that

---

[88] *See* S. BREYER [REGULATION AND ITS REFORM (1982)] * * *. *Cf.* Breyer, *Two Models of Regulatory Reform*, 34 S.C.L. REV. 629 (1983) (contrasting a favored "case-by-case" approach to regulatory reform, illustrated by airline deregulation, with a disfavored "generic" approach seeking improvement through a single, government-wide statute).

the market surely requires a considerable degree of "perfection" even on the terms of some of its strongest supporters. At a minimum, one must question whether market-based theory does not recognize so many exceptions to its rule against governmental intervention that the rule itself should be considered the exception.

Furthermore, the market-based conception is persistently criticized for seeking to reduce all matters of public value to issues of individual, subjective preference. On its own terms, can the market be counted upon to realize important public values, given that presumably it is driven largely by the self-interested motivations of producers for profits and of consumers for lower prices and better goods and services?

* * *

One possible response would be that the market's products by definition are expressive of the public good, and therefore one ought not to be overly concerned about, and ought not to argue on the basis of, premises concerning what is or is not a public value considered apart from decisions of the market. This response is subject to serious question by those who hold to a vision of moral and social values that is in any basic respect independent of the subjective choices of hypothetical rational actors in the market.

In addition, the market-based model constricts considerably the terms of public debate by seeking to reduce issues of administrative choice to questions of economic rationality. This tendency is reflected, for instance, in the model's criticism of existing schemes of federal regulation on the ground that they embody "irrational" political compromises and predilections. Regulations also are condemned on the basis that they reflect "irrational" institutional tendencies to rely on precedent and to achieve enforceable, if not pristinely rational, standards. These objections * * * tend to reveal as much about the limited premises of the critique as about the matters being criticized.

These and related concerns have been debated in an extensive and expanding literature that continues to produce new calls for deregulation and economic alternatives to regulation, on the one hand, and summonses to a wider conception of the administrative process, on the other hand. Whatever one's attitude toward particular debates about the approach, it seems plain that it does not exhaust the possibilities for redirecting energies devoted to administrative reform.

V. The Third Major Ideal Reflected in the Contemporary Debate: The Democratic Process Ideal

A. The Nature of the Democratic Process Ideal

The third of the three competing ideals of the administrative process reflected in the contemporary debate is the democratic process ideal. The basic vision underlying this ideal is of a highly participatory, representative decisionmaking process in which relevant officials are held accountable for the extent to which they actively take into consideration the views of affected groups in formulating and implementing agency policy. This vision derives its intellectual force from democratic theory and its critique of nonrepresentative decisional processes.

A number of contrasts may be drawn between this third ideal and the first two. Unlike the public purposes ideal, the democratic process ideal does not place primary emphasis on the purportedly expert status of administrative agencies or on the instrumentalist character of their decisionmaking. Rather, the third ideal conceives of administration primarily as a political process. * * *

The relationship between the democratic process ideal and the rule of law ideal is somewhat more complex. On the one hand, the democratic process ideal, unlike the rule of law ideal, does not attempt to separate the sphere of politics, as reflected in legislation, from the realm of legal decisionmaking, as reflected in administration (and judicial decisionmaking). Rather, the third ideal, in assuming that the administrative process is inherently political, basically borrows the guiding legitimating conception of democratic politics as the normative perspective from which to judge administration. In sharp contrast, the rule of law ideal confines the democratic ideal of interest representation to the legislature itself.

On the other hand, there is a certain affinity between aspects of the democratic process ideal and of proceduralism as a variant of the rule of law ideal. Both share the rhetoric of "fair" procedures and "open" decisional processes. Nevertheless, the highly individualistic conception of fair process underlying proceduralism is profoundly different from the picture of the collective pursuit of plural interests that informs the democratic process ideal. The former is directed at protecting the interests of discrete individuals on whom the force of government has been brought to bear. The latter, by viewing agencies essentially as surrogate legislatures, emphasizes the affirmative project by which agencies are to represent the interests of major groups in society. * * *

The most direct expression of the democratic process ideal in the contemporary debate is the commitment generally to expand public participation in administration. "Participation" is viewed primarily as the opportunity to present opinions and recommendations to agency officials regarding pending matters that will directly affect the public's interests. Underlying this commitment to participation is a pluralist vision of political life as consisting of the competition among various groups or interests in society. The task of successful administration, on this view, is to implement public law by selecting a compromise position that will be acceptable to the agency and a sufficient range of affected interests, such as consumers, producers, labor, and industry. Participation is seen as a way to foster necessary conditions for compromise and agreement, to inform officials about the relevant issues and views of affected interests, to allow concerned groups to become involved in decisional processes in which they have a stake, and to endow the administrative process with the appearance and as much as possible the reality of democratic responsiveness.

Various methods for promoting broader participation have been suggested. One is to foster a significant minimum degree of openness in the administrative process itself so that members of the public may become better informed about matters of importance to them, such as evolving enforcement policies. This approach basically assumes that when the public has access to such information, its members will be able to make their views known to the agency. Such a perspective is reflected in several laws enacted during the 1970's, including the Federal Advisory Committee Act (1972), amendments to the Freedom of Information Act (1974), and the Government in the Sunshine Act (1976).

Related contemporary reforms call upon agencies to broaden efforts to inform the public of proposed actions that may affect their interests. For instance, President Carter's 1978 Executive order on regulations required agencies to take specific measures to notify the public about upcoming rulemaking proceedings in advance of the publication of a statutory notice of proposed rulemaking. Another way to expand opportunities for public involvement is to fund intervention in agency proceedings by groups that otherwise would not be in a position to participate. Richard Stewart has discerned further examples of the participatory ideal in judicial decisions involving the doctrines of intervention in agency proceedings and of standing to challenge an agency decision in court. As Stewart noted in 1975, such areas of the law saw considerable judicial innovation during the preceding decade. He argued that, at least in part, the innovation in that period reflected a judicial commitment to increase the opportunities for interest representation in administration.

All of these examples have in common the effort to broaden public input into agency processes. Like the underlying notion of participation itself, they are largely process-oriented, for they do not purport to instruct agencies in substantive terms about the basis on which decisions should be reached. Rather, they seek to hold agencies to a relatively high standard of openness and responsiveness in their dealings with the public.

It might be suggested that, in the last few years, the core of the democratic process ideal has fallen on hard times, for the energies behind much of the contemporary debate have not been directed at opening up and making more participatory the administrative process. Nonetheless, this ideal exerts continuing influence, as it speaks to fundamental values in our administrative system. * * *

B. *The Limitations of the Core Embodiment of the Democratic Process Ideal*

* * *

The participatory vision underlying the democratic process ideal requires for its full realization that the institutions in which it operates be governed by premises of responsiveness to the sentiments of the participants. Although imperfectly, Congress may be said to be so structured, for at least its membership finally depends on the continued favor of the electorate. However, as is well-recognized, the administrative process is not similarly structured either by law or custom.

Administrative decisionmaking occurs chiefly in hierarchical bureaucracies charged by law with making choices about public policy. * * * To be sure, * * * [agency] appointees are subjected to a variety of political forces, including the views of significant groups of the public. But at bottom, agency decisions must be legally and bureaucratically justified, not grounded principally on the specific goal of representing the views of the affected public. Indeed, when agencies arguably have come to act as mere representatives of certain groups in society, they frequently have been sharply criticized by members of Congress and the public itself as "captured" agencies. * * *

Given these realities, it is fundamentally difficult to achieve the goals of the participatory vision. Certainly, agencies may be made more aware on an *ad hoc* basis of the views of significant societal interests, such as by the importuning of members of Congress or of the President or his subordinates. Also, steps may be taken, as discussed in the previous section, to provide for a somewhat more open and participatory process. However, despite the continuing power of the democratic process ideal, the gap between its core embodiment and the existing process is so profound that the core, if fully realized, would radically transform rather than merely reform it. The core embodiment simply does not account for the practices of the hierarchical, specialized bureaucracies in which administrative action centrally resides.

In this light, the grand terms of the participatory vision inevitably seem only thinly realized in the proposals to reform the administrative process in its name. The creation of formal rights of participation, which basically are rights to express views to decisionmakers who remain as free as before in substantive terms to do as they will, seems hardly an adequate means of capturing in its fullness the power of the participatory model. Given the present institutional realities of administration and the norms and rituals of the adversarial process that they foster, however, this may be all that can be expected.

Furthermore, the program of the participatory ideal is undermined by the constraint of limited resources of both affected interest groups and agencies. In practice, the interests that appear to have the greatest access to the administrative process tend to be those with reasonably significant standing in the broader community and thus the political savvy, informational sources, and financial backing to organize when necessary to protect valued positions. Is it realistic to expect society to invest the resources that would be necessary to subsidize other groups in order to make the administrative process truly as open and participatory as possible? * * *

Moreover, strong institutional pressures almost certainly will continue to be exerted by agencies themselves against opening up and making more participatory the administrative process. In part, such resistance is a perfectly understandable reaction to the likelihood that such reforms may prompt delays in an already cumbersome process. Criticism by agency officials of the Federal Advisory Committee Act, for instance, reflects in significant measure a desire for a more efficient administrative system. At the same time, agency opposition to a more participatory process is likely driven, at least in part, by self-protective and self-serving commitments. In any event, administrators are bound to continue their resistance and thereby to contribute to the cumulative difficulties encountered by the participatory vision of administrative reform.

Even more basically, the core of the democratic process ideal, by requiring that the administrative process represent a full range of interests and views on a particular matter, necessitates a bureaucratic decision about what interests and views are worth representing. Thus, in order for the ideal's core to be implemented, it is necessary * * * that an essentially nondemocratic decision be made about what democracy ultimately requires. To this extent, the attempt to realize the core of the ideal in the administrative context seems self-defeating.

C. The Alternative Expression of the Democratic Process Ideal: Political Oversight

The limitations of the core participatory conception are substantial enough to prompt many proponents of the democratic process ideal to reach for an alternative, if derivative, way to realize its values. In the contemporary debate, the major alternative expression of the democratic process ideal is the commitment to more active oversight of the administrative process by politically responsive officials.

What may be called the oversight model retains the ideal's underlying belief in the democratic process and its basic conception of administration as an essentially political process. At the same time, it abandons the emphasis on the ideal's direct realization through public participation in agency proceedings themselves. Instead, the oversight model relies on national political authorities—principally, the President and members of Congress—as the intermediaries whose job it is to impose the public's will on administrators. The basic project of administrative reform on this view is, put briefly, to promote greater control by the President and Congress over agency action.

* * *

The first major application of the oversight approach is the proposal to strengthen the role of the President and his immediate staff, located in the Executive Office of the President, in overseeing and, when necessary, checking the rulemaking decisions of agencies. * * *

Proponents of Presidential oversight of the regulatory process have argued that since the President is the single nationally-elected political official, he is uniquely qualified to impose on agencies the will of the public. Therefore, it is argued, the President should be given more power to do so. Opponents of the expansion of centralized executive oversight have urged that existing laws will not permit it, for it may undermine the intended role and powers of particular agencies under given authorizing statutes.[116] More-

---

[116] *See* Staff of the House Comm. on Energy and Commerce, 97th Cong., 1st Sess., Report on Presidential Control of Agency Rulemaking (Comm. Print 1981). For a contrary

over, opponents have asserted that such expansion is unwise because, in practice, it would encourage *ad hoc* political intervention in the administrative process that would impair a rational, coherent, and fair decisionmaking system. It also has been noted that, in reality, Presidential oversight largely means influence by subordinate, appointed officials in the Executive Office who are not themselves politically accountable to the extent the President is. Since the present Administration apparently is committed to increased Presidential oversight of the regulatory process, the debate over these issues is likely to continue.

The second basic application of the political oversight model is found in proposals to expand congressional power over agencies. Traditionally, these proposals have stressed such mechanisms as more rigorous congressional oversight of agency behavior. Although such an approach has received some attention in the contemporary debate, particular concentration has been centered on the legislative veto mechanism. * * * The term "legislative veto" refers to a statutory provision that purports to authorize the legislative branch to disapprove or mandate an agency action by adopting a resolution—which may be passed by one or both Houses of Congress or even a committee of Congress—that is not presented to the President for approval or disapproval. Scores of federal statutes contain such provisions.

A longstanding dispute between Presidents and Congress over the constitutionality of such provisions intensified significantly in recent years, during which time numerous such provisions were enacted. * * * [In 1983] the Supreme Court dealt with three cases raising the constitutional issues. In all of them, resolutions under legislative veto provisions had been adopted in order to nullify executive actions, and the courts of appeals had held that the veto provisions in question violated constitutional requirements.

The first case involved a one-House veto of the Attorney General's decision, following an administrative adjudication, to suspend the deportation of an alien under a provision of the Immigration and Naturalization Act.[125] The second case involved a one-House veto of a regulation adopted by the Federal Energy Regulatory Commission that implemented the "incremental pricing" provisions of the Natural Gas Policy Act; the thrust of the regulation had been to shift some costs of the deregulation of natural gas prices from residential to industrial consumers.[126] The third case involved a two-House veto of a Federal Trade Commission rule regulating warranty and disclosure requirements in connection with the sale of used cars.[127] In these three cases, opponents of the legislative veto argued that it violated both the general principles of the separation of powers and the particular procedures for legislative action set forth in article I, section 7, of the Constitution, calling for bicameral passage of bills and resolutions and their presentation to the President for approval or disapproval. In turn, proponents urged that the legislative veto mechanisms, admittedly not contemplated specifically in the Constitution, nonetheless were authorized by the necessary and proper clause of article I, section 8, and that they were consistent with the flexible precepts underlying the separation of powers.

In its decision in the immigration case [INS v. Chadha], the Supreme Court ruled that the bicameralism and presentation requirements generally do apply to exercises of legislative power under article I and that the challenged nullification of the suspension decision itself was such an exercise of power. The Court's language was quite broad, indicating that it would be difficult indeed to distinguish between types of legislative veto provisions in applying the controlling constitutional requirements. In a vigorous dissent, Justice White decried the breadth of the Court's opinion, suggesting that it would have far-reaching consequences for the distribution of powers between the two branches in view of the large number of statutes containing analogous provisions. Shortly after this decision was reached, the Supreme Court summarily affirmed the lower court rulings in the natural gas regulation and used car rule cases, lending further credence to the view that legislative veto provisions as a class run afoul of constitutional dictates.

Although the long-running debate about legislative vetoes has now entered a new stage, one may anticipate continuing discussion of alternative mech-

---

view, see Memorandum of the Department of Justice, Proposed Executive Order entitled "Federal Regulation" (Feb. 13, 1981), *reprinted in* Report on Presidential Control of Agency Rulemaking, *supra*, at the appendix.

[125] Immigration and Naturalization Serv. v. Chadha, 634 F.2d 408 (9th Cir. 1980), *aff'd*, 462 U.S. 919, 103 S. Ct. (1983).

[126] Consumer Energy Council of Am., Inc. v. Federal Energy Regulatory Comm'n, 673 F.2d 425 (D.C. Cir.1982), *aff'd mem. sub nom.* Process Gas Consumers Group v. Consumer Energy Council of Am., Inc., 463 U.S. 1216, 103 S. Ct. 3556 (1983).

[127] Consumers Union of Am., Inc. v. FTC, 692 F.2d 575 (D.C. Cir. 1982), *aff'd mem.*, 463 U.S. 1216, 103 S. Ct. 3556 (1983).

anisms for increased congressional oversight of the administrative process. Indeed, as representatives of the executive branch themselves stressed during the recent years of heated exchange about the legislative veto, there is no shortage of such alternatives. These include placing time limitations in statutory authorizations and thus forcing periodic reauthorization of various administrative programs, confining the use of agency funds in a manner consistent with particular legislative objectives as expressed in appropriations legislation, and, of course, the familiar techniques of legislative oversight. Although such alternatives require Congress either to use the plenary legislative process in order to make its will legally effective or to rely mainly on advice or threats to agencies in the oversight context, they nonetheless constitute a formidable array of powers.

Even though the political oversight model, with its emphasis on Presidential and congressional supervision of agency action, has demonstrated considerable vitality in the contemporary debate, the model has significant shortcomings. In its essentials, it is an indirect and incomplete means of realizing its ultimate ideal. The guiding ideal is to achieve democratic responsiveness to public interests within the administrative process itself. The oversight approach does not seek to accomplish this directly, but instead attempts to rely on the President and Congress to make the public's views known to agencies. This reliance presupposes that the President and Congress are themselves responsive to a full range of public interests, but that presupposition is subject to serious question.

Relying on the President to oversee the administrative process is problematical on the premises of the democratic process ideal because the President has his own policies and programs that themselves are not necessarily designed to express the full range of the public's views and interests on particular administrative issues. Indeed, the President is an explicitly political actor with specific constituencies, preferences, and predilections. To rely on such an official to monitor the administrative process on behalf of all public interests is to risk ignoring that the President's political commitments reflect a subset of those of the polity. Moreover, even if it were possible to conceive of the President as * * * bringing to bear the full variety of public views and interest in the oversight of administration, one would be justified in asking why such a representative is necessary in the first place. If such were the case, why not simply rely on direct representation of the public's interests in the administrative process?

Similar concerns are raised by proposals to enhance the power of members of Congress over the administrative process. Such a method for achieving democratic responsiveness by agencies also is inherently an indirect one. It might be thought initially that Congress may be more capable than the President alone of representing the public's collective views and interests, if only because Congress itself is a collective body. However, in practice actual influence over the administrative process is wielded by specific members of congressional committees or their staffs. Like the President, members of Congress have particularistic political commitments that cannot be assumed to be equatable with the full range of the public's attitudes concerning matters of administration. Thus, as with the President, reliance on Congress as an indirect means of realizing the underlying democratic process ideal creates a definite potential for frustrating that very ideal.

Moreover, * * * one may doubt whether many arcane issues that come to the fore in administrative decisionmaking are likely to generate broad-based political attention that will be channelled to the President or Congress and, through them, to agencies. The problem is not merely one of mobilizing public interest. More generally, the problem is one of communicating to politically accountable officials the full range of the public's views in the absence of special efforts to broaden participation in the administrative process.

In the end, it is not unlikely that political officials acting under strengthened mandates of oversight will function significantly as conduits for particularly influential societal interests, such as important constituents of members of Congress or major supporters of and contributors to the President's party or allies. Even though this may not raise eyebrows from the perspective of realpolitik, it is inconsistent with the broad normative commitments of the democratic process ideal underlying the oversight model. That ideal, again, calls for channelling broad-based political views to administrative officials in order to make the process more truly responsive to the democratic will—which is not the same as the heightened influence of a few of the most directly interested and powerful social groups.

VI. Conclusion: General Perspectives on Administrative Reform

* * * [T]he contemporary debate about administrative reform does not consist merely of specific controversies about a plethora of discrete proposals or initiatives. Rather, there is a basic pattern in the debate that may be obscured if one considers it on a purely particularistic plane.

There are three major, competing ideals reflected in the debate that advance fundamentally different visions of a well-regulated, legitimate, and rationally-functioning administrative process. The rule of law ideal imagines a restrained and ordered process governed by norms of law; it seeks to achieve statutory aims in a manner consistent with the protection of private entitlements and adherence to legal limits. The public purposes ideal posits a more policy-oriented vision of administration; it prescribes the efficient and rational achievement of valued public purposes, or at least an effort to foster their realization by private economic actors. The democratic process ideal takes to heart the precept of democratic theory that choices among warring values in society should be made as the result of a basically participatory, representative process; it seeks to achieve this standard even in the context of hierarchical, bureaucratic institutions.

These three competing ideals reflect deep normative commitments that are central to the contemporary debate. At the same time, the ideals are in sharp conflict with one another. In particular, the core embodiments of each ideal, which reflect the most direct means of realizing the ideal within the operation of a reformed administrative process, are fundamentally critical of each other.

Thus, the core of the rule of law ideal rejects the open-ended character of the public purposes ideal and its tendency to emphasize policy-oriented, as opposed to strictly legal, decisionmaking by agencies. Conversely, the public purposes ideal refuses to accept the rule of law ideal's commitment to formalism as the basis of agency action.

At the same time, both the rule of law ideal and the public purposes ideal reject the democratic process ideal's notion of an open, participatory, and responsive administrative process that is seen as essentially political. The rule of law ideal rejects this conception by maintaining that administration is significantly apolitical in character and that duly-enacted laws are the bearers of values to be implemented, not created, by administrators. The public purposes ideal attacks the democratic process ideal by stressing the technical nature of expert administrative decisionmaking and by highlighting the irrationalities of a decisional process governed by political compromise.

In response, the democratic process ideal views both of the other ideals as misguided and illegitimate because they do not focus on the achievement of a democratic justification for the use of considerable public power by unelected agency officials. In particular, the democratic process ideal objects both to the bureaucratic and extremely rationalist propensities of the public purposes ideal and to the highly legalistic orientation of the rule of law ideal.

Despite these differences, each ideal, when viewed from an "internal" perspective, may be seen to encounter a common concern, albeit in different ways. Stripped to its essentials, each core embodiment appears to take for granted certain conditions of administrative life that seem substantially at odds with the possibilities of the existing administrative process. At the same time, each ideal is essential to understanding and justifying the administrative process in terms of the contemporary debate. Accordingly, a movement occurs in each ideal from a core embodiment to an alternative expression. The latter retains the ideal's basic theory of legitimacy, but it seeks to realize that legitimacy through some means other than one demanding the most direct transformation of the existing administrative process. In turn, however, each of the alternatives is subject to the charge of failing fully to achieve the ultimate ideal of which it is an expression, and each one has its own specific limitations.

The framework developed in this Article can account not only for deep clashes among the three ideals, but also for limited alliances among some of the ideas inhabiting more than one ideal. Certain aspects of the core embodiment of one ideal and the alternative expression of another ideal may be seen to "work" together in reformist discourse. It bears noting that the cores of different ideals do not combine with other cores; only alternative expressions combine in certain respects with the cores of other ideals. Moreover, these makeshift alliances are temporary and unstable because the alternative expressions ultimately are traceable to underlying ideals at odds with the competing cores. While not in any way denying the separateness of and competition among the three ideals, these *ad hoc* relationships highlight the complexity of the contemporary debate considered in terms of the framework put forward here. * * *

For instance, there is a degree of overlap in some of the ideas advanced on behalf of the formalist core of the rule of law ideal, on the one hand, and on behalf of the market-oriented model, on the other hand. Even though these two approaches ultimately posit very different justifications for administrative action, they both adhere to the notions that the public and private spheres must be kept separate, that legal norms help provide the necessary boundaries between the two realms, and more particularly that public laws should preserve private entitlements from undue impositions by the state. These themes often are linked together in reformist argument. For example, deregulation is defended chiefly in terms of a return to a "free" market, but also in terms of the need to eliminate legal intrusions on the "private" sphere that are said to be insufficiently confined by rules of law.

There also is a certain congruence between aspects of the core of the public purposes ideal, on the one hand, and of the political oversight model, on the other hand. Even though they represent distinct underlying visions of the legitimacy and character of administrative action, they both stress the multiplicity of goals and interests that must be balanced in the context of administrative decisionmaking. This shared theme frequently is found in arguments on behalf of an expanded role for the President and his staff in overseeing agency regulations. Such an expanded role is, of course, one means of pursuing the goal of political oversight of administrative decisions. But it also may be defended under the core of the competing public purposes ideal: the Executive Office of the President could be said to be the most competent institution for undertaking the government wide balancing of costs and benefits of contemplated agency actions necessary to achieve the most instrumentally rational result.

In addition, there are certain connections among the ideas contained in the core of the democratic process ideal, on the one hand, and the proceduralist expression of the rule of law ideal, on the other hand. Although the ideals underlying these perspectives fundamentally differ, both approaches emphasize innovation in decisional processes, the language of fairness, and the interests of affected parties in becoming involved in administration. These notions commonly are relied upon in arguments on behalf of expanded public participation in administrative proceedings, which is claimed not only to enhance the openness and responsiveness of an essentially political process, but also to control agency discretion and to protect private entitlements by imposing procedural constraints on agencies in the name of the rule of law.

* * * In light of the limited overlaps among aspects of the cores of certain ideals and the alternative expressions of other ideals, is it possible to suggest that the conflicts reflected in the contemporary debate may be harmonized? Or given the fundamental tensions among the three ideals, is it more accurate to perceive irreducible normative tension underlying the contemporary administrative process?

It could be suggested that a degree of harmony might be achieved in terms of the alliances just noted among certain ideas inhabiting more than one ideal. The notion would be that such alliances may establish ways to bridge the gaps among the ideals and perhaps may point to a unified theory of administrative reform. This suggestion ultimately cannot succeed, however, because it fails to deal seriously with the fundamental clashes among the cores of the three competing ideals. The three ideals embody distinct visions of the legitimacy of administrative action and the character of administrative decisionmaking, and at these basic levels they are at war with one another. The ideals cannot be magically harmonized—even if aspects of them can be compared and combined on an ad hoc basis—without ignoring, or wishing not to notice, these deep conflicts.

For similar reasons, two well-established portraits of modern administrative theory cannot be accepted as fully adequate perspectives from which to understand the contemporary debate. The first portrait suggests that there is a continuing crisis in the American administrative process that should be resolved by developing an embracing theory of the legitimacy of administration in our political system. This portrait aptly notes that the problem of administrative legitimacy is a longstanding one and that present concerns reflect recurrent dilemmas and doubts. However, the suggestion that the crisis of legitimacy should be resolved by a harmonizing theory or vision simply is inconsistent with the existence of deep normative conflicts at the root of the contemporary debate. In fact, the debate reveals major clashes among three competing ideals, which advance their own forceful claims on the basis of distinct and to a large degree mutually incompatible premises.

The second portrait is one in which a traditional model of the administrative process, which might be assimilated here to the rule of law ideal, is seen to have disintegrated, leaving in its wake an array of alternative conceptions tending to lack overall structure or patterned relationships. In analyzing the contemporary debate, however, it is not possible to say that any one "traditional" model is significantly more disintegrated or limited in its conceptual or programmatic promise than the other competing ideals. In some ways, the rule of law ideal and its expressions are among the most robust sources of reformist criticism. More generally, one cannot disregard any of the three competing ideals, for all of them are central to the contemporary debate. Furthermore, the different ideals, viewed as a group, do not lack structure or pattern in their relationships with each other.

In the end, the contemporary debate reflects major clashes among three competing ideals of the administrative process, as well as a parallel internal development within each ideal from a core embodiment to an alternative expression. No single conception at any level seems sufficiently moribund to permit the conclusion that any is necessarily much less vital than the others. Similarly, none appears particularly preeminent or in the ascendancy, either in theoretical or practical terms.

The contemporary debate about administrative reform * * * is enmeshed in the complex dynamics surrounding the elaboration of and competition among deep, preexisting premises. A degree of self-consciousness about this predicament seems essential for a full awareness of the character and constraints of the main arguments advanced on behalf of administrative reform. Moreover, this understanding leads one to conclude that the contemporary debate is not likely to come to an end * * *. The debate about administrative reform exhibits fundamental tensions within reformist discourse that are likely to continue to fuel new proposals for change. * * *

Additional Sources

Brian N. Barry, THEORIES OF JUSTICE (1989)

Paul Brest, *Further Beyond the Republican Revival: Toward Radical Republicanism*, 97 Yale L.J. 1623 (1988)

Stephen Breyer, REGULATION AND ITS REFORM (1981)

Harold H. Bruff, *Legislative Formality, Administrative Rationality*, 63 Tex. L. Rev. 207 (1984)

James M. Buchanan & Gordon Tullock, THE CALCULUS OF CONSENT (1972)

Ronald M. Dworkin, LAW'S EMPIRE (1986)

Christopher Edley, Jr., *The Governance Crisis, Legal Theory, and Political Ideology*, 41 Duke L.J. 561 (1991)

Daniel A. Farber & Philip P. Frickey, LAW AND PUBLIC CHOICE (1991)

Kathy E. Ferguson, THE FEMINIST CASE AGAINST BUREAUCRACY (1984)

James O. Freedman, *Crisis and Legitimacy: The Administrative Process and American Government* (1978)

Daniel J. Gifford, *The New Deal Regulatory Model: A History of Criticisms and Refinements*, 68 Minn. L. Rev. 299 (1983)

Amy Gutmann, *Communitarian Critics of Liberalism*, 14 Phil. & Pub. Aff. 308 (1985)

Samuel Krislov & David H. Rosenbloom, REPRESENTATIVE BUREAUCRACY AND THE AMERICAN POLITICAL SYSTEM (1981)

Howard Latin, *Ideal Versus Real Regulatory Efficiency: Implementation of Uniform Standards and "Fine-Tuning" Regulatory Reforms*, 37 Stan. L. Rev. 1267 (1985)

Theodore J. Lowi, *The End of Liberalism:* THE SECOND REPUBLIC OF THE UNITED STATES (2d ed. 1979)

Arthur Maass, CONGRESS AND THE COMMON GOOD (1983)

Jonathan R. Macey, *Promoting Public-Regarding Legislation through Statutory Interpretation: An Interest Group Model*, 86 Colum. L. Rev. 223 (1986)

Jerry L. Mashaw, BUREAUCRATIC JUSTICE: MANAGING SOCIAL SECURITY DISABILITY CLAIMS (1983)

Sam Peltzman, *Toward a More General Theory of Regulation*, 19 J.L. & Econ. 211 (1976)

Richard J. Pierce, Jr., *The Role of Constitutional and Political Theory in Administrative Law*, 64 Tex. L. Rev. 469 (1985)

John Rawls, A THEORY OF JUSTICE (1971)

Thomas O. Sargentich, *Teaching Administrative Law in the Twenty-First Century*, 1 Widener J. of Pub. L. 147 (1992)

Steven Shiffrin, *Liberalism, Radicalism, and Legal Scholarship*, 30 UCLA L. Rev. 1103 (1983)

Richard B. Stewart, *The Discontents of Legalism: Interest Group Relations in Administrative Regulation*, 1985 Wis. L. Rev. 655

Richard B. Stewart, *The Reformation of American Administrative Law*, 88 Harv. L. Rev. 1667 (1975)

Cass R. Sunstein, *Beyond the Republican Revival*, 97 Yale L.J. 1539 (1988)

Cass R. Sunstein, *Changing Conceptions of Administration*, 1987 B.Y.U. L. Rev. 927

Roberto M. Unger, KNOWLEDGE AND POLITICS (1975)